SYSTEMATIC POLITICS

OTHER BOOKS BY GEORGE E. GORDON CATLIN

Thomas Hobbes as Philosopher, Publicist, and Man of Letters: An Introduction (Oxford: B. Blackwell, 1922)

The Science and Method of Politics (London: Kegan Paul [Routledge & Kegan Paul]; New York: A. A. Knopf [Knopf-Croft]; 1927)

A Study of the Principles of Politics, being an essay towards political rationalization (London: George Allen & Unwin; New York: Macmillan; 1930)

The Story of the Political Philosophers (New York, London: McGraw, 1939; George Allen & Unwin, 1950; New York: Tudor, 1947)

Rules of Sociological Method by E. Durkheim, edited with introduction (Chicago: University of Chicago Press; Cambridge: Cambridge University Press; 1938)

Preface to Action (London: George Allen & Unwin; New York: Macmillan; 1934)

The Anglo-Saxon Tradition (London: Kegan Paul [Routledge & Kegan Paul]; New York: Macmillan; 1939)

One Anglo-American Nation, the foundation of Anglo-Saxony as a basis of world federation (London: A. Dakers Ltd.; Toronto: Macmillan Company of Canada; 1941)

Above All Nations, an anthology compiled with Vera Brittain and Sheila Hodges with foreword by Victor Gollancz (London: Gollancz, 1945; New York: Harper, 1949)

On Political Goals, University of North Carolina Weil Lectures, 1957 (New York: St. Martin's Press, 1957)

The Atlantic Community (London: Coram; Toronto: Macmillan Company of Canada; 1959)

Systematic Politics

ELEMENTA

POLITICA

ET SOCIOLOGICA

GEORGE E. GORDON CATLIN

University of Toronto Press

Preface

This book is concerned to do two things. It seeks to restate the position in political theory taken by the writer in the years 1924 to 1930. This might seem an idle occupation were it not the case that the pioneer position then taken—both as touching the nature of politics and the appropriate area of its field, and as to the importance of the study of power, precisely defined, as a clue to the systematic interpretation of this area—has been massively enough sustained by the work of subsequent students of politics, some of whose work is of indisputable weight.

Secondly, and consequently, while recording my debt to earlier writers such as Professors Graham Wallas and Robert MacIver and to deeply valued colleagues such as Professor Harold D. Lasswell, the task has been undertaken of reviewing this subsequent relevant work and of refashioning and giving increased body to the theme, thanks to the labours of these many other students. This is indeed the fourth volume of a series which, taken together, seeks to outline a Systematic Politics.

In many cases, naturally enough, the other workers in the field are not to be supposed to agree with my theories nor always I with theirs. If, in the supporting and critical material, here printed, I have perhaps written out my own theme too little and, in the opinion of some, in almost scholastic style quoted too much, my defence must be that, in building a science, what matters is not to claim or dispute about originality, but to build up the structure, brick by brick, on well-laid foundations.

However, since it has been suggested that what was perhaps the distinctive approach in the campaign 'to take political science seriously,' instead of apologizing for the subject as inherently unscientific, was an approach exclusively conditioned by the American historical and political scene, it is perhaps desirable to state uncompromisingly that most of my personal contribution to this work was first drafted in England, even if it was developed (with every encouragement, for which I am immeasurably grateful) in Cornell. It owed its origin primarily to a very ancient and Old World source, to wit the writings of Thomas Hobbes (upon whom the author wrote a monograph in 1922,[1] being an Oxford University prize essay), vivified by consideration of the clinical work, on the interest in power, of Alfred Adler. Assuredly, Thomas Hobbes was not a tree that grew in Brooklyn. I hasten to add that the political philosophy of the writer neither was nor is Hobbesian nor positivist. This my *History of the Political Philosophers*, being the third volume in the connected whole, amply shows.

The present book is not, of course, limited to the two themes above mentioned, the nature of politics and the study of power. Other discussions, already outlined in the original work, are elaborated further, such as the stress upon the methodological identity of Political Science and Sociology, the separation in political theory between Political Science and Political Philosophy, the stress upon quantitative measurement, the functional approach, equilibrium theory and the theory of the political market, the importance of recurrent patterns, the concern for power expressed through pressure groups, and so forth. Perhaps, above all, the enunciation should be mentioned of what is hoped to be a coherent and systematic theory of the relation of freedom and authority, from which any notion of schematic 'laws' in politics must stem. The idea of such laws is, it need scarcely be said, very old in political theory. And, when it has been possible to call attention to the sober simplicity and clarity of Aristotle as a model, this has deliberately been done. At least Aristotle was not the victim, like nineteenth-century jurists, of obsession with theories about the modern nation states, taken as unchangeable data, and their sovereignties.

It is not, however, the view sustained in this book that the political theorist has completed his task when he has sought to advance

[1] *Thomas Hobbes* (Oxford: Blackwell, 1922).

empirical political science and has made a study of means alone. There are indeed many competent theorists in the field of political philosophy and here pioneering undertakings are less rare. Nevertheless, in an abbreviated form and perhaps rather as headlines for later discussion, a number of suggestions, some Thomistic and some otherwise, about the valuational issues of today have been put forward. The final problem of power is that of the transcendence of power, without ignoring reality. This is discussed in the concluding chapter.

I am, of course, well aware that there are many matters, legitimately the concern of the political theorist and even of the highest importance, which for reasons both of space and design, have here been omitted. It is perhaps proper to add, autobiographically, that I have personally been more concerned with political and ethical philosophy than with political science. I may also say that my interest in this last, and in the analysis of social structure, has sprung from very practical considerations of issues of peace and war, meditated upon in 1918 outside Mons. It has not been my view that practical and effective solutions can be offered without a far more fundamental structural analysis than obtained in academic quarters, at least at that time.

An attempt has been made to acknowledge and fully advertise the work of the many authors who have, in this last quarter of a century, made their contributions to the structure of political science. Many others, unfortunately, have undoubtedly (and to my regret) been omitted; but there was a risk of making the *apparatus criticus* too burdensome for the book and of weighing down the main theme. For such omissions of reference to work of value I apologize to authors and publishers alike.

In one case, however (apart from those already mentioned by name), I feel that especial reference must be made. When I first drafted this present book I had not seen the book on Sovereignty by my friend, M. Bertrand de Jouvenel—to whom I am indebted for reading the present work. My agreement with so much of what he has to say is so profound that I feel I must here make a personal acknowledgement.

I also wish to express my deep appreciation to a few very busy scholars, Professors Harold D. Lasswell, Robert M. MacIver, Henry Habberley Price, and K. R. Popper, for their great kindness in having read through, in whole or part, an early draft of the script. Whether, of course, they agree with the conclusions is quite another matter, and certainly not one in which I would venture to take their names in vain. Their own contribution in this field or in that of philosophy, as everyone knows, is immense; and I am honoured by having had at least the advantage of their comments. To Professor C. J. Friedrich of Harvard I am much indebted for the suggestion of the title of this book. With these names I would like to couple those of early Cornell friends to whom I owe so much, President Livingston Farrand and Professors C. L. Becker, R. E. Cushman, E. B. Titchener, and W. Notestein. I further wish to thank my colleagues at McGill for their kind tolerance of my diversion of time and energy to this book, both when I was Bronfman Professor and, especially, when I was departmental chairman. I am likewise greatly indebted to President R. C. Pratt and Professors Andrew Hacker and Francis Wormuth and to my son-in-law, Mr. Bernard Williams, sometime Fellow of All Souls and New College, Oxford, and now of London University, for reading parts of this script and for many helpful comments; and also to the editors of the University of Toronto Press for unstinted and quite invaluable work on the text.

GEORGE E. GORDON CATLIN

4 Whitehall Court,
London,
October, 1961

Contents

Prologue

It has been suggested that it will make for the convenience of readers if the Propositions stated in this book be listed in order. This is here done. Students are, however, warned that the meanings and implications of the Propositions are, in many cases, only fully intelligible if read in connection with the context in which they appear.

Chapter 2

1. Broadly, Politics is the study of Society as organized; and hence cannot be divided from Sociology.
2. Politics is divided into three parts: the Art, and (within the Theory) the Philosophy and the Science.
3. We need to find some function or form of activity or process in terms of which the whole field of political data can be seen to have a common principle.
4. The crux of the science of politics lies in the isolation and study of the Political Act.
5. Political Science is concerned with the function in society of Control; with the Acts that issue in Control; with Wills; and with the structures resulting from the control relationship of Wills.

Chapter 3

6. There is a general will to execute one's Will, which is the agent

for realizing one's particular Wish or End; and for Freedom for that realization. The condition for such execution is Power.

7. Those who hold power will gratuitously sacrifice neither their freedom to do what they choose nor their established liberties.

8. So soon as political means have in fact been chosen, they and their structure will condition, and even severely condition, the human and actual achievement even of the most divine, categorically moral, or ideal ends.

9. All politics is by its nature power politics. This analysis is more fundamental than the Marxist.

10. The desire for Domination is one species of the desire for Power, which is caused by a confirmed fear of frustration. The inclination towards Co-operative Power is another species.

11. Education may not be the pious answer of bad faith but the authentic answer to the key problems of Politics.

Chapter 4

12. Although the impulse to Freedom is fundamental and instinctive, no one particular expression of Freedom (which may be determined by the local culture) is instinctive. Those demands arising from the changing situation, which the local culture or its established institutions and conventions recognize, are called Liberties; and collectively are a recognized Liberty.

13. The urge to Freedom, moreover, is in a quite explicit, technical, scientific, and not only rhetorical sense an instinct.

14. Freedom, of its own inner logic and necessity, involves (to protect itself) Power, objective Control, and (in particular phases of the sequence) recognized Authority.

15. The whole of Political Science springs from the logic of the Law of the Correlation of Freedom and Authority.

16. The basic and harsh (though not unadaptable) Law of the Political Alternative is that one has to choose between obtaining goods and paying for them, or not having them.

Chapter 5

17. The Law of the Market needs to be stated: that all security involves an exchange of some general freedom in return for some security which we value more, as assuring a particular liberty to realize what we wish.

18. Authority is not the contradictory of Freedom, but springs from it and is its polar contrary and complement.

19. No Government Bureaucracy or similar Producer, civil, industrial, or ecclesiastical, is likely to welcome Pure Democracy, which is an extreme form of consumer control, unless it is assured that effective power still lies in government hands.

20. The democratic system and the sovereignty of the particular people under the present state system are irrelevant *pro tanto*, or at least indecisive, where the issue is one of 'external' and not 'internal' sovereignty.

21. Democracy conforms, in theory, to the type of a consumer's market, with freedom maximized.

22. All Democracies, save those which readily tend to change into Oligarchies or Dictatorships (or which have a tradition of aristocratic leadership), have difficulty in raising, to cope with competition or emergency, the Costs of Government to their supporters.

23. A Democratic Government has difficulty in restricting the freedom and customary liberties of its citizens, even where this reduces its own power to preserve elementary liberties of the society and individual in international competition.

24. No man voluntarily sacrifices the power of freedom of expressing his opinion, he regarding himself as the equal of any other elector and his opinion as being as good as his neighbour's, unless some advantage to himself (or loss of penalty to himself) can be shown if he does so. Complementarily, all those who have unchecked power to enjoy freedoms tend to use it—which also includes the abuse of it.

25. Those that have the power will tend to use it.

26. We have in Dictatorship the extreme case of a sellers' or producers' market, where authority is expanded and liberty diminished.

27. All government tends to be government by minorities or government by oligarchies.

28. Internal Liberty will tend to vary inversely with estimated External Pressure.

29. Every Tyranny will be suspicious of possible enemies, will tend to invent them until they exist, and will be, by its nature, expansionist within the limits of its powers.

30. A Tyranny is never more in danger (unless it be by arrogant miscalculations in external aggressions) than when, the sense of crisis being reduced, it begins to relax its internal restraints.

Chapter 6

31. The satisfaction of the perennial demand for institutional authorities, and for the social goods of authority and security in power-

competition, always tends to give preponderant power to limited groups of a few who are prepared, persistently and at costs, to organize and sustain these authorities.

32. No regimes, their mechanisms apart, will be stable which do not supply the mass of consumers with the goods for their particular major wants; and a prime method to achieve this stability is to shape consumer opinion to demand that which one is fitted or considers that one ought on long-range considerations to supply.

33. It is those who feel strongly, articulately, and steadfastly, and who are correspondingly organized around this common purpose, whose will is likely to prevail.

34. All men, even bureaucrats, have an appetite for power which, *ceteris paribus*, grows as it feeds; and no man who has the choice between converting a subordinate into a possible rival and multiplying subordinates, over whom he remains magnified as master and arbiter, will readily choose the former. Hence all bureaucracies, being jealous of power, tend towards growth in personnel.

35. It is dangerous and dishonest to found a proposition in Political Science of major practical importance, to wit, unqualified Human Equality as distinct from the ethical imperative of Human Fraternity and Partnership, on a demonstrable falsehood.

36. The doctrine of equality is not a scientific doctrine of human biology, but is fundamentally a religious doctrine of fraternity, connecting intimately with the notion of community and what we mean by it.

Chapter 7

37. Aristocracy has not only a role but a functional role, which Constitutional Democracy has tried overtly to recognize, in the political system.

38. Community is the area in which, with rational confidence, men have the power to enjoy the co-operative goods resulting from trust.

39. The Church has a political function bearing on the civil authority.

40. To take the specific instances of the Latin Catholic and Greek Orthodox churches, there is a cultural anaemia in failing to recognize that they not only were, but in their culture and community are, the primary specific bearers of the Judao-Hellenic and Roman (or New Roman) tradition, not so much of European (the recently Christianized Nordics have inadequately felt themselves to be part of it) as of Mediterranean civilization. To ignore or divorce oneself from it conduces to cultural poverty. This contention is not incompatible with

emphasizing the human vitality which springs from diversity and mutations of views.

41. For survival under conditions of crisis, community goods, requiring by their nature education rather than coercion, must be inculcated positively, even at costs to alternative wishes; this is educationally possible and will be politically successful so far as the common commitment rests upon a more profound satisfaction of our human nature, and a greater accord with Natural Law, than does the alternative.

Chapter 8

42. The concrete individual is never merely forced into, and lost without residue, in society.

43. We may hold the fundamental nature of Sovereignty rather to be Judicial than Executive or Legislative.

44. In the twentieth century an effective supra-national institution must be constituted, sovereign *ad hoc*, and superseding in its own functional field the archaic political inventions of the seventeenth century.

45. The present State, in so far as it is machinery, is obsolete, decrepit, and dangerous. It is itself provocative of friction and war. The test is that, far from efficiently performing its civil function of maintaining peace, it creates explosive dangers of its own, like any other outworn machine. The appropriate forms need to be rethought.

46. The State in its present form must be abolished. It is the prime threat today to peace (whatever its past utility) and an instrument of domination menacing peoples.

47. Political functions being adapted to actual human wants and being improved by the need to fulfil them, it follows that, where the prime function is the maintenance of actual civil peace, only a system of organization which is wide enough, as sovereign arbiter, in fact to fulfil the function is rational as to ends and tolerable as to means.

Chapter 9

48. Political Philosophy is concerned with the ends and values men pursue (including *pro tanto* the intermediary ends), as distinct from the means as such. No Political Theory, since its subject matter is also practical, can be complete without consideration of the ends of action and the discussion of values.

49. Philosophy is one.

50. It can be argued (and is here argued) that there is a grand tradition of civilized values, as displayed in history.

51. The criterion of goodness lies in the beauty for us as end-satisfaction in itself, and not in the power.

52. In this alignment of means with the profounder human judgement of ends, which is the categorical aesthetic judgement, lies the reconciliation of Power with the Good.

53. The naive judgement of beauty is capable of Education.

These Propositions are not to be understood as summarizing the entire argument of the book nor are they dogmatic. Even the theses of Luther at Wittenberg were not originally dogmatic. Rather these are to be understood as hypotheses or theses, as in the mediaeval disputations of the schools, put forward for examination and argument or test.

Part I: POLITICAL SCIENCE

1. Introduction on Method

§i. *What is Science?*

"The proper study of mankind is man." So wrote Alexander Pope. Socrates, against the too dominant prestige of the physicists of his day, had thought the same. It is today's issue also. The study of institutions is derivative from this study of the nature of man, unless—like Marx—one would make man to be flotsam on the material stream and the creative spirit epiphenomenal or, as would perhaps be countenanced by Hume, one would make institutions and social habits or conventions some kind of causeless, arbitrary factor and unmoulded moulder.[1]

The present unbalance of culture and material civilization—an inversion and perversion of the concerns of Socrates which makes physics the prime study, which indeed increases the powers of the human race —has not had uniformly fortunate results. Especially is this true where the disposition of the fruits of physical research often remains a matter of political decision, concerning which physicists have neither pro-

---

[1]"Habit soon consolidates what other principles of human nature had imperfectly founded." (*Essay on the Origin of Government*) However, (*a*) Hume admits "other principles"; (*b*) provides a psychological analysis of habit in terms of association; and (*c*) rests all these principles upon a postulated 'human nature.' "Politics admit of general truths." (*That Politics may be Reduced to a Science*) It is a central theme for Hume that there is 'a science of man.'

fessional competence nor, in this alien field, better common judgement than other men. We need to have recalled to us the judgement of Plato, from which substantially Aristotle does not dissent, that Politics is architectonic, not only (as *The Statesman* indicates) in its art but in its professional study. The practical importance to humanity of Pure Politics, which we shall explain later, is not less than that of Pure Physics.

Mr. John Plamenatz has recently argued (in his *German Marxism and Russian Communism*, 1954; hereafter cited as *German Marxism*) that "the proper study of politics is not man but institutions." This dictum, rightly calling attention to the need for the objective, quantitative, and comparative study of institutions, is probably no more than reaction against profitless speculations by academic theorists about dead philosophers with dead theories of social contract and the state of nature. The tradition of Mill, Sidgwick, Bryce, and Wallas (as will be shown) is yet different in emphasis from the quoted remark. We must beware of what A. F. Bentley calls "evading the very central structure of [the] study." The downright statement of Professor Wright Mills is valid and should be digested: "the facts . . . are . . . about the success and the failure of individual men and women" (*The Sociological Imagination*, 1959, p. 3). However, we can cast the judgement in more social terms. No one denies that a vast subject has to be subdivided for pedagogical purposes, if there is to be any mastery of it. It may well be professionally desirable to specialize in Municipal Government, Trade Union structure, or the constitutional structure as interpreted by the Supreme Court. But, on principle and scientifically—and this is the condition for vital advance—we must agree with Professor Martin Lipset that "the independent study of the state and other political institutions does not make theoretical sense" (*Political Man*, 1960, p. 23). This has been one key theme of the present writer for these last three or four decades, although for traditional reasons it has not commended itself to political students in some countries until recently. It is a pleasure to cite Professor Lipset's quite remarkable and outstanding recent book in support. The tide is turning.

The demand is incessant in the popular press, and indeed among responsible writers, that "man's political and social genius should catch up with his scientific genius." But the complaint has been the same for thirty years. Little indeed, either by way of expenditure of money or of concentrated thought upon scientific method, is done about the matter, since in politics every man regards himself as an adequate authority. On the other hand, as Lord Attlee, sometime Prime Minister of Britain, has remarked, eminent physical scientists on the matter of politics display less judgement than that usual with the ordinary voter. It is not who manufactures the hydrogen bomb but who decides to throw it and why, that we have to consider.

The rewards of the Nobel Committees go to physicists and chemists for exact research but, where peace is the concern, they go traditionally to those responsible for good works or to practical statesmen. Were the concern in social and political research as serious and hopeful as in physical and chemical research, the reward could be directed into comparable channels. It is a matter for satisfaction that the 1959 award was made to Mr. Philip Noel-Baker, for a very fine technical study. The incessant identification, alike in the press and among politicians, of all science with physical science does harm at all levels, including that of the financing of research, and bastardizes the social sciences.

In considering Political Science, the first question that arises is whether or not it exists. The reply depends upon what is meant. Some may prefer to call it Political Sociology; and then add that Sociology is a science, in a specific sense. But 'Politico-Sociological Science' is a cumbersome form of words. Can there be a 'new science,' *nuova scienza*, born from political theory? Should it fight its way against the ever-conservative scholasticism of the 'establishment' of the universities? 'Science' may, as a term, be used so widely that, like the German *Wissenschaft*, it becomes a word describing any body of logically systematic knowledge, such as is philosophy. In this sense we can (as it has been called) 'scientize'—this being just an obstinate and consistent method of thinking—about anything at all. But such scientizing will be devoid of predictive value.

Duns Scotus writes: "Scientia est de mutabile, secundum quod est immutabile" (*Quaest. in Post. An. I*). "And so from necessary and appropriate principles it proceeds to necessary conclusions, and thus in this respect is science." (*Quaest. super Univ. Prophyrii*) It is the element of constancy which is of the essence. Both Windelband and Rickert use 'science' in an extended fashion, to which reference is made above, on the supposition that 'events' can profitably be described as able to be ordered into a 'science' (*Ereigniswissenschaft*), although it yields no 'immutable' laws, but is only subject matter for a discipline. So the crafts of palaeography and heraldry are called 'sciences,' not to speak of pugilism and law. So also we may speak of a *Geisteswissenschaft* of art or history or of culture; and even a *Literaturwissenschaft* is discussed. This view, common in German Sociology, is here challenged. The late Professor Karl Mannheim (in *Ideology and Utopia*, 1929, ed. and trans. L. Wirth and E. A. Shils, 1954, p. 146) asserts that "a political science is possible and can be taught"; but he did not mean by it what we mean here. According to the perhaps excessively severe judgement of Professor Arnold Brecht (*Political Theory*, 1959, pp. 10 ff.), the chief offenders here are "the professional escapists," who either "ignore the problem" or who refer the whole matter to the historians, or for original thought substitute—what, of course, is of indisputable importance in its different sphere, as this writer has elsewhere asserted—studies in the history of other people's ideas. It is with some slight surprise that the writer finds himself listed by Professor Brecht in the brief category 'Machiavellian.'

The term 'science' may also be used, as it frequently is in the English-speaking world, to mean a connected body of knowledge or the knowledge of a system of relations based upon observation and, as Lord Kelvin said, preferably upon quantitative measurement. These, together with exactitude and an agreed language of definition, are the requirements. Lord Kelvin's preference here is as old, in the history of thought, as Pythagoras. In this context such a phrase as 'Moral Sciences,' like 'Experimental Philosophy,' is to be regarded as an archaic oddity. 'Science' is, moreover, here thought of as yielding through its studies empirically testable 'laws,' or conclusions about constants, which give to man, or to the professors of these matters, some hope of powers of prediction and control. These are much needed if indeed man's intelligence in the ordering of his own society is to keep pace with his dangerously "uncontrolled control" of the physical world. When we refer to a 'law' we refer to a formula which, like Solomon's signet ring, gives the secret of useful control. We are not committing ourselves either to a Kantian view of laws, or to a Hegelian or realist view of the nature of this law as immanent. To this topic, however, we shall return. Patently those who have this knowledge will concretely modify their own future conduct (as they also modify nature) in the light of what most surely would have happened if they had not possessed it. (This, for example, is a commonplace of economics.) Their science must, hence, be propositional, hypothetical, abstract, and a matter of *als ob*, 'as if.'

Dr. James B. Conant, sometime President of Harvard, in his *Modern Science and Modern Man* (1952, Anchor ed., pp. 106–7) writes: "Science is a dynamic undertaking directed to lowering the degree of empiricism involved in solving problems; or, if you prefer, science is a process of fabricating a web of interconnected concepts and conceptual schemes arising from experiments and observations and fruitful of further experiments and observations." He adds, in agreement with Professor M. Polanyi (quoted *infra*, p. 387) and in a sentence relevant to certain false distinctions often drawn between the natural and the social sciences, "the activities of scientists in their laboratories are shot through with value judgements." "These conceptual schemes have been essential for the advancement of science." (p. 120)

In his excellent booklet *The Present State of American Sociology* (1948), Professor Edward A. Shils—of Chicago and Cambridge universities, and himself an excellent example of the international quality of this whole scientific movement—writes of the specialized studies of Professor R. E. Park that "they were however still not science. They might have become such had [Park] seen the need to relate concrete indices to general abstract definitions, and the indispensability of general and not just particular explanations." (p. 11) This comment applies to many British 'mass observation' and detailed 'area' surveys, illuminating although they may be. (Conversely, it may be added, a concrete social problem often has to be broken up into components, each subject to its own generalizations, which component factors are not perceived by an enthusiastic or alarmed public opinion. Cf. the present writer's analysis in *Liquor Control*, 1931.) "Sociologists have lacked the concepts, the first-hand knowledge and the observational techniques and even more important they have not been able thus far to isolate the problem which should be studied. . . . Certain basically important problems and hypotheses which should have been common to all [sociology, economics, law and political science] were neglected by all." (*The Present State of American Sociology*, p. 22. *Vide* also p. 55.)

It is important in regard to predictive utility in the social sciences that all students, including critics, should note the importance of the conditional 'if,' and the 'as if' of the schematic models, as distinct from dogmatic prediction or prophecy about historic facts of a time and place. As Professor Joseph A. Schumpeter says (*Capitalism, Socialism and Democracy*, 3rd ed., Harpers, 1950, p. 416): "Any prediction is extra-scientific prophecy that attempts to do more than to diagnose observable tendencies and to state what results would be, if these tendencies should work themselves out according to their logic." This warning is peculiarly important when we come to the alleged sciences of History, on which *vide* Professor Karl R. Popper's *The Poverty of Historicism* (1957).

It is noteworthy that, as shown by recent scholarship, Herodotus was concerned, not with literary talks, but with the illumination of cause and consequence, even if the beginning of the wars which Herodotus records was no more than a riot about women. Herodotus, if unscientific, was here as right in supposing an order as the astrologers, in their unscientific way, were right in supposing that the heavenly bodies influenced the tides. Science begins this way, with conversion of unscientific thesis into critical hypothesis. The Father of History is here followed, in very significant words, by Thucydides, who writes that his object as an historian was "to give a true picture of the events which have happened and which, human nature [τό ἀνθρώπειον] being what it is, are likely to be repeated at some further time with more or less exactness." His *History* of the Peloponnesian War finds that the major source of the trouble was "the pursuit of power, animated by covetousness and ambition." Elsewhere (i, 23), he ascribes the cause of the Peloponnesian War to fear by Sparta of the growing power of Athens. Those who, on the contrary, for a variety of causes arising in the mental climate of certain periods and connected with scepticism about the powers of the analytic reason, doubt whether politics or economics can achieve any degree of exactitude have preferred to use some such non-committal, tepid, or ambiguous phrase as 'social studies.' We must, of course, anyhow only expect, as Aristotle warns us, from any science such exactitude as is apt to the subject matter. The issue is: how much?

Thus, the Professor of Political Science in the University of Cambridge, Dr. Denis Brogan, despite the title of his chair, said in his Inaugural Address (1946): "We may doubt today whether any such academic discipline as political science exists, a doubt practically unknown to earlier ages . . . Politics may have all the potentialities of the atomic bomb, but those potentialities are not [*pace* Marx] the

8

result of the activities of political scientists . . . This university has wisely provided for the case of any professor holding this chair who might be tempted to deny the historical character of the studies by attaching him to the History Board." It is doubtful indeed if one can sit in a chair if it does not exist. There is irony in the fact that Principal John Caird (*University Addresses*, 1898), in an address given to the University of Glasgow in 1884, inquired whether History ought to be permitted to rank as a fit academic discipline, and commented that the expediency of putting it into the curriculum "turns upon the question whether history is capable of scientific treatment . . . submitting itself to the grasp of principles." How different was then the mental climate—and doubtless it will be again. In a somewhat different sense to Principal Caird, it may be pointed out that, in the most recent historical work, statistical analysis, for example of electoral rolls, has been introduced to check the too rash generalizations of earlier historians.

Professor H. D. Lasswell, indeed, and the present writer have been selected and coupled by Professor T. I. Cook, of Johns Hopkins University, as two children pursuing a road that must lead to a "dead end" (although he also has referred to these children as "founding fathers"); and this writer alone has been isolated into pre-eminence by Mr. William Esslinger in his *Politics and Science* (1955) as having this undue faith in a science. (The different view of Professor David Easton, in his full discussion in *The Political System*, 1953, is cited later.) Indeed, in the present tractate, the writer is not saying new things but reiterating old things said thirty years ago and re-emphasizing them. Esslinger does, however, attribute to the school of thought, here defended, and specifically to the present writer, the position of being "one of the first in our time to treat systematically the question of linking theory with practice in politics"—so the science is not too impractical. Those engaged upon this work can say, as did Machiavelli in his Introduction to the *Discorsi*: "I have resolved to open a new route." Perhaps it is only fitting to add the warning context which Machiavelli supplies to this remark: "The envious nature of man, so prompt to blame and so slow to praise, makes the discovery of any new principles and systems as dangerous almost as the exploration of unknown seas and continents."

It will be noted that, some time ago in his *Human Nature in Politics* (1908), that great and inadequately honoured man, Graham Wallas, wrote: "We must aim at finding as many relevant and measurable facts about human nature as possible, and we must attempt to make all of them serviceable in political reasoning." However, although the attention of the student, when discussing such heady abstractions as 'socialism,' 'capitalism,' 'sovereignty,' should always be directed to 'what actually does happen' and to the objective, nevertheless let us always remember that no amount of discourse on facts as such about political institutions will *per se* answer any theoretical questions or practical ones either. In this sense alone we can say that it is a learned frivolity and exclaim with Rousseau against its professors, "Ecartons les faits."

It is of secondary importance (and not essential) that experiment shall be possible of a precise kind, although this experiment is indeed only possible in a limited fashion in not only Politics and Economics, but also Astronomy and Geology. Whereas experiment is important, what enters into the definition of 'science' in that more precise sense in which we shall here use it is the possibility of empiric verification of general statements. Frequently this can involve the possibility of prediction, certainly not in the sense that, like crystal-gazers, we can prophesy in detail what is going to happen, but in the sense that we may predict what will happen upon the contingent hypothesis of certain circumstances recurring, and 'as if' they recurred. This recurrence may be sufficiently close to give practical validity. There are indeed those who not only would restrict all *scientia transmissibilis* to that which is capable of empiric verification, but who would choose so to limit the word 'knowledge' itself. This, however, represents the opposite, positivist extreme to that described above, and there is no need to embrace it, as we shall see in our final chapters. It would have the interesting, if perverse, consequence that most philosophy is not knowledge.

This last theme, concerning *scientia transmissibilis,* is defended by Professor Arnold Brecht in his *Political Theory.* However, he admits a "non-transmissible knowledge," and with much of his argument I deeply agree. In this pertinacious and monumental defence of a particular methodology in political and social science, to which all students will be indebted for its argument and for its massive review of the literature, it may be felt that Professor Brecht has not only proved his point but gone beyond what the argument demands. The exactly opposite argument will be found in Dr. Bernard Crick's *American Science of Politics* (1959) of which it may be thought that the relevant criticism lies in the very title itself. The odd view is here entertained that the modern approach to political science springs entirely from the (supposedly homogeneous) local American scene. Professor Jan Barentz (International Political Science Association, Fifth World Congress, "Some Notes on Political Behaviour") described this as "an outspoken, interesting, but after all somewhat shallow book." However, it contains philosophical speculations of some virtue, and better things can be anticipated from this pen.
  In the field of social prediction, attention is called to the writings of Professors E. W. Burgess and Paul Horst and to work done in the field of juvenile delinquency. The great but enigmatic work of Durkheim on suicide is not entirely out of date. Some of these things are, of course, commonplaces of the insurance companies. In a general sense, too, all judgements are forecasts. However, when Napoleon said, "to govern is to foresee," he did not mean what we mean here; his trust was in particular domination.

Although we must agree that, in the words of Professor Brogan, "a bogus neutrality" in the social sciences is to be condemned (as bogus, although not as neutral)—an issue of professional integrity and of descriptive accuracy which we shall discuss later in this book—the confident, but possibly reactionary, denial of the scientific character of these studies has not been the tendency or habit of the great masters of the subject in 'earlier ages.' This is true of Aristotle who, in his *Politics* (ed. Bekker; 8. 5), says: "Speaking broadly of politics in general we may say that these are the causes which have resulted in revolutions." (Lenin, in a famous passage, remarked these also.) It is true of Machiavelli, with his fundamental thesis in his *Discorsi* that, "men are born, and live, and die, always in accordance with the same rules. . . . Anyone comparing the present with the past will soon perceive that in all cities and nations, there prevail the same desires and passions as have always prevailed." Thus he pursues his quest into "the effectual truth of things," and explains the utility of History. It is true of Hobbes, with his exaggerated belief that this architectonic subject "consisteth in certain rules, as doth Arithmetique and Geometry, not (as Tennis-play) in practice only." "The object of man's desire, is . . . to assure for ever, the way of his future desire . . . So that in the first place, I put for a generall inclination of all mankind, a perpetuall and restlesse desire of Power after power, that ceaseth onely in Death." (*Leviathan*, chap. xi) Hobbes then discusses "the *means* to have the assistance and service of many."

Likewise, Spinoza maintained that there were exact rules; and Jeremy Bentham, following Helvétius and d'Holbach, maintained that there was 'a logic of the will,' which John Stuart Mill discusses as the basis of his Economics. Mill sought for a firm psychological foundation here. He adds (*Logic*, bk. VI, chap. x, sec. 4): "the problem of general sociology is to ascertain these [empirical laws], and connect them with the laws of human nature." Earlier, Hume had, without the geometrical illusions of Hobbes and Spinoza, restated the theme: "It is universally acknowledged that there is a great uniformity among the actions of men, in all nations and ages, and that human nature still remains the same, in its principles and operations. The same motives always produce the same actions: the same events follow from the same causes." (*Enquiries concerning the Human Understanding*, ed. Selby-Bigge, 2nd ed., 1927, p. 83) Hume must not be supposed to be asserting here, as some rush to conclude, that human nature does not change culturally, so that we shall, for example, always have slavery, cannibalism, wars, or Scottish clan feuds; but that it does not, within terms of practical reference, change 'fundamentally,' biologically, psychologically, and rationally.

Indeed the quest for uniformities, patterns, and constants may be posited as a characteristic of the human mind in pursuit of knowledge; and what Aristotle calls 'the eye for [actual] similarities,' amid the concurrent actual confusions and diversities and secondary divergencies, is the mark of all scientific genius. The evasion of it is the mark of the second-rate and the unimaginative. Karl Marx notoriously made it his life-work to expound, not only the abstract rules of a science, but a complete social determinism, in the exploration of which he held himself to be the new Darwin of the social sciences. In rejecting this dogma of material dialectic, as it is the argument of this book to do, we should not reject his massive affirmation of a science. The tradition of Bentham is maintained by such late Utilitarians as Henry Sidgwick in his *Elements of Politics* (1891). It is also appropriate here to refer to the scientific work of systematizers such as Bluntschli; and of the great Austrian, German, and Italian sociologists, such as Ratzenhofer, Simmel, Max Weber, and Pareto; of the jurist von Ihering (in terms of juristic logic); and of too little esteemed writers such as A. F. Bentley, whose *Process of Government* (1908) remained for twenty or more years so largely uninfluential and in eclipse. Although imperfectly developed, the supposition is plain in Sir John Seeley's *Introduction to Political Science* (1896) where the technical term 'politicist' is introduced, even if writers of the last century as eminent as Walter Bagehot were confused by pseudo-scientific biological analogies. It is a great pity that the solid if prosaic Utilitarian tradition has, on its sociological side, been so completely forgotten or repudiated in the British universities, although Bentham's verbal analysis is one element in a philosophy now (perhaps excessively) in high honour.

In a recent and illuminating book, *Accent on Form* (1954), L. L. Whyte truly remarks that "Science starts with an assumption . . . There exists a simple order in nature; a simple way of representing experience is possible; the task of science is to discover it." Moreover, what Bacon called "the subtlety of nature" is not less than the subtlety of man; nor should it be more difficult to find reason in the affairs of men (and even in their dreams) than in the vast chaos of the universe itself whereby it can be turned to intelligible cosmos.

As Arthur Livingston, the editor of Pareto, remarks in his Introduction to Gaetano Mosca's *Elementi di scienza politica* (in English, *The Ruling Class*, 1939): "Probably no human being since Adam has been without an approximate knowledge of the law of gravity; but no one till Galileo's day thought of centering his whole attention upon the falling object and making it the pivot of a scientific revolution. No human being since the day of Cain and Abel has been unaware that people preach moral principles and then use such power as they have often, if not always, without regard to moral principles." (Newton's apple, it will be noted, does *not* always fall.) However, to surmise, intuit, and hint is not to state alike the hypothesis and its limiting conditions. As Galileo himself observes in his *Dialogue*, "every one knows that it is gravity;" but the fact that the matter is "generally" common knowledge is irrelevant as an objection to making it specific scientific knowledge. This can scarcely be over-emphasized. That the sun goes round the earth is also the most common of daily common-sense observations. (It happens to be false and superstitious.) And, as Hayakawa (cited later) truly remarks, "politics is full of superstitions."

There are, moreover, indications, to which reference will be made later, that the reaction has now run its course against the over-confident excesses of Hegelian dialectics and nineteenth-century rationalism, a reaction which often only confounded the clarity of any empirical science and which was illustrated in economics by the sceptical criticism by J. A. Hobson of 'natural economic laws,' as the subjective prejudice of dominant groups. It is now the case *per contra*, and by antithesis, that the exaggerated relativism of Mannheim's 'sociology of knowledge,' tracing from Weber, has been discredited; and that the confusion induced by Croce and Collingwood between the 'concrete reality' of history, to be understood empathically, and the instrumental use of scientific abstraction is ending. A *systematic, empirical, observational, objective, and (in some measure) quantitative[2] study of politics may be developing*, thanks to an immense amount of recent detailed work in the field. This work initiates the revolution of taking Political Science seriously again, as it has not been taken since the collapse of the Utilitarian school. We have seen, indeed, the development of *the controlled experiment*.

The immediate question at issue is not that of the present utility of the controlled experiments (in the sense mentioned below) which have been carried out, but (in reply to dogmatic denial) that of their practicability, even with limited resources. The particular instance may even be trivial. The methodological principle is all important. Such work has in fact been done, for example, in Chicago by Professor Harold F. Gosnell in *Getting out the Vote* (1927) and, along with Charles E. Merriam, in *Non-Voting: Causes and Methods of Control* (1924), using experimental and control groups, and by Kurt Lewin with "experimentally created social climates." Similar control studies in authoritarian techniques were conducted by Dr. Ronald Lippitt (University of Iowa Studies, 1940). There is no inherent reason why enquiry should not be carried out upon the nature of obedience, for example, and whether human beings are more inclined to obey if there is a multiplication of laws and regulations, traffic controls, and comparable factory regulations or whether, as some have thought, the fewer the laws the better. This, of itself, is not unimportant. Professor George C. Homans provides other instances in *The Human Group* (1950). Cf. also (with

---

[2]Cf. this writer's article, "The Delimitation and Mensurability of Political Phenomena," *American Political Science Review*, XXI, 1927, p. 255. Along with the work of Stuart Rice and Rueff, this was quite an early statement of a point of view.

an answer in favour of the second alternative) Mr. Chester I. Barnard's *The Functions of the Executive* (1938). The mundane modesty of the examples must not deter us. Law and ordinance are issues basic for political science.

Methods in Social Science (1931) edited by Stuart Rice, carries comment by the present writer on Gosnell's work; and by Professor W. Y. Elliott of Harvard on the work of Professor W. B. Munro and of the present writer on the possibility of political science. The issue of objectivity, as raised by Weber and by Karl Mannheim, in the latter's *Ideology and Utopia*, is discussed *infra* p. 41. Both Weber and Mannheim, with their 'sociology of knowledge,' well criticized by K. R. Popper and Morris Ginsberg, illustrate the reaction against intellectualism to which I have already referred.

As touching the test of precision and *measurement*, here also striking work has been done, almost undreamed of thirty years ago. We do well to bear in mind such measure of legitimate weight as the remark of Kepler may indeed have—Professor R. M. MacIver wisely warns us against exaggerating it—when all has been said about universal or eternal values (and what we shall ourselves say, in this book, later on): "The mind is made for understanding not qualities but quantities." Fontenelle had the same inspiration, expressed in a more positive form: there is a profound aspiration of the mind to cosmos and quantitative harmonies. On the one side, mathematicians and statisticians have become curiously interested in these political patterns, as is shown in the work of L. F. Richardson; on the other hand political scientists and sociologists have had a considerable practical interest in the new statistical study of voting now called psephology.

Extensive work in quantitative analysis in politics was done by Stuart A. Rice, in his *Quantitative Method in Politics* (1928); on its basic theory by Jacques Rueff, in his *From the Physical to the Social Sciences* (1929); and more recently in *Sociometry* and in the work of Jacob L. Moreno. This line of exploration continues from the work of André Siegfried, before the First World War, on to the work of Herbert Tingsten (1937) on election statistics, and to the contemporary work of Gabriel Almond, Stein Rokkan, and Karl W. Deutsch.

The social sciences owe much, from the twenties onwards, to the work on measurement by Professor L. L. Thurstone and others of the brilliant group of the then Chicago school, which included C. E. Merriam and H. D. Lasswell, and to the work of Professors Emory Bogardus and F. Stuart Chapin. Some work was done in Cornell. It is noteworthy that today even the historians are utilizing statistical methods—for example, in studies of voting and social distribution—which give precision to earlier generalizations. A major contemporary need is for the illustration of social regularities and patterns by mathematical graphs and formulae and, hence, for the close collaboration of mathematicians and statisticians with the relevant departments of the social sciences. This is happening in economics and psychology, but (illogically) not in politics. Cf. *Mathematical Thinking in the Social Sciences* (ed., Paul Lazarsfeld, 1954). Of a more extreme character in psychometrics is the work of Professor H. G. Gough, of the

University of California, while in politics new lines have been explored by Lasswell (now of Yale) and Ithiel de Sola Pool (working with Norbert Wiener in
the Massachusetts Institute of Technology) in their team work on content
analysis in the Hoover Institute Studies done at Leland Stanford University.

Comment will be made later on the extraordinary implications of
the polling technique of Dr. George Gallup and others, who have
achieved an accuracy of prediction, in many cases to a decimal point,
not indeed perfect but yet also far exceeding that of the commercially
and aeronautically important work of the meteorologists. The more
important work is perhaps not always that done at election times,
but lies in giving on the issues of the day a true and proportionate
picture of 'the general will' (or even of the confusions and schizophrenia of that will) instead of mere partisan rhetoric about it. From
such an analysis the 'need for leadership' may, of course, emerge yet
more clearly.

Party politicians, in charge of 'party machines' designed to secure
victory at the polls, were at first inclined to dismiss this inconvenient
revolution of numbers as arbitrary, preposterous, and a mere superstition of numerology; then to condemn it as immoral and subversive
of sound principles of congressional (and party) government; but
have now come to regard the predictions with scarcely concealed
anxiety, coupled with applause and attention-calling when the diag-
nosticians are favourable to their own futures at the hands of the
electors. The polls have, indeed, become among the most important
items in contemporary practical political calculations, promoting
some candidates and serving to exclude others. The withdrawal of
Governor Nelson Rockefeller from competition for the U.S. Presidential nomination in part turned on the prognostic message of these
indices.

The notion of the party as the sole guardian of knowledge of 'what
the people think,' and uninhibited rhetoric about the people's supposed
interests, have been greatly restricted and sobered. Moreover, these
polls, content analyses, and mass observations (the last more common
in Britain) have revealed unexpected and curious popular views and
prejudices, of extreme political importance, which could not hitherto
have been guessed, let alone accurately assessed, by any previous
technique. A new light, with exact shades, is thrown upon the actual,
and often unexpected, nature of 'the Will of the sovereign People.' As
an example, a majority of the British people (a) thought that the continued explosions of hydrogen bombs would damage the health of
mankind; and also (b) declared that they were "not worried" by this

consideration. . . . Semantically, 'worried' perhaps here, for many, signified 'flustered.' Such analyses often show perchance that, not the law, but the public "is an ass." Incidentally they have shown that, in the United Kingdom, the House of Lords is more popular than the Trades Union Congress.

Other statistics show the extraordinary 'cussedness' of human nature, which has to be demonstrated to be believed. Long ago Mr. Peggotty, in the pages of Dickens, commented on its 'rumness.' Thus, when professional statements, officially confirmed, have indicated a probable connection between smoking cigarettes and lung cancer, after a brief delay the figures showing the consumption of cigarettes in the United Kingdom *rose*. Likewise, after Mr. Khrushchev had made it very clear that he would be unwilling to negotiate with Mr. Richard Nixon, the polls showed that Mr. Nixon, not preferred by the American electorate on other counts, headed the poll as the man best suited to negotiate with Mr. Khrushchev. The motivation, one supposes, was one either of obstinate disapproval of negotiation or of canny suspicion of negotiators favoured by Mr. Khrushchev.

§ii. *'Taking Political Science Seriously'*

It may indeed seem strange that Politics, acclaimed by Plato over two millennia ago as a master discipline, with a prestige comparable to Theology or Chemistry (Alchemy) later, should have taken so long to mature as a system of Pure Politics, as distinct from an art, craft or practice of Applied Politics. When Edmund Burke wrote, "no reasonable man ever did govern himself by abstracts and universals" (although, since he was reasonable, presumably he did by some principles, such as Burke's), Burke was clearly speaking only of that most applied form of all thought, the application we make in judgements about our own particular conduct and our own casuistry in our own *casus*. (Incidentally, Burke was probably better philosopher than politician; and his own practical judgements in the art, on the French Revolution for instance, have by no means generally been acclaimed as sound . . .) Not only do practical engineers, including social engineers, shape applications by the test of universals, but this is the presumed basis of any government "by Laws and not by Men." The restoration of a serious Political Science yet proceeds; and one object in this tractate is to spread the view that we "must take political science seriously"; and must distinguish it from anecdote, pamphleteering,

superstition, and political rhetoric. The present writer would be the
first to concede that undue concentration on Methodology may prove
merely sterile. He would emphasize this. Nevertheless, a wrong method
(perhaps due to regarding attention to methods as trivial) is liable
to issue in misleading results—which is worse than sterility.

The reasons which may be suggested for this tardiness are various, although
it will be noted as ground for optimism, that, despite the early work of Aristotle,
Biology only achieved systematic status in the last century, Economics a little
later, and Psychology yet later—perhaps it is best to say with Wundt in 1879.
Only in the last twenty years, after centuries of conspicuous failure, have the
alchemists succeeded in transmuting the elements, as they aspired to do so long
ago.

For one thing, since Aristotle himself, with his teleological method and discussion at the beginning of his work on the vast theme of the universal *summum
bonum* of mankind, there has been a grave confusion between (Political) Philosophy and Political Science. Politics and Sociology (not least in Germany) had
academically almost as much difficulty in emancipating themselves from Metaphysics, an emancipation still incomplete, as Philosophy had earlier academically
in separating itself from Theology in order to achieve a distinguishable sphere,
as a condition of systematic work. As Plamenatz writes, in his *German Marxism*:
"The natural sciences are now free from philosophy, but the social sciences are
still tainted with it." The resistance of the schoolmen of the universities to the
new learning of Humanism is a commonplace for the students of history. However,
it will be noted that, for example in the case of the work of Abbé Mendel, the
natural scientists have occasionally shown themselves no less reluctant to admit
new ideas which seemed to conflict with their prepossessions.

For another thing, the methodology and systematic data of Politics were both
inadequate, so that the subject matter was treated majestically like that of
Alchemy and Astrology, as highly complex and to do with 'the Emperor,' 'the
State' or even with under two score 'Civilizations,' themselves largely unique and
non-recurrent in history, and so vaguely known in detail as to defy exact analysis.
Instead of analysing calcium, nothing less than the chalk cliffs of Dover in their
entirety, as it were, concrete and poetic, would satisfy the romantic enquirers.

A cynical reason for the delay was long ago provided by Thomas
Hobbes, in his *Behemoth*: "If any man had been so singular, as to have
studied the science of justice and equity, how can he teach it safely
when it is against the interest of those who have power to hurt?"
Today, could a student show that the sovereign national state was a
dangerous anachronism, belonging to the epoch of the stage-coach
and directly conducive to war, and were the demonstration taken
seriously, the same question might be asked. And yet to gain peace
without totalitarian monopoly of power is as serious a problem in
Politics as to have full employment without inflation is in Economics.
Who can tell a Sovereign Parliament, or a Congress that is perhaps

one-third of a sovereign, that it is not a democratic system at all in the traditional, plebiscitary sense of the word where the Sovereign People is all? Or tell a member of the Soviet Supreme Praesidium that his system is not 'a fuller democracy'?

In discussions of social justice this difficulty often arises; and indeed the comments of physicists and natural scientists, natural science prophets, alchemists, and astrologers are more readily tolerated on issues of peace and war than are those of social scientists, especially as the latter, too often without practical experience themselves, do but put the politicians on their mettle. There is always a demand that the professor of the social sciences shall become a political eunuch. Nevertheless, the philosopher of Malmesbury adds thoughtfully (and we may, with a more fit modesty, do the same): "The rules of just and unjust sufficiently demonstrated, and from principles evident to the meanest capacity, have not been wanting; and notwithstanding the obscurity of their author have shined, not only in this, but also in foreign countries, to men of good education...."

However, the climate of the age has now so far changed that, on the one hand, there is today as almost embarrassingly a large demand, if still popular and confused, for the study of Politics as humanly important as once there was for the study of Economics. It is even beginning to be grasped that, as had been said above, Pure Politics[3] is as important to the direction of Applied Politics as Pure Physics is to Applied Physics. By Pure Politics is here meant the theory and analysis of the general political structure and functions.

That man's chief need today, amid technological development, is for 'the conquest of himself,' for a consciously directed development and for the rational control of his social order is almost a platitude, used alike by preachers, philosophers, and poets. On the other hand, although there are still many who wish to write essays or emotion-charged partisan pamphlets in a tradition which has lasted from the seventeenth century, or from Rousseau, to some more contemporary

[3]Not to be confused, as a general term, with the work of certain psephologists who have (perhaps rather pretentiously) adopted this name. However, the value of these studies of what might be called 'micro-politics' is of indubitable importance. M. Bertrand de Jouvenel also usefully adopts this term 'pure politics' in the sense used in the text. He speaks of the study of the circumstantial *eventum* and of the theory of 'représentation schématique de phénomènes ("Théorie politique pure," *Revue française de science politique*, vol. XI, June, 1961, pp. 365, 379). I agree that "le terme 'pure' exprime que les relations posées sont formelles, propres à recevoir différentes données empiriques." The results of micro-politics constitute, he adds, the data of macro-politics.

work (such as some of that of Laski or Cole, or of certain Conservatives), and who wish to call this 'political science,' the careful student and increasingly the general public will no longer be willing to accept this pleader's oratory or prostitute argument. Nevertheless, the desire to have full scope to promote party propaganda without calling it such, and to assume for it such names as 'Marxian science,' or 'the defence of economic laws and free enterprise,' or 'self-evident' political theory, may explain both some of the animus that exists against the development of a scrutiny of politics which cares for none of these things and which perhaps is not in enough of a practical hurry, and also the tendency to affix to it words of dispraisal.

§iii. *The Rape of the Terms*

In order to discuss any subject satisfactorily, it is preferable to have a clear idea about what one is talking. We shall never learn to think correctly, nor will learning and science be advanced, unless we humbly seek to call things by their proper names. Indeed, Economics has been happily described as "the science which enables one to understand that one did not understand what one thought that one understood all along"; and such a pedagogic technique, against the presumption of those who, to vary Locke's phrase, claim to know because they do not know how little they know, may have much to commend it. Politics has been peculiarly infested with the bombast of vague words— what Bentham called "bawling on paper"; nor is it a defence to reply (as has been attempted) that grand words always move in a perpetual condition of historic flux, a semantic mist. Patently, words do not tell us everything. (We need to look to the object; and language, with its stereotypes, may confine and prematurely check exploratory thought, its very grammar carrying unanalysed assumptions.) But words should tell us something, being signs symbolizing something precise.

Although over-preoccupation with words may lead to a decadent scholasticism such as makes men Dunce-like and triflers, lack of caution about words, too easily taken as indisputable in meaning, may lead to the misdescription and abortion of an entire science. All our discourse is conditioned by linguistic habits and twists of meaning. With perpetual vigilance we have to guard against political superstition. How indeed we need a linguistic analysis, in the good tradition of Bentham—and of Copernicus! One of the most persistent occurrences in political language and propaganda is 'the terms technique,' whereby one acquires favourable names such as 'progressive' or 'worker' or 'patriot' for oneself, and identifies the opposition with unfavourable ones.

A useful distinction is made by Professor Andrew Hacker between professional Political Theory and Ideology, not in the pejorative sense as 'the other man's theory,' but as a system of ideas designed to persuade to a given conclusion. Confucius it was who said in his *Analects* (XIII, iii): "The one thing needed is the correction of terms . . . If terms be incorrect, then statements do not accord with facts; and when statements and facts do not accord, then business is not properly executed . . . then justice becomes arbitrary . . . the wise man will on no account have anything remiss in his definitions." And "he who does not know the force of words, cannot know men" (XX, iii). Jeremy Bentham in his *Book of Fallacies* (written c. 1810, published 1824), Sir George Cornewall Lewis in his *Treatise on the Methods of Observation and Reasoning in Politics* (1852), John Plamenatz, and, in numerous important books, Harold D. Lasswell (not least in conjunction with Nathan Leites and others in *The Language of Politics*, 1949) have given attention to the same fundamental semantic theme.

The new interest in semantics, stimulated by the work of Ogden and Richards, Carnap, Alfred Korzybski, and others, has found expression in a literature more fundamental than the older studies, such as Arthur Ponsonby's *Falsehood in War-Time* (1928), and than that of propaganda in the pejorative sense, with which Walter Lippmann (a pupil of Graham Wallas) concerned himself in his *Public Opinion* (1922, reprinted 1960) and Harold Lasswell, more systematically, in his *Propaganda Technique in the World War* (1927).

Among recent more popular studies one may mention S. I. Hayakawa's practical *Language in Action* (1941) with, for example, his happy distinction in political speech of 'purr' words and 'snarl' words, to which we might add consideration of politically useful, deliberately undefinable words such as 'snollygoster' (used by Harry S. Truman), 'swizling neutrals' (Kipling), 'mugwump,' and so on. In the words of Robert Merton, "a basic requirement of research is that the concepts, the variables, be defined with sufficient clarity to enable the research to proceed." More broadly, we are concerned to develop for the social sciences what Professor G. C. Homans has called 'a common language' (or maybe 'an uncommon language' accepted by all professional students), to which task Professor Lasswell has also directed his great abilities. However, perhaps the classic guide here, the indispensable *Politics* of Aristotle, remains among the best, and shows that poetry and even humour need not always be excluded. Our task, here as elsewhere, will be 'to get back to Aristotle.'

The elementary precaution of making our definition, as the necessary prelude to any precision, is not always taken on the ground that everybody knows in politics what is meant in popular usage anyway. Hence, popular superstition is always common sense; and common sense is right. In politics, as in economics, people feel that they know too well about common experience to need to be taught. However, the economists have advanced further in combatting superstition, and in insisting on the exact, technical use of words than have the politicists or sociologists. Nevertheless, because the public inadequately appreciates the objective realities of Economics and Politics, though it appreciates well enough the objective realities of Physics, "within a considerable range," as Professor J. K. Galbraith remarks in his *The Affluent Society* (1958), "[the individual] is permitted to believe what he pleases. He may hold whatever view of this world he finds most agreeable or otherwise to his taste."

It is easily supposed that the meaning of such words as 'liberty,' 'independence,' 'equality,' 'democracy' (along with the very practical obligation to be killed or imprisoned for them), 'socialism,' 'the workers,' is a meaning self-evident. This is not the case and conduces to lack of integrity and to what Bentham called "nonsense on stilts." There is scarcely an abstract noun in frequent use in political discussion which is not also a clap-trap word of ambiguous meaning. The practical politician naturally hesitates pedantically to disturb his electors about words which each thinks he understands as well as, if not better than, he does himself; or to throw doubts upon the credentials of what have been called 'purr' words, with which he may stroke them, or of 'snarl' words, which have emotive or magic power in declamation. Popular usage, however, may be emotional, vague, multiple, and for scientific descriptive purposes quite unsatisfactory. It is not enough for political theorists to go around labelling events "good things" or "bad things" and all that—it is not good enough. Hence Bentham contrasted 'descriptive' language, approaching mathematical symbolism in accuracy, and language 'evocative' (sometimes called 'prescriptive'), both by appraisal and by dispraisal, as in advertising and in platform oratory designed to get out the vote.

Economics, Psychology, but especially Politics, since it touches the nerves of power, have been affected by this disadvantage, although it is corrected in Law. It should, for example, give us cause to pause when we note that Aristotle, the father of systematic empirical politics and *maestro di color che sanno* (Dante, *Inferno*, iv, 131; "master of them that know"), the sponsor of much of our technical terminology, describes 'democracy' as "a perverted form of government," in accordance with an attempted formula of precise definition. This issues from his rejection of any equality which "renders equals to unequals," and also of unqualified majority rule in its own sovereign interest.

The opposite error to that of inattention to definition—so that (as is remarked in *Alice in Wonderland*) "When I use a word, it means just what I choose it to mean—neither more nor less. . . . The question is which is to be master—that's all"—is the error of supposing that to every word, especially one scholastically defined, there must correspond an object. Thus it is supposed that, because there has been a weighty amount of learned disquisition about 'a supreme, irresistible, uncontrollable authority,' or 'sovereign' (Sir William Blackstone, *Commentaries*, 1769, II) which satisfies a certain desire for logical elegance, therefore such a Sovereign Power must *eo ipso* actually exist. Sometimes, as Hobhouse pointed out, the State itself takes on, in some measure, this same metaphysical and ghostly character, as an organic something, incubus or succubus, separable from human flesh and blood, the irrelevancy of which vampire superstition to politics is not observed. This may be called 'the error of false hypostasis.' As Confucius also said: "Do not hypostatize that which does not exist."

Here we may ponder the words of John Locke: "Vague and insignificant forms of speech, and abuse of language, have so long passed for mysteries of science; and hard or misapplied words with little or no meaning have, by prescription, such a right to be mistaken for deep learning and height of speculation, that it will not be easy to persuade either those who speak or those who hear them, that they are but the covers of ignorance and hindrance of true learning." It will, moreover, be noted that not only do men abuse language but, owing to obsession with abstractions and with comfortable or established stereotypes in their minds, they become incapable of perceiving freshly and accurately the facts of experience.

S. I. Hayakawa, in his *Language in Action*, writes that "the willingness to rely on words rather than on facts is a grave disorder of the (scientific) evaluative process." At every stage the student needs to have his attention directed to check words and theories by empirical observation, and to look from the party argument to the active practice. Conversely, 'behavioural studies' should not be confused with 'behaviourist studies' (as by J. B. Watson and Arthur Bentley) which may be bad psychology and worse philosophy. Further, just as Max Weber's psychological 'types' tend to be at once vague and yet static, so Bentley's 'interests' tend to be impersonal and without basis in the individual to the extent of becoming, like 'groups,' in the hands of some writers those very metapolitical entities that Bentley himself professed to condemn.

As I have said elsewhere (*Science and Method of Politics*), we should "base ourselves on observation of social behaviour" and study the objective. However, Hayakawa concludes, as emphasized above, that we have always to repeat "cow$_1$ is not cow$_2$; cow$_2$ is not cow$_3$." We must define and distinguish.

To the importance of emotive words in political Magic and Propaganda, thanks to which whole commonwealths may by power of this Word be overthrown without war, as Joshua by his trumpets overthrew Jericho, we shall return later. It is enough here to emphasize this 'terms technique,' or what I will name 'the Rape of the Terms.' The appropriation of certain terms, of a laudatory character, as by the Soviet propagandists—usually beginning the most controversial statement with the words, "as is universally known" (cf. "as every schoolboy knows")—can be decisive in policy and propaganda. Moreover, there are many nouns in the language which carry an emotional overtone of praise or blame, and few adjectives which do not. Indeed they are far fewer than is generally supposed. The Greeks were among the first to shape the character of political theory by their use of terms such as Aristocracy. But the process can continue as one that conduces, in propaganda, to victory or defeat. The task of the policy-maker, or his subordinates in public relations, is to explain his policy through emotionally sympathetic formulae. It is elementary in the study of Opinion and Reporting that precisely the same event can be truthfully described in emotionally opposite fashions. On all of this we can say that, whether or not Logical Positivism or Analysis can be argued to produce an Occamite 'Termism' or decadent scholasticism in philosophy, its application is most seriously required in the study of politics.

Many political thought-processes are of a semi-hypnotical (magical) order. Thus many simple folk reason (within the direct experience of this writer): "The Soviet Union is a union of the Socialist Republics. Socialism is on the side of the workers. I am a worker. Therefore I must support the Soviet Union." No term is analysed. In our contemporary culture 'worker' is a magic word, meaning either 'not an idler' or 'a manual worker earning weekly wages.' 'Private enterprise' can be either the laudable effort of the adventurous individual or the operation of a monopoly, so long as it is not a state one. Even such ordinary adjectives as 'high,' 'low,' 'red,' 'black,' 'yellow,' all have emotional coloration in certain contexts or by their suggested analogues. Hayakawa cites the following opposite British descriptions of guerrillas in the Boer Wars: "They [Boers] were sneaking and skulking behind rocks and bushes," or "our fellows [British] were cleverly taking advantage of cover." Again: "the Senator was obstinate"; "the Senator courageously stood by his principles"; "the Senator was the only one who voted against the bill." Again, in epitome: "I am firm; you are obstinate; he is a pig-headed fool." A recent journalist has added a further illustration. "Those who support the leader (or dictator) are loyalists (or lick-spittles) who are proud (or bribed) to fight (or persecute) the furtive (or underground) Communist (or Liberal) renegades (or dissenters) and their henchmen (or colleagues) who plot (or plan) to impose (or impart) lawlessness (or democracy)."

§iv.   *Back to Aristotle*

As touching the word 'politics' itself: 'it is all politics,' 'playing politics,' 'I have never yet been called a politician' (from a United States Secretary of the Interior), "confound their politics," 'the politics of the Democratic party,' 'politic' (a thirteenth-century adjectival use, in contrast to 'despotic,' but also meaning 'diplomatic'), 'going into politics,' 'British imperialist politics,' 'politics and economics,' 'ecclesiastical politics,' 'Aristotle wrote his *Politics*,' 'the study of politics'—all have different shades of meaning, quite subtly interconnected. Many of them are derogatory, which will be a matter for curious interrogation when we come to deal with resistances to power. Since we cannot fall back here upon popular usage for clear guidance, we are well advised to turn to etymology. In this book we shall understand by Politics roughly what Aristotle understood by it; and the implications of its connection with the word *polis* or City-State (as distinct from what R. M. MacIver calls *The Modern State*, 1926, in his book of that title) we shall discuss later.

An interesting and perverse usage will be found in Mannheim's *Ideology and Utopia* (p. 170): "Politics as politics is possible only as long as the realm of the irrational still exists (when it disappears, 'administration' takes its place)." One has travelled far since Plato, and not for the better.

§v. *The Simple Elements*

It is generally accepted that the maturity of any science is indicated by the condition of its general theory and by the ability to discover formulae which will subsume the whole field simply, demonstrably, precisely, and in a manner that relates to other fields of human knowledge. The vision, which is the act of true genius, which can see a pattern in the objects of knowledge which was always present, which was not seen before, and which once seen can never be overlooked again, is usually an astoundingly simple vision. The mathematical formula of the structure of the universe can be written on half a sheet of paper. Locke thought the same was true of political principles, an assertion either very true or very false according to the context. Sometimes the layman mistakes these formulae for statements about commonplaces which everybody knows. Newton's law of gravitation is the formulation of a most commonplace experience—apples had fallen for centuries before Sir Isaac—but to the commonplace facts are added an intelligible law of uniformity, amid the infinite confusion of the atomic universe, with a precision upon which one can build. Man's mind makes that universe simple or apprehends an immanent simplicity within it. ('Some men,' that is. Other men temperamentally prefer to dwell on 'a big, blooming, buzzing confusion.') No accumulation of descriptive social studies (important although the Linnaean work of truly scientific and accurate cataloguing may be) or numbers of essays on values or pamphlets on reforms can of themselves, however erudite, produce such a theory, comparable to the general theories in Sociology. Maybe we cannot better Marx until we can be more simple than Marx. The truism has to be reduced to exact truth. Sometimes indeed the formula does not confirm the most patent commonsense observation made every day, such as that the sun goes around the earth, but offers an alternative pattern of explanation (just as in an optical illusion of cubes we see first one pattern obsessively, then another) and an explanation more complete. The major advances are indeed often made, not by examining complex conclusions or like an Euler studying the irregularities—this comes later—but by attending to the so-called axioms too uncritically accepted by a Euclid, a Kepler, a Newton, a Marx, impeding a wider theory and emerging in some exaggerated form of error as logical deduction proceeds.

To recapitulate, we may suspect that only small scientific advances can be made, and all measurement and experiment will be frustrated, if we take as our data something rare, highly complex, and intermixed, such as some eighty or so instances of states and their sovereignties, their laws and wars, peaces and police, full of dangerous analogies from past history, or (with Arnold Toynbee) some twenty odd civilizations or cultures, and suchlike dignified, subtle phenomena; or even take Max Weber's 'types and roles,' which have had on the whole an inflated reputation and confusing influence on much sociology and are even sometimes open to the accusation of substituting jargon for insight. Rather we should take things commonplace, frequent, simple, and comparable. We must beware of what I will call 'the error of grandeur.'

In the past the 'architectonic' study of Politics shone with some of the greatest names of learning, not least Anglo-Saxon, from Aristotle to Machiavelli, Hobbes, Locke, Bentham, Marx, Mill, Spencer. Today it is noteworthy that, speaking of outstanding masters in all the social sciences, Professor David Riesman in his *Individualism Reconsidered* (1954) cites Durkheim,[4] Simmel, Max Weber, Marx, and Freud. Only one of these can be called a political scientist. Something has clearly gone very wrong. Likewise, *The Making of Society, an Outline of Sociology* (ed. Professor R. Bierstedt, 1959) provides excerpts from Plato to

---

[4]Durkheim's work Professor Talcott Parsons was good enough to allege that I had made "respectable in America," in a little introduction to Durkheim's *Rules*

Mill, but then very significantly turns its attention exclusively to sociologists from Comte to Parsons, as if substantial and relevant political theory had ended with Mill and Marx. My distinguished Cornell colleague, Professor Andrew Hacker, following Professor George Sabine among Cornell historians of political theory, also terminates his excellent survey, *Political Theory* (1961), with these last worthies. However, indeed, political theory continues. It may yet be that some of us have been talking sociology all our lives without knowing it.

A definition in science must be useful and more than an arbitrary verbal scheme. Politics as a theoretical discipline, or Pure Politics— just as one may speak of Pure Physics, which is indeed Physics with the physical left out—I defined in the second book of my Systematic Politics (*Principia*, 1929, chap. II,[5]) as "the study of the control relationship of wills . . . the study of society in so far as it displays the control relationship of men with men." This definition, because it is unusual, is not therefore wrong and may be precise. It will be noted that what is here involved is a study of a *Function*: that of control in various forms. And attention is directed to a dynamic *Process*, the endeavour to maintain or change this control, involving a regularity of pattern perhaps susceptible of being expressed in terms of formulae, hypotheses, and laws. The Conventions and Institutions and rules, legal or otherwise, and values, which issue from or are shaped by the needs of the functional process are derivative areas of study.

"It is possible to say that every society and every social group, capable of consistent action, may be regarded as an organization of the wishes of its members." (R. E. Park and E. W. Burgess, *Introduction to the Science of Sociology*, 1921). The *wish*, however, must have reached the stage of translation into action by *will*, degrees of which we shall have to analyse. Again it is possible to treat our subject as "the science of institutions . . . or more specifically of institutional structure," as does Talcott Parsons (*Essays in Sociological Theory*, p. 235); and indeed our concern and curiosity have to do with the Structure of Society, as has physical science with the structure of matter. However, the issue of this institutional stress, taken incautiously, may be the underestimation

---

of *Sociological Method*, written as a reply in an argument of mine with Professor C. J. Friedrich. Earlier work, however, of introducing Durkheim than this and the translations by my friends and students, Professor George Simpson and Miss Solovay, both of Cornell, was done at Chicago.

[5] *An Introduction to the Principles of Politics: A Study of Political Rationalization* (London: George Allen and Unwin; New York: Macmillan; 1939), henceforth in the text called *Principia*. *The Science and Method of Politics* (London: Kegan Paul; New York: Knopf-Croft; 1927) is henceforth called *Science and Method*. (This was in substance produced in thesis form in Cornell in 1924). The third volume of the Systematic Politics, *The History of the Political Philosophers* (New York: McGraw-Hill, now Harlem Press; London: George Allen and Unwin; 1938), is henceforth referred to as *History*.

of personality and its motivations, the ignoring of psychological problems of human dignity, the unconcern with rights, and the begging of fundamental questions, so that a theory logically emerges of social communism, pseudo-community, or pseudo-*Gemeinschaft*. On the contrary, the unit for our subject is (as Talcott Parsons, following Weber, most truly says, *ibid.*, p. 228) "the human individual as actor"—or rather, the socio-political 'act.' Few contemporary sociologists have made a greater contribution than Professor Parsons or even a comparable one; and his use of terminology deserves the closest and most respectful attention. There are always the gravest risks when we get away from the observable individual, Smith or Jones, as a basis of study, and start talking about Russia and what 'she' did, America and what 'he' (Uncle Sam) did or, more basically, of 'us' and 'them.' This easily ends in those collectivist and even totalitarian dogmas or fictions which, if the political scientist must study, the political philosopher is tempted to condemn. In order, however, that we may abstract from all the concrete or historico-poetic richness of human personality that with which we are scientifically concerned, the words 'will' and 'act' are less dangerous than the 'richer' words 'person' and 'actor.' The theses of Control, Market and Equilibrium (this last stated only inadequately by Spencer), maintained in the *Principia* and also in *Science and Method* (part II, chap. III), will also be found interestingly developed in Professor G. C. Homans' *The Human Group* (chaps. XI, XVII) and is discussed later.

Frequently, instead, some such phrase as 'study of Government' is used. Thus, Arthur Bentley, to whom reference has already been made, speaks of the need to "plunge into any phenomena or set of phenomena belonging to the roughly recognized field of government." This admonition is good in so far as the stress word is 'any'; but the implication is yet that, although 'rough,' *what* this field will be is something self-evident. But this use of terms implies that, were the State "to wither away," which Marx and Bakunin (and apparently Mannheim) agreed upon as goal, then matter for political study would be eliminated, which is at least what has to be proved. Any definition which begs the fundamental questions at issue is itself faulty, superficial, and dangerous. Today we are overloaded with immensurable observations, too few of which have undergone any Linnaean tabulation: the problem is to introduce order out of a complexity of history nearly as vast as in the infinite universe of the natural sciences, for which purpose we have to study both the nature of the science, if it be such, and its method (which I attempted in an earlier book).

Political studies may be regarded (as indicated earlier) as being just the study of 'institutions' or use of public administration, without regard to political structure or functions. The unsatisfactory nature of this description has already been commented upon. It leaves us preoccupied with the accidental. Politics, like war, is indeed an arena of chance and luck, but we must not become submerged by reflections on the prevalence of these chance and irrational factors. A definition in terms of 'Government' is certainly better than this, especially if we construe government widely in terms of its essential, and not its conventional, characteristics. This means that we set out, discarding conventional prejudices and apologia, to study (with an adequate multiplicity of data) the phenomena of the control of men, just as the economist studies the phenomena of production and distribution of wealth.

An attempt has indeed been made to define the field as that of 'Legal Government.' There are certain objections to this which, if we are to be intellectually thorough and not arbitrary, we may hold to be fatal. (*a*) The first and obvious one is that we should also, under democratic theory, be concerned with 'the governed,' whether we are thinking in State terms (which has additional difficulties mentioned above) or otherwise. (*b*) The introduction of the adjective 'legal,' supposedly a reinforcement, in indeed question-begging. One of the major issues in political studies is that of the critique of positive law (itself a product and not a canon of organized society) in terms of natural law. What then, precisely understood, is 'legal'? We should not put into our definition or axioms the very thing we have to discuss and explain. (*c*) Is tyranny legal government? And, if not, should our anaemic discussion of politics exclude reference to a Lenin, a Mussolini, a Hitler—or our discussion of parties exclude the Communist party? This would be a fantastic pedantry. (*d*) The so-called classical theorists were preoccupied with issues of the good society, freedom of speech, human equality, the democratic pattern, and the class structure. How far are these items of 'legal government'? (*e*) Would any political theorist from Plato to Machiavelli have accepted this definition of the field—or would even Hobbes, with his elaborate psychological preoccupations and basis in discussion *de homine*, have been content with it? Is it not in fact a prejudice of men brought up in post-seventeenth-century western European national states and, moreover, propaganda (if unconscious) for the *status quo*? (*f*) How far are contemporary parties, pressure groups, status groups, public opinion polls properly brought under the caption of 'legal government?' (*g*) Is not the most enterprising and fruitful work today not being done by scholars precisely in those studies which only by the most forced construction can be called those of 'legal government'?

The student is here referred to the quite admirable and indeed indispensable survey, subsidized by the Carnegie Foundation, made by Professor Charles S. Hyneman and published as *The Study of Politics* (1959). Professor Hyneman explicitly suggests that, if some teachers limit themselves to the description of institutions and object to others going further—no one objects to the valuable departmental specialist—it is because of their own training. They feel that they would be incompetent and at sea in these other areas, from which they therefore 'head off' students. Were this indeed true (and among major scholars of integrity I am not at all satisfied that it is true), it would be a very sordid reason. It would not, however, be without many precedents in academic history from the days when a decadent and nominalist scholasticism, with its logical preoccupation with terms, sought to head off the ambitious 'New Learning' of the Renaissance. And it may, of course, be admitted that even the best scholars have a prejudice in favour of teaching their pupils what they themselves can display to best advantage. Also, university teachers must beware of 'playing the examination game,' and preparing subjects 'for examination' where, as with 'facts,' the answers can be quickly ticked off by an examiner—'yes' or 'no'; 'right' or 'wrong.'

In his significant article, "World Trends in Political Science Research" (*American Political Science Review*, June, 1954), Professor C. Brough Macpherson of Toronto writes that "the bulk of the research being done by the institutions is the collection of data about the actual functioning of the political process," of which "the potential value is undoubted." However, (*a*) no amount of collection of data of itself produces a theory or a synthesis; (*b*) actually this research is often motivated by a patent and acknowledged anxiety about the genuine validity of accepted democratic theory; (*c*) "work in the direction of systematic theory is so far rather limited, but . . . there is increasing awareness of the need for it." In the United Kingdom there is more attention to value judgements, "perhaps because they are fairly sure of their values." The political parties are allegedly founded on value principles. It may be added that the political parties and their defenders are usually in fairly violent conflict about the value of the respective values. Partisan pamphleteering results.

The point about systematization is made with force by Professor D. Easton, of Chicago, in his *Political System*. He is not alone. Cf. "Knowledge of an isolated 'fact' may be quite useless erudition; the isolated 'fact' must be related to a larger theory of political behaviour before the significance of the 'fact' may be perceived" (V. O. Key, *Politics, Parties and Pressure Groups*, 1945). Cf. also R. M. MacIver, *Community* (1917, p. 5): "*Wherever living beings enter into, or maintain willed relations with one another, there society exists.* All such willed relations are the primary social [? political] facts." It may be submitted that *any* aggregate is, at one level, a society, but (lacking the element of control) is not a *political* society.

Sometimes systematization is limited to 'the machinery of government.' It is on this basis that many academic departments of Politics are called indifferently departments of Political Science or of Government. To refer, then, to the subject as 'government' seems to imply a loaded relationship of 'governor' and 'governed' or what Professor Karl Loewenstein chooses to call 'power-addressees'; and it might indeed be more democratic to speak, at this level of the common man, of a Department of Citizenship . . . Patently 'government' is but one species of 'control.' Likewise 'decision,' and the study of this executive act, although important indeed, is different from 'control' and its study.

In Britain the field of discussion tends to be especially preoccupied with argument, not about 'machinery' as distinct from history, principles and elements, but about 'political obligation' and "Whether Will, rather than Force, is the basis of the state" or "Is the State prior by nature to the Individual," which the late T. D. Weldon of Oxford, in his *Vocabulary of Politics* (1953), suggested were 'nonsense questions' (we discuss this issue later) or related to 'pseudo-axioms,' for which alternatives in method of approach should be discovered. It is noteworthy that, in his vast *Study of History*, although this is based upon the relationships of 'cultures,' following F. J. Teggart in his *Theory of History* (1925), Professor A. J. Toynbee makes his elucidation of 'laws' a matter involving human 'wills' and a matter of 'a psychological explanation of regularities in human affairs' (*Study of History*, vol. IX, p. 327). In the words of Professor V. O. Key of Harvard, "the main concern of the political scientist is the discovery of these uniformities in political behaviour." We do not require what A. F. Bentley, in his *Process of Government* calls "a dead political science . . . a formal study of the most external characteristics of Governing Institutions." This criticism is endorsed by M. Bertrand de Jouvenel, in his brilliant book, *Sovereignty* (1957, English ed. only, p. 295).

There is indeed no theoretical reason why the study of controls in the relations of wills should be confined to the relationship of human wills. In Biology human beings are rightly seen as of a wider animal family, and not as absolutely *sui generis*. We need to leave the door open to biological contributions. Extremely interesting studies of practical importance could be made of "the ants' republic, and the realm of bees" (what Toynbee calls "an apian social science," in which 'wills' or 'choices of the unit' might take a very unfree form); of the social relations of totalitarian termites, and of anarchic swallows; and of the order of discrimination and of domination, not least sexual among apes; and, in pecking, among fowl. Much light can be shed by such studies, as also by anthropology, proto-history and the study of dreams, upon the largely instinctively determined and obscure conduct of human beings (described by Taine as *bons gorilles*), whose society is usually presented merely in terms of their articulate, rationalized, and formal, or even legal and 'blue-book,' social arrangements.

Thus, as Spinoza says, writers have "chiefly conceived of men, not as they are but as they themselves would like to be" in theory or according to the law or according to a bureaucrat's dossier, and hence "have generally written satire." Indeed we do well, as in Proverbs, to "consider the ant" (as does Bergson). It will aid, rather than hinder, an exploration of 'Human Nature in Politics,' by giving an impersonal *point d'appui*. Economy of space alone, and not any arbitrary distinction, imposes limitation here. The imperatives of survival, of power, and of adjustment between the pleasures of reproduction urging societies to grow and the pains of hunger operate also here.

§vi. *Pure Politics and History*

The fields of History, including Proto-History, and of Anthropology, are quite distinguishable methodologically from that of Politics as an academic discipline. It is inexcusable to confuse them—although we may most truly say with Aristotle (and thereby avoid pedantry) that "Politics is the best of the sciences," embracing all the unspecialized field of controls. This distinction holds, even if it happens to be true that much of history has been concerned wtih the conduct of kings, generals, and rulers, and with foreign wars and peaces. The task of the historian is to record ('natural history' apart), in von Ranke's often misquoted phrase, what particularly has come to pass in human affairs or to relate to us, descriptively and critically, what the chronicler has already recorded in detail, or even to show it as saga with the amusing arts of Clio, herself a Muse.

Professor C. E. Merriam referred to history as concerned with *miranda* or the sagas of a nation's heroic and Homeric achievements in some memorable age and with the glorious traditions of a people. History may indeed, as Dionysius of Halicarnassus suggested, be "philosophy teaching by examples," and may nobly enrich thereby our education in the humanities; but it is not the task of the historian as such to philosophize (weighty though his informed general judgements must be as a man) or to generalize; nor is he, again, a scientist. We may say with the singular candour of such a historian as Mr. A. J. P. Taylor, following Hume, that "I am a historian because it is fun"— a kind of competition with the entertainment trade—or, with Professor Raymond Aron in his *Introduction à la théorie de l'histoire* (1938), may hold that historians are concerned with the sequence of particular causes and particular effects, but not (as with science) with a system of such sequences. Beyond the particular sequence lies a realm of individual judgements. History is sometimes a photographic and sometimes an impressionist art; but it is an art. It is impossible, in one sense, to write definitive history, since history by its nature is infinite.

The classical statement here of Schopenhauer, following Aristotle, holds good. It would, moreover, be entirely erroneous to suggest that History should not exist on its own educational account, but "*only* as a fact-gatherer for the social sciences," a contention which (despite one respected critic, Professor C. J. Friedrich) has never been that of the present writer, who, trained as an historian, began his own original investigations from the problem of the practical meaning of History, and who, nevertheless, was in revolt against the precious fun of seducing students into studying at dedicated length the Norman origins of the English jury system or the seals of the Plantagenet kings. Mr. A. J. P. Taylor himself, a distinguished historian but weak as a political scientist, is prepared in his quite remarkable book, *The Causes of the Second World War* (1961), rather contemptuously to hold that, apart from such general causes as (I cite his own instance) that automobiles are the cause of an automobile accident, only particular historical or occasional causes deserve attention. The instance seems to be singularly ill chosen and the approach amateurish, particularly to the causes of war, and not that of a contemporary sociologist. The view maintained here is the opposite—which is yet no criticism of the actual acumen of Mr. Taylor's historical survey, with its Oxenstjerna-like philosophy, *Quantula sapientia mundus regitur.* This may inspire poets such as A. E. Housman: it is small consolation for the war-dead (or for those killed in the road carnage). Political Science is not dull; but it is not just 'fun.'

It is sometimes suggested, on the other hand, by philosophers that history *alone* gives the correctness of the social whole, without which a full and even 'empathic' understanding is impossible. The Neo-Hegelians, Croce and Collingwood, and the Holists, are inclined to this error (in the particular context) or 'fallacy of misapplied concreteness.' On the contrary, every science deliberately uses abstraction as a tool for clarification, for further empirical research, and for the production of results applicable in controls of, or power over, the concrete. On the plane indeed of 'the facts of history,' every 'fact' has its material causation in a myriad other impinging facts, and the quest for the efficient cause becomes the hopeless one of infinite regress. If we were fish always swimming in water, instead of having evolved as men walking on dry land in three dimensional space, we would probably not be as prejudiced about individual efficient 'causes' striking us or propelling us from without. Our world would be one of flux. It takes all history to cause all history. Admittedly the political theorist and sociologist require the work of the historian of the past and of the social student of the present to provide the material for the Linnaean work of classification. But political theory is no more the mere exact discipline of the history of institutions than it is a matter of essays and party pamphlets, or, as Laski held, 'a branch of ethics.'

It was Schopenhauer's judgement that there could be no such thing as a Science of History, although there could be a species of quasi-science, a more or less accurate scholarship by the historiographer in the technical use of records. (Cf. also H. A. L. Fisher, *History of Europe*, 1935, vol. I, p. vii). The issues of the relation of the Philosophy of History and the Science of Politics I have discussed, at length, in the first volume of Systematic Politics, *Science and Method*, part I; and they need not be rehearsed here. If, however, (the theodicies of Bossuet and Vico and the reversed theodicy of Comte apart) it were empirically proved to be correct that there were, as Spengler and Toynbee (in his monumental *Study*) suppose, large-scale cycles or static patterns in history, of known and variable or unconditional recurrence, then this judgement would have to be changed. The criticism of all such 'scientism' by Dilthey is important. See also Professor Raymond Aron's illuminating study, *Introduction à la théorie de l'histoire*.

The supposition (significantly less emphasized by Professor Toynbee in his later work) is that history directly displays the operation of the laws of a social science which is one, not of individual recurrent acts, but of entire societies with patterns cyclical in epochs, entities integrated in the form or *Gestalt* of cultures), and perhaps explicable by Jungian psychology. This position, which awaits proof, is not to be confused with the very sound judgements, to which reference has already been made, (*a*) that there are indeed constants or patterns in individual human behaviour and 'a patterned system' based thereon, in group behaviour, when and if human nature is confronted in society with difficulties or inducements of a recurrent order; and (*b*) that past history is for the sociologist, like contemporary history, one vast storehouse of data for his science, as 'natural history' is for the biologist and ecologist. I would not wish to deny that the world may move on a cycle of extremism and reaction. (*Vide* my article, "Toynbee's 'Study of History'" in *Toynbee and History*, ed. M. F. Ashley Montague, 1946; and Professor Toynbee's replies in his *Study of History*, vol. XII, together with my review of this volume, *Contemporary Review*, July, 1961.) This, however, does but reiterate Lord Acton's theme: "History does not repeat itself, but historical situations recur"—which is basic truth.

It is in many ways remarkable that, when some historians cease to be men of detail, they tend to precipitate themselves into historicism—or belief in dynamic sweeps of history, subject to some fate or what Professor K. R. Popper has called an 'Oedipus effect'—and to indulge in long-range prophecies. There is to be some kind of 'science of impending developments,' which, even in their detail, are necessarily such. This joins well with a Weberian holistic theory of 'roles'; but has been criticized admirably—though I would not commit myself dogmatically to his nominalism—by Professor K. R. Popper in his excellent and astringent *Poverty of Historicism*. This work also (pp. 24–6) carries an attack upon doctrinaire opposition to quantitative methods in political science. For the 'historicists,' says Popper, there is a "denial of the applicability of the experimental method" and an assertion that "history, political and social, is the *only* empirical source of sociology" (p. 39).

I need scarcely underline my agreement with Professor Popper's view of "a methodology [that] would lead to the study of the general laws of social life with the aim of finding all those facts which would be indispensable as a basis for the work of everyone seeking [to conserve or] to reform social institutions (p. 46) . . . I have in mind the existence of sociological laws or hypotheses which are analogous to the laws or hypotheses of the natural sciences (p. 62) . . . I do not admit that the situation described [leading to the conclusion that we must never assume a universal law] is in any way peculiar to the social sciences, or that it creates any particular difficulties . . . there seems no reason why we should be unable to frame sociological theories which are important for all social periods." (pp. 100, 101) For a discussion of what is meant by a 'social fact' and an 'event' *vide* the writer's Introduction to the English translation of Emile Durkheim's *Rules of Sociological Method* (1895, trans. 1938), commenting on Durkheim's own discussion.

Much of the treatment, by contrast, of Pure Politics, outlined above, makes use of abstractions, such as the 'Political Act' and even, more tentatively, the 'Political Man,' and the derivation of Authority from Freedom. The term, indeed, 'Political Man,' used by me in my *Science and Method* and recently adopted by Professor Lipset, is a Latin one (as *homo politicus*) of the age of Hobbes. It anti-dates 'economic man,' and is most useful as a concept. It cannot be too much emphasized, not only that we are entitled to use hypotheses, if they will conduce to satisfactory experiments and fruitful results, but that abstraction itself is not a distortion of science (unlike concrete history) but is of its very essence. Without abstraction there can be no science; and advance comes with the subtle and fit choice of abstractions. Whether we are philosophical determinists or not, we must agree that, so far as our knowledge goes in the world of history and reality, there can be no set deterministic logic of Historicism. But we can agree with Bentham that, at least within the field of hypothesis and abstraction, we have a logic of the will and we find Professor K. R. Popper, in an invaluable discussion, admitting what he calls a 'logic of situations' and what is here called a logic of means. As M. de Jouvenel has pointed out, in his important recent writings, the achievement of specific values apart, there are such permanent structural considerations as the maintenance of the stability and the survival of the society. To say this is not for a moment to deny that, when we come to practice, political scientists, precisely like economists, must adjust themselves to the 'total situation' or that, as in economics, grave practical errors may develop if they do not do this.

On the methodology of hypothesis the classical book by Henri Poincaré, *La Science et l'hypothèse* (1916), still merits consultation. Professor D. Riesman *et al.* in *The Lonely Crowd* (1950, p. 279), dealing with such measure of abstraction as is involved in sociological 'types and roles,' after the school of Weber, writes of, "in Max Weber's sense, 'ideal types,' that is, constructions necessary for analytical work." Although the remark made by Edward Westermarck that German metaphysics gave "the impression of depth because it was muddy" is grossly unjust and displays contemptible national animus, it may yet be doubtful whether all the work of the German sociologists who have been led by Max Weber has helped clarity of treatment. An 'abstract model' and an 'ideal type' are not identical concepts. It must always be borne in mind that Max Weber was an economic historian with radiating interests rather than a professional sociologist, great though the impetus was which he gave to the development of modern sociology. As Professor Lipset (*Political Man*, p. 19) suggests, as a historian he probably exaggerated the factor of religious ethic. His self-chosen task was rather one of classification by types than of constructing hypotheses, psychological or otherwise, for empirical tests. These types themselves, part neutral scientific model and part factual norm, are too imprecise to be invariably useful instruments of research; and can be gravely misleading, because they are imposed upon the material rather than derived from it. As Raymond Aron (*Introduction à la théorie de l'histoire*, p. 327) points out, he inadequately distinguishes here 'the existential' and 'the desired.' Weber's honour is rather that he was a pioneer, who began almost from scratch and from whose vast and erudite (if not unprejudiced) works his disciples have posthumously developed coherence. Professor Talcott Parsons has done this with singular distinction. For some of these comments I would record my debt to Weber's sometime student, Dr. A. W. Stonier.

In the present work the direct debt to Hobbes and Machiavelli is clearly acknowledged, but diverse debts are also owed to Bluntschli, Ratzenhofer, von Ihering, and Simmel. The scheme offered here is not derived from Bentley, and is in opposition methodologically to much of that of Rickert and the Webers. Reference should also again be made to the discussion in J. S. Mill's *Logic*, bk. III.

§vii.   *The Identity of Political Science and Sociology*

The task of Anthropology is to describe human customs and the past habits of peoples. The distinction between Sociology and any form of Anthropology concerned with contemporary conduct, unless we either choose to attribute a higher degree of scientific synthesis and system to the former or to limit the latter to studies of 'primitive' peoples, is arbitrary and a matter of verbal usage. The work of such a writer, for example, as Malinowski on warfare is of the highest relevance for a sociologist or politicist.

R. R. Marett, in his *Anthropology* (1923), says: "Anthropology is the whole history of man as fired and pervaded by the idea of evolution." This, of course, imports a philosophy or at least a hypo-thesis into the treatment. F. J. Teggart in his *Prolegomena to History* (1916) goes so far as to write: "The formulation of a theory of progress is the aim of a branch of philosophy, known as Sociology," here basing himself on Professor T. N. Carver of Harvard. This is not the view taken here, which distinguishes apocalyptism from science. It may be added that, according to Professor Shils (*The Present State of American Sociology*) the scientific plight of Anthropology and of Psychology is worse than that of Sociology. Cf. also the article by R. Firth and G. P. Murdoch, in *American Anthropology*, vol. 53, Oct.-Dec., 1951.

Sometimes a distinction between Social Anthropology and Sociology is made on the ground that the social anthropologist, unlike the sociologist, draws as it were a circle, selects a unit, and studies all social phenomena within the selected unit. However, this is an arbitrary distinction and rather one between the 'micro-sociologist' and the 'macro-sociologist.' The great work of W. I. Thomas and F. Znaniecki, *The Polish Peasant in Europe and America* (1918–20) is always regarded as a great work of sociology, although it 'took a unit'; and the same remark can apply to the sociological work of Tom Harrison in Britain, in Bolton and Black-pool, as well as in North Borneo. The conclusion would seem to be that 'Cultural Sociology' might just as well be called 'Contemporary Cultural Anthropology'; whereas the sociology of social inter-relations—and this enters into the definitions of many sociologists—even beginning (as did Morgan and, earlier, Aristotle) with the kinship group and its constant pattern, is, as 'Political Sociology,' something else again and is the theme of this book.

It is sometimes stated that Sociology is only concerned with 'social positions,' structure and institutions and, bluntly, "does not concern itself with individual people" (G. Duncan Mitchell, *Sociology*, 1959, p. 36, who adds [p. 37] that "we should avoid introducing value judgements."). Were this so, Sociology is indeed sharply divided from Political Science since political scientists, Marxist and non-Marxist, while students of 'society,' have not been prepared to accept the social position or the institution passively, as mere datum, but have sought to show what caused the institution to develop. Most of the better of them (including even the early Marx himself) have never forgotten the concrete and real basis in the relations of individuals. They have concerned themselves, also, with the individual sources of initiative and decision. The opposite course leads to the dangerous 'metapolitics' of pseudo-entities. Even in dealing with such a 'social fact' as alcoholism, the first step (with Durkheim) is to survey the obdurate characteristics of the data without preconceptions, but the second is to break down the situation analytically (cf. the writer's *Liquor Control*).

A possibly useful distinction, however, can be made between the formal or specific sociology (of Human Organization and Controls and Institutions, and their conventions or habits) and the general sociology or anthropology (of Arts, Crafts, and the like, and their conventions, and of Civilizations and also of Cultures). This latter, *Kultursoziologie*, is, superficially and in the present state of our knowledge, on a distinct plane, not fully integrated with social organization. (The final validity, as we shall show when we discuss cults, of this distinction of discipline is dubious; and useful border work is already being done on those relations of politics and art which Plato noted. In 'a general theory of action,' according to Professor Talcott Parsons who speaks with authority, culture is one of the three expressions or elements, along with personal psychology and social organization.) The distinction between Politics and Physical Anthropology—or, again, Cultural Archaeology—is clear.

The close connection between Sociology, often in this connection called Cultural Anthropology, and the study of Politics in primitive societies is well illustrated by a comment by Mr. G. Duncan Mitchell. "If in any particular society we fail to find clear developed legal and political organizations, we should examine its kinship system to see in what way it replaces them. Social order, then, is our point of departure." (*Sociology*, p. 77)

Sociology and Politics, however—or, more precisely, the Sociology of Organization (or Political Sociology) and Political Science as one aspect of Pure Politics—are indistinguishable. We may, indeed, choose to introduce the term 'Political Sociology,' especially if we wish to rescue Sociology from being an *omnium gatherum* of the academically dispossessed, who range in their studies as far afield as vital statistics and matrimonial habits. But here either we are using the word 'political' in the old sense, in which case we mean the sociology of the state— which is not the customary outlook of contemporary sociologists who usually repudiate any such emphasis on distinction—or (which is usual) we mean precisely the study of society as organized and the study of the rules of that organization. The residue is the study of *un*organized activities or of society from some other aspect. If, with so many sociologists, we introduce the concept of organization into the definition, then Political Science is Sociology. The profitable study of political life can be nothing less than the study of organized human society; and any alternative concept—for example, study of the state exclusively or of state government—leads to narrow error. It is a waste of academic time and energy to divide the two disciplines, as well as being a methodological error and an incident in the strange histories of university administrations. This does not mean that some students will not study Municipal Government and others (with Sir Henry Maine) patriarchal rule in primitive societies. Questionable margins are reached when we start academic studies of how to organize boys' clubs.

Political Science is Sociology. Most attempts to draw distinctions between Political Science and Political Sociology are bogus and gravely obstruct the advancement of learning, since they conduce to mutual ignorance about related sections of what is one field and hence to sterility. This is not, of course, to depreciate the importance of detailed studies of Civil Government, e.g., of Municipal Government or even of sanitary departments, sewage disposal, and what Hans Zinser called the theme of 'rates, lice and history' as a municipal affair. But it is surely a waste of academic time deciding whether discussion of the political élite, the class structure, or the party system are matters of Political Science or of Sociology, or which subject has been most benefited by the work of Michels, Mosca, Pareto, MacIver, Lasswell, or de Jouvenel. The competent scholar must be fully at home in both

fields. The utterly deplorable and artificial thing is the mutual ignorance that prevails. (One very recent textbook on Sociology omitted
all reference to political scientists in the index . . .)

"Human society, to the philosophic inquirer, is political society; and therefore
the 'social science' or 'sociology,' of which Mr. Mill [*Logic*, VI, chap. ix] has so
well described the limits and object, and for the investigation of which he has
laid down the conditions with so much precision, appears to be in fact no other
than political science." (Sir G. C. Lewis, *Treatise on Methods*, bk. I, p. 51).

For reasons of a historico-academic, rather than of a logical, order,
Economics and Political Theory have appropriated the prime cuts
in the subject matter of social sciences, leaving to Sociology, as a new
claimant, the rump. Thus Professor David Riesman speaks of himself
as having, as a sociologist, studied "movies, comic books, magazines";
and there are the classical 'sexological' studies of Kinsey and Havelock
Ellis. The grand themes of affairs have been those to do with *raison
d'état*, so that even economic factors were neglected until the last
century and the coming of Marxists and demi-Marxists; and Sociology
was either left with the apparent trivialities such as surveys of voting
polls or industrial group relations—which have since become patently
so important—or with, as its speciality, unspecialized social theory.
Likewise Astrology and Alchemy had to do with the grand destiny
of man, the philosopher's stone, and other premature attempts (realized in our own days) at the transmutation of the elements; and
were for a long time abortive until they produced exact Astronomy
and Chemistry. Sociology, freed from a hampering tradition of the
magnificent, metaphysical, and complex, has been able to study
detail, such as conditions of obedience to factory rules or local by-laws,
or family and kin groups, or human relations in industry, or voting
and public opinion, which are of high scientific and practical interest.
Voting is certainly a political phenomenon. So is the class structure.
Aristotle, it is noteworthy, most properly begins his *Politics* with
studies of the regulation of the phratry or clan, and of the nature of
the family as basic—and concludes without providing his readers
with any metaphysic of sovereignty.

It is, of course, possible to argue (as do some sociologists) that there is a
social science, but no such thing authentically as political science, so that "it is
highly questionable whether 'political theory' in a scientific rather than in an
ethical and normative sense should be regarded as a fundamental element of the
theory of social systems. It is more logical to regard it as a field of application
of the general theory of social institutions, but one which is insufficiently differen-
tiated to be treated as an independent discipline for many purposes." This
is merely a matter of verbal convenience; and, if this contention by Talcott
Parsons is accepted, then what we are here concerned with is 'social science.' The

rest is ethics. Nevertheless, in practice this can lead to discarding from consideration the rich work of political students of many centuries (certainly not excluding the great work of Meinecke on *raison d'état*), who certainly did not regard
themselves as mere *a priori* speculators—a far more opulent treasury than a
sociology, still jejune and ill-recognized, as yet has to offer. Conversely, we
can allege that "political science has the mind without the body, and sociology
the body without the mind"; but most sociologists would object to having themselves regarded as mere hodsmen of trivia, devoid of a general systematic theory.
The contrary was the view of Comte, Spencer, and of modern German and American sociologists, such as Talcott Parsons, Homans, and Merton.

The story of the carve-up of subjects in France has been interestingly different.
Sponsored by the anti-clericalists, in the days of the Third Republic, the academic sociologists got support and respect, whereas *science politique* (which was
not a science) was until recently left to the usually conservative and traditional
lawyers.

Sometimes indeed, as with Max Weber and Dilthey, the concern has been with
'type,' *Gestalt*, and historical development, rather than with recurrents and
constants (that is, with behaviour that always recurs under given intermittent
conditions). But this is a subordinate distinction of method. Weber's preoccupation, for example, was with something as near to the core of contemporary
politics as the class structure; so was Mosca's. It is more prudent merely to say
that any political scientist today will be a very poor one who is unacquainted
with work done under the captions of 'sociology' and 'social psychology.' A quite
admirable study of British political parties is the work of the Reader in Sociology
at the University of London, Dr. Robert T. McKenzie. But few people would
therefore assert that political parties are not within the proper ambit of political
science . . . It is to the disadvantage both of the political scientists who too
often are professionally complacent in not reading the works of the sociologists
and of the sociologists who find it unnecessary to read those of the political scientists!

It was the great work of Professor R. M. MacIver, at Columbia University, to
bridge academically the two disciplines and to introduce order into the then
chaotic data of Sociology. This would be a sound technique for new chairs in
the British universities, although there is little probability that this judgement
will be acted upon unless the government establish Regius chairs. The philosophers, who dominate the scene along with the historians, have different views.
M. Jacques Maritain's comments in his *Reflections on America* (1958, p. 151)
on the academic conservatism of the University of Paris can be read with profit
and amusement. Professor Theodore Abel's study of the emancipation of Sociology from academic swaddling clothes in Germany also merits notice.

§viii.   *The Psychological Basis*

Of all these inter-disciplinary relations which are of practical importance for Political Science, the most important is that between Politics
and Psychology. For the present writer it is fundamental. The imma-

turity of Psychology in developing an adequate general theory of human motivation has had until recently a retarding effect upon the development of the ancient discipline of systematic Politics, even more than has the paucity, in some fields but not all, of the historical and sociological material (costly although much of this itself is to collect in any useful form).

The early works of W. H. R. Rivers in his *Psychology and Politics* (1923) and especially of Graham Wallas in his *Human Nature in Politics*, if informal, was authentically pioneer. Wallas' work, acclaimed repeatedly by Mr. Walter Lippman in America, has for a variety of reasons, not always creditable, received far less than its due acknowledgement in Britain. Professor H. J. Laski did less to praise his great predecessor than he should—a compliment returned in kind by Professor Michael Oakeshott. The tradition in approach which traces from Wallas is one of the most impressive contributions in Politics made by London University. The academic students of society had their attention turned to psychological issues by Tarde, Gustave Le Bon, and others and, later, in certain respects by Pareto. Recently an immense amount of valuable work has been done on this approach by entire schools of social psychologists and in the academic schools of political science by the writers of the (then) Chicago school. Especially reference must be made to the fruitful collaboration of the sociologists Talcott Parsons and E. A. Shils with the behaviourist psychologist Edward C. Tolman in *Toward a General Theory of Action* (1951). Professor Tolman's little study in peace and war, *Drives towards War* (1942), with that of E. Durbin and J. Bowlby (in *Democracy and War*, ed. G. E. G. Catlin and E. Durbin, 1938) certainly deserve attention.

Some ambiguity here is created by the suggestion that politics or sociology, so treated, should be called Social Psychology; and, again, that all psychology, since human beings are born to be social, is indeed social psychology. Neither position can be maintained. The facts that human beings are born within the material and economic limits set by geography, and again are also determined in experience by population factors and by the plurality of human beings, now called the facts of geopolitics and of demography, are certainly facts most important (as Plato argued) for the developing psyche; but they are external to it and its dynamism, and have their own specific consequences, which can be abstracted and distinguished. The distinction between Sociology and Psychology is rightly emphasized by Emile Durkheim. On the one hand, then, it is unprofitable to minimize this harshly non-subjective, non-volitional element arising from the objective quality of the social order as an external condition (as was too usual with individualist theorists before Hegel) or to fall into the anti-sociological error of 'psychologism.'

On the other hand, although human psychology may indeed (even, although negatively, with a Crusoe or the Desert Fathers) be shaped by the social factor, there may yet be scientifically different emphases, so that clinical analysis no less than physical psychology cannot (as Gordon Allport stresses) usefully be reduced to Social Psychology, a term held by many psychologists such as E. B. Titchener to be itself misleading and illegitimate. There is at present an excessive and unfortunate tendency under behaviourist influences, and fraught with specific political consequences of a totalitarian order, to resolve the psychology of the ego and person into the sociology of institutions, despite the obstinate facts of biology. It is not an attempt likely to be successful, any more than that of the Marxists, after the work of Engels, to resolve everything whatsoever into the dialectics of physical matter.

Certain objections to professional study by political scientists of those inter-relations of psychology and politics, first elaborated by Plato, are stated by Professor K. R. Popper (*The Poverty of Historicism*, pp. 65, 157–9) and in an excellent book, *John Stuart Mill* (1953, pp. 79–86), by Professor Karl Britton. As against Mill's contention that all phenomena of society are phenomena of human nature, Professor Britton argues: "What happens in society commonly depends on ways of individual behaviour which are never observed in any other context, and on effects of human conduct which would be completely trivial were it not for the fact that they are multiplied a million-fold in the lives of the masses . . . evidence that men in general have such appetites and ambitions [as Marx supposes] is simply that they work together for the exploitation of nature." Society, social behaviour and institutions are all. Here Karl Britton goes too far. This is a materialist behaviourism beyond the limits of Marx himself and is, in my view, nonsense. It also discards the structural method of Hobbes, who deduces his arguments *De cive* from the themes ultimately set out in *De homine*, and assuredly connects the two. The opposite method evades the most fundamental problems on the nature of freedom and of human values. It also omits the sensible evidence for men's appetites taken from the study of the men themselves and their common nature.

It is erroneous to assume that the study of men (and so also of their institutions) is the same thing as 'a great man' theory of history and the study of the biography of particular individuals; or, again, that it is the same as a discarded rationalism (which contemporary sociology has even excessively rejected) which would falsely suppose psychology to be the study only of conscious intentions, and institutions to be solely rational and contractual structures.

Further, this thesis is guilty of 'the error of grandeur,' upon which we have already commented. 'What affects human beings is trivial,' and beneath notice; and only when multiplied by masses does it become important. This theme is a major barbarism. Politics is indeed, in one aspect, the study of society or of 'masses'—but of masses of sentient human beings with consumer wants. Population problems are of course very real. Population relations shape possible individual choices. But the deduction indicated here is a basic anti-humanist error. Also, we must not confuse the truism that all human beings are born into a society with (to use Dr. K. Britton's own term) the 'falsism' that nothing a man does need be studied by political scientists except his behaviour in relation to the pre-existing institutions of a particular and historical political society. If all that matters is "the correlation of one social fact with another social fact" (an ambiguous term; cf. my Introduction to Durkheim's *Rules*), hypotheses concerning the 'out-going' creative element in human nature, as distinct from the 'impress' of materialistic environmentalism and determinism or the Humean cult of irrational habit, are wiped out. I fail to see how, for example, the basic political problem of Freedom can thus be adequately studied. I doubt whether this is what Professor Britton here intends in his minority view. This view is yet actually encouraged (*a*) by the preference of some political scientists for a narrowly descriptive study of institutional facts *without* a general theory; (*b*) the sensitivity about all psychology of many professional philosophers who fear that the foundations of their scholastic logic might be upset. These professional views are human, but they are not sound.

The present writer is in no way inclined to seek to reduce logic to psychology or even to indulge in 'sociologies of knowledge.' He abjures a rigid and determinist psychologism as he does a dogmatical determinist institutionalism. Professor Popper truly writes (as against Karl Britton) of "the quite unassailable doctrine that we must *try to understand* all collective phenomena as due to the actions, interactions, aims, hopes and thoughts of individual *men*, and as due to traditions . . ." (italics mine). He is, however, so far attached to the values of *individual* freedom as not only (rightly) to fear a dogmatic psychologism, but also (surely wrongly) to distrust all general psychological hypotheses as explanatory of human conduct, almost as much as he distrusts historicist dogmas and apocalypses. Freedom is hence paradoxically found in positing the rational individual as providing the irrational or "wayward" element in social life. Here the individual's especial actions are not, as with Britton, "trivial" but are the nemesis of 'plansters'—and this so much that instrumental hypotheses about a common human nature become unsound. A strange thesis—truly directed against psychologism (as dogma), but perhaps founded on a misunderstanding of what some of us have proposed in the social hypothetical method here, which allows for, and stresses, human motivations springing from the depths of human nature, while in no way denying the utility of derivative piecemeal approaches and changes. We could end by denying any 'human nature' as 'false realism'; and by denying psychological uniformities along with it. And we could end also by denying the most human quality in man, his reason and the predictability of rational conclusions, along with the statistical probabilities of mass emotions. On the contrary, we return to the conclusion: "Are these hypotheses fruitful?" and not "May they upset particular philosophies, whether of extreme environmentalism or of extreme individualism?"

Neither Psychology nor Political (or Sociological) Science can without residue be resolved into the other; nor again can study of the conduct of Politics be resolved into comparative observation of institutions and remain guiltless of a hypothesis or theory of motivation. To say with Bentley that "we know men *only* as participants in [social] activity" (italics mine) is an error or else a sophism on the word 'to know' as implying plurality. These are not the sole 'manifestations.' To say that "there is no idea which is not a reflection of social activity" (such as the poems of St. John of the Cross . . . ?), or to commit one-self to the Marxist view, so much contradicted by Marxian history itself, that ideas are only "the torches in the procession," sounds like a bold and brusque truth but indeed involves an unscientific distortion. The best guide for the politicist, as touching this relation of Politics and Psychology, is perhaps to be found in the outlook of that great and too little honoured man, Graham Wallas, and in the pregnant remark of Lord Bryce (to which he himself, maybe from lack of equipment, paid too little attention), in his *Modern Democracies* (1921): "Politics has its roots in Psychology." Certainly this is the understanding which H. D. Lasswell and myself had thirty years ago; and which has been abundantly illustrated since.

Our particular approach as well as that of Merriam, and, rather later, of Russell, de Jouvenel, and others was discussed in the UNESCO Report of 1950, *Contemporary Political Science*: "the attempts to apply the findings of psychology to political science . . . the use of the power concept" (cf. pp. 82, 83, 180). The UNESCO Report of 1956 added "a 'political' point of view had come into acceptance and use in an area of political science where it previously had been absent" . . . "two decades of continuous advocacy of the view that power is the central concept of political science—as wealth is of economics—have had an effect in forwarding the politicization of political science *and in determining its nature.*" (*Political Science in the United States*, pp. 24, 77; italics mine.)

It may perhaps be added that reports on 'Political Science in the United States' or 'Political Science in Western Europe,' while useful (and Professor Jan Barentz' book of the latter title merits careful consideration), are all too traditional and may yet be held to offend against the fundamental spirit of all science, which knows no national or regional boundaries. The true scientist, like the true humanist, is as such an international, whether he reside in America, Europe, or (as often) both. In the words of Professor Barentz himself, "Political indictments against [or for the benefit of] any nation are never wise." In the sciences they are deplorable.

2. Definitions and Functions

§i. 'Homo Politicus'

Within the field of the social sciences it is methodologically sound and not practically difficult to distinguish between: (a) Social Genetics, Demography, Ethnology, Vital Statistics, and those studies broadly concerned with the factors of time and of the relations between the human generations, with studies of the family, if made with biological emphasis, falling on the frontier; (b) Economics, Geo-Economics, and studies primarily concerned with the distribution in space of the raw materials of human production, and with the production, distribution, and exchange of material wealth and with the Technology here involved; (c) Politics, and the Sociology of the political structure and its changes and of human group organization and controls, with, for example, the study of the organization of industrial manpower, as distinct from the technology of production, on the frontiers of Economics. Economics moves on the frontiers of Psychology when it emphasises acquisitive desire; and on the frontiers of Politics with the study of social organizations dominantly shaped by economic production and exchange.

The study, for example, of trade union structure and of personnel management is, in our sense, essentially political in character. It is of contemporary importance indeed, and certainly not a mere matter of 'hands' for production of 'things' (ambiguously called 'goods') and of the assimilation of human beings to 'objects' ('objectification') or to the fluidity of money capital. It is of extraordinary practical importance, in our study of the State or of International Organizations, to recognize that the State or indeed these Organizations are not segregated; and that the study of union organization, business structures, and ecclesiastical obedience is political in its fundamental nature. This approach involves a new and important advance and school of thought. The technical production, however, of industry on its organizational side is primarily a matter of economics and is so to be measured. A project, again, may be physically feasible and popular politically in terms of votes, but be unsound economically in terms of measurable wealth.

When the sovereign electorate of a country persistently elects a government which is unwilling or unable to increase a production upon which the standard of living of the country eventually depends, here we have a nominally political situation patently limited by economic factors. Where we have an industrial concern increasing production by technological methods which yet arouse, as interfering with the rights of labour, the hostility of organized trade unions, then the situation is a primarily economic one, conditioned by political organization. Concretely the two situations are joined. But to clarify, say, the first situation, we shall have incontrovertibly to undertake a sound and economic analysis and then convince by its truth the holders of political power. On the other hand, the error of the so-called Vienna School of Economists is that in dealing with unemployment they have been hesitant about reversing this legitimate abstract process of exposition, and about treating holistically the unemployment problem as also a practical political one. Hence they become dangerous *political* guides who, for the sake of doctrine, could provoke revolution. A legitimate abstract economic analysis, owing to an inadequate political one, has been applied to a concrete situation which is largely political without being recognized as such.

Much recent experience has tended to show that research investigations made by economists, for an example, in aid to underdeveloped countries, were far more appropriately matter for research by politicists and students of government. The case of the Belgian Congo shows how mere economic development alone proves an abortive experiment, and how political issues tend to run away with economic. The economic test of efficiency in production yields to political tests of power. As to the investigation of industrial organization, which is really rather a matter of political than of economic structure, but still yields to a quantitative approach, attention is called to the distinguished pioneer work of Professor Philip Sargent Florence, and to the recent work of J. G. March and H. A. Simon, *Organization* (1958).

Politics claims scientific status on precisely the same basis and by the same arguments as Economics. And most of those arguments which seek to demolish Politics as a science would demolish the theoretical basis of Economics also, whose founding fathers in a great age made progress by the bold abstraction of an 'economic man.' Hence we may care to say that we are concerned (to use with caution a seventeenth-century term) with *homo politicus*. His use, if at all, will lie in his pragmatic convenience in explaining what happens.

All working models, such as *homo politicus*, must be used with common sense and recognition that they have no blood but are only convenient abstractions, which the philosopher and historian can correct to get the whole, concrete, incarnate man. Based upon psychological hypotheses, they are themselves plural and postulational, not dogmatic. Marx certainly used such models (even if dogmatically) as the Capitalist and the Proletarian. However, in *Das Kapital* (ed. Modern Library, I, p. 668) he writes, with wit: "To know what is useful for a dog, one must study dog-nature. This nature itself is not to be deduced from the principle of utility. Applying this to man, he that would criticize all human acts, movements, relations, etc., by the principle of utility, must first deal *with human nature in general* [italics mine], and then with human nature as modified in each historical epoch. Bentham makes short work of it. With the dryest naïveté, he takes the modern shopkeeper, especially the English shopkeeper, as the normal man."

BROADLY, POLITICS IS THE STUDY OF SOCIETY AS ORGANIZED; AND HENCE CANNOT BE DIVIDED FROM SOCIOLOGY (Proposition 1). An unorganized crowd, without leadership or common motivation, is not political. As a led herd it is political. The propositions stated here are instrumental hypotheses, not dogmas. The reservations to this proposition, which check us from regarding the human individual as entirely social, have already been made. The individual is not only 'a member of the group,' but a member of a plurality of groups, and not totally a member of any one of them. It is the virtue of the school of Political Pluralists to have established this. He is also a psyche with an inheritance in part (as with other animals), but not entirely, biologically determined, apart from social education or environment. The poet and mystic, the individual *an sich*, is not solely a creation of the current and particular social environment. Aristotle, for all his Greek social emphasis, does not make this dangerous error, and even Marx (who, unlike some totalitarians, was not a social pantheist) refers back the case for social reforms to the benefit of the individual. In the words of the official exposition (*Textbook of Marxist Philosophy*, 1937, Leningrad), "the individual does not exist merely to serve the interests of the community." Conversely, however, the interests of the community cannot be resolved into those of one generation of individuals in one particular place, as Burke well recognized. "Why should I concern myself," as one cynic said, "about posterity? What has posterity done for me?" References to 'society,' a monistic 'social environment,' or to 'social forces' and institutions, such as those made by Marx, Engels, Mannheim, and other exponents of determination from without inwards, and even made apparently, in some passages, by Plamenatz —man as a concrete individual being flotsam on a social or material sea (an error avoided by Plato)—must always be judged with this in mind. It will be considered further in our discussion of Society and Community. What it is true to state is that, as Plato saw, Individual and Society eternally react upon each other in a continuum; and that any abstract dichotomy of the two is fruitful only of error.

There are industrial and (as Hooker said) ecclesiastical, as well as civil, municipal, and international, politics. Any other construction of the subject matter is dangerously narrow and, it should be emphasized, may heavily prejudice the practical conclusions reached. More precisely, as stated in my *Principia*, we may say that *Politics is a study of all the plural relations of controlled and controller. It finds its core in these social problems of the objective control relations of human beings and wills,* and unlike Economics, not in production and distribution relations with economic materials. Social activities, such as free play and art, not involving control, lie outside the primary ambit of Politics. To the role of Art (*mousikē*) in shaping education in ends and values we shall return.

This definition of the political field will be amplified later. It is interesting to note that Mr. Chester Barnard, in his *Function of the Executive*, uses 'political' in this wider sense, as above, in connection with industry. Most industrial relations are more the politics of men than the economics of 'hands.' Later, also, we shall see that certain methods, such as the Marxist, tend to minimize the differences by resolving politics into economic or material determinism or dialectic, deifying or reifying History, or, conversely, by resolving in practice economic activity (as Dr. Peter Drucker points out in his *End of Economic Man*, 1939) into issues of social and political controls. This first point, the resolution of politics into economics, was rightly noted and challenged by Dr. Eugen Dühring, Friedrich Engels' victim and antagonist. Dühring's contention deserves more study than it has received. According to Marx himself (as de Jouvenel points out) what is fundamental in economics is the control of manpower, rather than the specific consumption goods or play of the market price. With the development of nationalized industries and of public bodies as employers, an awareness of this fundamental function becomes increasingly momentous.

The views of John Plamenatz referred to above will be found in his *German Marxism* (pp. 309–17, especially p. 316) where the comment occurs: "Every man . . . is, indeed, conscious of himself as a unique individual *only because society has made him self-conscious*" (italics mine). The fact of self-consciousness would seem, however, to arise from the existence of an objective world, including that of other individuals and of physical objects, and to be not exclusively social. Fichte is a dangerous guide here. The character of the self-consciousness could be ascribed to many factors, including hereditary urges (or are these to be called social?). This is compatible with Mr. Plamenatz' respect for institutions as objects of study, but I cannot believe it to be his final judgement or compatible with much else that he says. It could end in a sophisticated form of praise for 'organization man' (cf. p. 104 *infra*).

The importance of including, within the field of Politics, social, industrial, ecclesiastical, international, and familial activities of control, in terms of that function of human activity, will be shown later. It amounts to something that is nothing less than a revolutionary change in the approach to Political Science. It carries it away, not only from partisan pamphleteering and *belles lettres*, but also from technical juristic studies on the state and journalism on institutions. This inclusive definition of the field is called, by some writers, 'politicization.' The character of the subject takes a new and clear shape. We are confronted at present with an epoch of political forms in transition. A political theory will be not only worthless but misleading that can only deal with them in static terms. Such a theory, to be worthy, must probe beyond the conventionalities of the routine textbooks.

In the UNESCO Report of 1956 on the teaching of the Social Sciences, to which reference has been made, the author says: "Not only are concepts and techniques being absorbed from other 'behavioural' disciplines, but these disciplines, increasingly and importantly, have been turning to the study of political phenomena. . . . This matter deserves emphasis." The technically political aspects of activities is perceived, where of recent centuries (partly under the influence of economists and of the lawyers) it has been ignored.

Geopolitics and the practical sciences of strategy and logistics also move on the politico-physical border-line, mixing the elements of will and of determination with non-human factors such as those of geography, upon which indeed the historians Buckle, Mahan, Mackinder, and Haushofer placed such stress. It is not beneath notice that, even in such a severely practical art as strategy, von Clausewitz takes time to emphasize the importance of having a basic theory.

§ii. *Practical Politics as Craft*

Politics is sometimes regarded in two ways: as a Practical Art or craft—including statecraft (with its implication of 'power' or *Kraft*); or as an academic and theoretic study, Political Theory. The former thesis is especially espoused by politicians who have been brought up 'in the university of life' or by 'the hard way.' Rather: POLITICS IS

DIVIDED INTO THREE PARTS: THE ART, AND (WITHIN THE THEORY) THE PHILOSOPHY AND THE SCIENCE (Proposition 2). It may be suggested that the practical use of the theory is to train politicians in the wider ranges or, again, in the immediate techniques of action, bearing in mind the dictum of that great practitioner, Benjamin Disraeli, that a merely "practical man is one who practises the errors of his fore-fathers." If this training is not given, it may be suggested that it is because the theorists do not understand their own task and have not adapted their product to their true customers. They are content to train schoolmasters and not politicians. It is also subsidiarily useful that political theory shall inform citizens about the context within which they have to live their lives and which is called 'the Web of Government.' Indeed, in the great controversy discussed by Sir Charles Snow between natural scientists and humanists, it may well be that university administrators should consider whether political theory, including at once social science and humane philosophy, does not provide the necessary middle term for a sound education.

It may further be suggested that, just as no economist can well talk about his own subject who is innocent of all knowledge of the methods of work of factories, banks, and the market (and is indeed dangerous if he tries so to do), so no political scientist is competent who has not served a personal and immediate apprenticeship in the actual stresses of practical politics, and may also even be a bad guide. Up to the present, universities preoccupied with the task of instructing the subgraduate[1] young, as distinct from the advancement of learning, have tended institutionally to ignore this. On the other hand politics is not (according to that worn *cliché*) "the art of the possible," for this description does not explain a Napoleon, a Lenin, a Hitler, a Churchill, or a de Gaulle. We cannot know so accurately at any given moment what human nature is capable of in the conquest of means to attain its ends; and we should not deceive ourselves by identifying the practicable and the mediocre. Rather we may share the view of the Cardinal de Richelieu that statesmanship is the art of making possible that which is necessary.

On this issue cf. this writer's McGill Inaugural Address, "Political Theory: What is it?," *Political Science Quarterly*, March, 1957 (now published, by permission, separately by the McGill Bookshop); and his paper before the Triennial Conference of the International Political Science Association at Rome, 1958, on "The Relations of Theory and Practice in Politics" (published in the same

---

[1]The word 'undergraduate,' like the word 'sociology,' is etymologically a bastard term. This tends to be forgotten by captious linguistic critics of the latter term alone.

pamphlet); and his article "The Function of Political Science," *Western Political Quarterly,* December, 1956. In the useful words of Professor Harvey Wheeler (*Natural Law Forum,* 1959, no. 1, p. 163): "To be worth the name, political theory must direct itself to the solution of real problems." (This article carries a most interesting review of M. de Jouvenel's *De la souveraineté,* 1955.)

It is not surprising that Mr. H. S. Truman (in an address to the Pilgrims in London, 1956, of which the theme was not, significantly, repeated in his address to the American Political Science Association in September of the same year, when he merely suggested that no 'impartial' scientist could be a Republican . . .) supported the view that politics is an art only. The superb political artists will always be likely to take this view. The task, however, of the scientists is to analyse the work of the artists and to show what they are really up to and, maybe, "to frustrate their knavish tricks." A magistral analysis, so effective that this easy view of politics can scarcely be maintained any longer, will be found in the great work of Schumpeter, *Capitalism, Socialism and Democracy,* pp. 256–89. Conversely cloistered academics, who hold that political theory should be exclusively a matter of imparting a kind of Rochefoucauld-like or Burkean wisdom, should reflect what personal experience they have to presume to instruct politicians brought up, for example, in Kansas City or in the Roman Curia. Indeed, I can forsee instructional courses on the theme: "How does one 'square the Pope?'" (a dictum attributed to Cecil Rhodes, a practical statesman) or "How many divisions has the Pope?" (apothegm of Stalin, a practical revolutionary).

The educative and ethically normative value of study, through *Political Philosophy,* of 'the grand tradition' in human thought or 'traditions of civility' (such as I have attempted in my *History* and which have been so maturely set forth by Professor Sir Ernest Barker) we may indeed grant, if, as I believe, such a tradition exists. We may add, as a value of humane studies, "the broadening of civic intelligence and the extension of civic knowledge," the making of the 'urbane' and 'civil' man, as distinct from the barbarian and Philistine of power and material engineering. The engineer, unless educated to check professional bias, tends to reduce 'souls' to 'hands,' 'men' to 'objects'; to produce (as said above) the current disease called by the French *objectification;* to defeat even his own assigned ends; and can be accused, whether he is Russian or American, of being a natural fascist or totalitarian. This danger in training is today admirably recognized in major institutions and not least in the great American engineering schools.

The utility of *Political Science,* on the whole a more 'modern' development, remains to many obscure, although the hopes of such men as Machiavelli and Hobbes, Bentham and Sidgwick, Comte and Spencer, Ratzenhofer, and Max Weber in this and allied fields are clear enough. What, we may ask, is the utility of Economic Science? The reply would be, to take but one instance, that the work and hypotheses of such men as Lord Keynes enable us to cope with the hitherto insoluble problem of recurrent economic boom and slump, called the economic cycle, a problem once regarded as inevitable, in a fashion that can save not only billions of dollars but also much human misery and social unrest due to indebtedness and unemployment.

Our answer, in the case of Political Science, is analogous. To take but one instance, if we could so far analyse (as Ranyard West has urged) the concrete and practical problem of collisions of group powers, following the periodic upsets of the balance of power, and could discover some system more stable than that of more than eighty sovereign states, we could advance far towards solving the puzzles of international war (while gaining insight into the 'rigid-group' or 'class' causation of industrial war). We could advance towards decreasing armament expenses and the vast conditioning of civil policy, including trade and even scientific education, by fear of war and by the needs of armaments; and towards increasing production and the reduction of human misery. The question, like that set to Lord Keynes, is hypothetical but very practical. A few decades ago the answer would have been that these difficulties lie in the nature of things and that the puzzle is miscalled, since it admits of no solution. "War always has been, and is, inevitable." It is proper that man, in the needed social study of man and in mastery of his own affairs, should attempt the social and human solution, lest he be damned and destroyed by his own progress in the physical and non-humane sciences. There is a further point. In the cause of clarity of system we have used the phrase, 'back to Aristotle.' But do not let us repeat the remarkable blindness of Aristotle in failing to perceive that the political system which historically he was describing was passing away under his eyes. It is more than likely—it will even be a major contention of this book—that our current political system is doing today precisely the same.

Our times also are different from past times. They need political systems as different from those of past centuries as an aeroplane is from a wagon. We need to be prepared to discard the rag-bags of conventional political ideas about means, which we inherit from the days of William of Orange and Victoria, and to rid ourselves of constitutions dating from the horse-and-buggy age. Even the American Constitution and the eighteenth-century doctrine of the Division of Powers may not be sacrosanct and beyond critical discussion in a smaller world, where not isolation in experiment, but the fiercest competition in power, is a practical reality. Perhaps the entire American Constitution is due for a revising convention, and not only the Eighteenth Amendment, which this writer in some small measure contributed to change. We may indeed *desire* one thing, but we may *need* another. We should have the moral and scientific courage for this criticism, not for the sake of novelty as such or 'action,' but because we may suspect that old means must always stand in need of new testing in new circumstanses. If it be said that this is revolutionary, and that inherited national systems or the orthodoxies of Left and Right are sacrosanct, the reply is that the world today, unless it has audacity in new adaptation to new inventions, is speeding to its own destruction in very fervent heat. It is a radically new system of means, well based on tested principles and natural law, which may alone be competent to preserve the inherited values that may be worth preserving. To insist on treasuring old political machines in a new enterprize with new demands is to guarantee an explosion. Too many holders of academic chairs, content to mull over with their examinees three-centuries-dead theory, seem incapable of making this calculation or of wishing to contribute an efficient answer. Leaving the metaphors of engineering on one side, this need for fresh, new means to express new insights into old truths is recogniezd in the pictorial and poetic arts. If Aristotle could be blind, how much more can our own academicians be blind, who are not Aristotles! We have to encourage a new spirit in the young men and a new school.

§iii. *Pure Politics as Science and as Philosophy*

If Politics then divides into Political Practice and Political Theory, in turn Political Theory divides into two parts: (*a*) Political Philosophy or (more accurately) indivisible Philosophy in its political and social emphases, and concern with the analysis and evaluation of *ends*; and (*b*) Political Science, concerned with the analysis and selection of *means*. Sometimes, when the stress is upon selection and recommendation (approaching an art), the term used (perhaps unhappily, since 'choices' have no 'science') is 'Policy Sciences.' Means severely condition ends. It is the hall-mark of the doctrinaire to refuse to recognize this.

Professor Hans Morgenthau, indeed, seems to include all political theory under Political Science: but this would seem to be a hard position to maintain. As will be emphasized later, the distinction between ends and means is an abstract and convenient one, and not a concrete and historical one. The ends, by conditioning the selection of means, tinge these with their own values; the ends achieved may be means to other ends; certain means, such as the hydrogen bomb, restrict ends since they may be inappropriate (as Aldous Huxley has argued in his *Ends and Means*, 1937) to other values. The distinction, nevertheless, if propositional and hypothetical, is sound. It is best stated by Professor

Morris Ginsberg, in his *Reason and Unreason in Society* (1947, p. 126): "The true distinction seems rather to be that economics deals with ends hypothetically. It answers the question: if the end were so and so, what must be done in order to attain it? Ethics, on the other hand, is concerned with the more radical question as to what ends ought to be chosen. If confusion is to be avoided the two questions *must be clearly distinguished*" (italics mine). When the organization of men "n'est plus un moyen subordonné à une fin quelconque, mais . . . est lui-même considéré comme fin," we have what M. Bertrand de Jouvenel (*De la souveraineté*, p. 32) calls *politique pure* in a distinction which would yet seem to exclude all speculations of Political Philosophy (but see *ibid.*, p. 25)—I think inconveniently—from 'pure politics.' Certainly not all theory can be placed under the heading 'Practical or Applied Politics.'

To the discussion of Political Philosophy, we shall turn in the final chapters of this treatise. It is important to discuss radically the ends, and also alternative ends with other characters and consequences, to which the study of means hypothetically relates. There are also two other approaches besides those of Political Philosophy and Political Science: (*c*) the Institutional (including that of Comparative Government), where political science moves over to applications—this study can be also conducted descriptively, without a general theory, atomistically and area by area, country by country, and we shall return to it in a later chapter—and (*d*) the (related in that it also uses description) Historical approach, on which we have made some comment and which, somewhat unexpectedly, frequently connects through historicism with political romanticism. Those, incidentally, who deny that there can be a political or social science will have to cover the entire field as philosophy or by historical narratives, descriptions and anecdotes about institutions and politicians. The immense importance of this historical work on institutions, even when static, but also in the classification and comparisons of dynamic events, has already been stressed. There can be no political science or sound political philosophy without it. But it is not departmentally separable and, if separated, ceases to be Political Theory or propaedeutic to it. It becomes either Ancient History or 'current events'—or perhaps talk about 'great issues.' It should be noted that no quantity of accumulation of 'facts,' whether comparative or otherwise, without literary form, theory or ordinary hypothesis, constitutes knowledge—not to speak of wisdom. This may be elementary, but, alack! it needs to be restated. The late Harold Laski rightly pointed out the genetic importance of the historical treatment as against the contemporary or comparative discipline, just as Mannheim has stressed the role of 'perspectives' in judgement; but neither history nor comparison can undertake the entire task. The attempt to display a continuity or tradition in political philosophy I have made elsewhere in my *History*. The negative and critical attempt to explain specific political theories in terms of the limitations of their historical context (for example, that Marx was in reaction against, but also a product of, the Manchester school of economists with its crude, aggressive psychology, and that therefore he becomes 'dated'), is of not great importance in science when the question is "what is analytically true?" but is indeed highly relevant to a political philosophy not destitute of historical sense, which must take into account nuances and syntheses of values and the value of the valuer.

The distinction between Political Science and Political Philosophy is, then, broadly that between the study of means, and their empirical investigation, and the study of ends, and their evaluation. It raises the vexed issue of values, which will be dealt with amply enough in another final volume. But the theme is totally different from "whether Ethics can be a science," to which the answer is (in our sense) "no." The confusion, however, is common between ethical values (as norms of choice) and functional norms of efficient process. Sound medical techniques constitute functional norms; but they are not directly ethical values. The point would not be worth making were the error not frequent.

Professor Lionel Robbins wrote in his *Essay on the Nature and Significance of Economic Science* (1932, p. 24): "the economist is not concerned with ends as such." Those who insist upon the inherent inseparability of means and values or ends would do well to concentrate their attack upon the economists who share Lord Robbins' view. It may well be that, at the present advanced stage of Economics, subtler hypotheses should be constructed which will take into account political, sociological, and ethical alternatives of wider range than those usual in the nineteenth century. There can be an economic science of means to Marxo-Bolshevik ends; indeed, there is. Moreover, the distinction has always to be borne in mind between abstract theory and practical application in history. An engineer would be a poor one who allowed for no factors beyond the principles of pure physics and mechanics. Nevertheless, no illuminating and useful schema can ever be constructed which ignores the first rule of scientific method: the duty of abstraction. The test lies not in the measure of concreteness in what William James called (in a phrase already quoted) "a blooming, buzzing world"; but the measure of utility in the methodological tools.

§iv. *'Ta Politica'*

The term for our subject used by Aristotle is *ta politica* (τὰ πολιτίκα). Examination of its implications gives a refreshing novelty of approach, stimulating criticism of stereotypes and exposing the begging of questions by those intoxicated by the current spirit of the age. There is no need to try to improve upon it by substituting some such loaded terms as 'civics,' which rather refers to instruction in the rights—and, one hopes, the duties—of citizens. 'Politics' etymologically derives from *polis*. This was a city-community, such as was general in much of the ancient world from Spain to the Indus (as distinct from empires such as the Persian), not a state in the modern sense of the term or a nation, and without any developed theory of sovereignty as distinct from one of actual force. Witness the history of the Athenian Empire in the contest with Melos. Whereas the *polis* was frequently and ideally a homogeneous community, the modern state often springs from the feudal superimposition by war of one tribe or caste (Frank, Lombard, Norman) heterogeneously upon an earlier civilized population, which only later merges into such a novel homogeneity as, by analogy, to be called a nation (*natio*, 'the group of those born'). Philologically all members of a nation should be blood kin. However, among 'Britons,' there is little blood-kinship between Celtic Welsh and Teuton Englishman; although even this 'nation' is not as much an educational or cultural artifact as the American 'nation,' melted into unity by the schoolhouse, or as the Canadian 'nation,' which has scarcely even accepted the schoolhouse philosophy but rather respects a provincial approach, and where heterogeneity as such and variety are esteemed.

Aristotle, in his discussion, begins with a study of the family, of the household, and also of slavery. It is the more remarkable that he thus began with the small or face-to-face group, since an epoch of disruption of the patrician clan-family had been followed by one in which the social whole of the *polis* was exalted, to be superseded within a few decades by the developing concept of a *cosmopolis*. Study of origins is part of Aristotle's treatment. If followed today, we shall avoid the secularist and even totalitarian error of regarding Politics as merely the study of the State and its Government, or of taking the Nation-State as if it were something unique, eternal, static, of metaphysical essence and to be reified, instead of being a particular social form that has evolved and can change. (Later we shall see why this static approach, not least in legal quarters, has been preferred and elevated to levels of what Hobhouse has called a 'metaphysics' and Peter Viereck a 'metapolitics.')

As Sir Alfred Zimmern, in *The Greek Commonwealth* (2nd ed., 1915) and other Greek scholars have pointed out, the Hellenic *polis*, smaller in area, was much wider in embrace than the nineteenth-century 'state' (what Professor R.

M. MacIver calls, from the sixteenth century on, 'The Modern State'), including aspects of social life and political economy other than those preoccupied with the machinery of voting and of making and executing state laws and with local, state and federal league government. Fustel de Coulanges, in *La Cité antique* (1876), emphasized the religious origins of much of the apparatus of this organization and the ancient fusion of clan, church, and state. In the words of Ernest Barker, the *polis* "is a small and intimate society; it is a church as well as a state." To treat *polis* and state as synoymous terms, each being translatable without residue into the other, is a fruitful source of confusion among students and of dangerously erroneous theory. Politics is precisely *not* the study of the state in the modern sense. Traditional reverence for Greek thought, coupled with this gross mistranslation, had an immense impact upon European thought during the last two centuries (cf. F. M. Watkins: *The State as Concept in Political Science*, 1934). The confusion is promoted tendentiously by such German writers as Treitschke, in his *Politics*, with his deliberate state-worship, and by some modern disciples including Professor Hans Morgenthau, a no less distinguished exponent of traditional German theory who has, however, significantly mellowed his views in his recent work, especially in his recent *The Purpose of American Politics* (1960).

Professor Morgenthau writes (*Politics among Nations*, 1948, p. 400) in words that recall the distinguished Hegelian Bernard Bosanquet, "the [sovereign] nation is, as we have seen, the recipient of man's highest earthly loyalties" (. . . until he is dead). Unlike Bosanquet, who re-read Hegel after 1914 and found (in the introduction to his new edition of *The Philosophical Theory of the State*) a place for the League of Nations, Professor Morgenthau does not recant, but, posing squarely the problem of peace, finds a way out in "the revival of diplomacy" and avoiding "the vices of publicity." Morgenthau here uses 'nation' in the American sense, as equivalent to the European 'state,' and not in the sense of 'the Ukrainian nation' for example. The argument would, of course, either way have had small force before the recent rise of Nationalism with the French Revolution. Professor Morgenthau's work is an incisive criticism from the traditional German standpoint—or what was that standpoint until Adenauer's United Europe thesis—of American liberalism, as especially expressed by Woodrow Wilson. As it has been put to this writer, "it is doubtful whether Morgenthau will ever understand the American tradition," despite his championing of "the national interest," as he expounds it. This defect, it should be added, he has nobly endeavoured to remedy in his last book, where he finds the American purpose (*The Purpose of American Politics*, 1960, p. 34) in the equalization of opportunity and the minimization of political control domestically.

As Professor C. J. Friedrich says, in his *Constitutional Government and Democracy* (1937), "the polis was really a church as well as a 'state.'" Perhaps the two most important healthy developments in formal political science in the last thirty years have been (*a*) the general adoption again of the power hypothesis; and (*b*) the 'politicization' (as already said) of much of the social field, that is the treatment of political activities functionally, and the rediscovery and study of them in fields arbitrarily set aside as industrial, religious, and so on. It is doubtful whether any competent political scientist expects this trend to be cancelled or reversed or imagines that it can be ignored. However, Professor Edward Shils rightly deplores (*The Present State of American Sociology*, p. 34) that "the internal structure of the church [has] not been studied either for the Catholic or Protestant Churches." Here is a fruitful field for investigation, hitherto pre-empted by pamphleteers and partisans.

It is not enough to pick on some concrete objects, such as 'horses,' if we want to develop a science of Biology or Psychology. Biology is the study of all life. So Lord Russell rightly insisted, in *Power: A New Social Analysis* (1938), that he proposed to treat Politics as a science with a fundamental field, just as one treated Physics as the science of energy. The concrete study of men as a species in evolution, with which some sociologists have concerned themselves, is sufficiently covered by historical Anthropology. To take 'states' as our object, which rather constitutes one sub-group or instances of a particular social form, distracts us at the very beginning from attention to funda-mentals, and inevitably tends to issue in the kind of theory called *étatisme*; nor is this the better or necessarily redeemed because it may, for some, have state socialist or collectivist implications. It encourages not a socialism of the community, but a mechanical and bureaucratic socialism of the state. WE NEED TO FIND SOME FUNCTION OR FORM OF ACTIVITY OR PROCESS IN TERMS OF WHICH THE WHOLE FIELD OF POLITICAL DATA CAN BE SEEN TO HAVE A COMMON PRINCIPLE (Proposition 3).

The Harvard study, *The State as Concept in Political Science* by Professor F. M. Watkins of Yale (and formerly of Cornell and McGill), referred to above, begins with a defence and development of the argument that political science must be a study of more social organizations than the state, and for the 'politici-zation' of a wider field, which he delineates in this work. He cites the present writer as having "in particular, ventured to question the desirability of making the state the focus of special scientific inquiry" (p. 1). Professor Watkins re-states the case that no authoritative science of politics can develop from the narrower field, and supplements it by an admirable historical study. One must further agree with him that many social organizations, families, churches, asso-ciations, and unions use an effective *vis coactiva*, although I am more conserva-tive than he in feeling that the state, as primarily concerned with the civil peace, and with repression of violence in disturbance of it, exercises a characteristic *vis coactiva*, or at least claims to exercise coercion over coercers which is practi-cally distinctive enough from the *vis directiva*. (It is a great source of regret to me that I was not earlier acquainted with this weighty reinforcement, made in 1934, of my views, which Professor Watkins was good enough to quote at the beginning of his argument.)

Professor Watkins' polemic underlines, moreover, that the views about the state, which he here advocates—that we should direct our attention to the function of power rather than to a static concept of the state or even to its institutions—were far from being commonplace, platitudinous, or "merely a re-hash of Machia-velli," but were in fact views repudiated by the leading authorities in vogue at that time, a repudiation emphasized by some British reviewers. I have also recently had the opportunity of seeing M. de Jouvenel's remarkable *De la souveraineté*, a sequel to his *Du pouvoir* (1945) to which reference is made in the text. (The English translation by J. F. Huntington, *Sovereignty*, contains material not in the original French version.) Here M. de Jouvenel makes this interpretation of the range of Politics, as given above, fundamental. "Personnellement nous considérons que tout ensemble humain organizé pour une coopération régulière est un corps politique, et que l'objet de la Science Politique est l'étude de la cohésion de ces corps, comment créée, comment maintenue et perfectionnée" (p. 13) . . . "un des obstacles s'opposant jusqu'à présent au développement de la science politique était qu'elle n'attachait qu'aux aggrégats nommés États." (p. 39. Cf. also pp. 7 and 10.)

§v. *Society*

That Politics is a study of human society, as controlled and organized, we have already offered as a first or general approximation in the delimitation of the field. Control involves a plural relation. Hence the concept of group or society is politically fundamental. The word 'Society' itself, however, is full of ambiguities. First, there is a distinction between what may be called its 'intensive' and psychological use, and its 'extensive' and organizational use. (The word 'intensive' must not here be misunderstood as referring only to area.) Its treatment by the philosophers of the *polis*, and the philological implications of the word *socii* (and also *comites* and *genossen*), emphasize the idea of a common spirit or sentiment. Emphasis upon this idea culminates in the notion of the Community, as having much more to it than mere social interaction, a crass underestimation of its potentiality. Of this idea the classical and pregnant description is that of Plato, its especial philosopher: *Hē tēs hēdonēs kai tēs lupēs koinōnia*, 'a common-sharing of pleasure and pain.' It becomes congruent with the churchly notion, emphasized by Toynbee, of a 'brotherhood.' It has sharply to be distinguished from that conventionally imposed society which we may term 'pseudo-community.' But the appeal of the Nation, to be discussed later, is also made to a like sentiment of sharing whether a common birth and inheritance of blood (as by the philology of the words *natio*, *nasco*) or a common tradition and history of activity together. It will be noted that the idea of the homogeneous Community not only predicates a sharing within the group of sentiments, conventions, and spirit or patterns of value, but also, latently, an exclusion of those who do not share. This will later be seen to be of crucial importance.

To this distinction between a community and a (political) society as an (organized) human aggregate, which plays an important role in Greek thought, and again in modern nationalism, we return in chapter VII. It is discussed in the *Gesellschaft und Gemeinschaft* (1888) of the Hobbesian scholar, F. Tönnies; and by R. M. MacIver in his *Community*, and in portions of his valuable *The Web of Government* (1947) where, however, he tends to identify community with 'the people' or 'the country,' 'a limited area of society,' and not with that 'perpetual plebiscite' stressed by Ernest Renan. This, however, is to suppose that which may or may not be present: a sentiment of unity in 'the people' or 'the country'; consider Korea, Germany, Ireland, Jews, and Zionists. It is, however, valuable as stressing the contrast between the 'intensive community' and the state as the mechanism of administration or rule. This latter is the Metternichian concept (which we can also detect in the work of Professor V. O. Key) of the state, where government is detached from communal sentiment.

In all these points it is of prime importance not to beg questions, before we begin, by our very use of terms. On the ground that it is not 'organized' by any official institution or machinery of rule, some philosophers such as Bernard Bosanquet have denied that humanity, taken collectively, can be regarded as 'society' to which obligations are owed. But the relevant issue is whether there is a reasonable sentiment of a human community, as of like emergent values, making it something more than a mere temporary aggregate, in a socially inter-dependent world; or whether such a sentiment can only be directed towards 'a delimited area.' We may also ask whether any society, short of humanity, is indeed today fully autarkic and self-sufficient, a question raised by Watkins in *The State as Concept.*

The word 'society,' as used here, carries none of that connection with the integrated community which is implied in the Greek word *politeia*. Here, again, an ambiguity of translation, putting twentieth-century meanings into third-century B.C. arguments or the converse, may mislead us. Thus Professor Paul Weiss, of Yale, in *Our Public Life* (1959) writes: "In fact no one of us knows at what point a group can no longer be properly termed a family, a village or a tribe, and should instead be called a society" (p. 32). The context shows that Professor Weiss, when he uses the unanalysed term 'society,' is here thinking directly of the Aristotelian *politeia* (which Aristotle himself, in *Politics* 2. 1, characterizes as a 'community,' *koinōnia tis*) or what Dr. Weiss immediately afterwards qualifies as 'a mature developed society,' leaving it to be assumed that what 'mature' means is self-evident, alike to a follower of Locke and a follower of Hegel. This society may be homogeneous, and stress this fact, or heterogeneous and proud of it.

Society is often discussed in a fashion in which the greatest differences in conclusions are drawn from a confusion of terms, and sometimes even from an elementary failure to distinguish the abstract from the concrete and to watch the use of the indefinite article. Neo-Hegelian writers, having demonstrated grounds of obligation to Society, then by verbal legerdemain apply the benefit of their demonstration to 'a society' of their choice, without showing that it could not equally well be applied to any other group or association, such as the Society for the Propagation of Christian Knowledge. In innumerable cases in political argument the simple substitution for 'a society' of 'Society' (undefined, but what Hayakawa calls a 'purr' word) or 'Community,' or for 'some people' of 'the People,' will produce amazing changes in the conclusions. There has been no lack of political conjurers to effect these changes.

'Society' in the second, extensive, mechanical, or organizational sense usually means, as with Tönnies, any society (Gesellschaft) which is political where, however widespread or however narrow, there is either a system of durable interdependence or organization—what the French call a quality of éternalisme—and relevant Institutions, or —and this is sufficient—the mere translation of a social sentiment into objective habits or Conventions of expected co-operation in the aggregate. The word 'society' is used here throughout in this second sense, since it is the simpler use, less burdened with emotional overtones; and it permits the reservation of the distinguishable word 'community' for the first sense or meaning. The usage is determined by an Occamite economy which suggests that an ambiguous or multiple-meaning word should never be used when a clear and unambiguous word, empirically delimitable, can be used instead. Wherever the society is more than an assemblage perhaps with common preoccupations, like enthusiasts for a sporting team who are themselves unorganized, and is organized so that a relation of control or rules is established, it should properly be described as a Political Society, peculiarly where it is this function of control or institutional order which is predominant in interest. When the organization is of a State character, the society is a Civil Society.

Particular societies are Groups or groupings which are societies for the purposes of sociology, although they may be only culturally such, and do not need to be organized and still less to be societies recognized or incorporated in law. In some cases these groups or societies are brought into being for a specific or limited purpose, and are conveniently to be described as Associations. In other cases, and these among the greatest, they are rather organizations fulfilling a permanent or quasi-permanent function, and involving for those organized a pattern of life for which no termination is visualized. Where such organizations are not regarded as being dependent for their existence upon the will of another, they were described by mediaeval writers as juristically societates perfectae. They are yet, in so far as they are mechanical and extensive, to be distinguished from spiritual and intensive Communities (Gemeinschaften), although some may be both. Those patterns of life which shape the behaviour of the groups can be called Conventions; and the specific organizational systems for the performance of specific functions, through which these conventions are preserved and maintained, Institutions.

A Group is, then, a limited or particular society, of whatever degree of organization, within human society. A Political Group, however, involves organization. Abram Kardiner and his colleagues in *The Psychological Frontiers of Society* (1945) originally defined 'institution' to mean "a fixed mode of thought or behaviour which can be communicated, which enjoys common acceptance and the infringement of or deviation from which creates some disturbance in the individual or group." Subsequently modified in comment on the basic structure, on a point here irrelevant, this definition identifies institutions with *mores*, except as touching the depth of roots of 'disturbance'; and makes them synonymous with what, for the sake of differentiation and economy of terms, we here prefer to call Conventions. Purity in attitude, it may be suggested, is an ethical principle: chastity in conduct is a Convention; and marriage is an Institution (involving certain Organizations such as registrars' offices and marriage advice bureaus).

The word 'Association' is also used by some sociologists, such as Professor D. Truman, in another fashion from that chosen here. In this text it is used to mean a group organized with a specific and determinable object that can be achieved finally or recurrently (such as to achieve a Conservative victory or to protect the interests of car manufacturers). Professor Truman uses it as a species of federation or group of groups or (almost) an Althusian *communitas communitatum* (in which case the state would be, as in the Althusian philosophy, an association)—"a group, a continuing pattern of interactions, that functions as a 'bridge' between persons in two or more institutionalized groups or sub-divisions thereof" (*The Governmental Process*, 1951, p. 40). This would seem to leave us without a term for the group or, to use the French commercial term, *société anonyme* with specific objectives, but with a plenitude of names for a society of plural or confederate structure. Significantly Professor K. R. Popper (*The Poverty of Historicism*, p. 157) writes: "Institutions . . . must be . . . properly manned . . . We can never be sure that the right man will be attracted . . ."

'State' is a term, of no earlier use than in the Italy of the fifteenth century, which we will discuss more fully later, since the implications of almost any definition cut to the bone of controversy. Philologically it is almost synonymous with 'the Establishment.' Provisionally we shall define a 'State' (in the sense of political science, but not in that of American and Australian constitutional law) to be the organization of certain human beings, whether a precedent group or those shaped into a group by its organizing action, for the primary function of repressing violence and itself, therefore, alone enjoying the right to use directly the *vis coactiva*, physical coercion or violence, or finally to authorize its use. Those so organized are described as its Subjects or Citizens, and the instrument of organization or rule is called the Government or Administration. For those who object to this rule it is, as by Marxists, entitled an instrument of domination or oppression of subjects by their class (or other) rulers. Lenin called it "a club"— and he did not mean an association for good fellowship. These rulers need not always be of superior caste or class: they can be low-caste adventurers, as often was the case in India. Of the Modern State we may still say, as Aristotle said of the *polis*, that "it came into being for the sake of life," and to ensure organized social survival, although of course it may add to this those activities of 'the good life' which can, in some respects but not all, be achieved in the welfare state or, to use Gunnar Myrdal's term, 'Beyond the Welfare State' as a further addendum or development.

§vi. *The Political Act Defined*

The most crucial point of intuition and vision in the study of a subject is the detection of the fundamental schematism, the abstraction of the function or activity in its simplest form. As we have said, the maturity of any science is indicated by the condition of abstraction and coherence of its general theory. Moreover, the most striking advances in sciences are made when we re-examine the axioms, as of Euclid or Newton, and become freshly alive to the danger of having packed into those axioms errors which plague us later. No advances, moreover, will be made if we ambitiously make a beginning by choosing very grand or highly complex instances, subtle organic compounds (such as would be an ordinary clod of turf for chemistry) or instances of a rare and very dignified kind, or activities which offer few or no precise repetitions in history. No advance can be made by taking, for example, as our *prima elementa*, eighty or so states or twenty or so cultures or social complexes, by which history offers rather analogies than instances substantially alike; and in which the key to the explanation of their activities may lie precisely in the differences.

Although it would be admirable if we could learn the laws and cyclic movements which govern 'civilizations' and 'cultures,' it can be argued that these are susceptible of no such precise definitions as to admit of comparisons which would reveal laws. Merely we have the illusion of comparison because thousands of human beings in these various civilizations have behaved and do behave, in recurrent situations, in effectively the same way—as Machiavelli said—as human beings. That there is a 'human nature' we posit. For the *prima elementa* what we require are activities repeated many millions of times every day and, therefore, genuinely capable of comparison and scientific study, with observation and experiment. Nor must we be shocked by the banality of some of the instances; much may be learned, as Darwin knew, from earthworms. THE CRUX OF THE SCIENCE OF POLITICS LIES IN THE ISOLATION AND STUDY OF THE POLITICAL ACT (Proposition 4).

The student brought up on political grand drama and on enquiries about "thy mortal god, Leviathan" may be startled when Kardiner illustrates a basic theme by the words: "The principles which psychoanalysis can give to the social sciences are best illustrated by the following case history . . . A man of thirty complains of having great difficulties with women . . . His relations with men are hardly more successful . . ." (*The Psychological Frontiers of Society*, p. 17). He continues with studies of the Comanche and Alorese Amerindians . . . Nevertheless, to the anthropologist, the learned laughter may be as "the crackling of thorns under a pot" (Ecclesiastes 8: 6). Professor David Easton, in his *Political System* (p. 118) says, commenting on my own earlier work (which he is good enough to describe as "blazing a trail . . . along which political science must ultimately follow"), that Political Science can be argued to be "largely interested in political institutions, but unfortunately these appear with relative rarity in the world. If we study the so-called state, there are less than seventy in the world . . . the reason for this relative backwardness of the study of politics as a science lies largely in failure to isolate a political phenomenon which is repeated with a frequency sufficient for it to be studied exhaustively. Political data must be so repetitive that their functioning can be understood from the unlimited variety of available cases." Cf. also F. Watkins, *The State as Concept*.

The attempt to take 'civilizations' or 'cultures' as the units of study is illustrated in the monumental *Study of History* by Professor A. J. Toynbee, which yet has a tragic aspect to it since (though possibly right in its conclusions) its methodology, essential to the valid impact of the whole, is almost casual, questionable, and incomplete. Having the deepest personal respect for Professor Toynbee, being of the minority that agrees that 'church' or voluntary social forms will supersede those 'state' or coercive forms which will 'wither away,' and agreeing that humanity is more deeply concerned in comparative history than in 'micro-history' and in the detailed doings of clerks to the Mediaeval English Privy Council or in the history of particular royal seals (and even requires men to read the history of their own countries as written by their countries' critics), nevertheless I am unable to do other than express the opinion that Toynbee's method is quite basically wrong and liable to confuse the student. Nor is this judgement altered by the fact that he may be the most massive historian in the world and that he, like Spengler and Wells and Marx and Bossuet, is doing what the common man craves to have done and is determined that historians shall be thrust into doing—that he provides, as hierophant, a clue to the labyrinth of history and declares an apocalypse. I would add, parenthetically, that I sometimes entertain far warmer sentiments for Dr. Toynbee as a contributor to the comprehension of civilization, than I do for, as example, Mr. H. A. L. Fisher, who brought to the judgements of history a chill mind. This does not yet mean that

I do not agree with Warden Fisher's judgement in his *History of Europe*, bk. I, p. vii.

Also, while being unhappy about Professor Toynbee's laws of history, I can by no means agree with Mr. Richard Wollheim, who states that he has "always regarded it as a sign either of a weak mind or of a dull imagination to show an excessive interest (and no one ever shows a moderate interest) in the large-scale laws or trends that are supposed to determine the lives of human societies." This sweeping generalization seems to me to be unwarranted, harsh, unseemly, and too clever.

Max Weber (who was in party sympathies a liberal socialist, if an ineffectual one) wrote: "Interpretative sociology considers the individual and his action as the basic unit, as its 'atom'—if the disputable comparison for once may be permitted . . . In general, for sociology, such concepts as 'state,' 'association,' 'feudalism,' and the like, designate certain categories of human interaction. Hence it is the task of sociology to reduce these concepts to 'understandable' action, that is, without exception, to the actions of participating individual men." The myths of Social Contract and (even more misleading) of Social Organism do not yet come within the field of reference of the present argument. That *how* men act is governed, even in 'the state of nature' of the most primitive societies, by rules, tabus, and conventions, and that men are not born as Crusoes but rather as Topsies, is not here in dispute. What is at issue is *where* we should begin our study of acts, and how we should select *what* acts. Should we follow Aristotle and Machiavelli? Should we look at the repetitive patterns in men's political behaviour? Should we regard our study as primarily one of process? Should we consider the impulses and functions that give rise to these patterns? Can we rely, with Montesquieu, on all of human nature being in each man? I submit that we should and can.

It will be noted that, in respect to what is objective and extensive, not subjective, Politics is concerned with society as organized, that is, with society in so far as its members have certain relations to each other and in so far as these relations are established and so maintained by certain controls. A mere human aggregate, save that it is under some controls or acts collectively as a led herd, is not its concern. A herd in peace or war, shaped by a common controlling instinct as described by Trotter, provided that this instinct is not transient in operation but tends to conventional and institutional expression—in other words, is calculable—is its concern. The mere act of control indeed goes beyond the individual and his psyche, and implies an objective social relation. Further, in order not to enrich the terms with historical or poetic irrelevances beyond the requirements of the subject, instead of referring to the 'person' and the 'actor' who,

64   SYSTEMATIC POLITICS

besides his 'role' as 'king' or 'administrator' (or even as 'old man' and the like), is also an artistic, religious and economic human being, it is preferable—as we have said earlier—technically to refer to 'the Will' and (here with Weber) to 'the Act' following from this Will. For like reasons, of danger of ambiguity, we shall not adopt the collective, neuter, and too often anonymous and unanalysed word 'Interests' (with Gumplowicz and Bentley) to describe the primal factors or relations.

The field of Politics is one of the study of innumerable Political Acts. In brief: POLITICAL SCIENCE IS CONCERNED WITH THE FUNCTION IN SOCIETY OF CONTROL; WITH THE ACTS THAT ISSUE IN CONTROL; WITH WILLS; AND WITH THE STRUCTURES RESULTING FROM THE CONTROL RELATIONSHIP OF WILLS (Proposition 5). Whenever Smith gives an order to Jones or, more precisely, by any act controls him, no matter how many millions of acts there may be, each is the fundamental Political Act.

More forcibly (and, for reasons which will become clear, far more controversially) Professor H. D. Lasswell, in his incisive book of this title, isolates the fundamental political act and theme as 'Who gets What, When, How?' What are the political goods and who gets them? The Webbs saw the matter as a theme of 'Who gives orders, who rules whom, why, how?' However, for Politics, as we shall see, there is also a subjective, intensive issue of psychological response on the part of the ordered to this act, which, assent or dissent, in turn will bring us to the unavoidable philosophical themes of community or 'like-minded group,' and of shared ends. And we can here understand what is meant by describing 'the political man' as nuclear: he is the man or 'actor,' in fact or abstraction, peculiarly preoccupied with political activity and controls.

It is Sir George Cornewall Lewis, in his *Treatise on Methods*, bk. II, p. 310, who says: "All political conduct is resolvable into a series of political acts." The present writer, in his *Principia* (pp. 71, 92), wrote: "In the political act . . . the primary object is to procure some personal adjustment of the will of another man to my will . . . We have defined Politics as the study of the *control* relationship between willing beings." In his earlier *Science and Methods* he wrote: "of man in his relation to the wills of his fellows in control, submission and accommodation . . . [this] is the characteristic of the 'political situation,' and the man whose experience is dominated by it, and who thinks and acts especially in terms of it, is the 'political man.' "

Concerning the danger, with many contemporary sociologists, of taking the group as the beginning point of studies, *vide* the article by Stanley Rothman, "Systematic Political Theory," *American Political Science Review*, March, 1960.

3. The Power Hypothesis

§i. *The Power Theory of Politics as Hypothesis*

The dynamic study of a subject must go beyond its abstract definition and *formal delimitation*, as stated in Propositions 1 and 5, or even the detection of the nucleus or core of its subject matter. We should not, with Georg Simmel, make Sociology solely the study of abstract social relations, suggestive although Simmel's work is. The distinction is important. Admittedly the definition of the field is, in part, an arbitrary matter of convenience. If we define the field of politics as 'state government'and then empirically get no fruitful results from this, we must change this definition. But it is also a logical matter, arising from careful analysis of the common factors in the conventionally agreed field. To be distinguished from this are the various theories we may adopt (which are even more emphatically to be judged empirically) of what is *the character of the operations or functions* which unite the field. Biology is the study of life; but what 'life' is, as an operation or function of growth, is a much more controversial question. Why, then, do men require or desire Control? Why are they interested in having it? And what social formations are produced in order to give operational effect to their desire for it?

Moreover, in our hypotheses about this latter, we must beware of the unicausal fallacy, even when we are feeling as proud as an Einstein of having reduced multiple operations to one formula. Not only must we have what President James B. Conant calls 'the bold working hypothesis,' but we do well to bear in mind that, as Dr. Conant tells us, chemistry for long worked with at least two hypotheses about the molecule which, at one time, superficially seemed contradictory. It depended on the working model. Admittedly (a) we must always be ready to change our model for one that works better, and (b) as we work in to specific studies of this or that time or place instead of one model we must patently have many more limited and specialized ones. Nevertheless, our first concern is with the more permanent social structure and functions, and only later is our concern with the subsidiary structure of local, temporary, and conventional institutions.

When Lord Russell writes in his book *Power*, "in the course of this book I shall be concerned to prove that the fundamental conception in social science is Power, in the same sense that Energy is the fundamental concept in Physics," I venture to suggest that he fuses or confuses the defining concept of Control with the operational hypothesis, which has to be tested, of Power. Beneath the phenomenon of control, which we define, we have to investigate what *causes* control situations so generally to arise. It is a distinct issue. It is at this point that imagination is required to supply 'a working hypothesis' which can subsequently be tested experimentally to see whether, as Darwin demanded, 'it does work.' Moreover, the whole history of science indicates that this fundamental hypothesis is likely to be characterized by extreme simplicity, not by complicated description or by confusion with secondary and concessive principles. Classical economics were so built. The most vital thing in science is the capacity for the brilliant guess.

Marx and Engels occasionally ventured upon specific and refutable predictions. Thus they prophesied that the social revolution was destined to take place first in countries of the most advanced capitalism. Marx and Engels were wrong and the prediction false. Usually, however, their system is so stated as to explain everything, if we take on faith its initial assumptions, and hence not to be capable of refutation because a subsidiary explanation can always be found. Such explanations are not science, as used here. If, however, we state that the power hypothesis offers an explanation of national action which is not, except by introducing without elegance or economy species of 'explanation by epicycles,' to be interpreted by Marxist orthodoxy, then we offer a scientific challenge which can be shown to be true or false. We do not say we have a panacea which can assuage all difficulties. We may say we have an explanation which covers more of the data than any other—or at least offers an alternative of significance. In Britain, however, perhaps inspired by academic modesty, there has been an unexpected but embattled repugnance to this procedure, itself typically in accord with the English tradition since Bacon.

Professor E. H. Carr in his *Twenty Years' Crisis, 1919–1939* (1939, p. 97) points out that "the *homo politicus* who pursues nothing but power is as unreal as the *homo economicus* who pursues nothing but gain. Political *action* [italics mine] must be based on a coordination of morality and power." In this passage he seems not only to say what is quite true, but to indicate that I hold a different view. I do not. Surely to resolve all political theory, ideals, ends, and action into affairs of power is one thing. To suggest that, in the abstract theory of political science and means, power may be one of the widest and profoundest clues to interpretation yet found as a hypothesis, among other possible clues, is clearly something very different.

As touching the aspiration to reduce multiplicity to simple formulae and the secret of successful hypotheses, Professor J. Bronowski writes (*Science and Human Values*, 1961): "All science is the search for unity in hidden likenesses ... (p. 24); "there never was a scientist who did not make bold guesses" (p. 72). Perhaps the qualifications of a great scientist are nearer to those of an artist than a scholar or schoolmaster.

Hence we can advance beyond the notion that our field is that of society as organized (possibly teleologically, as a matter of ends shared and already projected in the community). The issue is not only of the 'how' and the static or of a definition; but also of the 'why' and the dynamic, and of what urge (which may be in addition to, or may be presenting itself as, the final end or intermediate end) causes these formations of like phenomena, which we gather together in our definition. Moving beyond the notion of organization, and the more precise and simple notion of control and the act of control, we arrive at the hypothesis on action that, whatever may be the *various conscious or rational ends* (teloi) to which sentient beings individually or communally aspire, they all alike intermediately desire power, whether they have it or not, in order to achieve those ends. THERE IS A GENERAL WILL TO EXECUTE ONE'S WILL, WHICH IS THE AGENT FOR REALIZING ONE'S PARTICULAR WISH OR END; AND FOR FREEDOM FOR THAT REALIZATION. THE CONDITION FOR SUCH EXECUTION IS POWER (Proposition 6). Power, although not a particular primary end, can thus become a general intermediate end or can be alternatively described in its less self-conscious condition, not *ad finem* but *a tergo*, as a common urge or inclination. This issue of motivation is of prime importance. Further, and to complement this proposition, we may say: THOSE WHO HOLD POWER WILL GRATUITOUSLY SACRIFICE NEITHER THEIR FREEDOM TO DO WHAT THEY CHOOSE NOR THEIR ESTABLISHED LIBERTIES (Proposition 7).

Any man, in dictatorship or democracy, who has a particular power to achieve his ends will not yield his power except from fear, from a conversion of his desires to other ends, and for the particular power to attain these new ends; or because he is offered yet more of what he has always wanted in exchange. (Clearly, indeed, where there is no felt obstacle to achievement, there will be no conscious desire for power.) In the words of Thomas Hobbes, "I put for a general inclination of all mankind, a perpetuall and restless desire of Power after power, that ceaseth onely in Death." And for this urge there is indeed no rest but proceeding. It does not indeed follow that men, who have freedom in the gratification of their immediate desires, may not be indolent or improvident about guarantees which they think tedious or about the irrelevant liberties of other men which they think of little immediate interest. As Hobbes also truly says (as did Bryce later)—and this, with fear, explains much compliance with efficient tyranny—"Desire of Ease and sensuall Delight disposeth men to obey a common Power." The sense of possessing power, like money, may be indeed a present enjoyment for the imagination and an active pleasure. It may provide a deeper, more exciting and more inclusive pleasure than money. Power in its exercise is indeed always a matter of human relations, but it is *substantial* in its enjoyment and something which only some men possess the gift to achieve. Where the control pursues over an appreciable time a distinctive and articulate continuity of direction, we may refer to it as a *policy*. Nevertheless, both general power over men and general wealth in things are primarily necessary *means* to specific control or to consumption. There can be an imperative desire for certain things, lustful or ideal; but the technical problem is how to get them.

The *Principia* of the present writer, dedicated to Graham Wallas and whose sub-title was 'a study in political rationalization,' was described as a study of "the nature and utility of this science of power and the physiology and anatomy of social groups," putting "the state in its true place as one instrument of social organization" and discussing "the nature of the like-minded group and the future of community life." And, again, "we shall then define Politics, not in terms of objects, such as states, but in terms of an activity, that of establishing control . . . the genuine political act . . . All political conduct is resolvable into a series of political acts . . . In Politics we are concerned to study the power of the will to change the objective world . . . of willing beings . . . The general political will is, then, the desire to control." It is not merely a supposition in the sense that Rousseau's general will is so frequently such, and is moreover factitious and bogus. It is open to empiric investigation.

The distinguished pioneer work of Harold Lasswell, especially his *Propaganda Technique in the World War* and his *Psychopathology and Politics* (1930), owes much to his early training in Freudian psychology. That of A. J. Toynbee has been stimulated by the work of C. G. Jung. The present hypothesis, first stated in my *Science and Method*, springs from the mating of the philosophy of Hobbes with the psycho-analytical theory of Alfred Adler, especially in *The Neurotic Constitution* (1912, trans. 1917). (This matter of method is something quite separate from the author's philosophical position as to ends, which has been broadly Thomist.) In *Individual Psychology* (1918, trans. 1925), Adler writes: "A thoroughgoing study has taught us that we can best understand the manifold and diverse movements of the psyche as soon as our most general presupposition, that the psyche has as its objective the goal of superiority, is recognized."

Professor T. Cook, in an article in the UNESCO publication, *Contemporary Political Science*, distinguished the method here adopted (as distinct from that of the valuations of tradition in my *History*) as 'postulational' and the parallel work of Professor H. D. Lasswell as 'psychological.' Although Professor Lasswell, in his *Psychopathology and Politics* and subsequently, has made greater use of case methods, it would appear that both techniques of interpretation can properly be described as 'hypothetical' and as concerned with 'controls.' Certainly Professor Lasswell cannot be charged with being a psycho-analytical dogmatist, and his later works are rather semantic or quantitative and behaviourist in character. The 'hypothetical' or 'postulational' technique is a mere matter of caution, in an immature field.

The fundamental hypothesis of the Power Theory of Politics, later expanded by Professor C. E. Merriam in *Political Power: Its Composition and Incidence* (1934) and still later by Lord Russell in *Power*, has now become almost a commonplace and a platitude, appearing in innumerable titles, and is itself in sad need of a new critical analysis. However, the most powerful work, verging on a pioneer genius, remains that of my colleague for many years in this undertaking, Professor Lasswell, now of Yale, not least in his *Politics: Who Gets What, When, How?* (1936), *The Analysis of Political Behaviour* (1948), and (with A. Kaplan) *Power and Society* (1950). The argument of this present book, while bringing up to date, in some measure presupposes acquaintance with, the argument of the two earlier books in my Systematic Politics, *Science and Method* and the *Principia*.

One form of power is, of course, military power, studied by the theorists of strategy, such as von Clausewitz. Thus Professor Denis Brogan, in his introduction to Leopold Schwarzschild's *World in Trance* (1943) writes: "Power, military power, is as important in world history as it has ever been; it has not been and will not be

abolished by pious opinions, by moral boycotts, by sermons and reso-
lutions. There is little risk in England that the place of moralized
sentiment will be neglected . . . But the place of power is very likely
to be neglected, or stated in terms of a bogus realism, which means
backing the current winner with a great but not deceptive air of
magnanimous free choice."

The importance of this argument should certainly not be ignored:
it is highly topical also today. In this connection Professor N. Spykman's *America's Strategy in World Politics* (1942) still merits consultation. But it would be an error—into which von Clausewitz himself
assuredly did not fall—to suppose that the *only* decisive form of power
is military. Spykman certainly does not so write. Nor do the highly
power-conscious Soviets make this mistake. The well-armed forces of
Chiang fell away, not because of lack of munitions, but because of
lack of morale and the influence of a skilful propaganda of ideas.
General Eisenhower has been among the last to underestimate these
non-military forces. (The present writer can state this on the basis of
personal discussion.) Hence 'power' has been given by political
scientists a meaning both wider and more fundamental. It is in this
technical sense that Professor W. A. Robson wrote, in a UNESCO
Report: "It is with power in society that political science is primarily
concerned—its nature, basis, scope and results . . . The 'focus of interest'
of the political scientist is clear and unambiguous, it centres on the
struggle to gain or retain [not wealth or ownership of production,
but] power, to exercise power or influence over others, or to resist
that exercise." (*The University Teaching of Social Sciences: Political
Science*, 1954, pp. 17–18)

Professor C. J. Friedrich in his *Constitutional Government and Democracy*
(pp. 583–4), has offered some criticism of the theory of power. But (*a*) he has
made considerable use of it himself; (*b*) he selects for criticism the writing
of Professor C. E. Merriam, who is not the strongest representative of the
school, and who is stated to attempt entirely to dissociate political theory from
values—which is (*c*) emphatically not the position adopted in the text. It may
be added that "a human relationship in which the leader and the led are
banded together for the accomplishment of some common objectives . . . partly
by constraint" (p. 19) is *not* an instance of "common values and ends" permeating
what political science has to study, but *may* even be a case of that "using man
as means" to an alien end which Kant condemned as a blasphemy against values.
This consideration stresses the need to distinguish study of the two fields. It may
be added that Professor Friedrich lays full emphasis on both the significance of
psychology for political science and upon 'politicization' of the social field, as distinct from the lawyerly stress upon the state and its sovereignty—both positions
adopted in the text.

For the student a perusal of the suggestive *Study of Politics* by the current President of the American Political Science Association, Professor Charles S. Hyneman, is almost required reading, especially pp. 142–50. Mention should also be made of Professor Vernon Van Dyke's *Political Science* (1960).

It has perhaps been a distinctive weakness of some American political theorists that, unlike Professor Friedrich, they have too much concerned themselves, like Talmudic scholars, with the Constitution and with comments on its interpretations, whereas the Constitution is indeed not Holy Writ, and criticism, for example, of the First and Eighteenth Amendments, could with advantage have been more radical. Jefferson was perhaps right, that constitutions were meant to be changed.

One other aspect of the traditional discussion requires note. A well-known dictum by Lord Acton, in a letter of 1887 to Bishop Mandell Creighton of London—"Power tends to corrupt; absolute power corrupts absolutely"—imports an ethical valuation into power itself. It is stated more succinctly still by Archbishop Fénelon: "power is poison." It is comparable to the maxim that the love of money is "the root of all evil." Two comments can be made on this. First, it may be granted that power, like physical strength or any other outstanding and pleasurable attribute, tends as a matter of immediate imaginative enjoyment to intoxicate certain men with arrogance, as does strong drink, and hence has its sibling dangers in what the theologians call 'pride.' Not as a relationship, but as emotionally substantial, like the possession of wealth without thought of consumption, it can be 'enjoyed'—and the taste for it may grow. Briefly, a Lincolnian modesty may be held to be a virtue, and pride the especial attribute of Lucifer. It is perhaps not beneath note that in commenting on the collapse of the Summit Conference of 1960, the French press explained (May 19, 1960) that the root of the complexity of foreign affairs lay in "the pride of individuals and of nations."

Secondly, and of more theoretical importance, the extent to which power inherently corrupts (apart from the defects of weak, vain or megalomaniac characters) much depends upon the meaning that we are here assigning to 'power.' If we mean 'control' itself (which is the very structure of authority) and, precisely because it is control, something more than momentary, and something having a certain element of futurity and permanence, then the judgement is untrue. It is *lack* of power which has been the corruption and cause of decline of many a state and party. Indeed we should note the Platonic judgement that potentiality for much is intrinsically good; and indeed that the increased power, over physical nature but also in ordering itself, of the human race is a major condition of progress. Thus far, then, 'power,' like the use of 'talents,' has an overtone of praise. This is, incidentally, the position of orthodox theology. Concupiscence, of itself, is not evil. Further, only Divinity has almighty power, *omni potentatui dominans* (Esther 14). What is essential to, or contributes to, the power of the whole race, for example, to reach the stars, *pro tanto* is to be accounted beautiful and good.

If we mean, however, *dominatio* ('domination') as a specific kind of power or *potestas* (in which consent plays a small role and force a large one), or being 'over' when the other side is 'under,' or what Adler calls 'superiority,' then the allegation may indeed be true and this domination corrupt. Indeed, in his treatment of individuals, Adler sets as his goal "the conscious destruction of the will-to-power" by an elaborately psycho-analytical technique. Merely uncritically to identify power and a Nietzschean domination as synonymous is to assume what would have to be proved and what is (rather indeed) a basic error. *Power has many species*, which we do well to analyse. We shall not understand our social structure unless we do. We must not be misled or hypnotized by the cliché 'power politics,' which usually refers to that traditional relation between states which Hobbes described as "gladiatorial."

In the writing of many political theorists 'Power' and 'Domination' are habitually confused or identified; and this fallacy of *pars pro toto* has to be watched for, since the erroneous consequences are grave. Thus Max Weber states (*vide* Reinhart Bendix, *Max Weber*, 1960, pp. 296 ff.) that "all administration means domination"; and indeed he uses the words 'authority' ('autoritäre Befehlungsgewalt') and 'domination' as synonymous (*Wirtschaft und Gesellschaft*, vol. II, part II, chap. IX, p. 544). Patriarchalism was taken as archetype. Beginning with a comparative study of domination, he concluded, not unexpectedly, that a system of bureaucratic rule is inescapable. And, granted the wrong definition, as in mathematics, the more the erudition the more the error.

As we have said earlier, saints and sinners alike desire power, because they aspire to control the means to achieve their ends, pious or impious. The little postmistress, without necessarily having to be a Jill-in-office, is as interested in power on her own scale as the prime minister. Inspired by the desire to 'play safe,' the bureaucrat working to rule becomes the incarnation of the ruthless, the picayune, and the unimaginative. The impulse to power touches something deeper even than the desire to acquire wealth (when this is not itself rather political than economic) and the control of the means of production or to avoid poverty. Strong convictions, indeed, and ideas about ends have shaped and can shape history; but the stronger the convictions the more the determination to acquire power to realize and effect them. If a man is asked whether he would like to have power for himself— not for the other fellow—he will usually find that there is much morally to recommend it, as there would be were he asked whether he would like to have wealth. Whereas, however, Machiavelli tells us that the thorough-paced sinner can adopt many means, including hypocrisy and religiosity, to achieve his ends—and so may any man who, as a military man or engineer, has a single assigned end which he is under mandate to achieve without professional regard for other consequences that may be the by-product of his action—the saint is in a more difficult position. Evil, unlike virtue, is protean. Occasionally the saint's aim may be specific, as to drive the English from the land of France but, as saint, the higher task is to display an integrated pattern of general behaviour with which the choice in adopting particular means must be compatible.

Again, the soldier under mandate—or even the prince in a condition of autocracy amid a general individualistic anarchy—may be solely concerned with victory and may use even apocalyptic weapons to win a battle for Babylonia and, going beyond "breaking the will," to effect the unconditional surrender of the opponent. But the statesman has to consider the wider consequences of the use of these weapons upon his diplomacy and upon the political relations of his country as a state which is going to last into the future. He cannot move in abstract isolation. He has to make some contribution towards building Jerusalem. The implicit dogma of Machiavelli that the moral law, understood as the principle for the happiness of all human beings, is less important than what some individuals of power think may be desirable for the better security in their ways of the few thousands of the people of Florence, has but to be stated to be seen to be a fallacy of misproportion of means and ends; and, indeed, a sophism about the nature of enduring power. This is a particular instance of a general principle. And, as applied by Machiavelli, it is a lie.

The choice of apt means conditions the actual achievement of chosen ends. The choice of particular means limits the character of the ends which can be chosen and achieved. A scientific study of means can throw a new light on what structure of means is apt; but it will also penetrate into the very realm of ends, as indicating what ends are alone realizable by a particular structure of means. It will, for example, shed light upon the compatibility of the pattern of social co-operation among all, as a human end, with the adoption of intrinsic means of domination and tyranny of some over others. It may indicate that, with the adoption of these means, as Lord Russell says, a utopia of love will not emerge out of a fanaticism of aggression or hate or, to put the matter more narrowly, only a close co-operation of *some* can emerge. What may emerge may be what St. Augustine called *magnum latrocinium*—'a vast brigandage.' This limitation of achievable ends by their selected means (and conversely this necessity to select the particular means in accordance with, amid a variety of possibilities, the hypothetical or chosen ends) will especially concern us when we turn to political philosophy and to—if there are any—ultimate values. For the moment we can state the matter summarily: So SOON AS POLITICAL MEANS HAVE IN FACT BEEN CHOSEN, THEY AND THEIR STRUCTURE WILL CONDITION, AND EVEN SEVERELY CONDITION, THE HUMAN AND ACTUAL ACHIEVEMENT EVEN OF THE MOST DIVINE, CATEGORICALLY MORAL, OR IDEAL ENDS (Proposition 8). Each particular apocalypse carries with it, inevitably as it descends into history and the web of means, its own particular fires of destruction, unless its horsemen have first chosen solely to ride in a fashion actually compatible with blessing to men upon earth. Moreover, angelic or rational ends, when pursued by human beings, have to accept the colour of the limitations of humanity as their agency. This applies even to Churches.

Like so many words in the terminology of politics, 'Power' has not escaped abuse and usages that have been vague and conflicting. Discussion of definitions and vocabulary may be tedious but it is quite essential, if scientific progress is to be made. As will be seen, great practical errors of human consequence have flowed from distorted ideologies and idea-patterns, based upon the confused or the oversophistical use of words about our political choices. Demagoguery flourishes owing to precisely such carelessness. The matter is more important since one main charge of Bishop Butler against Hobbes (who was no mean philosopher) is that he left this central term, 'power,' ill defined. "Could anyone be thoroughly satisfied that what is commonly called benevolence or good will was really the affection meant [by love of power], but only by being made to understand that this learned person had a general hypothesis, to which the appearance of good will could not otherwise be reconciled? . . . These are the absurdities which even men of capacity run into" . . . Undoubtedly some men pursue power itself as an end (and Hobbes may cynically have emphasized this, along with "fear of violent death"), just as a miser pursues money. But the accumulation of coins is not what an economist understands by good business, and the accumulation of power as end-in-itself, and not as means, is not the object of our scientific study here. Yet, for all this, men desire a power to realize their benevolent plans and fear an impotence in the means to do so. Power is just as much the preoccupation of the small man or of the liberal who fears negatively to be ruled by others and who wants rights, securities, and defences, as of the big man or of the totalitarian, who wishes to regulate others, positively, in accordance with his own wishes.

It must yet be conceded that some writers, especially those following well-established German traditions (of the pre-Adenauer epoch), have introduced not an analysis, but a kind of *mystique*, of power. Thus, Professor Karl Loewenstein of Amherst College in his *Political Power and the Governmental Process* (1957) with some indebtedness to Gerhard Ritter and explicitly attempting to establish "a conceptual framework," initiates his work by reference to "a Mysterious Triad" of love, faith, and power, and to "the Demonology of Power." While firmly asserting that "Politics is *nothing else* but the struggle for power" (italics mine), he yet asserts, of the members of the triad, that "the cognition of their inner reality escapes [man]. His logical endowment is insufficient to penetrate into their essence." (p. 3) The all-important factor, it seems, is like God on Sinai, the all-incomprehensible. Merely commandments emerge.

Professor Loewenstein states, indeed, that "more and more, power is being considered the dynamic infrastructure of sociopolitical institutions," and that this (which could betoken, in its context, a not wholly healthy return from Bodin to Machiavelli) has largely superseded the earlier interest in sovereignty. But this does not deter him from concentrating his attention on the state—"in certain historical cases, the exclusive organization"—or declaring, without reservation, that "institutions are the apparatus through which the power process functions in a society organized as a state," and that ideologies are the values and value systems that underlie these institutions. Logically it would follow that 'the State' is society organized; and that churches and industrial movements have no native ideologies, since these are "the 'spirit' of the political dynamism of a particular state society" (p. 10). The student should yet note that Professor Loewenstein's work here contains many shrewd and wise observations and is by no means to be dismissed lightly. Many of its chapters are excellent.

Within the ambit of this same German tradition (not that of Kant, despite his over-sharp distinction of substance and phenomena), which influences the work of Hans Morgenthau and Loewenstein, some of the political work of the distinguished Protestant theologian, Professor Reinhold Niebuhr, also falls. There is always a tendency in these writers, as also with Gerhard Ritter, to regard 'power' as some kind of Gothic demonic force, rooted indeed in human nature, but not to be understood in its essence or reduced to any classic comprehension by political science (cf. H. Morgenthau, *Scientific Man v. Power Politics*, 1946); and as escaping from the maxims which guide the moral man. In the opinion of the writer this is a doctrine not just erroneous, but catastrophically erroneous and corruptingly erroneous.

Departing from the common professional language of political science, Dr. Reinhold Niebuhr makes 'force' and 'prestige' ('power' and 'influence' in a less satisfactory form) the major factors of politics.

'Force' or 'coercion' is closely associated with 'domination' or 'dominion,' and then again with the essence of power. 'Prestige' is identified with 'majesty,' which probably involves a *double entendre*. The *maiestas* of Bodin is translated by himself *souveraineté*; and 'sovereignty' is assuredly something very different from 'prestige.' As we shall later see, 'justice' is put into antithesis to 'order,' for which Marxist class-survival explanations or those hinging on 'social survival' may be offered. Hence Dr. Niebuhr writes: "Force, while always minimal in a well-established state, in comparison with 'prestige' or 'majesty' [e.g., of a Napoleon or Mussolini], may itself be the source of authority, at the beginning of a reign or after a revolution. Coercion enforces obedience until the authority of the government has been established, when it may win uncoerced consent by its prestige." (*The Structure of Nations and Empires*, 1959, p. 8. Cf. also p. 242.) This passage illustrates the grave danger of taking 'the State' as the sole example of political activity. It could scarcely have validity in the case of an industrial management, a trade union organizer, all of these exercising authority in terms of functional organization and results, or of a church, which may have prestige but does not usually begin with force. It does, of course, apply in the case of a dynastic king in relation to territories other than his traditional ones, for example, to Frederick the Great in relation to German territories other than Prussia. Force is indeed *one* species of power and, if recognized, of authority. But it is not the *source* of authority as such, which is precisely distinguished from it by the essential element of recognition, habitual or rational. That authority rests on mere power, especially power-as-domination (*Macht*) is a fruitful source of error. Cf. also the work of the distinguished Munich professor, Dr. Erich Voegelin, *The New Science of Politics* (1952).

§ii.   *Power, Potentiality, Force, Domination, and Influence*

A distinction of some subtlety, but important in our work of classification, must be drawn between *potentia* and *potestas*. The former is actual power. *Potestas*, for Cicero, is legal power and authority. English imperfectly renders the difference by distinguishing 'power' and 'potentiality.' The distinction, which is of great importance, manifests itself when we come, with many political writers, to discuss 'influence.' Briefly, 'influence' indicates a 'potentiality' in shaping decisions; but it is not, by common usage, itself the 'power' to decide.

The so-called British Establishment is an excellent instance of what has recognized influence without yet unity in decision. Often influence shows itself, negatively, as the effective power to suppress.

The opposite, and more dangerous, confusion arises between 'power' to decide and 'force.' The German word *Macht*, with all its overtones, as does perhaps the English term 'might,' embraces both concepts and confounds them. 'Force' is indubitably 'power,' if exercised; but not all—or maybe not some of the most important—forms of power involve physical force, which may be marred by its temporary and unstable quality. It may be true that 'fist-right' police-power and army-power are inadequately discussed by theorists with a democratic or liberal bias; and that more attention in our textbooks should be given to the very frequent historical phenomenon, especially outside modern Europe and North America, of army rule. It is yet not the case that we should identify 'power' and 'force,' genus with species. A further profound and frequent confusion (as has already been indicated and which will be a matter of comment later) is that between the genus 'power' and the species of power, often non-physical, which is 'domination' (*dominatio*). Much bad theory rests on this inveterate confusion. Indeed, much of political theory has been concerned with the problem of how to have power, domestic and foreign, in order to avoid domination.

Finally, it is desirable to ask whether 'power' can be 'potential' or, by its nature, must not always be actual. The answer depends upon our chosen use of the words. Thomas Reid wisely wrote, "Power is one thing: its exertion is another thing. It is true that there can be no exertion without power, but there may be power which is not exerted." (*Works*, ed. 1843, vol. I, p. 43) *Pouvoir* and *puissance* are not exactly the same. 'The act of control,' as manifest, patently is 'actual.' "This Power is other than Vain-glory"; and it is other than Influence. We may have a full and actual power to do something, which is not a matter of influence but of competent decision to do or not do something, which we may yet choose not to do. *Power is, therefore, present ability to be free in effecting our own will and to control, whether exercised or whether not exercised but potential.* However, not every Act of Control may require Force or Domination. Control, indeed, unlike Force, implies an element of stability or (limited) permanence; and projects itself into the immediate future of reference. Also the potentiality to control, at wish and will, is more than Influence. As Mr. Alan Bullock says in *The Life and Times of Ernest Bevin* (1960), "influence, unlike authority, is not susceptible of constitutional definition." Further, as George Washington remarked, "influence is not government." Influence produces of itself approval rather than power, although adequate approval makes power. Ambiguity here can confuse the entire argument.

In an important book, *Presidential Power* (1960), Professor Richard E. Neustadt adopts a different terminology. "Command," he writes, "is a method of persuasion, not a substitute." Accepting this slightly unusual meaning attached here to the 'command' (for instance, is it only persuasion that occurs on the parade square?), this statement is consonant with the present theme that Co-operative Power is as much power as Dominative Power. "Power," Neustadt adds, "is persuasion and persuasion becomes bargaining." Granted his use of words (which, under a Hitler or Stalin, could be ironic), this also can be accepted. The affair, in Co-operative Power, is one of the reconciliation of interests, on 'a two-way street.'

However, Professor Neustadt passes over to the identification of 'power' (as persuasion) with 'influence' which has "no guarantee attached." Here we must step carefully and make a vital distinction. 'Persuasion' or 'influence' is power when we mean that the persuasion is 'effective,' that is, we have assurance that an act is under control and will assuredly take place. Professor Neustadt rightly introduces this crucial word 'effectiveness'; and here is the key. But this is quite different from 'influence' regarded as no more than 'the potentiality or opportunity to persuade,' *without* assurance. Admittedly the *vis directiva*, while designed *à diriger*, is not coercive. It may create an atmosphere of 'influence' such that the *effective* course of action becomes highly probable. Nevertheless, the *vis directiva* is only power when it is 'recognized authority,' and moves on such a basis of established co-operative understanding that a breach of its directions would amount to a breakdown of agreed or habitual social controls.

Professor Neustadt's concentration of the power problem on the theme of 'personal influence' can come very near to stress upon the importance, for success and prestige, of a good public relations organization. Power, in a democracy, is this: but it is in essence more than this. We may yet agree that it is other than 'formal powers.' Professor Neustadt, however, with his discussion of 'trading stock' in power, is most right in warning us against textbook triteness: "the probabilities of power do not derive from the literary theory of the Constitution." The Webbs in Russia did not always avoid this error.

It may also be added that men's actions may often be objectively regulated, even by other human beings or social systems, because, for example, of habit, without any person or group of persons aspiring to, or deliberately and consciously exercising, power. The critique of some of the work of Durkheim and Duguit, with their emphasis on the mass reaction of 'the vast anonymous,' is relevant here. The anarchist theorist assumes the possibility of general regulation of a habitual or instinctive character, without control (let alone domination) being displayed by any. This may be utopian; but some parts of the animal creation, such as birds in their flight, seem to show that the supposition is not absurd. What such movements, however, are not is what, in our sense, we call 'political.' Politics has here withered away. A Bergsonian instinct or *élan vital* has replaced it. Perhaps it would be more cautious to say that, if not indeed all political habits and conventions (so that we know what is going to happen), yet political institutions and personal authority and command, have withered away.

Further, we may advance the hypothesis that: ALL POLITICS IS BY ITS NATURE POWER POLITICS. THIS ANALYSIS IS MORE FUNDAMENTAL THAN THE MARXIST (Proposition 9), since it rests on the supposition and the problem of a certain *permanency* of social controls. Today's conflict between Russia and China is not primarily an affair of economics. Even Anarchism does not entirely deny this permanency on the social level, while tending to rely rather upon instinct and habit than upon deliberate action, although it does deny it on the level of governmental dominance. Patently, as a matter of controls, power is relational. But, as a matter of a gift of 'drive' or as a felt need which some individuals have more than others and have perfected in technique, it is 'substantial' (as well as in the actual emotional enjoyment of its exercise by the individual), so that some have gifts for assurance in leadership—and this by consent as well as by coercion—which others, even if institutionally no less endowed and authorized and provided with its forms, yet substantially, that is, in actual enjoyment and gift to animate the efficient relationships, lack. Power is not *only* relational as a matter of act, and dissolvable without residue into a web of institutional relationships or even of reactions of the social organism or mass, since the act still stems from the personality of the actor and the strength of his impulses, irrelevant or prior to the immediate relational scene. We need not therefore disagree with the statement (whatever his interpretation) of Professor Hans Morgenthau, in his *Politics Among Nations*, that "international Politics, *like all politics*, is a struggle for power"; or of Lord Russell in his *Power* that "I shall be concerned to prove that the fundamental concept in social science is Power"; or of Max Weber in his *Politik als Beruf* (1918) that "Politics is the struggle for power or the influencing of those in power, and embraces the struggle between states as such and between organized groups within the state." Subject to the explicit reservations that we have made and shall make about 'unicausalism' and about scientific (or merely rhetorical) dogmatism, and while admitting that it is not yet complete as a science and may well be a science of more than this, we can yet provisionally say that *Politics is the Science of Power*. Our real difficulty and problem has been rather how, with exactitude, to define 'Power' and to remove loaded interpretations.

At the risk of wearying the reader (but inexactitude here can offend against all scientific construction later), it may be pointed out that, when Weber writes that power is the "possibility of imposing one's will upon the behaviour of others even against opposition" (*Wirtschaft und Gesellschaft*, translated by M. Rheinstein and E. Shils in *Max Weber on Law in Economy and Society*, 1954, p. 323; cf. discussion by Bendix, *Max Weber*, p. 294), he is guilty of culpable slackness in phraseology. Power is not a "possibility" or an opportunity (of which one may be impotent to avail oneself when it 'raps at the door') but a potentiality of effective action. And Weber here (as earlier mentioned) further confounds 'power' and 'domination,' which latter indeed 'imposes' its will, with or without opposition and coercion. Weber's German text (*Wirtschaft und Gesellschaft*, vol. II, part II, chap. IX, p. 542) reads: "Herrschaft in dem ganz allgemeinen Sinne von Macht, also von: Möglichkeit, den eigenen Willen dem Verhalten anderer aufzuzwingen." It will be noted that the word Weber uses, translated as 'power,' is 'Macht,' with all its peculiar overtones. An alternative translation in English is 'Might.' The very ambiguity of meaning (and translation) tends to set the tone of a tradition—which can (or which its users suppose can) influence statesmen.

Force, it may be said in summary, is one kind of guarantee of control and, where durable, of power. 'Violence' is the pejorative or 'snarl' word by which we describe the force we condemn. But not all control (or perhaps the most stable and scientific) is by force—which may rather "smash the watchwork than adjust it" and, for reasons given in the text, will provoke the psychology of frustration and counterforce. And not all power is coercive; but Domination is only one species of Power, and Coercion one species of its exercise. Force is only one species of control where it offers such prospect of continuation as to give the guarantees about future action which lie in the very meaning or definition of control. Not all displays of force are even truly defined as control. A Donnybrook Fair is not control.

Influence, on the other hand, is at the opposite pole. Influence, like education, may contribute to build up a control system, especially of a consensual, habitual, or co-operative order, as distinct from command and coercion. It has a potentiality. But the word is so used as to imply an imperfection or margin of uncertainty which is not yet rightly called 'power.' To be brought within the category of potential Power, much less actual Control, we need to add the qualification 'successful influence.' The control lies in the success, not the influence which is one modality of endeavouring control. Unsuccessful power is not power. Successful influence is a name for mental control; and propaganda is a species of it. Certainly it must not be supposed that the prayers and influence of the saints or the force of ideas and of propaganda, whether *de fide* or otherwise, are politically negligible. A realistic view will be the opposite, despite Stalin's famous gibe. But, nevertheless, influence alone is only a swaying of those who have power, not a control of them. It can, if so institutionalized through church or education or press that it *has* to be heard, become a 'directive power.' But it cannot be described as more than power at a second remove.

Dr. Georg Schwarzenberger in his *Power Politics* (1941; 2nd ed., 1951, p. 14) writes: "Power is the mean between influence and force. All three are different ways of establishing a social nexus on a footing considered satisfactory by the active agent in such relations. Power distinguishes itself, however, from influence by reliance on external pressure as a threat in the background, and from force by preference for achieving its ends without the actual use of physical pressure. Thus, power may be defined as capacity to impose one's will on others by reliance on effective sanctions in case of non-compliance. It also follows that power is both a subjective and relative phenomenon." The comment may, however, be made: (*a*) that non-compliance implies *pro tanto* non-power (a point brought out by Professor Felix Oppenheim, in his "Analysis of Political Control: Actual and Potential," *Journal of Politics*, vol. XX, 1958, who also elaborates a distinction between 'the [negative] power to control' and 'the [positive] cause of action'); (*b*) that to speak of power having a 'preference' is to import meanings into the word which may prove unacceptable and 'loaded'—the only scientific 'preference' of power is to be effective; (*c*) that these definitions would exclude *all* species of both force and of influence from the genus 'power'—which seems unacceptable and paradoxical. Incidentally, Professor K. R. Popper (*The Poverty of Historicism*, p. 62) posits a sociological law, "you cannot make a revolution without causing a reaction," which bears upon the unstable or explosive character of force as power, although this 'law' itself needs to be put into the context of a systematic exposition.

Peter H. Odegard and E. A. Helms in their *American Politics; A Study in Political Dynamics* (1938) quote from Harold Lasswell's *Politics*: "The Study of Politics is that of *influence* and the influential," and continue "what there is to get may be summed up as power." The observation of George Washington, already quoted, will be recalled here: "influence is not government." Also, *eo ipso*, it is not control. But the objective activities of pressure groups are of course relevant to politics, and also the subjective values which cause the application of pressure. 'Power,' as has been said, is indeed to be distinguished from mere present 'control,' which formally may be ephemeral, since it, of its very nature and desirability, implies *potentia de futuro*. However, 'control' is more, in our usage, than 'influence' since it implies, at least *de praesente*, assurance, whereas 'influence' only implies a probability.

Professor Georges Gurvitch (*Twentieth Century Sociology*, chap. x. "Social Control," p. 291) lists 'ideals' among 'controls'—which are "the sum total or rather the whole of cultural patterns, social symbols, collective spiritual meanings, values, ideas and ideals, as well as acts and processes directly connected with them," that is, not only 'controls' but the entire scheme of enduring relations and influences. M. Bertrand de Jouvenel properly adopts a less sweeping usage. It is perhaps relevant that the English verb 'to control,' with its sense of *diriger* or *maîtriser*, is itself more rigid than the French verb *contrôler*. M. de Jouvenel (*De la souveraineté*, p. 29) uses a subtle ambiguity when he writes: "politique [est] l'action qui incline des volontés étrangères." 'Control,' in this book, is used in a fashion which looks to the empirical result rather than to the mode; and hence tends to the French sense of the verb.

In the work of Mr. Chester Barnard, *The Function of the Executive*, the crucial study for political science is rather seen as that of *responsible decision-making*. Here the appropriate comment would seem to be (*a*) that some decision-making, as of an engineer, is not distinctively political; (*b*) that such as is, undoubtedly is of key importance and always involves will and control, *but* it is set in a social web of interdependence, conscious and unconscious, not least in a free democracy. Not all controls involve any single focus of decision, responsible or otherwise, and many of our most difficult political problems arise precisely from this fact.

Interestingly enough, whereas Odegard, Helms, and Lasswell add on, to our definition, 'influence,' which may be at best rather a species of power diffusely organized and not institutionalized as such, Dr. V. O. Key of Harvard restricts the field, as more limited than that of power or control, to "those power or control relationships having to do with the machinery of *government*," in a book which is nevertheless called *Politics, Parties and Pressure Groups*. The difficulty here lies (*a*) in the risk of *petitio principii* about just what is 'government,' an activity still to be analysed, and (*b*) the risk of excluding by definition all discussion (as certainly not 'machinery') of 'the community,' with its valuational overtones, which constitutes much of the substance of political philosophy. Doors of investigation which should not yet be closed become closed. Here I must deprecate that tendency of some definitions to fall into 'spiritual naturalism,' with which Dr. K. R. Popper so courteously taxes myself in his *The Open Society and Its Enemies* (1945, pp. 208–10). The valuational and philosophical field cannot be disregarded, by an exclusive preoccupation with 'objective' institutions and machinery: there is always, as Rousseau and Mill knew, a 'why' as well as a 'how.'

Apart from the work, already discussed, done in Chicago and Cornell between 1924 and 1935, and the (at this time) almost unnoticed work of A. F. Bentley, the student will note the preoccupation with power of so many recent authors in these disturbed times such as F. Wieser (*Das Gesetz der Macht*, 1926), Bertrand Russell (*Power*), Gerhard Ritter (*Die Dämonie der Macht*, 1940), Georg Schwarzenberger (*Power Politics*), Guglielmo Ferrero (*The Principles of Power*, 1942), Bertrand de Jouvenel (*Du pouvoir*), Edmund A. Walsh (*Total Power*, 1946), Alfred Pose (*Philosophie du pouvoir*, 1948), Lord Radcliffe (*The Problem of Power*, 1952), Thomas I. Cook and Malcolm Moos (*Power through Purpose*, 1954), Louis J. Halle (*The Nature of Power*, London ed., 1955), Karl Loewenstein (*Political Power and the Governmental Process*), Barrington Moore, Jr., (*Political Power and Social Theory*, 1958), David Spitz (*Democracy and the Challenge of Power*, 1958), and Mr. Secretary Dean Acheson (*Power and* [in smaller letters] *Diplomacy*, 1958), as well as Professors Hans Morgenthau, Nicholas Spykman, and others already cited. Several of these authors are not concerned with a general theory of politics but rather with historical discussion, although the mere concentration of professional interest since 1930 is remarkable. The list of those who, since the work of the twenties, have given their attention to the problem of power is certainly impressive. It would, however, be distressing if so many of these eminent writers had operated, as central to their thought, with a fundamentally unclear idea; but I cannot indeed believe this to be the case.

The remark of my friend and sometime colleague, the late Professor Carl Becker, in *Making a Better World* (1945) in the chapter "Can We Abolish Power Politics?" is worth noting: "The simple fact is that politics is inseparable from power." It is perhaps relevant to add the remark of President Conant of Harvard in his *Modern Science and Modern Man* (p. 130): "Which one of the common-sense fuzzy ideas about consciousness, love, or the zest for power will be picked up by a rare genius and be the basis for a vast expansion of fruitful scientific work?" The challenge should be taken up. Political scientists must rise to the height of their professional opportunities and of a reasonable public demand.

It is sometimes objected (as already noted) that power is a complex, elusive notion, especially in the context of contemporary society. This is, of course, true—but, except for loose thinkers, this states the beginning and not the end of the problem. The term has, as above, to be defined and used with care—not discarded and its analysis abandoned, as is done by some who are more political philosophers than, save as amateurs, political scientists. After all, if 'power' is a complex and elusive term, if used in lay fashion, so too is 'wealth.' Usually this objection indicates a desire to return to the discussion of politics in the older terminology of the lawyers (but not in the terminology, for example, of the more modern sociological schools of law). Our task is the practical one of finding how far what we may now term the 'Power Hypothesis' provides any useful key—more useful, and fundamental, for example, than the economico-materialist hypothesis of Marx—or one key of major utility among many, for unlocking the door to a General Theory of Political Action, such as Adam Smith, Ricardo, and Keynes have provided in Economics.

§iii. *Towards a General Theory of Power*

If we are to follow the good example given by Graham Wallas in his *Human Nature in Politics*, we shall not be afraid of investigating the actual psychological causes which add to that appetite for power which political philosophers from the days of Machiavelli and Hobbes have alleged, and which Lord Acton himself found Machiavelli to be justified in remarking as a dominant factor. The 'small man' may not be moved by it or, more accurately, may be moved by desire to have the power to avoid the responsibilities of decision in the greater conflict; but those who shape society are so moved in the more overt sense. A Gandhi, a Capone, and a Hitler, all desire power to achieve by such means their chosen ends. Power of itself is neutral (subject to what we have said above).

The investigation is empirical, conditioned by the limits of contemporary psychological research (and hence to be undertaken hypothetically), and can only here be stated in a most abbreviated form. Its interest, however, lies in its possible confirmation of our central hypothesis; in the vitality which it can give to the whole formal treatment; in the unexpected lights and insights which its speculations can give; and in its illumination of the fundamental connection between Will (as used in our original definition of politics) and Power. By Will, I understand a resolution of mental powers towards action. First is the Idea and the emotive Wish in its free dream-world; then is the active Will for Freedom to realize objectively the Wish;

then is the demand for Power, as means to assure this Freedom in the act. The first demand, it will be noted, is not for power but for freedom for oneself—to which may come to be added fear of the freedom of others. Of the later demand for Domination, Fear is the converse. Some, indeed, may rather say that in the beginning is the need. But, unless the need is recognized and a wish established (which, in most of the centuries of human customary existence, may well not be the case), the sequence of action which we here have to discuss may well not be set up. What moves men, perhaps unfortunately, is not the real need, but the felt need. Pleasure, as Hobbes said, counts, as well as Need and Fear.

The matter can be set out in a brief summary, adequate for illustration and without pretence of psychological finality. At least this has the virtue of enabling us to turn from perhaps tedious commentary about the correct definition to a fresh statement of fundamentals. It begins in our scheme with the Wish. The newly born baby is full of wishes concentrated upon its mother. When satisfied, it has what some psychologists have called a sense of 'oceanic omnipotence.' More accurately this might be called a 'sense of oceanic being,' as of those unborn and still 'at one'd' with their mother. Here no problem involving power has yet arisen. The infant, again, does not yet doubt that the moon could belong to it, if it wanted the moon. It has not confronted a doubt or fear. It does not clearly distinguish between subject and object and objective limits, between itself and what is not itself, or between wishes than can be fulfilled and wishes (as for the moon and stars) which are too contrary to the *real structure* of things ever to be fulfilled, so that the will is impotent. The God who is the principle of reality and the unlimited principle of the limit has as yet imposed no veto in Paradise. This area of Wish is indeed not at all so unimportant for political action as might be supposed.

A vastly larger area of political behaviour than is academically supposed takes place on this plane of the wish-fulfilling imagination. Not only the Utopian literature of politics, but much of that dreaming about the Good Society which may suddenly descend dynamically, as a revolutionary movement of freedom, into the frustrated world of affairs, sometimes to end in disillusionment, sometimes by faith to prove creative, belongs to this unchecked world of Wish, this world of dream freedom. Good folk, moving in such a blissful world, are usually ineffectual folk—unless they become fanatics obsessed with the idea that the Almighty or the Dialectic is on their side. Then they become prophets of power. Some political parties—or their dedicated party workers—rather think of themselves as churches inspired by the revealed dogma of a future apocalypse, which will transcend all material obstacles and historical limits; and occasionally this dream apocalypse indeed becomes a historical, if terrifying, reality. Indeed, the greater the obsession with the dream utopia the more the tendency, when confronted with the actual social structure of the time (which certainly may have only an inadequate basis in permanent social reality and natural law), to react by means of violence of an apocalyptic order, 'a last judgement.' This may issue creatively in progress and success for the visionaries, confirming and justifying their rationalized and elaborated ideology, or may be doomed to failure and amount to obstinacy equivalent to a death-wish. (Politics, let us repeat, is not limited to what mediocrities think to be possible.) This can happen with the dedicated members alike of political parties and of churches and of intransigent reformist groups.

Like comments also apply to much sectarian churchly literature which, in a perfectionist 'other-worldliness' of freedom, can develop its hopes unrestricted by mundane history and human nature (but also sometimes even unrestricted by the rationality of God) so that it comes to deny, as against the orthodox faith, a rational Reality in favour of the caprice of 'Jehovah's will' or the 'cruel will' of our own super-ego. Leibnitz, like St. Thomas earlier, although he was a Protestant, avoided this heresy. Here, however, also prophetic ideals may gather conviction, later immersing themselves in reality by true vision, to descend upon the actual world, its priests and rulers, to denounce or to exhort.

It is indeed well that we should dream, since when we cease to dream we only sleep—a condition indeed to which Freud said that, thanks to some law of psychic thermodynamics, we ever seek to return. Apathy is a very real political factor and its actuality offers the revolutionary his best excuse. Even in the best of democracies the self-satisfied citizen often has to be pressed to reflect on the matters on which he votes by the stimulus of a little violence—or of 'non-violent' illegal action. This is regrettable but true, and has been noted by both Bryce and Bentley.

As I have said in my article, "Authority and its Critics," in the symposium *Authority* (1958) edited by Professor C. J. Friedrich: "it is a mistake of old-fashioned liberalism to ignore how much of political action takes place in close connection with the emotion-shaped Jungian world of imagination—in identification with Hollywood-style princesses, and with fantasies of national omnipotence—a world of various opiates (including the Marxist predestination to victory), with attendant sedative or intoxicant dreams." (A critical review of this contribution will be found in the *Mid-Western Political Quarterly*, 1959.)

However, Walter Bagehot took up this element of fantasy and imaginative identification (howbeit with a typical nineteenth-century attitude of patronage towards the intellectual limitations of 'the lower classes') in his classical description of the English Constitution and Monarchy. Cf. also my article "On Liberty," in the symposium *Aspects of Liberty*, edited by Professor Clinton Rossiter and Milton Konvitz (reviewed in the *American Political Science Review*, June, 1959); and Raymond Aron's valuable book, *L'Opium des intellectuels* (1955).

If the child has a good inheritance and good nurture, its original satisfaction by the mother will be transferred into a condition of trust in the mother; and the rational or social wishes which, without difficulty, it will be formed, educated, and habituated to express will be those which the mother will be able and desire to satisfy. The shaped or rational wishes so satisfied, the will to satisfy them will have no ground for becoming self-conscious; and the child will pass from satisfaction and trust—which the Greeks called πίστις, usually translated 'faith'—to easy confidence, first in the world of its mother; then of its parents; then of generalized 'reality,' that is, as the theologians say, of God; and then (which comes later) of actual multifarious human society. His benevolence in the affairs of human interdependence can be relied upon. His trusts and also his distrusts will be 'rational,' the latter derived from the logic of specific experiences, approached originally upon the basis of Trust, and from the discovery that there are knaves in the world. The attitude can be called 'theist,' in the specific sense that the universe is regarded as created to be the bearer of good values. It has been a singular satisfaction to me, and a confirmation, to discover that M. de Jouvenel makes *amitié*, in his book *De la souveraineté*, closely corresponding to what I here call 'trust,' the central theme of his argument on social stability, authority and sovereignty.[1] The limits will be seen as no more an 'obstacle' than a mountain is to a climber; but as facts of nature or life to be overcome by competent skill—and which will be overcome because one is competent. The ordinary man, and not only the lame, will easily abandon the wish to be an Olympic runner, and will turn his energies elsewhere. It is a nonsense question to ask whether there is a deprivation of freedom to be unable to obtain that which, by hypothesis, we do not wish to obtain.

However, the limits on freedom and on what the will can command

[1] A critical review by Professor William H. Harbold of Washington University of M. de Jouvenel's work, on the theme of power, and my own will be found in the *Western Political Quarterly*, vol. VI, no. 4, December, 1953.

in the satisfaction of some wishes, although untested, nevertheless remain in the actual structure of reality, and not merely in unlucky accident or an ill-wind or in the malice of some unfriendly neighbours. Hence some philosophers have developed the doctrine of the enlightened will and of 'real' interest, that is, approved, unfrustrated, and 'free,' thanks to a humble, habitual conformity with the more enduring realities, and indeed the doctrine of "the perfect law of liberty," only challenged by a lawless 'pride.' In political science, however, as distinct from political philosophy, we have primarily to be concerned, not with moral education, but with actualities and with the actual will, whether right or wrong.

The small child, on the other hand, may not be so psychologically fortunate in his development of trust as to move on into confidence in parents, God and Society, and then into confidence in his own skill to overcome all that should be overcome. The career of what we may call the 'right-handed' or 'good' child may not be his. Factors (perhaps no one of them decisive) of 'bad seed,' bad nurture, environment, and bad actual social structure or an 'insane society,' of luck or bad choice and bad will, may decide against his remaining in this Eden of natural innocence or maturing as 'a child of grace.' Every child is going early to discover that there are certain acts which it is forbidden in Eden, certain wishes that it is not allowed to fulfil. With the child fortunate in temperament or good in nurture, they may be few. Another kind of child may say, in the words of the Capeks' *Insect's Play*: "I want, I want, I don't know what I want." However, it lies originally in its very nature, as a physically separate being, fighting for survival, not only ideally 'to wish,' but existentially 'to will' to execute or achieve whatever may actually be its wish.

The condition of a static, enjoyed Eden of Freedom is more primitive or basic than the *élan* or energy or dynamic drive of Will or the condition of struggle for Power. It is a state of Nature in the dream-world of the subjective mind. But in an objective world of change and action, the one imaginative and solipsist condition passes over inevitably into the other practical one of relationship. This emergent Will can indeed be shaped and changed by a sense of the superior wisdom of authority or by a maturing appreciation of 'facts' (as Walter Lippmann advised in his *Preface to Morals*, 1929) and of how reality is structured, which increases with maturity. Even so, where there are obstacles to a contemplated freedom in the achievement of the rational and willed object, the mind first becomes preoccupied, losing natural innocence, with the *power* (of whatever kind) to overcome them, and with *cupido dominandi* ('ambition for power'). Will is not Power but, moving into action, can require it. First is the wish, the thought, the contemplation of freedom to enjoy the object of the want; but then comes the contemplation of the obstacle. Then comes the will to power; the power; and the realization in actual freedom of the wish.

But another development is possible: that the child becomes wedded to its self-will as such, and becomes obstinate and proud about its own egotism and insistent on its freedom to have 'its way.' It discovers the need for actual power. It looks at the tree of knowledge, aware both of the commanded limits and of what the sweet-smelling fruit of success can give, and makes a choice. In the struggle to survive, generate, dominate, it is tempted by the apple of lust for power for its own will as such and because it is its *own* Will, growing with the *fomentum carnis* and uncontrollable passion. In pride, it is tempted to demand power to rebel and to consume the fruit. There is a gradual hardening and interacting process. The wish is not fulfilled, and the wilful child refuses to understand the reason why. Or perhaps in a bad society or, with bad nurture, parental egotism, and deprivation of affection, there *is* no good personal reason why the child is both perverse and frustrated, and the sin is the parents'; or, since the nurture as distinct from the economic aspect of life is peculiarly the mother's, the sin is especially the mother's, even if the full genetic blame cannot be hers alone.

The frustrated will takes on the attitude of mistrust in the particular case, which enlarges itself into a general distrust or suspicion of mother, parents, reality, God, and society. It confronts its world with fear and defensiveness. Every opponent, and whole classes and nations of opponents, are seen as incorrigible knaves, full of 'knavish tricks.' This is a commonplace of contemporary psychology. All counterbalancing emotions of charity or judgements of decency are held to be aims of an inept political or social or personal 'sentimental-ism'; and reason is converted to the task of 'hardening the heart.' As Hobbes says, fear and, above all, "fear of violent death," becomes (as in this atomic age) the key to policy. There emerges what Harrington calls a *libido dominandi*. We get what I will call the 'left-handed' or 'bad' child. (I use the term 'left-handed' not, of course, literally, but to indicate a structural graining of brain and personality which neverthe-less does not prevent as yet the overcoming of the handicaps by choice or by that environmental factor in reality or society called 'grace,' which can overcome the original disposition, latent in all, to pride of will.) Not only does the child act out its adolescent revolt in public, and not only is there a pleasure in naughtiness which adds a mischievous spice to life; the adult acquires a pleasure in destruction.

The work of Dr. Melanie Klein and Dr. Susan Isaacs on small children has stressed the element of aggressiveness in their conduct which has, as factual data, to be taken into account by those who would construct their optimistic political philosophy with Rousseau, the greatest of all philosophers of wishful thinking, on the basis of the 'naturally good' child (until corrupted by civilized institutions), the child that is the father of that 'Common Man' who is romantically never himself 'a dirty fellow' or Caliban. Those students who require a more elaborate psychological study than that which it would be relevant to give in the lay sketch provided here should consult J. C. Flugel's *Man, Morals and Society* (1945). It will yet be clear from what is said here that the ordinary trusting man has to learn rationally to protect himself against interested and aggressive power groups, with occupational axes to grind.

It is noteworthy that, according to Marxist philosophers, the grave fault alleged in the work of psycho-analysts is, disregarding objective reality, to encourage every bellicose or primitive instinct to claim a right to express itself. Here Marxist and Catholic philosophy are far closer than is customary or than is conventionally thought. What, however, the Marxist (and pre-eminently, the follower of Engels) tends to underestimate is the impulse of creative man to shape his world from his soul and maybe rational spirit outwards, and not simply to be epiphenomenal to the Ganges-flood of the dialectic of objective matter, shaping him from without inwards.[2] The Logos-movement is not objective matter, but consubstantial with our own creative spirit. It need scarcely be pointed out that the Marxists do not object to certain bellicose emotions, but are (as will be noted later) themselves the chief proponents of an elaborated philosophy of Mistrust.

As the attitude of suspicion of *mis*trust becomes general and settled, so does the feeling of frustration and of fighting a fearful battle for one's will in an inevitable conflict, which one has 'realistically' (that is, neurotically) got either to win or lose. There is the pattern of 'domination or submission,' 'over or under.' This specific and new form of the desire for power will be noted. Fear of *loss* of freedom

[2]It is but fair to say that some of the early writings of Marx have an apocalyptic or prophetic character with different philosophical implications of an individualist and an anti-determinist character, although this involved contradictions in his own (or in his and Engels') thought. See George Lichtheim, *Marxism: An Historical and Critical Study* (1961) *passim*; J. Plamenatz, *German Marxism*, pp. 76, 310–15. It indeed appears that, thanks to modern scholarship, the young Marx will emerge as the great individualist, although this is unfortunately not yet recognized in all quarters of the world.

complements the great and original importance attached to freedom *for* survival. Concentration of will upon power as such grows with this fear of loss. There is an original bias to self-will which can become 'hard-of-heart' and proud; an Original Sin, a bias or tendency present, not in *some* men, but in *all* men, nations and societies, however righteous they account themselves. Not only has the egoistic will become highly self-conscious, obstinate and 'proud,' by a compensating arrogance, but all of one's environment becomes something with which one is in competition and which has got to be controlled by dominative power, of which there is (as Hobbes says) never quite enough. Assurance of the future is not by co-operation with one's fellows, which one can expect and be confident that one will in turn receive—they can never be trusted—but by dominion, where the safeguard of yet more dominion can always be wished. There is lack of confidence except in an unceasing struggle, in which one has got to be either 'on top' or 'under.' The kind of Power called Domination is (as Marx shows) what one requires.

The feeling of frustration becomes the habit of 'defensiveness,' of 'the chip on the shoulder,' and of the look-out to take the opportunity oneself for aggression and victory in the real fight. There is what Adler calls the quest for "the goal of superiority." "War is the father of all things." Competition is the secret of progress, and the devil takes the hindermost in the race for Power and Success. The social life is one of *Kampf* or fight. The attitude to reality becomes one of an aggressive atheism and the monitions of religion are to be regarded as monkish weakness or as old wives' fables. Perhaps as the man matures, with his own group, nation, or class he may establish some basis of common interests which are the Hobbesian intelligent self-interests of all, such as the calculated avoidance of violent death. Even here he may win advantages by competitive smartness. But at least towards other groups he is hostile. Indeed, his aggressiveness, having been transferred over to his group, may receive (as Ranyard West insists) against aliens the reinforcement of group sanction and morality.

In more marked cases, he is hostile towards most members of his own group; he has become "Ishmael, for his hand is against every man." Desire, as Aristotle said, is unlimited. It is, therefore, condemned to innumerable frustrations which, from the point of view of the suspicious personality, will be malicious frustrations. Any breach, therefore, of the moral law, here regarded as the convention of the more powerful, will be reasonable, including kleptomania or the egoistic taking of the property of others, or violent assault. Above all, the distrustful man moves to the belief that the so-called rules of morality or decency are merely the customs supported by one lot of clever fellows, in defence of their own position, which a really more clever and pragmatic lot of fellows will know how to get around either for their own several power and advantage or (with an element of contradiction involving 'honour among thieves,' but enforced by vendetta) for that of their gang or class.

It is not so much that hate is a more powerful motivation than love, although in an animal history of the prey and the preyer this must be allowed for, as that fear and appetite for assuming power have replaced trust. A step further, and we have reached the medically neurotic type, in which distrust is a recognizable disease. Every new experience presents itself as a challenge in which the question is not 'How can I best shape my will to reality?' (or 'What is the more eternal reality in the name of which I might be right in challenging this local custom or transient injustice?') but 'How shall I make this challenger yield to me, accommodate himself to my pride and sovereign will?' In this last phase but one, it is not enough to have physical power; one is under the emotional compulsion of the inferior-feeling to display it. Hate has turned in as self-hate, a diffused hate of *all* reality, a psychological atheism. The man so possessed is unable to love himself or anyone else: "he that loveth iniquity hateth his own soul" (Psalm 10: 16); and he that cannot enjoy himself will not enjoy his neighbour. The phase is that of Sadism; nothing so satisfies as displays of cruelty, even of blood and Mexican human sacrifice, displaying 'virility.' The mood is that of the pathological murderer. The type is no longer Ishmael but Cain. And the brand, it will be recalled, of the potential Cain, who carried the original sin to its logical end, is upon every man. No man here, and (whatever the philosophers of the State, or of men as beyond good and evil, may say) no nation is wholly exempt from this original sin.

The final desperate manifestation of power, after sadism, is the display of the power to annihilate in suicide. But ideally, and for some who have the calculated self-interest to survive, there is the phase of the deliberate intellectual choice of evil *because* it is evil, as a sweet revenge on humanity and reality, which is Satanism.

Recently psychologists and sociologists have given attention to the case of the recessive types, men who seem not so much to be apathetic to desire for power (and indeed to most desires) but to seek to avoid it. It is not here necessary always to assume a desire to be dominated, although of this last Erich Fromm in *Man for Himself* (1947) writes that its mood is: "if I submit to the stronger person he will give me all I need"—his power will become, by parasitic symbiosis, mine. We may find, on closer analysis, either an empathic or hero-worshipping identification with aggressive types or an alternative technique of power, on the part of those inferior in strength, by submissiveness to woo those who have the power to achieve for them their objects. Again, the substitution of passive resistance for aggression may be a calculated technique of power.

There remain yet a large mass who, in the struggle for power, have neither overcome distrust by rational co-operation nor accepted defeat and yet found a route of escape, but who have accepted defeat as their lot from lack of energy and from habit. It is here that the inculcation of a *greater* rational aggressiveness and rational discontent, which we shall later discuss, inspired by education and moral ambition (that is, will directed to reasonable objects and skills), become relevant. One interesting and frequent compromise is that of the persons who gratify their desire for power, while protecting themselves against exposure of their absence of personality and vitality, by ensconsing themselves, pseudo-democratically, in some small official or bureaucratic position from which they can display authority (as 'the Government' or the like, or even as governesses) over all who come near their chosen web. One of the greatest menaces of our contemporary age, substituting the 'official' attitude for the 'co-operative,' is the psychology of the defensive-aggressive Bureaucratic Mind, "drest in a little brief authority."

§iv. *Civilization and Its Discontents*

The classical analysis, in neo-Hobbesian terms of human nature, as it manifests itself in its struggle against the authority and Confucian good manners imposed by civilization and culture, will be found in Sigmund Freud's great work, *Civilization and Its Discontents* (1927–31). In his later work, when he operates with the 'death instinct' and impulse to self-destruction, Freud draws nearer to the analysis, in terms of power, of his disciple Adler. All Rousseauite philosophy about man, with his heart always good, being frustrated by social institutions which are inexplicably wicked—by kings, priests and capitalists (as exclusively power-obsessed)—is discarded in favour of a more ferocious exposure of the human heart which finds within itself murder, primal since the days of Cain, although it is less disquieted when it finds release rather in the satisfactions and dreams of tragic or, at a lower level, criminal literature. Freud writes: "The bit of truth behind all this—one so eagerly denied—is that men are not gentle, friendly creatures wishing for love, who simply defend themselves if they are attacked, but that a powerful measure of desire for aggression has to be reckoned as part of their instinctual endowment

. . . In all that follows I take up the standpoint that the tendency to aggression is an innate, independent, instinctual disposition in man, and I come back now to the statement that it constitutes the most powerful obstacle to culture . . . The natural instinct of aggressiveness in man, the hostility of each one against all and of all against each man, opposes this program of civilization."

Psychological studies of the lust for power will be found, not only in such works of Freud as *Civilization and Its Discontents*—where the full dramatic force is given to the fundamental challenge of one aspect of man's character to civilization itself, and to man's active preference for barbarism—but also in the work of R. Dodge and E. Kahn in *The Craving for Superiority* (1931); of Thouless; and of D. W. Harding in *The Impulse to Dominate* (1941). Harding writes, "our civilization has a long established faith in the social techniques of domination and submission as the chief means of handling disagreements; many people indeed can conceive of no other way." Edward Glover in *War, Sadism and Pacifism* (1933) says in effect, in criticism of the rational arguments of Sir Norman Angell, that the bias which can lead to aggression or protest "is dictated by individual unconscious needs and not by rational conditions of social necessity," a view in accord with that of Pareto, but raising the issue of group demands for superiority and *gloire*. Dr. Karen Horney in *The Neurotic Personality of our Time* (1937) remarks on "the secret insistence" of the neurotic "that the world shall adapt itself to him instead of him adapting himself to the world," while Dr. Susan Isaacs in *Social Development in Young Children* (1933) points out the desire in children to play the role of power, which has to be guided into co-operative channels. Dr. Ian Suttie (*The Origins of Love and Hate*, 1935), Dr. Karl A. Menninger (in his *Love against Hate*, 1942) and Dr. Erich Fromm (*The Art of Loving*, 1956) stress the need for affection by lonely man as a fundamental drive, needing corrective satisfaction; but Menninger goes further than our text in thrusting Eden back into a pre-natal condition, and in alleging that every child is born in a condition, not of fear, but of rage and hate. The view in the text is supported by M. F. Ashley Montagu (*The Direction of Human Development*, 1955), who, however, also sums up the evidence for primitive innocence, that "the child is born good."

These views of psychologists and educators are carried over to a basic socio-logical analysis by Dr. John Dollard of Yale and his sociological associates in their *Frustration and Aggression* (1939) with its theme that "this study takes as its point of departure the assumption that aggression is always a consequence of frustration," (a point challenged by Karl Menninger), while comparisons of aggressive cultures, such as the Mundugumer of New Guinea, and the Kwatiutl Indians of the North West of America, studied by such an anthropologist as Dr. Ruth Benedict, in *Patterns of Culture* (1934), in contrast with pacific religious cultures such as the Pueblo of New Mexico, illustrate the theme. So does the work of Professor R. Linton, in *The Cultural Background of Personality* (1947), and that of Dr. Margaret Mead. We shall return to consideration of this.

Mr. Walter Lippmann, in *Preface to Morals*, stresses 'facing facts' as a sign of maturity; while a study of the psychology and logic of 'pride' will be found in *The Nature and Destiny of Man* (1941) by the theologian, Dr. Reinhold

Niebuhr. The universality of the tendency to this 'original sin' is patent, unless checked by 'grace.' It is left for such a political scientist as Professor Lasswell to insist in *World Politics and Personal Insecurity* (1935) that there is "an unbroken line connecting personal insecurity with the outbreak of war among nations"; and for Dr. Ranyard West, who has more recently developed his theme in the Walgreen Lectures in Chicago, to urge in his *Conscience and Society* (1942) that "only by abolishing power units which can cross [without authoritative controls?] the path of other power units shall we detach the loyalty of normal man from a point of danger, where it can breed dangerous hostility."

In an imaginative book, *Dominations and Powers* (1951) George Santayana speaks of "uncontrollable circumstances," more than mere 'Powers,' frustrating, "and all the latter, when they cannot be escaped, will become Dominations." The distinction here is reaffirmed, with a slight variation of language, between power and domination, although genus and species are elevated into two separate genera. The two species (at least) are Dominative Power and, on the basis of Trust, Co-operative Power. THE DESIRE FOR DOMINATION IS ONE SPECIES OF THE DESIRE FOR POWER, AND IS CAUSED BY A CONFIRMED FEAR OF FRUSTRATION. THE INCLINATION TOWARDS CO-OPERATIVE POWER IS ANOTHER SPECIES. (Proposition 10) This distinction is overlooked by many writers; and confusion of theory, leading to belief that the notion of 'power' is incurably 'elusive' and to dangerous confusion in practice (explaining the moral animadversions of Fénelon and Acton) results.

It will be remarked that, whenever in human history we find a parallelism or concurrence of new conclusions arising in several distinct scientific disciplines at once, such as we have illustrated in these last paragraphs, a significant revolution in the climate of thought (as at the Renaissance or with the theory of Evolution) and a great change in the affairs of men may be anticipated. It is our theme that such a mighty revolutionary climax can be expected in the understanding of politics today, urged on by critical dangers to the whole human race. Also, with Weston LaBarre, in *The Human Animal* (1954) we may note that the greatest advances are often made, scientifically, from points on the border-lines of the recognized disciplines, such as politics, sociology and psychology, not to speak of anthropology and economics. The 'Power Theory,' therefore, with its light on the shape of the demand for trust, fraternity and the satisfactions of community, and its frustrations, as well as the 'Redefinition of Politics,' may be expected to mark a substantial change in the nature of political science and an advance in approach. Neither the economico-materialist approach of Marx (which bears the typical but out-dating hallmarks of the early nineteenth century and of the crude aggressive psychology of laissez-faire, however inverted) nor the popular-idealist approach of Rousseau penetrate, it may be submitted, so deep nor are they so scientifically satisfactory.

It is not unamusing to note that the head of the great conservative House of Hapsburg, the Archduke Otto, in his stimulating little *Soziale Ordnung von Morgen* (1957) discovers the poisons of our age to be Marxism—and old-type Capitalism. Anglo-Saxon political theorists, with their old-fashioned Liberal background, should please note. Of recent years the term (publicized by President Eisenhower) 'competitive co-operation' has come into use.

§v. *Science v. Determinism*

The implication of the theme of the last section is that political organization, although shaped as social by external circumstances of geography, economics and customs and early institutions, yet flows from a drive towards control coming from within (Proposition 6). In the beginning is the individual atom, without which 'society' is an abstraction, even if his mental pabulum from infancy comes from without, especially from maternal tradition. This will bring us close to Plato's position that the remedies of political evils lie in psychological education, the social order being the personal character writ, by many, out large, although social 'pasturage' and psychological appetites interact. Further, the need is, instead of an 'eristic' method, 'knock-out arguments' and the typical eristic techniques of the prosecuting or defence lawyer, to have the modesty to apply in politics those 'charistic' principles of co-operative power which we have already learned to be sound in educational discipline and psychological therapy. *What we have learned in Education we should apply in Politics.* This conclusion, in terms of *eros*, not *eris*, about the correct approach to the basic political problem is one drawn by Bertrand Russell and is perhaps basic to traditional Greco-European or Greco-Christian culture, as distinct from the frequent American 'other-directed' engineering mentality and the Russo-Marxist materialist monism.

In his *Human Society in Ethics and Politics*, Lord Russell says: "If politics is to become scientific, and the event is not to be constantly surprising, it is imperative that our political thinking should penetrate more deeply into the springs of human action . . . The only theory that will redeem mankind is cooperation, and the first step toward cooperating is the heart of individuals . . . it must be by an understanding of man and his impulses, and of the discovery of the ways in which his impulses can be led to happiness and contentment." And, again in his *New Hopes for a Changing World* (1951): "For these reasons the war of man with himself is that which at the end of human evolution assumes supreme importance." On this point, Mr. John Plamenatz, on the contrary, talks rather in terms of 'institutions'; of their mutual reaction with morals, these being in part "the moral codes prevailing in their communities" (*mores*); and of rights and obligations as preconditions of both governments and classes. Hence 'institutions' emerge as prior to 'power'—which here seems to be equated with institutional authority. *Vide* his *German Marxism*, p. 314.

It will be noted that this interpretation of politics rests on the hypothesis that, although external events condition society and individual, and biology determines the existence of social aggregations and even of the parent-child relation with human infant dependence, nevertheless the impulse towards survival, assurance, power, control, and order comes creatively from within, *ab interno*, and that man and his society are not mere flotsam, directed like objects *ab externo*, by facts of determinism, of matter, of economic need to eat, even by factors of 'what is expected,' and by technical development. The power impulse to have power to live, survive, and not be eaten, is even more vital, immediate and profound than the economic need and impulse to eat; energy is more basic than matter; life is earlier than the animal; consciousness is more primitive and diffused than the brain; nor is (*ist*) man what he eats (*isst*), to correct Feuerbach—and Pythagoras. It is possible, with individual self-respect, to be "Beyond Marxism." It is the only successful way to meet it.

This statement repudiates a large cluster of misconceived arguments which assume that political science and economics involve philosophical determinism. Men—even Tolstoian men with their cult of the mystic anonymous—are not lemmings. It is true that many sociologists and psychological behaviourists, of the school of Watson, have talked in this fashion; but they have been guilty of abandoning the scientific route of hypothesis in favour of dogmatic fallacies. Because a human being's activities are conditioned by the psychological make-up of himself, as by the geographic or economic conditions of his society, that certainly does not dogmatize either for determinism or against it. Nor do we dogmatize that man is not free to will (and in this issue the 'learned ignorance' of Lord Samuel is perhaps most satisfactory) what he chooses, when by reason in his choice utilizing his psychological urges and faculties. He can even do this better if he is fully conscious what those urges are, and what are their conditioning limits and constants. Saints and sinners, Mohandas Gandhi and Al Capone, alike desire power; and some desire it to assume responsibility and some, Dr. Erich Fromm maintains, desire power to avoid responsibility. The position, then, here taken is the precise reverse of that taken by Karl Marx and Friedrich Engels with their dialectical material determinism, although Marx and Engels are also upholders, even passionately, of the existence of a precise sociological science, which is Marx's own; and our position is not entirely dissimilar, at least in emphasis, from that of the maligned Dr. Eugen Dühring.

This issue is discussed in my *Science and Method*, part I, chap. I. We are also able to agree, by this route, with the contention of Professor Sir Isaiah Berlin, in his thoughtful Comte Memorial Lecture, *Historical Inevitability* (1957). Determinist views, Berlin says, rest on the assumption that belief in the importance of motives is delusive, and that the behaviour of men is in fact made what it is by factors largely beyond the control of individuals. Their holders are committed "to placing the ultimate responsibility for what happens on personal or 'transpersonal' or 'super-personal' entities or 'forces' whose evolution is regarded as being identical with human history." This pseudo-science deals in terms of vasty structures of concrete history; aspires to predict concretely "every detail in the life of every single human being"; and ascribes what is bad to "ignorance of *ends*" [italics mine], scientifically demonstrable; and offers what is "*never a scientific, that is, empirically testable theory, stated in quantitative terms*." Supposing such to be seriously contended, this refutation is indeed admirably said, and is also the argument of this tractate.

It is important to stress this agnosticism on the issue of philosophical determinism, neither Calvinist in dogma nor Arminian (but perhaps suggesting that we are dealing with 'a necessary ignorance' of motivation, of which the opposite gnosticism transcends all our practical and moral references), since this attitude, consonant indeed with the better theological tradition, is often distorted by controversialists, opposed to the development of political science as 'anti-democratic.' The development of medical science could also be held to be 'anti-democratic' as restricting free choice of rational regimen. Indeed the medical profession can easily, as it explores the 'unknown land' of the brain, offer the greatest practical threat of all to the free moral choices of the individual—a drug or 'personality reconstruction' will do it all for him . . . Other controversalists I have heard, at Oxford high-tables, deny all scientific basis to Psychology and to any Economics founded on it—and Politics is on the same basis—on the ground that 'the psyche is subjective.' To such dogmatism it is perhaps best sharply to oppose Professor James Burnham's counter-dogmatism: "There is a political science." Or, in the blunt words of Freud: "I do not argue: I expound."

It can indeed be urged, owing to a misapprehension, that the hypothesis here used is guilty of the same scientific fallacy that infests Marxism—although it does not affect Marx's very proper stress upon the neglected economic factors in history—namely, that of 'unicausalism,' that is, the explanation of all events by one factor. On the contrary, this argument we have already rebutted (chap. II, §iii). The concrete world of experience and history is indeed conditioned by a million causes, of greater or lesser degree, even including the magnetic influence of the stars and of the moon and tide upon behaviour, in one vast, and bubbling stew of events. This gives a melancholy satisfaction to some philosopher historians, who call the resulting existential confusion for man by the name of 'the human predicament,' and feel that it has some peculiar relevance to super-historical grace and salvation. The works of Berdyaev and of such a historian as Professor Butterfield of Cambridge merit attention here. The Marxists, as dogmatists rather than (to use their own comparison) Darwinians of the social sciences, are indeed guilty of such 'unicausalism,' because while Engels, with one hand, concedes the existence of other factors, with the other he draws back the philosophic concession on the ground that 'basically' the economic (or, as Kautsky, being more logical, says, 'the material') factors are ultimate. A dogmatic materialism, however refined, is the result—from an argument which the uncommitted student (who is uninterested in waging a Leninist war on clericalism) might even deny, in so far as it was 'dialectical,' to be what is commonly meant by 'materialism': and might identify with 'objective realism' or 'monism.'

It appears as if some movements in contemporary Communism, especially in Yugoslavia, are emphasizing elements of revolutionary freedom in the young Marx, of attention to creative change, and of stress on psychological factors. These would end in a repudiation of Stalinist totalitarianism and even of something of the dogmatic materialist determinism of Engels. This hopeful evolution towards common sense is, politically and philosophically, worth watching.

Whereas Marxism maintains dogmatically that an 'external' cause, be it one of metaphysical ('dialectical,' not mechanical) 'matter' or 'economic' (whether or not including the element of human creative genius in technology), determines personal conduct—even if the person later sets out not to speculate but to change—here we are investigating empirically the extent to which our hypothesis (among many possible others) of a motivation springing from within, from the depths of human personality (although primitively sprung from the biological urge to survival), explains the observed facts and apparent motivations of social conduct and the recurrent social patterns, including especially the observed phenomena of control. Whereas Marxism, despite reservations in words, is 'unicausal' and comes back to reiterating that the one 'basic' cause of the 'concrete' social structure (even, for example, national relations) is materio-economic, it is yet embarrassed, as one can see in the classical statement by Plekhanov, to explain the personal factor.

Here, however, we are maintaining a 'multicausal' position, and that a multitude of causes are at work to explain social controls, among which the economic is one, and so also is the psychological (not material) desire to avoid poverty and acquire wealth; but that this last economic urge is only one species of the deeper and more vital desire to acquire power which both sets up the need for control (which does not arise out of nothing) and shapes those forms which the social controls take in accordance with its own character.

Indeed, as has been wisely said, a wealthy man does not seek to acquire more wealth in order to have warmth and clothes, but in order to acquire more power, status and prestige (even by wasteful consumption). In the words of Ernest Bevin (Bullock, *The Life and Times of Ernest Bevin*, p. 552): "The landlord does not fight to retain his land merely because of the money it yields him, but because of the power it gives." Likewise, it is notorious that nations tend to go to war *despite* their better economic interests. Although his story shows the illuminative value *also* of economic determinism, it is well to recall the words of Cecil Rhodes: "I never tried to make money for its own sake. It is a power, and I like power." In brief, the Power Hypothesis, although not exclusive, is to be preferred to the Marxist hypothesis because it is more embracing and scientifically more elegant.

Further, we maintain that there are many political phenomena, such as nationalism, which cannot be adequately explained economically; and that, as with the hypotheses of classical economics, so this hypothesis of the desire for power should be explored by developing an 'abstract' or schema of action, until the limits of its utility are discovered. It is in this sense, and with this emphasis, that, passing beyond the delimitation of the field as that of social controls and of the Science of Social Controls, whether customary or more specifically and deliberately organized, some proceed (as we have said) to refer to Politics as the subject of the Science of Human Power, or 'can-do' (as distinct from 'power' or 'force' in other forms of energy, such as water), which is not only economic.

Schumpeter (*Capitalism, Socialism and Democracy*, p. 235) points out that "individual and group-power cannot be defined in purely economic terms." There is an ambiguity in Marxism between a useful 'economic' interpretation—which yet, in so far as it pivots on the acquisitive impulse and, also, on the instruments of production and their control (that is, inventive Technology and the socially arranged control of it), involves important non-economic factors—and a strictly logical, but also dogmatically metaphysical and not useful (because 'all-explaining'), 'material' interpretation, which positivistically resolves everything into material determinism. This issue is discussed by Karl Kautsky, who decides in favour of metaphysical 'materialism' not 'economism,' in his discussion of the Materialist Interpretations of History. Nor does it help to deny that the 'dialectic' (as distinct from mere exposition of a process) is metaphysical by redefining metaphysics and denouncing old-fashioned 'mechanical materialism.' The 'dialectic' cannot be 'touched or seen'; nor is it 'natural' or 'material' in the sense of the common man. How do we know that matter *must* follow a particular Hegelian course? And what is to be the test proof that it does or does not? Either here we have a (not illegitimate) 'act of faith' or a hypothesis, or we delude ourselves with a metaphysical proof of the empirically unprovable. As John Plamenatz (*German Marxism*, pp. 81, 84–5) says: "This does not mean that there are no sociological laws," but "the Marxists have not yet done the first things that must be done before their kind of fundamentalism can be proved."

The Marxist reification or deification of history Dr. Weston LaBarre (*The Human Animal*) dismisses as 'nonsense,' perhaps justifiably in some of the forms in which Marxists have stated it. The embarrassments of Marxism in dealing with the reconciliation between the personal, creative factor in revolutionary history and the inevitable material dialectic and determinism will be seen in G. V. Plekhanov's *The Role of the Individual in History* (1898) to which oddly Sir Isaiah Berlin does not refer in the treatise on historical determinism cited above. In the critical passages Plekhanov's argument becomes sophistical. The comment is relevant by R. M. MacIver (*The Web of Government*): "The individual is never wholly absorbed in his society, wholly responsive to it, wholly accounted for by it."

It may here be suggested that the fundamental criticism of Marx is that he is too much of a capitalist; that (as Marxism must admit) his thought was shaped and dated by his place and time, and by the environment of capitalist laissez-faire and the Manchester School of Economists from whom he learned, as well as by the inveterate (if often self-contradictory) philosophy of mistrust, sponsored by Bentham and James Mill; that, for individual economic competition à *l'outrance*, he merely substituted a *Kampf* of liquidation of other classes. The *fundamentally aggressive psychology* of intelligent pursuit of self-interest, derived from Hobbes through the French hedonists, Marx does not *reject* as 'capitalist' but, under his new socialist dispensation, uncritically *accepts* and indeed exalts into almost a prime principle of action. Lord Russell is right that it is educationally improbable that a utopia of love can be evolved by emphasizing a gospel of hate. Any effective propaganda against Bolshevist Marxism will probably win if it can explode this fissionable and unstable thesis of hyper-aggressive Marxism by logic from within in terms of modern psychology; but most so-called 'free world' propaganda is an affair of radio-technicians, superficial, hesitant, or too noisy, and too often (in the comment to this writer by President Eisenhower) "very ineffective." Incidentally, it appears that equal claims to have initiated the phrase "the struggle for the minds of men" can be made by Senator William Benton and (according to a letter from Sir Percy Spender, sometime Minister of External Affairs in Australia) by the present writer.[3]

§vi. *Dominative and Co-operative Power*

A distinction has been drawn (which will later be elaborated) between the desire for, and will to, power—the power-to-execute-one's-will and to achieve one's particular wish—and the specific desire for domination or 'to be over.' (See Proposition 10.) We have indeed drawn careful distinctions between the cognitive or imaginative Contemplation; the emotive wish; the Will which moves towards action to fulfil the wish; the mental consideration of Freedom, which is an enjoyment of our Will, such that if we have it there is immediate gratification by the act of appropriation; the Power (which is later than this consideration of freedom, but which is the first characteristically *social* stage) by which we have the potentiality, if we choose, to overcome obstacles; and the Executive Act through Force or Concurrence. In view of the complexity of the issues here, which is so great that the answers which have been given range from Tyranny (which Hobbes called merely an evil name for 'strong government') to co-operative Anarchism, as preached by Prince Kropotkin, to dismiss the problem on the ground that it is idle "to write a book to show that men like power" (as is stated to have been asserted by Professor Laski) is merely silly.

Later we shall find reason to suppose that many of the problems of politics can be solved if we can substitute a deliberate discipline of Co-operation instead of the cruder but more direct technique of solving issues through Domination. The former political technique, however, is not 'natural' to man but is one, centred on certain chosen principles (or ends), in which, by the reduction of fears and by approaching freedom from fear, he has quite deliberately to be psychologically and socially trained—as Plato and also the Indian Mahatma said. This alternative has sometimes been referred to, with a slightly different emphasis, as the distinction between 'mutuality' and 'coercion,' to which we shall return. The phrase 'mutuality' or 'team-spirit' overlooks the element of 'direction,' by some detached principle in the choosing mind or from an accepted authority (*vis directiva*), which is 'guidance,' as distinct from 'coercion' (*vis coactiva*). The techniques

[3]There is, however, evidence that a similar phrase, "the battle for the minds of men," was used by Creel during the First World War. See W. P. Dizard, *Strategy of Truth* (1961), p. 30.

used individually in educational psychology have to be applied here, educating political man, educating politicians. EDUCATION MAY BE NOT THE 'PIOUS' ANSWER OF BAD FAITH BUT THE AUTHENTIC ANSWER TO THE KEY PROBLEMS OF POLITICS (Proposition 11). How one may compel politicians to be educated is something else again; but the answer, as usual, probably lies in educating them at public schools before the age of seven, or educating their parents. Fascists and Marxists, with their aggressive obsessions, like the chauvinists, contrive to miseducate their 'black guards,' 'élites,' or 'vanguards.' There is yet, it will be noted, a natural wilfulness and an assertiveness in man (which Gandhians underestimate) distinct from the acquired modes of social trust or of social mistrust, which is not unhealthy or 'wrong' and which can both be enervated by clumsy or dishonest customs of co-operation or of 'other-direction,' or perverted by invitations to co-operate upon wrong grounds.

By the use of the word 'wrong,' as distinct from 'inefficient,' we indicate a stage where the problems of political science pass over into those of political philosophy, to which we shall later turn. It is today in vogue to maintain the sophistical position of the conventional nature of ethics and of moral relativism; and to deny the validity of moral absolutes. This confronts the logical difficulty of the question, in 'other-directedness': "if relative, relative to what?" We cannot answer "relative to each other: relative to what is relative." 'Being the same as the Joneses,' as a basis of morality, on which W. H. Auden comments, shaped neither by trans-cendental religion nor by immanent duty, can only be acceptable, as an alternative to ethical scepticism, if we hold that ethics is what some society absolutely (and not again relatively), although represented by 'the Joneses,' determines. Beyond this, the answer seems to run that the ethical is 'that which it is pleasant or useful to do in the light of the Joneses' adaptation to environment' (as in the philosophy of Herbert Spencer), or—in other words—adaptation to the survival of those who are fittest to survive. The 'other-directedness' of contemporary cosmopolitan civilization, on which Professor D. Riesman comments in *The Lonely Crowd*, has to be balanced by an 'auto-nomy,' which yet involves the concept of a rational and universal *nomos*, if it is to be distinct from individualistic *anomie*. Cf. M. Gins-berg, *On the Diversity of Morals* (1956). This is a point often overlooked in the liberal cult of autonomy.

A vital assertiveness which may be healthy, and which civilization should not suppress, unless a disease of what Freud calls 'discontent' is to supervene, is remarked by Dodge and Kahn (*The Craving for Superiority*) who discuss how it can be canalized in socially useful fashions. "The craving for matter-of-fact superiority is a wholesome and useful personal characteristic. It may, and often does result in significant achievement. The craving for a *feeling* of superiority, irrespective of the *facts*, is conspicuous in many psychopaths. Craving for pseudo-superiority is always unfortunate. It is hard for a person with such a craving [and inferiority feeling] to square himself with the real world." Several educational psychologists, such as Isaacs and Horney, stress the need for training in skills, such as give objective superiority and the sense of objective achievement. So also does H. D. Lasswell in most of his recent work. In commenting on Gandhi, Mr.

W. H. Morris Jones (*Political Studies*, February, 1960) remarks that, in a campaign of non-co-operation with evil, the Mahatma looked to "the ethically disciplined resister," and did not rely upon "the conscience of any random person" (or his private and spontaneous judgements).

The answers to the problems of power in terms of Co-operative Power have thus their own difficulties, since Co-operation is not (as sometimes supposed) good *in esse* but a limited good, as will be seen more clearly later. Nor indeed is it yet clear whether Affection or Love is other than a limited good, or in what fashion it is a good, or what is meant by it. Against it has perhaps to be balanced zeal for Justice. Charity does not abolish the individual. These issues involve ethical choices of values. Co-operative Power, more complex and subtle to establish as a political instrument than Dominative Power which has the seeds of violence in itself, may yet be more stable, efficient in the long run, less explosive and less liable to evoke resistances "as Enceladus turns in revolt under Etna." Nevertheless, adaptation alone, co-operation as in a lynching mob, cannot be supposed to provide our final answers, as indeed is said in Exodus (23:2): "Thou shalt not follow a multitude to do evil." The task of building our society, in time, upon Co-operative Power may be encouraging; but it would be idle to suppose that this answer, taken by itself, will present the political scientist with no difficulties.

The dangers of that excessive stress upon 'co-operation,' 'team-spirit,' 'belongingness,' and 'mutuality' which omits any analysis of ethical value or any guiding principle from above, is that it becomes merely a 'social ethic' so-called and bogus, because shaped as *means* for the convenience of the ends of particular organizations or institutions, be they the commercial corporation or the state. It has rightly been exposed and castigated in Mr. William H. Whyte's brilliant *The Organization Man* (1956). The different position, which is philosophical, that man *totally* finds his ends in *a* particular society or even in human society as equivalent with *the* Society (which is the embodiment of all social values), and has no non-social values as check on social claims, is a species of atheism (as in Marx) or at least of complete theistic immanentism, and is defensible, but, as it is hoped to show in the final chapter, deeply wrong.

Reference may again be here made to Professor R. Neustadt's *Presidential Power*. The whole argument here tends to show how far in a constitutional democracy power is a matter for negotiation and *bargain*; is limited by its own requirements as co-operative power; and does not conform to the supposed automatic chain of command (it may be gravely doubted how far it is really so automatic, cf. p. 122 *infra*) which obtains in an army. It is the experience of many a Minister that he cannot rely upon the automatic co-operation of his civil service subordinates (or a Colonial Minister on that of Her Majesty's Governors and their Chief Secretaries), unless he exercises patent persuasion. It is not the man who *wants* power (construed as dominative) who gets it where the structure of power is co-operative.

4. Freedom and Authority

§i. Freedom and Liberty Defined

Few words are used with less precision and in fashions more loaded with overtones than the words 'Freedom' and 'Authority.' These are words frequently put into opposition as contraries, if not construed as contradictories. The emotional literature about them is vast; but the logical analysis is too small. Little progress will be made until they are stripped down to essentials and the definition of them cleared up. As Lincoln said, "we have never had a good definition of the word 'liberty.'" For convenience, and with some precedents, those kinds of 'freedom' which are specifically enjoyed within the framework of civil society or indeed of political conventions we shall distinguish as 'liberties.'

Professor D. Brogan, in his *Study of Politics*, says: "The study of politics . . . is . . . the study of the means whereby liberty and authority may be best combined . . . When the whole problem of politics was the combination of liberty and effective authority and while there was still apparent agreement on the meaning, both of liberty and of effective and legitimate authority, the mechanisms of politics could be studied with the same optimistic attention as the mechanics which were transforming the industry and commerce of nations." James Madison referred (rather as James Mill did in the case of Representative Government) to "this great mechanical power in government, by the simple agency of which the will of the largest political body may be concentrated, and its force directed to any object which the public good [as understood by the majority] requires." On the other hand Ernest Barker, also quoted by Dr. Brogan, says that Liberty is "a part or element of the social aspect of goodness." The not dissimilar classical description by Montesquieu will be recalled, to the effect that "dans une société où il y a des lois, la liberté ne peut consister qu'à pouvoir faire ce que l'on doit vouloir . . . la liberté politique ne consiste point à faire ce que l'on veut" (*Esprit des Lois*, ed. 1777, book I, p. 308). It is *not* what Kant calls "a wild, lawless freedom."

For Spinoza freedom becomes identified with reason: living "according to the dictates of reason alone" (*Ethics*, book IV, prop. 67); for Rousseau it is obedience to self-discipline: "l'obéissance à la loi qu'on s'est prescrite est liberté" (*Du contrat social*, book I, p. 8); for Kant it is conformity to the moral law as limit: "independence of anything other than the moral law" (*Critique of the Pure Reason*). Hegel, needless to say, goes further and finds freedom in the consciousness of, and in the obedience to, law. All these are attempts to sophisticate the meaning and to moralize what humanity praises but what is often immoral and inconvenient. The issue will be discussed later, as political philosophy. The boldest attempt to have the matter both ways is by Milton (*Sonnets*, XII):

"Licence they mean when they cry libertie;
For who loves that, must first be wise and good,"

Which means, in effect, my liberty is liberty but yours is licence. A modern variant of this will be found in the statement that "Freedom is the facility for achievement by someone sincerely in quest of the good." This is noble, and has a Thomistic ring—but it is wildly out of touch with what, in contemporary society, is popularly meant by freedom. It can (and would) be attacked as moral *snobisme*. Lord Acton's definition is probably in no better case, that freedom "is not the power of doing what we like, but the right of being able to do what we ought."

Opposite to this is the unguarded definition which Lincoln in fact supplied in a speech at Baltimore in 1864: "liberty for each man to do as he pleased with himself," which is freedom to fulfil his *actual* wish, however immoral, according to his own choice and opinion; according to his own reason, however ill-informed (unless, with Sartre, he regards reason as a 'tyrant'); and his own conscience, however odd. An excellent anthology of usages will be found in Maurice Cranston's admirable *Freedom* (1953) which, however, discards the useful distinction between Freedom and Liberty in so far as this is adopted by Sir Herbert Read.

The profusion of the definitions or descriptions of Freedom is one indication of the mental confusion which reigns about this subject on which men feel so passionately that they will die for it—but think with so little clarity and in a fashion so little logically positive that they are not clear that they know what it means. For primitive peoples, living in a tribal life of community or *Gemeinschaft*, the problem of the glories of liberty as freedom from fear of the aggressive competition of the neighbour or of governmental authority so far scarcely arises that Professor A. Kardiner in his *Psychological Frontiers of Society* writes: "No Comanche or Alorese would have any conception of freedom in the sense [not accepted in the text] in which it is commonly used in our society." One of today's major problems is that some of the traditional liberties of 'the West' have little emotional resonance in 'the East,' and lack meaning for much of 'the South' (the southern hemisphere). On the other hand, in a yet more basic sense, Freedom is always attractive. *Liberté* spells 'more power for me and fewer *costs*.' Who could dislike it—for himself? "Great is Diana of the Ephesians" for the Ephesians, who can shout about it for the space of many hours.

On this issue of Freedom and Authority, reference may again be made to the writer's article, "On Freedom," in the symposium *Aspects of Liberty* edited by Professor Milton Konvitz and Clinton Rossiter (Ithaca, N.Y.: Cornell University Press, 1958), and his article "Authority and its Critics," in the symposium *Authority* edited by Professor C. J. Friedrich (Cambridge, Mass.: Harvard University Press).

To put the matter briefly, since freedom is "like 1066, a good thing," the philosophers have felt under an obligation to praise it. But that which these wise men have praised has usually been almost the opposite (that is, self-control) of what the man in the street means when, in his simpler fashion, he talks of freedom: freedom from governesses, freedom to get drunk himself as well as freedom from annoyance by other drunks, freedom to be lousy and not to wash, freedom to sing in the streets and also to sleep well o' nights. He means what Lincoln meant but more than Lincoln meant it. He means all freedoms he wants, including ignoble freedoms, whereas the philosophers mean (but do not say) 'noble freedoms.' The real issue (discussed by Isaiah Berlin) is whether we here should be led by the general teaching of 'the philosophers,' especially those mentioned.

For the purposes of what Bentham calls 'description,' as distinct from 'evocation,' science as distinct from homiletics, the most satisfactory and aseptic definition of freedom is that by Thomas Hobbes: "Liberty [or freedom] signifieth the absence of opposition." By some it may be felt to be too negative, bare and prosaic; but at least it raises no ambiguities of value about the difference between freedom and 'licence' (with its adjective 'licentious'; or with its link with the word 'libertine'). We may, if we choose, call this 'Freedom A.' It weights no balances and passes no false coin. The definition by John Stuart Mill is equally bald and honest, if not so precise: "Liberty [freedom] consists in doing what one desires."

At the other end of the gamut of definitions is that of the Stoics: that 'real' freedom is freedom from the bondage of vice and one's own evil wishes. Most men are pitiful slaves to their own passions and idle opinions. Only the philosopher is 'free' and not the vulgar. Men's actual wants are unimportant or due for correction by the authority of reason, ruling the passions. This is "the perfect law of liberty" (James 1:25)—what we here call 'freedom'—in doing the works of righteousness. This usage we can speak of as applying to 'Freedom B,' sometimes (but again with a bias—for who shall say that St. Paul and a 'scientific humanist,' so-called, would agree?) called 'rational freedom' or 'spiritual freedom of the real self.' Or we could speak of a so-called 'freedom' (as in legal usage) which is only understood as 'liberty' conforming to the *actual* civil rights (or recognized permissions) under a particular political constitution ('Liberty *A*'), as distinct from those under alleged natural rights which *ought* to be constitutional ('Liberty *B*'). There is liberty under law as actually set forth in the Constitution and interpreted by the courts. "Equal justice under law" is its maxim. But a Constitution which violates equal justice may be held to be contrary to Liberty *B*. Correct definition here is of fundamental importance: it crucially matters that *A* should here always mean *A*, and not A^1 or *B*. Nor need such definition therefore be sterile and inept for the scientific purposes of exploration. For the present, however, and for the precise needs of Political Science, we shall proceed to mean for Freedom what we here distinguish as Freedom *A*. "The prefect law of freedom" (*sic*), imposed by reason or revelation, we shall discuss later, as part of the philosophy of ends which can shape our wishes.

Politics we have described as the study of the control relationship of wills (see Proposition 5). Wills, limited as 'human' only if only human beings have wills, we have stated as wills to execute one's will, active wills objectively engaged to realize the wish or the 'passive will' or 'want'. Tönnies gives to his sociology the same basis in will or the decision to make the effort for satisfaction. Emotional wish, then a dream with or without intellectual debate or resolution, then practical will-as-to-direction or commitment, whether or not following from reasoning—such would seem to be the sequence. After this there can arise the fourth phase: the question whether we are free to achieve. At this point, at least, of questioning, if not earlier, enters the intellectual pondering (which itself *non movet*) when we debate whether Wish and actual Will should, according to temperament or conscience, be reaffirmed as practical Will-to-be-executed. We may decide that, although we would actually 'like to do this,' we are, all things considered, 'not *decided* to do this, having counted the difficulties.' We will not take the step from the subjective direction to the objective will that demands freedom for its accomplishment.

This practical will, it may be noted, may be merely potential and does not become explicit if, as soon as the wish is formed (for example, of the infant for the breast), it is gratified without opposition. It also does not become explicit if we are satisfied that our wish—for example, to fly like a bird in the air before the invention of the aeroplane—from the nature of the case cannot objectively be gratified, although the adventurous may be left with a legitimate doubt about what is 'the nature of the case.' (Even the 'contradictory' is not 'impossible,' if we have some reason to suspect that our experience is not adequate to decide what is contradictory 'really,' as distinct from appearances.)

The transition in the former case from the wish to the gratification is, in effect, instantaneous and without problem. Clearly, if a condition of willing is so shaped that all wishes are of the kind to which reality offers a *nihil obstat*, then one is in a condition of grace, in which there is no politics, and the fortunate man, quit of taint of original sin, may say that this righteous "service is perfect freedom." Here, in the words of Duns Scotus, freedom "is a perfection of the Will." St. Paul says we can recapture this condition by conforming with spiritual passion, and without fear of the limiting Law, to God and reality. The Hobbesian definition does not deny this, but rather refers us to the highly complicated quality of a problem which it is not concerned to solve, but to state.

T. H. Green, in his lecture "On the Different Senses of 'Freedom' as Applied to Will and to the Moral Progress of Man" (1879; published in *The Principles of Political Obligation*, 1895) after rehearsing the views of the Stoics, St. Paul, and Kant, on an ethical or value-bearing Freedom *B* (not habitually distinguished from Liberty *A* or *B* under law positive or natural), admits that their usage, although popular (which we may question), is metaphorical, as distinct from the bare usage of non-restraint, which Green himself calls "the primary meaning of the term." Kant indeed distinguishes, from a "wild, lawless freedom" (which is nevertheless freedom), that tendency to self-realization or even, as T. H. Green puts it, "self-improvement," which is only free because—as we have said, in the text, of 'innocent' and 'rational' trust—it has aligned itself with God or reality, or with what Green calls "the law which determines where this self-satisfaction [or 'fulfilment of possibility' in 'self-realization': Goethe's and J. S. Mill's 'harmonious whole'] is to be found."

Since Kant is pre-eminently the philosopher of freedom, the ambiguities in his own position especially require attention. Freedom is one of the highest of moral values for man, but it is circumscribed within the rational moral law. In his popular essay *Über den Gemeinspruch*, u.s.w., Kant preaches the importance of men thinking for themselves (except, he adds, when they occupy an official position such as a Lutheran pastor); but almost immediately we find him using the claims of the scholar *ex officio* to speak out. The issue here, then, is not of the right to have thoughts (as Hobbes said, no man can prevent it; but they may be of no value), *but of the duty to think rationally*, and to think with a cultivated and disciplined *responsibility*. Reason and the moral law remain objective and capable of imperatives to the individual.

The residue of the argument seems to be an Aristotelian and not unimportant one: as everybody ought for his health to exercise his muscles, so everyone ought to endeavour to think in a disciplined fashion and to *use* his right judgement, whatever that may be. Here the liberty, to be socially recognized, of Free Speech, seems to be based upon a natural law principle. But it is *not* the entire abstract freedom to be, in thinking and speech, entirely uninhibited by considerations of responsible thought. The real trouble arises when the holders of power become the interested upholders of bogus thought and mental authority, which responsible and professional thought has to overthrow in the name of the disciplined and cultivated tests of truth if, indeed, they can show what truth is. Briefly, Kant is the apostle of a disciplined Freedom *B* and also Liberty *B* under reason and not of an absolute spontaneity of Freedom *A*, as urged either by the untutored impulse or the unexamined conscience of the moment.

In political philosophy we have indeed to evaluate the often uncritical desire for 'autonomy'; and analyse whether any particular *nomos* is rational and indeed valuable. But, in political science, we are not prepared so far to go, with St. Paul and others, beyond 'the primary meaning' as to equate Freedom with Self-Improvement and, on the other hand, to find the very 'servitude' of men in their doing democratically what they actually will to do. Bosanquet calls the will which accommodates itself to profound degrees of reality "the real will"; but psychoanalytical usage (cf. J. C. Flugel, *Man, Morals and Society*, Penguin ed., p. 62), on the contrary, equates this with the 'ideal,' and puts the actual will, here perhaps misleadingly called 'real will,' into opposition and strain. Our concern here, in political science, is with the adjustment of *actual* power-bearing wills to ends which are data, or hypotheses, upon which we are not yet called to pass philosophical judgement of *value*, as distinct from judgement of their degrees of *support* and *power*. The argument of Professor K. J. Scott, in his article, "Liberty, Licence and Not Being Free" (*Political Studies*, vol. IV, 1956), that the concept of 'licence,' or immoral abuse, must be included within the neutral meaning of 'liberty,' must be accepted, but only if we translate 'liberty' (defined by us as 'within the law') into 'freedom.'

Just as no definition of politics is tolerable that evades the Pluralist issue, which raises the problem of the plural forms of organization that human society may assume, or that omits from purview the rich fields of political organization in industry and in what Richard Hooker called 'ecclesiastical polity'—leading to the anti-social error that ecclesiastical matters are solely 'other-worldly'—so no definition is satisfactory which, talking about 'machinery of government,' brusques the argument about freedom of the anarchist philosophers. Indeed the two are connected, if we agree with Marx that the State-form and 'rule of men' will ultimately "wither away"; or with those, from St. Augustine to Arnold

Toynbee, who hold that the movement is from the State-form as coercive towards a more perfect Church-form of society, as one of moral choice and moral authority, with the *vis coactiva* reduced and the secular sword, first exercised by that great hunter Nimrod, being sheathed beneath the spiritual sword.

Attention to the anarchist philosophy of Prince Michael Bakunin, magistrally surveyed by Professor E. H. Carr, marked by the veritable pathology of an Oedipus complex (as was perhaps that of Laski) in its relation to authority, tends to distract attention from the constructive work of Prince Peter Kropotkin and of Earl Russell. (For reasons of status it may be that aristocrats tend to the utopias of anarchism, themselves not needing protective securities or wage guarantees.) It would be erroneous to suppose that Anarchism cannot join hands, as in Catalonia, with a positive philosophy of the Co-operatives, as distinct from the philosophy of 'the Red Prussian,' Marx, a figure as superauthoritarian in personality as Moses and, fundamentally, himself (at least in his later days) the great conservative or Byzantine (as Stalin perceived) or, if the current colloquialism may be permitted, "Red Square."

Anarchist philosophy, at more than a superficial level, does not equate with Nihilism or indeed deny the importance of cosmos or order; but aspires to a condition when, by co-operative training or by nature, this order shall be achieved as an immediate gratification, aided by some intuition about co-operation or by the instinct of creative craftsmanship. In the animal world (which we should never overlook) we observe this condition in a flight of swallows, which wheels in the heavens without rulers (such as have the apes and baboons) and without a word of command. That psychotherapy has discovered the curative effect for the wounded psyche of the free dance is perhaps a support of this philosophy; and to the issue of sacred ritual, as having custom or habit, not statute and police, we shall return. It is interesting to note that some primitive acephalous people seem to have social habits that conduce to an easy co-operation, although this objection to having recognized permanent chiefs appears to be due to an association of personal power with dangerous witchcraft.

Professor S. De Grazia, in *The Political Community* (1948), comments on the *anomie*, distintegration of political and religious systems, and 'sense of drift' which arises, first (as Durkheim indicated) from the division of labour and increased 'alienation of the worker' from a sense of being wanted in a community or pattern, and later in the anti-teleological moral nihilism or denial of objective valuations indicated, for example, in Joseph Wood Krutch's Bergsonian *Modern Temper* (1929) or, more thoroughly, in the thought of Netchaev and Sartre. It will be noted that, unlike these writers, the leading anarchists were all Rousseauites and optimists who believed that man, left to himself by any external law, Mosaic or otherwise, would from his very good nature develop, unaided by compulsive education or sacramental (i.e., social) aid or grace, a laic spirit of benevolent and productive co-operation, in the fulness of everybody's native powers as they *actually* are (or, at least, are optimistically supposed to be).

If we go further and stress the importance of disciplined education to shape freedom, then we confront the problem which beset James and John Stuart Mill. Who then are to be, not the educated in an 'educated democracy,' but the educators? It is a question that James Mill answered almost naively. If there are higher and lower pleasures, who is to make the distinction? If self-regarding and other-regarding acts, who is to judge which is which? Shall interminable discussion, rhetoric beyond rhetoric in endless waves, the din of unending popular discussion, decide without confusing common men (and when)? Or are not rather all opinions, of free men, themselves "born free and equal"? Certainly Mill did not think the majority should decide. Many American sociologists—but also a progressive socialism (which, despite confusion in some Congressional quarters, is not the same thing)—tend to answer that the priority lies with co-operation, 'mutuality,' 'a team-spirit.' This is 'the right education.' Progressive liberalism, with the successors of J. S. Mill, tends to give priority to "the full development of powers." But is not a principle or principles required to judge on *what* we should co-operate, and *which* powers we should develop?

In his inaugural lecture, *Two Concepts of Liberty* (1958), Isaiah Berlin raised the issue whether there is any one principle or one pattern of values or public philosophy, in the light of which reason will compel us to decide that this freedom is good, disciplined and educated, as against that. Perhaps there can be no agreed Freedom *B* and indeed—although this is arguable—as the legal positivists since the days of the Han School in China have said, that there is no Liberty *B* at all. The doubt is well taken. Nevertheless, the excess of toleration ends in the imposition of law; and all law marks the limits of toleration and the beginning of persecution under law. In the words of Justice Learned Hand: "Never forget that law is violence." Too sceptical a doctrine about 'rational freedom' historically tends to end in the arbitrament of force.

Berlin himself, however, prefers to affirm that there *are* indeed "ultimate values," to some one or other of which we ought to pay honour —one of them yet being "the ideal of freedom to live as one wishes." Between these 'ultimates' there is an individual obligation of moral choice: "men choose between ultimate values" (p. 37). Or are they only penultimate, with abstract freedom-for-whatever as ultimate? At least the exact contrary basic proposition of the Soviets here demands consideration in assessing a true philosophy for our age. The Marxists, as determinists, have no especial respect for freedom to choose; the Catholics, Augustinians with semi-Pelagian practical leanings, respect on principle moral freedom to choose but are convinced about what should be chosen; the Voltaireans, being optimistic voluntarians, both exalt freedom to choose and do not pretend to know or give united advice about what will be chosen. The question, then, (which we defer) is one for political philosophy. For the moment (with Professor Berlin) we must be content with empiric balances.

§ii. Freedom as Instinct

It is sometimes rhetorically said that "the desire for freedom is an instinct," like the desire to drink. This claim, however, can probably be justified in a quite precise sense, using the word 'instinct' exactly, as a drive expressed in a conditioned reflex. It remains consistent with the Hobbesian definition and enriches it, although at this point we must insist that: ALTHOUGH THE IMPULSE TO FREEDOM IS FUNDAMENTAL AND INSTINCTIVE, NO ONE PARTICULAR EXPRESSION OF FREEDOM (WHICH MAY BE DETERMINED BY THE LOCAL CULTURE) IS INSTINCTIVE. THOSE DEMANDS ARISING IN THE CHANGING SITUATION, WHICH THE LOCAL CULTURE OR ITS ESTABLISHED INSTITUTIONS AND CONVENTIONS RECOGNIZE, ARE CALLED LIBERTIES; AND COLLECTIVELY ARE A RECOGNIZED LIBERTY. (Proposition 12)

We may consider the analogy of filial piety, beloved of the classical lawyers of Natural Law. As Herodotus insists, the expression of the deep impulse towards filial piety (in which perhaps human nature, as said Ulpian, does *not* change) is discovered in all those so different cultural forms which indeed change, "custom being king" (Pindar), taking shape as the funeral custom of burying, of burning, or of dutifully eating one's parents. Where the demands are in fact, not only permitted, but guaranteed in the positive law of the State, they are called Civil Rights. The forms of power to be free in achieving one's wishes, are multiple: the substantial demand for power generically is not.

What we can say here is that total denial of the instinct of freedom, to the point of the muscular strait-jacket, is unhealthy and ultimately kills life. It may reasonably be supposed that all suppressions of this kind, psychical as well as physical, are *pro tanto* unhealthy and, as we shall suggest later, 'contrary to instinct and Natural Law.' The extinction of life indeed has—other things being equal, and despite the Buddhists and followers of Schopenhauer—the flavour of the unethical and bad, which we shall note against the time when we come to valuations. It will also be noted that what is fundamental is, first, the Wish which is the sign of life, even if subconscious as touching articulate, or logical, mental life; and then the Wish as (in Schopenhauer's terms) it moves from *visio* or Dream-Idea to become, not merely subjective, but active Will concerned with obstacles and with Freedom.

The social issue of *Freedom is, therefore, secondary*, although instinctive, and only arises by reflex, as a negative demand (although the contemplation of this gratification for the will may give positive joy), whenever the primary deliberate *will* of the individual, or 'orientation to action,' is thwarted or frustrated and stands in need of power. Politics can be considered in its activities as an affair of a conditioned variable—as the functions of the dynamic desire for Power, which is *tertiary*. Freedom as a negating urge, and the desire for Power as a positive guarantee, are functions of the primary and active but checked Will. Where the Will remains always unfrustrated, as in utopia, Eden or heaven, there is no emergent desire for specific freedom or personal power (whose fruits are already being enjoyed by the saints) and no disobedience, although there may be desire for knowledge of necessity and omnipotence and for the general 'perfect freedom' of identification or 'at-one-ment' with Omnipotence. Neither democracy nor parliaments obtain and God, who may be a Trinity, is not a Committee.

It is an error to suppose that men initially want obstacles in order to enjoy the sensation of being free and powerful, beyond the point where, like mountain-climbers, they have the confidence that they will surely gratify their want and overcome them. They later, maybe, want a piquancy of opposition to enjoy, with this sauce, the meat of power unopposed. At this point, however, where it is frustrated, the will lights up in struggle and aggressive postures—as Hobbes says of sovereigns, "in the posture of gladiators." There is then a struggle for Freedom. From the experience of the struggle and of the sweets of Freedom and maximal gratification, the appetite for Power is born, as the potentiality of sure gratification and assurance of enjoyment. THE URGE TO FREEDOM, MOREOVER, IS IN A QUITE EXPLICIT, TECHNICAL, SCIENTIFIC, AND NOT ONLY RHETORICAL SENSE AN INSTINCT (Proposition 13). It is inevitably stirred into activity (or 'touched off') by certain conditions.

In his great work, *The Conditional Reflexes* (1927), Pavlov writes, perhaps not without irony: "It is clear that the freedom reflex is one of the most important reflexes or, if I may use a more general term, reactions, of living beings. This reflex has even yet to find its final recognition. In [William] James' writing, it is not even enumerated among the special human 'instincts.' But it is clear that if the animal were not provided with a reflex of protest against boundaries set to its freedom, the smallest obstacle in its path would interfere with this proper fulfilment of its natural functions. Some animals, as we all know, have this freedom reflex to such a degree that when placed in captivity, they refuse all food, sicken, and die." (The human being is not among these excessively freedom-loving animals . . .) This is to carry the issue (as it is intellectually satisfactory that it should be carried) beyond politics into psychology; and beyond empirical psychology into empirical physiology. It does not, of course, in the least affect valuational issues of how freedom *ought* to be used. It does yet imply that *if* health and individual life are ethically good, then *total* repression of physical and physico-psychological freedom is ethically bad. Granted the premise (which objectors need not grant), an ethical conclusion does follow—just as, in the art of medicine, which joins the study of animal physiology teleologically to social well-being or welfare in the common weal, the unspoken ethical presupposition (which Plato criticized) is that life should always be preserved.

§iii. *The Deduction of Authority from Freedom, and Their Polarization*

The realization of Freedom, for the execution of my Will and actual wishes (however foul), involves either the absence of or overcoming of obstacles to the will, or power at any convenient time to overcome and control such obstacles, including those, social and human, created by other wills. Freedom is not so much a 'power' or a faculty such as will; but a condition or a facility. This Freedom is frequently a human and social freedom, that is, a freedom from restriction, not only from the physical world but from other human beings; and political Power (cf. p. 85) is the assurance of such Freedom. Briefly, it must be noted that, except under Eden-like conditions of 'pre-established harmony' or co-operation: FREEDOM, OF ITS OWN INNER LOGIC AND NECESSITY, INVOLVES (TO PROTECT ITSELF) POWER, OBJECTIVE CONTROL, AND (IN PARTICULAR PHASES OF THE SEQUENCE) RECOGNIZED AUTHORITY (Proposition 14). Also, my own freedom, as being freedom for my own wishes to be achieved, is usually and primarily regarded as good, although a like freedom for the other fellow, since it can involve a restriction, may well be bad. It will, therefore, be noted that it is not to Power that men really object, as corrupt, or to Wealth, but to Freedom—the other man's unqualified freedom. But they usually find it imprudent to say so.

In this tension of Freedom and Authority lies *the dialectic clue to the whole matter*. It is as fundamental as the early enunciation by the classical economists of the Law of Supply and Demand. The relation may be polar. It is yet not contradictory; but complementary. That there is a paradox here, which leads to much confused thinking, is shown in the phrase of Lincoln, that there can be "Liberty according to the wolves' dictionary," or in the phrase that "freedom for the pike is death for the minnows." What the minnows demand is objective Authority, for their frustrations are many and (as also Thrasymachus indicated, in Plato's *Dialogues*) the pike's frustrations are few—unless there comes a stronger pike to master him. Likewise the manual workers are perhaps ultimately (and, some would say, 'after the revolution') the most conservative body in the world, and what they also tend to demand is increased Authority (with its security, and maybe a touch of violence against the other fellow), provided it be regarded as their own.

Authority we shall, therefore, define as a Control which is not transient but enduring, objective, recognized by consent, assent or habit, limiting (without suppressing) autonomy; and which is not only a power (*potestas*) at any moment actually exercised, whether by Force, Assent or Consent, but is a potential which can at any convenient moment be activated and executively exercised, as a 'Power Habitual.' As one species of control it is more than solely the facility to gain consent or support, although, being a recognized power, it implies a measure of support adequate to this control. (It may have its inward mirror or counterpart in a trained auto-nomy, an educated super-ego or disciplined conscience, guided through reason and tradition to a *nomos*.) Such a habitual power is, explicitly or passively, *not only a social but a socially Recognized Power* (*potentia*); a Power far more even than the force of any one man; and not (because it is social) contingent on the wishes, opinion, private 'reason,' conscience, or caprice of any single one.

On this Hume has commented. It has recently been suggested by Professor Herman Finer that Power is an abstraction; and, moreover, derivative from Authority. On the contrary, I would submit that, by definition, nothing is more actual than power in our confrontation with the world; and that all authority as such is, or claims to be, a limited species of it, unless the cause of confusion here is simply because the reference is solely to 'legal powers.'

Authority as *legitimate* is *pro tanto* recognized to be advantageous to one's own social bargain, even if but the lesser evil; and is so assented to in law. It delimits liberties. Authority which is solely constraint, not serving a preferred choice, and not recognized as legitimate by the individual, is better called, according to Hume, bare Power and, if temporary, is a mere exercise of Force. An Authority *de iure* is an authority which some, officially or otherwise, think that they ought to recognize as a potentiality.

Attention has already been called (*supra*, p. 76) to the idiosyncratic derivation of authority provided by Professor Reinhold Niebuhr (*The Structure of Nations and Empires*), of which the consequences can be grave. Authority is provided with sources in 'force' and 'prestige' or 'majesty,' of which the former may be the initiator. This does not, however, at all mean that Dr. Niebuhr visualizes the social order as primarily under the domination of coercive power. There is a dichotomy (very typical of, especially, Lutheran thought). The 'civil dominion,' indeed, is preoccupied with 'order' and this, it is to be noted, is put into antithesis to [? spiritual] 'justice.' In part 'justice' is here a preachment of that 'perfection' which we shall later discuss; and it is not quite the same thing as the legitimate distinction between the ideal prescriptive norm arising from Natural Law, and the rule of positive laws. (The distinction between 'natural justice' and 'justice as distributed through the civil courts' we can accept, without positing any antithesis at all in tendency.) But, in part, 'justice' is more precisely defined, over against the 'order' necessary for social survival, as "the rightful relation of the various vitalities and forces in the community." These demonic vitalities and forces are not themselves evaluated here as "rightful"; and it is not clear whether the "rightful relation" is subjective, in terms of private judgements of perfection, or objective, in terms of some kind of Platonic or pragmatic social balance.

Obviously any man prefers the exercise of his own freedom (unless it seems to him wrong, which is rare and in which case he can change it by reason and will) to the sway of any authority whatsoever which can be exercised over him against his wish and without giving reasons, unless that authority also is serviceable to him, as lesser evil, by controlling another. His own will he subjectively tends to regard as good like himself—unless by an act of faith he is converted to regard it as bad and himself as 'utterly corrupt'—although objectively we can regard it, in Kant's famous term, already quoted, as involving "a wild, lawless freedom." Indeed the use of Authority to each is precisely that it, in some worthwhile measure, protects his own Freedom. As the urge for Freedom is instinctive and natural, so too (as St. Thomas affirms) the growth of Authority is natural, and not artificial, arbitrary, or by deliberated contract. It may be discovered in some rational and objective reality (and Natural Law is of this character) *or* it may be constructed by actual majority or other consent, on utilitarian grounds. But its recognition as legitimate is social and in defence of rational freedom.

One man controls another, eristically, by direct force or by imposed rule, which control only arises from fear by the other and gives no stable habit; or, charistically, from love, which the other recognizes as binding in trust and fully reasonable; or from a reason, mutual convenience (of short or long range) and agreed control which becomes stable and habitual because, if one party default, other parties and authority will uphold it. This last is the condition discussed by Kant, last and best of the theorists of the Social Contract school. Indeed, when its doctrine has been stripped of a mythology fundamentally discussed by that school itself, nevertheless the school tends to ignore that some Authority, as of Reason, *in esse* is not itself by compact or only from deliberate consent of men and by calculation of sovereign individuals; but it is only the recognition, passive assent, and active consent and support of it that comes from individuals, from which last springs, in operation, the social *power* of it. Most controls, for example in British social and constitutional life, so far depend upon habit in consent that they are frequently described as 'organic' (a term which we shall discuss when we consider community life) rather than as contractual. The ideal authority of Reason or God does not derive from consent, but from reality; and ideally upholds and justifies only a reasonable freedom.

This condition of compact, which Kant also applies as basis of his 'World Republic,' is advantageous, he says, to men "even if they were devils," provided that they are intelligent devils. This is a theme the more interesting in that it comes from the pen of the writer who was pre-eminently the philosopher of individual duty. The moral basis of allegiance (and allegiance to what) we cannot discuss yet, although there are those in our universities who would seek to found political theory upon that of which the discussion has never yet ended, but where men "came out by the same door wherein [they] went." The habit of obedience, although tinged with interest, nevertheless need not be a creature of constant intellectual calculation, any more than is most people's use of their wealth and funds.

Authority is, therefore, distinct alike from Force (which is actual and of this instant) and even from Power (which is potential as well as actual, but seeks stability for my specific use, as when we speak, in another context, of 'electric power'). It is a form of Power, potential and actual; but one socially recognized, consented to or 'legitimized' as reasonable by some others (not necessarily or often, *all* others) as having a social general function, with its institutions for specific purposes. It carries with it at least such passive recognition or assent as is to be found in habitual mass obedience to its rule, with some alleged rational claim to such obedience. That freedom which authority itself recognizes as consonant with its rule (such as there was even in Eden under the Almighty, and which perhaps lies in the nature of things, if these be sufficiently known) we may call Liberty; and the exercise of it is said to be part of our recognized and legitimate Claims or within our Rights. What rights these be, and how defined, depends upon the nature of this authority, as well as of the claimant, man; so that some are called civil, others spiritual or ecclesiastical, and others industrial or again domestic, and some universal, natural or human (such as a constitutional morality and civil or ecclesiastical law prudentially must recognize in order to remain naturally sound) as springing from the basic nature of the claimant and native to his dignity or character as man. At the present time, especially in many underdeveloped countries, there is a profound and revolutionary antipathy to all authority, rule, government, and leadership as such, alike civil and ecclesiastical, as incompatible with this dignity; and, instead, there is a simple demand for educational guidance which is (falsely) supposed to be something quite dissimilar. This was recently expressed articulately by a distinguished Indonesian minister. This we shall discuss later, especially with reference to the diverse functions of *vis coactiva* and *vis directiva*.

Immanuel Kant, in a late statement of the once famous doctrine of Original Contract, points out that this is indeed rather a logical than (if it were ever so imagined) a historical construction. Our present construction is true because it is psychologically true, from which truth derive the problems of human choice. No question arises here about the character of some historical 'state of nature,' whether it were, as Locke imagined, one of Arcadian sociality "as with the North American Indians," or of some primitive peoples living in clans, perhaps full of customs, tabus and values but prior to the use of civil organization; or as individual Crusoes, noble but very savage, as Rousseau said in his *Discourse on Inequality*; or, as Hobbes maintained for his own purposes, a society where life was "solitary, poor, nasty, brutish and short," and where Natural Right was no more than Natural Power. Nor need we examine the nature of this Social Compact, fictitious anyhow, beyond remarking that the recognition of authority offers general mutual advantage; or enquire who provides that which is not specifically advantageous to me with a morally valid sanction.

It can, of course, be said (as by recent critics) that men grew up as social like the piccaninny Topsy, whether or not this condition offered mutual advantage —Nature provides the suicidal lemming with no right to life and with few natural advantages—and that there is an obligation, as well as a habit and convenience, in a moral being to behave 'socially,' such as renders all talk of 'natural' right redundant. The reply to Sir Robert Filmer, however, here still holds: that a man is actually born into *particular* societies or group organizations (sometimes overlapping) with different and sometimes conflicting claims; and has to make *choices* about his obligations. He will choose, if he can, that which leaves him on balance most free—that is, most free to do what he wants *actually* to do, and to follow his own ideas and dreams. There is the subsequent question, indeed, of what he ought to want to do or dream, which will obligate him in what he does. But to this we have to return later.

§iv. *The Bifurcation of Power*

Power bifurcates into two expressions. On the one hand, there is the Will demanding, positively, its freedom to fulfil its actual self and, in reverse, to have Power-for-myself to be free, to thrust aside all obstacles. This is the simple 'Robinson Crusoe' situation, which yet in practice exists a thousand times a day in things indifferent. Perhaps its enjoyment may be due to the unimportance of any obstacles; perhaps to some kind of pre-established harmony or intuitive (or calculated) co-operation, so that nothing is wished which will actually be refused. It gives powers for myself which, when socially allowed, are called Rights. Such freedom (to repeat), when socially recognized, is Liberty.

On the other hand, there is Power in the form of potential Power-over-others, in rule of men and administration of things, which can be advantageous in guaranteeing our (own) freedom and power, and which can be activated, to achieve our wishes, through permitted or enforced actual executive acts. But here the plot develops, because this form of power, as Authority, also guarantees the liberty of others, and does all this on terms. It guarantees, to each, freedom as a liberty in some respects, but on the other side, justly restrains for each both his abstract, total freedom and also some very concrete, actual activities, which Kant embraced under the term of "lawless freedom." To both Freedom and Authority there can be a rational attachment, and also with them both a pathological obsession. I can no longer appropriate Naboth's vineyard (or Uriah's wife) if I have a common law, to which I also am subject, which forbids another to steal from me; or change, by law of force and 'right of the victor,' the ruler of another state if I need a general authority which will define and protect my own sovereign rights. I can do these things by privilege; but at my own risk, unless the *lex* is one also generally recognized. Liberty and Authority, then, although polar, are not mutually exclusive or contradictory. They trace a common derivation from power, or from the wish-expressing and power-desiring Will, which first and formally wills to be free. Likewise, the Will wills both freedom and authority. Their tension is the source of all political dialectic and science, just as in Economics the balance of demand and supply is the dialectical axiom.

§v. *The Political Exchange*

Out of this exchange arises the notion of Political Goods, which we understand not in the ethical sense (as yet) but as we do Economic Goods. The whole of Economic Science, we have said, springs from the logical connection expressed in the law of demand and supply. It was the achievement of the classical economists to have enunciated this and its consequences with clarity, although subsidiary considerations had to be introduced later. Not for a century yet in Politics can we expect to make the equivalent of the modern refinements (of such vast practical use) of Economic Theory. But we can achieve the basic insights of pattern of the classical economists. And we may make some advances such as theirs by study of their methods. To reformulate what we have said above: THE WHOLE OF POLITICAL SCIENCE SPRINGS FROM THE LOGIC OF THE LAW OF THE CORRELATION OF FREEDOM AND AUTHORITY (Proposition 15). Liberty is freedom within the ambit of authority, exercising jural discretion.

The concept of a *Political Market* was outlined in *Principia* chap. v. Although scarcely elaborated, and rather used merely as showing a similarity of operation, the idea was also picked up by so eminent a political theorist as Ernest Barker in his recent books. In his *Reflections on Government* (1942) he writes: "The material to be handled is man: the problem to be solved is the government of man. It is the never-ending problem—always being solved, and never finally solved— of making, repairing and maintaining an adjustment of human relations which satisfies (or is generally calculated to satisfy) the moral claims of right made upon one another by human individuals and by groups of such individuals." Barker then proceeds to a discussion of duty (to which we shall come later) as alone providing the data to be surveyed by a 'scientific method.' The words 'material' (with its discouraging, if unintended, implication that man is being treated here as a 'thing,' not a 'will') and 'moral claims,' assuming that this is known as definitely as the 'actual claims' (or the legal claims), are loaded words.

In his *Principles of Social and Political Theory* (1951) Professor Barker writes: "Rights are not to be had for the asking, or as a matter of pure gift. There is always a sense in which they are bought; and they are only sure when they are fairly bought by an honest bargain . . . The necessity of reckoning gain and loss between different classes or sections is a still more obvious necessity, daily forced upon our attention by the process of class debate . . . The argument seems to result in a paradox: 'The greater the liberty of the individual, the greater the interposition of the activity of the State in declaring and enforcing law.' The statement of the paradox suggests a reflection. There is always a price to be paid for rights. That price, as has already been noted, is partly financial, or a matter of payment in money; partly spiritual or a matter of payment in the acceptance of control." What Barker here calls 'spiritual,' since the control is not of the mind, thought or wish, except most indirectly, I here call 'political.' Some of the 'financial' payment is also 'political,' since parties and churches have fallen and risen on issues of taxes and the budget, or, indeed, of trade union fees and of the sale of indulgences or the collection of tithes.

Professor G. C. Homans, in an enumeration of political goods in his *The Human Group*, writes that the groups which he studies have "even tended, as we have seen, to produce a surplus of the goods which make organization successful: moral leadership, cooperation between increasingly large numbers of people. Cohesion has been produced at a price." Two of these items seem rather to be part of the general mechanism of the market than goods (i.e., the potential satisfactions of human wishes) *in se*, although there are doubtless some direct satisfactions or pleasures in both. Old age insurance payments, hospital nursing and veteran payments, all given by law, community centres civilly established, trades union holiday homes, church feasts, are direct satisfactions. It may be argued that at least Professor Sir Ernest Barker, if not Professor Homans, is only talking in terms of metaphor or general analogy. This may be. But I am not so talking. I am discussing a new method of talking which can shape the very subject itself and its interpretation.

In a very relevant book, *The Functions of the Executive*, Mr. Chester Barnard ties together what he calls "the principles of co-operative action" (cf. *Lord Stamp, The Science of Social Adjustment*, 1937), stressed in chap. II *supra*, with the notion of a market, interestingly enough illustrated by comments upon the basis of obedience in an army. "Our definition of authority, like General Harbord's democracy in an army, no doubt will appear to many, whose eyes are fixed only on enduring organizations, as a platform of chaos. And so it is—exactly so in the preponderance of attempted organizations. They fail because they can maintain no authority [cf. certain churches], that is, they cannot secure sufficient contributions of personal efforts to be effective or cannot induce them in terms that are efficient. In the last analysis the authority fails because the individuals in sufficient numbers regard the burden involved in accepting necessary orders as changing the balances of advantage against their interest, and they withdraw or withhold their indispensable contributions." It is understood, at this time of writing, that Professor David Easton is engaged upon a further study of equilibrium theory (cf. Barnard, *The Functions of the Executive*, pp. 56 ff.) and that Professor Talcott Parsons is translating his study of the economic market, in *Economy and Society* (1956) into a new study of the political one. It may be added that one of the prime practical tasks of political science is to level out the oscillations between excess of authority and excess of licence. Cf. also the interesting comments of Professor Felix E. Oppenheim in his *Dimensions of Freedom* (1961).

The general institutions and specific organizations of authority, and their members, are the Producers of political services and goods. Those who are the recognized and formal functionaries or agents of authority, in terms of that function acquire a certain institutional status. The man who wants those services in order to provide him with the means to achieve his wishes in society and to satisfy his wants is the Consumer. Political Goods are various. The demands of consumers change from time to time and vary from person to person, and from consumer group or type to consumer group or type. As Hayek indicates, we cannot tell how much, subjectively, his demand may mean to one individual compared with another, except in terms of intensity and persistence of demand and of what *costs* he is prepared to pay. To be so governed by mental stereotypes as to expect absence of change in tastes is political ossification, however disguised by talk about 'principles': to expect all consumer demand to be 'good' is utopian romanticism.

Much confusion here has arisen from supposing static or ideal perfection in politics (unlike economics); or from concentrating all attention upon some one good or social *summum bonum*, disconnected from demand, or even upon a local 'pattern of life,' as static; or from elevating some supposed 'good' which everybody *ought* to demand, such as unrestricted free enterprise and its defence by society or the nationalization of all industries, abstract Capitalism or abstract Communism, into doctrinal dogmas to be thrust down the public's throat. Both economics and politics are dynamic, or at least manifest change. Marxism here (itself yet characterized by an eschatology of final goods) is useful, by stressing the detailed technological factors which contribute to shape and condition the scheme of living, and the changing ideas, of particular ages.

Thus the Roman of the equestrian order, such as Cicero, wished freedom to enjoy the privileges of the Roman Republican Constitution, in which a balance had been reached with the patricians; and with this he frequently coupled free trade and opportunity to exploit the provincials. The proletarians found, under the dictatorial or bureaucratic Empire, the advantages of all to enjoy equally the rights of citizenship (fiscally dubious although they were), relaxation of the restrictions of poverty by grants of land to veterans, circuses, and the free distribution of corn.

The mediaeval churchman, member of a powerful corporation with ideal ends which he felt morally ought not to be challenged, demanded freedom for the church and the suppression of subversives of the public philosophy and pattern. The Renaissance merchant, already with ideas of large-scale finance, had small use for the goods of a feudal system admirably adapted to the military protection of the rural village and the walled town; found the system one of burdensome cost; and turned, discovering greater freedom of trade, to the new monarchs, patrons of adventure, as his providers. The squire and lawyer of seventeenth-century England wanted his freedom from what he regarded as unconstitutional taxes to sustain the navy and national defence, and the right to produce uncensored political pamphlets. The American colonial retained all this objection to paying taxes to cover the cost of wars, and resisted any executive authority which was liable to impose restrictions, even on smuggling, to which he was ill-inclined to assent. As independent farmer and pioneer, he had little need for any controlling authority to provide him with security, except perhaps in the Indian wars. He valued freedom high and authority's services low. His was a consumer's market with light demand. (Cf. A. de Tocqueville, *Democracy in America*, World Classics ed., p. 75: The American "never thinks of soliciting the cooperation of the Government.") Professor Martin Lipset (*Political Man*, p. 305) points out that the Hamiltonian wing of the Federal party "passed legislation largely connected with the needs of the urban merchants and industrialists, ignoring the fact that ninety per cent of the electorate were rural farmers," and that, whether this was for the 'real' or 'ultimate' good of the country or not, this led to the demise of that Party.

The industrial worker, on the contrary, is concerned for freedom from fear of ill-health and freedom from want and unemployment, such as welfare insurance can give. But he is, on the whole, indifferent to the right to publish pamphlets of which he never expects to be the author, nor is he gravely concerned about mental monopolies in broadcasting or suspicious of an executive which expresses, against the few, that majority will which is, on the whole, his. Cf. E. H. Carr, *Conditions of Peace* (1942, p. 127): "The transfer of authority is not unnaturally resented by those who once exercised it as a deprivation of their liberty; and this explains why liberty has readily become in recent times a conservative and even a reactionary slogan. But it is not so resented by the masses, who do not necessarily see in the increased authority of the state a loss of liberty for themselves." In some quarters, then, the legislation demanded will be that which will increase consumer prosperity, preserve full employment, and raise the standard of living of the manual worker. In other quarters the demand may be for raising of the standard of national prosperity measured (as until recently in the U.S.S.R.) in terms of capital goods or (as in some Western countries) in terms of favourable balance of trade, perhaps with low wages or import restrictions but possibly with pecuniary advantages to the merchant class.

In the current press one reads of "estimating the cost in civil liberties of the demand for social securities." The Marxist talks, as an ultimate, of that 'classless society' in which the dynamic dialectic of struggle in the universe will apparently have ended. And others regard 'democracy' as ultimate, static, and beyond criticism, but cannot decide what it is. To the Marxists some of the very presuppositions of this democracy may seem to be instances of political 'bourgeois infantilism': the freedoms talked about are insubstantial. What particular groups want varies: what, in any given age, any particular group is likely to be strong enough to secure varies. The wishes of the skilled and of the unskilled industrial workers, of industrial workers, of Soviet bureaucrats, of Party officials and of peasants, will not be the same. To speak of the 'class war' is sociologically far too great a simplification. And, as Professor Leslie Lipson has commented: "if government consists of services provided by the rulers to the ruled, it is wrong to

think only of those who produce the services and to ignore the consumers." It may, of course, be said that this is merely "a fashion of
talking" (just as indeed mathematics is a symbolic fashion of
talking, which to begin with does no more than express in precise
terms what is common sense), but the question is whether this is not a
fashion of talking and thinking which, if we use it, gives us a new
insight into action and its motivation.

§vi.   *Absolute Liberty*

Do men 'want Liberty'? With the rise again of Tyranny as a form of
government, once classical and now revived in the twentieth century,
there has been much alarmed and sorrowful discussion of this question.
There have been suggestions that modern man, and especially the
industrial worker, is not as interested as he should be in these political
goods of antique liberty and of the actual rights of man; and is content
to abandon old rights, once bled for, in a flight from adventure and
responsibility. One may even ask melancholically, with the Emperor
Tiberius, "How shall I restore the ancient virtues?", adding with the
tired and sophisticated Pilate and some modern philosophers, "What
is truth?" The argument clearly demands critical analysis, especially
as the prizing of adventure and the prizing of responsibility are
scarcely synonymous. There is a difference between apathy about freedom to do as one likes, and apathy about the civil freedoms, such as
of free exercise of the right to vote and to carry civil responsibilities,
which *other* people think one ought to have, even if they have to be
paid for by oneself (for example, in personal military service or exposure, in civil defence, to atomic or other 'liquidation').

The answer would seem to be that Society is plural in its wants;
but that human beings never at any time cease to be interested in the
freedom to acquire what in fact specifically and adequately *they* do
want (See Proposition 7). The error is in supposing a similarity in
these wants, which the market does not in fact exhibit.

Not only can there be a dissimilarity in wants, objectively expressed, but
also (as Lord Robbins has pointed out in the comparable field of Economics,
and as Professor Michael Polanyi has indicated in his remarkable *Logic of Liberty*,
1951) a subjective dissimilarity.

This error, in turn, is due to a false identification of liberty with
freedom from regulation by civil government. As we shall see, much

unchecked regulation may indeed have its oppressive costs; but it may yet be the case that (as might be expected) an increase in authority in particular directions may offer attractive compensations and advantages. There is, as distinct from 'freedom,' no 'absolute liberty,' since liberty functions within law and is relative to it; nor is it, therefore, (as Lippmann has said, in his *Public Philosophy*, 1955) any unqualified or simple, monolithic, civil good. It is always qualified. Freedom for themselves men always want in general. Not all freedom in particular is socially desirable or 'good.' Liberties in particular men want according to the cost. It will depend on what kind of a market it is. Excessive stress upon authority and upon the normal 'authoritative pattern' or condition of the political market favouring government and the producer, we call 'authoritarianism' or (the better to avoid confusion) 'despotism,' and, where this is total, so far as this may be humanly practicable, 'totalitarianism'; and excess of freedom, beyond the 'liberal pattern' or condition of the market favouring the individual, small groups or the consumer, we call 'libertinism' and those who practise it 'libertines,' or to use a more neutral-tinted and less derogatory word 'anarchism.' It will be noted that it can be both possible and desirable to be authoritative without being authoritarian; and to be at liberty without being licentious or libertine or anarchist.

It is frequently stated, especially in time of international crisis, that it is pointless "to fight to preserve one's liberties if, first, one is going to impair liberties." This is not so much a platitude as a logical deception. All liberties involve *some* sacrifice of freedom to authority; 'liberty' is not an all-or-nothing structure, but a balance; and in time of crisis more freedoms may have to be sacrificed, as a cost, to preserve the preferred and prior liberties. For example, we may say that the United States preserves a desirable balance of liberties and the Soviet Union gives a quantum of goods which fails to balance the losses. This can be argued. Those who, with Patrick Henry, prefer freedom to death, must be specific on the freedom. One permanent problem with liberty is how to retain enough authority to guarantee its own survival. Poland perished, as a state, from too much (baronial) liberty. Freedom to do as one likes is not the best guarantee of victory. What yet is profoundly true is the psychological maxim that, to get men to struggle at all, they must be given a lively expectation of retaining or achieving what *for them* are keenly desired political goods or retained liberties of independent action.

As Professor C. J. Friedrich has pointed out, in recent lectures delivered in London, the maximizing of private freedom and of public freedom, including 'freedom of participation,' may be alternatives. Or, in the words of Lord Attlee, speaking in Toronto (May 21, 1961), the only way to preserve freedom [liberty] can be to accept restrictions on personal freedom.

An effectively majority-controlled government or group authority is likely to please the hopes of the majority, 'the wishes of the common man.' It may sacrifice many ancient liberties, from trial by Peers (as distinct from peers, *pares*) to freedom from detention (as under recent British security regulations) without trial. Whether this is 'a good thing' may carry us beyond discussion of means by political science. For the moment our concern is to point out that 'the irresponsible desire for security' is itself a form of desire for Liberty, as we may actually view liberty, not perhaps 'bourgeois-demanded liberty' but 'proletarian liberty,' to get what we want by law and to remove obstacles. That this is 'irresponsible' is a sectional valuation, whether right or wrong, by those who want other incompatible liberties such as reduction of taxation. It is not repudiation of freedom, but a repudiation of what other people, whose interests may not be ours, have the presumption to tell us that we ought to want. It is unscientific to confuse this issue and not platitudinous to say so. It may be found more useful to survey what men actually do want and to enquire why and how. The 'have-nots' in their quarters of the world, with small expectation of the satisfaction of abstract demands, are obviously likely to be more tolerant of or even in favour of what Hobbes called 'strong rule' and others have called tyranny than the 'haves,' with their elaborated traditions of civil and individual liberties. Their preliminary 'leftish' demand for change satisfied, they frequently have what Lipset calls "authoritarian predispositions."

The two most famous orators in history, Demosthenes and Cicero, both praised liberty, the one the forlorn liberty of the city-state against wider Hellenic unions, the other the liberty enjoyed under the free Roman Republic for the equestrian order, to which he himself belonged, but which was coupled with great liberty (despite all his efforts) to exploit the provincial for gain. Great patriots, champions of past and obsolescent liberties, whether of the small municipal state or of the equestrian order or middle class—how tragic was the catastrophic failure of those good, liberal, constitutional men, Cicero, Brutus and the rest, who have their compeers today. As against this the international Empire of Alexander and the dictatorship of the Caesars and the Roman Empire offered political goods to the small man, including a new and equal freedom for the provincial. The goods were, of course, obtained by costs, and ultimately cost the proto-feudalism (with limitation of free movement, as in modern Russia) of the Byzantine Empire.

Professor F. A. Hayek quotes the saying of John Milton: "They who seek nothing but their own just liberty, have always the right to win it, whenever they have the power, be the voices never so numerous that oppose it." (Milton clearly felt that 'the just' was self-evident; or evident to the miraculously ever-right private conscience.) It is the mood that inspired the heroism and the collapse of the intransigently libertarian Polish Republic. Hayek also writes: "there are few of the political views in the [Victorian Age] regarded as characteristically English of which the majority of people in this country [Britain] do not now seem ashamed, if they do not positively repudiate them" (*The Road to Serfdom*, 1944). The electoral collapse of the Liberal party generally may be taken as a comment on this.

Deploring the collapse of Liberalism, in what yet is significantly entitled "a conservative approach" (and in many countries of Europe the 'Liberal' or 'Free Democratic' parties are highly conservative of Manchester economics) Dr. Peter Drucker writes commenting on an anti-dictatorship slogan, 'It's fun to be free': "The mob of Imperial Rome at least never pretended that circuses and freedom were identical. It had the courage to admit that it preferred circuses . . . Freedom is not so much a right as a duty . . . Unless there are decision and responsibility there is no freedom. There may be happiness, security, peace, and progress. . . Freedom is not only possible, it is inevitable on the basis of the belief that every single human being *has* to choose between good and evil" (*The Future of Industrial Man*, 1942; italics mine). In this same sequence of thought Dr. Erich Fromm states: " 'Freedom from' is not identical with positive freedom, with 'freedom to' . . . Modern man lives under the illusion that he knows what he wants, while he actually wants what he is supposed to want . . . It is necessary to realize that to know what one really wants is not comparatively easy, as most people think, but one of the most difficult problems any human being has to solve . . . the powerlessness and insecurity of the isolated individual in modern society who has become free from all bonds that once gave meaning and security to life . . . positive freedom *insists* on the *spontaneous* activity [*sic*] of the total integrated personality." (*Escape from Freedom*, 1941. Italics mine.) Beyond this, again, in the libertarian ethic, lie the Nietzschean and Sartrean excursus, with their distrust of the tyrant Reason, from which it is almost possible to complete (through moral and rational nihilism) the circle into 'negative freedom.'

The comment on the exchange of the potentialities of (morally recognized) Freedom *B* for the indirect power over others of security, made by Dr. R. E. Money Kyrle (*Psychoanalysis and Politics*, 1951) is relevant. "If the super-egos of a people are on the average becoming harsher . . . in the end they will make the state stricter than it was before, and compensate themselves, for their actual loss of freedom, by identifying themselves with it and so acquiring the sense of vicarious power . . . An insidious influence in this process is the increase in the desire for power which accompanies a decline in the desire for freedom" (i.e., for particular liberties, perhaps archaic or of 'antique virtue,' as praised above).

What is described by some writers as 'positive freedom' (*B*) or 'real freedom' is a highly complicated condition, sharply distinct from that Freedom *A*, with instinctive basis, which we have already discussed and which is the condition of absence of restraint upon the realization of wishes and empirical will. We are here concerned with *actual* wishes and wills and (as Mill said) with men's interests *as they suppose them to be*. The comments as cited are concerned with so-called 'real' wills, aiming at self-improvement according to some ideal scheme, self-development, autonomy of choice and the like. Here human 'perfection' in autonomy, or maybe *Islam* or entire obedience to divine will, or 'self-improvement' or 'productive development' (*not* direction by common wishes or passions) are ideals of the personality, to which only a few can indeed attain. It is, as the Stoics said, an escape from vice (or, in theological terms, sin); a very difficult and burdensome decision in choosing the good, supposed to be known (and perhaps *summum bonum*); ultimately a 'service' of the good, and a 'duty,' or even an autonomous, existential activity destined to decide us according to our own private (or, as the Greeks called it, 'idiotic') *nomos* or 'law'—or choice (as the Greeks called it, 'heresy'), and to plunge us into 'commitment.'

It will not be useful to discuss further this philosophical or valuational use of the word 'freedom' at this stage: although this is by no means to suggest that political philosophy will not have to discuss it. An even narrower interpretation of 'positive freedom,' verging (despite statements to the contrary) on an extreme moral relativism, anarchism or nihilism, is given by Mr. Archibald MacLeish, poet and close personal adviser of President Franklin Roosevelt, in his *Freedom is the Right to Choose* (1952).

"If freedom," writes MacLeish, "ceases to be the American faith in man and in man's unqualified right to find the truth *for himself*, it will shortly express a faith in established truth, in the rightness of official opinion." "The American Proposition is the proposition, advanced at the beginnings of the Republic and enacted into law when the Constitution was adopted, that a man's freedom *to be a man*, and to find and speak *the truth that is in him*, is more important than the protection of any accepted belief. Those who have offered their lives precisely to defend the prejudice that freedom has a supreme and *absolute* worth . . . our willingness to think for ourselves, and to say as we think, and *do as we say* . . . The American Proposition is the proposition that if men are free to think for themselves and to believe as they think and to say as they believe—if men, all men, are free to make their own way *by their own means* to the truth that is true *for them*, for each one of them—the world in which they live and which together they compose will be a better world: juster, stronger, wiser, more various" (italics mine).

The question may be asked how moral freedom can be both so free and yet 'absolute' about anything. Here freedom becomes either a purely formal freedom to think, say, do, *anything*, or it becomes attachment to a *particular* tradition or 'pattern' or 'American faith,' shaped indeed in part by Tom Paine although constitutionally opposed, for example, to all other traditions or 'established churches' (U.S. Constitution, §i). This is yet the pattern which every man, who reaches truth strictly by his own means on his own, will necessarily, it seems, come by some protestant pre-established harmony to endorse. The truth is strictly individual and relative ('truth for them'); yet in each man there is 'a truth,' which seems to be absolute although not to be tested by any objective criteria, as of rationality. Anyhow, the freedom to achieve it, and socially to act on this untested revelation, is of "absolute worth."

Mr. MacLeish adds, with perspicacity, "ours is a time of extreme personal insecurity and private frustration"—perhaps due to excess of such unsecured freedom. "Until we have learned how individual human beings can recover *a measure of control of the conditions* of their lives in the world which science and technology have created, the will to peace will be merely a hope" (italics mine). Also, slightly contradictorily, Mr. MacLeish talks about the collaboration of intellectual workers in progress, so that it looks as if, to reach the truth, before we "do as we say," a certain amount of consultation, instruction, illumination, humility about *how* we 'think for ourselves' and (as the saying goes) 'shoot our mouths off' may be advisable, so that we 'think what we say before we say what we think.' Freedom means, it seems, fewer 'public philosophies' but more controls . . . Here, then, we return to a need for increased controls as means to the substantial liberty never enjoyed under conditions of war—not at all a matter of every *enragé* chauvinist, who (in Locke's phrase) is "sure because he is sure," finding the truth for himself. It is of some importance that the protestant conscience, as thus made over by secular interpretations of private judgement and of what is 'the truth-for-him,' in the Bible itself comes to an entirely bad end. "The way of the foolish is right in his own eyes." (Proverbs 12: 15) Nor are the Israelites commended for doing what was right in their own eyes. Their way led to destruction. About such concrete peace and control, at least, political science is competent to make a few observations.

Before, however, proceeding to these, one comment may be made in anticipation of the discussion in political philosophy. The notion of Freedom *B* as self-development according to an objective moral or rational law is intelligible and merits examination. In contemporary Western civilization, however, this is almost habitually identified (contrary to the highly rational principles of Goethe and Mill, who insisted upon a 'harmony' and even upon discipline) with 'self-development,' as something self-evidently good without any norm, directive, or *nomos*. This is, of course, not a humanist philosophy in the great tradition but a Renaissance heresy, clear in writers such as Alberti, egotistic, megalomaniac, and anarchist. It is arguable that, if we wish to discover the kernel of the weakness or decadence of much of Western philosophy and of the Western pattern of living in confronting, not so successfully as is to be hoped, the Soviet world, it lies precisely here, even if the attitude is often only semi-conscious and inarticulate.

In the case of young people this attitude is sometimes naively expressed as "we are against everything but, literally, against everything . . ." Logically this is nonsense; psychologically it can be a condition—nor, where a vote is given at eighteen, need it be politically negligible in demand. However, the resulting problems in education and in juvenile delinquency are not novel nor are they unknown in the Soviet Union, which copes with them by more than Victorian severity.

§vii. *Absolute Authority*

To balance what we have said about confused ideas on absolute freedom, it may be well also to clear the undergrowth and brushwood a little from a jungle of ideas about absolute authority, regarded in secular politics as a moral imperative. We are not here discussing whether there is or is not an unqualified imperative to accept the rational law of contradiction, the conclusions of mathematics or logic, or the demonstrations of Euclid, or like alleged truths. The issue is that of the imposition, by authority and by law, of particular securities and plans. If we knew the moral and social *summa bona*, would we be entitled to impose these goods by law?

If it be said that this is an ethical issue of philosophy and not one for political science, we can restate the problem. Is it not absurd or misleading to talk of any 'market' of political goods, when in fact the issue is not at all one of what people actually want, and of what they are prepared to pay, but of what they *ought* to want and for which they should be ordered 'to make sacrifices'? In Cromwell's phrase: "It's not what they want, it's what's good for them; that is the question." In the words of a great Cromwellian admirer, speaking on behalf of an electoral minority view in terms typically Jacobin, Mr. Michael Foot, M.P.: "opinion is made." This may be true. Is it a question of converting them to the true faith, known and held uncompromisingly by a few, of civil and economic salvation; and indeed (some would add) of imposing upon them, by law and coercion, what is the rational and good panacea? In the last resort it may be argued that human beings, left to themselves, will not make sacrifices, are short-sighted and untrustworthy about their wants, and should be ordered about for their good by 'vanguards.' Also that, in the end, they like it that way—so that, even empirically, the technique is justified. Masses in one generation are liquidated; and, in the next generation, the standard of living of the slaves goes up and everybody (save a few) is happy. In the words of Halifax 'the Trimmer,' "it is true in government, if sad, that it is necessary to treat men scurvily."

We shall discuss this further when we come to political and civil Parties, and their techniques of persuasion or pressure. Can it yet be truly said that these Parties *want* power and are hence reduced to exploring the means for *support* to obtain it? Call it 'dream-politics' or call it 'death-wish,' is it not the case that some political Parties, far from wanting power or to provide goods in popular demand in any so-called 'political market,' are prepared to suffer extinction as movements or conventicles rather than change one iota of what they believe to be the true political or economic faith? Their attachment to a creed or collection of 'principles,' and their resistance to criticism, is obsessive.

To restate the matter in our own terms, we have here a political producer, whether he claim 'divine right' or only dialectical certainty, thrusting upon the market political goods which, according to the supposition, the consumer public does not want. Such a statement is no distortion of the position. We are not concerned yet with the moral or rational worth of the goods, but with the demand and support. We may, then, reply (a) that the vendor certainly *on principle* (if not in paying the realistic electioneering costs) wants power to achieve the realization of the programme, with seats of authority for the vending and high-principled group, who will doubtless fight in due course for ministerial posts; (b) that such an enterprise, so conducted without attention to support, will end in the bankruptcy of the vending party. Such bankruptcy happens often enough. Indeed, political bankruptcy we can describe as inability to produce the goods and inability to gain adequate support for their production.

We may suspect that analysis will show (a) a confusion, due to emotion or interest, between an empirical matter of means to desired change, such as free trade or temperance regulations or nationalization of the means of production, and an article of faith about ends, such as human fraternity and its supposed consequences; (b) a confusion between the functions of a state and a church; (c) hence the desire to impose by *vis coactiva* (by coercion) principles of faith and moral choice, whereas what should be imposed alone, to get results, should be practical regulations, susceptible to the empirical observation of their consequences in terms of what people actually want. A Party such as described chooses *not* to give the people what the people wants, perhaps because it mistimes its activities—its turn, if it lived, would come later—or because it will not pay the cost in changing its traditional ways of doing business, bound up with the vested interests of the old management and veteran leadership or with the fanatically loyal enthusiasm of the indoctrinated but inexperienced.

In reply it may be urged that it is precisely by the intransigent faith of the 'true blue Economic Bourbon,' or of 'the Old Bolshevik' (liquidated by Stalin) or of the fanatical or 'true' Socialist, Liberal, Conservative, that the masses are converted and support won to this uncompromising authority. This however, is to destroy the supposition that we are dealing solely with a problem of minority rule. Rather it is one of how majorities are swayed to accept authority. We have not abstract absolute authority, as distinct from ultimate brute force, but a technique for claiming active consent and passive assent. The magnetic influence of fanaticism or of what David Hume calls 'zeal' in amassing power and victory—no matter how much it is detested by some and no matter whether this is chiefly motivated by faith, lust for power or by the obsessive vanity of individuals in the movement who would 'lose face' by change—will be discussed later. But the present suggestion is that, under the right conditions, it will prove to be an effective technique to rally support (by persuasion or intimidation, marketing of ideas or by monopoly of goods).

This comment is not to deny that abuses and corruptions, bedded in apathy, should not be rooted out with idealistic ruthlessness. It is to suppose, on the contrary, that consumer support *can* be attracted. (Some would add that the prime interest has become one in direct political goods, not for the public but for 'the army of active party workers' themselves—but this is usually hotly repudiated.) It becomes, now, a calculation of the time it may take to attract consumer demand; and of whether the process can be speeded up by the use of force, as against education and propaganda, at least so far as the occupancy of commanding positions (from which the rest of the consumers can be directed, monopolized, and made captive) is concerned. Indeed, behind dictatorship there may be political faith; but there is almost always also an immense power-impulsion, historically followed by the enjoyment by the dictatorial circle of uncircumscribed political goods for themselves. The power analysis, then, holds.

It can, of course, be argued (and has been argued, in May, 1960, by Viscount Montgomery) that it is better that some millions of human beings should be exterminated than that hundreds of millions should be delayed in their gratification with goods which, it is alleged, they actually want and, moreover in the opinion of some, should want. This offers justification for terror. It must further be admitted that a minority (even a large one, beneficiaries under *ancien régime* or *status quo*) occasionally opposes promptitude, not on grounds rationally articulate, but on grounds—even if excused as some local pattern of life—marked by apathy or obstinacy and in contempt of reason.

§viii. *Political Goods*

Political Goods, then, may concretely include peace, social security, employment insurance, government-subsidized food and housing, the guarantees of liberties (as distinct from the condition itself of freedom unassured), the guarantees of employment, wage and trade, and indeed all those things procured or promised by political parties in election addresses or by industrial or ecclesiastical organizations for the loyal and faithful. These goods require, to get them, social organization; and, for them, the fact of social organization, or at least consensus, is primary, as distinct from those economic goods in which technological production is primary. It requires social organization to produce pig iron or a ship, but these would not be regarded as other than primarily economic activities although, secondarily, bad or good labour-power organization of the steel trade may affect the entire political structure and human relations of a steel-producing country. Both aspects, then, are valid and necessary for study. It is a dangerous error to suppose that, in industry, only the economic activities of production of what may oddly be called 'goods,' such as bombs, by what is no less oddly called 'hands,' i.e., human beings (*politica zoa*), are involved.

When the words 'Political Goods' are used, *a measure of effort* in production of these wares is supposed. Many control relations are so habitual, as in domestic activities, that no cost is noticed in acquiescence or in paternal insistence upon them, just as articles in free supply, such as air and (often) water, even if vital, are without price. Even so, these customary habits or goods may suddenly demand attention and become matters of conscious criticism, as for example, with the decay of the patriarchal or Confucian family. Usually, however, there will be no goods produced through organization without *costs*. Also, where there is demand by those ready to go to the effort of paying the price, there will be a variety of competing producers, for example, organized in rival parties or denominations (or even unions), seeking to attract to themselves support and power, with its advantages. The theorists of Social Contract and of Governmental Contract at least grasped these things better than some of their more ambitious successors, who dealt in philosophies of history and false analogies of the organic. Nevertheless, the theory of the Political Market is something considerably more sophisticated than the much-discussed one of the Social Contract.

§ix. *Consumers' and Producers' Interests and Pressure Groups*

An entire school of political scientists, following in the train of Arthur F. Bentley and his *Process of Government*, have seized on the scheme of picturing politics as a chaffering of 'interest groups.' Within the broader market of the national or international community, with its concern about some kind of equilibrium or even 'just price,' attention has been directed to groups or associations—sometimes with the danger (along with Marx, in the case of 'classes') of regarding these abstract 'interests' and their concrete organized groups as atomic, unanalysable, and final. Actually Arthur Bentley's usage of the term 'groups' is subtle and elusive. These groups are integrated for the execution of a general or common will directed to a common object, to which they are 'committed,' this 'will' being here called an 'interest.' These 'interests' are shaped subjectively by the wish and will, as 'my interests,' but they are also delimited by the object, apart from achievement of it. (There is here an ambiguity which is misleading between the objective and the subjective, so that a man may be said to have 'interests,' involving a complex of relevant means with their obligations, in which he is 'not interested' or which he neglects.) We have, then, to ask what are the stronger consumer groups in the competition—and also what are the producer groups; and how are these organized. The study becomes one of 'Interest Groups,' covering society in their network or web and making it plural, instead of undifferentiated and homogeneous.

The recent work of Wright and Hyam, in the *American Sociological Review*, of Peter Odegard, in the *Western Political Quarterly*, and recent work in the *American Political Science Review*, all point to the need for caution in this field. The majority of American citizens, Wright and Hyam have shown, do not belong to any association (or union) but operate as individuals.

It will be noted that our own theoretical basing has been upon the individual and upon the 'political act.' On the other hand, some of the most powerful asssociations, such as the Federation of British Industries, are not made up directly of individuals, but of companies (admittedly not devoid of human interests and decisions). The groups themselves, as we shall note later, tend to be 'managed' by a few, rather than being all voluntary associations of democratic citizens equally sharing in decisions and using their group pressures for self-protection against, say, bureaucracy. Some do, some do not, some 'do a deal.'

That the play of Political Parties can be so regarded is obvious enough, although a closer analysis will show these Parties to be rather organizations of Producer interests in providing goods in return for office and power, than indeed Consumer interests. Not, however, only Parties but also organizations behind Parties can be Interest Groups, demanding Legislation—such as the Corn Law League; manufacturers' and employers' Associations pressing their particular case; and also Trade Unions, providing benefits for their members, both as ordinary producers of political goods, and also as pressing their competitors in the market in terms of soliciting legislation for their own advantage. In the same categories are agricultural and such sectional interests; churches which have legislation to advocate, such as for temperance, and are here organized in 'pressure' associations; and voluntary associations for like purposes, such as the American Legion and veterans' societies. They all come under this description of Interest Groups, who want power, competing in the market against other producers of goods, by pressure and propaganda, or making their joint demands as consumers of legislation demanding to be satisfied by legislators. In some cases they will be active as Parties, whether of the parliamentary or (as the Communist and Fascist Parties) of the conspiratorial order. In other cases they may be wealthier and no less powerful than the civilly recognized parties and political pressure groups. The examination of their electioneering methods, and techniques of attracting voting support, has been an object of study by psephologists.

Although there have been orthodox studies of Political (i.e., Civil) Parties from the days of Ostrogorski and Robert Michels to those of Professor Duverger, which have sometimes included the laying down of so-called 'laws' or, rather local and episodic 'rules of the game' (such as the so-called 'law of the cube' in British Parliamentary politics), in recent years there have been—as already mentioned—what the UNESCO *Report on Political Science in the United States* calls 'politicization,' that is, the adoption of the typical political treatment (as understood by Aristotle, Machiavelli, and the students of power) in other fields. Thus the work of Professor Peter H. Odegard in *Pressure Politics* (1928) took its rise in the study of the relation of the Methodist Church with the Anti-Saloon League, and there have been other studies of the power of the Catholic Church. The work of Professor Earl Latham, *The Group Basis of Politics* (1953), refers especially to the issues of price-fixing by manufacturers, the anti-trust laws, and, especially, to the Cement Institute. He clarifies his general position by stating that what "puts state and nonstate associations in the same category of forms is the common factor of power."

"Organized groups, then, are structures of power; they are forms of private government different from forms of public government principally in that public governments possess the characteristic of officiality . . . Groups are basic. It has also been pointed out that organized groups are structures of power and therefore within the scope of political enquiry. What is true of society is true of the communities of which the society is composed: the religious community, the political community (the state) [?the *civil* community, municipal, state, federal-national and confederate-international], and the economic community." However, as touching the 'basic' nature of the group, which has, in Bentley's work among others, obscurities of analysis, see Latham's comment: "Groups are devices by which the individual fulfills personal values and felt needs."

In the case of A. F. Bentley, in his pioneer book *The Process of Government*, a quite remarkable thing happens. Although his entire argument rests on the importance of the behavioural interplay of interests ("pseudo-scientific behaviourist superstition," Sir Julian Huxley has called this) as distinct from the influence of ideas or what he calls 'mind-stuff,' Bentley nowhere stops to define, as touching these all-important entities, what he understands an 'interest' to be. However, thrust away in an aside on p. 444 we get our clue. Bentley here writes: "The term 'own interest' here may again be understood in two ways. Either it may indicate a specialized underlying interest of the individuals who compose the group in question—so, for instance, the 'selfish' [*sic*] personal interests of a despot or of a boss and his henchmen—or it may mean the tendency of the representative group to persist, i.e., its inertia, whether the case is of a belief or of a governmental form." His lapse here is comparable to that of Marx himself, who nowhere precisely and consistently defines "class." In brief, when the analysis of these metaphysical entities called 'interests,' to be yet behaviouristically observed in mind-stuff-less social interaction, is carried through, we are left with what the eighteenth century used to call the 'enlightened self-interest' of individuals (admittedly multiple, as Bentley insists) and the stupid apathy of the sluggish masses who hope not to be disturbed or 'pushed about.' Bentley's philosophy will not allow him (any more than in the end did that of Lincoln Steffens) to remove the ironic quotation marks from 'selfish.' The immixture of the moral indignation of Wright Mills is not yet.

The work, more preoccupied with the impinging of pressure groups on the orthodox civil process of law production, is also important of E. Pendleton Herring, in *Group Representation before Congress*

(1929), and of V. O. Key, in *Politics, Parties and Pressure Groups*. The most wide-ranging and detailed survey, however, of this theme will be found in Professor David Truman's *The Governmental Process*, with its argument that "organized efforts to influence and control attitudes [in politics] are inevitable," and can be observed by study of Interest Groups. Especially relevant is the comment: "We shall not begin to achieve control until we have arrived at a conception of politics that adequately accounts for the operations of political groups. We need to know what regular patterns are shown by group politics before we can predict its consequences and prescribe for its lapses . . . Our first step in the development of a workable conception of political groups will have to be *away from formal government* and [civil] politics as such" (italics mine). Despite a certain fluctuation of terms, we have here a clear programme of 'politicization' by function in the social field. As touching the psephologists, the work of H. G. Nicholas and David Butler should be noted, with their attention to measurable quantities.

It is interesting to note that American writers have in the past (perhaps thanks to the influence of constitutional lawyers) been less ready to recognize the play of pressure groups as 'normal' in civil politics than have British theorists, despite (or, perhaps, because of) the greater virulence of some of these groups in North America than in Britain. Alarm, a late prejudice against giving official recognition to any such groups, even political parties, and an individualistic philosophy, substituting a stereotype for the actualities, may offer some explanation.

At present, a new attention seems to be given to these issues by North American scholars. See the comment of Professor C. Brough Macpherson, "World Trends in Political Science Research," (p. 435) about "the whole range of phenomena (parties, public opinion, the democratic control of administration, etc.), which are now regarded as central to the understanding of the political process. . . . Hence the traditional university structure offers no encouragement either to research in these fields or to the development of an approach or method designed to produce a systematic theory of politics."

The issue is not only that of competing on the market, both to provide *goods* which the political public wants, such as voluntary health insurance (being the brand recommended by the professional Medical Associations) or national health insurance, and of attracting that *support* which will enable the producer to achieve victory at the polls or in wide party membership and, hence, effective control; but also is one of the packaging of these political goods, through skilful advertis-

ing and propaganda. In this art some pressure groups are more successful than others equally meritorious in product but not in the art of
'making friends and influencing people' at home and abroad.

There have been several studies in this new field, in which attention should
especially be directed to the survey of the activities of the American Medical
Association and the Republican National Committee made by Stanley Kelley,
in *Professional Public Relations and Political Power* (1956). It concludes with
an interesting, if exaggerated, quotation (*vide* p. 238 *infra*) from a public relations man: "The people are not interested in politics. They are too busy earning
a living. They think you can get a political education 'on the fly' from headlines.
But someone will find a new way of campaigning, some kind of new strategy. I
think people are already tired of the 'baloney' we feed them about our candidates being great men. There are few men of any stature in public office."
(p. 235) The fact remains that, on the record, the electorate is preoccupied in
large measure with 'bread and butter concerns,' does collect its political information 'on the fly,' and does accept 'the baloney'; and this has to be set in the
balance, when we come to judge democracy as efficient to public ends, against
Aristotle's estimate of the sound judgement of his free farmer-elector. Reference
must also be made to Mr. Vance Packard's book, *The Hidden Persuaders* (1957)
which is discussed later.

§x. *Political Costs*

The costs of political goods, resulting from laws or rules, civil, industrial or ecclesiastical, have to be paid for in terms of restrictions of
different degrees. They are of two kinds: direct, in the sense that the
advantages I get from the security that another will not conduct himself in a vexatious way, guaranteed under a general law, rule or
custom (as distinct from privilege), also has to be paid for by limiting
my like freedom; and indirect, in the costs, military, economic and
social, of security organization. If I substantially want the assurance of
being safe in my house at night from murderers and thieves, as Adam
Smith himself suggested, I must abandon a freedom, for which I
might abstractly wish, to murder my mother-in-law, although in the
early stages of law and privilege this would depend, as touching the
penalties, upon her caste and upon mine. In an almost hackneyed
phrase, 'rights have to be balanced by responsibilities.' These are
specific consequences of 'the Rule of Law.'

Further, to secure enforcement of law as distinct from anarchy,
there has to be a particular organization of police and judiciary (or
of episcopate and power to excommunicate; or of trade union and
management organization); and also a general integration of the

society which has, not only to be 'paid for' in economic terms of tax and budget, but also 'paid for' in the political terms of a society with obligations and 'duties,' and with restraints whether more 'liberal' or more 'socialistic.' Indeed there must be an organization in which some specific powers or privileges have to be allowed to, and recognized in, those who do the organizing. Societies vary in the degrees to which their members are prepared to pay costs, and this not only in terms of such habits as evading income tax and customs dues.

If it be assumed that a Common Market will greatly benefit, on the balance, a whole group of countries, nevertheless in particular countries it may be to the grave disadvantage of groups, such as farmers and others, able to exercise pressure and who are unlikely to be forced or bribed into consent. The individual or even some of the group may indeed emigrate, rather than pay the costs, just as wealthy land-owners have left Britain for Kenya to avoid heavy surtax—but, then, they have to pay other costs in Kenya. One of the greatest problems of our day is where an entire generation, or most of it, in a country can have to pay punitive costs, to enable a minority to deliver, in disregard of individual natural rights and the rights of other minorities, goods of unprecedented material advantage to a subsequent generation. The Soviet Union and China come to mind. Here the payment of costs is imposed by *force majeure* ('rather starve than be shot,' 'rather Red than dead') and is successfully induced by concentrated and centralized propaganda. This is a matter of the 'actual' working of a monopoly market—unless the monopoly is broken. Whether it is 'right' is a matter for political philosophy.

Also it must be insisted that, for our present purposes, at this general and non-particular stage, no generic distinction in costs can be drawn between the enforced customs or common law of a tribe, the statute law of a sovereign state, the 'shotgun law' of a pioneer community, the canon law or *regulae canonicae* of a church and the rules laid down in the thousands of instances of planned industrial management, or even the mutually agreed (or not agreed) rules entered into in matrimony and domestic life and for the prevention of delinquency in children. All that is relevant is the precise cost, the assurance that it will be exacted, and the balance of advantage of obtaining the goods visualized over the costs.

Against such cost the innate human dream-desire 'both to eat one's cake and keep it,' what Freud calls "the discontent" against civilization and its order, protests. The average human being desires to pay the minimum costs in restrictions: as with much of the American electorate during the Korean War, he wants to have, first, a splendid victory; secondly, no new taxes; and, thirdly, reduced military service—and he is peevish when he does not get all these. An electorate can desire to avoid personal military service; to maintain national defence and prestige by preparation for 'scientific' or 'push-button' warfare; but yet also to keep its hands clean of the guilt and its skin free from the disadvantages of hydrogen warfare. There is the desire to have the whole department store for one's own, even although one has no money, nor will politicians be lacking who will suggest that it can indeed be acquired (or wars won and paid for) on the principle of what is called hire-purchase, 'never-never,' or additions to the national debt. There are indeed occasions when what is here termed 'deficit financing' may be sound; but bankruptcy and sound credit are seldom compatible. Against this desire must be set a principle which can be formulated. THE BASIC AND HARSH (ALTHOUGH NOT UNADAPTABLE) LAW OF THE POLITICAL ALTERNATIVE IS THAT ONE HAS TO CHOOSE BETWEEN OBTAINING GOODS AND PAYING FOR THEM, OR NOT HAVING THEM (Proposition 16). It is a truism that is yet true, a political platitude too often practically forgotten in the heat of electioneering.

At the time when American scientists were outdistanced by the financially well-supported Russian scientists in the launching of 'sputniks' (outdistancing an American model which might be called 'Rearguard'), and when there was alarmed enquiry why the Western ballistics programme was falling behind, to the grave danger of the security of the Free World, the retiring Secretary of Defense, Charles E. Wilson, popularly known as "Engine Charlie," whose task hitherto as a great capitalist had been competitively to 'deliver the goods' by private enterprise, explained that he was "not alarmed" and, in a revealing phrase, added: "That would mean more taxes. Not very popular, eh?" (New York Herald Tribune, October, 1957).

'Freedom' too often becomes synonymous, in a civilization hedonistic and materialist, with having fewer taxes to pay and more money to spend on consumption and 'more automobiles for junior.' Heavy demands on manpower, as the alternative to the use of morally repulsive if not suicidal and unusable instruments of war, are peculiarly uncomfortable and undesirable for high-living civilizations, while not objectionable to very primitive and 'have-not' cultures, although these have until recently lacked technical 'know-how.' (Actually the manpower of the United States and Western Europe, often described as inferior, exceeds that of the Soviet Union.) Hence so often in history luxury civilizations, where men were too well off, have fallen a victim to sterner and more primitive ones.

As touching the Law of Choice or of the Political Alternative, Professor C. J. Friedrich (Constitutional Government and Democracy, p. 73) well remarks: "There is the desire for peace, and the concurrent insistence upon things which cannot be had without recourse to war, because someone else's vital interests are involved." In the 1930's Roumania was able to hold up 'peaceful change'—a formula so attractive to the hopeful mind—affecting the revision of frontiers by threat of war, just as Japan, by the same technique, could expose the weakness of the compromise demand for economic sanctions in the Manchurian aggression.

The concept of Cost here has the merit of exposing the error of placing Freedom and Authority, not only as contraries, but as contradictories, so that the one can be supposed to exist, *in vacuo*, actually either without, or in no systematic relation to, the other. Hence we get rhetorical laudations of Authority, as a species of manifestation of nature and of the will of Jehovah carried over into human affairs in a fashion not related to natural law, but arbitrary and inexplicable; and on the other hand, laudations of Freedom (or laudations, yet more contradictory, by our definition, of Liberty, which is socially recognized Freedom), which in practice can only end in decay into *anomie* and unco-operative anarchy. We get, beyond an 'authoritative' pattern, a 'despotic' stress; and, beyond a 'liberal' pattern, a libertine or 'anarchic' stress.

§xi. *Political Price and Its Measurement in Support*

Although the concept of Cost follows fairly closely that in Economics, *homo politicus* here being like *homo economicus,* the concept of Price in Politics does not follow this analogy. Price, however, fundamentally is to be measured by the units we are prepared to assemble to meet a Cost. Incidentally Price is always regarded as quantitatively measurable, and attention has already been called to the importance attached, even by critics, to quantitative analysis in the social sciences. What, then, are the units?

In Politics Price has, with a certain neatness, to be reckoned quantitatively in terms of units of support, that is, in terms of those who will 'stand up to be counted' in terms of support of certain legislative restrictions or of certain liberties in need of protection. The numbers of the apathetic (with reservations to be made later) do not count in politics in reckoning price. Price is the number of units we can command that are prepared, for the sake of the goods, to support the costs. The price to get the legislation through will be the sum of so much support. It is Hobbes who says, in *Leviathan,* that the price of a man is "so much as would be given for the use of his power." This could be changed to read: "political price is so much power as can be raised in support of a political item or project." The price, not of this or that political good or piece of legislation, but of the whole concern is the quantity of support which is behind the institution or system in the particular market of the moment. Where the political support is lacking to do the main things which a government or directing body plans, it may, in Professor Karl Deutsch's phrase, be described as 'politically insolvent.'

That the might of chieftains, to enforce their law, has to be reckoned in terms of so many 'spears' or 'swords,' and the power of states in relation to their neighbours in terms of military statistics of 'men under arms' or some superior combination of quantities of men with quantities of arms, is not new. Likewise, in Economics, there is an economy of barter and, again, of cowrie shells, as distinct from that compounded by high finance. Nor is the slogan new that 'ballots must replace bullets' in a democratic society.

The highly conventional measure of economic price, often without intrinsic value apart from the sanction and credit of the law, is money. The Vote, as socially recognized, is an obvious conventional unit of civic and other support, with all its complications of organization and compounding. We must indeed always remember that back of the conventional vote can be the unconventional (and frequently majority-disregarding) bullet. In peaceful Switzerland every elector is issued, as his democratic right, with a gun. The Second Amendment to the United States Constitution inconveniently affirms the same principle. Rule of entire cities by the violence-practising 'under-world,' sometimes interlocked with the 'over-world,' is always a practical political possibility. The vote need not be a ballot. The question is: How many people are prepared (and, as we shall later see, to what degree), not necessarily in a parliamentary vote but, for example, in a poll of opinion, where opinion can be effective on actual controls, to support a given measure of restriction in order to procure a particular advantage? A politician without support is like a manufacturer without money; he may be a bankrupt or he may be a millionaire, but, if the latter, only potentially.

Attention has already been called to the controlled experiments of Professor H. Gosnell of Chicago. The richer field of measurement of width of support in general (although not always making clear the issue of *Intensity of Support*, frequently neglected in democratic politics) has recently been tilled by Dr. Gallup, of whose polls I shall later suggest that they indicate the most potentially revolutionary route of change in constitutional government in this century. They provide the technical opportunity for what Renan demanded as a perpetual plebiscite of the nation, and indicate the state of the stock in the political market from day to day. Mention has already been made of the work of recent psephologists in studies of voting. Fundamental studies of the more purely democratic poll, as measure of Opinion, including the liability of poll-voters to vote for things desirable but incompatible, have still to come. It is regrettable that no collective and comparative statistical study of these opinion polls, national and international, has yet been made. It could provide an admirable survey of the vagaries of actual public opinion much of the world over.

The notion of a Political Market or Exchange takes shape, following the assignment of precise meanings to Cost and Price. On this market some goods which were highly prized, some items which were advertised in party and like programmes (as it were in Sears Roebuck and Marshall Field catalogues), are sacrificed and exchanged for new goods, which now acquire sufficient support to bring them into production. Occasionally the old goods and new cannot be held by the same group at the same time: a choice in general has to be made. More frequently incompatibilities are only slowly recognized as the costs work themselves out. Not only legislative bodies, but all assemblies of decision, provide such markets for goods which it is the business of executive bodies to initiate, to shape into production and to supply concretely to the customer, under general directions or prescriptions. The law or order-on-paper, without the execution of it in actual controls, offers no goods. Further, with the women's suffrage achievement for example, a large mass of influential new consumers may be added to the market, being worth a great amount of votes to the credit of this or that party.

The austerity or self-denial of political science prevents us, as yet and in the present state of the schematism of the Market, from following, for example, Ernest Barker into his discussion of the honesty of bargains or of who may be its judges, unless it be the makers of the law, who are producers, or the market of people who are consumers; but we are here much concerned with the logical mechanism and with the actual political mechanism of the 'paradox' of choice to which he refers, which is fundamental and too little appreciated by partisan enthusiasts, either for old freedoms or for new welfare. Control may be well paid for, if it provides the precise security which we want. THE LAW OF THE MARKET NEEDS TO BE STATED: THAT ALL SECURITY INVOLVES AN EXCHANGE OF SOME GENERAL FREEDOM IN RETURN FOR SOME SECURITY WHICH WE VALUE MORE, AS ASSURING A PARTICULAR LIBERTY TO REALIZE WHAT WE WISH (Proposition 17). Liberties are controlled freedoms. The motorist on the road, following the Highway Code, knows this. This formula can sometimes usefully be expressed in mathematico-symbolic terms. Again, following from Proposition 14: AUTHORITY IS NOT THE CONTRADICTORY OF FREEDOM, BUT SPRINGS FROM IT AND IS ITS POLAR CONTRARY AND COMPLEMENT (Proposition 18). It is the necessary complement of any assured liberties. To praise Freedom or Authority *in vacuo*, or in the empyraean, is as if an economist were to praise Consumption or Production (some people indeed do, in an 'affluent society') as goddesses or ideal abstractions. This leads to 'metapolitics,' and to mental stereotypes adorned with capital letters.

§xii. *Equilibrium Theory*

The study of the course of exchange in the political market leads on to the theoretical problem of the Political Equilibrium. This matter is perhaps best approached by asking the question: what in politics is to be regarded as the norm? This can mean the ethical norm or *summum bonum*, which *ought* to be—an issue which we shall defer. But it can also mean, in a mixed society of human beings of different ethical standards and a great variety (possibly to be ethically approved) of consumer demands: to what condition—if to *any* particular one—as norm, does this system tend, so as to produce general contentment and be stable?

Here again we must distinguish. We may mean: under what condition would some lasting stability be achieved, *if* everybody did that which was most prudent (I do not say necessarily 'good in all respects') from the contemporary view of individual and social health. It may be that there is no actual agreement upon what is social health or—more probably—that our knowledge of it is very incomplete. This theme also we shall discuss later when we discuss Natural Law. Finally, we may mean: what is the condition of actual stability such that, empirically, there is no discontent or movement for the overthrow of the actual social system. (Whether, here, there ethically *should* be no discontent, e.g., whether traditional acceptance of an autocratic system is humanly healthy or ideally good, is a different question.) We must beware, no less in Economics than in Politics and vice versa, of being misled by a Newtonian tradition of physical models into constructing (as perhaps Ricardo did) our practice of equilibrium or even our models too mechanically or with naive trust in "an invisible hand." The model is never quite the same as the historical reality.

That Political Science or Sociology *as such* is not ethically normative is a common if controversial argument of Leopold von Wiese (*Systematic Sociology*, 1932, chap. 1) and of Max Weber. Reference has already been made to this issue.

The answer would seem to be that, under the social and educational habits of small demand, a quite meagre supply by a government, whether in fact monopolistic or merely enjoying the credit advantages of 'monolithic' tradition, will produce contentment. Social demand for services may be made but (since in parts of Asia and Africa, for example, there may be no standards of comparison with systems built up to correspond with greater demand) a one-party Bolshevik or oligarchic system, a religious paternal directorate as under the Jesuits in Paraguay, or a paternal autocracy, as under Indian maharajahs, may seem varieties of government without, for the masses, spelling a decisive difference. Such contentment may abruptly be broken up by the insurgence, thanks to imitation or to propaganda by a few, of newer and highly stimulated demands, such as for rule in accordance with nationalist or tribal principles.

On the record, however, supporters of maharajah government in South India may change over to being supporters of 'the benevolent autocracy' of Communism. There is actual contentment as practical norm, because in each case a low supply (or, more precisely, a low *variety* of supply, and possibly, as with the Jesuits, a very specific supply) is in equilibrium with a low or unvarying demand. During most of the centuries of history the equilibrium has been of this order, and relatively static. So long as the equilibrium was maintained (neither the traditional demand changing nor the supply), contentment remained. And towards contentment (even to what Freud called, in terms of the third law of thermodynamics, inertia or 'deadness') society groped to move—or to move back.

The extent to which human intelligence is only developed to overcome unwonted and unwanted difficulties is a problem outside our range here. It is, however, politically illuminating to read such a remark as that, to the present writer, of an official who had served under the British *raj* in India as the loyal servant locally of a highly conservative, if efficient, maharajah-governed, Indian State regime, but who is now pro-Communist. He writes: "Democracy can never be a success in the Asian countries with a tradition unique in its nature for monarchical benevolence"; the goods of communism are not dissimilar from those of the desirable old monarchies or *raj*. There is no restless discontent. Lord Bryce, in his *Studies of Sovereignty*, emphasizes the great political role played by indolence or apathy which, up to a point, provides a dam to needed or revolutionary change—and hence is politically significant and enters negatively into price: "those who will not support"—but, beyond it, makes forcible revolution a necessity and increases the head of water of the down-pouring flood.

The principle, however, of Equilibrium is shown most clearly where, owing to new ideas about demand, or to technological or natural scientific changes, which remove inhibitions about the possibility of their natural gratification and owing to fluctuations about their nature and the demand and the quantity of their support, the equilibrium itself has to be 'dynamic' or, more precisely, in constant readjustment.

This will especially obtain where a large variety of people are asking competitively for a large variety of potential goods, with some expectation of being satisfied. Thus, there is a market where the demand of the Consumer, rather than the supply agreed to by the Producer, is dominant. Liberalism, it may be remarked, has here the same effect in the economic and in the political spheres—an effect of favouring the consumer. Conversely, under dictatorships, both fascist and communist, we have politically as well as (in the U.S.S.R.) economically, almost entirely a Producers' market, of a monopolistic character. However, statesmanship consists not only in pleasing the immediate consumer and voter, but also in balancing 'long-range' considerations about political goods against 'short-range.'

Here we have the problems of equilibrium in what we can call the 'Potential Free Market.' Contentment will never be complete, since always new unsatisfied demands, instead of habitual ones, will be arising. Moreover, as in economics, so here there will always be imperfect competition and a measure of monopoly in political supply owing to the tendency of authority to substitute a monistic for a pluralist system, subsuming weaker authorities. Nevertheless, there will always also be an aspiration, at least as touching the naturalistic 'ideal' *model*, for the optimum satisfaction of demand by the optimum provision of goods, subject to limits of supply by high costs. This last will be met by competition for supply of goods. A constant of contentment will be approached, resultant from a rapid transition (or 'dynamism') of adjustment in changing supply to changing demand.

The concept of Governmental Balance, to check the monopolistic tendencies of the Executive power, is old enough and expressed by Locke and Montesquieu. The different concept of a Balance of Power in external affairs, so that the competitive satisfaction of one country's demands for the goods of territory and suchlike shall not be achieved disproportionately at the cost of other countries (who might be the allies of the future), is as old as Cardinal Wolsey. The student here will find Sir Harold Nicolson's brilliant book, *The Congress of Vienna* (1946), helpful. Notions of an adjustment of Social Classes will be found in the writings of Edmund Burke; and the idea elevated to a greater generality, as a philosophic principle, by Spencer.

Instances of its precise development as a clue of interpretation in sociology are more rare, although such a writer as Mosca makes play with the notion of 'social adjustment' and Professor Talcott Parsons, in succession to Max Weber, has made the subject very much his own, in *The Social System* (1951), on the basis of shared ends.

Later we shall discuss whether the word 'class,' here used, is sufficiently precise to be useful. The notion of division of labour, economic or social, as in Adam Smith and Emile Durkheim, is different. It seems improbable that the Principle of Equilibrium can be fully comprehended except in connection with a developed theory of the Potential Market. Otherwise, it tends to be vague, unsatisfactory, and even misleading. It must be emphasized that the equilibrium theory with which we have been especially concerned has been one of a moving equilibrium, such as has its analogies in Economics, rather than with any physico-Freudian theory of a tendency to return to equilibrium in conservative inertia.

Care must be taken in utilizing this principle of Political Equilibrium to make it clear within what framework it is being applied. For example, some recent students have used it, in their interpretations of foreign affairs, as a refinement upon the doctrine of Balance of Power. It is, therefore, important to note that, valid as this may be within its own assigned framework, there is nothing incompatible with the Equilibrium Theory in supposing (and even advocating), in a yet wider potential market, the total overthrow internationally of the regional Balance of Power.

The 'Balance of Power' conventionally makes the usual assumptions about the continuation of 'the Modern State,' i.e., sixty or a hundred individual and separate 'sovereign and absolute' States (or a smaller number of 'Great Powers') confronting each other in a very loose international aggregation. But it is entirely possible, theoretically and actually, to suppose a general, constant, and insistent demand for the potential goods of peace; and also to suppose that these would be held to be so incompatible (for example, in western Europe) in political choice with this traditional state system (elsewhere sometimes called, as by Lowes Dickinson, 'international anarchy'), that an intolerable imbalance between political demand and supply would be set up. This would occur if no authority arose to satisfy this insistence on peace; and if politicians confined themselves to providing discredited remedies and balances, and antique goods of the seventeenth-century state machinery, instead of a radical reform of that political system which was shaped by the Peace of Westphalia.

Professor David Easton, in his *Political System*, writes, of my *Method* and *Principia*, "the fact that the concept of general equilibrium pervades his work shows how close he was to the basic currents of thought in empirical research." Professor George Liska in his eminently suggestive *International Equilibrium* (1957) writes in a passage reprinted in James N. Rosenau's *International Politics and Foreign Policy* (1961) that "perhaps more explicitly than any other systematic theorist of society and politics," I regard "the equilibrium and equilibration of wills, as the fundamental condition of social order and integration." This may be true of my general Theory of the Market. To some extent I must, yet, utter a caution, if not a disclaimer. Professor Liska's book is a most interesting and worthwhile investigation into international relations, in which he makes considerable and advantageous use of Equilibrium Theory. It is, nevertheless, necessary to emphasize my reservations upon the case instance of this theory discussed in the text above.

It so happens that my view is very sympathetic to those who hold that, if any lasting peace is to be established, the balance of power between states must be utterly unbalanced; and the orthodox system of so-called 'independent sovereign states' must be re-formed in the interest of the growth of Unions (as recently, with unexpected speed, in western Europe and in the Arab Countries) of, at least, vast regional extent. This last is indeed a private judgement; but it seems to me to emerge clearly from any scientific analysis of the conditions of peace, a conclusion to which Professor E. H. Carr also inclines, in a more restrained fashion, in his *Conditions of Peace*. This, of course, does not preclude wider balances of power in the world system. The final balance, however, must always be between Producer (even if it be a World Government with monopolistic tendencies) and the Consumer market of humanity.

§xiii. *Producers' Profits*

Mention has been made of the consumer, who is entitled to be served. He is entitled to ask whether the proffered services, for which he will assuredly have to pay, will be of utility to him and how much.

The collapse, in the Anglo-Saxon world, of the attempt to take political science seriously coincided with the rise of the neo-Hegelian school and with the defeat of the Utilitarian school, which underwent fission between the older strict hedonists, followers of Bentham, and the 'softer' school of John Stuart Mill, who satisfied their consciences by absorbing the humanistic philosophy of Goethe and Wilhelm von Humboldt. The Utilitarian school decayed under the solvent question: "Utility for What End?" It must yet be noted that Bentham himself was a practical law reformer, and that the utilitarian slogan of his school retains all of its force if we avoid final questions and simply enquire, within the limits of such a given end as 'enforcing civil justice,' whether a specific means benefits most of the citizens or bears marks of utility chiefly for the benefit of the legal profession. Not for nothing did Bentham go around probing with his stick for 'vested' and 'sinister' interests. Within the assigned limits we can still be good utilitarians. 'Useful as Means for What?' 'Who Rules Whom?' or (in Professor Lasswell's phrase) 'Who Gets What, When, How?' 'Where does the Common Man come in?'—all this is relevant and 'useful.'

The reward of the Producer politically has yet also to be considered. Unless he is prepared to undertake his task of organization of support, to do his work of providing authority, law and government, these will not be maintained, as is the case in many parts of the world. That his pay in terms of personal prestige and power may be far too large we can all see readily enough in terms of the perquisites of the dictator and political monopolist, not only in Latin America. What is not equally recognized (but can be impressed upon us by the marketing style of argument) is that the rewards of the Producer of political goods may be far too low.

In America, but also especially (until recently) in France, the title of politician may carry so little respect that no reputable men will take time for this labour; and those who do are tempted by corrupt adventures and kickbacks. In France hitherto the smallest licensee of a government tobacco store may exact respect, but not so a Minister of the Republic. The situation may change under the Fifth Republic— indeed it could change so much towards policy monopoly as to produce swing and reaction. There could set in again what (familiar to economists) in politics is sometimes called 'the swing of the pendulum.'

In the United States, in connection with the investigation into Federal Agencies in 1958, a situation has been shown to have arisen where comparatively unknown men for quite modest financial rewards, under a system of equalitarian-democratic pattern (where nobody is supposed to be recompensed by 'honours' or superior respect) are entrusted with responsibility on matters affecting vast financial negotiations. It is not remarkable that a system which, for reasons of an ignoble economy, asks too much for too little tends to break down. The whole issue is much emphasized and developed by de Tocqueville, in his *Democracy in America* (p. 154; also cf. C. Wright Mills, *The Power Elite*, 1956, pp. 357–61). In France it is credibly stated that the Fréjus dam burst, with ensuing disaster, because the cement layers had not been adequately bound together, because the cement supply for them was spasmodic, because the governmental credits were spasmodic, because the politicians of the Fourth Republic were too busy changing governments to vote the supplies . . .

There are Party machines which hold their power over the poor and ignorant by acting as benevolent societies (of more concrete use to their clients than the formal liberal politics of 'the stiff shirt'—who is also often 'the stuffed shirt'—and the public meeting for good, well-heeled citizens), sometimes in direct alliance with the criminal underworld and to its profit. *Why* this power alliance is *so* frequent, however disreputable, requires a study: it probably lies in the Emersonian disrespect for the producer-politician in non-aristocratic or non-civilly-minded societies. Respected citizens of ability, contrary to the sage Platonic notion about the reasons for remaining in political life, have quit the political field. We have also the case of quite worthy but underpaid legislators in a world which expects success. They are well aware of the sums and prestige they could earn by ability or energy in other professions, and may 'sell out' (on the whole less often than might be expected) as delegates to patrons in the great 'respectable' corporations and unions. They may also be brought, by greed or by over-weening ambition and a cynical sense of so-called 'political realism,' to connive, as 'front men,' in the operations and instructions of the 'Invisible Government' of men who use politics and its controls as the tools of highly organized *Mafia* or crime. They may seek 'the fast dollar' this way. Sometimes, of course, the payment may be to vanity and in terms of publicity. As with Communist Party fronts, the 'front men' may be naively unaware of how they are being used. But even the most genuine, far from having the status Plato gave his governors, do not even find that they have that of respected citizens. In the hurly-burly it would be thought to be somehow 'undemocratic' and pretentious . . .

On the other hand the old German Imperial Civil Service was wisely assigned great personal respect and power within the established limits of their office; and a brilliant Indian, the Sardar K. M. Panikkar, has truly commented that for a century India was governed, not by men who expected great monetary rewards, but by an inexpensive system, which he describes as that of 'Rule by the Knights Commander' of honourable orders of chivalry—'Knights Commander of the Star of India' and the rest. It was not equalitarian, but it was not hypocritical.

Incidentally, it must not be presumed (as is apparently done by C. Wright Mills, in his remarkable *Power Elite*, p. 17 and pp. 242–68) that a practical normative Theory of Equilibrium or of the Market in any way excludes, at any time in history, a specific tendency to power monopoly or to producing or brokering organizations, such as political parties, having sometimes a highly oligarchic structure. But, needless to say, my agreement is profound with his statement (provided that it is put into a perspective of concrete history and of the real influence of ideas and of Natural Law): "For every epoch and for every social structure, we must work out an answer for the question of the power of the élite. The ends of men are often merely hopes, but means are facts within some men's control. That is why all means of power tend to become ends to an élite that is in charge of them. And that is why we may define power-élite in terms of the means of power—as those who occupy the command posts." Incidentally, when this élite talks, not in terms of the market as here, but in military revolutionary terms of "occupying the commanding heights," a mood of enthusiasm, intolerance, sacrifice, and obedience is produced, to the advantage of that élite, in the rank and file of 'followers.'

§xiv. *The Mood of Negotiation*

One general observation may permissibly be made about the state of
mind likely to be engendered by full consciousness of the Law of
Political Choice and the Law of the Market. It can perhaps best be
noted, as a fruit of long years of intuitive statesmanship, in the life of
Lord Melbourne, as described by Lord David Cecil. Lord Melbourne
found the great Reform Bill (and not this alone) to be in accordance
with the party programme of his own party and also, it seemed, overwhelmingly demanded by the country. (Later Party leaders in Britain
have, even today, found themselves in not dissimilar positions. The
great "political broker" was perhaps Disraeli, who had a detachment
which most—for example, American Republican—leaders lack in dealing
with a national health programme, old age pensions, and other political
items where the American outlook can be denominated as, in the eyes
of the rest of the world, pre-Bismarckian and archaic.) And Melbourne
therefore, as promised, proceeded to advance the Reform Bill in its
early stage, later completed by Lord John Russell. But he had a happy
scepticism that it could ever produce the costless advantages visualized
for it by its enthusiasts. Consistently, through his long and philosophic
life, he declined to believe that gains, either in politics or by human
nature, were as easy to come by as others supposed, while never
deflecting from a humanistic view of how civilized men should conduct themselves by sentiment and thanks (as the Chinese so wisely
thought) to manners.

  The object of a moral crusade or movement is to persuade enough
men freely to adopt a particular view about what is a good and a
laudable end, desirable 'in reality' even if not desired—although there
will always be 'graceless zealots' urgent to persecute those who disagree. The object or function of a political party is to rally and
consolidate enough support for some agreed programme to assure
actual victory (although there are indeed times when present victory
is best passed up for the sake of later popularity); and, incidentally,
to get for this purpose enough people to change their minds and
demands to obtain the decisive vote, while asking for what the party
or government is prepared to produce and supply. The two activities
indeed overlap in programme and personnel. Nevertheless, a moral
crusade in some respects bears the character of the activity of a
church. It seeks to convince without coercion; and its members are
supposedly not concerned with their own gain but with procuring the
acceptance of a worthwhile end. A political party is concerned with

victory and the means thereto. Hence it can properly engage in compromises. Its test will be whether it has satisfied demand better than its rivals. It is for the public to make the moral assessment and give the mandate. And when such a party gains office it proposes to legislate and, in the last resort, to coerce. Thus it is important that it should only coerce within the limits for which force is appropriate in civil affairs, and not within those of a far wider moral pattern. Not every excellent cause is appropriate for the activity of a secular political party. We should distinguish the generic functions of church and state. And a secular political party does well, without moral pretences, dangerous fanaticism, undemocratic claims to be infallible or multiplying absolute principles like rabbits, to limit itself to its proper marketing functions as broker between the common man's actual wants and those competent to make provision.[1]

We may observe that men would be far more cool and tolerant in political affairs and there might be fewer wars and unsocial fanaticism and strife, if men accustomed their minds to distinguishing between, on the one side, imperative moral goals and, on the other, advantages yielded by political means, goods of a lesser order, the demands for and prices of which must be expected to fluctuate, and should not alarm us if they do fluctuate, in the higgling of the political market.

It was part of the liberal tradition of the last century, as expressed in the great German *Aufklärung* and by John Stuart Mill, that variety of itself was 'a good thing.' We should possibly see with tolerant pleasure around us variants (valuable to civilization, like the biological variety of species), eccentrics, hooligans—for did not Durkheim emphasize the sociological similarity of crime and genius?—and decadents who shape popular taste to vulgar passion. It can, more soberly, be enquired whether what the sociologist is not more likely to detect and expect than stability are social booms and slumps. There will be epochs of 'morality' and of the austere 'rule of the saints,' sometimes ending by burning books and men, the rule of puritans, temperance reformers, religious orders, even of the Red Puritans of Victorian severity and of devout Marxist religion; and there will be epochs of 'adventure' and of tolerance, laxity, libertinism, even decadence in the precise sense of repudiation of moral rules generally accepted by the majority of elders, so that low standards, fraud, pornographic stimulation, contempt for duty for the sake of success, mass hysteria, tasteless vulgarity called 'being democratic,' and playing up to the adolescent

[1]See my article, "Political Parties: Instruments of Government or Religious Conventicles?" (*Contemporary Review*, October and November, 1961).

and immature for cash become commonplace. Balance, see-saw, fluctuation, and higgling of the political market must not surprise us. Rather we may conclude that authoritative systems are likely to follow liberal systems and despotic to follow libertine; and that, in turn, to the libertine will succeed the reforming (even if not benevolent) despot and to the liberal the collectivist. Not only 'co-existence' of different consumer demands but Fluctuation of Markets is to be expected.

In recent evidence (September, 1961) on Capitol Hill, Washington, General Don Flickinger of the U.S. Air Force stated that the reason why American missile development lagged behind the Russian was that this had been entrusted to private enterprise and not to the army. The attitudes of doctrinaires of exclusive private enterprise and capitalism guided by the profit motive, and of doctrinaires of the public ownership of *all* means of production, distribution, and exchange (with accompanying bureaucracy, as distinct from the co-operative principle), such as does not obtain in Yugoslavia or even in contemporary Russia, are equally objectionable from the point of view of the empiric approach. Here concern is for actual efficiency in the production of economic and political goods according to demand, subject to decency of ends and appropriate means.

The secret of successful reform measures lies not so much in the theories, which must be tested, or in the legal forms, which can be changed, but in the factual analysis and in the tempo and timing. We would expect, then, to see in human history a rhythm of periods of excess of freedom and of excess of authority, of laxity and of austerity, of individual brilliance passing into stable and conventional restraint. We would be better served by having fewer uncompromising enthusiasms, choosing them better and then holding to them more resolutely. Political 'principles' casually multiplied become fragments of secular ideologies, rigid, dogmatic, doctrinaire, fanatical, and bigoted—all in the manner of the utopian 'good,' and disconnected from the actual market of human wants. It is not at this moment maintained either that Pareto and Michels were right in urging that revolutions in the end make no fundamental differences (a matter for separate and more precise debate) or, to use Professor Denis Brogan's phrase, that "the Costs of Revolution" are often (and, under some circumstances, necessarily) too heavy. But, in this present new age of tyrants and of religious wars, it becomes the part of the statesman, not rigidly obstinate in the conclusion that a particular price or surrender is one too heavy to pay for one particular political good in demand, yet to conduct himself upon the reflection that no particular goods, whether luxury and bauble or the latest necessity, is likely in the concrete to satisfy fully or to be permanent. He will consider that estimates are subjective; that the offers of the other side are unlikely to be quite without value; that human appetite, stimulated by new technologies, demands change; and that, within the limits of decency and natural law, men are best left to learn from experience the short-comings and inflated prices, in the brokerage, of the realization of their dreams.

Such tolerant reflections about the market, less pecuniary and cynical than Walpole's, conduce to the avoidance of much barbarism and cruelty. They also contribute to training the better type of politician and civil servant. The mood they induce in the body politic is alert to the dangers of an obstinate apathy, such as is unwilling to facilitate peaceful change, but is inimical to fanaticism. Hence government becomes neither lethargic in providing political goods save for the markets of a past age and for past power-holders, nor obdurate in thrusting upon the unwilling the perhaps already outmoded goods of government, which were possibly approved by the revolutionaries of yester-year, but which younger nations and newer classes of emergent power do not want.

5. Forms of Government: Democracy and Tyranny

§i. *The Aristotelian Categories*

As touching Forms of Government and Control, the classical distinctions are those made by Aristotle (and less fully by Plato in *The Statesman*). Nor can anyone as capable of so masterly a description of revolutions as Aristotle be accused of sacrificing a dynamic to a merely static approach. One object, as stated earlier, of this present tractate is to recommend a return to Aristotle. In his *Politics* Aristotle says: "As supreme power must be vested either in an individual or in a few or in the many, it follows that, when the rule of the individual or the Few or the Many is exercised for the benefit of the community at large, the politics are normal, whereas the politics which subserve the private interests of either the individual or the few or the masses are perversions" (6. 2).

The discussion of these generic forms appropriately precedes discussions of State, Church or industrial or family organizations, since both logically and historically we may make statements about the forms in which power is exercised, *de facto* or also *de jure*, before we proceed to discuss the particular and historical organizations of society for that exercise, such as the Modern State or denominational churches or the small companionate family.

It may indeed be argued that Aristotle's categories are both archaic and mechanical; and that it would be more illuminating to discuss the growth of historical forms, such as the kingdom from the clan chieftain's rule, or to suggest an economic or class basis for the different species of governance, which many early writers such as Harrington and Madison (and indeed, as we shall see, Aristotle himself) have indicated. Many political theorists who are primarily historians have pursued this route, usually with much addition of anthropology. The historian tends always to prefer the concrete and particular. However, the prudent political scientist, in considering his material, will weigh the merits of the quantitative, and of what lends itself to abstraction. The Aristotelian definitions have the merit of being 'stripped,' are not guilty of question-begging, and allow for some measure of debate about what 'subserves private interests' and about the rights and authority, in morals and power, of majorities as distinct from organized and even armed minorities or the personal rights of individuals.

The criticism is frequently made of Aristotle's categories that these are merely superficial and quantitative, with a cross-division of 'good' and 'bad.' They certainly have the merit of simplicity and, therefore, form an admirable and, on the whole, objective start for analysis. Even the cross-division may not be entirely subjective, since some governments admit and proclaim their class basis, and refuse to be also representative of any loyal opposition (or declare that it is known dialectically that it cannot be loyal). To the argument, 'How do we know who are the best?' or 'Who decides the interest of the whole?' we shall return later. The most frequent criticism, therefore, to the effect that Aristotle ignores the class basis of governments is not warranted by the text: he merely dislikes such governments and denies the condition to hold for all governments. It is not inevitable that all government must be class government. The opposite criticism that he minimizes the role of individual rights, and of divisions of powers to protect these rights, is more apposite when directed against any Hellenic philosophers of the Golden Age. That it is impossible to crib the multitudinous governmental forms within the Aristotelian categories is merely the contention of those who decline, in analysis, to proceed by stages.

These categories are of superior validity to those, in terms of monarchy and republic, of Montesquieu, which can be highly misleading—the ideological fight sometimes being between (heredity or dynastic) 'monarchy' and constitutional 'republic,' and sometimes between 'republic' or commonwealth and 'dictatorship.' The former issue, once regarded as vital, today has become of negligible importance, except perhaps in an argument concerning social precedence and the charge of (non-intellectual) snobbery. Of itself, it produces small difficulty in India and South Africa, although Burma was lost to the Commonwealth because the eirenic formula was found too late. The issue could arise again in connection with the union of Europe, monarchical and republican.

Even these formal distinctions must yet be distinguished from mere discursive descriptions of organs of government, without Linnaean classification. Such description (a) offers of itself no basis for criticism or functional understanding; (b) tends to take transient forms as permanent political data; (c) can especially fall into error where the institutions or constitutions (as Karl Loewenstein, *Political Power and the Governmental Process*, pp. 23, 55, points out) have a propaganda character, deliberately intended to mislead—an error of which such eminent sociologists as Sidney and Beatrice Webb, in *Soviet Communism: A New Civilisation?* (1st ed., 1935) were not guiltless; (d) tends to excessive legalism. No successful science fails to ask 'why?' or is content with this superficial technique. Even discussion of 'structure,' as distinct from 'process,' begins to break down and atomize, and only trees are noted, instead of the wood.

The three sound forms of politics we are told by Aristotle to be Monarchy ('rule of the one'—although formally of a non-hereditary type, based upon virtue and wisdom, which would seem rather to provide a theory of Papacy), Aristocracy, and Constitutionalism itself (*politeia*); and the three perverted forms we find to be Tyranny, Oligarchy ('*rule* of the few') and Democracy ('*power* of the people'). It is beneficial that the contemporary reader, nurtured in the free world and accustomed to regard Democracy as beyond at least overt criticism, should be startled to discover Democracy classified as a perverted form, to which Aristotle adds (*Politics* 8. 5 and 10) that Tyranny is peculiarly likely to spring from Democracy. We who, in this century, have seen unprecedented developments of democracy, for which the world was to be made safe, but also the successful establishment of indubitable tyrannies, such as the world had forgotten for at least four centuries, may have to pause to consider how far the detached and scientific observations of *il maestro di color che sanno* may not have noted a connection in politics which we have, in our wishful enthusiasm, been unwilling to admit. Neglect here in examining fundamental principles has been too rife in the West, is no service to its civilization, and is unprofessional from the point of view of political science.

As Professor Robert A. Dahl in his excellent brief *Preface to Democratic Theory* (1956) says: "It is anomalous, perhaps, that after so many centuries of political speculation, democratic theory should continue to be . . . rather unsatisfactory." That this is an understatement he makes clear in the next paragraph. "One of the difficulties one must face at the outset is that there is no democratic theory—there are only democratic theories." (p. 1) For reasons that will become clear in the sequel, he adds (p. 23): "If a natural right were defined, rather absurdly, to mean the right of every individual to do what he wishes to do, then every form of government must be tyrannical." All civil government contains an element of coercion or authorized force and sets a limit to the extremes of our tolerance.

Regular, free *elections* are sometimes held to be the defining characteristic of democracy. But this element of definition is not as clear as would superficially seem to be the case. 'Freedom' may or may not be held to require a multiparty system. We need to know who is the electorate, and whether any rights are secured save those of its majority, according to its absolute will, which majority may without reserve opt for a dictator. The regularity of elections and the breadth of the electorate are indeed important; but the crux seems to lie in the actual responsibility of the government to the electorate and in the effective *control*, by the latter or through constitutional safeguards approved by it, actively or traditionally. There is no reason to suppose that, in their heyday, the governments of Stalin, Mussolini, and Hitler were other than 'popular' or would (at their zenith) not have received the free majority endorsement of their peoples, as much as ever did Senator Joseph McCarthy or Governors Huey Long or Jimmie Davis, however artificial the majority actually recorded. It is not the dictators, such as a Stalin or even a Khrushchev, whose assassination is attempted, but a de Gaulle and an Adenauer. It was the Duc d'Enghien and not Napoleon who was murdered. *'Popular Government' is then not identical with Democracy* (whether or not it can be born from its matrix), where this latter signifies *not only* majority support *but also* formal responsibility of the government to the electorate, so as to assure the 'power of the people,' and indeed actual constitutional control by the latter. The very phrase, 'the people,' is highly ambiguous, since it may or may not mean all the inhabitants or native-born. However, it may be that the one, even when assuming the form of Dictatorship, can proceed, as the Greeks suggested, from some inherent weakness or opportunism in the other. As touching the Aristotelian suggestion of a connection between popular government and tyranny, the comment (Jean Campbell, *Evening Standard*, London, Oct. 17, 1960) on the impact of Mr. Khrushchev on world opinion when he was in New York in 1960 is worth quotation. "As Prime Minister Macmillan once said to [Mr. Khrushchev]: 'Mr. Khrushchev, you are a born demagogue. If you had popular elections in your country, you would be voted in every time.'" The commentator, who happens to be a daughter of the Duke of Argyll—and the Campbells are always shrewd politicians—continued, turning to the American elections: "Perhaps the 1964 election will throw up a demagogue or a clown. The circumstances of television may produce such a man." The 1960 candidates, the commentator felt, disappointed popular viewers by being perhaps sincere statesmen but, compared with Mr. Khrushchev, very inadequate actors in the political circus. One complaint against both as campaigners was that they were "too much gentlemen."

In a Communist society it is regarded as a form of blasphemy, as well as treason, to criticize Marxism in any fundamental sense which affects the social constitution. In the Representative Democracy which obtains in much (although not all) of the geographic area of what is conventionally called 'the Free World,' it is often regarded as in at least bad taste, if not sacrilegious, to discuss freely criticisms of Representative Democracy, although Democracy is always busy with criticism of the Executive, which seems to be part of its very nature. It must be insisted that, in the interest alike of the vitality of Democracy itself and of the integrity of political science, this discreet censorship must be vigorously repudiated. We may even find that it is not our temporary administrative expedients, with which so many academics exclusively occupy themselves, but our fundamental political education which requires reconstruction. The avoidance of radical discussion constitutes both a hypocrisy and a disservice. Such discussion is the very pragmatic justification for the existence of political science. Admittedly such professional criticism may arouse passions as vehement as criticism of Capitalism in parts of America or of Communism in Russia.

It is perhaps not without reassuring significance that, speaking in Boston on October 5, 1959, multimillionaire Mr. Averill Harriman said: "Capitalism in the minds of the people of Asia is almost synonymous with colonialism. It seems to me that we should not permit Mr. Khrushchev or any other Communist to write us down as the standard-bearer of capitalism. Our economic system has little resemblance to the century-old Marxist concept of capitalism and we should abandon the word." An equally open-minded approach to the sacred terminology of democratic politics might be no less beneficial.

§ii.   *Classical and Pure Democracy*

Democracy, unlike Tyranny, is philologically clear in meaning. The word *demo-cratia* signified the 'power' (not *archē*, 'rule') of 'the people.' It will be noted that the Greeks, by their very use of words, did not ascribe the work of government to the *demos*, as they thought it might be ascribed to the few ('olig-archy'); but only the power or control ('demo-cracy')—the power 'to hire and fire.' When today we speak, for example, of a 'meritocracy,' we have changed this usage.

In certain contemporary Constitutions, such as the Belgian, it is laid down that all power comes from the people as sovereign. Although this is neither stated nor true under the United States Constitution, this document yet begins with the words 'We, the People,' and not 'We, the States.' The dangerous distinction, made by Thomas Hobbes for the benefit of Leviathan but also by some contemporary sociologists for the benefit of their own views, between the state or *res publica* or even 'the public,' and the so-called 'masses' (which also corporally consist of human beings, with two legs and a brain) or 'the mob,' is not here made. Where mob-rule or ochlocracy is referred to, it is called by that name. If the public votes into power a 'popular government' which, as in Germany, ends in dictatorship or, as in Italy, confirms it, or if it resorts to extra-constitutional mass action, it is the 'public' nevertheless (except under conditions of minority terror, as in the case of Germany) which must carry the responsibility. The 'mass' can be an organized group of thugs. But it may be, not the 'mass,' but 'the public' that is given a bad name by some writer who disapproves, like Coriolanus, of their majority views. 'The mob,' 'the public,' and 'the sovereign people' can be terms of condemnation, neutrality, or laudation for the same thing. What matters is the relation to recognized authority.

In all early discussion of the matter it was assumed that Democracy means the direct, plebiscitary power of the people, say, in civil government. Ecclesiastically this inspired the Congregationalist movement. It was what is called direct or Pure Democracy. The people might, as under the Roman *tribunicia potestas*, transfer this power. But the classical world had no system of representative assemblies. It is important, then, to bear in mind that Democracy, when first developed, was marked by the environment of simple and small communities, and was as pure. It was indeed insisted that, for success, it must consist of potentially a 'face-to-face' group. Its problem today is to control a very complex society and very complex bureaucracies. However, the complexity of the problem is no excuse for political scientists to confuse their terminology. Whether, indeed, Representative Democracy, through representatives who are not delegates, is indeed authentic Democracy at all is a question that we shall have to discuss. All we can say is that liberal philosophers such as John Stuart Mill certainly had this illusion, but (a) modified it by the role that they allocated to 'responsible' educational leadership and educators, and (b) sought to justify it by defence of strict proportional representation, making 'the representatives' thus mirror exactly the views of 'the represented.' By Marxists 'representative democracy' is called 'bourgeois democracy.'

Admittedly the number of recent manual workers in the United States House of Representatives or among the Conservative Members of Parliament in Westminster is few.

Although, as Ernest Barker has shown, certain of the more 'democratic' Friar Orders approximated in the Middle Ages to such a system —the origin of much of the theory of civil government is to be found in the ecclesiastical field—the philosophy of Representative Government as a complete system for legislation based upon a wide franchise comes with the Utilitarian school, especially the Mills, father and son. Its advent had been acclaimed by the Gironde. Agitation for it had been continued by the Chartists. So remote, however, is this from the concept of Aristotle that the philosopher contemplates curtailing the population of all democratic or constitutional *poleis*, so that an assembly of all the people could be addressed at one time, just as their habitations could be 'viewed well at one time' (*eusynoptos*). With too large a population a politician would "require the voice of Stentor" to address them. The objection seemed to be founded on brute fact, and final against further argument. Not only with Montesquieu, but as late as with Rousseau, the discussion is whether a large country is, as touching civil government, compatible with Democracy, by which was meant 'pure' or 'plebiscitary,' as distinct from 'representative,' Democracy. Certainly such a country would (it was supposed) lack ethical *homoinoia* or 'like-mindedness'—the very basis, as Cicero insists in *De re publica*, of authentic community life. De Tocqueville discusses, with grave attention, this quite new modification of the problem of any democracy in states of great territorial magnitude, as changed by the technique of representation. That democracy spells "the sovereignty of the majority" he has no doubt. Madison, however, it will be noted, in *The Federalist*, no. 10, argued in favour of large democratic countries because, according to his distinctive use of the word, it was necessary to frustrate the tendency towards tyranny of the people's majority, and this 'multanimity' or diversity of factions and interests within the majority did. *Divide et salva libertatem.*

Not only must we bear in mind the distinction, as explained above, between formal 'Democratic' government and 'Popular' government. It is always possible that the populace, for example in Asian or African countries of less set tradition, may only insist upon popular government and may actually want only this. What matters here is not, in terms of the market, that the citizen consumer should formally control government, but that the political producers should actually and quickly satisfy their public, at a quick if inhumane tempo, by whatever technical means. The major substantial issue between Conservative, constitutional reformer, and Communist then becomes this of tempo.

It is also essential to note the distinction of meaning, in the civil dominion, between (a) the 'Government' (whether or not considered as including, along with the party Administration, the permanent civil service and officials; but always as set over against, and distinguished from, the 'governed,' whether called citizens or, more miserably, subjects); (b) the 'State,' which includes both elements as formally organized, whether considered as expressing its authority and its influence only through a representative body or through other constitutional, legal, and even 'establishment' channels; and (c) the 'People' or 'Public' (made up of private individuals), which may under the constitution express themselves in whole (or, as in South Africa, substantially in part) in formal fashion in politics—but which yet also politically exists as a nation or society, even if only on the level of social controls (and hence, despite Hobbes, no mere unrecognized or thug 'mob') and of pattern of living, but without formal civil powers. When we speak of 'France and Germany speaking, acting, deciding,' it is quite vital to remark which of the three actual meanings, behind this rhetorical hypostasis, we have in mind. The conclusion of our argument may be sharply different according to this choice of meaning.

It is arguable, even if paradoxical, that one of the oldest existing democracies of all, that of the Swiss Confederation, is as yet not such at all, since half the inhabitants, the women, are excluded from the Confederate franchise. It is yet more remarkable that, as stated to this writer by a Swiss ambassador, one reason for this exclusion is that, in the cantons of direct democracy, the number of people entitled to be present is already almost intolerably large; and that a widening of the franchise, it is alleged, would produce the breakdown of an honoured and traditional system.

Comment may be made upon the exclusion from the franchise as citizens of a considerable portion of the *inhabitants*, not minors, as in South Africa and, in the past, in the Southern United States. A British ex-M.P., in a recent book, *Curtain Up on South Africa* (1960), can describe legislation as having been "based on the democratic theory of the minority loyally abiding by . . . the decisions of the majority," where he means by "the decisions of a majority" the majority of the oligarchy entitled to vote, and certainly not a majority of the country's residents or inhabitants. (If we restrict the citizen or voting body, as is reasonable, to civilized men, and not to *all* interests of human beings, as such, and make the test educational or aristocratic, then we may have to exclude semi-literates who have hitherto regarded themselves as the very white backbone of the community.) Actually what we have here is an oligarchy, with attempts to justify it—which is, of course, arguable—as an aristocracy. But this is not said. This issue is, in the States, the spear-head programme of present reform.

The question is also under debate whether a serving soldier and married man should be regarded as a minor, which also raises the issue of 'democracy' and mirroring of interests, as against an 'aristocratic' notion of 'maturity' which, carried too far, could exclude so many. In the Union of South Africa and in the State of Georgia the voting age has been reduced to eighteen. It cannot be said that either in Nazi Germany or in Soviet Russia the political conduct of youth inspires confidence. The 'appeal to youth' can be a demagogic appeal to inexperience and passion as much as one against crabbed selfishness. On the contrary, it might be better if politically the claims of youth were 'cut down to size,' and the wisdom of the Greeks recognized to the effect that the qualifications of the soldier soldiering and of the citizen exercising political wisdom are not the same. This does not mean that those who take decisions ought not to be fully informed, by objective polls and the like, concerning what the specific interests and views (if different) of those within given age limits may be.

As Professor D. V. Verney has re-emphasized, in his impressive little book, *The Analysis of Political Systems* (1959), neither the Parliamentary nor the Presidential systems, upon which political students have spent so much time, any more than "alien systems without the law" (such as those of the older Orient), were systems, "in origin, of participation *by* the people" (p. 95) in principle, even if, over against restricted franchises, Thomas Jefferson defined a true republic as a "government by its citizens in mass, acting directly and personally, according to rules established by the majority" (p. 100).

The distinction between Pure Democracy, classically held to be the sole valid form, and Parliamentary or Presidential and Congressional Democracy is not customarily discussed adequately. The location of sovereignty in the United States, if not a theoretic solecism (since the Founders intended to give it no abode there), is at least a conundrum. It may be held to lie with those who have the amending power; but it cannot be said simply 'to lie with the People.' In the United Kingdom it explicitly lies with Parliament (or 'the Queen-in-Parliament'); is complicated by ministerial exercise of 'the prerogative'; and does *not* lie with the Electorate or People. Certainly it does not lie with Party Conferences. The distinction is not pedantic but vital. All issues of 'privilege of Parliament' apart, Parliament can resist and does tend to resist plebiscitary demands, such as those yet recently favoured in South Africa and offered to the U.S.S.R., as a challenge, by President Eisenhower. The favourable comments made by Earl Balfour (A. J. Balfour) on plebiscites, and even Sir Winston Churchill's famous pun and slogan, made when, as a Liberal, he waged war against the House of Lords, 'refer and end 'em' (he also, according to Lord Attlee, raised the same question in 1945), represent a distinguished but minority view. Broadly, impassioned opposition to the plebiscite tends to come from strong Party men who are moreover radical or even Jacobin-minded. Thus Dr. Konrad Adenauer is on record as favouring a plebiscite in Berlin, but Professor Harold Laski was strongly opposed to so ascertaining the opinion of the sovereign people on the abdication of Edward VIII.

Sometimes, instead of 'Sovereign Parliament' (and the Cabinet as a committee thereof, being Privy Councillors of the Queen and technically "Her Majesty's confidential advisers" [cf. Sir Ivor Jennings, *Cabinet Government*, 2nd ed., 1951, p. 71] or alternatively as a committee of Privy Councillors, being Parliamentarians), the word 'State' is written. Sometimes 'the State,' as active agent, concretely and pragmatically involves not only the Queen-in-Parliament and the apparatus of law, but also the Bureaucracy and that vaguer web, sometimes called 'the Establishment.' But at least it does not mean the People as over against, or distinguished from, these. To this extent what emerges is more an oligarchy, whether 'representatives' of the masses or not, rather than any conception of a Pure Democracy. It would be both sad and ironic were the United States and the Soviet Union to go to war in defence of Democracy, whether or not 'fuller,' since in the eyes, for example, of Aristotle, neither of them are democracies.

Yet what has to be noted is that Aristotle's supposed factual objection to Pure Democracy, for any large territorial state, such as worried Rousseau and de Tocqueville, when considering 'the Great Experiment' of America, is entirely a matter of the past. Technically, Pure Democracy is possible. Moreover, it may be asserted that it is sound democratic doctrine that, not king or leader, parliament or party, but Reason and the People itself (these being balanced) should have not only the ultimate but also the decisive voice; and this at the decisive moment, by referendum, plebiscite, or poll, and not only through representatives who may be years away from their election mandate. For example, decisions of peace and war do not wait for a Congress or Parliament to be re-elected. Nor should the inhabitant People be other, under democracy, than the registered adult Electorate. It does not, of course, follow (nor is it here said) that reason and the voice of the people, *vox populi*, will agree. But at least the true issue will have been stated, between immediate wants and possible ultimate advantage or good. (It may indeed happen that a changing public will be hereby educated to laugh at itself.) After the issues have been so clarified, the more rough and ready 'rules of the game'—which can, for example, substitute representative or electoral college vote for popular vote—can go into effect.

The very real jealousy between sovereign parliament and sovereign people, I have discussed in an article, "Considerations on the British Constitution," in the

Political Science Quarterly, vol. LXX, no. 4, December, 1955. To anybody who thinks in terms of political producers (including their brokers, the party machines) and political consumers such observations will seem platitudinous enough. In a speech in New Delhi, of December 11, 1959, which must be regarded as more than merely casual (directed perhaps chiefly, but surely not exclusively, at countries under dictatorships), President Dwight D. Eisenhower said: "Governments have a way of obstructing the feelings of people. They sometimes create problems and then say they are trying to solve them." Conversely, writing on divorce and moral issues in his diocesan magazine of December, 1959, Archbishop Fisher of Canterbury, a senior member of the English Establishment (in its precise sense) wrote: "It is the State which decides what it will regard as criminal offences. In doing so it cannot travel very far ahead of public opinion; but if it takes its responsibilities seriously it will always be thinking ahead of public opinion and helping public opinion to realize where the true welfare of the community lies." Here we find a clear distinction between an impersonal 'it,' the State, and public opinion; and the implication of an aristocratic concept of personal leadership by particular human beings (unspecified), which we shall discuss later. Whether, for example, before a State enters into union with a confederation of other states or even into a common market there should not be a plebiscite *ad hoc*, as distinct from a general election on a variety of party issues, is at least a question inviting grave consideration.

The customary objection to Pure or Plebiscitary Democracy is that it is not practicable in gatherings too large for Stentor to be heard or in great territorial States. Aristotle denies, to those lands where vast numbers prevent all being consulted, both the very title of States in the Greek manner and all capacity for good political life, thus rejecting not Pure Democracy but the Modern State as a tolerable political form (*Politics* 4. 4). De Tocqueville entertains the same classic fear. Stress is placed upon the role of the 'pure democratic' town meeting in the moulding of American politics by de Tocqueville, in his *Democracy in America*, p. 57. He also then (p. 103) develops the traditional theme that "it may be advanced with confidence that the existence of a great republic will always be exposed to far greater perils than that of a small one," a point on which, however, David Hume, like Madison, expresses an opposite view.

However, owing to modern technological progress it is now entirely practicable to present statesmen on television at any time; by simple electrical devices to record the poll of opinion; and by computers to make the exact picture of national opinion available more rapidly than it is at a General Election. It is not facetious to suggest that, with the will for it, a small polling board for every voter, with three buttons, red, green and yellow, would provide the means . . . A polling board in every house is as reasonable as a telephone or a motor-cycle or car. There is now reduced excuse, in theory, for control through a Party in a Legislature, which Party may be a minority or (which is even less defensible) a majority endowed with formal power but only representing a minority of the voters, a not infrequent situation. Dr. George Gallup, using much slower methods, yet has effected a potential constitutional revolution, as yet little understood but already politically effective and disturbing to nervous politicians, as sapping the foundations of Party machines.

If we do not constitutionally use Pure Democracy, it is because we fear or *distrust* it or because we regard an Elective Oligarchy, based upon Parties (which under our Pure Democracy could be abolished), or a limited Aristocracy, however clumsy and imperfect, as practically better. Granted constitutional balance by a Council or Committee (such as is at this moment under consideration for that new form of political organization which is the European Common Market), this seems to me to be an uncritical and inadequately analysed prejudice. It is of importance to know, in statistical detail, not in General Election party packets but on each issue severally, the exact opinion of the people. It is important to know how it varies—as distinct from what party orators tell us it must be or ought to be—not least in time of crisis. That the People is ill-informed is an observation that will apply in other quarters than this and even to politicians. There remains a strong and even revolutionary case for Democracy; and an irrefutable case at least for knowing what Democracy would do, be it stupid, prejudiced, or wise, were it practised.

Conceivably, even the case for expert or non-elective politicians (as in the British House of Lords, an excellent if powerless system as now set up)—or for a Civil Service such as that set up by Richelieu and Napoleon and now still dominating France, which tends to be anti-democratic and far too powerful and Byzantine a bureaucracy—might be strong did we know more accurately how dangerous (contrary to the Aristotelian optimism here maintained) an unbalanced but authentic majoritarian democracy might be. It is not here argued that the political producer can afford to give the consumer whatever he likes. It is argued that, were the (unAristotelian) assumption true that the public is a fool or confused or schizophrenic owing to incompatible desires, it is highly desirable that its government (and political scientists) should know this and not deceive themselves.

It is noteworthy that today in the State of Oregon (the historical home of the plebiscite and recall as devices of government) the law requires the State Secretary to enter as Presidential candidates to be voted upon at the party primaries the name of every citizen who has not signed an affidavit that he is not a candidate and who can, in terms of public opinion and discussion, seriously be regarded as a candidate. Moreover, here the quantitative method in judging support is supplied: 'a serious candidate' is one, discussion of whose potentialities as candidate has occupied so much measured space in the national or state press. The Press here, perhaps rashly, is regarded as the disinterested organ of representative public opinion. Nor are the citizens of Oregon to be regarded as more backward, naïve, or preposterous than most in political matters. Quite the contrary. Cf. also the work of S. M. Lipset on the Oregon primaries. On the other hand *vide* Cortez A. M. Ewing, *Primary Elections in the South: A Study in Uniparty Politics* (1953).

The objection to plebiscites, therefore, takes the new ground that pure democracy is undesirable. It would indeed possibly involve the termination of the party system, including conspiracies such as the Marx-Leninist, and the establishment of an executive of the Swiss technical type. It is not self-evident that this must be a bad thing, although it might be surprising to the conventionally minded. At the present time, 'polls' operate, like 'the press conference,' extra-constitutionally as a powerful influence on politicians parallel to Congress or Parliament, although this truly popular system is still inchoate. Professor H. Sidgwick wrote, in his *Elements of Politics*, a classic of its day: "No private Englishman will suffer any legal penalty for disobeying a resolution passed by the most decisive majority of the electorate; and no law court would admit such a resolution as a valid excuse for disobeying a law laid down by Parliament" (a view only conditionally true in the United States, thanks to the nature of the Power of Amendment, possible through conventions). The difficult issue of 'offences against civilization and humanity,' which may be committed under the instructions of the national sovereign or constituted authority but for which high officials may be sentenced to hang, cannot be discussed at this point.

The argument that an 'unguided' public opinion of common men, expressing their views through polls and plebiscite, will be, not only ignorant in detail, but unstable, capricious and revolutionary in character, must be regarded with caution. Some relevant experience, chiefly Swiss, seems rather to indicate that plebiscites tend to display conservatism and indeed ingrained prejudices—in part to be regarded as reactions against supposed rivals for a share in control, such as women and Jews. Radicalism, whether 'enlightened' or otherwise, would not seem to be the normal condition of public opinion, which tends to apathy except in mass-revolutionary situations. The charge, not of radicalism but of probable caprice, especially were public opinion polls given any species of constitutional validity, has more force and makes them objectionable to any established Bureaucracy (whether Administrative or 'Party'), just as, in the Soviet Union, officials argue that the economy of the country cannot be exposed to the whims and free trade demands of short-sighted consumers.

Against all this has to be set the patent defects (however much conventionally ignored) of the present customary method of control by periodical elections, conducted on party lines. Here the governmental claimants present their public, through the brokerage of the political parties, not with individual goods upon which to pass a clear judgement of demand, but with combined packages which they have to buy as a totality. Hence, under this system (as distinct from poll-guidance) the consumer does not get only what he wants, but also what the rival producers choose to offer him as a market compromise.

In the British elections of 1959 it was alleged, pre-eminently by Mr. Aneurin Bevan, M.P., that a majority of the electorate voted against the Conservative programme; and twelve million in favour of 'nationalization' of industries. But (a) those opposed to the Conservative programme were divided, chiefly between Labour and Liberal, so that a minority programme (by the above reckoning) won the approval of Great Britain. However, (b) of those who voted for the even more minoritarian Labour ticket, some may have had strong views about Suez policy, some about African colonial policy, some about the social services, and some about public ownership (whether nationalization or otherwise). Nevertheless, the partisan for nationalization, who knew little about colonial policy, and the progressivist in African policy, who was tepid about the public ownership of all means of production, were both taken as supporting the total set of proposals.

This defect seems to be inherent in the Parliamentary Election system on Party lines (about which Rousseau made his famous comment on the spasmodic quality of the freedom of the British to control their Parliament). It is not so prominent where, as in the United States, the Election is not so much on a programme as on personalities, although the citizen's control is not thereby strengthened. In effect the consumer is buying a brand product in a tin on the strength of the reputation of an established firm. It is a little better than the older system of "open your mouth and shut your eyes and see what King George will send you." But it is idle to pretend that the system is perfect.

That no existing electorate, be it in Switzerland or South Africa, is likely to welcome the extension of its powers to new groups, except where overriding factors intervene—such as the logic of the emphasis on nationalism, economic appeals, or ingrained democratic sentiment—follows from what has been said earlier (Proposition 7). We may now add: No Government Bureaucracy or similar Producer, civil, industrial or ecclesiastical, is likely to welcome Pure Democracy, which is an extreme form of consumer control, unless it is assured that effective power still lies in governmental hands

(Proposition 19). On the other hand, it (and public opinion generally) will regard it as blasphemous to criticize any system, called 'democratic,' which is apt for rallying Maximum Support; avoids the weakness of oligarchy and aristocracy of having quantitatively a small base, even if sometimes it is a stable one; and so is flattering to the consumers in the sense that each one counts equally in his voice, at some level or other, for one. On the one side, it is an idle error to suppose that any public or 'powers of public opinion' can run the administration themselves, although President Jackson and the Jacksonian Democrats tended to this error of simplicity. There must be, if not 'leadership,' at least what Aristotle called 'a Council.' On the other hand, it is desirable to recall that Pure Democracy was once held to be the *sole* valid form. There can be no better corrective of a major contemporary danger, a growing Bureaucracy, an entrenched producer mediocrity protected by the complexity and Parkinsonian proliferation of its own rules, or of the cabals of professional politicians, than the clear and direct democratic expression of consumer opinion through specific polls, whether formal or otherwise, but anyhow actually influential. The emergence of such Polls over against Bureaucracy, and concurrently with its growth, is a major, novel, and (for the democrat) beneficial political change of the mid twentieth century.

§iii. *Definitions of Democracy*

It is here desirable to draw distinctions between, at a minimum, five different usages of the word 'Democracy,' as well as between (as we have just said) Constitutional Democracy, whether Pure or Representative, and Popular Government, which is not at all the same thing.

a. One of these usages is too ancient and universal to be dismissed but, as with Plato, rather concerns a *pattern* or matrix of moral living in society, as a desirable end, than a means or *method* of social control, with which it yet undoubtedly connects by common sentiment. This usage (which we shall call Democracy A) considers democracy, not as a form of control or government, but as a valuable moral pattern of social life. Parenthetically, it is important to note that a highly oligarchic society, as in South Africa (in contrast here to the Southern States), may pride itself upon its sturdy democratic equality *within its own ranks*. Aristotle (*Politics* 7. 2) also refers to this pattern when he describes one characteristic of Democracy as being stress upon personal freedom, of which a mark is "that every citizen lives according to his own pleasure," that is, he seeks to fulfil, and is justified by the constitution in seeking to fulfil, his own *actual wants*, however 'materialist' or hedonistic.

It is a pattern frequently condemned by philosophers of the rational, as Spinoza and Hegel, or of the moral law. (The position of Kant here, as already shown, is ambiguous.) In so far as emphasis, in this pattern, is placed upon 'mutuality,' then there is a tendency to a mood of 'self-expression' current in many contemporary societies as a matter of social ethic, especially where a 'consumptionist hedonism' obtains, only held in check by the expediency practised by 'organization men' and by deference towards the neighbours. On the other hand, that this democratic pattern may emphasize authentic human qualities of fraternity, which are in every human community entitled to categorical respect, will be pointed out later. The stress here is upon the dignity of man; not upon organizational efficiency, and upon the fitting of well-oiled cogs into the cogging, or upon the desire of no man, without calculation, to offend his neighbour in the common pursuit whether of mundane success or of the quiet life, such as does not arouse his neighbour's envy. Its defenders can point to it as especially the pattern of a 'co-operative system of power.' Discussion of philosophical and technical comment on this 'pattern of living,' especially in its more extreme or anarchistic contemporary forms (which the Greeks antici-pated) is deferred to chapters VI and IX. However, it seems relevant to quote here the comment of Dr. Norman Bentwich, distinguished some-time professor of law in the University of Jerusalem (*The Religious Foundation of Internationalism*, p. 287): "What is new in the revolu-tionary world is the massive character of the dissolution of authority in the spiritual and temporal order." It could be contended that this is far more characteristic as a weakness of the Western democratic 'free world' than of the 'revolutionary' world of Russia and China.

As distinct from this moral usage, we may distinguish between the form of Democracy in which (*b*) the κράτος or 'power' is held by the many, whose popular will, or rather—they being only the majority—whose chance or actual majority will (what the Greeks called *psephismata* or 'votes,' as distinct from *nomos* or fundamental law) is to be entitled to prevail in all political decisions (Democracy *B*); the form in which (*c*) a few, who hold that they understand better and more responsibly than others the 'true' basic interest or 'real' general will of the majority or, indeed, of the socially virtuous whole, i.e., the ideal will as supposed by them, are thought to be justified in demanding and ensuring that their own will as *valentior pars*, or that of a 'politically conscious vanguard,' shall prevail (Democracy C); and the form in which (d) each is held to be, naturally or civilly, entitled to political rights or Liberty B, whether he be of the majority or of the minority, and where, by these fundamental rights and liberties and by respect for them, the constitutional power of the majority, or of any directive minority, is limited and confined (Democracy D). The minority or individual is personally so 'entitled' in terms of reason, custom, Natural Rights or Natural Law, beyond arbitrary veto, and *not* by majority concession. Democracy D seems to be committed to some such philosophy, for example, of Natural Law.

These three last types of Democracy in the control of power, we may (speaking generally) call the Girondin or Menshevik; the Jacobin or Bolshevik; and the (chiefly) Anglo-Saxon concept of Democracy, to which last St. Thomas in some measure, with all subsequent Whigs and also most Catholic teachers, inclines. Democracy A involves a philosophy of living. Democracy B we may call Majoritarian Democracy. Democracy C we may call Guided Democracy, guided by an oligarchy or aristocracy of Guardians (or even by a tyranny or monarchy) in some cases selected from 'the vanguard of the proletariat.' That the essence of Democracy lies in choice and change of government is here denied. Democracy D we may call Constitutional or Natural Rights Democracy. We should perhaps also add a category, Democracy E, as the Democracy of Unanimous Consent.

It is, however, rare for the general public to grasp the importance of these major distinctions or to be so instructed by its journalists or political leaders, who rather leave the impression that democracy is always something 'self-evident' as 'rule by all'—"of the people, for the people" and even "by the people"—thanks to a unanimous or 'general' will, apart from a few unhappy and probably immoral dissidents. (Lincoln, in the midst of the Civil War, presumably can have had no such delusion.) An illusion is even created by producers in international affairs (as once, in Poland, in domestic affairs) that democracy spells unanimity. In effect, however, this (Democracy E) means the *liberum veto* of the smallest minority, and of any one government in a confederation—a patent recipe for those who desire inaction as the alternative to chaos.

In the face of all historical experience, it was supposed at San Francisco in 1945 that a Security Council with five Powers (more than a 'troika' of three) holding an absolute veto could and would work harmoniously and even efficiently—or it was politely assumed that this could be so. Alternatively statesmen can argue (politics being allegedly 'the art of the possible,' e.g., in educating the American Senate) that this harmony may work for a while before breaking down, and will work better on the basis of the formal and diplomatic fiction that it will not break down. Indeed, if every interest and claim of individual sovereignty, however unreasonable, is to be put forward as a democratic natural right, then Democracy D would readily pass over into the negativity of the 'Rule of Formal Unanimity' such as might obtain in Quaker meetings or among the angels in Heaven were it not for the unfortunate dissension of a Lucifer or Devil. From such formalism the reasonable common 'sense of the meeting' is not likely to emerge with speed. We might call this illusion that of Democracy E. We are not yet scientifically entitled, a priori and without analysis, to reject any reputable claimant to the title 'democrat,' whatever may be our distrust of what can amount to an arbitrary minority tyranny.

Realistically, we have never had 'the Rule of the People.' What we do have is either (a) the rule of the majority at the expense of (and, in case of crisis, by coercion of) the minority. (This position the minority may not actively consent with, but passively assent to, as 'the lesser evil.') Or we have (b) a minority, controlling by propaganda the majority and hence, in fact and amid popular hallelujahs, other minorities. Or we have (c) a Constitutional Democracy, under which the rights of the majority are limited by the assured rights of minorities.

In terms of Aristotelian usage, the fourth or Anglo-Saxon form (D) is not exclusively Democracy, but precisely Polity or Constitutional Government, which (as not only Polybius but also Aristotle himself indicate) may be improved by a certain balancing mixture of *aristocratic* elements in the constitution or balance of governmental powers. It follows, also in terms of Aristotelian terminology, that the Soviet claim to have provided, in both the Menshevik (B) and Bolshevik (C) variants, an authentic and more marked Democracy than the traditional one of the 'Free World' is correct; but *also* that they are both perversions . . . Of the Jacobin variant of Democracy (C) de Tocqueville yet said (*Democracy in America*, p. 158), "To style the oligarchy which ruled over France in 1793 by that name [a democratic republic] would be to offer an insult to the republican form of government." The claim was, however, passionately made.

As touching the first type (A), it is noteworthy that an eminent champion, Professor John Dewey, in his *Philosophy of Education* (1956), writes: "Democracy is much broader than a special political form, a method of conducting government . . . [This] is a means, the best means so far found, for realizing ends that lie in the wide domain of human relationships and the development of human personality. It is . . . a way of life, social and individual . . . It is a form of idolatry to erect means into the end which they serve. Democratic political forms are simply the best means that human wit has devised up to a special time in history. But they rest back upon the idea that no man or limited set of men is wise enough or good enough to rule others without their consent (pp. 57–8) . . . *Asking other people what they would like* . . . is an essential part of the democratic process" (p. 36; italics mine). We have here a heavily 'loaded' definition or description.

Also we have to divide between the attitude of those who will maintain that "accepting the responsibilities . . . for realizing ends that lie . . . in the development of human personality . . . the necessity for the participation of every *mature* human being in formation of the values that regulate the living of men together" (italics mine) is a Public Philosophy, as expressed in the views of Walter Lippmann on Natural Law, which has to be taught, even to the unwilling, if liberal systems are to survive; and that of those who maintain that what we have to consider democratically are men's *actual likes*, actual opinions and passions, actual judgements as grown men (or adolescents) and citizens 'born equal.' If, therefore, the popular majority decides to install and maintain a dictatorship—or what Aristotle calls a tyranny—as a popular government, it is their undoubted democratic free right to do so and their judgement *est toujours droit*. It would be dictatorial "to compel them to be free."

Cf. Chester Barnard, *Organization and Management* (1948, p. 192): "A new description of democracy might well be that in a democracy people have to be only as free as they want to be." Cf. also his comment: "the imposition of freedom may easily be a severe form of coercion, involving boredom, frustration, or persistent worry" (*ibid.*, p. 192). This latter view conforms to the Aristotelian and Platonic descriptions of democracy A.

Incidentally, if democratic forms are merely the best forms of government discovered in the *past* or, as Sir Winston Churchill more drastically puts it, a bad form but one than which no better has yet been found—elsewhere, however, described by him (as touching parliamentary government) as "a very good plan . . . based on trial and error"—this constitutes a scandal in Political Science and a reproach for their complacency to political scientists, even if we may fully concur that no better form has *as yet* been found of political machinery. That the business of political scientists, as of engineers and architects, is always to be suggesting something new and professionally better, does not sometimes occur to them, who are too often *laudatores temporis acti* or armchair critics. The same radical comment may be made upon the entire party system, and upon the failure of political scientists to disengage themselves from mere historiography and description and to suggest needed improvements. It is absurd to suggest that no improvement is possible upon a system where (unlike, let us say, rival oil companies) rival groups, at least at the popular level if not that of the committee room and bar, regard each other as composed of very wicked men, if not actually devils incarnate. The psychology, with its 'will to conflict,' is archaic and obstructive, and the ethic not so much sporting as malignant. Criticism must not come to a stop because we have fallen asleep on the chance of doing better (cf. R. Michels, *Political Parties*, 1915, p. 407). An engineer who, instead of concentrating upon building a good machine for its purposes, largely concentrated upon preventing anticipated explosions blowing the machine up, would be held to be a very poor engineer.

Parliamentary politics remains primarily, unlike science or business, an amateur affair, of wealthy squire amateurs or of trades union amateurs, and not of professionals. Nor is it an affair of the actual popular will. One can dismiss one's physician overnight and (usually) with promptitude change one's engineer. One does not have to wait four years to make the change—and then only as between amateurs. Indeed, the day for amateur politics, so condemned by Lenin, may be over. The free market may have to choose amid professional producers or career men, not spoils men or preachers and prosecuting attorneys.

It can also be argued that classical Democracy *D* is too much animated, with its technique of checks, by distrust of the executive, and by each group of other groups. Under the British (as distinct from the American) system, the first point in analysis cannot be sustained. There was indeed, at a time when the constitutional tradition was taking shape, much distrust of the Crown. Today there is extensive Cabinet and/or national Party machine control. In Britain, the Premier rather than the Queen can be held to be, in some sense, a monarch. The substance, including the aristocratic influence of what is vaguely called 'the Establishment,' is not as the form. However, for both the United States and (in different fashion) for France under the Third and Fourth Republics, the objection has held and will be discussed later. The French system approaches permanent bureaucracy, traditionally exercised since the days of Cardinal de Richelieu through the *Conseil d'Etat*, disguised by unrestrained and often irresponsible faction fights in the name of democracy, equality, and the rights of man. The British system approaches one of partially elective aristocracy, claimed to be pragmatically successful owing to the local constitutional *mores*, and the so-called organic character of the whole.

It is arguable that Democracy as a system of government, which supposes the acceptance of constitutional measures as against the use of force, counting all votes as equal, "each to count for one," that is Democracy B and D, is only viable under the condition that there is a large measure of shared values of a community and 'a constitutional morality' which effectively discourages the use of force and, be it noted, of enthusiasm or fanaticism ready to resort to force. Indeed it may be asserted that Democracy operates, not only within a general political power system, but also solely within one specifically of a 'co-operative' power type or on a mutual trust basis (cf. chap. III), despite the formal and perhaps superficially contradictory mechanism, in Democracy D, of distrust and 'checks.' There has to be a measure of agreement on fundamentals.

Hence we can say that: THE DEMOCRATIC SYSTEM AND THE SOVEREIGNTY OF THE PARTICULAR PEOPLE UNDER THE PRESENT STATE SYSTEM ARE IRRELEVANT *pro tanto*, OR AT LEAST INDECISIVE, WHERE THE ISSUE IS ONE OF 'EXTERNAL' AND NOT OF 'INTERNAL' SOVEREIGNTY (Proposition 20), that is, where it is an issue of foreign affairs; where many of the bargainers and the factors are outside the control of any one community or sovereign people; and where the presuppositions of a co-operative principle may not hold under the contemporary State system. What matters is the externally determined relation of the political producers. *The priority here lies not with the democratic system; but with survival as an independent state.* What the human beings think *en masse* is subordinate, subject to one consideration, stressed by de Jouvenel— that the goods to which they still give priority are those of social survival as an organized set-up (which may not be at all the same as individual survival) or of independent national survival in the international power system. (An alternative here can be, on the contrary, to opt for union—such as that between England and Scotland—instead of independent survival, as giving increased power: *l'union fait la force.*)

Debate by the consumer electors on this issue, however, of what is *meant* by 'survival' may be most real; and the need for consumer control, in a matter of life and death, over the interests of the producer governments, with their long-range interests, may be of unimpaired importance. However, the decision taken, the means are subject to the international market and are not within the sovereignty of local opinion. "If only Ireland could be put under the sea" (or Germany or Russia or China or the Negroes) is, fortunately, dream politics. In comment, it may, indeed, be said that an international co-operative system ought, for the efficiency of political functions, to be created; that 'national independence' is relative and a matter of policy for the population, to be judged by polls; and, further, that since the whole people is affected, the whole must be consulted and (so far as strategic technology any longer allows time for it) their actual will or, at least, passive acquiescence ascertained.

Is it just, it may be argued, that, not merely taxation, but the very life and death of millions in Western Europe at this minute should be utterly in the hands of a President of the United States, whom their representatives did not elect? Is it yet practicable, under conditions decided by the realities of technology, not the legalisms of popular sovereignty, for the decision to be placed anywhere else? This issue, and whether here an authoritative but limited leadership is not required, will be discussed in chapter VIII. The extent to which the internal affairs of societies organized primarily to maintain the peace, such as Sovereign States, are determined by their external affairs, beyond the exclusive determination of their electorates, can scarcely be over-emphasized. The quest for peace may determine an election, but the result of the election cannot alone or sovereignly determine the success of the quest for peace, which can rest with statesmen and with *other* peoples in their own interrelations as would-be peace producers, as well as with less personal factors.

Professor K. R. Popper makes the fundamental distinction about whether a regime is democratic turn on the blunt fact whether government can be changed without bloodshed or not. This may indeed prove to be a matter of the lethargy of the many when opposed to change and of the resolute determination of the community of the few. The traditional Liberal supposition is that reason alone can change anything, even interest. This itself is an act of faith. Professor Popper's distinction would rather seem to apply to 'constitutionalism.' The statement, interesting in its bearing on foreign affairs, is made by Mr. Chester Barnard (*Organization and Management*, p. 26) that " 'democracy' relates to behaviour *within* a cooperative system."

Under a democracy (save perhaps *C*) it is assumed, as axiomatic for the system, that the distribution of power by 'ballots' roughly equates that distribution by the use of 'bullets,' which it is supposed to supersede. It is yet important for students of non-parliamentary political systems, especially non-European, to bear in mind that junta or Army (or, in Siam, also Navy) regimes merit study in their own right; and that these regimes are not automatically 'reactionary,' e.g., those of Generals Chiang and Mao in China, considered in the context of their place and time. It is quite possible, in a semi-literate country, for an ostensibly 'representative parliamentary' and 'Liberal' regime in fact to be under the control of the few wealthy or of merchant and banking interests; and for the Army and 'young officers' (as in Turkey) to offer the only opportunity for the landless peasant, peon, or industrial worker classes to exercise power and to set up a 'popular' government and make material 'progress.' At least one Central American government has considered financing a study of how to transfer a dictatorship into a stable democracy. It should be an interesting search.

The issue debated above relates to the question whether Democracy B or D can effectively go beyond giving a general mandate about ends, purposes, demands, while leaving the details of production (or short-range activities—and we live in the short range) to be worked out by the Executive council, as Aristotle suggested, or by the Executive in collaboration with legislators who here are deliberative men of judgement, and *not* only delegates or representatives. This distinction is complicated by the fact that the Council or Government is likely, as producers, to have a better grasp of the 'real, long-range interests' than the short-range preoccupied consumers. In the area of foreign affairs, where immediate or short-range decisions may often turn the balance, and where there is, on the hither side of catastrophe, little margin for error, the importance of the issue must be emphasized. Indeed, an important distinction may be drawn between strictly Representative Government and Responsible Government (it being tacitly assumed that what is 'responsible' is already known).

Here there is often a contradiction in the thinking of democratic writers. On the one hand, the responsibility for every decision (according to the degree of its importance, not according to its generality or quality of end-product) is claimed for the electorate and press, which has 'a right to know,' however inconvenient in the international game of power-poker. Likewise, 'a right to speak' is sometimes claimed, even if the majority decision has been to the contrary. On the other hand, with a view to the efficient transaction of business (often best by methods of private negotiation), a limited political group or administration will be responsible—and responsible for what goes wrong . . . An attempt is made to reconcile the two positions by holding the politicians to be 'representatives.' But indeed, so far as they are perfectly representatives or delegates, they may have no more expert judgement than their electors; and, so far as they do have expert judgement, they may decide to depart from current average opinion and certainly not be delegates. The question arises, for short-range important decisions, what allowance must be made for an electorate in part uninformed or, even if with facilities to be informed, yet not interested. A distinction here emerges (which has its bearing on Democracy C) between the total electorate and the 'educated' or the 'politically concerned' electorate—by some writers tendentiously called 'the public'—or even 'the active Party members.' Again, among 'the politically concerned' a distinction may be drawn between a few (or so-called professional 'élite') with expert knowledge, and a much larger number of self-nominated 'élite,' who are active party workers.

It may be argued that there would be no harm in ascertaining, through perpetual poll or plebiscite, the actual demands of the electorate in its different percentages, while leaving decisions to professional politicians or members of the Executive. It could be argued that this would produce a quantitatively more accurate picture than by the method which M. de Gaulle explains that he himself adopts, of ascertaining the opinion of France "by looking within myself." (Clearly the Referendum or the Plebiscite are constitutionally to be preferred to the Sample Poll—but they are vastly more expensive—and might be adopted chiefly when the Poll is challenged.)

However, as Joseph Schumpeter, sometime Austrian Minister of Finance, said (*Capitalism, Socialism and Democracy*, p. 264): "Politicians presumably know why they are almost invariably hostile to that institution [of referendum]." In this impressive and incisive book, Schumpeter writes: "once they have elected an individual, political action is his business and not theirs . . . few people realize that this principle clashes with the classical doctrine of democracy and really spells its abandonment" (p. 295). Politics is expected to be a kind of sporting ball-game, calculated to excite and amuse, a matter for opinionated argument and generalizations, but not comparable to business or craft matters in which one has seriously to know detail and form careful judgements. "In the other case [the elector] has *not taken the trouble* to qualify (italics mine); he does not care to absorb the information . . . without the initiative that comes from immediate responsibility, ignorance will persist . . . He argues and analyzes in a way which he would readily recognize as infantile within the sphere of his real interests. He becomes a primitive again . . . if for once he does emerge from his usual vagueness and does display the definite will postulated by the classical doctrine of democracy, he is as likely as not to become still more unintelligent and irresponsible than he usually is. At certain junctures, this may prove fatal to his nation." (p. 262) "Normally, the great political questions take their place in the psychic economy of the typical citizen with those leisure-hour interests that have not attained the rank of hobbies, and with the subjects of irresponsible conversation." (p. 261) "So far as this is so, the will of the people is the product and not the motive power of the political process." (p. 263)

Indeed the study of Rousseau's fraudulent theory of the *volonté générale*—not to be confused with that of the inculcated 'community pattern'—so ardently pursued in some of our ancient universities, can be not only irrelevant, like undue study of phlogiston or of the Ptolemaic theory, but actively misleading, whatever the *bonhomme* of Geneva may have thought. How far is a democracy entitled to enjoy its gamble in error; and who decides what error is? In the Canadian Elections of 1958, according to a March poll, 25 per cent were *neither* 'very' *nor* even 'moderately' interested. Interest in politics here ranks long after the interest in entertainment ('circuses'), homicides, sport, advertising and economic needs ('bread and butter'), in that order, in an affluent society. The United States (as M. de Jouvenel points out) has the lowest percentage of voters of all countries where adult suffrage now obtains. Its citizens, 'sent' by Mr. Elvis Presley, are politically bored. Recent Gallup polls in the United Kingdom have shown that (*a*) the great majority of the public is much opposed to South African *apartheid*, but (*b*) believes—and especially those in the lower economic brackets—in reintroducing flogging for certain kinds of crime (*vide* also p. 14 *supra*).

Nevertheless I prefer the Aristotelian view of the people's competence to Schumpeter's. Schumpeter does yet both underline the seldom noticed rivalry between democratic popular sovereignty (*B*) and democratic parliamentary sovereignty (*D*), and brings out the importance, to be discussed later, of the issue of political leadership, decision and responsibility.

§iv. *Polity*

Among his political categories Aristotle lists, as least ideal of the good but yet akin to what is best of the bad, a political form called 'Polity,' balancing what he calls 'Democracy.' Technically it is the form where, not indeed the whole (which is seldom unanimous, even in intention, whatever our views about a General Will), but the many are concerned for the good of the whole. It is assumed, in typically Hellenic fashion, that there is such a 'common good,' and that it can be discovered by reason: propositions both of which can be denied. Where a section or class has obtained power and refuses all effective share to the defeated portion—and this would apply to distinction by race and colour among those once admitted to citizenship—what we have, according to Plato (*Laws* 4. 1715) is not a polity at all; "and their notions of justice are simply unmeaning." It would be inappropriate here to name those states of our contemporary society to which this damning criticism applies.

This political form is, of all the Aristotelian categories, most akin to what we have called Democracy *D*, in which the government or controlling authority is obligated to respect certain minimum and natural rights, social but pre-civil, of each single individual and *a fortiori* of minority groups, so that the art of government becomes that one of balance and of compromises, based on the philosophies of Locke and Montesquieu, so vigorously defended by James Madison. This assimilation can only be made subject to the reservation that the fundamental philosophy of what we may call Anglo-Saxon Democracy is individualistic and quite non-Hellenic in outlook. It will, however, be noted that, in his actual treatment of this form of Polity, Aristotle (despite the strict and majoritarian terms of his definition) comes close to a notion of social balance, and to that theory of mixed or balanced constitutions which is praised from Polybius to Montesquieu and Voltaire. Incidentally, the word used by Aristotle, 'Polity,' could quite appropriately be translated 'Constitutionalism' (although *not* in the precise, legalistic sense in which that word is often used today) —and this word 'Constitutionalism' can also be used for that (somewhat different) political form which we have hitherto called Democracy *D*. Both accept the notion of a fundamental good law or system of human rights. (They are hence, it may be incidentally remarked, incompatible with a radical scepticism about the existence of this 'good' or these 'rights.')

The Whig scheme of civil government, sometimes described in this connection as 'Madisonian' (for example, by Professor Robert A. Dahl, *Preface to Democratic Theory*, chap. 1), assumes the fundamental role of factional or group actual wishes or interests, as of factual individual wishes or interests; and that, this being taken as datum, freedom against the tendency in other men or groups to tyrannize can only be assured by balances. Professor Dahl argues that the Madisonian error lay (other contradictions between equality and individual freedom apart) in attaching too high importance to institutional checks in the civil structure of government and too little importance to the balance of groups holding power in a pluralistic society. Nevertheless, it was precisely owing to the multiplicity and diversity of its groups that Madison was more hopeful about a widespread democracy than one of small territory. It was yet a Madisonian assumption that loyalty to the Federal Government, based upon a certain unanimity in interest, would continue to take precedence of any inclination between factions to 'fight matters out.'

Professor R. Neustadt, in his *Presidential Power*, raises (as also does Professor Karl Loewenstein) the question whether in fact a 'division of powers' obtains as between the organs of government of the United States, or in any co-operative 'web of government.' The anomalous position of the Vice-President, whose executive functions today grow while he remains president of the Senate, would seem to support his argument. "The constitutional convention of 1787 is supposed to have created a government of separated powers. It did nothing of the sort. Rather, it created a government of separated institutions *sharing* powers." (p. 33)

There are indeed writers of weight who, against the background of the American scene, have held that Constitutionalism as characterized by the Division of Powers in the Governmental Process (and even of what Professor Galbraith calls 'countervailing powers' between social groups) is the critical test of the existence of a democratic system. However, this contention flies in the face of Aristotelian usage, under which Democracy *du sang pur* is a majoritarian system, even if a perversion; and also begs ethical questions, about the role of the individual in a Democracy, in a fashion that would probably not be accepted in France, with its Rousseauite or even Girondin tradition, and certainly not in Russia. We are only entitled to say that we have here, under the Whig traditions and under the semi-sacred aegis of the American Constitution, *one form* of Democracy which (as against Marxist writers) can persuasively be contended to be indeed such and which has its virtues.

Whereas the British system offers an authentic example of a 'mixed' constitution, including non-elective elements, the American system typically puts elected authorities, such as Congress and President, into apposition within the framework of a Constitution not determined by simple majority vote. The defects, however, of this kind of Constitutionalism are logically clear enough. It is stalemate—even if frequent division of control of the Legislature and Executive between the Parties may, under Presidents Truman and Eisenhower, today seem a novelty acceptable to the electorate and offering enlivening possibilities in bipartisanship. Provided that there is general consensus upon the constitutional *mores* and upon rational and natural rights, the basic difficulties may be avoided. But, otherwise, arbitrary minority vetoes, even when disguised as by Calhoun under the claim for 'concurrent majorities' (including majorities of minorities), can inhibit all new governmental action. Minimalism becomes the official philosophy. Political goods and securities may disappear from the market, until such time as a reaction sets in and the consumers are prepared to pay a far higher price. Checks, due to local state rights, prevent the provision of, for example, education goods for all, for which a majority or even a potent minority sees no need; and the central government may be defied and internationally humiliated. If there is not deadlock with the Executive or the throwing-out of legislation by the Supreme Court, then there is filibustering in Congress or conflict between the two houses of Congress.

The American Constitution, it has been argued, by Mr. David Lawrence among others, is best interpreted, not by the courts, but by the popular plain common sense of the folk of the respective confederated states, enjoying all rights which do not seem to them to have been pooled. A premium is put upon nothing being done and, in a plural society, upon the active provision of social goods being left in the hands, not only of the federated States or (in Canada) Provinces, but of non-civil organizations, such as voluntary societies or industrial business, with a consequent new orientation of the entire market. The problem thus becomes one of, say, how far there will also be effective checks and balances against cartelization and unrestricted company control of labour (or closed union domination, such as is not tolerated in the U.S.S.R.) in the economic-industrial field.

Professor David Spitz, in an article, "On the Abuses of Power in Democratic States" (*Midwest Journal of Political Science*, November, 1957), not only comments on "the abusive practices" of "groups who exercise power through control of primitive organizations." He also interestingly develops certain logical rights from and under a Democracy D (assuming this to be invaluable), such as freedom of assembly and speech, instead of attempting, as is more usual, to defend Democracy D, as good, in terms of certain natural rights which it protects.

Apropos of the interpretation of the American Constitution, the United States Federal Court of Appeal, in the Little Rock case (August 18, 1958), seems to have held that conduct supported by a State Governor and a conspicuous majority of State voters can be the conduct of 'a mob,' contrary to law. This interesting (and perhaps legally inevitable) decision is indeed entirely compatible with the principles of Democracy D (and C), but scarcely of Democracy B.

It may be argued that Constitutionalism is possible, strictly in accordance with Aristotle's usage, which moreover is not weakened in what it can provide by "a Madisonianism gone mad," i.e., by the vetoes of too many component and mutually checking elements. For example, it can be urged that the so-called British Constitution provides a firm tradition of 'constitutional morality,' assuring wide liberties for the citizen against governmental actions which public opinion is habituated to reject; substantial legal (not 'constitutional') safeguards; the habit of communal co-operation; and freedom from excessive legalism with its inhuman delays (such as disfigures the American system of safeguards) where action is designed for 'the good of the whole.' It will be noted here that the real key to success is the firmness of the tradition and custom, within the limits of which the market is conducted. It is also arguable, and has brilliantly been argued by Professor Robert A. Dahl in his *Preface to Democratic Theory*, that what fundamentally matters, in maintaining those equilibria which guarantee freedom and a free market, is not, as habitually maintained in the American classical tradition, chiefly a legal and constitutional Division of Governmental Powers, but a social or 'polyarchic' balance of power, from which a constitutional morality is shaped. (Machiavelli, in his discussion of the relation of enacted laws to social customs, maintained a substantially similar position on the limits of institutionalism.) "In the absence of certain social prerequisites, no constitutional arrangements can produce a non-tyrannical republic." (p. 83)

Thus 'the Sovereignty of Parliament,' as distinct from 'the Sovereignty of the People' or 'the Rule of Law,' can mean something very different in the Union of South Africa from what it means in the United Kingdom. Restrictions in the latter can be heavy and authority strong, but the area of assent and even consumers' active consent is not only wide but of established and well-set duration. The dangers of this system lie, on the one side, in too great a growth of the power of the Cabinet Executive or, alternatively, of the Party Machine; and, on the other, of an excessive conservatism in demand, maintaining this traditional framework of the National Constitutional Morality (sometimes, if improperly, identified with 'Victorianism' or a 'class system'). We shall see that there is indeed much, from the point of view of a market in easy but dynamic equilibrium, to be said for such a stress upon popular tradition, modified by the innovations which a politically conscious vanguard, alert and competitive, is able and thinks well to provide. We might, indeed, here combine successfully all those major types, disparate though they may be, of Democracy in the contemporary sense, so that, instead of the perverted form, we have a satisfactory form for use for political ends.

Professor R. T. McKenzie, in his standard book *British Political Parties* (1955), seems to be open to one minor criticism (which I make on the basis of personal experience) in that he perhaps underestimates the influence of the local constituency parties and 'rank and file' (at least their negative influence, in preventing the selection of parliamentary candidates whom the Party Central Office may like, but whom they dislike). In brief, a constitutional polity of checks is more adequately maintained in democratic (*D*) fashion than Professor McKenzie might lead one to suppose. In the United States, the State Party organization is more permanent and more important than the national.

On the other hand, it will be noted that Professor H. J. Laski and G. D. H. Cole and others of their school tended to a doctrine of contingent revolution on the ground that the supposed common constitutional assumptions could *not* be presumed to persist—a position with profound (or what Laski, in one of his phases, would have called 'contingently anarchist') implications.

§v. *Analysis of Democracy*

Our immediate task is to analyze how the various Forms of Government or Control derive from what we had already said about the functions which this Control-activity fulfils in maintaining Authority, guaranteeing Liberty, and the like.

The common characteristic of the Democratic form of control, whether in family, industry, church, state or international organization, is stress upon the actual wants and pleasures of the individual unit. DEMOCRACY CONFORMS, IN THEORY, TO THE TYPE OF A CONSUMERS' MARKET, WITH FREEDOM MAXIMIZED (Proposition 21). From the point of view of government or production it has the merit that it potentially maximizes quantitative (as distinct from persistent) support. Perhaps for this reason the democrat, as captious consumer, is a habitual critic of democratic leadership. (The democrat intellectual feels that he has betrayed his vocation when he ceases to criticize.) The democrat does not perhaps venture to criticize the street-corner policeman, but he shows his small opinion, as of right, for the President of the United States. It does not always follow that it is actually the type of rule under which everybody is most free for most time. This may be true under the (often semi-aristocratic) species Democracy D; but under Democracy C this alleged maximization of freedom, for the majority, may be through authoritarian methods and institutions, oligarchic or even tyrannical.

This authority yet may be cheaply paid for by the many, since its regulations may scarcely restrict this majority at all—it may increase its privileges—but may be severe or liquidatory of the freedom and liberties of the few, and hence quite incompatible with Democracy D. Again, its freedoms may prove ill-balanced and short-lived. In a classical passage Aristotle, with primarily Democracy B in mind, with its tendency to be unrestrained 'popular government,' suggests that the policy of the poor as majority will always be to expropriate the rich; and this was a contention usually accepted (although as a warning) in the eighteenth century.

To take the political forms *seriatim*: under the Democratic form of society A, the stress patently lies upon men's *actual* wants. Aristotle makes this clear. People are so far entitled to express and to press their own opinions and judgements that they must be treated as entitled, each of them, to say what he does want and, in *his* view and according to 'his truth' ought to want, without being told what he should want, from some platform of superiority, by others. Hence, the political structure becomes a simple one of tolerant *accommodation* (on the free exchange) of men's actual wants and pleasures, as they themselves hold them to be; and spells intolerance of restraint upon these. The autonomy of the individual becomes an accepted maxim of the ideal, and also (except for some miraculous pre-established harmony) the multiplicity of ends or goods. Concurrently, variety is held to be characteristic of a high culture and has applied to it adjectives of laudation.

Thus 'variety,' instead of being an imperfection due to the limitations of human ignorance about the discovery of the truth, becomes, for J. S. Mill, aesthetically desirable in itself and a sign of mental robustness. This view Mill shares with John Milton, except that Milton makes quite clear that his is an aristocratic claim made from a platform of superior mental quality. Thus, for patience in dealing with criminals for example (who also may have their sociological defence) and in not 'plucking up the tares' *before* the harvest, is substituted tolerance of *all* moral variety that does not objectively and physically interfere with the like rights of self-expression in others.

Indifferentism follows as to contradictions of views, and applause of their variety. That the maintenance of civil peace, as against more adventurous pleasures, itself rests upon a certain unanimity of views or 'constitutional unanimity' is met by asserting that this civil good is 'self-evident' (except where the teaching of 'the violent overthrow of government' raises a doubt), whereas the goods of common morale and a public unanimity in morals are not evident. We have, therefore, what Dr. Crane Brinton, in his *The Shaping of the Modern Mind* (1959), calls 'multanimity,' and a market providing a great variety of demanded goods at cheap cost to the individual.

In the work of Archibald MacLeish (in his *Freedom is the Right to Choose*), where he discusses his so-called 'American Proposition,' it will be noted that the role of opinions as distinct from reason (*doxa* opposed to *epistēmē*) is not emphasized. This we shall discuss later. In the work of Fromm and Riesman there is, in the tradition of Goethe, stress upon 'self-development'; but Goethe's impatience with those who do not accept the discipline of tradition and costs of training in culture is absent. There is an appeal to the high importance of responsibility in forming our own judgements, but less indication of the objective *principles*, even existentially, in accordance with which responsible judgements should be formed. (It is indeed possible that Existentialism is *au fond* incompatible with 'principles' and is solely a philosophy of will.) Everything is corrupted by an antinomian subjectivism. It can be argued that this gospel of 'self-expression' (where there may be nothing valuable to express) is a quite misleading Rousseauite or romantic concept, founded on false psychology.

It is interesting to note the (somewhat extreme) view on the theme of tolerance expressed, in a recent review (*Observer*, London, September 1, 1957) by A. J. P. Taylor: "The truth is that toleration springs only from indifference." It may rather be suggested that true toleration springs from humility and charity. There is an interesting tension between the sense for Toleration (as among Hindu philosophers) and the active sense (peculiarly Semitic and Helleno-Judaic) for Justice. To admit this tension is not to deny that bigotry and injustice are usually associated—sometimes thanks to another antinomy or tension between Loyalty and Truth.

Of Democracy B, to wit, straight majority rule—which we shall call Majoritarian Democracy or (with Professor Dahl) Populist Democracy *—it can be argued with plausibility that this is the only authentic or terminologically precise form of Democracy, whether it take the Pure or the Representative form* and whether or not, in its machinery, it follows the French Convention type. *It can also be said that it is a very undesirable form of government.* Both points are made by Aristotle. It would seem to follow that caution should be exercised in commending it or in military campaigns to make the world safe for it. However, it may be urged that what is really here involved is the right of the majority of consumers generally to shape the market according to their actual wants; and that the matter of what consumers *ought* to want, in view of the needs of others, is no part of Political Market Theory or of sound practice in assuring clear popular controls. If, however, in a more primitive market, it is the organized military few rather than the majority who will have the actual power, this is (it may be said) with progress in civilization something that *ought* to be remedied, just as Free Trade is better than Mercantilism.

Democracy C, of which Puritanism or 'the rule of the saints,' Jacobinism or 'the rule of the patriots,' and Bolshevism or 'the leadership of the politically conscious vanguard' are illustrations, is not so much authentically of the democratic type, but rather an Oligarchy tinged with Tyranny, or according to another valuation, an Aristocracy. It certainly can claim to conform to the precise definition of an Aristocracy, as the rule of the few, inspired by disinterested values, for the benefit of the whole or vastly larger mass. As with all Aristocracies the question arises (a) whether 'the party,' be it Communist or National Socialist or Falangist, is indeed a few ruling in the common interest or is an oligarchy ruling for its own advantage or consolidation of power or for the benefit of a 'metapolitical' Moloch, antagonistic (as a monopoly of power) to consumer interests and all other rivals; and (b) whether the Aristocracy is indeed, like some clergy, a rule of the few best or whether, like the worse kinds of clericalism, it has a biased notion of what the best is, imposed on the passive *vulgus*, 'common man,' or flock.

Further, (on the evidence, in the case of the Bolsheviks, of such a representative as Nikita Khrushchev) this aristocracy of Bolshevism, in effect organized from the first under the predominant leadership of one man, Lenin, with the growth of 'the cult of personality,' can become, under Stalin, a most detestable tyranny. This school, especially in Leninism, is characterized by a marked contempt for what it terms the irresponsible 'Infantilism' of Left-wing Democracy. It accepts, without hypocritical appeals to 'democracy,' the oligarchic (or aristocratic?) structure of party machines, especially if conspiratorial. The task of the masses is to confirm the activity of 'the vanguard' *ex post facto*.

Aristotle writes, in his *Politics*: "As perverted forms of the constitutions just mentioned, we have Tyranny by the side of Kingship, Oligarchy of Aristocracy, and Democracy of Polity. For Tyranny is monarchical rule for the good of the monarch, Oligarchy is for the good of the wealthy, and Democracy for the good of the poor; none of them subserves the interests of the community at large." (3. 7) In an age when free criticism of Tyranny or oligarchic dictatorship in one part of the world is repressed and free criticism of Democracy in the other part is held immoral, this incisive and dispassionate comment by 'the Philosopher' is refreshing and, pulling the scientific student of politics like a horse on to his haunches, enables him to leap over the *clichés* of conventionality. Nor can it well be said that Aristotle's description of Democracy as a system under which the minority is taxed, according to full capacity to pay, without yet any grading of rewards according to community service (or even 'ability' or 'needs') rendered, is now obsolete and irrelevant.

Again, at a time when the liquidation of the other classes by the dictatorship of the proletariat (literally, 'those who have children') is being so widely urged, it cannot be well said that his distinction between 'the many poor' and 'the whole community' is meaningless, unless we suppose that, when the forcible liquidation of the property-holders and shareholders is complete, there will then at last be only 'the community' left, equal, classless and without (it is logically to be supposed) distinction between functionary and non-functionary elements. Hitherto, the liquidation of one set of functionaries (even if encumbered by the socially useless and functionless) has only led to replacement by a newer set of bureaucrats, yet more self-important than the rest. However, it may be that the Russians will claim that an aristocracy of ability, demanding leadership as such and rewarded according to social service, now disappearing from a decadent bourgeois and infantilely equalitarian world, is at this same time emerging to greatness in Russia, based upon assured popular or *demos* support. It is a novel thought.

On this issue of the emergence of a new aristocracy or oligarchy, far more in enjoyment of the services of 'directed labour,' uninterrupted by inconvenient trades unionism, than any present-day aristocracy in the West, the student should consult the indictments, based on experience, of Leon Trotsky in *The Revolution Betrayed* (1937) and of M. Djilas in *The New Class* (1957).

What, however, many writers omit to point out is the great attraction that this hierarchical organization of society has for men who aspire to belong to the political producing group, and this in many countries; and the consummate ideological skill that converts those who have never yet been within sight of satisfaction of their political demands to feel with enthusiasm that direction by the Party brotherhood is a regime proletarian, classless, and equalitarian and the 'fuller democracy' of satisfactions, whereas Individual Rights Democracy (owing to the antique nature of many of its goods, unrelated, for example, to Asian demand) is 'bourgeois.' The answer can only come in a radical reconstruction of the market, but raises the issue of different tastes in 'good' and 'goods' between the majority of 'have-not' countries and the lucky minority of 'have' countries. It will be borne in mind that, at present, the eighteen richest countries of the world, with only sixteen per cent of the world's population, enjoy more than seventy per cent of the world's per capita income. Moreover this discrepancy, far from growing smaller, tends to increase. Indices of relative income per capita for the U.S.A., Australia, Canada, and New Zealand on the average show (1949) a figure of 590, as against 214 for Western Europe, 133 for the U.S.S.R., and 20 for Asia.

As touching democracy *D*, we can without prejudice remark that this is especially suited to a pioneer civilization, whether of farmers or fighting men, where each member expects largely to be self-sufficient, to provide for himself, and to require little of the services from without of political goods or authority. The tendency is towards permanent suspicion of 'the encroachments of the Executive' and of governmental power; towards resistance to heavy taxation, even for defence; to a theory of the consent, at least in theory and so far as practical, of all the governed, with *liberum veto* and 'filibuster'; to legislative minimalism; and to the philosophy of Paine, Godwin, Humboldt and others that the country (usually both rural and under-populated) is best governed which is least governed. Even a tendency to deadlock leaves the supporters of such a system not disconcerted.

It can operate peculiarly successfully in a country isolated by its geographic condition, whether by an ocean which permits isolationism for the United States from the pressure of foreign affairs or even by narrow seas which have, more uncertainly, allowed a 'splendid isolation' for those in an insular position such as Britain. Indeed, the question may be asked whether this form of democracy is, not of general validity, but only suitable to countries fortunate, isolated, and protected by sea or mountain, such as the Anglo-Saxon democracies of Britain and North America, and Switzerland. Although not the view of this writer, it is arguable that it would have been incompatible with the development or survival of Prussia or even of France— indeed of the British Empire abroad. When psychologically isolationist areas of America (earlier known as also conspicuously pacifist, progressivist, and democratic) were dragged screaming into international commitments owing to the threat from the U.S.S.R., what emerged was the not-so-progressive popular applause for 'the fighting marine,' Senator Joseph McCarthy, who expounded to all listeners the story of the conspiracy thanks to which the farmers of Wisconsin could not do as they wished in their own farmyards and on their own dung-hills.

The desired norm is a weak central government with local initiative. It connects with the doctrine of Division of Powers. We shall call this Individual Rights Democracy. In the case of democracy *B*, to which industrial masses tend in search of security, by contrast a strong executive may be set up, corresponding to the stress on authority and authoritarian social plans. A condition, however, will be that this authority, arising to meet popular wants and wishes, shall not impose felt costs, of any onerous nature, upon this supporting majority. It has to take the shape of a party government, giving this majority what it wants. Under this system, in principle, orders travel upwards—except for the minorities. In Great Britain an interesting tension exists between the older Whig tradition of respect for unqualified Individual Rights and 'the dignity of the human person' and the trend, since Lloyd George, to Majoritarian Democracy.

As touching, however, the Division or Separation of Powers constitutionally, as under American Constitutional theory, although this is only one species (and a very rigid and formal one) of equilibration of the market between the claims of the producer Executive and of, for example, the Legislature as supposedly roughly representative of the common Electorate, the Judiciary being balance-holder, great importance is attached to it under a Constitutional System or polity, especially if of a 'Mixed' or even an 'Individual Rights' character. Thus Professor C. J. Friedrich, in his *Constitutional Government and Democracy* (p. 4) says bluntly: "This division of power is the basis of civilized government. It is what is meant by constitutionalism." This departs from the use of 'constitutionalism' as that which has basis in a peoples' constitutional habits and morality, i.e., 'legitimacy,' explicitly recognized by a people. Constitutionalism can, of course, also be used in a third and more limited sense, as meaning 'having a Constitution' or even 'having a written Constitution.'

Among constitutional lawyers and draftsmen of Constitutions, there is fundamental debate about whether (as Sir Ivor Jennings maintains) the Constitution should be brief and concerned only, or primarily, with the machinery of government, leaving (as in the Union of South Africa) large powers for the future to whatever may be the sovereign authority; or contain further articles and, primarily, a Bill of Rights limiting, apart from the abnormal process of repeal, the action of the legislators and eschewing doctrines of parliamentary or popular sovereignty. For adherents of any Natural Law school of thought there is a strong case (as against Jennings) for the latter principle and for an entrenched Judiciary. The crisis of South African politics emphasizes this. On the other hand it has to be confessed that a two-hundred-years-old Constitution, carrying a Bill of Rights with portions as 'period' and as philosophically disputable as part of the U.S. Constitution First Amendment, with its possible double meaning, can have the taste of flat champagne. Who knows whether this clause means that the United States is strictly laic, i.e., officially non-Christian, or only that it must not have 'a Church by law established,' as under the Queen of England, or like privileges?

From the point of view of political analysis Constitutionalism, when coupled with the principle of Governmental Checks and Balances and socio-political Pluralism, offers the ideal individual consumer's market or 'cheap' market. Restrictions upon the individual, whether in speech, writing or action, are at a minimum. Within a delimited field of constitutional rights or, more fundamental, of natural rights, authority cannot legally interfere, but is self-limited. Popular emotion, indeed, supported by skilful minority organization, can introduce such sumptuary and restrictive legislation as Prohibition; but when the emotional wave recedes this can be repealed. The defects, however, of this kind of Constitutionalism have already been indicated: political goods, such as employment security and business restraints under President Hoover, disappear from the market, until such time as a reaction sets in and the consumers are prepared to pay a far higher price. More and more contemporary American writers are querying on these grounds how far the American Constitution is in fact a 'good' one, in the sense of being suitable for the demands of the country.

It can be argued—although perhaps not successfully—that it is a bad Constitution but that the British one, with its hesitation between Cabinet and Party oligarchy and without the American elasticity of appointments under the Executive branch, is no better. The United States Executive system has, certainly, one major advantage, to wit, that the President, crossing party lines and for bipartisan purposes, can bring in to political activity men who neither have the mentality of civil servants, there primarily 'to administer the act' and not to ask the reason why, nor have spent their lives amid the hazards of party or even demagogic warfare. A premium then, in the case of American constitutional theory, is put upon nothing being done and, in a plural society, upon the active provision of social goods being left in the hands of non-civil organizations, such as voluntary societies or industrial business, with a consequent new orientation of the entire market.

It was the remark of Lenin that "nothing is so authoritarian as revolution." On the contrary, under a free democracy, where each consults his own opinion, one who 'runs for office' has to satisfy, if not all, then among voters enough numbers for victory, even among those who contradict each other. (Actually the candidate —or the politician, like Khrushchev speaking in India against the British, and then in London addressing the British with cordiality—is permitted to contradict himself quite freely if he does so to different audiences, each of which wants to believe him to be right.) Hence the problem, and even humiliation, of the independent candidate. As the *Observer* (April 1, 1956) remarked of the election campaign of Mr. Adlai Stevenson, the Democratic candidate, "if there is something sad in this determined search for personal popularity, Mr. Stevenson is none the less making a strong point. While behaving in this manner, he declares it wrong that the most responsible office in the world should be considered dependent upon the ability to shake hands." It is a corrupting element in our culture that under a plutocracy what is demanded is wealth; under communism it is power or domination; and under democracy it is personal publicity. Under none is it virtue or a "contribution to the benefit of the community."

There will yet be noted both the revolutionary demand, for practical reasons, for 'the strong man' and also the following for 'the film star,' who either by his power gives empathic or vicarious satisfaction for the powerlessness or glamour-lessness of others, and compensation for *their* desire for power and prestige, or who, being amiable, can be both adored and at the same time patronized. Some-times, as with General Nasser, the two roles can in large measure be combined. Healthier, but still of very dubious quality, is the following available for the charismatic leader of whom it is felt 'that he really cares.' This last concept, however, carries us over to discussion of Community. The constitutional hereditary monarch provides a more stable, formal, and 'cooler' figure for emotional transfers.

What is perhaps required are statistical or quantitative surveys of what the public, or its elements, actually wants, as distinct from what politicians or educators say that it ought to want. The result might be highly disconcerting; but it would be interesting in matters hitherto largely uncharted. Although allowance has to be made for the popular appeal to the adolescent of the drama of dictator-ship, especially if of a kind that fills them with no sense of inferiority, and the popular disapproval of the remote 'dignified figure' of the *ancien régime*, the future may well experiment not only in novel adventures in plebiscitary or 'public poll' democracy, involving that direct participation which Aristotle held to be the very test of citizenship, coupled with increased advisory use of the technician, but also perhaps (as in old China and also, in its own partisan way, in the modern Soviet Union) in deliberate mass education and inculcation of respect for the scholar (as moderator in humanism over against the technician), be he called *clericus*, philosopher, 'red professor,' or mandarin. This would produce a 'mixed' democratic-aristocratic constitution or 'polity.' Reference has already been made to the Swiss constitutional formula. Itself one of the lands of the plebiscite with government by executive council, Switzerland seems to prefer the form of a series of coalitions of Ministers with technical qualifications. There is much in its favour.

From the seventeenth to the nineteenth century the great debate was, not about Democracy, but about the respective merits of the Republican and the Monarchical forms of government. In retrospect we can see that much of this crusading fervour, which stirred great nations, sprang from an illusion and delivered small returns in concrete political goods for the consumer. The identification of all forms of Monarchy with Autocracy, as of the Tsars, was wrong. It had its justification in decadent forms of a despotism that was not benevolent, as in Naples; and its explanation, for example in America, in a con-fusion between the actual distribution of executive power in the days of George III, Chatham, and North and the powers attributed to the British monarch in the 'metapolitical' treatises of lawyers which were

read in New England without adequate context. The effort was made
to meet this latter bogey by cutting up George III (or William III)
into four-year periods, giving him two watch-dogs in Legislature and
Judiciary—and calling the product the Presidency of the United States.
On the other hand, it is quite certain that the Founding Fathers of the
United States did not identify Republicanism with a mass democracy
which they often distrusted and feared (even if they, and especially
Jefferson, gave approval to ideas from which it must logically develop).
The issue is today largely *vieux jeu* except so far as the question may
be put how far courts, peers, honours, orders of Lenin and of the Red
Banner, and public acclamation whether of heroes of the Soviet Union,
stars, millionaires, colonels, and Commanders of the British Empire,
is indeed compatible with Democracy A, for better or worse. The case
can be argued both ways.

§vi. *Democratic Weaknesses*

There are frequent political circumstances, and even circumstances
normal in the process of government in some areas, where the achievement of collective ends involves the overcoming of natural difficulties
(for example, the increase, in such lands as Russia and China, of
economic production under backward or unfavourable conditions) or
competition with other societies who have initial advantages or can
act more quickly and decisively. The achievement, then, of these long-
range ends involves immediate costs, unrelated to the fulfilment of
immediate short-range wants or individual human wants. One of the
harshest lessons of Politics about 'wishes' and 'ideals' (cf. Propositions
16 and 17) is that whatever one wants, involving social demands, also
has duties to be paid for, just as much as any 'customs duties.'
Peculiarly this is the case under circumstances of temporary crisis or
in what may be called lands of permanent crisis. A cost has to be paid
and this by the whole population, *including* the government's own
supporters. The form of government can arise as one designed ultimately to fulfil their actual wants; and yet these supporters, whether
from ignorance of facts or from deliberate human choice, may decline
to pay these oppressive costs. This reluctance can only be overcome
by fear (preferably presented as caused by an outside threat), or by
intensive propaganda, or by both. On the other hand, the supporters
may prefer to pay—as against an alternative of free consumption which
is merely potential—when their actual previous experience has been

of a monopolistic customary regime, such as that of the Tsars or of the Chinese Emperor, even more exacting. If all Asia and Africa were 'to go Communist,' it would be for these reasons of marketing and of limited expectation. In the West the force of the argument is habitually overlooked which may provide authentic grounds for more monopolistic forms of government in some (not all) of these areas. This is not in the least to subscribe to the erroneous thesis that "democracy is not for export," whatever may be the case with particular historical and traditional institutions. Even the British monarchy was found suitable "for export" to many parts of the world.

Bourgeois democracy has always had, perhaps because of the unpleasant menace of costs, a weak grasp of the weight of organized power. The Soviet and Communist Chinese governments, on the other hand, while sincerely striving for the reduction of poverty and for new controls over the means of economic production and wealth (not unaccompanied by the liquidation of millions of their citizens), have steadily been prepared to put affluence in consumptive goods and their advertisement in a subordinate position, in priority, to power. In this conflict Western democracies by structure are at a disadvantage in fighting a long-lasting 'cold war' with its sacrifices. Since it cannot be solely authoritarian in demand, the impassioned 'heating-up' of 'the appeal to the people' tends to come late and, when made, is difficult to moderate, cool or control. The acceptance of 'austerity' can indeed be induced, but is not natural to a consumer-dominated or inflationist political market. (Again, austerity, once accepted, may take the anarchic form of each individual neurotically building for himself ineffective bomb-shelters—even luxurious ones—and providing them with defences against his neighbours in best Hobbesian fashion.) On the other hand, the Communists are confronted with the clash between their propaganda of humane and even utopian *ends* and goods 'in the future,' and very present and unpleasant *means*.

"What troubled me was the disparity between the revolutionary objectives of the Third Five-year Plan and the mildness, the almost Victorian mildness, and the normality of the Indian political system. I asked myself whether the gigantic economic revolution can be carried out by Parliamentary politicians and civil servants without the dynamism and the discipline of an organized mass movement." (Walter Lippmann, "The Coming Revolution in India," *New York Herald Tribune,* December 15, 1959)

From the nature of the case authority, under Democracy *B*, has no reserves to compel the majority or successfully to raise the price against it. It may be termed, not in relation to its minorities, but in relation to its own supporting majority, a weak government. One which, under Democracy *D*, has also to woo all minorities, on any issue involving a *liberum veto* or their individual constitutional rights, is even weaker, unless there is some compensating constitutional or traditional factor, such as that power of a small Cabinet which exists in Britain and is now being considered in France—where indeed a 'constitutional dictatorship' (as in Republican Rome) for exceptional times of crisis is also a possibility. There may yet be decisive compensating advantages for the 'weakness,' in terms of popular satisfaction under conditions of peace, progress, and prosperity.

Thus the democracies of the West, their electorates and people, including the women electors, may succeed in preventing the military conscription of their sons in order to balance the (actually numerically smaller but relentlessly conscripted) manpower of the Soviet Union, and rely instead upon the diabolical power of 'push-button,' hydrogen-bomb warfare, which makes no immediate, non-financial demand—and, however diabolic, can even be urged (as in the case of the so-called 'civilian target' at Hiroshima) in the short run "to save American boys' lives." This response, here, does not indeed differ objectively from the old systematic *Schrecklichkeit* of German imperial militarism, except that the latter, unlike the former, was a military decision which pretended unemotionally to have calculated the full consequences. Also the women electors may succeed in checking trends towards war on the part of conventional or unimaginative politicians and in engendering a mood and climate of peace. In the case of the male electorate, determination 'to balance the budget,' without altering an earlier level of taxation, and reluctance to pay the charges and costs of defence—or, again, on a smaller scale, reluctance to pay the local taxes for an adequate properly paid police force—are more likely to be factors inhibiting the provision of efficient means by those with limited-range demands and small-scale interests. The fit fiscal limits within terms of the whole economy is a separate, technical question for economists. We are here concerned with the efficient means to hypothetically agreed ends. That the public should decide upon general ends, such as, 'to keep the peace,' or 'to safeguard national freedom,' is a quite different issue, not here put in question.

Alternatively, *a process of education and refashioning of actual wants* may be undertaken, which will issue in the moralization or idealization of wants, related to basic and objective psychological or social realities of health, prosperity or freedom; in a new, perhaps rational and, anyhow, consolidated support; and in a new enjoyment of social solidarity and 'belongingness' for those who shudder at isolation and loneliness in an atomic, liberal society. This can be balanced against the costs to be paid, at least during crisis, by democratic supporters in imposed taxes of wide popular distribution, as well as of high range. Beyond these may be costs that may be felt to be incompatible with habitual democratic rights, in the temporary 'freezing' of wages along with investment returns; in personal military service; in the restrictions of individual or group liberties, even (as in the Soviet Union) of the rights to strike or move one's location; in restriction of a free press or of exemption from confinement without trial (both as in wartime Britain); or in a centralized and co-ordinated national or party educational policy; and so on. None of these harsh restraints are likely to be welcome, but they may yet be tolerated where the sense of emergency or crisis is sufficiently widespread.

We may yet lay down that: ALL DEMOCRACIES, SAVE THOSE WHICH READILY TEND TO CHANGE INTO OLIGARCHIES OR DICTATORSHIPS (OR WHICH HAVE A TRADITION OF ARISTOCRATIC LEADERSHIP), HAVE DIFFICULTY IN RAISING, TO COPE WITH COMPETITION OR EMERGENCY, THE COSTS OF GOVERNMENT TO THEIR SUPPORTERS (Proposition 22).

To phrase the matter differently, a Democracy, being a consumer-dominated political system, can only become a so-called 'Strong Government' (or semi-monopoly government) by a perpetual re-education of its supporters about their actual wants in the light of what are held by the national educators to be 'real interests'; or (as in Italy, in Peron's Argentina, and in many Latin and Asian countries) by Aristotelian transition, through 'Popular Government' without effective majority controls but by majority will, to Dictatorship. However, the citizen's sacrifice of human ends (as in Germany, the Soviet Union, and mainland China) for the sake of the metapolitical 'enlightened ends' of a group concerned with the power of the regime does not of itself spell enlightenment. It can be *contra naturam*. The problem lies in the sound ethical assessment of priorities as touching ends and the common good; and hence is one of a humane political philosophy. By 'metapolitical' is meant here the substitution, for the satisfaction of actual human wants, of 'ideal' ends—"jam tomorrow"—rather connected with the maintenance in power of a group than with the rationally developed wants of human individuals in any society.

An interesting corollary follows from the last Proposition. If the citizens of a Democracy (other than Democracy C), will not readily submit to new, unhabitual, and authoritarian restrictions from which they see no immediate advantage in services to themselves, equally they will, by uncritical habit, continue to exercise their accustomed liberties of 'free speech,' 'journalistic enterprise,' and the like, however embarrassing this may be to a government in its competition in power with other governments. Recognition of the demands of a critical national situation will only come later—and, in an emergency, perhaps too late. A DEMOCRATIC GOVERNMENT HAS DIFFICULTY IN RESTRICTING THE FREEDOM AND CUSTOMARY LIBERTIES OF ITS CITIZENS, EVEN WHERE THIS REDUCES ITS OWN POWER TO PRESERVE ELEMENTARY LIBERTIES OF THE SOCIETY AND INDIVIDUAL IN VITAL INTERNATIONAL COMPETITION (Proposition 23). Essentially, as we have said, it operates in a consumer-dominated market. And here, without suitable education, the actual wants *may* be unenlightened, short-sighted, and in no wise characterized by the 'good judgement' postulated by Aristotle in democracy.

Contemporary illustrations of this will be found in the free enterprise of the American press and broadcasting systems, in catering for their own consumer's curiosity and demand for information, even if, for example, interviews with leading persons in the Kremlin, or perhaps television broadcasts from the boundaries of East Berlin (the last resulting in 'higher television rating' for Mr. Paar) may subserve the objective ends of Kremlin propaganda and embarrass gravely the American President and Department of State.

The maxim is "the public has the right to know and know now." It is a maxim which corresponds, not only with responsible judgements about the dependence of democratic control upon the public airing of 'the great debate,' but not less frequently upon public demand for some excitement each morning to relieve its boredom and gratify its curiosity and sensationalism.

Mr. Walter Lippmann has, on various occasions, pointed out the danger lying in the 'lag' in popular recognition of unwelcome political realities contrary to its conventional and comforting 'stereotypes' of thought; but the irresponsibility of particular agencies, unduly increased with 'scoops' and cash profits, has also to be allowed for. It will be noted that 'freedom of the press' is not a 'natural right' (being patently dependent upon the invention and particular methods and ownership of a press or broadcasting station) but is a civil liberty under law, logically justified for the specific purposes of, for example, the development of an objectively informed or intellectually vigorous democracy, and is hence a right limited to a 'responsible Press.' The question 'Who decides who is responsible?' is not prejudged here.

These two propositions 22 and 23 do not apply to Democracy C, which we can regard as a Democracy in transition.

Again: NO MAN VOLUNTARILY SACRIFICES THE POWER OF FREEDOM OF EXPRESSING HIS OPINION, HE REGARDING HIMSELF AS AN EQUAL OF ANY OTHER ELECTOR AND HIS OPINION AS BEING AS GOOD AS HIS NEIGHBOUR'S, UNLESS SOME ADVANTAGE TO HIMSELF (OR LOSS OF PENALTY TO HIMSELF) CAN BE SHOWN IF HE DOES SO. COMPLEMENTARILY, ALL WHO HAVE UN-

CHECKED POWER TO ENJOY FREEDOMS TEND TO USE IT—WHICH ALSO IN-
CLUDES THE ABUSE OF IT. (Proposition 24) This follows as a particular
case from Proposition 7. Indeed this desire to express one's free will,
with power over against others, is so general and pronounced that we
are entitled to say that there is a tendency to tyranny in every man.
The voter, of course, may well come to be persuaded that obstinate
ignorance, even if pleasant, is disadvantageous. It is the task of education to insist upon responsibility and to give direction to the sense of
proportion, which will otherwise be perverted, according to their own
interests, by pressure groups. It is tempting to add a positive proposition that: THOSE WHO HAVE THE POWER (be they Athenians on Melos,
emperors, admirals, or automobile drivers) WILL TEND TO USE IT (Proposition 25). They will certainly not (as Cosimo de Medici said) be
deterred by homilies, save when these homilies and paternosters constitute a genuine education and form habits. But the use will be restricted by the nature and the education of the wish. It is unfortunate
that recently so much of this education has been cynical and domina-
tion-obsessed or merely a matter of information or of verbal analysis.
The most we can say is that there is an *original* proud bias towards the
use of 'our' power, not necessarily bettered by subjection to the domination of somebody else.

§vii. *Derivation of Tyranny*

The derivation of Dictatorship or Tyranny can also be traced, with
a measure of precision. The advantages enjoyed by a dictatorship in
affairs of state are its ability to take rapid and secret decisions in
contempt of public opinion (not indeed, as Hume notes, in his *Essays*,
absolutely, but relatively); in its ability centrally to shape that opinion
by selective education, propaganda, and inspired fear; in its ability to
change policy for *raison d'état* without consultation; in its superior
willingness to go to war should it, at a given time, think it to be politic
or advantageous to do this—its citizens being 'expendable'—and in its
willingness to amass collective power thereby. It indeed remembers
(as von Clausewitz suggests) that every aggressor sincerely prefers
peace, to meet with no opposition, and to dominate the will of the
opponent without trouble. It frequently appears that it can act with
speed in providing easy political goods which its chief competitors,
afflicted by what Lenin called 'democratic committeeism,' by delays

for discussion with affected interests and persons, and by respect for individual claims, civil liberties, minority rights or by plain idleness or obstinacy, cannot do. This could become the contemporary problem in India and much of the Orient, although the adding up of accounts is now taking place in China. Impatience and the demand for urgency and for action now aid the rise of the efficient tyranny.

The position of a democracy confronting a dictatorship on issues of power is comparable to that of a poker-player, whose friends insist on reading out all his cards publicly and discussing them, in relation to a poker-player who holds his cards close to his chest. Only if the democrat's cards are *overwhelmingly more powerful* is he likely to win, although he may more cheaply produce a temporary stalemate. A 'cold war,' as we have said, is not a strong democratic suit. Historically on the record—and in the future, *unless* we can bestir ourselves with corrective measures—the odds in survival seem to lie, in a choice of two forms, clearly with Dictatorship. The supposition by some American scientists that Democracy has overwhelming scientific advantages is exploded. The democratic system, although much more pleasant, supposes much more good luck than its alternatives, in this being like free trade. Only where the international order is robust will it flourish. In human history the story of military and militant despotism, or of dictatorship 'normalized' as autocracy, is long—and this literally from China to Peru and from Memphis to St. Petersburg—and that of pacific and comfortable democracy, if brilliant, is fluctuating, over-optimistic, and brief. The ruin of Athens, in the Peloponnesian War, was not averted by the statesmanship of a Pericles and was made conclusive by the popularity-hunting of a Cleon.

If we consult the objective page of history, we will note that the political systems which have hitherto lasted longest have been the conservative, autocratic, and religious system of Egypt, the conservative and religious system of China, and also of the Papacy, and the conservative and (later) autocratic system of Rome, which last was actually concerned about the inadequate character of its religious basis. Athenian democracy flourished for under two centuries, and Florentine democracy for a briefer period. Whether these, in their brief lives, conferred far more on human civilization is not here the issue, although respect for the arts, for the artisan and for the technician, is not confined to democratic systems.

It would be an instance of the historical fallacy of false analogy to deduce from this past record, without precise analysis, that American democracy will not survive in competition against the disciplined tyranny traditional in Russia. It is yet essential to note that what, as a species within the genus of one-man rule, has historically endured longest has been, neither tyranny in the modern state nor dictatorship, but, as in old China, some kind of stable recognized authority, usually autocratic but conforming legitimately to a constitutional morality of the people (cf. my "Critique of Authority," in *Authority*) and such as could marginally be listed by Aristotle as a monarchy or 'best form.' The 'choice between two' (dictatorship or democracy) is not, therefore, the whole story. On this theme *vide passim* A. Cobban, *Dictatorship: its History and Theory* (1939).

In Aristotelian terminology a Tyranny is a regime dominated by one man, with his subordinates, which regime is directed primarily with a view to continuing the power of that man or of his dynasty (*dunasteia* or 'lordship'). Despite Aristotle's evaluation of this system as a perversion, the name 'tyrant' in ancient Hellas carried less condemnatory emphasis than today and Peisistratus could be regarded as a benevolent despot, as well as a contributor to the glories of Athenian civilization. The Medici could be regarded as tyrants, concerned indeed with the preservation of their personal power, but characterized by much of this moral ambivalence recognized in an earlier age. On the other hand, the term 'benevolent despot' as used of a Frederick the Great carries a more favourable moral evaluation. Hence, although a historical solecism is involved, in order to avail ourselves of a neutral term in our modern age of tyranny, the word 'dictatorship' is perhaps the best. This term does not imply that the dictator may not establish an extensive bureaucracy or circle of co-conspirators in his support. When there is any normal non-revolutionary, non-violent, and constitutional method, of practical utility, for changing the leadership, for example, of a Nikita Khrushchev, then the term 'dictator' will no longer apply. In this sense Chiang (who resigned once), however much in the saddle, to this extent is not a dictator, whether or not police power may be used extensively by his regime.

This, however, is modern usage, dissimilar from the precise usage of Republican Romans, for whom Stalin's Russia would have been not a dictatorship but a tyranny, whereas the system advocated by General de Gaulle might have been compared to the constitutional dictatorship of a Cincinnatus. A dictatorship in our sense, moreover, may be regularized where, for example, the interest of a dynasty is recognized and legitimatized under the constitution, with a set law of succession, as happens in certain absolute monarchies of a hereditary or adoptive, but non-elective, order. As has been found from Cromwell's day to our own, this question of the succession is a key one for dictatorships. Dictatorships, of course, may be 'popular governments,' and frequently are such even when there is no constitutional means of terminating the tenure of the dictator, as in Rome.

Dictatorship under the Romans of the Republic was a strictly constitutional and limited expedient, conferring emergency powers. The Dictator (speaking in that wider sense in which we can speak of the Roman emperors as dictators, 'with tribunician power'), when he comes to be both more permanent and more fully constitutionally recognized, becomes an Autocrat as under the Byzantine Empire (vide Ernest Barker, Social and Political Thought in Byzantium, 1957, passim), while the constitutional monarch can harden into the despot, perhaps 'benevolent.'

Where a number of people, amounting even to thousands, which yet constitutes but a minority of the whole, has alone the power to control policy, to the constitutional or actual exclusion of any other organization, we have an Oligarchy. This was the position of those privileged to be in the Golden Book of the oligarchy of Venice. Such is also the position of the Communist Party in the Soviet Union, emphasized by the peculiar position of the Praesidium of the Party. For many 'activist' or fascist-minded persons in the Communist Party, ambitious men, one of its attractions is its power to discipline other people and groups, including the free trade unions, and to break all strikes in the name of social production. When sufficiently narrow, an oligarchy can be described as a tyranny, as when one speaks of the joint tyranny in Athens of Hippias and Hipparchus. At the beginning of the Empire in Rome the Triumvirate was a form twice adopted; and we have seen it again in our own day in Russia. The aspect of a tyranny is emphasized by a personal cult, so that the Leader is not only surrounded by a band, as in Hitlerite Germany, but this élite goes in bodily fear of the Leader as under Stalin.

It is relevant, as to the advantages of Tyranny, to mention Stalin's remark to F. D. Roosevelt: "We neither of us want war, but our advantage is that you fear it more than we do." As touching the need for a despot to consider some public opinion—but by no means believing in the invincibility of public opinion in general —the words of David Hume (Philosophical Works, book IV, p. 31) are worth requoting: "The Soldan of Egypt or the Emperor of Rome might drive his harmless subjects like brute beasts against their sentiments and inclinations. But he must at least have led his mamelukes or praetorian bands like men by their opinions." In Stalin's day, we are told, many of his bodyguard were Georgians, not Russian-speaking. As to his entourage, we are also told that Beria danced in the council chamber around the body of his chief who seemed to have had a fatal stroke, but then grovelled when the face of the tyrant gave signs of recovering life. We find here, then, in terror, as also with Hitler and far more than in such a case as that of Peron, the precise distinguishing marks for tyranny.

In the cases of Tyranny, Dictatorship, Autocracy, and Despotism, since they are almost always used as words of dispraisal, 'snarl words' to describe perverted forms of government (as they were by Aristotle), the interesting question is why organically they should have been able to arise in the first case—and this not only in the distant past but newly in our own day—and how they can endure. In the case of Autocracy, indeed, its close connection with Monarchy, its limited degree of self-interest and the large influence of protracted habit may offer an explanation. Significantly, however, its citizens were described as 'subjects,' an archaic terminology which still also lingers in Britain.

The habitual claim of the eighteenth-century 'benevolent despots' or autocrats was that they were *patres patriae*, rising not only above party factions but also above the fractional interests of the various classes of their subjects, and performing a specific and beneficial function.

The case, however, of the origins of Tyranny is more remarkable, since these have no such constitutional legitimatization and usually spring from revolution. By definition Tyranny does not have the communal aspect of Monarchy, and is primarily concerned with the interest and preservation of its own regime. A clue here is given to us by Aristotle, who states that the Greek tyrannies usually were of popular origin. This contention seems also to apply to the emergence of the tyrannies of Stalin, Hitler, Mussolini, and even Peron in our own time. Some instances of violent 'boss-rule,' even among Governors in the United States, would certainly have claimed for them popular origin and approval. Mr. Huey Long, Governor and Senator, "spokesman of radicals of both parties" (Arthur Schlesinger, Jr., *The Age of Roosevelt*, 1957, vol. I, p. 417) rose as 'the people's champion' against the Standard Oil Company. In brief, not only (as Hume said) can tyranny be sustained by general popular acquiescence, timidity or terror. (As Mr. Khrushchev with humour pointed out to his critics, when asked why he did not protest against the rule of Stalin which he later denounced, nobody hastened to be first to rise to his feet even to criticize Khrushchev.) Dictatorship or tyranny can also actually arise from active popular demand.

In his *Politics* (7. 5) Aristotle writes: "It usually happened in ancient times, whenever the functions of demagogue and general [cf. South American conditions] were united in the same person, that Democracies were revolutionized into Tyrannies . . . the popular leaders [were able to establish a tyranny] in all cases by possessing the confidence of the masses [of freemen], the ground for confidence being their detestation of the wealthy classes." (He adds that, in more recent times, this type of change had been less frequent owing to the rise of rhetoricians to influence, and the military incompetence of such demagogues.) Cf. quotation from Lenin concerning revolutions, *infra* p. 206. When the prime concern of government had become economic distribution rather than any other principle, the many saw no reason why they should not advantage themselves against the few; but, for this political operation, they had to find a leader whose interests were of the same order. Aristotle's contention that Tyranny springs from organized Democracy, as distinct from popular demand (cf. the October Revolution in the Soviet Union), seems more dubious. A. H. P. Greenidge (*A Handbook of Greek Constitutional History*, 1896) remarks that the tyrants were "everywhere the precursors of a new phase of political life. The immediate effect of this rule may be summed up by saying that everywhere they left behind something approaching unity . . . they were the precursors of a popular government, which requires a collective will." This statement about them, as not only popular, but 'precursors,' is not borne out by the history of Rome or entirely of France. The Tudors, however, may have performed such a unifying function in England, precedent to parliamentary growth.

The problem, then, of scientific analysis now arises: why should a form of government by definition authoritarian, monopolistic, even oppressive, largely concerned with the interests and maintenance of its regime, yet (*a*) arise from popular movements, (*b*) by a slight adjustment and legitimatization, which converts it into an Autocracy, be able to maintain itself for longer periods in history than any other form of government? The question, on the basis of the analysis already provided, is in some ways analogous to that of how an economic monopoly is able to maintain itself and keep up prices. WE HAVE IN DICTATORSHIP THE EXTREME CASE OF A SELLERS' OR PRODUCERS' MARKET, WHERE AUTHORITY IS EXPANDED AND LIBERTY DIMINISHED (Proposition 26).

The Dictator guarantees the production of the "goods," and the estimate of cost is left to him. It is a situation which is a function of urgency in the time-scale; and tends to arise wherever there is a demand, not only wide but imperative, for the quick supply of goods whether economic or of security or of satisfaction in terms of injured pride or anticipated glory. The cost is not to be counted. Such a system, once established and having historically fulfilled its purpose, may be continued indefinitely by the interest of the power-possessors, the tradition of satisfaction, and the lethargy of the market or skill of the monopoly producers. It may be normalized and legitimized. The dictatorial system, however, will not itself spring up where there is an evenly spread social contentment and where men are in no activist or fanatical hurry to conclude bargains, which may be costly to their own power and short-sighted, for the sake of streamlined or inhumane efficiency in means and the urgent delivery of critical goods.

The first step in clarification here will come from putting the question: 'whose liberty?' It is facile to speak, in words of laudation, of 'unanimous consent.' But the theory of unanimous consent is that of the *liberum veto* held (as under the old Polish constitution and the contemporary and no more fortunate United Nations Security Council) by the most disaffected. It is an issue to which we shall have to return when we discuss Natural Rights. In practice Government, at any level and of any kind, is seldom by unanimous consent or even of 'concurrent majority' (which, if authentic and not indeed of a minority, contains some possibly useful safeguards), although in some circumstances it may approach to it. The authority of Government is sustained by the support of the majority of power, which is conventionally (but incompletely) equated with the majority of votes. In so far as this majority is decisive, especially when sustained by a strong community of sentiment about values in demand, it is likely to have little respect for the contrary demands and liberties of a minority. This still, however, does not explain why a majority should support a regime (a) primarily concerned with its own power, (b) making more demands on general liberty than this majority would actually have to suffer elsewhere.

In the words of Sismondi, in his *Etudes sur les constitutions des peuples libres* (1836), "nothing is more easy than to prove the sovereignty of the unanimous nation; nothing is more difficult than to prove therefore the sovereignty of the majority." But there is the further problem, beyond oppression of the minority, which was seen by Rousseau. What if the majority enslaves itself? How, with the sovereign people, shall we "compel them to be free"?

§viii. *Causes of Revolutions*

We have already stated that there is a logical absurdity and contradiction in supposing that those who hold power will sacrifice gratuitously their freedom to do what they choose and their established liberties (see Propositions 7 and 24). This does not, however, mean that they cannot be persuaded that it is in their interest, if they are to achieve their hopes and ends, to make this change. First, as touching Russia and to a far smaller degree Germany, there may be *an inadequate tradition of established liberties* and the enjoyment of these liberties as substantial may be too sectional and limited. Common men may find these traditional liberties to be, as it may seem to them, other men's liberties, in which they disinterest themselves, preferring both prudent avoidance of causes for fear and, for themselves, bread and circuses, entertainers and sports, "ease and sensuall Delight" (Hobbes). Secondly, the conversion of support by force into conditional support by vote may, under conditions of violence, be incomplete; and hence the numerical majority may be uncertain of its power and be afraid of the army. *Fear* is a prime human motive, being the converse of power; and is not the less fear for being disguised or rationalized by calculation. In the last resort, formal power is only formally power.

Thirdly, an issue arises not yet discussed. We have spoken of support in quantitative terms. But a thorough political analysis must assess, not only quantity of numbers in support, but also quantity of *degrees of support,* as indicated by such qualities as persistency, willingness to pay the cost of disciplined organization, the difference (often neglected by political scientists) between consent and assent or acquiescence. Majority support may only spell the counted acquiescence of the apathetic, the apolitical, the mass-followers, the timid, or those with no decided views of their own. When we distinguish between determined support or consent and passive support, assent, or acquiescence, and remove the latter from calculation, we may only find left, as political factors, two determined oligarchies confronting one another. As touching certain aspects of politics and power, we can loosely say that: ALL GOVERNMENT TENDS TO BE GOVERNMENT BY MINORITIES OR GOVERNMENT BY OLIGARCHIES (Proposition 27). This follows almost from the nature of the producer's function. It *need not,* of course, follow that consumer demand, instead of being spontaneous, is shaped by a few. In a contest, however, members of each oligarchy will pay highly and impose the costs upon the rest. To this issue of Oligarchy and of 'the compounding of power' we shall turn in the next chapter.

It will be noted that we have *not* committed ourselves here to Gaetano Mosca's so-called 'Iron Law of Oligarchies,' which does not by any means fully conform to our analysis of the Political Market—one could as profitably talk of 'an iron law of oligarchic industrial management,' which would provide no adequate analysis of share-holder controls—or to the general élite theses of Pareto and his followers. These are dogmatic and dangerous.

Fourthly (and decisively), a majority, even if in some measure power-holding, can be so moved by apprehension or *dislike of a possible alternative,* in the light of past or projected experience, that it may readily concede powers, at however high cost and approaching the dictatorial, to any oligarchy or 'leader' competent to oppose or prevent the actual (or propaganda-depicted) alternative. Hence we arrive at the Leninist doctrine of the revolutionary and ideological 'vanguard,' which will enlist the support of the majority to confirm *post factum* seizures of power that have already taken place. The objectionable quality of the alternative to the regime may not only be actually demonstrated but may be (and, in the case of most dictatorships, by propaganda certainly will be) projected; and this alike whether the menace is of a domestic or of an alien enemy. To overlook the realistic role of propaganda and its 'ideas' in influencing choice is to ignore a prime factor (the costs for which have to paid) in political action. The reverse side of the calculation, to this fear of an enemy, is a sense of need for protection, of common interest, of the goods of an enjoyed patriotic community, even if in a sense born of conspiracy or revolution.

In *"Left-Wing" Communism: an Infantile Disorder* (1920), Lenin wrote: "For revolution it is necessary: (1) that the majority of workers (or at all events the majority of class-conscious thinking, active political workers) should fully understand the necessity of a revolution and be prepared to sacrifice their lives for the sake of it; (2) that the ruling class should experience a government crisis which draws into politics even the most backward masses." Elsewhere, the conditions are stated succinctly as (*a*) an organized revolutionary core, (*b*) a loss of morale and self-confidence of the ruling group, (*c*) a crisis that has popular impact. The disasters of the Russian armies in the First World War provided the third condition. A corrupt Russian government, almost defeated single-handed by the Turks and certainly defeated single-handed by the Japanese, engendered the second condition. Revolutionaries from Herzen to Lenin supplied at length the first. A revolution emerged which not "all the king's horses and all the king's men" of the 'Western Powers' have hitherto felt themselves confident that they can, even together, hold in check. It may require the Chinese, single-handed, to do this . . .

The origins of autocracy would seem to lie, then, in lack of an adequate liberal tradition; fear (whether of the actual or of the imagined); a structure of power putting control into the hands of a few activists or men of ambition; no ready alternative; and community (*Gemeinschaft*), an emotional desire for the mutually protective, authoritative, 'loyal,' and trustworthy, symbolized by a 'leader.' If there is no *gain* on the market of immediate goods to be made by accepting the authority of a dictator and the superficially extortionate rate which he may charge for his services, there may yet be an avoidance of a supposed *loss* of freedom, individual or national, due to anarchy or to 'enemies of the state,' within the land or without. Fear of such enemies up to a marginal line will unite, freedom of the individual or individual group being sacrificed for the protection given by strong rule or collective security. However, beyond a point fear may disunite since no collective protection seems any longer effective, even the tyrant or Tsar has lost 'face' or prestige, and the principle supervenes of *sauve qui peut*. This, with a slight change of military fortune and a better German psychology, might easily have happened to Stalin's regime in Russia during the Second World War (as it happened to the Tsar's in the first), before unusually bad weather and Tennessee-manufactured rockets contributed to the saving victory of Stalingrad.

It is not, indeed, necessary that these enemies should exist or be active or their menace imminent: it is enough, for the calculation, that potential supporters should imagine them to be actual and menacing.

It follows that: INTERNAL LIBERTY WILL TEND TO VARY INVERSELY WITH ESTIMATED EXTERNAL PRESSURE (Proposition 28). Who shall ask for 'abstract freedom' or even traditional liberties in times of communal alarm and crisis? And how advantageous that they should not! However, to the factors above enumerated, we may add one of tempo: critical, urgent, and brusque demand for new goods, *novas tabulas*, not only eliminating old debits but lists upon which new requests may be written.

In order, then, to assure their own personally wanted and prized goods in crisis (as distinct from 'abstract freedom'), as a matter of priority men will tolerate the establishment of a strong executive or even dictatorial government, constitutional or innovating, with its claims. It must be insisted that, in areas such as Asia or Africa with a low standard of satisfied economic wants and a long history of autocratic rule, the superior ability of a tyranny or non-consulting oligarchy (especially if propagandized as Democracy *C*) to produce political, and economic, goods rapidly can outstrip any demand, by free debate, to control the human costs of this rule. We need not suppose only crude rewards to the greed or ambition of individual key supporters, as, for example, the offer of ambassadorial posts alleged to have been made by Mr. Lumumba in the Congo to Senators if they would behave themselves and support him. In such areas the market advantage may fall clearly on the side of a despotism, especially if it is in economic and social terms benevolent such as was the despotism of the Roman Emperors for the proletariat by comparison with that of the rich, liberal Senators of the Republic. It may also be well, at this stage, to point out that the discussion here is not about Communism (which, in its ultra-communist forms in the *kibbutzim* of Israel and in past communities in North America, may be unobjectionable enough and even, when voluntary, alleged to be 'too good for human nature') but about Dictatorship, as theoretically justified by Marxo-Leninism.

In *What is to be Done?* (1902) Lenin wrote: "The political ideas of the Germans have already developed sufficiently, and they have acquired enough political experience to enable them to understand that without the 'dozen' of tried and talented leaders (and talented men are not born by hundreds), professionally trained, schooled by long experience and working in perfect harmony, no class in modern society is capable of conducting a determined struggle . . . It was only by stubbornly and bitterly combating every symptom of demagogy" that this struggle can be conducted. "You will realize that 'broad democracy' in party organization . . . is a useless toy, because as a matter of fact, no revolutionary organization has ever practised *broad* democracy, nor could it, however much it be said to do so. It is a harmful toy, because any attempt to practise 'the broad principles of democracy' will simply facilitate the work of the police." These references primarily indeed apply to a struggle in Russia against autocracy, but not exclusively so (and the exceptions made by Marx were rescinded by Lenin, although there can be tactical adaptation).

"It cannot be seriously believed that it is possible to organize the majority of the proletariat under capitalism. Second—and this is the main point—it is not so much a question of how many members there are in an organization, as what is the real, objective meaning of its policy: does this policy represent the masses? Does it serve the masses, i.e., the liberation of the masses from capitalism?" (Lenin, *Collected Works*, vol. XIX, "Imperialism") As touching the duration of this phase, it will be noted that the Soviet Communist Party in 1956 is being urged to return from Stalinism to Leninism. As to service in 'the interest of the masses,' it will be noted that these interests will be defined by the vanguard until such time as the social war is finally won. ('Capitalism,' incidentally, is presumed to be static, unchanging, and a metapolitical entity or abstract counter like a mathematical symbol.) Likewise Adolf Hitler served the Reich in accordance with his own definitions of its interest, endorsed *post factum* by a vast acquiescent vote. One item of the condemnation of Stalin in the Soviet Army newspaper *Red Star* (April 2, 1956) is that his policy "resulted in the fact that in recent years serious works in military thought were not produced here."

In his *A World Restored* (1957), Dr. Henry A. Kissinger writes: "The distinguishing feature of a revolutionary Power is not that it feels threatened—such feeling is inherent in the nature of international relations based on sovereign states—but that nothing can reassure it. Only absolute security—the neutralization of the opponent—is considered a sufficient guarantee, and then the desire of one Power for absolute security means absolute insecurity for the others."

A tyranny that has artificially raised, by concentration of power and restrictions on freedom, the cost of such services as it gives must become highly alive to the danger of all competition which could destroy its monopoly market, and must seek to eliminate it, within and without (the 'within' and 'without' being frequently linked). Its 'cold war' of propaganda must go on. The costs of political supply hence are raised abnormally high; and a state of great instability for the regime is reached (in which it may either dissolve or 'normalize' into constitutional absolutism or autocracy; and in which, yet, it can only with the greatest risk relax or 'lift the flood gates' to popular demand, even if it would). Too much uncontrolled 'cultural circulation' can become a menace to it. Just as democracy can err towards anarchic excess of freedom, and of pandering to the vanity of people who make no effort towards excellence or to merit their liberties, so tyranny tends to a rigid and even totalitarian excess of authority. This is a major schematic or inherent weakness, upon which prudent opponents can fasten. Its human costs become vast.

This does not mean that, for the very issue for which it often has come into existence, to meet a foreign threat, it *may* not be more flexible, more subtle and with greater prospect of victory and survival in war, than democracy.

On the other hand a hedonistic Democracy, Equalitarian, Majoritarian or of Individual Rights, and perhaps especially a high-living Bourgeois Democracy, should it abandon both discipline and those who advise it on the harder paths, and concentrate solely on the satisfaction of immediate demand and emotion, may become extremely vulnerable. It may have a low prospect of maintaining the good of national survival—since urgency is usually costly and uncomfortable —in external affairs where no loud bragging about 'sovereign will,' without power, impresses the foreigner.

It also follows that, the more precarious or demanding a dictatorship, the more it will be inclined to a propaganda which instils into men's minds the notion that they have many enemies, and that the danger is proximate to them as patriots, and to members of 'the community of *us*, against *them*.' Not only are its people alarmed and feel distrustful, but the government wishes to continue this sentiment that they are encircled. Since the fiction must be made colourable by resemblance to facts: EVERY TYRANNY WILL BE SUSPICIOUS OF POSSIBLE ENEMIES, WILL TEND TO INVENT THEM UNTIL THEY EXIST, AND WILL BE, BY ITS NATURE, EXPANSIONIST WITHIN THE LIMITS OF ITS POWERS (Proposition 29). A military tyranny, with realistic objectives—except perhaps in the perpetual military fear that it is being outstripped in arms —may be easier to negotiate with than one held together by a party propaganda which knows no limits in reality. Plato further points out that a tyranny which begins by inventing enemies in order to secure the support of its subjects, continues by appreciating the hostility directed against itself, goes on to establish a Terror, and ends in a condition itself of terror by believing its own propaganda. Nevertheless an element of truth strengthens the propaganda, and dictatorship is least likely to be resisted by countries such as Prussia that, without natural or strategic advantages, have had to compete and fight every step for national survival or those, such as Russia, which have memories of frequent invasion of its open plains and of conquest even by nomad Mongols.

The final days of Stalin, marked by almost insane suspicion and, allegedly, by a busy imitation of Hitler in a threat to deport all the Jews (*France-Soir*, June 7, 1957), illustrate the truth of the Greek philosopher's observation. In commenting on the Bolshevik situation under Stalin, George Kennan in his *American Diplomacy, 1900–1950* (1951) writes: "since capitalism no longer existed in Russia, and since it could not be admitted that there could be serious or wide-spread opposition to the Kremlin springing spontaneously from the liberated masses under its authority, it became necessary to justify the retention of the dictatorship by stressing the menace of capitalism abroad . . . In 1924, Stalin specifically defended the retention of the 'organ of suppression,' meaning, among others, the army and the secret police, on the ground that 'as long as there is a capitalist encirclement, there will be danger of intervention with all the consequences that flow from that danger' . . . In this way, excess of internal authority leads inevitably to unsocial and aggressive conduct as a government among governments." (p. 139) In Hungary today Resolution 36 of the Central Committee of the Hungarian Communist Party reads: "The role of the Popular State as a political oppressor increases or decreases, depending first on the attitude displayed by members of the former ruling classes *and* the trend in international affairs" (Nora Beloff's "Hungary Today," *Observer*, November 29, 1959, italics mine).

It lies in the situation that those who, as monopolists of power, by the high hand take too much will be afraid of the day of reckoning; and indeed may be influenced in policy and reckless courses by fear for their own necks. In so far as it rests upon fear: A TYRANNY IS NEVER MORE IN DANGER (UNLESS IT BE BY ARROGANT MISCALCULATIONS IN EXTERNAL AGGRESSIONS) THAN WHEN, THE SENSE OF CRISIS BEING REDUCED, IT BEGINS TO RELAX ITS INTERNAL RESTRAINTS (Proposition 30). It is like a man who relaxes his reins with runaway horses. Nevertheless, it lies in the antinomy or contradiction of Dictatorship that, if the restraints are progressively increased, the limits of human tolerance will be overpassed and the issue will tend to revolt and military sabotage. This is perhaps the problem of Mr. Khrushchev today. It may be the problem of China tomorrow. A statesman may have lost interest in territorial ambitions; but a dictator under attack must either give immediate satisfaction or paint the pictures of present alarm and of future glory. He must make it clear to his supporters that he is more efficient than his competitors, is still on the winning side, and is frightening the rest. Further, since the issues are those of power over means as much as of ideologies, with their differences concerning ends, tyrannies as such—even when employing the techniques of ideological and cultural imperialism—are no less suspicious of each other than they are of the outside world.

§ix. *Supports for Tyranny*

If we have found here some reason why Tyranny or Dictatorship arises, it may still be worthwhile to elaborate the explanation of how, being a costly restriction of the freedom of the majority, it is able to *maintain* itself. It has been suggested that the majority may be so alarmed, and by propaganda kept alarmed, about the costs if the possible opponent achieves power, that it becomes docile as touching the actual day-by-day costs of the present regime. This is, hence, actually supported by assent or acquiescence. There are also the concrete material gains, especially in public works (from the Parthenon on to the Via Imperia), which dictatorships can give without fear of public audit or of individual protest about such spending. Some of these (such as Mussolini's very early provision of holidays with pay) are of indubitable concrete advantage to the workers.

There is, however, a further factor. We have said that the desire for dominating power is compensatory to distrust, and this also holds for nations. Thomas Hobbes put this more emphatically: that deeper than the positive desire for power in each man is fear, and especially the fear of violent death. Few prices are too high to pay to avoid this. This patently contains a measure of truth for our own 'atomic' times. Where this acute fear is lasting and has a substantial cause a dictatorship has an easy time. The people *not only* fear the dictator; thanks to its internal fears it is *also* behind the dictator. Where the people is educated in fanaticism they will suspect fanaticism in others; where they are educated in fanatical aggressiveness they will suspect aggressiveness in others. Pareto has indeed warned us about the elaborate intellectual rationalizations which men can devise to cover and explain less reputable impulses. Pericles referred, with Patrick Henry, to courage, which is closely allied to faith, as "the price of liberty." However, "skin for skin, yea, all that a man hath will he give for his life," remarked the Devil in Job.

a. For technological reasons, when the search is for 'the ultimate weapon' in *guerre totale* (originally a French theme), the dictum of Hobbes acquires a close resemblance to a description of present policy. In the resistance to Hitler, the United States, and Canada were not afraid and the people of Britain, without expecting the war to end in six weeks as in the First World War, yet remained optimistic. Subsequently an aggressor has come to have the advantage that, whether or not 'hot war' is any longer 'practicable,' its consequences are likely to involve such high costs for both parties as to leave victory itself as a debit. Peculiarly is this true as to democratic countries, with their philosophy of the non-expendability of life in the mass. They are, therefore, likely to regard, not only defeat, but war itself with abhorrence, while military men can make the calculation of the inevitable loss of national power and of that economic prosperity which checks demand for property-communism. Some people could regard the Battle of the Yalu River, following thirty years of civil war in the polity of Europe and the destroying of the balance of power there, as a decisive battle of the world and a Pharsalia in reverse, with the accompanying rise of Eurasia (not, of course, in itself a bad thing, but to be judged by its fruits in human good). Dictatorship gives a regime a peculiar power of manoeuvre in a situation of abnormal international fear, even while itself exacerbating it.

b. To destroy a dictatorship or tyranny it would appear to be necessary to do this with decision in its earliest stages, although other countries have only a motive for doing this in the case of a powerful country where the dictatorship (not as, for example, in South America, except secondarily as a strategic tool) will follow the logic of territorial or diplomatic 'defensive expansion.' Thus the tyranny of Hitler could have been destroyed at the time of the military reoccupation of the Rhineland in 1936; and it could only be destroyed, after that, years later at far greater risks.

Also, hopelessness in domestic resistance to tyranny is engendered for technological reasons. The politically apathetic from fear and curiosity will follow the regime, and respond to the stimulus it can provide. Even a murderer can be an exciting leader. For those who stand to lose there is the technological disadvantage that the days of the barricades are over. The sailors of Kronstadt were repressed without difficulty. A resistance indeed based upon guerrilla warfare is possible (especially with the support of the countryside and against a colonial or alien power) but even here an organized leadership (such as a quite ruthless tyranny can destroy) is required unless defeat is to be certain. Even St. Thomas does not counsel, as moral, an insurrection bound to fail. And an efficient modern tyranny, if it sufficiently adopts a ruthless policy of 'Thorough,' can destroy such leadership. Stalin understood this better than Hitler who, commanding more personal loyalty, yet experienced more conspiracies. Stalin had, further, the advantages of a better strategic position for his country and more manpower than Hitler.

It can indeed be argued that Hitler lost because he (*a*) did not push through his attack on Britain, but dreamed of negotiation; (*b*) gratuitously attacked the Soviet Union at the wrong time, for ideological reasons; (*c*) had too short a time to consolidate his regime and ultimately lacked manpower and economic resources; (*d*) was impetuous, and wilfully offended world opinion by openly proclaiming bellicose and genocidal intentions by his acts and even by his words; and (*e*) was prevented, by German civilized traditions and by the limited loyalty of his army, from being 'thorough' enough.

It is arguable that Hitler had never enough strength to win, or was unlucky, or was too spasmodic in his ruthlessness, or (as I think) had the wrong areas of the world, owing to their tradition, in which to be ruthless at that stage in the game of tyranny. That tyranny succeeds which is completely ruthless, completely shameless, does things (including murder) on a sufficiently wholesale and thorough scale, and has the resources, economic and in manpower, to carry matters to a conclusion. It should be added that, whereas fascism from its nature is only able to make a narrow appeal to those of the state or national community and later must convert itself into a romantic variant of *das Erste Reich* or into a traditional Roman imperialism—and hence suffers as an international system from a logical internal contradiction—for reasons to be given Sovietism has a wider appeal, especially when the prime requirement is for rapid economic change.

c. Allowing for such an appeal, and under conditions of great anxiety, a people's wish to confront what is unpleasant can give way to the wish to evade the unpleasant, to see 'something good in the end,' and to welcome a dictatorship as indeed 'a fuller democracy when properly understood.' To such persons, their moral sensitivities dulled by cowardice or bigotry, even to recall outrages against humanity is an offence against optimism and 'the longer view.' One technique of dulling moral responsibility is, by a pretence of being *tief* in moral considerations, to lump everybody together as "properly considered, *all* guilty before the tribunal of History." Some recent historians have tended to this.

There is yet a subtler reason for the continuance of Tyranny, beyond its rapid provision of prime material goods and its military competence —a reason connected with the alienation (especially in adolescents) of the real world or objective social world from that of men's immediate imagination and wish. The ensuing *frustration and loneliness* can be overcome by sharing a common dream with others, the dream of the community. Here is a political 'good,' giving a sense of personal 'wantedness' and significance, pre-eminently to be obtained in a society, party or movement, but often lacking in a 'liberal' culture. The emotion—one can call it a philosophy if one so chooses—shapes the contours of men's *wants*, and its satisfaction, indeed, becomes itself a major want. In a liberal society of excessive atomism, compulsion to assume free responsibility without adequate means, and competitive exploitation, there is a tendency—avoidable indeed in countries with an established tradition of civic co-operation—to turn by reaction to overemphatic community movements, stressed by intolerance and the cult of force. Instead of scrutinizing the nature of the political bargain, people prefer the easier way of having everything laid on for them. Whether it is more costly depends upon whether somebody else can be found, as scapegoat, to pay the costs or, at least, be exhibited as paying them.

Dr. Erich Fromm, in his suggestive *Escape from Freedom*, especially pp. 205 ff., discusses this issue of the psychological appeal of dictatorship. Whereas Stalin inherited, thanks to party manipulation, his regime from Lenin (Trotsky having sacrificed an empire to go duck-shooting), both Mussolini and Hitler had to create theirs by personal gifts or the *mana* of leadership. It was not merely a matter of leadership being 'a relationship,' but of the 'gift' to give a people what it was predisposed to receive. They were magicians of the community dream, as Lenin had been. Even so Jews or Ethiopians had to be found, as *kulaks* elsewhere, to be presented as a distraction, that is, as the people who were really paying the costs, while others shared *la gloire*. The sources, then, of the maintained success of dictatorship are popular fear; the dryness for the many of excessive individualism; national defeat of the old ruling class and its discredit in war, or like failure, and a sense of crisis; hoplessness about alternatives, including the absence or incompetence or self-distrust of alternative leadership; and the success and example of other plebiscitary or dictatorial adventures; and, finally, the quick delivery of present goods, issuing from its own competence, determination and audacity. These causes are not dissimilar from the conditions of revolution as analyzed by Lenin.

A revolutionary group or conspiracy (and hence so-called Democracy *C*) is, by its character, transitionally an aristocracy or oligarchy and, at least to succeed in the beginning, is likely to require some measure of the idealism, dedication, courage, and prestige of aristocracy. The West, owing to its material 'over-privilege' and lack of vital attention to psychological issues, is exceedingly likely to lose this prestige at the present time to the so-called 'materialist' but actually dedicated Soviet world.

§x. *Concerning the Instability of Tyranny and Its Transformation into Constitutional Autocracy*

By a conventional usage, as we have said, Dictatorship which began in Roman times, and which corresponds with what Hobbes calls 'strong government,' is to be distinguished from Tyranny, which violates, for some, Natural Rights (which we have still to discuss)— those very prior social values or 'goods' for which any regime is, at least in part, set up—or causes fear of the loss of them.

Hence the regimes of Colonel Nasser and of General Franco are not only to be distinguished from those of Adolf Hitler and Josef Stalin in military power or capacity for aggression. All in different degrees, indeed, are 'popular governments,' gratifying the community sense. But they are rightly distinguished according to the degree to which they habitually do or do not violate Natural Rights, and constitutional or rational morality, in their practice of rule. We may also, however, distinguish these (as will be seen later) on the ground of class basis, that is, the market for which they cater. Tyranny may indeed (Dahl, *Preface to Democratic Theory*, p. 6) be defined as ". . . severe deprivation of a natural right."

The causes of weakness, politically as distinct from morally, in a dictatorship have already been indicated by implication. If we assume, hypothetically, political ends in conformity with Natural Rights, then the means of Tyranny may be held to be adverse to, and adversely to shape, these ends. This criticism would not equally apply to all dictatorships. But, abstraction made of ends, Dictatorship presents difficulties of its own in efficiency for any ends, good or bad, although patently the successful achievement of adequately good ends will excuse *pro tanto* the costs of even irrational means. It has no normal criterion for judging the market of demand, since it itself regulates the market. Dictatorship, it has been said, is a species of political monopoly under which the dictator's government takes over totally, or in large measure, the entire task of control. A monistic or 'monolithic' system, and this without division of powers or constitutional limitations of functions, takes over the entire area of significant control, *et quod principi placuit legis habet vigorem.*

The Roman Empire, until it became in part, as the Holy Roman Empire, an elective monarchy (and although in the period of the Byzantine Empire it veered towards a bureaucratic oligarchy), was a dictatorship, but not habitually a tyranny. Its subjects were conditioned by education and habit to modest expectations, and the Emperor enjoyed, unchallenged, such benefits of power as an imperfect fiscal and dynastic system allowed him. Broadly the same is true of the centuries of the history of Russia, 'the Third Rome.' Where, however, people have been accustomed (or remember when they were accustomed, or mix with those accustomed) to have goods satisfying their actual wants at a cheaper price, there will be discontent and search for an alternative. The logical difficulty of a dictatorship lies in the fact that *either* it has to give way to a demand which will not stop until a natural balance is reached in the market, where the minimum is being paid for the political goods consistent with their actual production, *or* the power-holders must take yet more power to repress discontent by instilling fear. This, however, is a cumulative process—as Hobbes said "a striving of power after Power," until either the dictators are assassinated or the rebels dead. "There is no end, but addition." The price of the goods available becomes ever more exorbitant.

All that is required in a competent opposition is to start the explosive process of fission by 'dangerous ideas.' Therefore any opposition must be suppressed. A One-Party system follows. The rulers ever more have to frighten their subjects with the tale of foreign foes or enemies at home in order to sell to them the notion that the goods of dictatorship are worth while and the price in the long run not so extravagant as, in the short run, it seems. In the end, as has been said, they are deceived by their own propaganda, and frighten themselves.

A Tyranny or even a Dictatorship, then, being an extreme concentration of dominative power, is *inherently unstable* in its composition, not (as in a Democracy) from tendency to anarchy but from its difficulty in establishing a legitimate succession in governmental powers, and from pressure towards rebellion. If the Party dominates, as vanguard, the apolitical masses, and the Praesidium dominates the Party, the members of the Jacobin Committee of Security or of the Bolshevik Praesidium themselves go in fear of liquidation or have "to dance the gopak" at the whim of the tyrant, as in a performing circus. It would, therefore, seem that a Thermidor or some even more unstable Triumvirate, cabal or group must follow in a process of disruption of the Terror, given time. The tyranny begins to 'lose face'—of all things most fatal to it, especially among unlettered people—by providing hope to the discontented.

Moreover the false social ideas upon which the regime rests *can be ideologically exploded by an inner fission*: it can be shown, to those who are uncommitted but who may come to lead thought, that a cooperative human society cannot be built upon the inculcation of a deeply aggressive and distrustful psychology. The important role of this inner fission in a false ideology, this 'inherent contradiction,' is often ignored by political theorists. The Marxists themselves have grasped it. The inherent instability of Marxist political structures lies in the unstable combination of great stress upon the community with the persistent inculcation of suspicion of one's fellows—in brief, in its dependence upon this absolute or 'all-or-nothing,' unempirical psychology.

However, in the long term, a process of accommodation can set in (so skilfully carried through by the Emperor Octavianus Augustus, and to which Napoleon aspired) whereby the Dictatorship becomes an Autocracy, with attendant bureaucrats, or a dynastic or adoptionist (or even elective) Empire, consonant with the constitutional morality and level of demand of the time and place, a new equilibrium being achieved. The general level of popular political demand falls, with new and more conservative habits.

Dr. Vannevar Bush, in *Modern Arms and Free Men* (1949), writes that totalitarian dictatorship "is not adapted for effective performance in pioneering fields, either in basic science or in involved and novel applications." In view of recent developments, not least the Russian launching of Sputnik while their opponents were still talking about a complicated Vanguard, this political optimism shown by Defense Secretaries Johnson and 'Engine Charlie' Wilson, must be held to be very suspect. Unfortunately it seems that, being highly departmental and not necessarily humane, the physical sciences and their scientists (who are helped by dictatorial 'efficiency') can flourish very well indeed under a tyranny. It is interesting that Dr. Bush goes on to recommend world government and also says: "Here lies one of our opportunities. We certainly ought to be able to spread ideas, if we have them to spread."

As of the moment I see no reason to doubt, on the level of physical science, that the dominance of the world by Marxo-Leninist technicians or by Bolshevik Communism could be merely a matter of time. (This seems to be a view shared by Sir Charles Snow.) This will hold *unless*, at other levels also, we are able to invent a new political technique more resolute than any yet used. *L'union et la fraternité font la force*: a maxim which will involve the abandonment of many of the divisive selfishnesses of the *ancien régime* which still haunt us.

In the West many hope to improve their material condition by speedy means, and doubt, with H. J. Laski, whether these do not have to be revolutionary political ones. In Asia, Africa, and South America resentment against European dominance, imperialism, and colonialism is primarily a resentment against France, Britain, Holland, Portugal, and Belgium, although not unmixed with envy and jealousy of their backers in North America. Whatever may be the interesting case, stated even by J. S. Mill, for the value of economic experiments in communism (as in Israel, at Oneida, and in monastic primitive communities) and whatever the weight of the sociology of Marx and his predecessors, the denizen worker of 'have' countries has to be brought to realize that Marxo-Leninist dictatorship concentrated on the Urals will not improve *his* economic position; and the worker in 'have-not' countries has to reflect upon the advantage of addressing himself to new techniques, without losing his new found civil independence to the dominance of Russia, an old colonial empire of the most centralizing type, whose colonists are called 'technical experts.' Further, since the 'less developed' countries which especially the Soviet Union seeks to woo are especially agricultural countries, these countries will do well to reflect that it is precisely in its agricultural measures that Soviet Communism seems to be least efficient. However, the final harm lies not so much in Communism as in power-obsessed and world-planning Bolshevism. This discussion, however, leads us to questions in political philosophy, debated in the last part of this tractate.

Jeremy Bentham's definition of what, with a certain characteristic pedantry, he calls an 'undespotic government' is still worth recitation. "The characteristic, then, of an undespotic government—in a word, of every government that has any tenable claim to the appellation of a good government—is the allowing, and giving facility to, the communication [of opinion]; and this not only for instruction but for excitation but also for correspondence; and this, again, for the purpose of affording and keeping on foot every facility for eventual resistance—for resistance to government, and thence, should necessity arise, for change of government." It is perhaps important to say that Bentham visualized such change as being by non-violent means and by such amendments of the constitution as would permit change to be by constitutional means. It may be added that Bentham's 'resistance' can also involve resistance to other peoples' incompatible views of concrete freedom.

A stick of dynamite, however unstable, will only explode under certain conditions, of which "the communication" of opinion may be one. Contrary to Plato, it is evil men who will co-operate most actively when their own necks are in danger. Granted that the existence of a dictatorship can be protracted long enough, then by control of education it can become legitimized as a species of autocracy or oligarchy. Power once enjoyed, and this at many levels of party functioning, will not easily be yielded up. What can issue will be a regime less unstable and, by the same token, more permanent. It will be less aggressive only if its internal embarrassments in providing for the consumer or economic aspirations, technically demand delay rather than, to rally and unite the country patriotically, demand militant and Napoleonic postures. Success, moreover, even in this latter case, need not involve military invasion of a free world, but only such a concentration of power as reduces all will and independence, under fear of war, to its will. The object, after all, is not to win in war but, as von Clausewitz showed, to destroy the will and resolution to resist in others, and to dominate in power with or without war. This tendency can probably only be met by military counterbalancing forces, not potential, but actually available; by causing (which is no less important) diplomatic loss of 'face' and prestige to the tyranny, and the removal of subservient fear; by the exposure of its propaganda in areas sufficiently free for other ideas to circulate, even if under its civil control and persecution; and yet by maintaining such a diplomatic temperature that the opponent is not driven to cast the die for war.

The above themes, to which we return in the last chapter, are also discussed in my *What Does the West Want?* (1957; in U.S.A., *On Political Goals*), and in articles on Democracy and Propaganda in Professor Harwood Childs's symposia, *Pressure Groups and Propaganda* (1935) and *Propaganda and Dictatorship* (1936).

In summary, we note that a democracy (of which there are several kinds), despite its patent merits, suffers constitutionally as a system, especially in times of great international competition, from being the ideal system of the local immediate consumer. Nevertheless, it is meet and proper to ponder the remark of Mr. Justice Learned Hand that there must be grave risks which have to be taken in *any* open society. As Spinoza commented, most good things are difficult—or, as was said earlier in aesthetic terminology χαλεπὰ τὰ καλά ('the beautiful is not easily come by'). The risks have to be allowed for in the account, even if, with Norman Thomas, we recite the hope that "decent democracy will be victor."

We must yet beware of a euphoric optimism about automatic progress towards responsible democracy. In the words of Franklin Roosevelt (Schlesinger, *Crisis of the Old Order*, p. 482), "There is no magic in Democracy that does away with the need for leadership." As Alan Bullock, against a different background, says in his *Life and Times of Ernest Bevin* (p. 206), "Without leadership, democracy is an inert and feeble form of government, a truth still imperfectly comprehended by many who regard democracy and the exercise of power as mutually exclusive."

Likewise historically the demerits of tyranny are evident. Nevertheless, it is important to recognize that it tends in some parts of the world to be endemic and in others to recur. It recommends itself, on the hypothesis of power and in accordance with the mechanism of the market, to peoples who are not traditionally satisfied; who have become mentally alive to the possibility of the satisfaction of demands and who are not fortified by isolation or by power; who recognize a position of bitter power competition or urgent economic or other need; and who are content to make the sacrifice of ultimate consumer control to any political producer who will deliver goods here and now, which otherwise might be scarcely available at all. In such undesirable conditions and for such people dictatorship performs a function of recurrent validity, even if almost incomprehensible to those who are rich, self-sufficient, and perchance happy.

6. Forms of Government: Aristocracy and Oligarchy

§i. *The Compounding of Political Support*

The history of politics is, in large measure, the history of the conflict of Oligarchies, usually themselves representing wider Interest Groups competent to exercise pressures. It is the history of what has been called Polyarchy—many competing Producer groups. Sometimes these are associated with and especially cater for particular political Consumer publics. Among these Interest Groups are Social Classes; but Social Classes are not the only, or always the best organized, Interest Groups concerned with consumption. There are also producer groups.

A dictator often surrounds himself with a council or bureaucracy which becomes an oligarchy in its own right. At least one type of what is called democracy, (*C*), as we have shown, is in fact oligarchic or aristocratic in structure. Patent instances of oligarchy, which may yet be 'popular' in structure (and more popular than merchant or finance oligarchies, to which they may be opposed), are political structures which leave the army dominant—or parts of the army, such as the Praetorian Guard, Mamelukes, or paratroopers, with their special training, mood of the élite and *esprit de corps*. The same comment holds for all systems where great power lies in the hands of rival party machines or of active party workers. (There is, of course, no inherent reason why a group comprising a relatively few should not either itself be democratic in structure like the Model Army of Cromwell, or, again, be under a single dictator or 'boss.')

We have discussed political activities in terms of the political Market, of Costs and Prices, and of the Goods and Rights which the Producer in the Market can provide. We have also hitherto discussed this Price in terms of support for the exercise of power, reckoning all units as equal. As Mr. Tom Mboya has very persistently urged in Kenya, "One man, one vote"—the classical argument of majoritarian democracy, which yet assumes or posits the absence of all excessive pressures, not to speak of terrorism. In a Democracy or a Constitutional Polity (with balances and secured minority rights), this method of reckoning of votes remains formally true. Indeed, we might say that in certain countries of Europe and North America, television and the Gallup poll make true democracy possible for the first time since Aristotle and the days when Greek citizens of the *polis* gathered in the agora to be addressed by the unaided human voice of speakers. 'Ballots count instead of bullets,' so that the element of citizen force required behind ballots, even without (or as countervailing weight against) the more primitive method of imposing rule by the military force of the drilled few with their bullets or by terrorist oaths, tends to be forgotten. Locke (although he might, in view of his own life's experience, have had doubts) blandly states that the majority is "the greater force," embodying "the power of the whole." The bowman is yet not automatically an equal for cavalry, although knightly cavalry, in turn, may be overcome by the king's artillery. And the unarmed peasant is not a match for the bowman.

There is indeed, over large areas of the world, and especially in South America, a constant tendency, although recently less in evidence, of a 'ballot' democracy, which screens a struggle of oligarchies (in some countries even called 'Liberal,' that is, financial), to give place to an overt army oligarchy. Western social students have perhaps been too contemptuous of this frequent political phenomenon, occurring from Pakistan to Santo Domingo, to give it the attention it scientifically merits. This is the more odd since the prime political problem of our era is how those who, in the market, prefer a consumer's 'freedom' and the concurrent absence of force can, without force, prevail against those who opt for a monopoly authority and for the quick delivery of the goods. Naturally those who have what they want do not like the use of force against themselves; but this is not the issue. Rather it is that of constitutionalism, resting alike on majority assent or consent and upon checks and natural rights, as universally a desirable kind of market. Even in the British Empire, under difficulties such as those in Cyprus, civil governors have been superseded by military Governors. A democratic tendency under Cromwell's Parliamentarians and even in his Model Army, or in modern Switzerland, can be supported by the fact that each citizen is allowed to keep his own firearms. It is a permission from a bygone farmer age, consecrated by the Second Amendment to the Eighteenth-Century Constitution of the United States. In South Africa the Afrikaans own fire-arms and the Negroes do not; and this is basic to the political set-up.

It is also usually assumed that the citizen in fact exercises his voting rights. This, however, even in the United States, is notoriously not the case. The more normal part of the electorate voting, according to the character of the election, would be from one-third to one-half. In the United Kingdom it is higher, but still discouraging in local elections. In the national election of 1955 the percentage voting in relation to the eligible electorate, was 76.8 per cent. In the London County Council elections of 1961, only 31.5 per cent of those eligible voted. Mr. Tom Harrison's sociological survey (*Britain Re-visited, 1961*), especially of the Lancashire Farnworth constituency and the parliamentary election [? of 1935; Mr. Harrison does not say] showed 39 per cent voting at this election only; 32 per cent of men and 29 per cent of women voting at both the parliamentary and the subsequent municipal election; 21 per cent voting at neither; and the residue voting at the municipal only; that is, about 71 per cent of men voted in the parliamentary election. Harrison's conclusion is that fewer did not vote at all than was generally supposed, since the non-voter of one election (for instance, the younger group-member) was frequently a voter at another.

In most constituencies the result of the vote, for traditional reasons, is a foregone conclusion (cf. M. Lipset, *Political Man*, p. 271 ff.). A change of only 30 seats, out of 630, can give a Government a majority of 60. Professor V. O. Key (*Parties, Politics and Pressure Groups*, 4th ed., p. 625) shows that the British voting average compares favourably with that in the United States. Key points out, moreover, that non-voting is a phenomenon which frequently indicates, in a fashion to be expected on the basis of the Political Market, that some 'underprivileged' group is not being catered for by the political producers in this society: both their (unorganized) vote 'doesn't count' and, in response, they do not vote. As Professor Lipset, however, has insisted, non-voting is not to be counted as mere loss. It is especially totalitarian countries which insist upon a high rate of voting (*Political Man*, pp. 197, 219; also David Riesman, *Individualism Reconsidered*, pp. 414–25); and 'non-voting' may be a significant political act.

However, that, in a study of the British parliamentary election of 1950 (M. Benney *et al.*, *How People Vote*, 1956), 66 per cent of the lower economic group declared themselves 'uninterested' in politics, may show more than British phlegm or even (shown in another poll) a high level of contentment in the Welfare State, but an indifference far from healthy. (Poll analyses also show that, in Sweden for example, the character of the representative weighs as a factor in election as only 1 to 4 against the expectation of personal economic advantage. Cf. *New York Herald Tribune*, May 10, 1958.)

It has been suggested that, improving on the Australian position, the elector should be permitted to destroy his ballot but should be heavily fined if he does not vote. On the other hand, it has been suggested that the non-voter, after say six years, should not be compelled to vote, but should be deprived of citizen rights. What has to be allowed for (and here Aristotle did not comment) is that non-voting may even be a deliberate political act of warning. Conversely, modern dictatorships compel their subjects to go (to the extent of 99 per cent) through the plebiscitary demonstration of consent to the regime, even if the candidates are selected by an oligarchy (in the U.S.S.R. about 3 per cent) of the active political workers (in the U.S.S.R., in turn, themselves about 3 per cent of the citizen population). Again, the result in the 1948 Presidential campaign of Mr. Thomas Dewey was almost certainly reached, not by the turn-out of pro-Truman voters—eight years on, Mr. Truman attracted fewer voters than Wendell Willkie attracted in 1940, although Willkie was defeated—but by the last-minute decision of thousands of Republican voters not to vote. The failure of some predictions in the polls at this time was in part due, not to inaccuracy of statistics about the intentions of voters, if they voted, but inadequacy of check about their determination to vote.

Under all systems great masses of subjects are non-buyers; and conventional buyers, if left alone, are as politically inert as they are economically traditional or, to use Lord Bryce's phrase, 'fatalistic.' It is perhaps nearer the truth that politics without circuses, bread being assured, bores them in a way that horse races and football pools do not. Their political goods, one would argue, are wrongly packaged, so that no clear connection emerges between what, as in France, politicians have offered and what their public wants. But such 'packaging' usually involves highly coloured, emotional, mendacious, and dangerous presentation. On apathy in the trade union movement and non-attendance (between three and seven per cent attend on average) at policy meetings, with its consequence of putting power into the hands, e.g., of dedicated Communists, vide Julius Goldstein, The Government of British Trade Unions: a Study of Apathy and the Democratic Process in the Transport and General Workers Union (1952); and S. M. Lipset, "The Political Process in Trade Unions: A Theoretical Statement" in Freedom and Control in Modern Society (ed. M. Berger et al., 1954). It should, in fairness, be added that in the classical Athenian democracy about one eligible citizen in fifteen seems to have attended the meetings of the Assembly, and that hired Scythian archers were brought in to add persuasion (Gustave Glotz and Robert Cohen, La Grèce au cinquième siècle, 1931, p. 270).

It is, then, owing to an artificial convention (or to a theological or ethical dogma of equality, of which the religious character was overlooked) that Bentham can say that 'each to count for one' is the political rule, in order to attain the end in the greatest happiness of the greatest number, decided by each consumer in accordance with his own immediate, 'actual,' and possibly non-ideal wants, whether perverted and hedonistic or healthy and rational. It may be a 'useful' principle, conducing to contentment, absence of tension, and co-operative power; but it is conventional, arguable and not entirely 'realistic,' in the sense of corresponding to market practice. Notoriously it does not hold for power, although formally it may hold for voting.

A Tyranny is able, while requiring support, to rally it by a manipulation of opinion reinforced by fear and by the use of such entrenched power as it has against all competitors. An Aristocracy, if its authentic aim is the greatest good, must rely upon the education or shaping of opinion for its support, although an Oligarchy will have entrenched power, independent of persuasion and virtue or merit. But a Democracy, while aiming at a happiness issuing from a free market adjustment of men's *actual* wants (whatever, within conventional limits of the market, these may be), nevertheless does not, in assessing what goods to provide, rely solely on the principle of 'each to count for one.' The 'support of public opinion' can be considered as consisting of measurable units of support, which units are equal. Such measurement is basic in political science. But indeed the whole influences the units, even if quantitatively its volume may be reckoned by them; and the units are not equal in effective power to press. We have, therefore, to consider *the problem of Political Organization, compounding individual units*; and of the Construction and unequal hierarchy of Political Support, which conditions the provision of goods.

Jeremy Bentham denounces, as "bawling on paper" and as "nonsense upon stilts," the *a priori* affirmations of the American and French Revolutions, including that concerning the equality of men. But Bentham is no less guilty of *a-priorism*, since he arbitrarily posits that each is 'to count for one,' without justification save in his hedonism, which makes each Caliban wish, *at the least*, to be so counted, since he places his own pleasurable self-interest first. (Few Calibans object to being counted as among 'the damn-sight better,' in the slogan 'all men are equal and some are a damn-sight better.') As developed, the argument is that ballots shall count each as one, and that the majority (whether ethically or rationally right or wrong) will prevail as a matter of public *utility, because* the majority will be the more powerful. This is to suppose that, because in particular constitutions and under particular conventions, ballots can be equal with bullets, therefore realistically a number of ballots can be equal in force with bullets—which is an untrue statement, ignoring *inter alia* the structure of organization.

Human Society is formed of Groups, often overlapping, which usually, although not invariably, have their own internal organization, of different degrees of articulation and complexity. This is true of

Groups with no assignable purpose of association, as well as of Associations with a specific function or objective. Groups are not to be identified always as Pressure Groups. In some cases simple customs or Conventions unite and delimit the Group; in others more elaborate Institutions of organization, with officials and assigned duties, exist.

In the case of an Institutionalized Group, small or great, it is not the case that each human unit has equal power since, natural or nurtural gifts apart, the official or occupant of a key functional position and those whom he organizes have, *ceteris paribus*, more power than others. It is the position or status in the institution which gives power and prestige. In every case, therefore, Oligarchy *tends* to be the usual form of political power, owing to the requirements of production (see Proposition 27). There is, however, as already stated, no 'iron law' such as Mosca enunciates. There are tendencies and degrees. And the oligarchy itself may have, as in Venice and in the British House of Lords (at least as touching the respective 'orders'), a fairly strong sense of equality and that all of that community are peers, *pares*, and equals. Further an oligarchy (like a monarchy) may quite well be elective—just as Jefferson refers to (and condemns) "an elective despotism." The real issues are of the quality of, and checks upon, the oligarchy. Under an effective system of checks the power of the politicians as a group, which may take the form of being described as 'the sovereignty of Parliament,' may be very really subordinated to the sovereignty of the people, whose actual views can be discovered by elections, plebiscites, polls, or wide-based and authentically popular party organizations. Generalizations, apart from observation, are dangerous. But it is idle to suppose that this actual popular power either is easy to achieve or is at present formally recognized to be the correct and legitimate position as touching locus of power, even if it should be. It is difficult to define it. In the extreme paradox of John Chipman Gray, "the real rulers of a people are undiscoverable."

The oligarchical tendency of government, away from pure or plebiscitary democracy, or even majoritarian democracy B, is sufficiently stressed by the Italian sociologists, such as Mosca and Pareto, and is indeed a major theme of their argument. A recent and valuable survey and criticism will be found in Professor James H. Meisel's *The Myth of the Ruling Class* (1958). More discreetly it is stated by Marxo-Leninist writers. Understandably Liberals and Social Democrats have been reluctant to state it. However, so long as the doctrine of the sovereignty of parliament obtains, this serves to indicate those who are *not* sovereign. In the United States the device, in civil control, is adopted of checking functionally one established oligarchy or aristocracy—for example, the judicial aristocracy of nine of the Supreme Court, which alone can declare what is constitutionally law and is irreplaceable save by impeachment of members—by others legislative or executive, and by the amending power residing in part in the State legislatures or *ad hoc* conventions and in part in Congress.

The old basic Hellenic rule, that democracy meant every man walking up to forty miles to record his vote in person, no longer obtains. Napoleon III perhaps gave 'pure democracy' too bad a name. But his experiment was too perverted to be a proper test of the sole logical democracy. The problem always arising is: what is to be our democratic judgement if Democracy *B* actually wants to give away its power or control to some other popular rule, such as that of a Bonaparte? Are we, in this event, 'to force them to be free'? And who is 'we'? Is the issue Democracy *C*? In all these matters it is important for students to look beyond semantic disputes to objective situations of power. Thus we may deny that Menshevik Communism is a democracy because, as against Aristotle, we may choose so to define democracy. On the other hand Radio Moscow (May 11, 1958) can assert that Stalin, as exponent of Bolshevik Communism, was not a dictator, "because the very nature of a socialist [*scil.* 'Marxist interim'] society excludes the possibility of a dictator coming to power." Marxists alone understand the popular will; dictators are by one definition oppressive of the popular will; Stalin was a Marxist; *ergo* Stalin was not a dictator. Q.E.D.

Even as touching consumers on the political market, as distinct from producers, some consumer groups will give or withhold a support of greater worth to the producer than others. To a Government the support of a well-organized Party is of more use for producing in legislation the realization of a party programme than the support of the same number of unit voters unorganized. It is of more use because such a Government has assurance, beforehand, that the vote can be got out; the Government has support at various stages of the governmental process which the formal electoral vote for the legislature or executive personnel does not affect; and it has also some confidence of the persistence of this support into the future, assuring a formal vote and a stable market. In the words of the Comte de Tocqueville, "the skill of the actors in the political world lies, therefore, in the art of creating parties." (Incidentally, the works of M. de Tocqueville, little noted—his *Ancien Régime* apart—thirty years ago, are now being elevated into an exemplar of how shrewd political theory should be written, despite their repetitive quality and unexpected lack of reference to the concrete, for example, to the existence of the President of the United States, the scarcely inconspicuous Andrew Jackson. Like Adam Smith as touching America and like some of the contemporaries of Peter the Great as touching Russia, he had the prescience to forecast the dominant position of these two great countries such as has become clear even to the dullest eye today.) From the point of view of Quantitative Politics and measurability, not only the size of the vote but also *the persistence or stability* of the vote in the behaviour of particular voters, indicating the efficiency of the organization and the attractiveness of the programme, must be measured. Much of the problem here is to measure what may be called compounded support. (Marx had a rather similar problem in his Labour Theory of Value.) To a discussion of the political function of Parties we turn in a later section (§iv). Closely connected with the oligarchy of active party workers is the rival established oligarchy of bureaucrats, great and small.

Under the heading of Aristocracies and Oligarchies, it is appropriate to mention that these political forms are to be found not only in civil, ecclesiastical, and industrial life—such as in the control of great trade unions—but no less in musical, theatrical, literary and academic spheres, and indeed have been described by writers of eminence from Thackeray to Sir Charles Snow, including the brief *Micro-cosmographia Academica*. The issues are the usual ones of power and prestige, and the competition is as keen as elsewhere. Fascinating details of snobbery will be found in Sir Roy Harrod's book, *The Prof* (1959), about Lord Cherwell. Sir Charles Snow, in his Godkin Lecture at Harvard, *Science and Government* (p. 59), writes: "Put your ear to these meetings and you hear the intricate, labyrinthine and unassuageable rapacity, even in the best of men, of the love of power. If you heard it said once—say, in electing the chairman of a tiny dramatic society, it does not matter where—you have heard it in colleges, in bishoprics, in ministries, in cabinets; men do not alter because the issues they decide are on a bigger scale." In these matters few are deaf to the whispered intimations of fame and immortality. And power intoxicates as speed intoxicates.

In ordinary social life men in the street make a distinction between *nobiles* (or 'nobs'), those *sine nobilitate* (or 'snobs'), and 'cads' ('cadets,' etymologically 'little chiefs'—or juniors—not to be confused with the Russian moderate conservative party of that name . . .). However, to discuss these matters of sociology would take us too far from the central themes. It may be added that the man obsessed by particular power tends to regard the man as a bore who is obsessed by something irrelevant—a sentiment that will tend to be reciprocated.

We have seen that the gamut of the political market runs from the total monopoly of a centralized producer-dominated situation to the anarchy of a consumer-dominated one, so free in facilities without cost or responsibilities that production of authoritative guarantees tends to wither or dry up and some kind of underworld, with its own inverse authoritarianism, takes over. The first business of civil government is to see to it that the underworld, as ordinarily understood, never becomes the possessor over-world, while distinguishing the position (sometimes, but wrongly, held to be more dangerous) of political revolutionaries, authentically motivated by a desire to improve the condition of the human lot or its chances of salvation.

When, therefore, we speak (as earlier) of an Equilibrium of the Market, with different specific references, or to a Balance of Powers, we are not necessarily affirming, with Lockean political theorists and some contemporary writers, that such an equilibrium, balance, or check *ought* to be—which is a matter for argument—but we are speaking of a schematic norm to which the free political market actually *tends*. Hence the question does not arise whether this— allegedly like talk of natural law or rights—is a dishonest endeavour to justify the *status quo*, as argued by Professor Wright Mills. Liberals may in fact be justifying the bourgeois 'possessors'; but they also may be justifying the balanced free market, with minimum of appeal to force or even to pressurization.

The market is in a perpetual state of flux of actual demand, ethical imperatives being the shaping factors of some demands but not (any more than in economics) of all. On the other hand, just as one must not presume equilibrium as always obtaining (or even as something which *a priori* always ought to obtain), likewise the Theory of the Market offers us no ground at all for presuming that any permanent condition of total monopoly (i.e., Tyranny), or of semi-monopoly or centralized Oligarchy, will in fact obtain. There is no 'iron law' of one Oligarchy or 'Ruling Class' or 'Elite,' any more than (despite Marx and Lassalle) there is an 'iron law' of concentration of capital and of total cartelization. The theory of the Compounding of Power, to assure stable support and effective authority, carries no such inevitability of centralization. On the contrary, a pluralist theory is equally tenable.

An excellent survey, especially of the politics of the industrial structure (too much neglected), concluding that we require more empirical studies and exposing the weakness of *a priori* or sensational pamphleteering expositions, will be found in Professor Robert A. Dahl's article, "Business and Politics: a Critical Appraisal of Political Science" (*American Political Science Review*, March, 1959). Also *vide* Professor James H. Meisel, *The Myth of the Ruling Class*, pp. 355–65, with his discussion of the 'centralizing' theme of Wright Mills and the anti-centralizing argument of C. J. Friedrich.

§ii. *The Elite: What Is It?*

Much of the discussion in this field has turned upon whether there is a managing or controlling group, ruling class or élite—briefly, an effective Producer Oligarchy—or not; and what precisely is meant by these terms. *Omnis definitio periculosa.* There is a problem of exact identification. And, without pragmatic identification, the term is sociologically useless. The word 'élite' is a highly unsatisfactory one, because it is a 'loaded' term, replete in its very etymology with tacit assumptions. An 'élite,' like the Calvinist 'elect,' consists of a chosen few. But who chooses them, and for what? Not God, as with the Calvinists. But (it is suggested) perhaps Nature. Customarily the meaning oscillates between reference to a group that *does* rule or influence, and a select and superior group which, it is implied (as is the old argument of Callicles), *ought* to rule or influence. Hence Professor Meisel can appropriately refer to this neologism, now in fashion (but well established in French discussion of the theme), as 'the new snobbery'—or 'nobbery.'

Vide my article on this subject, "Élites politice," in the book of the same title, edited by Professor A. P. d'Entrèves (Bari, 1961). Professor C. J. Friedrich, in his recent London lectures, has also raised the question of how far the alleged élites (or the 'Establishment') are cohesive or in any wise approach an organized group, or are (as I would hold) multanimous.

There is the further ambiguity whether an élite is a group actually taking political decisions or whether a 'power-élite' (to use Wright Mills's term) is such a group; or whether an élite is circumambient, a reservoir of relevant ability, competent to 'influence' decisions. The old distinction between *puissance* and *pouvoir* (or *Macht*) reappears, as well as the somewhat different one between *potentia* (actual power) and *potestas* (legal power or authority). In Italian, Professor Guido Dorso has drawn, in his book, *Dittatura, classe politice e classe dirigente* (1949), a most useful distinction, indicated in his title, although the *classe politice* tend to be limited to the official civil government, in its multiple forms as 'government officialdom.' Perhaps, better, we should talk of 'the Control Groups' (which may rest upon a co-operative as well as on a dominative basis)—such as members of cabinets and party chiefs, senior civil servants and colonial governors in the civil structure, and senior 'executives,' industrial 'bosses,' members of the Sacred College and senior members of hierarchies elsewhere —and of 'influential people,' whose words, for whatever reasons, can sway those who take decisions. Of course, not all readers of the London *Times*, described in that great journal's advertisements as 'Top People,' have, it need scarcely be said, equal influence. Perhaps what a young man has especially to be advised to note as prudent is, not the importance of the exercise of power, which must rest with a few, but of access to those who do exercise it. But discussion of the question-begging word 'élite(s),' with its similarity to the Confucian usage, 'superior men,' is best left until we discuss Aristocracy. Those 'actually deciding' may be far from 'culturally superior,' nor is it proven that those 'culturally superior' are the people who it is wise should actually, as part of their role, order about and, at need, exercise coercion over others.

In the discussion of 'control groups,' integrated by the need to keep control stable and authority more than ephemeral in power, a vexed question arises about the relation between 'leadership' and the 'social milieu.' In some cases the social milieu is itself distinguished, as local, from the supposedly profounder levels of the 'national' social structure. This in turn, by one school, is regarded as a composite of 'institutions.' In the words of Professor C. Wright Mills, " 'social structure,' as the conception is most commonly used, refers to just that—to the combination of institutions classified according to the function each performs." On the contrary it may be suggested that (as Plato rightly held), if institutions indubitably shape the man, men also in the web of controls shape their institutions.

Further, the social structure is not merely an agglomerate of local and temporary institutions, whose characteristic is 'historic specificity.' The raw material of social relations, as we stated earlier, is a matter of the relations of individual wills; is shaped by men's needs, both those more basic and those more transient; and, from the major functions that are required even in a primitive society, with increased complexity of civilization increasedly complex institutions are thrown up. It is not the monarchy only that produces the king. A succession of strong war-leaders founds the monarchy. It is not only the Supreme Court, as we know it, that conditions the Chief Justices; a John Marshall and his successors conditioned the Supreme Court, as we know it. Attention only to institutions, and to local and temporary institutions, is a false track, tending to contempt for the individual person, his nature and wants, and duplicating the proper work of the historian, which is always specific (despite talk about 'types' among non-historians).

We need not adopt, in contrast to Tolstoy, any 'great man' theory—although a Caesar, Napoleon, Lenin (ironically enough a living confutation of strict Marxism and an ideological embarrassment to such theorists as Plekhanov), Churchill, de Gaulle do exist—in order to affirm that leadership is more than the inevitable product of some anonymous dialectic relation, web, or institution. What we have said is that there may certainly be wider *classe dirigente* or 'establishments' of influence—intermediary circles, as Professor Karl Deutsch suggests— connecting the decision makers with the consumer public, called by Professor Loewenstein 'the power addressees' and by Professor Mills 'the masses.' (Professor Mills apparently maintains that the only significant discussion or 'answering back' by consumers must be about civil party politics, in which these 'masses' are deplorably and, to him, rather inexplicably uninterested.) The political party itself, we further say, and comparable organizations are major networks of connection between producer and consumer.

The producer control-group, quite patently, does not produce or operate in a vacuum, apart from its public or its special factories or channels of operation, which are institutions. This last scarcely needs saying. All that we are entitled to assert is that, under conditions of quasi-monopoly, some decisions can be taken, for example, by the cabinet of a government, which it calculates that it can get its public to accept after the event. But the political scientist will be prudent not to see 'conspiracies' against the consumer or elector everywhere. It may be that some of the most foolish decisions, such as the setting up of these monopolies, can empirically be shown to have decisive public support. Human nature is like that.

What we have admitted and stated is that, human nature being what it is and as constant as it is, THE SATISFACTION OF THE PERENNIAL DEMAND FOR INSTITUTIONAL AUTHORITIES, AND FOR THE SOCIAL GOODS OF AUTHORITY AND SECURITY IN POWER-COMPETITION, ALWAYS TENDS TO GIVE PREPONDERANT POWER TO LIMITED GROUPS OF A FEW WHO ARE PREPARED, PERSISTENTLY AND AT COSTS, TO ORGANIZE AND SUSTAIN THESE AUTHORITIES (Proposition 31). *In this sense* all politics is in the hands of limited central groups; and we can speak, if we choose and according to valuation, of inevitable rule by Oligarchies, Aristocracies or (neutrally) by limited 'decision' or 'control' groups. This refers to organizations and does not at all necessarily imply that the market itself is monopolistic. It may be 'polyarchic' and comparatively free in choice.

These potential 'control groups' may be co-ordinated or may be (and frequently are) in trade rivalry for consumer demand, as mutually jealous systems. (Indeed, whereas 'the military élite' are assumed by some writers to be centralized and menacing, part of their menace to efficient defence arises from their deadly internal and professional rivalries. Likewise bureaucracies are riven by jealousies between diverse departments.) There is a balancing 'inevitable tendency' among oligarchic groups, as against concentration of power, for them to be rivals for the rewards of power, which upsets so-called 'iron laws' of oligarchy. What we can say is that each will tend to perpetuate itself by interlocking with other power-holding sections of the regime or 'establishment,' if it can thereby radiate and increase its own influence. But we are not entitled to say in satire that the sole essential characteristic of these groups of a few is that "they chance to be privileged" (C. Wright Mills). They or their substitutes have gained, and will gain, power because they perform a function. In the extreme anti-monopolistic case it is rather the *anomie*, the lack of 'responsible leadership' and the need for an Executive, *boulē*, Senate, or Aristocracy, which fills the sincere representative of middle-class democracy with concern and alarm. It may be that this alarm is misplaced. But that decisive powers tend to lie with a few is not necessarily and of itself alarming. What matters is the capacity of that few for meeting the needs of the many, as the many understand—or, according to another philosophy, should understand—those needs.

As distinct from the Elites or Control Groups, which are primarily political producers, consideration has also to be given to those pressure groups which are primarily representative of the consumer, although they may be (and usually are) pressing for a particular kind of legislation, of specific use to themselves and their wider membership. They have already been in some measure discussed (*supra*, p. 137). It has been pointed out that, described—with a certain anonymous impersonality which distracts attention from the individual actor—as 'Interests,' by A. F. Bentley for instance, they, like Elites and Classes, are less precise than is sometimes easily supposed. Nevertheless, the Pressure Group usually takes institutional form as a highly organized association; and as such admits of quite precise and objective description. Its more laudatory name is a Voluntary Society (even with restricted membership) for action, frequently legislative. As such it plays an immensely important role, peculiarly if a wide meaning is given to the word 'political.'

While the pressure group, in some aspects, is viewed habitually in the United States as a nefarious 'lobby,' Dr. Robert McKenzie has (rather surprisingly) pointed out that its especial home, where it is given recognition as part of the normal and even beneficial working of government, is Great Britain. It enables groups of consumer citizens to express themselves; and, by organization, to produce a kind of parallelogram of forces, which a successful government, or other producer institution, has to take into account. Thus regarded, pressure groups appear, not only as an immensely important subject for political study but as broadly beneficial in the working of a living democracy—and not as those "worms in the body politic" which Hobbes thought all organized groups to be. What is yet important is that their operations shall be public—and not an affair of secret societies.

In the case of the Communist Party, in Britain for example, it has been almost routine, when the Party line so indicates, to develop not only 'Popular Front' structures, but also voluntary pressure groups, upholding a 'principle,' with a respectable frontage composed of Liberals, artists, bishops, and peers; an executive committee, containing amenable personages; and either a general purposes committee dominated by party members or supporters, or an omnicompetent secretary. During the Second World War official Communist Party support in Britain for the war and civil defence was solicited, and publicly announced, along with that of the other Parties. This made the party respectable. It was almost certainly an act of bad political judgement on Sir Winston Churchill's part. It will be noted that the Communist Party is not so much preoccupied with being a Parliamentary Party as with strategically mapping out the militarily vital points of the economy (engineering, atomic research, electrical works and power stations, fire brigades, armed services, diplomatic and secret services) and placing its men in tactical positions of oligarchic power.

The Party is a very specific kind of pressure group, which will be discussed later, especially in relation with the alleged Class Structure of Society. Pressure groups, on the other hand, are almost infinitely heterogeneous, although also very diversely powerful. Much of the political progress of a country may be due to the enterprise of voluntary action groups. Although methods may be surreptitious and subject to criticism, their activities do more to guarantee than to frustrate choice; and ensure an active and democratic life and competition among the governors. Eminently they demonstrate that politics is not a matter of individuals, each counting for one, but (which shocked some enthusiasts of the French Revolution) of the compounding of power in groups—and not within the State alone. Their antithesis is the One-Party system—which has been known to obtain in Trade Unions and even Churches, as well as in States. A little heresy (the word means 'choice') does good.

On the subject of Pressure Groups, *vide* the works of Professor S. Finer (*Anonymous Empire*, 1958) and of Mr. Allen Potter (*Organized Groups in British National Politics*, 1961), as well as Professor V. O. Key's classical study and the earlier ones by Professor Odegard and others, already cited, and the work of Professors J. Meynaud and G. Sartori. Cf. also the study of British independent television (which gives, however, a picture which overemphasizes the play of commercial interests as distinct from the demand for freedom in the media of information, etc.) by Prof. H. H. Wilson, *Pressure Group* (1961).

§iii.   *Class and Status*

The concept of a 'control group,' or even of an 'élite,' has frequently been discussed in terms of a 'ruling class' and of the class structure of society. This is indeed a more traditional approach than the former and can be argued to be a more satisfactory one. The conclusion drawn by Marxists is that this class system can be abolished, although neither in the practice of rewarding according to service nor in the ultimate principle of a reward 'according to need' did Marx advocate any system of mathematical equality. Further, although the historical 'ruling class' of the moment came to be abolished by Bolshevik revolution (as the earlier feudal noble class had been abolished, although *not*, save in France, by revolution), what immediately was to succeed was the 'dictatorship of the proletariat,' operating through such authoritarian agencies as the restricted Communist party and the present regimes, with their political and technocratic élite, of Russia and China.

The objection to developing sociological theory primarily in class terms is that what precisely is meant by a 'class' is seldom stated. Marx makes this theme cardinal to his entire interpretation and campaign. Nevertheless, in his extensive writings, what is meant by class is more indicated by allusion than ever with care defined. Superficially, one is left with a clear-cut warfare between two classes, the owners of the means of production and those who do not own them and have been dispossessed. The idea is certainly not original with Marx. The origin of social evils, for Rousseau, comes with the claiming of 'private' property and adverse possession. Comments on the war of the rich and the poor will be found in Aristotle. Nevertheless, Marx also visualized a long succession during the centuries of ruling classes, each with specific characteristics but each, in the dialectic of history, replaced in its turn. Marx also recognizes, although more 'exploited' than 'exploiters,' a peasant class politically distinct from the industrial proletariat. There is, moreover, for him, a sub-political or recessive *Lumpenproletariat*. In brief, what Marx meant by 'class' varies with the occasion.

Contemporary sociology, in order to make an advance, has to assign more precise meaning to class, as a matter of social status and power, while not denying the importance of ownership and economic power—wealth—as well as of more patently political forms of industrial power such as the lock-out and strike. There is indeed today rather a tendency to see society arranged in an extensive hierarchy of 'occupations' (which is an objective and fairly easily definable term), each of which carries a certain status, by no means entirely replaced by free contract. Becoming a Senator of the United States may be a matter of election, but it is certainly not one of free contract—nor is becoming a banker or physician. These occupations still carry status.

The issue is not merely one of criticizing Sir Henry Maine's theme, in his *Ancient Law* (1861), of the transition from status to contract, or Herbert Spencer's transition from military to industrial society. Status, like the army, is still here. What interests the sociologist is the complexity of status. Berle and Means, in their *Modern Corporation and Private Property* (1932), and their successors, have shown that, even in the world of financial and industrial power, it is naive to consider the issue as simply one of owners *versus* non-owners. Effective industrial power may lie with a financial or managerial group, but legal title to the wealth and its ownership may lie with a collection of shareholders who have small effective power to decide and direct. A very few may legally 'own' a high percentage of the national wealth. But the further question arises: is this the same few, or another, as that which actually directs it?

Vance Packard, in his *Status Seekers* (1959), discovers in the America which has emerged from 'the Great Experiment' in equality, described by de Tocqueville, a hierarchy of five social strata generically, with special occupational sub-divisions, duly listed in accordance with gradings of respect. In Tsarist Russia there were about fourteen classes recognized in protocol. At the present time in the Soviet Union, according to Alex Inkeles (*American Sociological Review*, August, 1950) the sociologist can distinguish ten classes. That a new class system has emerged, and is in process of crystallization in the Soviet Union, is the theme of Leon Trotsky in *The Revolution Betrayed* and of Milovan Djilas in *The New Class*. It may be held that these are partisan books. Nevertheless, that modern Russia is a land of honours and decorations, where the humble soldier has less chance to mix with his officers than in the United States, cannot well be denied. The reward-spread by *average* of the classes is alleged to be greater in gamut than in the United States. In the industrial wage policy of all these societies 'differentials' matter and are fought for.

Indeed a 'hard-faced capitalist' might do worse than seriously consider whether he could not better himself by becoming a bureaucrat in a land of directed labour, no strikes, decreased income tax and increased indirect taxation, technological 'delivery of the goods,' and decorations to reward success. Much of the abstractions called 'capitalism' and 'communism' are stereotypes, legacies from a distant past, which require anew to be checked by empiric observations.

In Kharkhov the present writer was told that (as increasingly in America) the lad from the floor of the factory had little chance of promotion to managerial office, since efficiency demanded promotion through specialized schools.

The Russian and Chinese systems are tyrannical while claiming to be based on the will of 'the toiling masses'; but some at least of our present quarrels on economic methods (or that, philosophically, between Western agnostics and atheists in high places and the patriotic Russian Orthodox) are a beating of the air. Likewise, as to 'materialism' there is probably not a pin to choose, except among metaphyscians (but cf. *infra* p. 395), between East and West. All we can say is that the 'intention' may be different; and that Marx and Lenin, being strong anti-clericalists like the French Republican, M. Combes, chose to give a dogmatic atheist slant—Marx, of course, was wedded to his juvenile doctoral thesis on the matter—to a system which, in happier hands, could have been a 'Left Hegelian realism' of the Dialectic. The 'red professors' of Moscow are certainly less agnostic and probably substantially less atheistic than our current fashionable philosophers.

An interesting point, on the cultural aspect of society has recently been made by Mr. Richard Hoggart (*Observer*, May 14, 1961). Distinction by 'class,' he suggests, may not only be vague and currently misleading; it may also be definitely obstructive. The conventional distinction, he argues, is between the culture of the educated and that of the masses; but indeed it should rather be between a 'live' culture and a routine culture. We are left, then, as residue with substantial distinctions between, especially, occupations, economic strata, nationality, religious groups, and local, and other distinctions. (Cf. R. Bendix and M. Lipset, eds., *Class, Status and Power*, 1953.)

However, it must be added that Mr. Hoggart, almost certainly, to make his point about 'lively minds,' under-estimates the cultural differences in pattern of life *within* societies which, in matrimonial relations for example, sociologists have pointed out may be greater than *between* national societies. Cf. Lipset, *Political Man*, p. 120. This does not mean that, in some epochs, a more or less proletarian culture may not become fashionable throughout the entire society (cf. the rise of Christianity; the decade of Rousseauism before the French Revolution; the contemporary Angry Young Men) and reshape romantically its classical *mores*.

We may say with Packard: "Status is crystallizing; the boundaries between the various layers are becoming more rigid." We may deplore this. But also, while condemning anti-social prejudices and vulgarities in the chase for 'success' (which we shall discuss under the argument on Community), we may add, with him: "Status [? occupational *function*] distinctions would appear to be inevitable in a society as complicated as our own. The problem is not to try to wipe them out— which would be impossible—but to achieve a reasonably happy society in their framework." These are matters of ethical valuation, which we must postpone. That an increasing number of people in the West wish to regard themselves as 'middle class,' and to share typical middle-class wants and demands, as also that the 'middle class' itself may be dividing more sharply internally, seem to be warranted sociological observations. In the Far East we find an authentic proletariat, fertile, but uncertain even of the physical survival of individuals, so that sixty per cent of the human race lives on or below the Plimsoll line of hunger.

Democracy will or will not survive according to whether it does or does not supply the answer to wants by assuring a supply of the elementary goods. In the West, and especially North America, ever more may be becoming 'employees' compared with the free self-employed farmers—four-fifths of the whole—of Jefferson's day; but the effect of equalization would not be to make all their own masters but to make all, including university professors, into middle-class 'employees.' This mediocre status, however, being conjoined with economic high-life will not avert from them the envy of the proletariat of the East, *relatively* deprived, unless some sentiment of copartnership is engendered.

From the point of view of our preceding analysis we have to ask what effects social classes or stratifications have upon power-demand and upon political production. As we have said earlier, in chapter IV, the market changes with the emergence of new class demands, which general or local conditions and political rearrangements may make effective. The rarity of labour after a plague in an agricultural economy may lead to the relaxation of feudal dues. More purely technologically, the charge-hands in power stations or the operators in a telephone exchange or the skilled electrical technicians may, in a complex industrial society, be in key positions. It will enable them, as the Marxists insist, to give singular effect to their political demands. (The railroad men and miners, veterans of Socialism, may be technologically, conversely, in a declining position.) But *what* they will demand is a different matter. It may be the vote (of key importance to the American Negro); it may be a dictatorship; it may be higher veterans' pensions; it may be circuses. In some homes, in some times and places, a piano is a prestige symbol; in others not. The issue becomes that, not of the means in the political market (except for some authority to guarantee men much more freedom to have their wish), *but of the wish itself which shapes the goods in demand, within that market.*

However, there also then remains the technique of means. The market can be surveyed by astute politicians, aware of the respective class demands and of the numbers, prejudices, and stability of the different classes. A manual-worker group may have middle-class ambitions and effective demand. Why not? Strongly unionized labour may have a tradition or pattern of demand which may be keenly Socialist or Democrat. Nevertheless, the unemployed, whose demand is for the satisfaction of the moment, may be highly unstable supporters of long-range Socialist proposals. Within certain limiting borders the wants are not static but change—and, moreover, they can *be* changed. Here lies the task of the political salesmen, from the street-corner orator to the broadcaster, televiser, and Madison Avenue advertising man. This salesmanship may be criticized, in its methods and ends, in the light of moral judgements. Today, however, its existence is not a matter of morals, but *un fait social*: in Grover Cleveland's words, it is not a theory but a condition. In some cases it can be 'calculated,' and part of a financed campaign. In other cases it can be called 'emotive' or 'autonomous,' due to the normal tendency of orators—as Plato commented long ago—and of press-men to tickle the inattentive popular taste with exaggerations and headlines, and thus to 'project an image.' This lends itself to sensational and publicity-obtaining methods, if not indeed to riot and violence, instead of conventional democratic procedure, being resorted to by otherwise balanced and rational men, in order by a kick to attract the attention of a stolid, apathetic, and hedonistic public. It will be noted that, at this point, we have passed from the question of the individual or group will, and its available means, to the shaping of the wish itself. It is not an immediate matter of 'who commands?' but of 'what commands do I want given?'

The study of Public Opinion has rightly been a matter of much academic interest and attention since the First World War. Some of this, as by Arthur Ponsonby, Irene Cooper Willis, Harold Lasswell, and others, has been especially of propaganda which had produced such remarkable political results during that war. Some, such as Walter Lippmann's *Public Opinion* and Sir Norman Angell's *The Public Mind* (1926), had a more philosophic range. Yet earlier, Professor Alfred Venn Dicey had produced his *Lectures on the Relation between Law and Public Opinion* (1905) which was vigorously attacked by A. F. Bentley. (In classical days, when democratic legislation was by 'votes' or *psephismata*, the contrast scarcely emerged: the public opinion of the day was translated straight into the law. Nevertheless, rhetoric owes its rise to its influence, as propaganda, in popular assemblies and courts.) Reference has already been made to the studies upon the deliberate shaping of public opinion—or, more precisely, of the multitude of different group opinions—by advertising experts such as Mr. Stanley Kelley (*supra*, p. 139). The stimulating and most readable work by Vance Packard here again comes into prominence, especially *The Hidden Persuaders*. Under a democracy (A, B, or D) it would sometimes indeed seem that technical publicity is a necessary element, whether through the press, television or otherwise—a situation which gives a limited number of men great power. Earl Russell, the suffragettes, and many strikers have argued the desirability of calling the attention of a lethargic public by leaving an impression in its *corpus* where it hurts. So, however, have the fascists and Marxo-communists.

The social situation, then, is normally not one of a *single* ruling class or power élite. Even under the early rigid caste system of India, the power of the Brahmins was balanced by that of the warrior castes. There may indeed, in particular cases (as some sociologists have suggested), have been an interlocking and knit group of so-called 'power-élites' or, more frequently, a looser association of all those 'established' and of 'top' people, who are for most social purposes generally 'influential,' rather than actually 'powerful' in all fields. Power and prestige are not identical. Even so, there will be rival aspirants to power and influence. There is a danger here of exaggeration and of adopting too naively a crudely Marxist or 'conspiratorial' interpretation. That all men seek power is basic. That men seek influence and status according to a subtle social hierarchy, which varies according to time and place, is not denied—or that this is very important for the realistic interpretation of social conventions and their constitutional structure. Too much, however, of 'ruling class' theory looks at the market predominantly from the point of view only of the producer.

It is true that the political consumer always has to look to a few to produce. But these producers are plural. The greater danger of monopolies seems to lie, not in the absence of rivalry here, but in the excessive tendency of the consumers—not a new tendency at all, but one exaggerated by modern techniques—themselves only to ask for what the governing party, 'establishment,' or group eminently in control of press and propaganda, can best supply. The unsuccessful, especially, view with alarm that modern democratic elections have fallen into the hands, if not of Hitler's propagandists and of Lenin's *agit-prop* ('agitation and propaganda'), at least into the hands of advertising men, paid by commission on results. There is, then, a vast field of skilled political salesmanship, just as there is of industrial salesmanship.

Increased literacy should, theoretically, have greatly reduced in this century the suggestibility of the public; but appeals to emotion by new media seem more than to counterbalance the new education. The role of a so-called 'educated class' or 'educated democracy' diminishes as the very concept changes, of what is meant by 'educated,' away from its earlier aristocratic assumptions. *There is a Gresham's Law of Politics under which lower standards in political goods, which make small demands in costs and give much immediate pleasure, tend to replace those goods which give only long-range satisfactions—and do not 'give the public what it asks for'—at heavier immediate costs. What, however, we can prudently state is*: No REGIMES, THEIR MECHAN- ISMS APART, WILL BE STABLE WHICH DO NOT SUPPLY THE MASS OF CON- SUMERS WITH THE GOODS FOR THEIR PARTICULAR MAJOR WANTS; AND A PRIME METHOD TO ACHIEVE THIS STABILITY IS TO SHAPE CONSUMER OPINION TO DEMAND THAT WHICH ONE IS FITTED OR CONSIDERS THAT ONE OUGHT ON LONG-RANGE CONSIDERATIONS TO SUPPLY (Proposition 32). A Communist oligarchy, a bankers' regime, and a democracy of natural rights, checks, and balances, will each 'push' its respective preferred goods.

§iv. Parties

A Party is a specialized form of oligarchy of members, even if admis- sion may be cheap, or aristocracy of active workers. It may be defined as an association of men organized to pursue or promote a particular purpose or to procure the provision of particular political goods. This oligarchic character is especially clear in the case of one-party systems such as the Fascist and Bolshevik. Its function clearly indicates the importance of compounded, as distinct from simple, support. As indicated in chapter IV, a Party is an organization to achieve victory, by getting out the vote or support; by making that support persistent; and by rallying support even in other areas than the formal vote. A one-party system *precludes choice* (or at least permits no *organized* opposition to the official party); but it, as much as or more than the multiparty system, fulfils this political function which is as important under a monopoly as under a competitive system. It produces the formula of victory and negotiated compromise, so that even those who differ may appear to support the same thing and may agree to vote the same way. It obviates the awkward but recurrent situation under which the politician or producer Government, in order to hold the allegiance of one section of his or its supporters, has to alienate another section.

This is an observation which, since Disraeli, the Conservative Party of Britain has fully considered, but which both the Republican Party of the United States and even the Democratic Party have tended to overlook. Of course, in the States dominant balancing power may actually lie with the Southern Democrats, who *have* an alternative of supporting the conservative Republicans. This is possible thanks to slack national party discipline, so that Southern Democrats can, by seniority—thanks to being returned unopposed—still collect political spoils and key offices. Likewise the France of the Fourth Republic provided a comedy of parliamentary inefficiency because of weak party discipline. When the Party formula of compromise or articulation of agreement has been found, it must be adhered to, even by doubters who yet wish to remain within the organization. More exact definition in the formula might defeat its purpose and be divisive. Even direct contradiction will not be noticed, among believers, in the heat of the campaign. *Populus vult decipi.* This is what has been called 'the pragmatic approach,' or, by Franklin Roosevelt, "keeping the options open." However, the continuing search for a possible, yet not explicit, synthesis is compatible with bourgeois integrity. In the words of Roosevelt, "Let's concentrate upon one thing—save the people and the nation and, if we have to change our minds twice every day to accomplish that end, we should do it" (Schlesinger, *Crisis in the Old Order,* p. 455). Not least in the United Nations Assembly, the uses have been discovered of agreement by obscurity or equivocation. For this reason some prefer rather to organize support for 'personalities,' as in a football team, than for 'principles' which can later produce difficulties. Even this may be said heavily to reduce the prospect of any desired consumer goods being produced according to mandate, as distinct from entrusting the leader himself with 'a doctor's mandate.'

The party formula, indeed, should attract wide support. It does not follow that equal attention need be paid to all sections of the support. Ironically enough, in a close fight for marginal votes, provided that there is an adequate reservoir of keen and inexpensive workers, least attention (as has been mentioned) need be paid to those out-and-out supporters who have no alternative camp to which to go. The recent electoral policy of the Conservative Party in Britain has rested (very successfully) upon the formula that it can afford to ignore the 'Colonel Blimps' and Empire Loyalists who are unlikely to become Mosleyite. In the United States, Northern Democrats have spasmodically come around to the conclusion that the views of the South (which has few votes in the Electoral College) could safely be played down. The South will, it is said, not get a better deal from the Republicans. Politically, it is a dead-weight (except, hitherto, when it came to appointments). The validity of this calculation, the strength of the loyalty of the South to any Northern-controlled Democratic Party, remains to be seen. The political advantage of keeping seven or more States safely in the party fold before electioneering begins is a weighty counterbalance to any argument for straining loyalties for sake of a more consistent programme.

It can be argued that it is a better thing that electors should vote, even crossing party lines, for 'candidates of character'—perhaps voting differently in Presidential and State elections (cf. also Quebec)—than they should become involved in doctrines, dogmas, and pro-liferating so-called principles, which are more appropriate to a con-venticle or church of true believers than to a party performing its proper civic function of procuring, under democracy, for a people what it wants. Admittedly, the people may make foolish decisions about their interests especially in the field of long-range foreign policy; but, nevertheless, it is the people, the electorate, which has to be trusted, and not some self-elected élite. Dr. Kurt Hahn, the eminent educationalist, has remarked that the word élite "smells ten yards against the wind." It can, indeed, further be argued that the whole Party system and its machines are undesirable from the point of view of those who value a real working democracy in which every citizen is encouraged to take a share and use initiative. There is more weight in this argument than is sometimes admitted. The Party system can encourage a great over-evaluation of their own importance by 'active party workers' who, because they are voluntary, have to be kept enthusiastic. And its machine tends to crush out minority choices which impede its own work of achieving electoral (or dictatorial) victory.

Reference may here be made to the writer's "Political Parties: Democratic Instruments or Religious Conventicles?" *Contemporary Review*, October and November, 1961; and to Professor R. T. McKenzie's contribution. "The 'Political Activists' and Some Problems of 'Inner Party' Democracy in Britain," Pro-ceedings of the Fifth World Congress, 1961, of the International Political Science Association.

If the value of a party is that it expresses the transcendent convic-tion about ideals of some like-minded group, then clearly only a multi-party system, with as many parties as there are diverse social ideals, is satisfactory. The aspirations of the two-party systems, offer-ing an opposition, professional criticism, and a choice, are more modest—but perhaps better accord with civil politics. The confusion between Party and Conventicle is today frequent. On the other hand, if we do not accept the monopolistic dictum of General Charles de Gaulle—"The leadership of France belongs to those who are in charge of it. It belongs above all to me, and I say it without beating about the bush" (October 23, 1960)—then it is difficult to see how the free market is to be maintained, except through some Party Sys-tem which organizes viable political choices and marshals support for them. This specific and limited function does not derogate from the importance of Democratic Polls (including the electoral poll). There is a strong democratic or consumer argument for drastically reducing the importance of Parties, as potentially dangerous, as distinct from voluntary crusades for good causes, such as have produced the abolition of the slave trade, free trade, the enfranchisement of women, Prohibition, and numerous noble experiments.

The task is to obtain a producer who does not monopolistically impose his own tastes upon the political consumer, while at the same time educating a consumer who can admit that producer and salesman, if good, could have a more expert knowledge of the requirements to meet his needs than he spontaneously possesses himself. Whereas much public discussion has been given to the democratic system of the wide-franchise election, political scientists have spent inadequate time on the all-important process, in which the limited Party plays a decisive role, of selection of the persons of representatives. Even when the system of 'primaries' obtains (unkindly described by President H. S. Truman as 'eyewash') for purposes of selection, in practice Party and even 'machine' politics have played a major part. Patently the selection of the candidate, as distinct from the election of representatives of this or that Party (which alone is offered to the electorate), is of quite key importance if we are concerned about the personnel of the ruling body or group. In most constituencies in the United States and Britain the election is almost a foregone conclusion, as the simplest calculations will show; the selection equally certainly is not.

Representative Democracy is not the only or at all the most precise method of discovering the popular will in legislation, nor is the current method in Britain of choosing parliamentary candidates through a seven-minute speech a method of selecting executive efficiency that would be tolerated in any other field. It is a system under which the man with the aptitudes for patter and the insight into the minds of the public of a travelling salesman may be expected to win every time. Hence, as one British Secretary of State told this writer, the dominant characteristic of practical politics, as distinct from most other fields of responsible human activity, is the element of 'the fortuitous.' Decisions happen disproportionately by chance, luck, and demagoguery. This is a very grave charge indeed. It is perhaps the most unsatisfactory part, for a responsible democrat, of the entire political system. We are brought to the position that not only is all politics controlled by oligarchies but that, in one specific sense, Democracy (like the British Constitution) 'does not exist.'

The classical study of the history of Parties is that by Ostrogorski, taking an early step outside concentration on the field of 'legal government.' Perhaps, however, the most famous analysis is that by Robert Michels, of the University of Basle, *Political Parties*. The contemporary work of Professor V. O. Key, of Harvard, in his *Politics, Parties and Pressure Groups*, of Dr. Robert T. McKenzie, in his *British Political Parties*, of Professor Avery Leiserson, in his *Parties and Politics: An Institutional and Behavioral Approach* (1958), as well as the work of Sir Ivor Jennings, *Political Parties* (1960–61), are outstanding. Some of Michel's predecessors, whose thoughts he expounds, such as Mosca and Pareto, he terms "adherents of pessimism in sociology," and he concludes his own book by referring without dissatisfaction to "the cruel game," which he believes will have no end, under which oligarchy is perpetually and inevitably born from democracy and then uses the words of democracy to establish its power. This is, I submit, a highly coloured and over-sensational picture.

It was made clear by Aristotle and is patently true that the work of organization and administration, being specialized, can only be effectively carried out by a few. Not every one desires to be party organizer, a bureaucrat, or a civil servant. In this limited sense the paradox of J. J. Rousseau, in the *Contrat social* is, of course, right: "A prendre le terme dans la rigueur de l'acception il n'a jamais existé de véritable démocratie, et il n'en existera jamais." Great expectations, indeed, were once held out by the establishment of 'primary' elections by members of the political parties, with or without 'cross-voting.' This system has not produced the expected democratic 'machine-free' results.

Fuller examination of qualifications by responsible pre-selection committees, not only 'reducing the list' but taking their task conscientiously, although itself oligarchic, might constitute an improvement in the present amateurishness of government. It is, however, urged that, if not seven-minutes rhetoric before a delegate conference, at least a few minutes on television is enough to show the real quality of a man to all viewers. This may be negatively true. Industry, however, is not so casual in its method of selection. If industry or commerce were run, like politics, so that not only had the manager to be his own travelling salesman but the customers selected the managers or executive on the basis of their skill in patter and sales-talk, we should not get very far in economic progress. If the political field is taken to be (as it is) vitally important, then, instead of taking radical constitutional criticism (for example, of monarchy tied to a local established church and religious discrimination, or of parliamentary procedure or congressional rules) as a form of blasphemy, every decade or so we would be trying out new political experiments in method and testing the results empirically in the market. Incidentally, for such an attitude we should have the high authority among the Founding Fathers of the direct advice of Thomas Jefferson. These remarks are not to be understood as showing dullness of comprehension of the empirical importance of tradition and communal or public *mores* or cult, elsewhere stressed: their value has been demonstrated by time. What must yield is that not worth conserving.

Study of the functions of a Party (whether under the one-party, two-party or multi-party system) excellently underlines the theme that oligarchies do not operate in a vacuum apart from the consumer 'masses' or 'public' (here no distinction is drawn between these two terms, which are valuational). On the contrary, the wider oligarchy of the Party penetrates through to the local 'grass roots,' and is indeed designed to enable the producers of the upper hierarchy of politicians or of the bureaucracy to be kept aware of trends in consumer demand—as well as to persuade the consumer to accept and even to demand what the producer can, and desires to, produce. A government or hierarchy or union executive committee which loses touch with its people will as surely lose power as an industrial producer who loses touch with his market will go bankrupt. In this special sense government is "for the people" and even "by the people." As said earlier, a middleman or brokerage function is performed by parties. This holds true even of the one-party system. Oddly enough, it is perhaps least true of the multiparty system which claims to be most proportionately representative. Here the very variety of represented demands leads to compromises and agreements upon formulae at higher professionally political levels, and divorced from the electors' initial requirements. Thus, in the France of the beginning decade of this century, the majority of electors or largest single group favoured a policy both pacifist and anti-clericalist. However, the major party in the coalition representing this were more interested in delivering the goods of its anti-clericalism and, therefore, compromised for the sake of support with a minor faction whose views were more militaristic and were allowed to prevail in the field of French foreign policy.

The Party's valid and important task is to produce a market assured for the producer, while attractive for the consumer. In countries such as France under the Third and Fourth Republics (and, even more, Indonesia, where there were over forty parties, until a 'guided' system took over in the field of State elections), the parties may become rather concerned with negotiating for the goods of office among the producers themselves and having their trotters in the trough of spoils than with organizing and testing the largest vote. The party leaders are here rather preoccupied with the immediate rewards of being in office and engaged on production in collaboration with the established civil service, than inspired with any desire to challenge the long-range advantages of defeating all competitors for power in a general election.

It is the danger of a Liberal revival in Britain that, instead of the normal 'swing of the pendulum' between two major producers, it becomes possible for a minority party to remain indefinitely in power because the opposition, even if in a numerical majority, is broken between rival claimants. We may feel constitutionally suspicious of this without at all accepting Professor Martin Lipset's somewhat paradoxical thesis—however supported by Continental statistics or even

American experience—that the old-time Liberal (and supporter of laissez-faire for benefit of men of property) tends to turn into the new-time Fascist. Cf. my review of Lipset's *Political Man*, in *Contemporary Review*, March, 1961. Under the patently more monopolistic one-party system in the Soviet Union, where the Communist Party emerges as primarily a representative of the monopolistic producer and a persuader, scarcely even 'hidden,' of the consumer, it yet would appear to have to compromise about its monopoly with the army and the civil bureaucracy, including the police. However, under Stalin and even Khrushchev, it seems so much to have emerged as dominant partner as to be more collaborative 'producer' than public relations, support-collecting and selling 'agency.' The party members, in such a case, may share more than others in the benefits of power; but they pay for these goods, more than others, by the enforcement of the inhibitions of a rigid loyalty and of severe penalties for deviation.

Whereas the Party machine is the organization which imposes the formula, perhaps after complex negotiations appropriate for success, and sells the political product victoriously for the support of the wider consumer public, nevertheless the active party membership, just so far as it is itself an oligarchy to assure political production and 'the achievement of the programme,' and does not merely perform a brokering function, can notoriously acquire a mentality different from that of the average voting public and hence misleading to the politician. Perhaps few people are less representative of the democratic (A) average than the abnormally keen party worker who regards these party politics, not as a negotiation in government, but as a lay religion, whose very means are matters of absolute principles. The enthusiastic party optimists, with their rousing eloquence and rallying war-cries, may be convinced that the majority of the consuming public not only *ought* to like, but *does* like, something vastly different from what a poll would show to be the actual wishes and preferences. We have here indeed one argument despite all its defects—although of reduced importance granted adequate poll analysis—for the multi-party system, with its mutually contradictory enthusiasts, even where this is, at an election, selling not particular desired goods, but complex blocs of goods to the electorate for its choice. Only Pure Democracy would get rid of the middleman—although not of the executive and administrator.

The 'machine' tends to encourage, and even aims at securing, cross-voting when this will be to its advantage, although a potential majority party always has to consider whether it will not do better by 'scraping the barrel' of its own, normally non-voting, support. Hence, broadly, the 'machine' tends to be a moderating force, unless sure of a mass emotional surge, e.g., in times of national resentment, class resentment, or some particular campaign for redress and advance. To the extent that its role is important, it modifies the thesis of Senator R. Michels, endorsed by Professor R. M. MacIver (*The Web of Government*, pp. 216, 315), of a political party spectrum, running from extreme and revolutionary left to extreme and revolutionary right. The propositions are, of course, not contradictory.

The active party worker, left to himself, tends to regard parties as, not so much organs of government or of organizing opinion (or as a brokerage between the two), but as like church conventicles based upon faith (the delivery of the goods apart) and emotion. The 'active party worker' is nevertheless essential, with all his emotions and enthusiasms, if consumer opinion is to be cohesively rallied to demand this, as prior to that—even if the resulting practical package is often highly disappointing.

A party politician is a man who recalls that he is first a representative of those who may differ about almost all save the formula; and who will either speak to the formula or keep quiet. He will not, as party man, deviate beyond modest limits of individuality or impose unauthorized personal views. The honesty of politicians, as of lawyers, is often impugned owing to a misapprehension of their function. Under a constitutional system, such as the British, where Parliament shares in the executive work and responsibility, the views of Burke and Mill hold firm that they must, even to the limit of unpopularity, consult conscientiously their own private judgement. However, so far as the politician in a Legislative Assembly is regarded, in ideal, as solely the representative of the average or median opinion of his constituents, his task resembles that of a barrister stating a case for his clients, who is not 'dishonest' because he defends scoundrels or people of divided minds. Naturally, unless his approach is entirely professional, he is likely to do better if he is able to persuade himself that they are entirely in the right, a gift which, for example, Mr. Lloyd George had to a high degree. If he can persuade himself, like so many orators, that the public agrees with him, and then make them demand what he wants, his task will be still easier and his reputation for sincerity (or even fanatical loyalty) not in doubt. A clear decision will emerge from a semantic fog, which may disturb only the analyst and not the demagogue.

Speaking of Edward VIII, then Duke of Windsor, who expressed a desire to broadcast on issues of peace and war before 1939, the Right Hon. Herbert Morrison, now Lord Morrison of Lambeth, was reported at the time as saying: "If I agree with my Party on three points out of ten, and disagree with the remaining seven, I talk about these three points and keep quiet about the remaining seven. And the sooner the young man learns the same, the better."

That Parties are primarily connected with the production side, displaying political goods, rather than with consumer demand is shown by the fact that members are attracted to them as voluntary organizations, without many burdens and with some rewards or expectations, rather than regarding themselves, at least in their party capacity, as having especially, like ordinary electors, to pay the costs of new legislation. The One-Party governmental system is a striking illustration. It offers patent advantages in power to the active party worker. Often indeed Parties demand lower costs, and arise to press the cause of freedom. This can be to displace rivals in competition. A party man, however, as such tends to believe in what government (and his party in power) can do.

In the case of a One-Party system there is indeed, as in Russia, a nominal assertion that the Party is itself the producer, or 'vanguard' of co-operative producers; and that the State is a subordinate machine under control of its dictatorship. However, in fact the voluntary and church-like Party, with fanatical and crusading principles about 'what is right' (whoever wants it), tends to be brought under the practical discipline of the actual governmental regime, which has to be maintained in power, and is redirected to its functional task of rallying support for victory, and of keeping in touch with consumer opinion and warning of (and suppressing) danger. The fundamental distinction between Civil functions, affecting objective acts, and Church functions or 'ought' functions, with which those of a Party are readily confused by enthusiasts, will be discussed later. The consequences of the confusion can be grave.

As touching political statistics, it is alleged (although it seems to be most disputable) that, if a survey is made of place, age, occupation, financial status, and perhaps previous voting record, the vote of those surveyed can be predicted with a probability approaching certainty. (It is of course true that it is frequently easier to prognosticate the result of a political general election than the approach or depth of an economic depression.) This indeed raises a curious point of party technique, where the task must be to arouse enough interest to get out one's own party vote without arousing the kind of interest which, in a doubtful fight, could bring out the full poll of one's opponent.

It is anyhow desirable that more political statistics should be available, even if they need to be used with judgement, since (as Sir Ronald Fisher and Sir Roy Harrod have recently pointed out) it is only by such assemblage that one can constitute the basis for an inductive logic which will show 'mathematical likelihood.' Thus it can indicate inductively the probable course of particular events, as distinct from the deductive logic of general schematism, which begins with an hypothesis or *als ob*.

Without doubting that, in a developed culture, the political market will be a mass market, and while viewing the market as one of rivalry and accommodation both in the wants of groups and in the authorities that satisfy them, nevertheless one may feel that A. F. Bentley, in his analysis of parties in *The Process of Government*, although adopting a view comparable to that of Pareto, underestimates the extent to which "the interest groups of the masses" are shaped by (rather than shaping) oligarchies in possession of power, catering in their own way for demand, but still not widely 'representative.' Bentley verges towards a Tolstoian *mystique* of anonymous forces; and inadequately analyzes (except into an old-fashioned 'self-interest' and 'apathy'; cf. p. 444) those 'lower-lying interests,' upon which he relies so much. The theorists of Natural Law are more illuminating.

What Bentley does do is to emphasize the notions of 'intensity' and of 'persistence' of demand (as well as of 'balance'), upon which we have already commented. Both intensity and persistence are consequences of group organization which has this aim, although they may of course arise spontaneously. And honour should be paid to Bentley for his insistence, not least in his drastic attack on A. V. Dicey, upon the importance, in political science, of analysis of 'the political act' and of 'irregularities and tendencies,' instead of what, with Hobbesian brusque contempt, he dismisses as "ideal-stuff" and "brain-spooks." There is much 'pseudo-realism' in the work of Bentley; there is also much pioneering good sense. An atmospheric Marxism, smelling of the vintage of the decade of Sorel, is perhaps detectable, although not Marx but Spencer receives the greater honour. One recalls that the writing was in the period of Veblen and of Lincoln Steffens, himself, like Bentley, a journalist by occupation.

Sir Ivor Jennings, in his book *Party Politics*, vol. I, has been understood by some reviewers to argue that party membership can be explained in almost Marxist class terms, the Liberal Party deriving its membership from an entity called 'the lower middle class.' Apart from the fact that Sir Ivor is only concerned with the British (not, e.g., American or Canadian) statistical analysis, a careful reading of his important work shows that other factors play a significant role in 'getting out the vote,' not excluding ideas (coming, as in Marx's own case, from non-class quarters) such as those with provenance from the Fabian Society and from the climate of informed opinion. What, however, does emerge clearly is the extreme importance, for party voting, of 'the public image.'

Moreover, in a statistical study of immense importance (here confirming Catholic traditional educational theory as distinct from Liberal and intellectualist) Professors David Easton and Robert Hess show that this 'public image' is firmly impressed on the mind of future electors between the ages of three and thirteen ("The Child's Political World," Proceedings of the Fifth World Congress, 1961, of the International Political Science Association). However, even adults can change their mind, and attention has to be given by politicians to the *mana* or power of the 'public image' of the party. If particular pieces of unpopular legislation have to be carried, to symbolize the party programme as a whole a popular statesman will be put forward who will reconfirm the success 'image' and rally unified support, the business of politics being power.

The Party system, then, as distinct from Pure Democracy by plebiscite and poll, manifests the inegalitarian character of the political structure; and the importance of the role played by the intensity and persistence of wants, when reflected in organizational terms. Admittedly, this intensity and persistence, which can be organized socially, would probably be lacking if the wants did not spring from some 'urge' fairly 'low-lying' (to use Bentley's characteristically sardonic phrase) in the nature of man, although sometimes only effectively manifested in a particular market and in the character of particular men at a particular time with a particular nurture.

The Party is an oligarchic—or aristocratic, according to 'value-judgement' or 'mass-recognition'—organization of the many by the few, in order to join demand to supply and to produce more readily and efficiently the required legislation and regulations. It is a broker between Government, or any like producer organization, and the political consumer. On the one side its members feel, with the mass of electors, that 'something needs to be done.' On the other side, like an agent for producers, the 'machine' searches around for some new and politically rewarding 'issue,' some 'demand' which it can discover or induce in the electorate, and which it feels it can without too heavy cost (or need for support) gratify; or for a demand which well-organized groups of its members have an interest, public or private, in satisfying or pressing towards satisfying, as politically good business. Above all, it is usually felt that the demand, however treated, must not be of a 'divisive' character. IT IS THOSE WHO FEEL STRONGLY, ARTICULATELY, AND STEADFASTLY, AND WHO ARE CORRESPONDINGLY ORGANIZED AROUND THIS COMMON PURPOSE, WHOSE WILL IS LIKELY TO PREVAIL (Proposition 33), other things being equal, in a display of force or even of discussion, rather than those, however numerous, who want weakly or idiosyncratically and who are of uncertain opinion and demand.

It is such 'active' men which a Party first organizes as its solid core. And here the demand of one does not 'count as one,' but may be as decisive as that of two, three, or a thousand. It is important here to stress that the active party workers, some of whom are loyal citizens with an unusual degree of dedication and sense of political responsibility, some of whom are ambitious men and self-advertisers, and some of whom are fanatics or cranks, tend to think of themselves as 'the Party' but are unusually highly unrepresentative of the mass of the electorate. It is necessary not to be misled by the misuse of democratic terms; they are 'the few,' not 'the many.' The many may well be asleep: as was reported in a British by-election (1960), "Carshalton snores." It is the duty of a competent party leadership to recognize this distortion, while also recognizing the public functions performed by the limited band of loyal workers. We would again call attention here to the fundamental distinction between a Democracy *A* or *B*, comprising all adult inhabitants, and a 'democracy of an oligarchy,' i.e., a limited power-holding group (*C*), most of whom choose to regard each other as 'all equal in the cause' by reason of colour, class, doctrine, or pattern of living.

Whether this subjection of detached opinion, whether it be called 'disinterested' or 'idle,' or even 'sceptical' and 'tolerant,' to committed determination is a good thing or a bad, is a separate issue, depending upon our philosophy of the end to which the movement is determined. What one may say (with Plato) is that determination to 'evil' has to be met by like organized and active determination to 'good.' Unhappily it is usually the 'evil,' being individuals on the social defensive, who are most aggressively active about their ends and means, while others sleep, trusting in 'the God of Israel' that He will neither slumber nor sleep.

An interesting instance is to be found in recent British politics (Labour Party, 1960) of appeals being made to the elected Parliamentary Party to follow a policy line laid down by a National Party Conference of 1,273 delegates, mostly not parliamentarians, on the ground that this alone would be 'democratic.' (Trade union delegates had, in several cases, been instructed at their own Union Conferences *prior* to hearing the discussions at Party Conference.) A poll, however, (expressing the principle of pure democracy, if only by samples—and hence less than a referendum or popular ballot) indicates that, not amid the general electorate but amid the electorate voting for the Labour Party itself, five were opposed to this particular policy decision ('unilateralism') for every one supporting it.

The total active membership of the British Conservative Party is very generously estimated at three million, and that of the British Labour Party (which includes all Trade Union Members, active or not, who have not opted out and therefore pay political dues) is 6,436,986 (1958), of which, however, only 888,955 are 'individual members,' this in a population of fifty-two million. Three out of ten men (and four out of ten women) trade unionists actually support the Conservative Party.

Likewise, the active membership of the Church of England, by law established, sometimes indicated as being almost as extensive as the whole population of the country which it represents, is actually about five per cent. The active membership of Catholics in Britain (who are yet on grounds of religious discrimination excluded from the offices of monarch, consort to the monarch, Lord Chancellor, etc.) is about the same.

Under a Pure Democracy, parties (as already said) might be unnecessary in guiding the executive *boulē* or council of professional politicians or experts, which could be guided by mathematical graphs of polls on a chart. But, so long as they exist, all parties, even those of the widest membership, are by their function and resulting structure tinged with an oligarchic character and by a human interest in power. However, their pursuit of victory may be in the national interest and we may then call it aristocratic.

There is a danger in exaggerating the actual unity of Parties as of Pressure Groups. In Iceland the 'fishing interest,' pressing for a twelve-mile extension of territorial waters, has been internally divided between the keen 'small fishermen's' interest and the more hesitant 'trawler' interest. The extent to which the policy favoured by the left-wing of one party may go beyond that of the right-wing of its Left opponents is notorious. Incidentally the public may favour playing with both competing parties for office, and may view more with ironic satisfaction than with constitutional dismay having a Republican President balanced by a Democratic Congress or the reverse. It certainly illustrates a novel 'division of powers.'

If we accept Aristotle's very definition of a citizen as one who participates in jury or "judicial and deliberative office" (*Politics* 3. 1)— with a consequent more severely 'pure democratic' definition of Polity or Constitutionalism (Democracy *D*)—or accept the arguments of de Tocqueville, it follows (we may repeat) that *no* modern states are true democracies. They are rather qualified oligarchies or aristocracies of limited tenure, run by statesmen, politicians, and even advertising demagogues, who in congressional assemblies show great jealousy on behalf of parliamentary sovereignty, against all appeals to plebiscite or practical demonstrations of the permanent sovereignty of the people. The formal recognition of the plebiscitary function should be considered. On this indeed Rousseau commented, especially when he remarked that the British people was only free to express its general will at election times, every seventh or (now) every fifth year. Nevertheless, every party as broker has to allow, not only for the tides and fashions of popular consumer demand, but, under emotions of hope or fear, for its sudden uprush, for example, against excessive and destructive armaments or excessive lack of defence. As brokers, multiple and competitive—and, in a different way, monopolistic— parties perform a useful, and under certain systems a necessary, function. What they do not do is to perform the sole function, in estimating the market, which a pure democracy may require.

§v. *Propositions of Professors C. Wright Mills and Northcott Parkinson*

In this discussion about social science and specifically about oligarchy, Professor C. Wright Mills, in a series of books, including his *Power Elite*, has expressed distinctive opinions. On the one hand, he has repudiated the view that the social sciences should be concerned with control and prediction. Apparently this is done on the assumption that the prediction is alleged to flow from the specific act of control of some particular group—as perhaps, when Napoleon said that "to govern is to foresee." Napoleon may, possibly, have meant that he could foresee because he governed and found men to be 'highly manipulable.' Prediction here follows from detailed control by particulars of particulars. The sergeant can 'predict' what the squad will do. This is, of course, not the meaning implied in this book. On the contrary, one element in control is the frequent regularity in human behaviour, the 'patterns of government,' which *also* enables us to predict. Often then we can control in particular because we can predict conditionally, *als ob*, and in general: control follows from prediction. Nevertheless, in one passage of *The Power Elite* Mr. Wright Mills adopts the common-sense attitude that "the ends of men are often merely hopes, but means are facts within some men's control" (p. 23).

Professor Wright Mills appends to his *Sociological Imagination* a brief essay on English style and on how to influence people by it, which may explain his tendency to give punch to his arguments by exaggeration and paradox. Nevertheless, his own style is so far idiosyncratic that sometimes we are left in doubt about what precisely is meant. Thus there are references to what is called 'historic specificity,' with the apparent implication that no sociologist can safely make reference to human nature in general or to its characteristics. This argument is anti-humanist. Elsewhere, however, precisely such reference is made (pp. 171, 174, 193).

The theory itself, as well as the style, is idiosyncratic. Thus we are told (p. 135): "In our period, social structures [e.g., the Catholic Church, the World Bank and the United Nations, as well as the local club and my family] are usually organised under a political state. In terms of power, and in many other interesting terms as well, the most inclusive unit of social structure is the nation-state . . . all the institutions and specific milieux in which most men live their public and private lives are now organised into one or the other of the nation-states." There are here significant ambiguities between "usually organised" and "all . . . are now organised"; and between "social structures" and, "in terms of power . . . the most inclusive unit." There is an ambiguity in the author's own mind, coupled with a reaching after the arresting and extreme statement. "The history-making unit," we are told with a dogmatism reminiscent of Treitschke, is "the dynamic nation-state."

This is a statement, not of scientific assurance, but of a controversial nature which should rather challenge scientific exploration. "In our period," the social scientist might rather say that what is remarkable in Europe, Africa, and Arabia is the transcending of the old national state structure, which in Africa is largely meaningless and in Arabia has a quite different meaning from that in France and perhaps in Israel.

Indeed it is our author himself who, perhaps contradictorily but happily, corrects his *étatisme* by stressing human individual variety, and indeed altogether too much repudiates the basing of sociology on human nature by basing it, not even on nations regarded as entities, but on sharp 'periods' and local institutions and sometimes on 'worlds.' So separated out for attention are "Byzantine [*sic*] and Europe, classical China and ancient Rome, the city of Los Angeles and the empire of ancient Peru—all the worlds men have known now lie before us, open to our scrutiny" (p. 132). The reader must, then, not suppose that Professor Wright Mills is a chauvinist champion of nation-state power. Rather he adopts this vivid view, just mentioned, because it best fits in with his alarming conception of a conspiratorial inter-locking, at the national level, of military, industrial, and bureaucratic powers, by which he wishes to make our flesh creep. The nation-state must be regarded as all-powerful (this meaning 'having dominative power') and inevitable because a bogeyman, who was *not* powerful and inevitable, would not be nearly so good a figure in romantic drama.

Professor Mills presents himself as in the advantageous position of speaking for 'classical social theory,' with its old-world prestige. No one wishes to be unclassical. It is like being unscholarly. The locally accepted theory of American democracy, he argues, presents, on the contrary, "images out of a fairy story." The United States is merely a "formal" political democracy (rather as Professor Max Beloff told the assembled Liberals that contemporary Britain was "a police state") and, even so, "the formal political mechanics is weak." At the top there is "organized moral irresponsibility"—a saying not destitute, as we shall see, of a certain if very partial truth—which is only to be corrected by a "public" (as understood in Mills' sense), distinguished from the dumb "masses" by the fact that it will follow Professor Mills in "answering back." It has been stimulated by the right social scientists into having "sociological imagination." The mills of God, one gathers, usually grind wrongly; and most of the common run of social scientists have a spongey professional morality, little above the current "organized" immorality. If they do not actually conspire with the generals, industrialists, and bureaucrats to sow the seeds and causes of the Third World War (*vide* the author's book of this title), they yet are either extremists indulging in a pretentious 'grand theory' of futile abstractions or are one-track-minded would-be scientists engaged in the study of sterile and microscopic statistics about the trivial, like Dr. Kinsey on sex. Professor Mills, we are given to understand, here occupies a moderate and alone sane position, with classic stance, in the middle.

Professor Mills is scarcely in the classical sociological tradition of Comte, Marx, and Spencer, or in the behaviourist school of Bentley, although (however 'rumbunctious,' to use James Meisel's phrase) he may be in that of Max Weber. He may indeed be termed, in his general approach, Marxoid—since he would probably not wish to be called Marxist nor would the Marxists so call him. Indeed, he is rather, as I have said, in the American tradition of Veblen and (still more) of Lincoln Steffens and of the tougher 'muck-rakers.' It is admirable that, with Mills and Trilling, we should give our attention to 'the sociological imagination' or, again to 'the liberal imagination.' It is perhaps not quite so admirable that, with Burnham and Mills, we should give our attention to 'the élite,' since the idea itself is vague and unsatisfactory.

The trouble is that the tradition of Steffens, with all its moral rage and social satire, has itself about it an odd futility. It is more noisy than profound. Our attention is drawn to an intimate and horrible spectacle, the colours well painted in—a species of national 'Peyton Place.' Our human indignation is invited (by what, in this book, has been termed 'pamphleteering,' such as certainly provokes counter-pamphleteering). Nevertheless we are, at the same time, professionally assured that sociologists will see this unhappy development as almost inevitable. The 'masses' are themselves irresponsible and hopeless. However, the power-élite is worse. It could look as if the answer might lie in exploring some kind of authentic aristocratic principle—but this would, in turn, be contrary to democratic values. The common man and the common woman are our hope; but they, it emerges, are pretty common and ordinary—even (in the slang of Mark Twain) 'ornery.' We find ourselves, as it were, amid the rockets' glare of disasters.

As practical men, our imaginations made tense, we ask for the remedy. What should we do about this pest of political irresponsibility? The reply, however, of Professor C. Wright Mills (*Sociological Imagination*, p. 176) is that he "does not know the answer." There is a moral dilemma. And so the social scientist is advised to "get on with the work." He should, we are told, cultivate reason, and even discuss great "issues." But then so should every liberal man. We have a feast of imagination. But it ends in a nausea. "Democracy is a complicated idea, about which there is much legitimate disagreement." This surely is so.

Later in this book it will be suggested that the exact diseased nerve of the society of our period and place—which we must judge in the light of a wider humanism, such as is yet effectually denied by the historical relativism of Professor Mills' philosophy—is not either the moral irresponsibility of the few or the corruption of the despised 'masses' (Marx's *Lumpenproletariat*) but precisely the nihilistic ethic to which Professor Mills, in common with many of his contemporaries, uncritically commits himself. "What a man calls moral judgement is *merely* his desire to generalise, and so make available to others, those values *he has come to choose*" (italics mine). The altruistic or garrulous desire for what is sometimes called 'trans-communication' (when is it not 'trans'?) may be generous of him—but there is here no test of reason about it. It would seem to be about as much a moral judgement as whistling, which gives pleasure at least to the whistler. Caprice is king.

It may be appropriate, at this point, also to mention one other social scientist who is as fond of laws as Professor Mills is against them—Professor Northcott Parkinson. Perhaps he also is distressed by the impotence of professors of social science—who are, after all, not elected persons. The way out, indeed, of this impasse (which certainly troubles Professor Mills) through party activity was assuredly not found to be useless in the cases of Woodrow Wilson and even of Harold Laski—although Lord Attlee comments of the latter that he had "no political judgement." Anyhow Professor Parkinson also has found the use of literary techniques helpful in expounding *inter alia* his theory of élites. Any political scientist acquainted with the work of that great humourist, Stephen Leacock, will see the force of this.

It would be unkind to suggest that a Rochefoucauld might have chosen a better instance of the circulation of the élite than the official entertainments of colonial civil servants, where (we are assured) the superior guests leave early. (This discourteous habit, which surely is only to be found at the level of 'organization man' as distinct from polite society, Mr. Packard alleges is also shared by American college deans.) Professor Parkinson has himself to thank if a reputation for frivolity has clouded the influence of his wit. Indeed his 'law,' which has an authentic general quality of some real importance, which the theory of Professor Mills repudiates, remains unbased and 'in the air.' Nor has Professor Parkinson been entirely fortunate in his subsequent more ambitious work.

Parkinson's law is frequently so stated, as a disease of increasing expenditure on men and material, that it can all be summarized in one word, waste—a disease that for centuries has affected all enterprises with an inadequate system of accounting; with, in governmental matters, inadequate Treasury control of the purse; and of which Defence requisitioning departments have always been notoriously guilty both in buying and selling. Thus merchants dealing in army disposals are able to make considerable fortunes. A recent British newspaper headline runs: "Ministry sold £19,000 gun parts for £26" (*News Chronicle*, 29 February 1960). As the length of British navigable canals decreases, the number of officials engaged in their management has been found to increase. The Corps of Engineers, however, in the days of Kitchener's Sudanese campaign, being of high morale, was proud of conducting itself on opposite principles.

Further, as a corrective of this 'political Boyle's Law' of restrictive practices to the effect that lazy men tend to protract work 'to fill all available hours of employment,' empirically it can be pointed out that Governments tend (at certain levels) to pay low wages, even if this involves taking on employees of lower calibre and more idleness than would be tolerated in competitive industry—hence further adding to the drawbacks of bureaucracy. The scientific advance is not made by giving a name to an old scandal but by an interesting analysis of how and *why* men do not allocate work to personnel, but increase personnel and then expand, like gas in a new container, the work. This is an authentic phenomenon of the quest for prestige, influence, power (and higher salaries and honours). It is sometimes significantly called 'empire-building.' It may or may not be accompanied by solaces to national indolence or by 'feather-bedding.'

We can yet systematically restate the law. "ALL MEN, EVEN BUREAUCRATS, HAVE AN APPETITE FOR POWER, WHICH, *ceteris paribus*, GROWS AS IT FEEDS; AND NO MAN WHO HAS THE CHOICE BETWEEN CONVERTING A SUBORDINATE INTO A POSSIBLE RIVAL AND MULTIPLYING SUBORDINATES, OVER WHOM HE REMAINS MAGNIFIED AS MASTER AND ARBITER, WILL READILY CHOOSE THE FORMER. HENCE ALL BUREAUCRACIES, BEING JEALOUS OF POWER, TEND TOWARDS GROWTH IN PERSONNEL. (Proposition 34. This can also be cited as Catlin's Thirty-fourth Law . . .) It is a particular consequence of the interest in maximizing power. Equally obviously, those in control of other people's wealth will (subject to professional rules and public enquiry) be disinclined to curtail the blessings of expenditure so long as the fountain of supply continues lavishly to flow. It would seem to be unappreciative of public bounties. Also, as a protective device, bureaucracies tend to rigidity of rules, since their power is collective and of the office, whereas a dictator tends to contempt for rules since his ends are highly personal and to them he masterfully adapts his means. A high bureaucracy even when efficient typically is marked by the conservatism of the Byzantine epoch, whereas a petty bureaucracy is timid, sterile, stultifying, and odious.

In summary, however, of our digression in discussing these two well-known social scientists, we may conclude that the use of literary techniques as a route to influence tends to have results ephemeral, disappointing, and to be avoided. It ends in pamphleteering.

§vi. *Aristocracy and Equality*

Aristotle, in his list of political categories, describes one as "the rule by the many for the good of the whole." This category is simply called *politeia*, which can (as we have said) not inappropriately be translated as Constitutionalism A, whether it be of an altruistic majority alone or of a 'mixed constitution.' It must, further, be emphasized that Constitutionalism B which can guarantee any kind of rule from that of the Emperor of Japan to that of the People's Republic of China ("having an established constitution") is not the same thing as the specific use of the Constitutionalism C, in the sense of 'containing fundamental guarantees.' Incidentally Aristotle, it will be noted, in his discussion, comments upon the advantages of an aristocratic ad-mixture (*Politics* 6. 9) in the working of constitutional systems. Nevertheless, in his actual definition of *politeia* there is no intrusion of the idea of some limited number being put into a position of influence. The many are themselves inspired by an altruistic ambition for good citizenship.

The Aristotelian *politeia* A may, then, not be the same thing as that Democracy D, which we discussed in the last chapter and which, in contemporary usage, is sometimes called Constitutionalism C. The majority-will here, however altruistic, is negatively inhibited—some would argue in a conservative fashion—by certain specific Natural Rights or traditional civil liberties and rights of individuals—and the claim of the whole to be democratic rests upon respect for these rights (including veto rights) of each individual equally. It must always be remembered that 'government by consent' in effect spells 'government by the consent of some people.' Since an organized minority can impose a veto—not to speak of the constitutional use in the United States of such defensive techniques as the filibuster—there is an oligarchic colouration as distinct from the principles of straight and uninhibited majority rule. But, further, within the constitution in many cases there are positive aristocratic or oligarchic elements (such as the Supreme Court) which impose a constitutional restriction on the majority will, whether or not inspired by civic altruism. The Cabinet system, the Party system, Parliament and Congress themselves are among such elements. Indeed Bureaucracy can clutch the popular will as serpent folds did Laocoon.

The 'Sovereign Parliament' itself has some of the qualities of an exclusive, if elective, club. Constitutionalism, then, in the modern sense as distinct from the Aristotelian, in so far as it is maintained by institutions manned by men given functional power and authority, involves the existence of elements which we may specifically call 'aristocratic.' A few are constitutionally given powers (not by the majority of the time, but under the inherited constitution with its own system of change and amendment) for the actual advantage not of the few but allegedly of the whole.

It will be noted that, for example, in the case of sentences in London on Blake, *alias* Bihar, and others for spying, it has been suggested (*Observer*, May, 1961) that the sentences imposed by the judiciary (by making them cumulative and not concurrent) should not exceed the length intended under conditions of penal reform enacted by the legislature. But the notion that, 'democratically,' the judiciary should be elected has never been accepted in the British system as distinct from that of some American States.

We may conclude that, broadly, Democracy D is in fact a system of mixed constitution in which the aristocratic element is perhaps subordinate but is still fundamental. We can put the matter laconically by saying that the Anglo-Saxon peoples enjoy, not Democracy, as they suppose, but Constitutionalism. However the British system, despite Cabinet and Party oligarchy, is in principle more democratic, as touching its constitution, and less restricted by written limitations, than the American . . . More soberly stated, Democracy D requires that, amid the actual claims of all consumers in a free market, the established claims of each consumer for some purposes shall be publicly guaranteed and given proper priority. This guarantee is assured, in the United States, by the Supreme Court. To the theory of Aristocracy we must, therefore, now turn. It involves issues in human civilization so recurrent and profound that they can never successfully be evaded. Nevertheless, in recent decades they have received far less attention than they deserve.

Professor C. J. Friedrich, in his *Constitutional Government and Democracy*, writes: "by definition, a constitutional democracy is one which does not grant *all* power to the majority." Against the view taken above, de Tocqueville (*Democracy in America*, p. 182), clearly referring to what we have called Democracy *B*, writes: "The very essence of democratic government consists in the absolute sovereignty of the majority." Discussing the safeguarding of Natural Rights, Professor Spitz very justly writes: "The appeal to democracy remains an insufficient solution to our problem. We cannot say that the remedy for oppression is simply a return to democratic principles, for the very people who are guilty of oppressive acts often commit those acts in the name of democracy itself." (*Democracy and the Challenge of Power*, p. 108) However, Professor Spitz, in discussing guarantees and alternative routes, rejects what he calls "the never-never land of what they choose to call aristocracy" (p. 134).

Philologically speaking, no government could be better than that which is, by definition, 'the rule of the best.' The alternatives would seem to rely upon (contradictorily) substituting 'equality' as the highest social excellence to be achieved, or in denying the importance of excellence itself. 'Excellence' also, by its philology, indicates something ahead of the ordinary and not the possession of all. It is something to be achieved by choice. Continually it raises its sights. Aristotle, contrary to the view of some contemporary writers, connects the democratic stress on the principle of absolute equality (not that of 'equal things to equal people' or—with the Marxo-Leninists—'to each according to the degree of his service to the community') with the democratic stress upon personal freedom, in the sense of some absolute, metapolitical and individual quality, as test issue. Especially Democracy, for him, stresses the freedom of each man equally to act on his personal opinion (*doxa*), equated with knowledge (*epistēmē*); and emphasizes the repudiation of any political authority based, not on representation or delegation from 'the common man,' but upon alleged superiority in knowledge or excellence. Aristotle recalls to us the old technique of the lot (but not that lot of birth utilized for selecting the peerage) as the most logical method of assuring strict equality.

A political scientist, it may be added, professionally must beware of the kind of error of which Aristotle himself was guilty. Every commentator can point out the strange blindness of the great philosopher in regarding the structure of the *polis* as too sacred and full of communal values for radical criticism, at the very moment when the Macedonian hegemony of his own pupil was superseding it. Likewise, because the free democratic world can regard equalitarian democracy *A* or *B*, and free opinion, as so valuable and even beyond criticism, it may decline to consider the possible improvements of a mixed constitution and, especially, of educational leadership. It may do this at the very time when, perhaps within fifty years, the whole world might be destined to be given over to the ideological, political, and military triumph of 'fuller' Democracy C, which is called in the West the 'totalitarian' or Bolshevik variety of Communism. No political form whatsoever should be regarded as above criticism or improvement. What matters is, at the same time, to avoid a sterile cynicism and to be dispassionately clear about the virtues of the system under discussion.

In practice, the perennial problem of Aristocracies has been (a) to arrive at agreement upon what constitutes 'the best'; and (b), supposing we have arrived at adequate agreement upon this, at least as touching the time and place if not absolutely, then how to obtain enough support for 'the best,' i.e., enough for it to remain on the market, with support in specific power or in effective influence. The very maintenance of standards to which an aristocracy as such is dedicated arouses psychological resentment in the name of freedom. A third difficulty (c) also commands attention. Assuming that we took seriously the attempt to discover 'the best,' would it not be philosophically true that these would be the kind of good men who would insist on 'sharing power' and on mutuality; and who would decline for themselves, in state, church or indeed industry and unionism, *any* position of exclusive or preferential rule? Would they not be, more than Franciscans, a kind of political Congregationalists or Quakers, insisting on the real equality of men and (to speak in theological terms) 'the priesthood of all men'? Or would they, with Plato, find a motive for rule, as elect, in the determination to keep the worse and the profane out? The problem of Aristocracy is inextricably interlocked with the discussion of the meaning of human Equality.

We shall clearly make no advance here, and only end in verbal confusions, unless we first make precise our terms. By Aristocracy neither Aristotle nor Plato meant, and we do not mean, the rule of the rich. This will become abundantly clear. Such a rule is Plutocracy and, by both writers, is usually rather associated with Oligarchy and perversion. The poor may sometimes be such because they are idle and spendthrift; but also they may be sometimes such because they suffer from simple loyalty to the ties of their families and other duties or moral scruples and are not greedy for profit. The rich may sometimes be such because they are shrewder and more industrious, and sometimes because they are luckier gamblers, luckier in picking their parents, or more efficiently unscrupulous. There is no detectable constant correlation between wealth, ability, and social duty or what Aristotle calls 'virtue.' However, as Aristotle dryly observes, "since virtue is rare," many aristocracies are but a name for the power or, more exactly, rule (*archē*) of "ancient wealth." Here there is a deliberate contrast with "new wealth" and with the *nouveaux riches*. A pattern of behaviour and a legitimatizing respect are indicated. As Professor Lipset has said, an old aristocracy is often a liberal (or at least Whig) one. But this usage brings us closer into accord with that, in history, which has applied the title 'aristocracy' to the landed or noble 'interest,' into which an earlier military or knight rule has been converted. This is, again, explicitly not the sense in which we shall here use the word.

The argument for and against a peerage and monarchy is a different issue. We shall indeed have to ask whether, where titles are still conferred and a 'fountain of honour' still flows, public recognition of public service by titles of honour—such as also continues vigorously in the Soviet Union—is or is not relevant to the establishment of an authentic aristocracy. As to recent years, we have to make our own judgements whether, for example, the members of the Communist Party of the Order of the Red Banner are an aristocracy, concerned with the human and actual good of society; or an oligarchy, concerned in the establishing by any efficient means—or with the maintaining in power—of their own regime or that of their associates. The word 'aristocracy,' however, will be used here precisely in the sense of 'the rule of the best,' presuming that they are discoverable. This clearly involves a valuation; and, from this point, considerations of Political Philosophy, to be defended later, will have to be introduced. Nevertheless factual propositions can still be usefully discussed on the level of Political Science. As one passes from Political Science to Political Philosophy it is logical and appropriate to make valuations. As, however, these valuations may be attacked as prejudices, it is important and honest that the writer shall announce his valuations or prejudices in a fashion clear and explicit.

The persistence of Aristocracy rests upon popular or adequately widespread acceptance of the belief that certain men possess superior gifts which are politically relevant. This is balanced by a belief which finds expression in the word 'under-privileged,' a word in current use which, by its very form, is of high psychological interest. The implication is that *some* men have had *special* advantages ('privileges') to which others have no access; but that now more or all should have these advantages of civilization which yet shall continue to be special or outstanding, that is, to be achieved by special dynamism and endeavour. Older terms were politically offensive since they implied a static or stratified position of never achieving these desired social plateaux. These beliefs raise, along with the principle of Aristocracy, the issues of the principles of Equality and Status. Plato maintained that many inequalities or (more precisely) dissimilarities, such as the colour of the hair or sex, were politically irrelevant. They had nothing to do with the measurements relevant to the issues under consideration. Whether inequalities are by nature or are gains seized upon by ability (granting here equality of opportunity in nurture), is an issue not necessarily decisive as touching Aristocracy. Whether by gifts or by will, some men, it may be alleged, are better. We still have to ask: better for what? Aristotle, as we have said, defined Aristocracy as superiority of virtue, which is usually regarded as being a matter of choice and nurture. Nevertheless, what has to be borne in mind, at the beginning of the argument, is that the thesis of Equality—whether this here means that human beings are equal or at least that they are undifferentiable for all practical purposes of politics— and the thesis of Equality of Opportunity are not only not the same; they are *contradictory*. They may share one magic common word which pleases. If men all began as equal, it would be pointless to provide them with equality of opportunity in order that such as were unequal and superior in ability might, with unjust social restrictions removed, find the level which their qualities merited.

As is often the case when theorists, strongly attached to a position, are hard pressed, evasive semantic tactics come to be adopted. It may indeed be alleged that nobody ever held that all men were equal in the first sense; or, with Professor Paul Weiss, we may argue the more parodoxical theme than that they are indeed "equal, but not similar," i.e., equal for the matter in hand, which is what has to be shown. The former proposition, however, is merely not true. When Jefferson drafted the statement in the Declaration of Independence that it was self-evident that "all men are created equal," it is reasonable to suppose that he meant just what he said—and moreover proposed to collect in his support the full propaganda advantage of his statement. (It is true that at other times and in diverse places he did not say the same thing.) He had indeed added "and independent"—but the assembled Founding Fathers at the Philadelphia Convention had seen to it that this was cut out, as too patently *not* self-evident. That any child of man is *born* independent is flagrantly untrue.

The Declaration was made in consonance with the Lockeian theory of the child's mind as *tabula rasa*, like a clean sheet of paper unmarked by 'innate ideas.' There was here no Platonic 'recollection' and no heredity. Inequality came as children were taught to conform to this status or that, and subjected to the statecraft of despots. Fundamentally, however, all titles of distinction were, as the poet Burns sang, only "the guinea stamp"; and the plain man was fully man as much as his neighbour for all his clothes, titles and "a' that." When the French Revolutionaries at the beginning proclaimed *égalité*, they "in that red dawn" did not just mean "equality before the law." When the Revolution was over the view was to be changed. They meant what they said according to the plain meaning of words, which certainly had their political magic and power of bringing support. The sole question is whether what they said was true and in what sense.

While the complexity of inheritance is allowed for, so that it is well recognized that the offspring does not inherit, by primogeniture or otherwise, the bloc characteristics of the father—an idle male illusion—no animal stock-breeder believes that animal stocks are 'equal' in the qualities for which they are bred. Quite the contrary, as very drastic regulations show. It is odd that many natural scientists, who are ardent Darwinians and stress the animal and simian inheritance of man, are yet markedly anthropocentric and reluctant to apply the analogy of their arguments in the human sphere. The extremism of some eugenists has perhaps checked them. It is, however, refreshing to find an eminent biologist, sometime chairman of the board of the London Communist *Daily Worker*, Professor J. B. S. Haldane, writing: "In a scientifically ordered society innate human diversity would be accepted as a natural phenomenon like the weather" (*The Inequality of Man*, 1932, p. 23). As Sir Julian Huxley remarks in *The Humanistic Frame* (1961, p. 24): "Our new idea-system must jettison the democratic myth of equality. Human beings are not born equal in gifts or potentialities, and human progress stems largely from their inequality. 'Free but unequal' should be our motto, and diversity of excellence, not conformist normalcy or mere adjustment, should be the aim of education." Huxley's statement here goes beyond that in the text. What we have to condemn is the common, even if inarticulate, belief: All men are mediocre, and if they are not they ought to be. We may, however, also cite the significant remark, be it regarded as platitude or challenge, of Lenin: "talented men are not born by hundreds."

Recent biological research, while not excluding the possibility of deliberate interference with the genes, causing plasticity (and new inequalities), has tended rather to emphasize than to diminish the importance of dissimilar *biological* inheritance. The natural scientific trend is against equality as a dogma. This would be emphasized, in some ways, were it to be shown that there can be inheritance of acquired characteristics. What is false is the inequality, not of individual stocks, but of (ill-defined) races taken *en bloc*. This is so far discounted by contemporary social anthropologists that today they decline further to discuss the theme, dismissing it as unprofitable, despite its continuing appeal to some post-Nazi leaders. Even where differences of intelligence by race have apparently been statistically verified by psychologists, further studies by biologists have shown that this could be explained by inadequate nutrition.

Often the differences are cultural. Thus, at one time American intelligence tests showed unexpectedly low indices for North American Indians and Chinese. Further sociological research showed that their children had been brought up in customs of reserve and to regard it, unlike some New York East-Side *gamins*, as 'bad manners' to answer promptly in a style then approved by the intelligence testers. Two 'whites' or 'Nordics' may easily be more intellectually, physically, or morally dissimilar than a Caucasian and a Mongol. Authentically hereditary blood groups do not divide by colour of hair, eyes or skin—but these last differences are, of course, the most obvious to 'the man in the street.' To the Chinese the 'whites' are 'hairy red barbarians.'

It would appear that, biologically (and from the point of view of the human race as community), the most desirable thing would be entire racial miscegenation, as in Brazil, on the basis of uninterfered-with choice, except in the case of a few stocks so pre-eminent from the generality that, according to known principles, as well-bred they should be also in-bred. Experiments might be made here, in breeding for intelligence, physique, beauty, musical or mathematical talent, absence of hereditary melancholia, and (more difficult) general ability. It is quite unproven that some human types, for particular purposes, may not be superior; or that one could not breed types.

It may indeed truly be said that man is not solely animal, and has an intellectual and spiritual inheritance. As touching *mental* qualities, as measured by intelligence tests, the educational expert, Sir Cyril Burt, attributes twenty per cent of the difference among men to different early nurture and eighty per cent to hereditary factors. "The inequality of two brothers [in intellectual ability] with the same ancestry is on the average about half of that of two men taken at random." Admittedly general ability, like general intelligence, is more difficult to assess than specific abilities, in which the differences among men are extreme. Except among the most extreme predestinarians (who speak of 'the sin of Adam,' inherited alike by all his descendants) and those who emphasize externally communicated grace to the exclusion of all else, there has never been much doubt about human *moral* inequality, although stress on choice has tended, especially among Americans, to make this too much rather a voluntary matter of enterprise, with only occasional stress upon the unequal curse of 'bad seed.' And in the field of enterprise can the drone and the worker be held to be equal?

There are in the world—and among our electorates—really quite remarkably large numbers of people who, without being certifiable, have been or are potential inmates of mental hospitals. In England one person in a hundred is feeble-minded from birth. The *very simple* concept has immense hypnotic power, and such people are peculiarly liable to be affected. They can, for example, be hypnotized by the slogan, 'Keep Britain White,' whereas its apparent corollary, 'Keep Africa Black,' would startle them, did they reflect about it. (Cf. W. Sargant, *The Battle for the Mind*, 1957; and in this connection, Eugene Kirkhead, *Why They Collaborated*, 1959.) Whole nations, as we have seen, can be swept by mass hysteria which approaches mental instability, and even the leaders of great peoples, not only in Europe, seem sometimes to verge on the certifiable. The mental powers of the average British inhabitant, according to Professor Burt, is that of a child of about eleven; and there is no reason to suppose American citizens to be in any better case. So good a democrat as President James B.

Conant, of Harvard—although here unequal nurture may play an important role—separates out the student population by capacity into 3 per cent of high intellectual gifts, 15 per cent academically talented, and 82 per cent of others who are neither.

IT IS DANGEROUS AND DISHONEST TO FOUND A PROPOSITION IN POLITICAL SCIENCE, OF MAJOR PRACTICAL IMPORTANCE, TO WIT, UNQUALIFIED HUMAN EQUALITY AS DISTINCT FROM THE ETHICAL IMPERATIVE OF HUMAN FRATERNITY AND PARTNERSHIP, ON A DEMONSTRABLE FALSEHOOD (Proposition 35). To put the matter bluntly, human equality, however much used as a catch-phrase by politicians in pursuit of support, is a lie, even if to the envious or jealous a flattering lie. Black men may sometimes be superior and yellow men have always felt themselves to be. To insist that "they are all men" may be of immense importance; and we shall discuss this in the chapter (chapter VII) on Community. But to say here that 'what is really meant' is to call attention to the great values of Equality before the Law or of Equality of Opportunity or of the fraternity of the Human Community is, in the context of the present argument, an evasion. The Marxists here, as was emphatically stated by Stalin, are far clearer-minded than the bourgeois democrats. "Are Marx and Lenin right or are our bourgeois democrats? I say that Marx and Lenin are right." Accuracy is not merely a virtue; it is a duty. The argument of Thomas Hobbes, against Aristotle, that human equality rests on the equality of gambling chances in physical prowess, the weaker opponent of a seventeenth-century Thrasymachus perhaps having superior ability to draw a quick stiletto on a dark night, an Iago to his Othello, must be regarded as frivolous—although that sardonic philosopher could well perceive that it was flattering to human vanity and to all the Calibans. Further, inequality is not simply a matter of clothes and money, a depravity or flourish in the world of wealth and fashion. It may be true that "the rich are different—they have more money." This is not what here is under discussion. The rich may be the vulgar, if not the *vulgus*. Conversely, however, there may be the easy belief that every man could be a genius, if he wished to be, or that good manners consist in "keeping back with the Joneses."

We can, however, follow another route, supported by the authority of Plato, by saying that, when discussing politics, we are discussing equality *ad hoc* to political requirements, where differences of sex (for example) as of colour of the hair are irrelevant. Aristotle indeed distinguished common judgement from expert political or strategic knowledge. However, the rest of Aristotle's argument does not lead one to suppose that he regarded information or intelligence, among his ideal peasant farmers, as irrelevant to sound judgement. Within the genus *homo sapiens* there are different degrees of *sapientia*. This matter is of certain practical importance in administration. Plato certainly did not think that his citizens, of whatever kind or sex, could be exempted from the discipline of a carefully planned political training, even were they 'golden-born' enough to be apt for it. Size, sex, and colour as such may be politically irrelevant, but it does not hence follow in logic that there are no inequalities that are relevant.

A difficulty, however, arises which goes to the heart of the matter. Assuming that men are unequal, by what principle (and what method) are we to choose the politically better? In the first case, it may be found easier to decide how, and by what principles, we are to reject the humanly worse. On analysis it will be noted that much of the literature on Equality, and much of the political movements for its realization, have been rather *protest movements* against what was held to be a false and pernicious inequality, which gave superior status and power, without any beneficial political function being performed. It was the French nobility of the *ancien régime* (not lacking generosity at the eleventh hour) and it is the Italian nobility of today—and not only the hangers-on of Hollywood or the hoodlums of Brighton—of whom we are told that they disgrace themselves by the decadence of *la dolce vita*. There is a recurrent connection between 'high society' and crime, well known to sociologists and political students, wherever the former, like the latter, is governed by the principle of quick success. As Plato argued, plutocracy or the rule of the rich as such lacks any ethical or social justifications (since it has no direct correlation even with ability, much less with virtue). It is merely a historic fact of power, of frequent occurrence; and the best arguments for it will be found in the philosophy of laissez-faire or in the (more dubious) argument of Lord Hugh Cecil that we should not aspire to correlate the mundane order, shaped by law, and the moral order. Thus, it appears from this argument, in a satisfactory correlation there is no reason why a Diana Dors or her earlier husband (of whose life we have been told in full for cash) and a Winston Churchill should not receive the same rewards.

Even in the case of ability in private enterprise, we still have to ask, 'Enterprise for what?' Likewise resentment against specific inequalities may be aroused when a landed nobility claims privileges when it has ceased to provide military leadership or civic or social service of a beneficial kind; and has become merely a court-society, or what is today known as a café-society. Against this is developed the ideas of Equality under Law (so important, for example, for the Negro in North America) and of Equality of Opportunity, which latter we have yet emphasized is a notion *contradictory* to 'Equality' in the sense that it is affirmed to be a self-evident truth that all men are "born equal."

Lord Hugh Cecil, in *Conservatism* (1912), remarks: "The State never expressly nor by implication has contracted (in the supposed case) to save the man from starving. It breaks to him no promise, for no promise has been made (p. 173) . . . to estimate the true worth of services is altogether beyond human capacity." (p. 183) In his book *Equality* (1931), which has become a classic, the burden of the argument of Professor R. H. Tawney is not only that *any* differences of financial reward have no adequate social justification (on which *vide*, ironically enough, Karl Marx *contra*, in *The Critique of the Gotha Program*, 1891). Tawney also points out that marked difference of economic strata is spelt out in our society in scandalous differences of medical aid, of health, of inches of stature, and of life expectancy, even within one island such as Britain, as between rich and poor, *so that a schism emerges in the community* and, in the warning words of that great Conservative, Disraeli, "two nations" arise. Cf. also T. V. Smith, *The American Philosophy of Equality* (1927), and the writer's *Principia*, chapter VII.

The outstanding reflection here is that reward is based neither upon the social indispensability of the work in a full labour market *nor* upon rarity and individual civilized social value as with a starving painter or poet. It is based upon rarity of accepted supply, as with a pop-singer or members of other professions in relation to demand. Since reward is inevitably not without effect upon social standards, the result is a vulgarization—except where it is checked as by that puritan aristocracy manipulating the dictatorship of the proletariat which the Communists know so well how to develop.

It can be argued that we suffer today in the West from what could be denominated a shoddy adolescent Elvis Presley or Diana Dors culture, commented upon by Thomas Griffith in his *Waist-high Culture* (1959); and that this plague arises from specific views about social equality and about that particular kind of indifferentist democratic pattern which accords with it and is thought to justify it. A not uncommon species of 'payola' capitalism battens on it, following the easy profit principle. It can be argued that, when Plato satirized this pattern centuries ago and made a prophecy about its consequences, he was right. It can be suggested that historians have always tended to take these symptoms, since the days of Sybaris—or Sodom—as the certain signs of decadence in a civilization. We can find a standard of taste being set, not only by what sociologists might statistically separate out as the lowest social strata, but also by the richest and most licentious. We can find adolescent singers and singers for adolescents being paid ten times the salary of a Supreme Court Judge, and, in Britain, five times that of a Prime Minister or Archbishop. The phenomenon is not limited at all to North America. We can yet find a hill-billy singer and actor being elected, in 1960, Governor of a Southern State on a segregationist campaign. The election was presumably upon the basis of human equality (white) and not of the relevance of his acting or crooning to political success. In the words, however, of a past Republican President of the United States to this writer, the cause of the bitter racial hostilities in parts of that country may arise from economic jealousies and (I quote) "from the poor white trash."

It is possible to arrive at a civilization where men's minds are dominated by advertising men, explicitly concerned with appearances and rigged effects, not truth; and where men's conduct is a mixture of desire for the moment's pleasure, only restrained by social timidity and individual greed. The maxim of conduct may be set not by reason but by the passions and be that which was given by his mother to Nero, *Si libet, licet* ("If you want to, why not?"). 'Anything goes,' according to the Australian slogan. Men commit murder for publicity; and criminals sell their memoirs for substantial sums and find ready buyers. The most atrocious convicted murderers on parole threaten their critics with libel actions. Men change their wives, under our contemporary Western system of serial polygamy, as often as they change their registered dog licences, up to ten times or more, with the sanction of the law itself and, moreover, under the patronage of civic officials. The State looks after registration and then calls it solemnization. The newspapers can be shown to stimulate juvenile delinquency but, on the plea that they 'give the public what it wants,' they continue undeterred, provided that their circulations are increased. Detectable resemblance between economic reward and social service is absent.

It may be replied that excessive reward for the entertainment profession is as old as the Roman Empire or earlier; and that popular actors have always been paid more than professional nurses. For that matter prostitutes have habitually been paid more than priests. It may be said that "the press must be free," and that "the public must know" and is entitled to its coloured pictures of underworld life. So also television must be free so far as the commercial advertisers will pay. The connection of civil politics and crime, and of commercially successful literature with calculated pornography, is not new. All that is being said above is that common men in their wants prefer passion to reason; and that this bit of devilry is what makes the world alive. The Devil is a metaphysician, and himself a cultural necessity. The great French sociologist Durkheim discoursed upon the pattern under which the genius and the criminal both alike tend to be law-breakers. Each age thinks the following generation scandalous, and is found by historians itself to have been scandalous. But the answer is not satisfactory. It is too facile an answer to those who demand more social equality in protest against differences anti-social and scandalous.

There is what may be termed 'the politics of Nature,' which has its bearing upon attempts by deliberate biological control to separate out the better and the worse. It is usually avoided by party politicians, since it assures no votes and is too disturbing. It decides that the specific natural resources of a country, and even of the earth, are limited; that the water level may fall or rivers (despite the promises of politicians) change their courses; that, under certain circumstances of abuse, deserts creep in where fertile land had been. One item in the political problems set by Nature is the population problem. The ancient pagan Greeks had no doubt that it was part of the business of the *polis* to control population, whatever the individual might think, supplementing nature. Here yet they may have been wrong, since the Greek peoples died away in sterility. In human competition, as in animal, what breeds survives until maybe the whole human bee-hive will hive, under pressure, off to another planet. Lord Samuel, statesman and philosopher, in a recent statement (*Sunday Express*, London, January 24, 1960) discoursed upon the present immense untapped resources of the planet—where anyhow the population per acre of the Netherlands is higher than that of India and the birth-rate of the United States higher than that of Italy, and where the Chinese are opposed to restriction. The opposite fear, however, has been expressed that the more affluent peoples of the world are enjoying a recklessly too high standard of living and are improvidently using up natural resources. Legislation to prevent individual artificial control is, of course, also political control. Indeed, the debate may not be so much about control, including abstinence, as about *means* of, and *selection* in, control.

Professor J. C. Flugel in his *Man, Morals and Society* and Professor R. B. Cattell both suggest (as for that matter so does the Encyclical *Casti Connubii*) that more attention should be given to eugenics, from which we should not be deterred by the excessive optimism of some early eugenicists. Almost all birth-control propaganda ignores the consideration that those will heed it most who should, by standards of human racial advantage, breed most and that those who will practise it least, unless made easy and pleasant, perhaps in sugared pills, are those who should breed perhaps least, being indifferent to the maintenance of standards and their prudencies. Mathematically the future of the world would seem to lie with the Chinese to the elimination of the Catholics—although which (when different) are more admirable cannot be discussed here. The rearrangement of family endowment schemes or even taxation might be of aid. The great danger of coercive state regulations, interfering with all free will and preference, were horridly indicated under the Hitler regime: one murdered or sterilized one's political opponents. But public financial inducements might serve, if heritable delinquency could indeed be scientifically proven, to eliminate the 'bad seed' and the breeding of some, just as today legitimate marriage is, in some countries, forbidden to those having heritable diseases.

Already, in Madras, vasectomy is being officially encouraged, with financial rewards for those males operated upon. However, in China, with its 600,000,000 population and 1,700 hourly increase, since food production increase stands in a 9 to 2 relation to population increase, such population control is officially discouraged. It is part of the 'politics of Nature' of which the control is complicated by the politics of man. (However, some of the world's most brilliant figures have at some time suffered from diseases, conditionally heritable, such as tuberculosis, which a routine-minded medical profession might decide, without discrimination, to eliminate by law. Psychologists with a departmental concentration upon producing everywhere 'adjustment to normalcy' might prove an even greater menace to all genius and aristocratic personality.) It is needless to say that, unless the bribe were large and the policy prudent, the pursuit of such a policy, "to eliminate what some call the human trash," in the ancient Spartan fashion, would be likely to produce violent protest from the 'undesirable.' It could only tentatively be embarked upon until our medical evidence was more conclusive than it is at present about what is undesirable. It could be a ready tool of racial, national and political animosities. If the future breeding of stock were placed in the hands of a committee of artists and biologists, who would be confident of survival? Likewise, medical men must not practise without degrees, and perhaps politicians should not either—but who shall examine?

The new Columbus exploration of the century is likely to be in the field of heredity, in its relation to chemistry, and into the nature and determinants of the human brain. Here the medical profession can come to hold a frightening power in reshaping character. When we know more, the biological elimination of 'the worse' (so decided by objective test and general consensus) may be easier. For the present we have to continue with caution to ask: who are the undesirable? And are the 'unwanted' those whom wisdom, as distinct from hardness of heart, would not want? And are the pitiful and merciful "the salt of the earth" and the true elect and aristocrats, being considerate to the meek, and resolute to put down the powerful from their seats?

§vii.   *What Do We Mean by Aristocracy?*

At this stage we may turn from discussion of the elimination of the worse and undesirable, to the encouragement of the desirable and even excellent. From its very philological derivation and definition, as we have said, the excellent is not the ordinary. Our first problem is to discover whether, granted there is such a thing as 'excellence,' we can at all agree upon what it is in which 'excellence' consists. As Mr. Aneurin Bevan, sometime British Minister of Health, observed (House of Commons, February, 1958) about members of 'another place,' their Lordships would not suggest that they could be bred in exactly the same way as pigs. Sculptors may have some agreement about physical beauty (it is arguable) and, if we were breeding for physical beauty, doubtless Zulu, Malay and some Amerindian stock would rank very high—just as Negroes are outstanding, saving the American national reputation, in the Olympic Games. It is, however, more usually argued that an authentic aristocracy should be selected according to intelligence. There are yet difficulties.

General intelligence and specific intelligence for this or that function are different. Again, political ability, to handle the relations of human beings, and intellect are also different. As the Cardinal de Richelieu says, in his *Maximes d'Etat*: "Il n'y a rien plus dangereux pour l'Etat que ceux qui veulent gouverner les Royaumes par des maximes qu'ils tirent de leurs livres . . . Il y en a qui sont fertiles en inventions et abondans en pensées, mais si variables en leurs desseins, que ceux du soir et du matin sont toujours différens." One can name today British politicians of high intelligence of whom this is true. One is left, then, with the more difficult task of the selection of ability. Nevertheless, it may not be so difficult as is generally supposed and (assuming acceptance of the word according to the usage adopted here) there is indeed probably a substantial measure of agreement concerning who constitute the aristocracy, and what constitutes excellence, in the various vocations. What has yet to be recalled, as of key importance, is that they are indeed various. In the words of President Conant, in a Harvard address: "*Every honest calling, every walk of life*, has its own élite, its own aristocracy based on excellence of performance" (italics mine).

The test, then, of a wise theory is that it should require that respect be paid to each one of these excellencies, although an assessment has to be made of their bearing on, and significance for, the life of particular communities and indeed of civilization. It is improbable that the ordinary man, worker, or peasant wishes to be told that he is, without further effort, the equal of everybody else, or that his freedom does not have to be earned in terms of how socially he proposes to exercise it and to use his power. The trade unionist is not likely to be last in insisting upon the importance of wage differentials, in relation to responsibility. It may indeed be true that the trouble with the ordinary man is that, being governed by passions, he is not nearly sufficiently dissatisfied with his own ordinariness. Nevertheless, in however many cases it may be true that he can be flattered, he is yet not at heart deceived by such false democracy or demagoguery. What he wants is to be valued in terms of a *partnership*, where he is not a solitary and insignificant atom; and to be assured that, according precisely to the excellence of his contribution, he will be received and recognized. Public recognition is relevant, so that justice is seen to be done.

In the pursuit of excellence (rather than of happiness), it is frequently suggested in certain schools of thought that the democratic objective should be the development by each man of his full powers. The view of Mr. Archibald MacLeish about each man expressing what is 'the-truth-for-himself' has already been mentioned. This so-called 'American Proposition' reiterates a philosophy which, for the few, displayed itself during the Renaissance and was profoundly unchristian. For the many it logically ends in the assertion of the absolute right of, for example, the inhabitants of a township significantly called Demopolis, Miss., to assert publicly their detestation of Negroes exercising what the Attorney General of the United States holds to be their constitutional rights, on the ground that "this is what they believe," and that this presumably is 'the truth-for-them.' The bad influence of Kant (who also consigns the material-social world to the realm of determinism, egotism, and power) is probably at work here —not indeed in Demopolis, but with Mr. MacLeish. In this matter Marx and the Catholic Church are probably more similar in outlook than either are with Voltaire, himself a writer in a French tradition which had exacting standards of correct taste. Voltaire, at least, was far removed from the 'nature boy' philosophy of Rousseau.

Professor David Riesman, in his well-known *Lonely Crowd*, laments with his associates the perversity of people who are ready to shelve responsibility and to accept either tradition or 'heteronomy'; and exhorts them to desert bad mass-habits and to do as they ought by cultivating 'autonomy.' However, it is a grave difficulty in the argument that what is here meant by the 'law' or *nomos* in 'autonomy' is not developed, nor what is to be here the precise role of reason. Apparently it is all 'self-evident' like the adjudications, according to Protestant divines of the last century, of the conscience or private judgement. Professor Riesman does not even offer us, with them, the comfort of the allegedly 'plain word of scripture.' It is noteworthy that both Rousseau and Bentham rest such argument for equality as they offer on sentiment and feeling. "If you prick men, they bleed." If the deduction is made that, the rights of men (and animals . . .) being founded on their feelings and passions, not their reason, they have an equal right to demand freedom for the expression of these and for the satisfaction of wants shaped by them, then the conclusion is dangerous. What, however, has to be admitted is that philosophical aristocracies have competing views of what constitutes 'the rational' and of how wants ought to be shaped. This will be the problem of our last chapter.

One may agree with de Tocqueville (*Democracy in America*, p. 196) about "the courtesies of democracy," that "they assure [the plain man] that he possesses all the virtues under heaven without having to acquire them, or without caring to acquire them." Good manners, if they are exceptional, may be regarded as 'superior 'and objectionable and hence become bad manners. One Texan had the brilliant idea of lassoing President Eisenhower during his Inauguration Parade; and did it . . .

The motto, *aei aristeuein*, as involving that urge to the uncommon upon which human civilized advance rests, may become an 'unrotarian strangeness,' which stamps those who are 'not good fellows,' i.e., are 'bad fellows.' Cf. on this Professor David Riesman's discussions, in *The Lonely Crowd* and in *Individualism Reconsidered*, and the admirable satire in Mr. William H. Whyte's incisive book, *The Organization Man*. A neat criticism of what he terms Professor Riesman's "internal gyroscope" and an incisive general commentary will be found in Mr. Thomas Griffith's *Waist-high Culture*. "Equality is a trait we preen ourselves on, and when we violate its spirit we practice a careful hypocrisy, but I think we are its servant more than we know and more than we should be. Equality requires a closer look." (p. 177) "The dominant economic groups, which are in their own fields something of an élite, do not seek to erect standards for our society but set their course towards trying to please opinion." The 'aristocrat,' in this limited psychological sense, is the person whom, for better or worse, the totalitarian State cannot assimilate, except by the bribe of, as in Russia, putting him in its own privileged class (which is both large and without equalitarian pretensions) . . . It can, however, also liquidate him—until he re-emerges in the persons of his successors—as (such is the nature of the human spirit) he certainly will.

George Santayana, in his *Dialogues in Limbo* (1925), causes Socrates to ask: "Is there an intrinsic dignity in the freedom of a blind man when the degrading restraint exercised by the dog or the child leading him is removed, and he walks over a precipice?" In this Dialogue, the Stranger confesses, "Of course by self-government we do not mean the government of self." Contrary to the dictum of Campbell-Bannerman that "self-government is better than good government," the questionable conclusion here reached is that good government or "what e'er is best administered" is always right government. Moreover, Santayana argues, the skilled as ex-cellent (by the very philology of the word) are always the more rare and extraordinary and are, by definition, not the majority. The assumption is that we already can know *how* the self ought to be governed and *what* civilly is good government and the outlines of the agreed public philosophy.

Further, it will be noted that here the claims of the consumer to *choose* his goods are overlooked. To take Plato's instance of the physician, his professional prestige is determined not by popular election but by his compeers; but the patient (whether Plato admits this or not) has the right to change him if he distrusts the regime. Similarly with the manufacturer of goods, unless there is to be monopoly. This consumer right springs from each individual's basic desire for freedom and power; and issues in 'equality before the law' in 'a fair market' and in the convention, as touching support, of 'one man, one vote.' The individual, as a rational being, has to be persuaded about what is good, even when his reason accepts that his mentor is rationally in a better position to know. The alternative is the anti-rational domination of coercive force, not co-operative power.

It may be indeed argued that broadly approved aristocracy, rather than majoritarian democracy, is the most enduring form of tyranny. James Mill, in his essay *On Government* (1814), a classic in the school of Philosophical Radicalism, wrote, speaking of the middle class, of "that intelligent and virtuous rank . . . to whom [the poor's] children look as models for their imitation . . . as that portion of the community . . . of which the opinion would ultimately decide." The virtuous, who were the fully intelligent (who were the educated), were the guiding liberal aristocracy. Despite its obvious class naivety, a kernel of truth may be here, picked up again by later writers. John Stuart Mill, in his work *On Liberty*, with his deep suspicion of the domination of the original or initiating 'first-rate,' as bearers of the values of civilization, by the bureaucrat or the majority, by the routineer or mediocre and 'second-rate,' does not substantially alter the thesis about an *educated* democracy—and about the role of 'the educated' in control—save that he rather casts it in negative and self-protective terms. In the later words of Mr. Gladstone, "the principle of the Liberal Party is trust in the people, qualified by prudence."

The unspoken and uncritical belief here is that an agreement about what is meant by being 'educated,' and that the claim of the educated aristocracy to guide, will not be challenged. "Opinion must be enlightened," said George Washington. Education, not being part of the amusement trade, is aristocratically determined by its own inherent requirements. And one may, of course, say with Dr. Arnold Toynbee that the task is to give the people "the best possible life." But the question haunts us: what is that? And who decides what it is? The educated will show. They will show 'prudence' about what is good for other people, what goods should be provided and what wants gratified. This belief is, however, qualified in the case of John Stuart Mill and his successors by confidence in what is called 'the grand debate of democracy' and in an indefinitely prolonged and even endless discussion, in the course of which a supposed objective truth, it is hoped, will be sorted out. And, as arguments go, three logical arguments or thirty will be better than one . . .

Attention may again be called to the discussion by de Tocqueville (*Democracy in America*, pp. 6, 136). The vigorous criticism of liberal democratic assumptions by Professor Andrew Hacker (*American Political Science Review*, December, 1957) should also be noted here. On Mill's argument about interminable discussion, the comment is relevant of his biographer, Professor Karl Britton (*John Stuart Mill*, p. 105): "Here, surely, we do well to call nonsense by its name: to claim to be right is not the same thing as to claim to be infallible . . . It is not a question of absolute assurance: no public debate, however long-drawn-out, can provide that."

It may yet be urged that decisions should be reached by *all*, if they are of mature judgement, at least of the 'public' as distinct from 'the masses' (it is assumed that we agree upon what is meant by 'mature'); and that, to this end, we should train people in the full exercise of these powers and judgement. The wisdom of the outlook of the Enlightenment is frequently here cited. It is, on the contrary, very dubious (a) whether this loaded distinction between 'the public' (of whom I approve) and 'the masses' (about whom I entertain doubts) is valid: and (b) whether it is all so simple about what is 'maturity' and—as seem to have thought most of those sociologists who have followed in this popular philosophy—whether it is simple *what* 'powers' should be exercised, and whether a preliminary training and discipline is not required. Wilhelm von Humboldt and J. S. Mill indeed talked, in the style of Goethe, about the "full development" of men's powers, adding that it should be "into a harmonious whole." The exponents, however, of this philosophy should bear in mind the remark of Goethe himself: "What thou hast inherited from the fathers, acquire it and make it thine." A mature culture inherits a discipline.

It may be replied, however, that what is needed is that all men should exercise their private judgement. It is usually added that what is meant here is "a responsible judgement." A miraculous and all-wise conscience apart (and it will later be shown that intuition can indeed be instantaneous), 'responsibility' would seem to imply objective reason and information. We come back, then, to the need for the individual's deliberate training in these two. This will be the basis for judgement upon right behaviour. May it not yet be said that we have an agreed criticism of right behaviour in an advanced society, in that it conduces to respect for 'the dignity of man'? We shall comment on this when we come to discuss the nature of man and Natural Law. It need only be commented here that little precision seems to be exercised in the use of the term. It may be said that a Zulu or a Mohawk, a Spanish peasant or an Irish fisherman seem to display far more innate awareness of the natural dignity of man than most of the 'organization men' in a highly modern, technological, and commercialized civilization where one hears most about it. The dignity of man is not something automatic but, like the 'freedom' which is the 'self-discipline' of the philosophers, of Spinoza and Montesquieu and Kant, is something that has to be achieved, maintained, and cultivated.

While, therefore, we may and perhaps should applaud increasing Equality of Opportunity for the more able to develop and show their superior powers—the 'graduates' replacing 'the gentry' in the lead—the notion of an 'aristocracy of the educated,' a 'diploma élite,' or 'an aristocracy of intellect' presents greater difficulties than might be supposed. To put the matter bluntly, the highly intelligent are not liked—and there are good reasons why this should be so. The notion of 'the gentleman' (unless defined, as by Sir Thomas Smith in the sixteenth century, as one "who does no work") and of *noblesse oblige* is tolerable, but Confucian discourse on 'the superior man' is harsh to the ears. One sign of a superior man may be in singular imaginative understanding of his fellows, which yet in part must rest upon a shared experience—not that every surgeon has to undergo an operation, or every judge commit a crime, but that they should know what operations are about and why sociologically crime occurs. Even the undoubted ability and public spirit of Lord Curzon was unable to counterbalance the defect in him of what (to those who did not know that he was a man in constant pain) seemed an arrogant sense of superiority.

We revert to what we said (in chapter III) about pride. In the words of a Pope of the late classical period, St. Gregory the Great, the doctrine of inequality springs *ex fonte superbiae* ('from the fount of pride') which is the nub of the original sin of us all and of all nations, everyone. From it springs arrogance, contempt, and malice. There are indeed profound moral inequalities; but it is unwise for men, disregarding what they owe to a grace which is not theirs to command, to make judgements in their own favour. THE DOCTRINE OF EQUALITY IS NOT A SCIENTIFIC DOCTRINE OF HUMAN BIOLOGY, BUT IS FUNDAMENTALLY A RELIGIOUS DOCTRINE OF FRATERNITY, CONNECTING INTIMATELY WITH THE NOTION OF COMMUNITY AND WHAT WE MEAN BY IT (Proposition 36).

§viii. *Fraternity, Community of Values, and the Aristocracy of Influence*

If we, by hypothesis, wish to preserve a community, inequalities must be functionally justified in its interest, and equity and equality under the rules must be observed in giving satisfaction to the members. Further, it is contrary to the general moral judgement of mankind to suppose either that intelligence alone is entitled among all human qualities to be picked out for pre-eminence in respect or, still less, that the ability which displays itself in the pursuit and worship of the 'hot dollars' of success is functionally so entitled. Too often the highly intellectual gather together into arrogant cliques of mutual admirers. The highly intelligent and articulate, on the other hand, devote their talents, in their clubs and associations, more vigorously than most men, to the promotion of purely egotistic or narrow interests which, with the skill of briefed barristers, they know excellently how to defend. It is, again, the clever scoundrel who is the most dangerous scoundrel. This species of intelligence and ability is different from the concept of human excellence, in which reference proportionately obtains to skilful craftsmanship, artistic vision, the qualities of the admirable human character, initiative, rationality, saintliness, humility, and mercy—the development of which enters into the criterion of the good community itself, as well as fulfilling a rational function in it. To this concept of excellence we shall return in the final chapter.

Discrimination and inequality assessed upon the basis, not of ability, intelligence, character, and culture, but solely of colour of skin may seem obscene, and the sociologist will note it as especially a lower middle-class and proto-fascist phenomenon. Oddly some people, relying upon their private sectarian judgement and in defiance of that of the Holy See, can maintain that the constitution of their country will be that of 'a Christian Republic' and that they have Biblical support. Granted indeed their suppositions of private revelation, it is not of course possible to prove them wrong—or that the earth is round; or the prophecies of Joseph Smith and other Latter Day Saints excessive. The ordinary axioms of argument lapse. It is not possible, for that matter, to prove that local 'patterns of life' must not be elevated to moral standards, superior to criticism. This is also precisely what current anti-rationalism and moral relativism or nihilism seek to do. Here 'fundamentalist' and sceptic can shake hands. In the case of Bruderbond or K.K.K. neo-Nazism, it will be noted that it differs from Hitlerite racial Nazism in this respect that, whereas Nazism sought to persecute and abolish a minority, to wit, Jews, neo-Nazism seeks to persecute and abolish a majority, to wit, Negroes, unless prepared to accept permanently second-class citizenship and *Baas-kap*. It is proper to add that by no means all Nationalists in South Africa in any sense accept this view, even if they may advocate some form of 'Bantustan' development, perhaps with a multiracial Union Parliament.

As a matter of common sense we can in fact reach a considerable measure of agreement about what constitutes an aristocracy in the precise sense used here. We do not call in a physician to advise on house furnishing or an interior decorator to advise us on our health. But there will probably be a large consensus, first in their professions and then among the public, about who is an outstanding physician or an outstanding interior decorator. The issue is: what bearing has this upon politics? We can probably, even here, reach a large measure of agreement in a sane society about what human wants patently should be gratified and what particular ones, in the judgements of physicians, psychologists and moralists, spring from a diseased imagination. And, *in dubiis*, we can agree that a variety of opinion should be heard. We may have a very shrewd judgement about who is competent to express it, so that we become better educated in our wants and ends. Here indeed we must distinguish between the roles of the expert, professional, and craftsman who can tell us within a limited field fairly precisely what will provide satisfaction for our wants, and that of the philosopher (unless he regards himself merely as an analytical technician), not least the political philosopher, who should be able to suggest to us with weight the priorities and synthesis of our scheme of wants and satisfactions and hence to aid *in shaping the wants of the market.*

One consequence might be to educate men in the importance of civilized *manners,* as well as of economic *securities.* Perhaps the *Analects* of Confucius should be made required reading in all schools. In the expressed views of Mr. Justice Frankfurter, "morals are three-quarters manners" (*Felix Frankfurter Reminisces,* p. 12). If indeed all men were entirely equal, there would be no need for education. There is yet in many quarters an intelligible feeling that such teaching would produce obsequiousness, servility, and flunkeyism. Patently every maxim is capable of abuse; and, that "manners make man" can be twisted, as Bentham said, into the belief that "manors makyth man." We have already pointed out that snobbery, the peculiar weakness of some societies, is *sine nobilitate,* 'without nobility.' On the other hand the self-conscious refusal to seek out the better men, to acknowledge, respect, and learn from them, and to teach this duty, is a quality petty, vain, ignoble, and contemptible.

It is permissible to insert here the comment that the great Chinese people, ten times as numerous as those of some major countries and with (unlike the Russians) thirty-five centuries of a continuous and superb civilization, has a tradition to which, by all historical precedents, it may well revert—pacific, cultivated, and characterized by almost impeccable taste. (One exception lies in the almost Byzantine oddity of inserting photographs into ancestral paintings; and another in the provision of water-closets almost as objectionable as those in the Gare du Nord in Paris.) If the world has indeed to be ruled, for the sake of peace, by one people, it might do worse than choose the Chinese. But such a racial solution is, let us hope, unduly pessimistic. Certainly the system of rule by the classically cultivated and examination-chosen Chinese Mandarins had extraordinary survival value—which, in politics, is no small test. Our modern engineers with their technocracy and hypnosis of progress might take note—even if we grant (as does the writer) that sheer power, technically, for the human race is, abstractly, a good thing in itself.

The major argument of this book has turned upon the hypothesis that the structure of politics is a structure of power in various forms. We may indeed well distinguish between the desirability of men's wants and the mechanical market and means by which those wants are to be gratified. Nevertheless, it would be idle to conclude that political producers are entitled (and perhaps have a duty) to influence or educate the conception of desirability and of wants of their public, but that this task should yet actually be left in the hands, not of the political producers themselves, but only of philosophers, artists or men of letters, who, even if they have some influence, have no power.

That some guidance, however, on wants is required appears to be clear. To take a strong instance in the field of foreign policy. A not-too-hypothetical American might 'want' to fight Russians and 'Red' Chinese. An Englishman might want to fight Germans, Egyptians and Arabs, and Japanese. A Frenchman might be on excellent terms with the Germans and want only to fight Arabs. Supposing that these three countries are in military alliance, it follows that what some of these people want, being inconsistent with other wants, will have to be disregarded by government and their press clamour reshaped. Likewise, a doctrinal demand that Conservatives, Social Democrats or Christian Socialists or Socialites shall only enter into military (but no other) alliances of governments with each other—or that American Baptists may not, in the secular sphere, be diplomatically represented at the Vatican—may be contrary to national security and advantage. In the economic field it may be decided by the producers, or for them, that, owing to the need for conservation of resources or for national security reasons, it will not be good to produce certain articles or to meet certain wants. The popular demand of consumers for consumable articles may be checked by fiscal measures against inflation. An illustration is provided in the recent press comment by the economist, Andrew Schonfield: "Schizophrenia being the most common disease of nations, the Germans want both more export orders from the under-developed countries and thinner order books in general."

In politics we take one step further and have to decide about the goods of, let us say, the national survival and security itself. A dictatorship accepts the task of controlling opinion as a matter of course, so that the people are told what to feel from year to year: one year that they are to love all East Germans and hate all West Germans; the next year maybe that, according to the established precedents of Rapallo and of Ribbentrop, they are under command to love all Germans. Under a democracy a popular mandate may indeed be accepted to preserve, for example, the national power or to ensure peace with freedom. Nevertheless, a responsible government will have to retain power of control, to see that contradictory demands are subordinated to the over-all mandate. Just here may lie the distinction between Responsible Government (with the tacit aristocratic assumption that we know what is 'responsible') and purely and mechanically Representative Government.

Perhaps one of the most severe comments on the workings of practical democracy, in fields beyond its immediate range of responsible interest, will be found in the writings of a good liberal, Ambassador George F. Kennan. "Public opinion, or what passes for public opinion, is not always a moderating force in the jungle of politics . . . I also suspect that what passes for public opinion in most countries that consider themselves to have popular government is not really the consensus of feelings of the mass of the people but rather the expression of the interests of special highly vocal minorities—politicians, commentators, and publicity seekers [and recipients of 'payola'] of all sorts: people who live by their ability to draw attention to themselves and die, like fish out of water, if they are compelled to remain silent . . . I sometimes wonder whether a democracy is not uncomfortably similar to one of those prehistoric monsters with a body as long as this room and a brain the size of a pin: . . . you frantically have to whack his tail off to make him aware that his interests are being disturbed, but once he grasps this, he lays about him with such a blind determination that he actively destroys his adversary but largely wrecks his native habitat." (*American Diplomacy*, 1951, pp. 61–2, 66) Reference in this discussion should also be made to the work of an eminent educationalist, John W. Gardner, President of the Carnegie Foundation for the Advancing of Teaching, in his *Excellence* (1961); to John Wild's *Plato's Modern Enemies*; to the work of Professor J. Hallowell; and to George Kennan's *Russia and the West under Lenin and Stalin* (1961, p. 148).

It follows that the market has to be shaped. People must indeed be given, so far as maximum satisfaction permits, what they socially actually want. Perhaps the free market should be, without interference, allowed to fluctuate, in a rhythm, between laxity and austerity, and even between laissez-faire or old-fashioned Capitalism and the free choice—provided it is free—of Bolshevism. Nevertheless, people must also be encouraged responsibly to attend to the discussion of how the market should be shaped, beyond a mere elementary urge to declare immediate private wants. The crucial issue remains that of attending to what it is that they want, and of seeing that it is rightly what it should be. Anti-social wants will not be gratified—but, first, so far as practicable, they will not be encouraged to spring up. The consumers will not be encouraged to become opium or hashish addicts, or pornography and violence addicts, or exploiters of their neighbours. It is part of the marketing task of party organizations. It is the admitted task of a legislature and of an independent and uncorrupt court in dealing with the criminal world and in enforcing the law. Nevertheless, the *ideas* about how these controls shall be shaped and what shall be encouraged can come and, it may be alleged, ought to come, to politicians and to the higher ranks of the various hierarchies, from an aristocracy not of wealth or of intellect only but, nevertheless, from an aristocracy of influence. The ideas may be varied, but they will not be weightless or impotent. It is important that, affecting ends and choices, they should have access to the courts of power, where means are decided.

As touching titular and explicit rank conferred by authority, it is traditionally argued that a monarchy, acting as a 'fount of honour' is able, by confirming the social 'establishment' of influence, to give a particular tone and colour to a society which both checks the influence of a plutocracy and restrains political adventurers and over-ambitious men. It moves at the level where emotional mass opinion is especially able to be influenced, as it will not be by an *intelligentsia*. (It is the argument which Bagehot uses but exaggerates.) It may be that, had the Kaiserdom continued, Hitler could not have arisen. Today, the issue is not that of limiting the power of constitutional monarchy but of keeping a bureaucracy, of picayune imagination, to the performance of its assigned functions and free from petty abuse of citizen rights.

Over against this must be set the American 'dream' or stereotype of social equality, first shaped on the benches of the schoolhouse. We must beware of exaggerating, under the influence of popular satires on advertising men and status seekers, the extent to which this is out of touch with reality. It is still possible for a son of a banker, born 'on the right side of the tracks' in a small Middle Western town, to become a university president, and for three sons of a small farmer, born 'on the wrong side of the tracks,' to become respectively a bank vice-president, a university president and President of the United States. However, all these hold not only offices but excellent status titles, which John Doe is not usually, and without moral effort, able to attach to his name.

We are then left, in our discussion of Aristocracy, with a conclusion not dissimilar from one of Plato's. The doctrine that all men are equal, taken in the simple sense, is both false and dangerous. (Marx and Saint-Simon knew as much.) In the other sense, which goes out beyond mere equality before the law or even equality of opportunity, it is both humane and essential to the fraternal life of mutual respect in every authentic community. 'The best' are those who attach value to human fraternity; who have a sound judgement of ability and who esteem the equality of opportunity which gives ability its *carrière ouverte*; and who also esteem that ethical context in the light of which we determine what we mean by ability to be encouraged and what we mean by success. Such men may regard most 'wants,' in politics, as in economics, as indifferent and a matter for the free choice of the market. All that has to be watched is the thermometer of demand. Some, however, they may regard as of ethical and community importance and these they may aspire to shape—although they will recognize that other educators (with apparently as much public spirit and good claims as themselves) will be their rivals as to what should be the shape of more important wants and ends. They will desire to see that the means of power are effective to achieve the fulfilment of these moral wants. And some of them, disinterested as to the enjoyment of private power (and its troubles), will yet plunge into the fray of the power contest, as Plato says, to exclude others, an underworld of sophists and plain criminals, who must not be permitted, so long as moral values hold, to obtain power. This is the ethical justification of the power struggle, over and beyond the mere provision, for adequate reward, of such administrative goods as the public chances to want.

What, then, we have to conclude is that, if we are going to attend to the nature of actual wants as distinct from the market for them, we move in to this shaping in the market and, for the long-range consequences, to a work of evaluation. We shall not get national prosperity by popular election of industrial leaders. We shall not get the best medicine by electing physicians or the best law by electing judges. A statesman proves himself such by the judgement of his compeers—and, thus far, parliamentary and like systems, in fact marked by an oligarchic quality, are justified. But we must choose our economic producer or shop; and our physician; and our civil rulers and producers. Here it is vital to know, and not to be deceived about, both what the producers are competent to offer and what the political consumers actually do want—although the statesman may then take steps to educate them further in what is not only desired but desirable. He may have the duty to educate them to want something else.

However, as we shall see, the distinction is vital between the *vis coactiva* of government, which at some stage enacts law, orders, compels and terminates choice, and the *vis directiva*, which persuades. This is peculiarly important under any system of Co-operative Power as distinct from Dominative Power. It may yet be said that it is always the fault of the leaders if their people are not led; nor is it enough for the producer (or for the philosopher) to thrust the problem back upon the consumer. 'Aristocracy' is a term of evaluation; and the final aristocracy is composed of all those from expert and good craftsmen in their trade, men of skill, through to poet and philosopher, *savant* and saint, who are adjudged by co-option of their peers and by common intuition to have excellence. What perhaps chiefly distinguishes, as yet, the uncommon man from the common man, is sympathy of imagination. Essentially an aristocracy does not exercise power to control directly; but, primarily, influences in order to shape what is wanted before control begins, 'to shape the wish.'

ARISTOCRACY HAS NOT ONLY A ROLE BUT A FUNCTIONAL ROLE, WHICH CONSTITUTIONAL DEMOCRACY HAS OVERTLY AND SYSTEMATICALLY TO RECOGNIZE, IN THE POLITICAL SYSTEM (Proposition 37). *At the present time this recognition patently does not exist*; and a false antithesis is developed between aristocracy and democratic equalitarian thought. The cultural importance of a lead being given, against vulgarization of values, is not recognized. The channels of influence for an aristocracy are by access to the practical statesman, who has a professional duty to be available to 'initiators,' as distinct from 'routineers,' and to the play of ideas, and who should not be a member of a closed trade; and through education and the media of communication. There is no natural right of the press. An editor does not print every correspondent's letter in the sacred name of 'free expression for all.' Neither he nor his owner are ever 'elected persons.' There is, however, a derivative right of a responsible and public-spirited press not only to make cash for the oligarchy of owners and shareholders, but to circulate ideas and to enable the people to choose. And with the right there is, here also, a duty.

In Britain the rights of the Press to report divorce news is curtailed as is any attempt to report to the public on matters still *sub iudice*, for example comment on an accused person, as Lord Birkett pointed out in a broadcast comment on the C.B.S. film, "A Real Case of Murder." A British editor who commented on the Haigh murder case (although Haigh was later convicted) went to prison for three months for such contempt of court.

An active aristocracy of public service, Aristotle's practical men, must, then, be sensitive to the views, in all their variety, of that other speculative aristocracy of competent men, Aristotle's men of the theoretical life, men rightly of influence, who are *professionally* entitled to views about what wants should prevail. We cannot define precisely this aristocracy. Plato suggests that they are best competent to evaluate each other. Their societies are more comparable, we have said, to a multiplicity of Churches (both for better and, in their jealousies, for worse) than a multiplicity of States. As society becomes more educated and voluntary, and the States fade away with their force, their power not only to influence but to shape self-control will increase. They exercise, each according to his own capacity, a *vis directiva*, but (as Julien Benda rightly said, in his *Trahison des clercs*) they lose their vocation once they act as if the forceful *vis coactiva* were a substitute for it or enough. The Communist Party, influenced by a sense of immediate and crusading urgency in its time-scale, tends to obliterate this distinction. Its basic thesis in its Guided Democracy is that in detail the People does not know what it ought to want and should be told (and, moreover, compelled) by the Guardians.

The active few (engaged, as Professor Popper says, in their piece-meal reforms of means) will historically be judged by the extent to which they listen to this 'forceless' multiple aristocracy, which is the vanguard, interpreting with variety and abnormal sensitivity what the community means and should mean. (What measure of unanimity on ends there could be in the variety, we have still to consider.) Further, it is a chief and essential task of education to arouse the minds of the whole of those whom we educate to be able to judge the quality of its spiritual leaders and, having judged them, to respect those whom it has judged.

Part II
POLITICAL PHILOSOPHY

7. Community, Society, and the Individual

§i. Community and Society

If one of the major forms of the structure of power is that of co-operation, how far is this amenable to discussion in terms of the competitive political market? Can the relation of the individual to the community be discussed usefully in terms of political science and of means to his ends, or is the experience of community one of man's direct wants or ends for enjoyment? Is it a pragmatic matter of adjustment, existentially, of means to ends? Or is it an essential matter of 'what is Man'? And what, in Politics, can deserve more attention than precisely this relation, not of individual with individual, seeking like a housewife advantages on the market, but of the individual to the society or community in which he grew up, and the ideals and philosophy of which he shares?

The best and subtlest definition of Community, so fundamental to his concept of the ideal *polis*, is that provided by Plato himself: *koinōnia tēs hēdonēs kai tēs lupēs*, 'a having in common of pleasures and pains.' It is developed by St. Paul when he speaks of the comparison between membership of the Church and membership of a physical body. It enters into the whole Churchly notion of 'the brotherhood of faith' and *corpus mysticum*. The gathering of his friends around Epicurus in his garden is an instance of community life, recently rediscussed by Father A. J. Festugière, no less than the *ashram* of every Indian *guru* to the days of the Mahatma Gandhi.

Later, after misleading analogies of a totalitarian character had been offered by Hobbes, from whose pessimistic philosophy the sense of community is yet absent (Hobbes himself being too individualist or atomist in fundamental approach, even if also determinist, to have the makings of a modern totalitarian), Hegel developed a distinction between the *bürgerliche Gesellschaft*, which corresponds to Civil Society as described by Locke, and the State, which for Hegel was the true Community and indeed the temporal manifestation of the Spirit in history and the "march of God" in the world. In the last generation Professor Ferdinand Tönnies developed the notion of, on the one hand, Society and, on the other, Community, in his book *Gesellschaft und Gemeinschaft* (1887) with implications not only, in his own day, socialistic but also, as one can detect by hindsight, national socialistic and, according to general valuations, dangerous. More recently attention has been given to the issue of Community, not least in its smallest and more primitive manifestations as the 'face-to-face' group and—more complex—as the 'like-minded' group, especially by Professor R. M. MacIver.

Whereas, however, the great Greek writers of the Golden Age viewed the *polis*, as Community, as the highest expression of social life, nineteenth-century writers, thinking like many moderns of a community as primarily something like a primitive village, often saw the supposedly progressive movement of history as away from the community, with its social hierarchy of status, towards a civil society held together by contract and law. This is, of course, not true of the Collectivist school, initiated at the end of the previous century by Rousseau. For Rousseau the Commonwealth must inevitably break up or lose dynamism if, becoming unduly 'permissive,' it lost fundamental unity of wills and some species of civil religion or philosophy. The individualistic view is, however, especially characteristic of nineteenth-century liberalism rather than of the actual conservative views of some exponents of contract theory, such as Sir Henry Maine. They resented what may be described as the ubiquitous vulgarity and anonymous tyranny of public opinion, even when deified as a General Will. Defenders of 'the Open Society,' with their antagonism to anything of the nature of a public philosophy and a dogma on education, must tend to this view.

Since the above was first written (in 1955) I have fortunately had the opportunity of seeing M. de Jouvenel's important *De la souveraineté*, which discusses the issues raised by Greek ideas of the ideal *polis* as a small, homogeneous, and regulated community. Such regulation M. de Jouvenel holds must end in 'planning,' and planning end in totalitarianism, despite the views of Pericles. Hence, for M. de Jouvenel, the *amitié* (my 'trust'), on which he has based himself in his construction of authority, has to leave behind its original family and tribal form and to take new shape as the spirit of justice, among those of a non-face-to-face group, inspiring laws but itself shaped by *a common and traditional public philosophy* (*Vide* pp. 167–212; Eng. trans., pp. 126–65). In his *De la souveraineté* M. Bertrand de Jouvenel answers the major issue raised in the text by saying that the only community principle upon which an open society can operate is that of Mutual Trust (*amitié*)—which we indeed have found earlier to be the central principle of a non-Marxist co-operative society and of the co-operative interpretation of power. But the question then arises: *what society is the one which we shall trust?* To this Plato's answer is plain enough. But is it adequate?

The theory of Community, as discussed here, must be clearly distinguished from the erroneous doctrine of the Social Organism, developed under biological and neo-Darwinian influences, but by false analogy, even by writers as distinguished as Walter Bagehot and Herbert Spencer, not to speak of Schaeffler and Worms. It is discussed in detail in *Principia*, chapter VIII. It will be noted that the reference by St. Paul, and the Catholic theory emergent from it, most fully expressed in the encyclical *Mystici Corporis* (1943) does not—and indeed, consistently with stress upon the value of the individual soul, cannot—carry the implications of the doctrine of the State or of Society as a biological Social Organism.

In Hobbes' work there is a deliberate propaganda combination of the incompatible notions of a highly individualistic psychology, with *homo homini lupus*, with the organic depiction, on the frontispiece, of Leviathan as a totalitarian animal, with the head of Charles Stuart, and 'thy mortal God.' As touching the 'like-minded group'—a phrase then only just coming into usage—reference may be made to my *Principia*, p. 419 and to the writer's article 'Community,' in the Harvard symposium *Community*, edited by Professor C. J. Friedrich (1959) as well as to his *Thomas Hobbes*, where the criticism by George Lawson, emphasized by recent students of Hobbes, is mentioned.

The great philosopher, indeed, of Community remains Plato. Here the central ideas—and some of the central dangers also—will be found. They were restated by Jean Jacques Rousseau, but in a fashion complicated by his own earlier Lockeian and highly paradoxical views, and in a fashion ultimately more tending to obfuscate than to clarify the fundamental issues. The modern work of Tönnies, a close student of Hobbes, after initial neglect achieved *réclame*, in large measure owing to his onslaught on the typical nineteenth-century Liberal views of society. These views overlooked the significance of community values, as distinct from individualist and contractualist values. Tönnies, on the other hand, contrasted an association of 'organic life' with 'a mechanical structure,' leading to what was later to be called 'the objectification' or 'alienation' of man, who thus becomes identified with an article of economic transactions on the labour exchange or with a bearer of merely legal relations, rights, and responsibilities.

"Human wills stand in manifold relations to one another . . . The relationship itself, and also the resulting association [*Verbindung*], is conceived of either as real and organic life—this is the essential characteristic of the *Gemeinschaft* [community]—or as imaginary and mechanical structure—this is the concept of *Gesellschaft* [society]." (*Gemeinschaft und Gesellschaft*) Here the word 'real' as used by Tönnies, is itself loaded and tendentious. The Community is a field of "all intimate . . . and exclusive living together." There is no such thing as "a bad Gemeinschaft." It may here be objected that a criminal gang, as Plato recognized, may in some large part be precisely an intimate and exclusive living together, even if involved in a 'contradiction of principle.' Hitler most certainly provided the *Genossen* of his Storm Troopers with a *Gemeinschaft* of comradeship. Another name for a community, when small, respectable, and in a position of power, may be a clique. The Society of Jesus, the Fabian Society in its early days, and (in some measure) the Society of Friends offer instances of small communities.

The ambiguities also in Tönnies' use of the German *Gesellschaft* is shown by the fact that some English sociologists translate this as 'association,' and not as 'society.' Nevertheless Tönnies describes it as being "the world itself." Hence his usage allows us to speak of 'human society.'

In a much later, brief study of 1931, Tönnies added certain empirical and not very profound or convincing 'categories' of relationship, such as 'acquaintance-ship' and 'strangeness,' 'confidence' and 'mistrust,' and one of 'interdependence,' also much developed by Emile Durkheim, in his *De la division du travail social* (translated by Prof. George Simpson as *Division of Labour in Society* in 1933). Dr. Martin Buber, in his philosophy of 'I and Thou,' makes a comparable distinc-tion, between the society in which the relation is merely external, as of 'things,' and the more ideal group, where each stands to the other as one of 'we,' not 'they,' and as a full person or 'thou.' Unfortunately, the effect of forcing all relations into 'I-and-Thou-ness' can easily end, in fact, in what Aristotle calls 'wateryness'; and in debasing even the valuable intimacies into a uniform 'thing-relation' (because morally compulsive) of indifference or of distaste masked by hypocrisy. It tends to ignore the spontaneity of the emotions, and even their caprice, by subjecting them to a moral imperative of charity, applicable to the reason rather than the emotions.

Whereas Tönnies maintains a distinction between Society (which we have already sought to define, and distinguish from Association, in chapter III) and Community which is largely in terms of the nature of the sentiment involved—calculation as against loyalty—MacIver introduces a territorial aspect into his definition. This is the more remarkable because he describes the State, as also the Church, as Associations. The usage followed in the present book draws a distinc-tion between Society and Community as one between 'extensive' and 'intensive' forms of human grouping, while reserving the word 'association' for a society organized for some specific purpose. This distinction is not to be understood primarily as touching area but as touching emphasis. The Community is initially microcosmic, and best illustrated by the Family; but it is not necessarily microcosmic. It can be macrocosmic, like a world Religion or Church or like Communism. A Society can indeed be 'large,' as touching the numbers and width of distribution of its membership; but it need not be. Indeed a Community is a species of Society, which species has a certain 'extension' also and which, to its detractors, who have no sympathy with or empathy towards it, may appear to be merely an artificial and mechanical social grouping, imposing its authority by pressures. A Community may indeed also be of wide distribution *per accidens*; but in this event, as already said, it tends to become 'watery' and has specific diseases or dangers. It is 'authentic' in terms of its close-knit quality as something 'chosen' or at least 'habitual'; and by reason of the intensity of its feeling.

It follows that a Society can issue from compulsory or from voluntary, or even from accidental, aggregation. Unlike an Association, it need not have a specific and assignable objective, temporary or lasting; nor, like an Institution, need it always have developed Conventions which take instrumental shape in specific organizations of human beings for assignable functions. A Community, however, being a matter of common feeling, although it can be shaped by habit, nevertheless cannot be maintained *against* choice, deliberate or habitual. It does not, however, significantly issue from any kind of Social Contract of a calculated order. Clearly it enters, since we choose it as a good involving certain means, into the political world and the political market. But it tends especially to be chosen as offering a particular kind of goods of a non-concrete or subjective order, resting on a valuational element—goods assessed as 'good.' Briefly, we may say that Society is the area where men, whether characterized by trust or distrust, merely as human beings are organized by the division of social labour into the web of control relations. COMMUNITY IS THE AREA IN WHICH, WITH RATIONAL CONFIDENCE, MEN HAVE THE POWER TO ENJOY THE CO-OPERATIVE GOODS RESULTING FROM TRUST (Proposition 38; cf. Proposition 10).

It will be noted that some writers, beginning by thinking of the Community as primarily a face-to-face group, such as a 'greater family' or a village, and passing by the emotional ties of the Family (indeed an authentic if imperfect community, connected by birth) and even of the Clan, of the Caste and of the Class, proceed to stress identification with an area or territory. There may indeed be a strong emotional attachment to the soil and place where we were born and brought up. Nevertheless, the step is then short to finding instances of the Community in, for example, the 'community church,' which is a church serving *all* in an area—and hence, in some fashion, the opposite of 'a community'—or in the French administrative Commune or in similar debased communities or, indeed, even in the urban district or dormitory area in which one sleeps . . . But the classical (and, surely, the true) area of the Community is precisely that where there are waking and active thoughts and comradeship. Others verbally associate the Community, not only with the Commune but with Communication— but in the United States, seldom (though it is a connection which might yet have shrewd Platonic justification) with Communism. We must not be misled into supposing that what has like noises has like meaning. Nor must we be misled by vulgar usage in the West. If it be true that a deadly weakness of contemporary Western culture is its tendency to the alienation of the person from his world of activity— just as under the mechanical Roman Empire, when religion offered the only community outlet for human personality—and its inadequate capacity for understanding the meaning of Community as an area of trust and psychological partnership, then it is folly to trust to popular usage of the word, in its confusion, as a guide to what the enlightening meaning may be.

R. M. MacIver writes, in *Community*, ". . . all community is a question of degree . . . the degree and intensity of the common life" (p. 23). The concern of Sociology is with its development, beginning with "a tiny nucleus of common life." "Society," he writes, with an emphasis comparable to the work of Charles H. Cooley, "like the Kingdom of God is within us." (p. 83) "Community comes into being because interests are realisable only in common life" (p. 99; cf. Rousseau's well-known argument) . . . 'Community' properly signifies any whole area of social life, such as a village, or town, or country . . . any circle of common life." (pp. 8–9) Repeatedly he insists that the State is not to be taken as the sole or, as by Hegel, perfect expression of Community. He also distinguishes between the 'extrinsic' interests of power as means to ends or end, and the 'intrinsic' interests of *direct* enjoyment of goods or cultural good.

MacIver's second use of 'Society' (clearly corresponding to his first use of 'Community,' as 'relations of wills') is, broadly, adopted here for 'Society' (*supra* p. 58). With his definitions (*Community*, p. 22) we can agree: "Society . . . I intend to use in a universal or generic sense to include every willed relationship of man to man . . . By a community I mean an area of common life." But, perhaps because he has limited Sociology to discussion of Community, with its valuational implications (not indeed that Community *is* valuable *per se*: 'gangs,' as said above, are often authentic communities: but that communities *share* ends or what they *regard* as valuable), MacIver tends readily to 'concretize' his community, not only into face-to-face groups, for example, but into 'areas' such as 'a town or country.' But that 'a town or country' is actually a community, voluntarily sharing sentiments of sorrow, pain and values, may be just what has to be shown or even be created. It may, on the contrary, be a Peyton Place. Hence our use of the word 'Community,' although connected with 'intrinsic' enjoyment over whatsoever area of social life (maybe *not* face-to-face—and even here, a committee round a table may be one of enemies—and maybe not geographically contiguous), is not always the same as MacIver's.

Professor Raymond Aron, in his *Introduction to the Philosophy of History* (English translation, 1961, p. 296), wisely remarks that "the word *society* is not without ambiguity, since in one case it may designate actual collectivities and, in other cases, the idea or ideal of these collectivities"—which is especially true when it is capitalized as 'Society.' It will be noted that 'Community' may be thought to carry, as a word, the ideal overtones of 'society.' However, as used here, Community means any actual homogeneous 'society of pleasure and pains,' whether philosophically these pleasures are held to be good or bad. As always we must be aware of the intrusion, by legerdemain, into the definition of the word of redundant meanings, which will later be triumphantly brought out as logical conclusions of objective study.

Here, broadly, Tönnies' sharp distinction between *Gesellschaft* and *Gemeinschaft* is adopted, although all scholars must be indebted to Professor MacIver for the new dimensions of meaning which he has given to the word 'Community.' Professor Georges Gurvitch ("Mass, Community, Communion," *Journal of Philosophy*, Vol. XXXVIII, 1941) speaks of a 'Communion,' which for him carries many of the meanings of what is here called Community. Interestingly, he gives, as illustration, the 'communion' of international scientists. Other philosophers, who share a Protestant or secularist outlook, identify a Communion with a religious sect; put it into at least potential antithesis to *the* Community, which they tend to think of as the mayor and corporation; and then, regarding the former as less morally important, eviscerate this anaemic Communion of meaning by making it merely an aggregate, meeting in one place of assemblage, for each—except for such as are self-made men—to have a private monologue (not normally requiring reply) with his supposed Creator. The usage of the text is that communion is the relationship of the members of a Community; and a Communion is one, emphatic, form of Community.

A social Community, therefore, depends upon a psychological community of *ends*. What the political or economic consequences of its logic may be, and whether or not it issues in a voluntary or (which some will urge is self-contradictory) compulsive or coercive communism, is for the moment another story. It is itself a like-minded group, becoming a community in terms of the stability of its like-mindedness, and lapsing into becoming merely a group of society or Social Group so far as this like-mindedness dissolves. Professor Charles H. Cooley, in his sociological work in the tradition of Ward and Giddings, lays great stress upon the 'primary' or face-to-face group. It has been a great methodological error of old-fashioned Political Science, with its *idée fixe* about the State and with its unfortunate divorce from Sociology, practically to ignore the very primary groups in politics which Aristotle so admirably discussed. Here we adhere, as elsewhere, to the Aristotelian tradition.

In contemporary pioneer work in industrial psychology and relations, and in the development of the classless sense of community in terms of 'round table' and face-to-face conferences, engendering the 'co-operative of trust,' without anybody being suspected of a 'sell-out,' important stress has indeed been placed upon this personal relationship, with its ethical quality, of the face-to-face group. It must yet be emphasized that the face-to-face groups (or the Village or the Family) are notoriously *not* necessarily 'like-minded,' any more than those wider social areas which are not face-to-face such as the urban area and the country; and no facile identification must be made.

The Hellenic philosophers of the Golden Age, who were profoundly community-minded, so insisted indeed upon the importance of homogeneity (*homonoia*) and education in a public philosophy in accordance with the spirit of the constitution in the *polis*, that they even drastically tailored the *polis* to produce this result. They had little share in the mass enthusiasm which characterizes modern Nationalism, which they would have regarded critically. However, stressing those community virtues which made civic life 'worthwhile' and indeed 'the good life,' they were alarmed and defeated, not only by tyrannies which could put the duties, for example in family loyalty, of man and citizen into opposition (as in the U.S.S.R. and elsewhere), but no less by the problem of how the social virtue was to be retained if the society was diffused to the extent of a cosmopolis. They bequeathed this problem to the philosophers of the Silver Age who came after them, the simple-life Cynics, the Stoics, Marcus Aurelius, and the Christian Fathers who endeavoured to cement a Catholic community as wide as the inhabited world. The problem is with us still and is for us, in an age of great mass political movements, one of the most crucial of all.

Cf. Aristotle, *Politics* 8. 9. Actually the Athenian *polis*, since Cleisthenes, had broken down the old blood-community of the clan or phratry. Sir Henry Maine, in his *Ancient Law*, gave on the basis of Indian experience full weight to the community life of the village but, a man of the nineteenth century, he identified its habits with 'status' and put this into contrast with 'contract.' He sought to mark a development from one to the other—or from 'primitive' *Gemeinschaft* to 'Industrial Revolution *Gesellschaft*.' He regarded this as 'progress.' Walter Bagehot, in his reference to "the cake of custom," is more kindly to such a regime of stable social conventions, and also sees it (rather patronizingly) as emotional, contemporary, and functional. The issue raised is whether the extension of individual freedom and "the development of all one's powers" (unspecified and unevaluated) in a consumers' market of larger 'civil rights' is to be regarded as automatic human progress or as indeed a retrogression from community values to the mechanical atomism of *bürgerliche Gesellschaft*.

Recent political studies of underdeveloped countries, especially in Africa, show the extreme importance today of these tribal or group community structures, which political scientists of the West must not ignore. Moscow does not.

§ii. Loyalty and Choice

What interpretation, then, are we to give to Community, whether that of habit and blood-kinship or of developed, conscious and even articulate like-mindedness in values, in terms of the Political Market? Does the schema of the Political Market only apply to the world of Dominative Competition and Distrust, and not to that of Rational Trust and Co-operative Power?

This is a problem which we had already begun to confront when we discussed Domination and Trust. Spiritual and emotional satisfactions, such as comradeship—with its banishment of solitariness, of the feeling of 'not-being-wanted' and of *ennui*—are important values and ends of our contemporary civilization, which we put before ourselves in the choice of our actions. They are regarded by us as goods which we seek to achieve; and, to achieve these goods and to avoid their opposites such as the 'waste lands' of fear, loneliness, and isolation, we select relevant means. "Man is an animal of the *polis*." In terms of social or political means they are goods which we prefer, these against those, these of community warmth against those of cold individualist variety—or the reverse, those of individualist rich variety against these of herd-instinct and mob feeling. For their gratification we will pay and, as we count the cost of the means, they hence powerfully enter on the political market.

It is true that, once we decide to trust or to display a loyalty that counts no cost, we shall not calculate *within* the Community. Here our range of choice of neighbourly or charistic means, fit for *us* as mere members (although in no wise always means to be used by the Community or Nation or group, *collectively*, in relation to other Nations), may be heavily limited by the imperative and wide demands upon us of the ideal social ends. Obedience to the law, or rules, as chosen for the community good, may be no longer a matter to be chosen according to individual preference or even according to minor individual moral values. We accept, almost without reflection, what our community rules because *it* so rules. Its ruling is final, even if we may suspect that it is not always enlightened. The ruling may indeed be changed in the light of new demands, dictated by circumstances. The alleged high values of the ends penetrate down deeply to colour the choice of suitable means and the ritual and behaviour of common life. Statistical political analyses in Japan show how true it is that the individual follows community sentiment, at least in the rural areas of that country. Japan is not alone.

This, however, neither always affects the nature of our original *choice* of community or group as involving costs for these goods, which we are altruistically prepared to pay; nor does it negate the consideration that groups and communities, like less valuable associations that offer goods, will enter into the market of political ends. It will merely spell that we may choose different *Genossen*, and be perhaps members of a disciplined 'vanguard' or ascetic mission or 'teaching Church,' instead of rotarian fellows or members of a community church or of a 'pleasant Sunday afternoon' society. Indeed it may be argued that the more indefinitely high may be the common values which we choose, the more relentless or fanatical will be the competition and solicitation of support, by members who do not wish to be regarded as renegades, to carry out these aims and to implement these values. Indeed, the pressures may amount to denial of choice between groups. (How far one can be said, morally or practically, to 'choose our Village' or 'choose our State' will be discussed later.) The nobler the ends the more reasonable does intolerance of deviations seem to become. A State engaged on a war-crusade is seldom tolerant. However, the refusal of choice can be held to strike at the heart of conscious community.

Professor J. L. Talmon (*Utopianism and Politics*, 1958, p. 13) defines as Utopianism any attempt to postulate "at the same time the free expression of the individual and absolute social cohesion," as distinct from an equilibrium of compromise.

§iii. *Community, Autonomy, and Heteronomy*

The demand, not only for social organization, but for the experience of Community springs from the deeper nature of man, and from the desire for esteem from and union or 'at-one-ment' with his group. It also connects with the understanding of power as, in some species (including in some measure man, who is related to both the solitary and the social apes), a matter of co-operation where *l'union fait la force.* Hence it finds a basis in man's psychology and in Natural Law. However, the sense for community living, despite one of Rousseau's more misleading (or tautological) dogmas to the effect that only in society do men "taste the sweets of civic virtue," can have (as we have said) perverted as well as healthy forms. It is not solely a question, in Aristotelian terminology, of community being "good *in esse*" although "evil *per accidens.*" Rather the issue is one of the principle, end, or *telos* around which the community, as entelechy or at least woven into a common pattern, is organized. Community, as arousing loyalty, social sympathy and producing other goods, may be good *pro tanto* but, owing to the chance of perversion or failure of proportions of which it is still capable, it cannot be said to be good absolutely or unconditionally.

In a patently pathological form the sense of community can, under excitation, display itself as mob hysteria. In more customary forms, developing from the fundamental need to have trust, to be able to trust and to be treated as a full partner, there is the desire to feel oneself, and tangibly to be, part of some great forward-stepping movement, in which all comrades march together "in twos or threes"—or indeed four or sixteen abreast—full of experience of co-operative power and love of the comradeship. In more intellectually calculating conditions, this desire may be merely a wish to 'keep in step with the Joneses' or 'to keep up with the Armstrong-Joneses' or 'to join the "Establishment" or "Top-side,"' and in some democratic societies 'to keep back with the Joneses'; and a willingness passively and heteronomously to accept the local *mores* as the requirement for individual success and 'arrival' (as stressed by David Riesman *et al.* in *The Lonely Crowd*).

In a more emotional or altruistic environment, there will be a direct sensual enjoyment of the partnership of the mass or community movement, even achieving orgiastic satisfactions. (However, to call this satisfaction 'a phenomenological datum' is merely a pretentious way of saying that *for some people* it is, beyond doubt, a direct satisfaction. It was probably so for the early Christians in the *agapē* (or 'love') ceremony, for which the high formality of the corporate Mass was later substituted.) It banishes two of the deepest fears in man: that of loneliness or of 'not being wanted' or of failing 'to command respect,' of being 'treated as an inferior,' or of being 'below the salt'; and that of boredom or of emptiness, 'the look into the abyss,' *le néant.* The fascist, national socialist, and Bolshevik movements all provide exaggerated manifestations of community sense; nor do we have to look so far as to Hellenic Orphic rites or to Negro initiatory ceremonies. From their nature the element, with partnership, of initiation and even of conspiracy enters into all these fraternities. Their relation tends to be sacramental and their leadership, in Max Weber's phrase, charismatic. Indeed Weber himself, although a liberal socialist, thanks to his imprudent and misbegotten praise of such leadership tended to anticipate Hitlerite, instead of bourgeois and trades union or Social Democratic, developments in Germany. Cf. Franz Neumann, *Behemoth* (1942, pp. 73–85, "The Charismatic Leader").

The distinction between Society and Community has been, as we have said, much emphasized by German sociologists, who wanted 'a spiritual science' (whatever this may be) and had a Romantic interest in Community, although the distinction is not entirely valid since a Community is also a Society. In contrast, however, to Durkheim who observed in France that no social structure at all could hold together were some factors ensuring solidarity not present, members of the German school such as Max Weber and Tönnies (a student of Hobbes but in reaction from him) emphasized the distinction. To reiterate, for them Society is an association of men held together by individual assignable interests, including the economic and those interests of power from which the web grows of social controls, as indeed an association mechanical, extensive, impersonal, tending to "the objectification of man"; whereas Community becomes the social vehicle of spiritual qualities, or rather the intensive organism in which men find their personalities as members and from which they derive the ideas and standards of the moral life. Instances of Community thus range from the minute monastic community (termed by St. Benedict 'a workshop of souls'), the Utopian settlement, the religious sect or conventicle and social or Masonic club, to the massive Nation or oecumenical Church.

One of the most interesting points here is how far the Community, including the democratic community, to preserve its essence *must* necessarily be both intensive and small or microcosmic. It was objected by Rousseau, and by most writers of the Eighteenth Century, that the virtue which was characteristic of a Democracy could not be maintained in the macrocosm of a country-wide State, but could only flourish in communities such as the Greek and Italian city-states and the Swiss cantons. Democracy, it was contended, was unsuited to the country-wide realm, necessarily heterogeneous in spiritual character. (Much of de Tocqueville's interest in the United States was due to curiosity about whether here there might not be an exception to the rule). Various optimistic movements obscured this logical conclusion about the necessary limits on the homogeneity and community character of Democracy by reason of size. Madison, who praised variety and size, like most men of the Whig temperament, ignored this problem of Community and indeed is not the philosopher of 'Democracy' but rather of 'Constitutionalism.'

a. First, the rise of Protestant Liberalism produced the belief that

Democracy, far from being characterized necessarily by homogeneity of outlook and unity of pattern in virtue, would have no 'public philosophy' but would only admirably maintain the right of every man to form his own judgement, aided as little or as much as he chose from without. Every man, however limited, would have a right—some said as a rational man; some omitted this reservation—to express his own prejudices and pursue his own desires with entire freedom, subject to a veto thanks to the same right of others; and would have the right to act on whatever in fact were his views and beliefs, these matters being private to himself, subject to the like caution on behaviour. For an older school indeed this right was limited by revelation and conscience; but it later became open to each man to discard revelation and to analyse conscience into a private judgement, strongly held.

b. Second, there was the faith in Representative Democracy, as an improvement in principle upon Pure Democracy, its 'know-how' being regarded by James Mill and John Stuart Mill as almost like the semi-divine gifts bestowed on their societies by Lycurgus or by the demigods of old, such Representative Democracy overriding the need for a small community where all could assemble together, as in some Swiss cantons, in a face-to-face group for discussion and the shaping of a common mind. Here again, the earlier writers insisted upon the 'rational rights' of the minority of individuals (if not of group minorities), countering the view that *la volonté générale est toujours droite*: but later writers were sceptical about these rights, whether of individuals or groups, as distinct from rule by the opinions of equals assessed by numerical majorities.

c. Third, there was the rise of Nationalism, with its repudiation of the older theme, upheld by Metternich, that the State or Empire was a vast machine or instrument with the function of maintaining secular world peace or state-wide peace, rendered more easy in movement by the lubrication of personal loyalty to an emperor or monarch, a machinery of government which took into account, *not* the cultural nationhood of its subjects, *but* their individual civic duties. According to the thesis of Nationalism, size gave power, and the need for small size (to give intensity of community life) did not matter—since the whole supertribal or linguistic mass could be stirred by a common spirit of fraternal, patriotic, democratic, and mass enthusiasm. Aristotle himself, indeed, had said that size (for which he had little esteem) was a preservative of Democracy (for which he also had only an ambiguous esteem).

The issue here is whether these new movements did not vulgarize the older notion of Community; make it gross with size and compulsion; evade its real problems; and, from the point of view of political science as well as philosophy, leave problems of their own, such as those of the Nature of Public Instruction, the Limits of Toleration, and the Functions of Force as against Custom.

The student will note that, in fact, we are here passing, in this discussion, from the field of political science into that of philosophy. However, so long as we are discussing the structure of the like-minded community group, as distinct from that of a society (however habitual or 'natural') organized around interests that require no such like-mindedness, or from an unorganized society, that structure will impose on behaviour its own intrinsic conditions and controls, even of an elaborate character, which, irrespective of any philosopher's assessment of their value, are of scientific concern. De Tocqueville, for example, objectively suggested that American democracy worked thanks to a like-minded cult of equality over vast areas, while subjectively he retained doubts about the unqualified virtues of this cult. Again, we may desire a good society of peace, but how far massive deterrents contribute—as they may—as means thereto, is a matter of what are the appropriate and alternative means.

A distinction, different from that described between Society and Community, but illuminating in its bearing upon social allegiance, is made by certain American sociologists such as Riesman and, in some respects, Fromm between societies guided by the principles in behaviour of Autonomy, of Heteronomy, and of Tradition. There is here a valuational exaltation of Autonomy or 'self-expression' and of 'the mature assumption of responsibility' (not unconnected with Natural Law notions of psychological health) in the tradition of Goethe and the Liberals of a humanist stamp, in contrast to the laissez-faire Liberal economists. The assumption is also made that societies guided by tradition or Humean 'habit'—although this tradition may be imparted by living parents, priests or teachers—are clearly distinguishable from those whose direction in behaviour is taken from neighbours, whose own conduct is a matter of opportune adaptation rather than of tradition, but who in fact hold social power and influence.

Whereas the notion of Tradition—in the words of St. Paul to Timothy: "That which is committed to thy trust"—granted it is a living and shaping tradition, is compatible with that of Community, although distinguishable from it (societies which are not communities also being marked, if in a largely external fashion, by traditions), the essential notions of Autonomy and Community, both historically and psychologically, are antithetic or, at least, polar. Philosophically, of course, a reconciliation can be reached through free choice—one chooses not the "dear City of Cecrops" but the "dear City of God"—

and in the guidance of both by the norm of Reason or even of Tradition itself, intellectual or subconscious or behavioural. Autonomy indeed also involves a *nomos*; is in opposition to what Professor Sebas-
tian de Gracia, following Durkheim, calls *anomie*; and is not the same
as anarchy or even existentialist freedom. Heteronomy, even more
emphatically, is antithetic to the spirit of community, and is something
by definition imposed, dominatively, as an alien will without faith. It is
accepted, not from interior belief, but for reasons of calculation, owing
to recognition of the limits of personal power and of the facts of life's
controls; but, even if in detail these regulations may be heteronomous,
they may yet spring derivatorily from the constitutional will of a
Community which, as such and by definition, has been freely chosen
or is freely supported.

We reach, then, a position where, comparable to the contrast between Society and Community (these standing in the relation of whole
and part) but not identical with it, there is the contrast between
Heteronomy and Autonomy (which are mutually exclusive). In a
middle (and, for Fromm, primitive) position is a direction by a Tradition, which may be consciously chosen and intellectually deliberated;
or which may be non-intellectual, subsconscious and habitual; or
which may be partly both, in terms of a pattern or *credo* emotionally
embraced by the self in conversion.

In the area of Civil Society and of Heteronomy the role of force, of
Domination and calculated co-operation, and of the *vis coactiva* plays
a distinctive part. In the area of self-chosen or willingly accepted
Community, the role of choice, of that special kind of co-operation
we call Trust, and of the *vis directiva*, is distinctive. At the one
extreme Autonomy may issue in an individualistic (if contrary) rejection of a *nomos* and in 'anomie,' and in stress solely upon whatever by
chance may happen to be a man's actual opinions and desires. At the
other end, acceptance of community tradition may verge towards the
blindly habitual. Indeed, on the margin, the element of fear may begin
to enter in, as well as subconscious bias of will away from non-conformity. In between lies the voluntary choice of a community tradition
of values accepted, autonomously, in intellectual consciousness and
in emotional satisfaction. It will be noted that within the range of this
norm, the antithesis, posited by Riesman, between Tradition and
Autonomy disappears.

How far mass societies, guided by the chaffering of the free market, will in
fact have a public philosophy, unless more limited communities within them
form opinion by competitively propagandizing with vigour their own intensively
held public philosophies, is a key question. It connects with the teaching or

'influencing' function of true aristocracies. M. de Jouvenel, in his *De la souve-raineté*, meets the question by removing the distinction between *free Society* (in which *no* public philosophy is held, except for the benefit of what the members happen to regard as their wishes in the fluctuation of the market or their immediate requirements for survival) and a *limited Community* which, within that society, chooses voluntarily and deliberately to subordinate its members' actual wishes to a pattern of what, in that community, they rationally and morally *ought* to wish. We cannot presume that all members of Society, of their own initiative, will at all share M. de Jouvenel's views about Christianity and justice—and indeed he himself gloomily points this out, when discussing what he holds to be the errors of Darwinian so-called 'scientific humanism,' with its drastic implications. They can perhaps be brought to share them by education stemming from a community movement, sustaining a common philosophy of the good. The compati-bility between the order of Society and a more authoritarian—not necessarily more legalistic and certainly not more coercive—Community, held together by chosen values, tradition, and habits of service "expressing a 'true' Liberty," lies precisely in this element, in the Community, of free choice and concern for truth (*satya-graha*: 'search for the real') and grace.

§iv.   *Nationalism*

The Nation is, contemporarily and transitionally, the outstanding macrocosmic instance of Community. Allegiance to it, from its citizens and nationals, has sentimentalized and vivified the Modern State shaped in the sixteenth century, with its legal-mechanical notion of sovereign and subjects which, in turn, replaced the earlier concept of personal loyalty to a lord, who was liege suzerain among vassals and *comes* among his companions, equals, *pares*, or peers. The sacra-mental bond of the early Christian brotherhood and the conspiracy of the Communist Party (Bolshevik) can also be cited as instances. How-ever, unlike these, the Nation is usually (less so where there are ethno-logical patchworks such as Eastern Europe) almost universal in membership *within its territory*. Its form of community, as all-inclusive rather than primarily 'homonoiic' or 'like-minded,' tends to be 'demo-cratic *B*' or 'democratic *D*' in character.

Professor Johann K. Bluntschli, in his great and standard work, *Lehre vom Modernen Staat* (1852; English translation, 2nd ed., 1895, p. 100) remarks: "Nationality clearly has a closer and stronger connection with the State than with the Church, for it is easier for the Church to be universal . . . A People is not a political society [of itself]." The production, however, of a world culture, for example by the Catholic Church, and in regional measure by the Macedonian and Roman empires, is of the nature almost of a miracle, created contrary to the some-what static wisdom of some anthropologists who deny the feasibility and moral imperatives of world cultures, and who emphasize the local quality and 'parish-pump' patterns of cultures as *mores* and moral.

Objectors may urge that the concept of the Nation is now in decline: and that, after passing like a fever or infection over Europe after the French Revolution, it today only ravages Asia and Africa. It certainly cannot be applied to contemporary South Africa since, even if we accepted that the Afrikaans-speaking and English-speaking (but not the Coloureds or Indians) constituted a nation—a view unacceptable to the Bruderbond—the Bantu majority would be no part of it, although massively 'within the territory.' (Likewise, a city or 'community' like Montreal, in the eye of a sociologist, can be seen to consist of three non-intercommunicating communities.) The United States of America, it may be urged, is not, authentically and in this sense, a nation, although the federal or 'national' authority is often put into distinction from that of the States. The Nation is essentially a racio-cultural community, whereas the contemporary pseudo-Nation, built by immigration, is heterogeneous in composition, without racial unity, and the main emphasis of its culture is individualistic. The United States precisely bears the characteristic marks juristically of a State, even if in the weak or 'consumer-dominated' federal form; but (since the philology of the word *natio* indicates its connection with blood descent) it does not bear the marks of a Nation, except by adoption or legal fiction. On the contrary, stress upon any genuine sentiment of nationality, as in France, Wales, or indeed in Quebec (or upon what is misleadingly called 'race' by American official documents, although not by ethnologists) would disrupt the American or Canadian polity, which is fused by some measure of a common culture, imparted through education and the schoolhouse and ratified in law.

American official documents list the English, Scottish, and indeed Manx 'races,' although oddly enough not (at this time of writing) the Israeli. The fusion of the American polity into a certain minimal homogeneity is achieved through the 'melting pot' (which occasionally itself 'melts') of the traditional attitude to culture of the American schoolhouse. This attitude is reinforced by 'Middletown' community institutions of a socially uniform order and 'democratic A' pattern. On the other hand, in Quebec there is a compact, self-conscious culture, deliberately and also traditionally distinctive, largely based on blood and in complicated alliances with international religion. We have here almost all of the requirements for a Nation except, possibly, the wish and calculation. As to the connection between U.S. federal democracy and so-called 'weak' (i.e., consumer-dominated) government, cf. Walter Lippmann, *The Public Philosophy*, p. 34. "My hope is that both liberty and democracy can be preserved before the one destroys the other." (*Ibid.*, p. 19) "This devitalization of the governing power is the malady of democratic states." (*Ibid.*, p. 31)

The Nation, nationality as the character of its membership, and nationalism as the stressed concept of the nation, all historically connect with the notion of supposed common stock as providing ground for the 'perpetual plebiscite' of a will to remain together, and to make a community, as well as with that memory of common achievements which the members of any historic state, including even the Hapsburg or Austro-Hungarian Empire, have also possessed.

Not the least among the component, if not original or definitive, factors are religion and language. If there is a public philosophy, there is likely to be a common religion, although this does not hold true in certain modern states whose tradition is, as in the United States, libertarian and preoccupied with small sects. Even more generally there is likely to be a common language as vehicle of this culture. The claim to autonomy of culture is a basic claim. The present writer would be the last to underestimate the historic importance of the *mystique* of language, as both uniting force and as cultural vehicle. This has never been overlooked by the French, with their identification of France with civilization (or, rather, with High Culture); but it has been gravely neglected by the Anglo-Saxon Powers, whose outlook here has been less even than that of intelligent shopkeepers, short-sighted, unimaginative, and dull. The chief legacies of Rome have been her language and her law. The same may some day be true of the English-speaking peoples, unless from negligence the legacy is lost. This is not to deny that the unemotional attitude of the English-speaking may have, for a world language, over-all pragmatic advantages.

It is not, however, a language which alone constitutes a nation, although the German-speaking Swiss or the Walloons may here look to Germany or France. It is not race. It is not religion. It is not the land as self-defining, for there are few 'natural frontiers,' be they Rhine or Rhone or Elbe. The Pyrenees cut in two Navarre and the land of the Basque people, while a natural area such as an island can include English and Welsh, as well as Scots. The Nation is not the creation of the State organization, as the history of the Austro-Hungarian Empire shows. It is the resultant of a combination of several of these factors. The statement by Ernest Renan, in his *Qu'est ce qu'une Nation?* (1882) is well known. Among the major factors, "l'une est la possession en commun d'un riche legs de souvenirs; l'autre est le consentement actuel, le désir de vivre ensemble, la volonté de continuer à faire valoir l'héritage qu'on a reçu indivis . . . Avoir des gloires communes dans le passé, une volonté commune dans le présent; avoir fait de grandes choses ensemble, vouloir en faire encore, voilà les conditions essentielles pour être un peuple . . . L'existence d'une nation est un plébiscite de tous les jours . . . une conscience morale qui s'appelle une nation . . . un désir de continuer à vivre ensemble." For Rabindranath Tagore, in his striking book *Nationalism* (1917), the distinctive mark is a common historic culture. For some this creates a 'Nationality,' whereas for them the word 'Nationalism' is reserved for chauvinist expressions. In our own days it is interesting to note the part that language has played in the cases of Bohemia and of Israel, and religion in the cases of Pakistan and, to a lesser degree by far, Israel (here, ironically, reinforced by pure race) in shaping new nations.

The State, in so far as it is not regarded juristically as the basis of a machinery of government, holding a society of subjects together, but as maybe characterized by the common nationality of its citizens and tinged with a sentiment of nationalism, is *pro tanto* a community. It is true (and the objection is an early one) that it is 'extensive' and more preoccupied with civil order or even economic high-living than with like-mindedness. This, however, is balanced by its advantage in including, at least for certain purposes, *all persons within a stipulated territory*, even if this itself be, as in the cases of Luxembourg or Denmark for example, of mere pocket-handkerchief extent and no great empire. It should be added that a State can also be held together by a sentiment of community other than nationalism, either loyalty to the realm and its monarch or (as in the earlier days of the French Revolution) the sentiment of fraternity and patriot citizenship, or, as in the cases of Switzerland and America, by a confused notion of nationality and attachment to a particular 'pattern of life.' It will be noted that, as the Rhineland Germans found during the Revolutionary occupation, the sentiment of fraternity on the part of the French, as the propaganda fervour abated, soon restrained itself to the confines of the French nation of blood, together with a few French-speaking Bretons and Basques. In all cases the sentiment of community tends indeed to connect with a like-minded attachment, in part consequence and in part cause, to a distinctive and even exclusive or proprietary 'pattern of life.' The Southern States of the United States offer instances of such a pattern.

What has always to be borne in mind in discussions of the State as community is that the factor frequently held to establish its pre-eminence here, to wit, its universality (only, however, *within* its own territorial limits, i.e., the national sovereign state is *in principle not* universal), is a necessary consequence in the logic of its chief function. This is to maintain the civil peace between all within its area. If it is to be effective here, and in the last resort coercive, it has within the scope of this function to have authority over all in the territory or bailiwick. But it is precisely this distinctive hallmark of *vis coactiva* —not so much of power in general as of force or *Macht* in the last resource (so far as is authorized by the constitutional morality and by public approval, support, or tolerance)—which in fact restricts the State's claim to be pre-eminently *the* Community, based on like-mindedness. As Nation it may have some of this quality. But St. Augustine's comment holds true that, just in so far as the State does assume domination in an indispensable function, it may not indeed be pre-destined, as civilization advances, utterly to "wither away"—regulative powers of adjustment are required—but it yet is only a Community of a secondary and derivative order. Allegiance to it is not of absolute enjoyment of it as ideal, but is conditional on its performance of its functions as means. It is Community that is natural; and the State is only such (in a basic and distinctive respect) *ratione peccati et igno-rantiae.*

Several writers have laid great stress upon the national 'pattern of life,' as defining a Nation, among them Professor Sir Ernest Barker in his *National Character and the Factors in its Formation* (1927). The trouble here is that what defines is itself so difficult to be defined. What is 'the British national character'? And is it the same or different from that of the Irish, Welsh, Scots, English?

In his *The Genius of American Politics* (1953) Professor Boorstin picks up the same argument, but concludes it in favour of the *genii loci*, such as of Oklahoma. What matters is the local customs of the various American States; and the 'national character' shows itself by respecting these. Since, unlike the cantons of Switzerland, the frontiers of most of these states are artificial to a geometrical degree, why not (it may be said) rather praise the township or village life of the face-to-face group?

What are 'un-American Activities' may be known by legal or legislative decisions. The problem is: what are 'American activities'; and does Hollywood or Boston interpret them? In England the Anglican Church was established, by law of Elizabeth I, under statute to make the attempt to give precision to the national culture pattern (as Archbishop Laud, Coleridge, and Thomas Arnold so strongly felt); but the success has been imperfect.

It yet may be truly said that, although the United States is not a Nation in the sense of France or Spain by *ius sanguinis* and connected together by the tribal bond of birth, it is yet *made* into a Nation, not by legal registration of immigrants, but precisely by *ius soli* and by a common pattern impressed upon its people in 'the melting pot,' which is in fact education through 'the little red schoolhouse' and the morning secular religion of saluting the flag. This inculcates a secular uniformity and seeks to emphasize a sense of civic responsibility, however weakened, as Walter Lippmann points out, by confusion between moral education, belief in the infinite divergence of opinions as beneficial, and mere information and 'know-how' as distinct from 'knowledge.' The Canadian 'experiment' involves no such single melting pot of education (which indeed would be politically impracticable there); and is, therefore, even more ambiguous. In many ways *les Canadiens* have, with their homogeneity, all the strongest characteristics of a Nation.

A social contract based upon reciprocal economic interests and division of social labour does not constitute a Nation. As Renan says, "un *Zollverein* n'est pas une patrie." (It may yet be a contributory factor, like a military alliance or a 'union of crowns,' to shaping a community.) For a further discussion of the State, Nation and Society, the reader is referred to the author's *Principia*, chap. VIII.

Whereas, in the last century, under the influence of a secular religion of Nationalism, of which Mazzini made himself the prophet, the Nation, with its spiritual like-mindedness, was regarded as the Community *par excellence*, and this theme, with a racial and exclusive emphasis, was continued in Europe by Hitler and in its original fashion flooded over into Asia, it can yet be argued that the Nation can never fully conform to a genuine notion of Community. It is noteworthy that both Mazzini and Gandhi remained also fundamental internationalists. There is in the Nation an element, not indeed of mechanical compulsion as with the State, but yet of the organically non-voluntary. However marked may be the national habits, and however the 'national' or citizen may both habitually and voluntarily and *ex immo corde* patriotically conform to them, the fact yet remains that only exceptionally, and as 'an outsider,' does he join the particular Nation by free choice. (The Race he can never join—unless religious conversion, as with the Khazars to Judaism, can be said to be a 'joining.')

Further, he is not only a subject or citizen of the State—with a very hypothetical 'natural right' of emigration and immigration, on which Kant insisted so much. He is also a member of the Nation, which takes the coercive State organization as its institutional form, by birth and choice of his parents. And, however much he may be out of sympathy with the activities of 'his' people (rather he is 'theirs') or critical of them, he is a member willy-nilly, *volens nolens*. The 'contract' of membership is for him an 'original' one. If he is also member of their like-minded community by active choice (as distinct from passive assent), as well as partner by birth, it is either because he is docile and educated to this pattern, or because he is lucky in a kind of pre-established harmony, or because he has a strong moral sense of traditional history as a social fate. The 'plebiscite' went his way. But a Nation, unlike a plebiscite, is no temporary flux. The same argument, although less effectively—since the sentimental attachment is greater and the coercive power smaller—applies to taking the Family as the pre-eminent example of Community.

It will be noted that not only the individual may find the dominance of the Nation something compulsory and contrary to choice. Other authentic communities and, it should be noted, subsidiary or submerged nations, brought into 'the Nation' by a legal construction, may feel the same. The Irish declined to be part of 'the British Nation' (itself not a usual phrase). The 'whites' of the Southern States often do not consider themselves to be part of one nation with the 'blacks,' or the Ukrainians to be part of the Russians. Subject to what can be done by directed education or propaganda, only under coercion from above, legal or extra-legal, can they be compelled to change their pattern. The Nation as community fades away to reveal the force of the State and of Government. As Halifax 'the Trimmer' wrote, some-times to rule men you have "to treat them scurvily," even in the name of rational justice. The criminal courts, themselves, yield only an approximate and not an ideal justice.

§v. Weltbürgertum *or World Community*

The notion of a World Society, unless emphasized adequately so as to engender the sentiment of a world community, is embarrassed by the strength of the very feeling for community, often characterized by what Harold Laski called 'the will to conflict,' which finds focus in national groupings or like local 'patterns of life.' If the sentiment of a World Society (or what Graham Wallas called 'the Great Society') were taken seriously and the principle, under 'Democracy B,' added of 'one man, one vote,' a non-European dominance of the world would follow which, in the sacred name of national community values, many Europeans and Americans and even some insurgent Asian nationalities would, at present, find intolerable. Under an aristocratic principle of leadership, under a Soviet-Eurasian construction of 'Democracy C,' or under a tyranny, such as built the power of Rome, the difficulty might not be so acute. It may be that the world, with its many emotional communities, will only be united through fear of violent death; and peace will only be enforced under a resolute tyranny. To avoid such a tyranny, *prima facie* the rational course—well supported by the history of the growth of national states—would be to recognize that the United Nations principle of non-interference in the domestic affairs of States, *beyond* the legitimate state-rights of local government, if indeed a 'principle,' is a rotten principle; that the United Nations charter needs radical revision, since 'a sovereign assembly of free nations' cannot evolve out of 'a free assembly of sovereign nations' (or what Mr. Khrushchev calls 'a debating society'), any more than a diesel engine can evolve from a horse and buggy; and that the Secretary General, dedicated to 'maintaining and enforcing peace' and supported by massive force, should be given near-dictatorial powers, persistent obstructors to the formation of a like-minded community being expelled. The defects of alternative compromises may seem to have been highlighted recently in the Congo. The conundrum remains, largely in terms of public opinion, of the means to adopt for such a construction. We are forced to mix inadequate military power with the procrastinating techniques of negotiation.

Hence, although political scientists may demonstrate, with flawless logic, that the sole sure guarantee of civil peace through the world is some form of sovereign world government, practical obstacles to the acceptance of this unpalatable conclusion will be found in popular attachment to the psychological satisfactions of immediate national groups, each holding its own prestige bomb; to the values of the community sentiment; and to the traditional power, however picayune, which this gives.

That facilities under effective world peace organization could conduce to the development, not only of peaceful family life and of local communes (at present overshadowed by the State), but also, through devolution of power, of smaller National groups, Scottish, Welsh, and the like—strategic inhibitions being removed—is a consideration often overlooked. So also is the extent to which the treasure of the State itself and indeed its administrative machinery, direction of trade and even deflection of student education to the physical sciences, as well as all attempts to reconcile necessary politics and Christian ethics, are dominated by considerations of defence, more than all else, presumably as following from the civil and secular function of maintaining peace. On the contrary, what pre-eminently has to be preserved is the *patrimonium humani generis*.

In his *We Hold These Truths* (1960, p. 287), Father John Courtney Murray, S.J., writes: "I do not want self-interest interpreted in the sense of the classic theory of *raison d'état*, which was linked to the modern concept of the absolute sovereignty of the nation-state. This latter concept imparted to the notion of national self-interest an absoluteness that was always as illegitimate as it is presently outworn. The tradition of reason requires, with particular stringency today, *that national interest*, remaining always valid and omnipresent as a motive, be given only *a relative and proximate status as an end of national action.* . . . Political action by the nation-state projected in the form of foreign policy today stands with historical clarity (as it always stood with theoretical clarity in the tradition of reason) under the imperative to realize this structure of political ends *in the international community*, within the limits—narrow but real—of the possible. Today, in fact as in theory, the national interest must be related to this international realization, which stands higher and more ultimate in political value than itself."

§vi. *The Development of Regional Communities*

One of the wisest sayings of the late Professor Gilbert Murray was that there will be no pooling of sovereignty where there is no community of values. Assuming that the world does not accept the Bolshevik solution and that the actual inherent contradictions of Marxist Communism in time come to display themselves in concrete difficulties for consumers, then a European Union including even Poland (it is not culturally improbable) may develop; or Russian fanaticism may come to be balanced in power by Chinese. It must be frankly admitted that either such a Union or the Russian plan is likely, as its cost, to *reduce* the living standard of the British worker. In the case of a European Union, including Britain, this reduction to world-levels or to wider levels, might be corrected by greatly increased productivity. In the case of an Atlantic Union, including North America, it certainly would be. Russian Communist literature is full of exposures of the Anglo-Saxon workers' privileged and invidious position, as 'lackeys of capitalism,' if not 'running-dogs of imperialism,' while the British artisan has not the natural advantage of the American in being attached to a vast and almost self-sufficient land block. An economically acceptable way out, not culturally unacceptable except for those inflamed by anti-American jealousy or by *hubris*, could be found in the practical and realistic shaping of an open Atlantic community or even of a new, majority-based Commonwealth of the Free World, although these choices also will have their uncertainly defined limits and their costs. It may be added that those who would accept the greatest danger in the firing line, Britain and France (and, in logic, we must add Germany) must have a weighty proportion of influence in the shaping of policy which cannot be decided only in Wisconsin or Nebraska, any more than only in the Pentagon or White House. However, for the moment (and with a quite remarkable measure of unanimity of acquiescence, in professional opinion, concerning discriminations), it is the occupant of the White House who, absolutely, 'holds the bomb'—thanks to the time factor—for the Western World, even if this involves demolition without representation.

The route to world peace-enforcement, were men rational, might well be through regional nuclei and vast associations, such as the European, Soviet, Arab and (including the West European) the Atlantic, which achieve (even if provisionally and until authentic world organization is possible) a felicitious working equilibrium or pragmatic balance between national Community feeling and the calculations of individuals in Society concerning the solid advantages of peace. A habit of international co-operation can be engendered; a system of organic union and consultation developed, with interchange of plans and personnel; and that necessary experience in supra-nationalism, which would include the habitual mutual inspection and control of arms and of spying adventures—which, first practicable among friends, can later be extended to those in whom there is not like confidence. The immediate attempt to secure the *enforcement* of peace straight-away by one universal world organization (as distinct from the evolutionary selection of this as authentic goal), which organization does not yet correspond to any like sentiment, risks stretching the actualities of power too much and may lead to institutions actually devoid of force and to conference halls which are but whited sepulchres of a pious hope.

For further discussion of these issues, the reader is referred to my *Atlantic Community* (1959), and to my earlier *Anglo-American Union as Nucleus of World Federation* (1942) and *The Unity of Europe* (1944, commissioned by the Polish Government-in-Exile). Cf. also the writer's article, "The Commonwealth of the Free World," in the *Contemporary Review*, October, 1960; and subsequent articles, published for private circulation as *Atlantic Union* (1961).

It may be added that, if the U.S.A., acting for the U.N., and the U.S.S.R. had become involved over Korea—the Chinese supply lines were highly vulnerable and the issue that of the challenge to the reality of the Soviet-Chinese alliance—the showdown (equivalent to that which might have shaped, in 1936, with Hitler) would have taken place over Vladivostok and in the Far Eastern theatre, at a time inconvenient to the Soviets, and under one of the greatest of all American generals; and not, as with Berlin, in Europe. The avoidance, however, of such a trial of strength has possibly been beneficial both to the Asian and African worlds and hence, *pro tanto*, to civilization.

It may, of course, be plausibly argued (*a*) that the United Nations, for the present and for the immediately forseeable future, has and will have no power to enforce peace, at least where the interests of the Great Powers are affected; (*b*) that regional integrations, such as that of Western Europe, although moving on principle in the right political direction, are equally incompetent to enforce a world peace which is now at once urgent and indivisible, and could themselves become rival blocs, in addition to the World Powers, moved by jealousies, thinking of neutrality, and aspiring to regional prestige by entering into the bomb-race on their own account. Hence the only functionally satisfactory proximate solution, if it can be negotiated, will be a Russo-American *condominium* against all comers, pending world integration and government.

This was, of course, approximately the dream of Franklin Roosevelt in his handling of Stalin, in which policy Stalin out-played Roosevelt. Realistically and on a regional or dyarchic basis of agreed 'spheres of influence,' this policy, although it has its terrifying aspects, has much to be said for it. However, it is to be hoped that such U.S. hegemony will be organically united with a Free World Commonwealth or Atlantic Union grouping, in which the other members, besides the United States, would have full consultative rights and at least adequate, if not strictly proportionate (which could weaken leadership), joint political powers and representative democracy. This practical issue carries us beyond the theme of the present book.

It is, however, perhaps necessary to point out that all vital political theory is, and always has been, concerned with so-called 'great issues,' that is, with practical problems of urgency. This writer has been concerned with the practical problems, as central, of war and peace since 1918 (*vide* Preface). Thomas Hobbes wrestled theoretically with practical problems of sovereignty arising from personal experience of two civil wars—in the France of Louis XIII and the Fronde, and in the England of the Stuarts and Cromwell.

§vii.   *The Church as Moral Community*

The Church, as social form, offers a distinctive example of a Community, in its characteristics of like-minded sentiment, as well as in the manners and morals of the cultus, which distinguish it from any other organization of society. This remark applies alike to Catholicism and to the six hundred sectarian forms, listed in the United States under the title of a Church; and no less to atheistic forms such as Buddhism and Marxist organization, the last part-Church and part-Party. A Nation indeed can offer a share in certain values transcending the present, and inculcates, as under the pagan Roman Empire, a patriotic religion of dedication to its own community. There are circumstances under which Nationalism verges on a religion. But the element of deliberate choice of these transcendent values, accompanied by a ritual and doctrine concerning them, is lacking in secular organizations (as the words 'secular' and 'temporal' indeed imply). The Church lacks indeed certain (but not all the) pressure characteristics which, for example, Municipality, State, Federal Government, International Authority and, indeed, even Trade Unions possess in terms of their distinctive functions. But the membership of some churches is larger than the membership of many states; and, historically, the Church, alike Christian, Moslem, Jewish and Buddhist, has a more antique right to regard itself as a Community and indeed *societas perfecta* and *persona realis*, with attendant claims to allegiance, than the Modern State. The jealousy of Church and State is, of course, also a matter of the record, so that for Hobbes the Church is the Kingdom of Spirits and of Darkness, as distinct from the good Kingdom of Matter; and the Leviathan, of which Charles II was the sun or head and English *roi soleil*, could conjoin church and state in one 'mortal god.' It is, however, not until our own century that, as over against the Church, the local State has developed completely totalitarian claims as the *sole* Community.

The Church has the characteristics of a Community as like-minded, voluntary, homogeneous, intensive in social form, but also exclusive. This exclusiveness may amount to no more than an insistence, for those whom it freely welcomes, upon adherence to minimal requirements of creed or behaviour, and may be compatible, as in India, with the 'indifferentist' co-existence of one church with other churches or temples. Or, in accordance with the tendencies of *all* communities, it may be intolerant of intrusion and preferential in interest. As the Apostle says: "Do good to all men, and especially to those of the household of faith." Most benevolent societies conduct themselves in like fashion.

The position varies from the exclusiveness of Judaism and the militancy of Islam to the philosophical indifferentism as between "the many roads to truth," religious and moral, (but not ritualistic indifferentism) of Hinduism, and the practical philosophy of manners of Confucianism. Buddhism and Ba'haism can claim, with Christianity, to be religions of love, not only among the brotherhood but among all men of good will, although the former from India to Indonesia has shown low survival value and the second is a minor religious form. The interpretations of the dogma "I am the way, the truth and the life," and of the Power of the Keys "to bind and to loose"—"whose sins ye remit they are remitted"—have been various. Nevertheless, the Church as a community, in practically all its religious forms, has been based upon an articulate faith and attendant behaviour, and in principle upon a free private choice of that faith and behaviour. Civic order may be maintained by inquisition and coercion; but there is no salvation but by free choice. The Churches are voluntary communities by choice of the Faith or Idea. As such they are more ideal (or moral) communities than the States.

In the opinion of many political theorists (and, in the view of the present writer, correctly) the major political function of the Church is to check the State, as disorganized individuals cannot, and for this it requires power and acceptance of its own authority. Thus: THE CHURCH HAS A POLITICAL FUNCTION BEARING ON THE CIVIL AUTHORITY (Proposition 39). Moreover, a Church which is not a community, organized and with some form of 'book of discipline' (the Quaker term), is not for the political theorist a social or 'political' church, but merely an attitude towards life of aggregated individuals. It is without interest for the student of politics. (The polar opposite to this is a position according to which Christianity is defined in its teachings by the Church; and the Church is what the Pope says it is—although this last statement has to be conditioned by the authority of the Sacred College and by the very actual power of the local episcopate.) A church is subject to the general political rules of power even while (as we shall see, in chapter IX) being able to transcend them in its ends. There has, further, always been a churchly theory of hierarchy from the days of ancient Egypt to the present. That it existed from the days of the early Christian Church, despite prophetic and chiliastic elements, and is not a recent deviation, is made clear, in his *Social Teaching of the Christian Churches* (1931, translated by Olive Wyon), by Professor Ernst Troeltsch.

Thanks to this balance between ecclesiastical and civil organization (and to like balances established by other voluntary or industrial organizations), the individual is protected from domination and enabled to exercise a measure of free choice in social purposes, with a supporting public opinion. To perform this authoritative and directive function to the best effect, the powerful organization needs to be linked with clear conceptions of ideal purpose or ideal patterns of values. Industrial organizations have also been able to exercise powerful checking balance; but have usually put forward no like claims to ideal ends. (Marxist organizations have.) Thus Professor Troeltsch writes of the Catholic Church, monastic and papal, that it presented the structure of "World-flight in the service of the world-dominating Church: world-domination in the service of world-renunciation."

Calvinist writers have been equally clear (as Hobbes detected) about the authoritative function of the churches in limiting the secular sovereign, and in checking the excesses of ignorant or insolent kings or congressmen, by virtue of an established pattern of ideal values. Islam and Judaism have recognized a like task, although the distinction between legitimate authority and forcible power *de facto* has never been fully worked out under Islam (which means 'Obedience'), even under the Caliphate. Unlike a pious and admirable Confucianism, with its perpetual checks of a rational constitutional morality of manners, and unlike scholastic theses stemming from propositions of Reason, at once human and divine, in the case of Islam, with its philosophy of Will, 'the mandate of Heaven' could apparently be given capriciously and be withdrawn abruptly.

Two other views of 'the Ecclesiastical Polity' (to use Hooker's significant term) have been prominent. The first (1) of these is noncivic or 'non-civilly-minded.' We find instances ranging from negative Buddhism, as distinct from Lamaism, and from the primitive, persecuted (and, at first, chiliastic) Christian Church, down to contemporary Quakerism. Congregationalism has some of these characteristics, although not where it accommodates itself, in almost Rotarian fashion, to 'Community churches of civic works' (in another 'area sense' of the word 'community'). The Church here need not be 'acosmic' or entirely other-worldly, apocalyptic, or prophetic (although it is this for some): it can be concerned with the 'daily bread' and—as with the primitive Christian Church from quite early times—be so far orthodox in behaviour as to be (as the Church Fathers insisted) hierarchical and with a power order of command. But the feeling can be that the religious Community, emphatically felt to be such and to be a brotherhood, should be unconcerned with 'the world' as secular, and indeed be without power-connections with it.

In effect this has spelt in many cases (a) a relaxation of authority in the church community to a point where it does not attempt to control the secular order, except in the case of spasmodic 'moral' campaigns; (b) the atomization of the church to the point where it becomes, good-citizen relations apart, little more than an aggregate of individuals meeting for worship at intervals, because each individual is in private conversation with God and receives for his conscience private replies, if any, each individual being his own priest; (c) the utilization as individuals (along with other individuals, not of the communion) of, say, some secular Party, for purposes of achievements in the civil field—thus we can have 'Protestants and Others [possibly atheists or agnostics] United'; (d) the denial of any power structure or even repudiation of concern with effects in mundane History, as inconsistent with the ideal, since each achieves the good individually, and, as it were, in a dream-freedom (although Kant sought to show that all our *bad* acts are determined) or in some other-worldly state of the hereafter. The conclusion can be the effective dissolution of any Church as an organized entity, community or polity.

A second species (2) of Protestant political theory is best exemplified by traditional Lutheran theory (although it has influenced many political theorists who are not Lutheran). This makes a sharp dichotomy between man and mundane society, which latter is yet fully recognized. The moral man in a state of grace is not concerned with means, control, power, or the social or cosmic order, but with individual salvation of soul. (This can yet develop parallel with a Protestant economic theory of the individual pursuing his thrifty lonely way very keenly and industriously in this world under conditions of laissez-faire and despising social props.) This philosophy can grow along with a Kantian philosophy of pietism, which regards itself as free from all church rules. Grace is not regarded as a spiritual influence or education aiding the soul beyond its deserts from outside, through channels social, sacramental, or of individual agency, in a fashion compatible with the Platonic prototypes of the church in the ideal republic. Grace is strictly bilateral, not multilateral. There is no *corpus mysticum* exercising power, and (as Augustine thought) control for justice on earth, over the secular city.

In sharp contrast to the Helleno–Roman Catholic view, the secular city or, briefly, 'Society' operates under its own quite separate moral rules, or rather amoral rules, of power and *raison d'état*, although one may pray for 'a godly prince.' These rules may be those of Machiavelli or of Marx. Indeed we may recognize that there is much to be said for the Marxist position as touching these worldly rules of our ever-imperfect mundane society. Secular society, from the otherworldly standpoint, is necessarily utterly corrupt (as is human nature *in se*); nor is this corruption to be overcome by 'works,' social or individual. There is a 'Moral Man' and an 'Immoral Society.' Politics is not subject to the imperatives of ethics, which is personal, not social.

Along with the view that the moral individual should concern himself with more perfect matters than politics, the so-called Erastian will affirm that the secular society must direct the churches, where there is any overlapping of functions. The distance then becomes a short one to affirming that the state, for educational purposes, should develop a secular religion of its own. To meet the very practical demands of the secularist Third French Republic such theorists as the sociologist Emile Durkheim began to expound a social explanation of religion as the sublimation or hypostatic projection upwards of the tribal mind. The tribe, be it Neolithic or the Third Republic of M. Combes, these philosophers held, rediscovered itself as God by this cinematographic projection to the clouds, and duly worshipped itself —complete with Tricolour.

The false but widely prevalent doctrine that "ethics do not apply to politics" or, alternatively, that the ethics of the State (or Church or Trade Union or Class) and that of the individual belong to different genera rests usually either on a confusion of thought or definition or on a dogma which makes the achievement of individual ethical life something entirely other-worldly, not attainable in the present world in any exact sense (since 'works' are without value); the consequence of predestined salvation; and, hence, patently nothing fundamentally to do with the individual's behaviour in the present communion, and in social and political life with his fellows. The contrary principle is enunciated in the Lord's Prayer: *fiat voluntas tua sicut in coelo et in terra.* The issue is not to be confused with the quite different one whether it is prudent or honest to conduct the foreign policy of a great country by senatorial moralizings and homiletics addressed to foreign countries but with an eye on the home-voters; and criticism of situations where there is no readiness at all to pay the costs and assume concrete political responsibilities if the advice is taken. This, at the best, is a naive sentimentality (or a calculated vote-catching) and, at the worst, is hypocrisy.

It is noteworthy that, whereas Mr. George Kennan occupies much of his *American Diplomacy* with an analysis and denunciation of such irresponsible and immature tendencies in early American diplomacy, the actual conclusion of his book is the severely (and perhaps excessively) moral one that each nation must unilaterally set an example in its own territory and pattern of living which it would wish its neighbours to follow (pp. 127–8). In so far as what is urged is this unilateralism, the case is, at least, arguable.

As distinct from the senator or politician who moralizes to other nations about their conduct, without assuming himself political responsibility, it is important to note the harm done by the 'perfectionist' or 'other-world-er,' in the sense that, while insisting that man must strive towards the horizon of perfection, he affirms *a priori* that it is impossible that man should on this earth attain to the described perfection. It, therefore, lies outside the purview of mundane political discussion. In the words of Luther, "we know that reason is the devil's harlot." Against this we may state that a perfection which by hypothesis is impossible is by definition, since not realizable, therefore not a realizable good. That which we can never achieve in this world is no good in this world. Much trouble of grave import has been introduced into politics by this kind of theology, usually combined with escapism from the problems of power. And, because associated with the 'idealistic,' 'impracticable,' or 'humanly impossible,' ethical principles in politics have been degraded and associated with empty pieties and homilies—or the issue hypocritically evaded. Also, sound ethics are ethics that are imperative (and practicable) in the social realm of the practical. Otherwise, they are schizophrenic and therefore not sound.

In the days of the early Christian Church, and especially of Tertullian, there was among some a certain *non-civisme*. *Quid imperatori cum ecclesia?* This view did not prevail. The classical position becomes that of Ambrose and Augustine. Some of the Reformers, especially of the Lutheran tradition, in this respect embarking upon a deformation, emphasized a dichotomy between a 'civil dominion' which they admitted to exist and towards which their attitude sometimes verged upon the obsequious, and an other-worldly condition of grace to which the saved could attain, achieving perfection after this life. This emphasis upon transcendent individual values was different, but not dissimilar, from the exaggerated Renaissance emphasis upon the individual for whom, in Alberti's phrase, all things were possible. This mood is sometimes, by apologists, spoken of as the characteristic of the Modern Age. If so, we may say—so contrary is its mood to that of the present time—that the 'Modern Age,' no more than the 'Classical' or 'Mediaeval,' is eternal; that it is over; and that the new Social Age has overtaken it. In the words of Dr. Reinhold Niebuhr (*The Structure of Nations and Empires*, p. 138), "the Reformation was not very successful in relating these religious visions to the collective life of man." As to this last, Dr. Niebuhr characteristically comments that its "cohesion, always inconclusive, is ambiguous morally," history itself being contingent and of an "inconclusive character." Freedom has its "destructive" side; but we should cherish "an uneasy conscience" amid these chaotic doubts.

Dr. Reinhold Niebuhr as a theologian always deserves to be heard with respect, although as a political theorist he is (or was in his earlier books) perhaps an outstanding, if often ambiguous and sometimes contradictory, example of the traditional Protestant German heresy of dichotomy between man and constitutional or legal society, which is necessarily corrupted by the problems of power—or, to phrase this dichotomy as this writer would, the problems of necessary social adjustments between different men's ideals and ambitions. In his recent book, *The Structure of Nations and Empires*, Dr. Niebuhr has changed his position in significant respects. He maintains two theses. First, in *secular politics*: that the political form known as the autonomous nation is an enduring form in the existential political field; and that all discussion alike of such disarmament as changes the balance of power or of world government, or steps thereto, is visionary and misleading. All 'political universalism' is to be rejected. The United States is cited as an instance of an 'autonomous nation,' like France, although (apart from the query what 'nation' here means) it is explained that there can be 'multi-national nations'—a phrase which I do not understand. We are indeed told that "the rise of the modern nation . . . represents a victory of the more primal forces of community, particularly the force of ethnic kinship" (p. 289). This statement would be true of chauvinism, 'bruderbonds,' *Rassentheorie*, Hitlerism, K.K.K. xenophobia, and the like, but we are apparently invited to regard this as, if not 'the wave of the future,' at least an enduring and fundamental factor. It is an amazing concession, which makes the worst evils of 'universalism,' even the Communist authority, beautiful by comparison.

The second thesis (or prolegomenon about autonomy and individualism) is that, in the field of *transcendental values* or grace, there are personal perfections to which we must aspire and which never can be discovered in the actual life of any human society. "It may prove also that the ultimate truths of the Christian faith are acceptable *only to the individual,* and are almost bound to be misused by collective man and his majesties . . . only the individual can know of the impossible possibility of life transcending nature-history in some act of heroism and sacrifice which defies all rational calculations . . ." (italics mine). (It might indeed have been thought that statesmen were peculiarly acquainted with the heroism of armies 'achieving the impossible.') The universalism expressed in the Papacy (and in Communism) and its 'pretensions' (*alias* constructive work) are to be condemned. The doctrine of theopoiesis of the Orthodox Church would appear to be no less wrong.

Per contra, with this traditional Protestant heresy of the Lutheran school I disagree. In one passage, indeed, Dr. Niebuhr himself points out this great weakness (p. 291), even if his own dissociation is ambiguous and incomplete. The nexus between the religious prolegomenon and the political conclusion is logical. Dr. Niebuhr's analysis of the problem of power, which displays similarities with that of Professor Hans Morgenthau, and of that of human values, is not mine, although we agree about the conflict that lies in the nature of Man and of every man and nature. And the conclusion seems to me to be inappropriate as means to achieve the assumed ends of mundane peace —beyond recommending (as he finally does) the sanitary effects of a healthy fear of bombs and an increased use of traditional diplomacy. The perfectionist basis of argument, of itself and irrespective of the extent to which it is sustained by Dr. Niebuhr, would seem to be unrealistic in a fundamental sense, defeatist about human societies, and hence false and practically misleading.

Dr. Reinhold Niebuhr is a prolific as well as an influential writer. The evolution of his work (*Moral Man and Immoral Society*, 1932; *Christianity and Communism* [symposium], 1937; *Christian Realism and Political Problems*, 1954) merits careful study. In *Christian Realism* Niebuhr emphasizes "a sense of responsibility in the actual conditions of human existence" (p. 69); there is "a gospel of redemption" also for nations (p. 107); nevertheless "there is no way of transmuting the Christian Gospel into a system of historical optimism;" there is "an indeterminate character of human freedom" and fewer things than is supposed about which one can be sure that they must be done or not done. The dignity and the misery of man spring from the same roots. Owing to this central affirmation of will and indeterminacy, Dr. Niebuhr is an opponent of that assimilation of the Creation under the rule of law with human nature under the rule of reason to which the profoundly rational (if also empiric) Natural Law School tends.

With analogies between the relation of the West and Communism with Christianity and Islam or with Catholicism and Protestantism, leading to co-existence in later history, we have to be careful, since the nature of the balance was decided in arms at Tours and Lepanto, or in the seventeenth century, not least by Richelieu. One can, however, agree with Dr. Niebuhr and indeed go beyond him in holding that 'the cold war' should not be waged on irrelevant issues—both sides are materialist and contain many atheist intellectual leaders; the Communist economy may be more efficient (at whatever cost) in production than the Western with its restrictive practices; the technical education, puritan morale, and (one may truly say) religious dedication of the Communist world may be superior. The basic issues are, then, of relative power and of a blueprint to impose political monopoly (*alias* tyranny), not only upon those who like it, but upon those who do not. The 'struggle for the minds of men' (a phrase which there is documentary reason to think that Senator William Benton and this writer coined . . .) is about raising the morale of the free world commonwealth and making it receptive of bold leadership and of change of public opinion and capable of new ideas about outgrown political forms. Some of such ideas, alack!, Dr. Niebuhr with his traditional notions of power, rejects. As the Archbishop of Santiago de Cuba said (November, 1960), "Gold cannot buy or cannons destroy ideas." But it is yet necessary first to have them. Mental conservatism lagging behind the interdependence theme of the British Prime Minister will lead us nowhere—not even as far as an imaginative policy in Europe, under octogenarians, has already got Europe. America, one feels, must think again. Dr. Niebuhr himself is, of course, no conservative.

In considering the relation of the Individual to the Society or Community, it will later be argued in this book that there are transcendent values, whether we call them religious or metaphysical, intellectual or aesthetic. In the light of this it can here provisionally be asserted that the human ends of the developed personality are never merely the product of, and never merely subordinate to, any particular society or community. The proper means conduce to their increased realization *sicut in coelo et in terra*. So far there is, indeed, grounds for optimism. The person, whom Aristotle—and, in some passages, even some Marxists (*vide* Kenneth Ingram, *Communist Challenge*, 1948, p. 60)—puts first, judges between these social claims. We may go beyond judging *between* social claims. We may (and shall) affirm that there are aesthetic values which transcend—as being possible for the future 'in theory' ($\theta\epsilon\omega\rho\iota a$ or 'vision')—*any* social pattern of place or time. We shall condemn all presumptuous attempts, in the face of the record of cultural history and of humanistic experience, to elevate mere local and tribal patterns, even if resting on 'the basic affinities' of all Europe or of all the United States (as over against something called 'the East'), into moral certainties before the human and divine tribunal.

This does not mean that on this earth the central values are not realizable or have not for a while in particular places or times been realized, like some vision of natural beauty—but the force of pride and misplaced love of power compromise them. Who shall say that love does not exist, because domestically and socially it is qualified? The right social means also are means to making the transcendent more immanent among us. But daily and hourly and by strenuous individual and political work the two have to be brought together. If power is corrupted, it is *corrupted by men*, by choice, not by necessity—and not least by defeatist or escapist men, individual souls dreaming of individual pieties, who, not harnessing the spirit of the heaven-seeking monk to that of the social church, have not found their 'chariot of fire,' resolute to 'rebuild Jerusalem,' or who, having escaped on it, leave no Isaiah behind on earth and no Nehemiah.

It can be contended that 'the ethical' can be defined as behaviour which conduces, for the collectivity and for the individual within that collectivity as good citizen, to the victory of a State, Nation, or indeed

Class. This last is the Leninist contention. The formula in effect adopted by Machiavelli in *The Prince* (not the most serious of his works) is that the ethical principles of the human race or of the Christian religion are less important than what their rulers or tyrants decide is advantageous for the better security, *salus populi*, of the few thousand inhabitants of Florence. The paradox has only to be stated to be rejected. The truth is that the security of the people (or the right to the appropriate means by a class in the achievement of ends) is to be interpreted by what reason—and not the opinion or opportunism of the moment—dictates to be, in adequate perspective, desirable ends. About this there can be debate: but the debate is *within* the one field of ethics itself.

For example, it can be argued, and reasonably is, that a community has a proper right, resting on the freedom of its members, to preserve itself and to fight for the maintenance of that social authority which sustains its order. Hence a patriotic Scot could argue that Union with England was an abomination, as destroying this self-preservation. But there are many communities; and their rights have rationally to be weighed against each other in terms of human good and of these ends. Some can argue that there is a permanent plurality—and even conflict and *contradiction*—of rational goods. This we shall debate later. It is noteworthy that Aristotle, in his discussion of whether a good man can be a good citizen in a bad state, subjects such a state or *polis* to a general and common ethical criterion.

Much of the confusion is due to a certain moralistic *simplicisme*, and arises from a simple cause which need not be ground for controversy and is indeed a platitude in ethics as well as being the basis of casuistry. The instigators of the abandonment of moral imperatives in politics are often perfectionists, the men *qui veulent faire l'ange et font le bête*. The trouble here is a species of Montanist heresy which, if it cannot get personal religious perfection, throws away the reins of control; which insists that a priest is not such unless he is sinless or that a magistrate is not entitled to sit on the bench if he has ever privately committed an offence—whereas the saints themselves are not subject to the *dominium civile*, being in grace, and need no law. The perfect live apart from the world by good intentions of the will, by inscrutable salvation, and *fide sola*, without need to bear fruit *in fide caritate formata* and in the responsibilities of civic works.

Let us look at the issue concretely. For example, generosity is a virtue in the individual. But in the case of a family man, with the duties arising from his station, generosity beyond a certain measure becomes excessive, imprudent, and a vice. The same is true of a judge. A politician, or a prince, has human duties in terms of right and wrong like other mortals; but his behaviour is ethically limited by the rational responsibilities of his office. He has distinctive responsibilities *de regimine principum*. The morals of the business world, the official world, and of family life may and even should be different, not because of basic difference of ethical principle but because the fields of application, roles, and responsibilities are different.

For example, again, the ethical virtue of personal loyalty, laudable in all men (if sometimes liable to be at the expense of truth), is held —perhaps owing to its rarity—to be quite especially important in judging the quality of politicians. Likewise, political representatives, and under them civil servants and soldiers, may be held, like court lawyers, ethically to be obligated to conform in policy to the mandate given by their clients, the electors. To what extent they should conform as representatives or use their own judgements as legislators is a matter decided by the local custom and constitutional morality of the place. If the popular mandate is to fight any country at sight and on mere suspicion of 'knavish tricks,' if the representative thinks this mandate immoral or lunatic, he should resign. If the question be whether an electorate has the right to give such a mandate, the answer of the political scientist is that, in technical right about ends, they may choose any end or mandate they please. For the political philosopher they have no right to anything except what is moral and rational, whether it be to preserve the end product of their state (e.g., of Scotland as against the reasonable union of England and Scotland) or to preserve their individual lives (e.g., as Hobbes said, to run away in battle if that were the more expedient course) or to achieve something better. The empire of the ethical judgement cannot be abrogated. But the ethical imperative is adjusted to the situation, since actual duties are the duties of the situation. The Ten Commandments depend upon definitions.

Under an Erastian theory, indeed, the realms of 'the Dominion of Grace' and of 'the Civil Dominion' can be brought into closer association but, so far as all those worldly activities are concerned (which exist in a different compartment from the Sabbatic affairs of individual salvation and prayer), the State will be in charge. This philosophy, incidentally, fits well in with those schools of thought which conceive of the State as a metaphysical entity and as *the* exclusive Community —in contrast to Maritain's correct distinction of "State" and "body politic"; and of its priest, the statesman, as sharply apart alike from the morals of the common man and from any laws springing from the psychology of human nature. This is a repudiation of the view that these rules also obtain for man as man-in-society (as Plato said), and even for rulers, politicians and statesmen, who both can and do err and sin. It is a heresy, profoundly anti-Augustinian and condemned by orthodoxy, of which the consequence is to remove from this world and its rulers the shackles or limits of the moral law, as enforced by a highly organized ideal opinion and by practical political support or withdrawal of support in accordance with its authority.

That the checking function of the Church, when not organized with an adequate discipline, is incomplete is shown in contemporary Eastern Europe, although the work of such Lutherans as Bishop Dibelius (practising a very conditional 'passive obedience' . . .) must not be underestimated. As a check the Church appears to be, on the record, more politically effective than Trade Unionism, which is more easily subverted. (However, in the case of the Eastern Orthodox Churches it would be true to say, not that they were made political by Constantine, but that—with distinguished exceptions—after Constantine they either were content to be 'other-worldly' or were used as political tools, losing any independent civil politics of their own. Of ecclesiastical politics, they had enough and to spare.) The alleged remark of Stalin, "How many divisions has the Pope?" although cynical, was more stupid than most by that statesman, and tends to echo its laughter back.

The received Lutheran tradition of the recent past, dividing the spheres of Church and State, not in the manner of the Gelasian formula, but on the basis of the Church being 'only other-worldly,' will be found in the address of the Rector of Berlin University, Dr. G. Rümelin, *Politics and the Moral Law* (translated by Rudolf Tombo, Jr., 1901) before the First World War; and indeed in the more notorious but doubtless sincere writings of a pious layman, General von Bernhardi (quoted in *Principia*, p. 395).

The separation of Church and State, generally received as part of American constitutional doctrine, is ambiguous in character. It can spell no more than the repudiation of the notion of having any national church 'by law established,' such as the Anglican Church under the Statutes of Elizabeth I. In the views of Paine and indeed of such deists as Jefferson (and even of Franklin) it is almost certainly meant much more—and indeed is a sentence of death on orthodox Christianity by the 'hundred cuts' of sectarianism, the sects ranking legally on the same level as golf clubs. Some of this purely secularist philosophy, in lieu of empiric accommodations, will be found periodically in decisions of the Supreme Court of the United States, as well as in a certain species of American secularist and 'national-pattern-of-life' philosophy.

The right of children (Protestant) to be instructed in the schools in their own religion has interestingly been held in Canadian courts to be a matter of Natural Law and unsubvertible (Mr. Justice Casey in *Chabot* v. *Commissaires*, 1957, Court of Queen's Bench, 707).

For the Society of Friends (Quakers), who have their Book of Discipline, the highly selective and small community is held together by a maximum of 'sharing' of pleasures and pains, and a minimum of coercive social discipline. We thus have an authentic community of a very high voluntary level. The theoretical difficulty that the doctrine of 'the Inner Light' is highly individualist, and even anarchist, is met by a selection of like-minded souls, which collection discovers that a common light from a common source, welling from the divine spirit in the profoundest human nature, is shared. (A sympathetic interpretation of this view, and of its basic soundness, will be found in Bertrand de Jouvenel's *De la souveraineté*, chap. XXVI.) The society in Utah of Latter Day Saints or Mormons, also an authentic community, is for more authoritarian and territorial in focus, and hence resembles old Geneva Calvinism politically.

The Church politically provides not only a valuable political balance, ensuring, as against communal totalitarianism, a range of choice. Patently it also offers to the individual chooser its own cultural goods of direct enjoyment. A German school indeed, represented by such writers as the historian Heinrich von Treitschke, in the wake of the more cautious Hegel, has expressed the view that today the State is the primary bearer of cultural values. It is an error into which the Marxists, who have traditionally viewed the State as an instrument of class oppression (Lenin), have not blandly fallen. On the contrary: TO TAKE THE SPECIFIC INSTANCES OF THE LATIN CATHOLIC AND GREEK ORTHODOX CHURCHES, THERE IS A CULTURAL ANAEMIA IN FAILING TO RECOGNIZE THAT THEY NOT ONLY WERE, BUT IN THEIR CULTURES AND COMMUNITY ARE, THE PRIMARY SPECIFIC BEARERS OF THE JUDAO-HELLENIC AND ROMAN (OR NEW ROMAN) TRADITION, NOT SO MUCH OF EUROPEAN (THE RECENTLY CHRISTIANIZED NORDICS HAVE INADEQUATELY FELT THEMSELVES TO BE PART OF IT) AS OF MEDITERRANEAN CIVILIZATION. TO IGNORE OR DIVORCE ONESELF FROM IT CONDUCES TO CULTURAL POVERTY. THIS CONTENTION IS NOT INCOMPATIBLE WITH EMPHASIZING THE HUMAN VITALITY WHICH SPRINGS FROM DIVERSITY AND MUTATION OF VIEWS. (Proposition 40) If this Judao-Hellenic tradition is to be ignored on the ground that the more youth severs itself from ancient tradition the better, then European-American civilization becomes a very raw and recent thing compared with that of the Chinese, the Indians, or even the Arabs. The habitual Chinese claim receives justification.

There is indeed another tradition, a flowering of Anglo-Saxon Puritanism, with its integrity and *raide* austerity, still best found in Boston (not the city, but the mood). There are, of course, other great traditions, including the Rabbinic one, tracing from original Judaism—although culturally the Old Testament, taken in isolation, is an unpleasant book. Perhaps the only great cultural tradition comparable to the Catholic which the history of mankind offers is the immensely wealthy and respect-worthy one of China, until this last ephemeral minute of its history pacific and only disfigured by a certain indifference, in that over-populated land of the Yellow River, to the claims of human life and the pursuit of happiness.

§viii. *The Community and the Market of Wants*

a. From the point of view of political science, a Community, regarded as means to an end, offers a close combination, providing an alternative and even intoxicating increase in power for the whole and for its leaders against those less organized. It is able to achieve this result owing to the willingness of the consumer members to sacrifice a large measure of their material and political demands, which might require divergent action, in return for *the prospective rewards of a close, organized co-operative partnership.* Hence an authentic Community is a striking instance of the action of trust and co-operative power within its group, which by no means excludes ambitions of dominative power over the heathen and Gentile without. (A Machiavelli was indeed prepared to urge that religion, as a strong bond of community, should be used for a similar end.) The correction of this last difficulty may be expected to be found in the development of co-operative power as between communities or nations, which in turn means the emergence of *both* sentiment for some adequately rewarding, larger form of community, *and* suitable institutions, together with some transformation, although not necessarily decay, of interest in the earlier community as exclusive and as having claims in excess of the national values and rewards which it can supply. One can, of course, imagine the evolution of a world state and complementarily of a world church from existing traditions.

A disadvantage with Democracy B and, especially, with Democracy D is that these, approximating to free consumers' markets, cannot readily adjust themselves to competition from a disciplined community, with directed labour (popularly sanctioned) and with its small demands both for itself and upon its leaders, who can accumulate the powers of tyrants or dictators. The Constitutions, under Democracy D, tend to enshrine demands that became fixed even two centuries ago, perhaps under conditions of isolation and which are not elastic to change in a new international situation. Such a Constitution can be a millstone around the neck of its citizens. Even at a military level (not to speak of the prolonged mental discipline of a 'cold war,' which seems contrary to the entire temper of a hedonistic and consumer-satisfying democracy) it is difficult to secure assent for the necessary sacrifices from those brought up to believe that only their own opinions and desires matter, especially if they can collectively call themselves 'sovereign.'

The Civil War in America was greatly prolonged, according to competent military testimony, owing to what was termed 'democracy'—the custom in the Northern armies of electing the officers like the judges—and owing, hence, to the incapacity of these officers to enforce discipline. It is yet noteworthy that Lincoln seems to have thought of himself (Edmund Wilson, *Eight Essays*, 1954, chap. VI) as destined to exercise powers of 'strong government' that might well end in his own assassination. A dictatorial government, further, can maintain a secrecy which a populist one can only correct by dangerous spying.

The alternative is, first, the route of appeasement or compromise with those who actually hold organized power; secondly, to permit (as under the Vichy regime in France) the swing of the market across from excessive freedom, through defeat in diplomacy or war and with a winnowing of established stocks of 'rights,' over to an externally imposed authoritarian or even tyrant regime, with the prospect of a later swing back to more sober freedoms; thirdly the establishment of a successful leadership, with voluntary surrender of hurtful freedoms excessive or too cheaply obtained; or, fourthly, the abolition of war and the reduction of the pressures of competition in defence, hostile to any wide freedom (cf. Proposition 28). The first choice is the usual result of negotiations with tyrannies, 'lest a worse evil befall.' (What is in particular the lesser evil depends upon the resources which resolution and discipline, and the restriction of the licence of what may be termed 'Elvis Presley democracy,' can summon up.) As touching the second choice, the drawback is that, on the record and despite the opinion of Aristotle, tyrannies, especially if they pass over into paternal despotisms, are a singularly long-lived form of polity. Men are ever ready to establish a tyranny through their hopes and greeds; and to be unable to terminate it owing to their fears. One constructive method of self-discipline, as in the third choice, is the establishment of a wider order, as it were by a social contract of sovereigns, to *enforce* peace, with powers (as in all law) *against oneself*. Patently it has costs . . . Another method is, during crisis, the restriction of the competitive brokerage or salesmanship of the multi-party system, with its over-exploitation of the free market. It is a one-party community system which has to be met in competition—perhaps by increased bipartisan approaches in matters where agreement on techniques or ends is feasible. The issue here is one of a clear perception of priorities among needs. It has, of course, also costs.

b. A Community, however, in its common behaviour of the members, provides for its members a direct object of enjoyment. To this extent it is not political means, but an end in itself. Sometimes indeed (and this must be stressed) the bonds of community offer means to ends less laudable, as we have seen in our own day. A community may be Rousseauite and virtuous, or it may be repressive and indulging in such practices as ostracism. It is Janus-faced. Again, its emotional extremism can take many forms, whether national or class. Durkheim and Duguit have indicated how organically it can press the individual. Sometimes, its own principles of co-operation may be false, and it is a gang or what Augustine called a *latrocinium* ('a brigandage'). Nevertheless, within these reservations, a Community offers certain direct values, as ends or enjoyments by the individual for their own sake, not purposive beyond themselves. Those who choose may say with Rousseau that here man enjoys "the sweets of civic virtue." Certainly, there are offered the removal of the fear of loneliness; the prospect of aid, companionship, and a charistic relation with its gratified *libido* or love; fraternity, solidarity, and that 'moral equality' which arises from the assurance of authentic mutual respect; and, consequently, the increase of self-respect by the endowment of life with meaning and dedication or purpose. These values may be those which a rational community could yield, such as were discussed by Plato and Aristotle. Or, again, as indicated above, they could be less rational, less laudable, and more sectarian.

It may seem too trivial or frivolous for serious discourse but to the ear of a psychologist it will not lack interest that a customary form of popular salutation in shops in Southern England is 'dear' and in the North 'love,' except for certain persons addressed as 'sir' or 'ma'am' (not 'mum') who are presumably honourable but not lovable. In the United States the phrase tends to be 'honey.' This democratic equalitarianism is disliked by some pompous persons. Perhaps it should rather be regarded as a demotic manifestation of Christian democracy. It is novel and significant. It may indeed be said that this is mere idle and routine behaviour. To this the behaviourists have something in the reply that the behaviour stimulates the sentiment. The best Confucian ethic is insistent but neither pompous nor cold.

One parenthetic comment here may be important. We have seen the importance of the Co-operative Principle in the interpretation of Power, itself intrinsic to all political structures. We have seen that in the Community peculiarly that Principle is allowed free and uninhibited play. Wants are fully gratified, with a sense of freedom, because there is like-mindedness on the wants to be gratified and on the requisite authority, discipline, and costs needed for their gratification. In the previous chapter we distinguished between false and intellectually indefinable notions of Equality and those which are tenable. Patronage and 'Big-Brotherdom' are not true equality. An authentic humility is a necessary component. It is incompatible with ill-founded and ill-defined talk about an élite. However, just as fear of total insignificance is for each man a real emotional fear, a matter not of humility but of humiliation, so an assurance of significance, in the eyes of God or man, is a deep need. There is not only an emotional but a metaphysical 'fear of the abyss.' By this I mean a fear of thoughts that ineluctably confront us on a cold analysis of the human situation. It may, to reason, seem more probable that man's whole story is "a tale told by an idiot, full of sound and fury, signifying nothing." There is a theological answer and there is a practical social answer (and the two, in a church, can be combined).

In protection from the cosmic chill there is a need for a human brotherhood and community, with its consequent 'equality' in membership, and for an act of faith in man's dignity as an ideal which each can achieve or which we can detect in the face of another as something he might achieve. It will be noted that this is a human predicament, not one of some State or Tribe; and its answer has to be a human answer. No doubt there are some who will add to the glory of humanity more than others and some who have more ability to add to the race's power. A Lucifer or a superman can stand apart, proud of 'not being dependent,' proud of a defiance Promethean if futile, of being 'self-sufficient.' But the actual want for brotherhood and mutual respect and, moreover, the belief that human power will grow most thereby, returns.

In 1960 in Nyasaland some white settlers are reported as calling to Negro crowds, "What do you baboons know about responsible government?"—adding that they were "just down from the trees." It would be 'responsible' for them to reflect that, like the French planters in Haiti, they may find that it is they themselves who may be hanging from the trees by other suspension. Responsibility is not for mobs, white or black, who have to be brought under law. It was responsible that, in South Africa, the British Prime Minister should point out that India was a country of high civilization when the ancestors of the Dutch and English were miserable barbarians—so stupid that, as Cato said of the British (Welsh), as slaves they were best not preserved but used up. The great Chinese people which, not without cultural justification, had regarded itself for ages as superior to all others, is bitterly resentful of all species of colour exclusion such as ignorant and inferior men exploit. Ignorance or obstinacy on these things, alike in race matters as in those economic class matters which the Marxists harp upon, cuts athwart community, brotherhood, equality—as does also violent and reckless haste. Such obstinacy can also wilfully distort the orthodox Christian faith to its own ends.

Should there, then, be no aristocracy? We reply: are lynchers the aristocracy? In a technological society those of more ability will always be in demand for direction. It is those who have nothing but the colour of their skins and their prejudices to count as assets who have something to fear. It is arguable that, for such people, a general miscegenation might be a eugenic kindness. Rome had less hesitation in practising it than the moderns and thereby built a great empire. The Soviets, with their unpleasantly class-divided and harsh society, have talked much but at home have practised less. The talk can be part of a technique of power. Those, on the other hand, who wilfully divide communities racially, weaken power.

The rise of importance and valuation of the Community, in contrast to more economic forms of Society characteristic of the last century, is one of the most remarkable changes of our times. We see it in the role played by the active membership of Political Parties and their discipline; in the rise of Trade Unionism and 'closed shops' against the abstractions of free contract; in the revitalization of certain Churches;

in the uprush to historical prominence of the comradeships of fascist and communist organizations and orders; as well as in the modest forms due to the improvement of communications. The political market is one today which shows, not only an increased value placed upon social security together with a willingness and capacity to pay for it, but, specifically, an increased value placed upon those goods and enjoyments which the close partnership of a community can offer to social masses which feel confused and without purpose.

The Community is indeed built up upon the sense of Trust, upon which in early chapters we laid stress as related to Natural Law and a healthy society—although, in its external relations, it may display a confident aggressiveness and a heightened distrust. In so far, however, as the Community is not co-operative means to further ends, but an area of direct enjoyment of sought political goods which are ends in themselves, its assessment is an affair, not of Political Science, but of Political Philosophy.

The Good Community is not such by reason solely of co-operation, but in terms of the ethical principles or pattern of conduct about which we co-operate. Here the individual person, unless he is prepared to be 'heteronomous,' 'brain-washed,' and 'Butlinized,' has the capacity, as ever-solitary, to remain the judge. Education is (and should be) compulsory in form. As touching moral, religious and experimental content, there should be choice. It is true that compulsory education may conduce to hypocrisy—which may yet be better than *anomie*, anarchy and contentlessness. But it need not so conduce if the teacher is judged by the pupils. Their faculty of choice, among goods, is one of the most important faculties that they have. The *whole* of the individual (as even the atheist Hobbes admitted) *need* never be, and perhaps *should* never be, totally socialized and absorbed in that "mortal [or maybe immortal] god," Society. He is free to contemplate the vision of, and to wish for, a more ideal society. A man's primary allegiance is to his own rational vision of truth. And, even if this contemplation begins as free dream, for the creative individual with power it need not remain such.

It is with this key reservation concerning what transcends actual present life that we can say that the achievement by each of his own fit community is the highest joy in life. His quality as man bids him to transcend the actual, historical, and human community. The present cannot swallow the future within its claims. But the spirit that can transcend is also the spirit that can return to create the co-operative whole, to control the obstructions of the world, and to enjoy the fellow-ship. What matters is whether the fellowship, in turn, is totalitarian or respects this transcendence of the spirit: in brief, what is the character of the Communion.

The grave cultural and political weakness of the democratic West is that, whereas Communism, thanks to its close and authoritarian party discipline and resort to local intimidation by determined and committed men, can subvert governments from within, the West, without resort to the disciplines of war or of reactionary tyranny, has no such political instrument wherewith to oppose it. Without a self-chosen or inculcated discipline and faith comparable to that of early Christianity, it has no agreed public philosophy, except it be, per-chance, that of local nationalism and self-determination.

This last, unfortunately, does not aid but rather can (taken in a narrow context) impede the prime political task of engendering and *enforcing* international civil peace of a liberal social character, by new customs indeed but also by a specific supra-national and co-operative authority. Some indeed of the so-called ideological and 'cold war' differences between the Communist and Western systems may be arti-ficial, bogus, and hence unlikely to conduce to success for their pro-ponents. The Communists have the no small advantage today (as distinct from the times of Lenin) of upholding a 'Victorian' morality, against social atomism and moral nihilism and what Mr. Khrushchev, in Georgia, called (apologizing for his 'vulgarity') any sort of "degene-rate bums." The substantial differences are on issues of domination, and of final purposes—not least that of what role coercion, as distinct from free co-operation, shall play in society and in providing certain securities. The question is whether the society moves to more use of 'force' as its pattern (not one of whether the pattern is more posi-tive) or to less use.

What is required is, not the depreciation of community sentiment (although not without its mass abuses), but a new and intense com-munity sentiment—because intense, therefore with the risks of intoler-ance under law of subversion of its rules—positively inculcated and based on the common ground of respect for human personality. That personality has to be understood, not as atomistic but as a concrete expression of the human spirit that finds formulation in natural law and which, in the last resort, appeals to the discoverable characteris-tics and entelechy of human nature itself, as over against all super-ficial or pseudo-scientific systematizings. In brief, the study of the

Community would seem to conclude with the proposition (cf. Proposition 23): that: FOR SURVIVAL UNDER CONDITIONS OF CRISIS, COMMUNITY GOODS, REQUIRING BY THEIR NATURE EDUCATION RATHER THAN COERCION, MUST BE INCULCATED POSITIVELY, EVEN AT COSTS TO ALTERNATIVE WISHES; THIS IS EDUCATIONALLY POSSIBLE AND WILL BE POLITICALLY SUCCESSFUL SO FAR AS THE COMMON COMMITMENT RESTS UPON A MORE PROPOUND SATISFACTION OF OUR HUMAN NATURE, AND A GREATER ACCORD WITH NATURAL LAW, THAN DOES THE ALTERNATIVE (Proposition 41).

There can, indeed, be debate about the time-scale and the degree proper for the sacrifice of the present for the future; but those who degrade, or are opposed to, this rational development are clearly no friends of humanity. There are some licences and egotisms, tolerable in another condition of political relations, which in a time of sterner discipline become contrary to the self-determination of the community, hostile to morals, and intolerable.

The virtue of a Civil Society is the freedom of the market and tolerance or indifference about purposes which it allows, within the law, to its members. The sense, however, of common purpose will come as an inspiration from another level. This freedom of the market is preserved if individuals retain a choice as between the directions tendered, the goods offered, in society. The advice may indeed be tendered by individual leaders. But, where a movement of the whole particular society is concerned, this movement—even in so individualistic a matter as the Cobdenite Repeal of the Corn Laws—will find force in a prior movement of active members around a leadership which will have a community character. However, at such a stage of civil society, the community may scarcely rise above the level of a temporary association with a limited and specific end, although the individualistic and liberal Free Trade Movement, for example, was passionately alleged to rest on a *principle* of human progress. More usually we find some Party or Denomination with an active programme which yet is regarded as inexhaustible, and which moves forward by the support of thousands who feel themselves to be bound together, in giving direction to and providing goods and protection of interest for the political mass, by a comradeship. In the final stage we find the work of direction assumed by a nucleus or few, which is assured of its own close-knit durability by being itself an authentic and full community. These communities have, in the immediate sense, a purpose and, in the wider sense, a principle or moral pattern around which they are organized. In this realm of ends, which is that of Political Philosophy, we have now to discuss the criteria by which we shall differentiate the better polity from the worse. The means, which we have hitherto discussed, will be selected, as efficient, according to the goods which we primarily desire.

M. de Jouvenel (*De la Souveraineté*, Eng. trans., pp. 299 ff.) in one of the most thoughtful books on these issues, greatly emphasizes the function of leadership in the exercise of authority, as distinct from the functions of any automatic equilibria or impersonal 'rules of the market' which may emerge, for example, under committee forms of direction. Hence we get stress upon the gathering of active membership around a leadership of prestige. This position, although it contains much emphasis on 'trust,' nevertheless has indeed certain dangers, as has Max Weber's praise of 'charismatic leadership.' It would yet be unfair to M. de Jouvenel, who is more concerned (and rightly) with a rational ethical principle, to identify the two. In words which it is the thesis of the text to emphasize, he writes (p. 299): "The essential freedom, as I see it, is the freedom to create a gathering, to generate a group, and thereby introduce in society a new power, a source of movement, and change." Comment has already been made upon the important insight of Dr. Arnold Toynbee—in which, nevertheless, he has Marx *and* St. Augustine as fore-runners—of the transition in the highest civilizations from the State form of politics to the Church form.

The matter here discussed in the text has a very urgent importance since the gravest weakness of the contemporary liberal West, which has lost some traditions without discovering new ones equally compelling, is its failure to produce any adequate sense of community, and—still less—one that is rationally and morally satisfying. The United Europe movement is, on the secular plane (although greatly inspired by non-secularist statesmen—incidentally all Catholic so far as the European Continent was concerned, with memories of the Carolingian tradition), the outstanding exception to this vacillation and the noblest experiment of our generation. Perhaps some day men of courage, with a like common outlook, will do the same for the Atlantic Community and for the yet wider Commonwealth of Free Nations.

It may perhaps be said, not improperly, that today the two outstanding illustrations of Community are the Church and the Party, both of which have greatly grown in importance, although North American experience is eccentric to this generalization and conforms more closely to nineteenth-century models of a Civil Society balanced by Individualism. The generalization, however, holds for Western and Southern Europe and Islamic lands, and more specifically for the Catholic Church and the Communist Party. In Asia and Africa, what is temporarily dominant is the fever of Nationalism, which is in some cases merely a reconstructed tribalism. In Poland a most interesting, but possibly temporary balance has been reached—one yet comparable to many concordats, as an immemorial solution, achieved in the past between Church and Empire.

The dangers of the Party as Community, even more than of the

Nation as such, have already been stressed. It is tempted, owing to the very strength of its convictions as community, to do that which is a sacrilege against the spirit of community, that is, to use force to compel others to come in. It is difficult for men with strong convictions, in possession of coercive force, to restrain themselves (cf. Proposition 25). Hence the greatest contemporary danger lies neither with Communist economic theories nor with Russian soldiers, but with the fanatical Messianism, never doubting whether they may not be fallible, of power intoxicated Parties, Sovietic and Chinese. Nevertheless, the confusion between the Church form (be it theocratic or so-called 'scientific,' as with Marxism), where men like physicans seek through eminent authority to persuade men in their wants, and the civil Party form, where by the use of force (because civil) new positive law is contemplated, is one not limited to the Sovietic world.

The temptations to confuse the two functions, to transfer the ideals of a church illiberally into the compulsions of a state 'without waiting for any,' to idealize a pragmatic negotiation, to compel first and to persuade afterwards, to substitute Domination, as quicker, for Co-operation—these temptations are endemic in political thinking. And as the function of churches is devalued the confusion, by compensation, increases. The sense of direction gets lost amid the pragmatic, and indeed opportunist, calculations of party-men in the market of power. Machiavellianism, parading as dedication to the human race, takes charge.

8. Law and Sovereignty

§i. *Positive and Natural Law*

In the two chapters on Democracy and on Aristocracy, we discussed systems of control, especially (but not exclusively) civil control, with focus upon the issue of where power lies. It is now logical to discuss *those systems of control which have become so far conventionalized, established, and indeed institutionalized as to provide a general political framework, within which power is supposed to be exercised in so far as it is legitimate.* Thus we separate the impersonal laws from the wilful men who first, even without deliberation and by habit, created these rules in accordance with their own deeper instincts or patterns of thought. In part, we have to consider law within the agencies but also, in part, the basis of law for the agencies. Here, indeed, we have the product of political activity; but in some measure, in politics (like the economic system as a whole), the laws provide shape for the subordinate political activities and for the higglings of the market itself.

The product is so far conventionally accepted that the future political market moves within the conventional and institutional terms of that acceptance and of those rules. What was dynamic as political programme and legislation comes now to wear the appearance of being static as law: and this is not without cause, in view of the durable nature of some kinds of law for which the deepest spirit and nature of man itself is the legislator. Further, the Community is indeed a society of men of common will and sentiment; but every society, so far as it is political and one of stable controls, not only should be, but *pro tanto* is, a society "of laws and not of men," and the Community is not only a society of personal feeling but also of that feeling conventionalized as law and rule. This does not mean that it is not better to control men through communal habit and custom where practicable, and to avoid the bureaucrat's error of multiplying legal restrictions. Let us, therefore, turn our attention to what we mean by these laws.

The money market and the corn exchange are the results of economic activity, shaped in part by the nature of the article dealt in, but which yet could well be conceived as shaped otherwise than it is. But the particular activities of this market or exchange move within the accepted frameworks dictated by the logic of the material and the situation of time and place. The same comment holds in the political field.

Natural Law or *ius naturae* is the name given by the Roman civilians, and later by the canonists, to certain fundamental rules or principles underlying Jurisprudence. In the case of some lawyers, such as Gaius and Paulus, it is identified with, and by others, such as Ulpian and Florentinus, it is distinguished from, the Law of Peoples (not to be confused with International Law) or *ius gentium*. This was originally the pattern of laws actually and generally accepted by the folk of the Mediterranean basin with whom Rome traded. For some jurisprudents slavery might be according to the customs of peoples but not according to Natural Law (*contra naturam*); and others, interestingly enough, put private property into the same category. Whereas the character of the *ius gentium* was, as it were, anthropological, or matter of empirical observation and indeed of statistical average, the *ius naturale* was regarded, following the Stoic philosophers, as primarily arrived at by reason. How far, owing to the fall of man and the hardness of men's hearts, what obtained in mundane affairs was rather the *ius gentium* was a matter for debate among the later canonists and civilians who received the principles of Roman Law.

For Chrysippus "the common law is the right reason pervading all things." For Cicero (*De legibus*) "Law is the highest reason, implanted in nature." Gaius (quoted in the *Digest* i. 1) says, "quod vero naturalis ratio inter omnes homines constituit, id . . . vocatur ius gentium." *Vide* R. W. and A. J. Carlyle: *A History of Mediaeval Political Theory in the West*, vol. I (1903), *passim*. Of especial interest for the present argument is the dictum of Tryphoninus (third century, A.D., quoted in the *Digest* xii, 6): "Ut enim libertas naturali iure continetur et dominatio ex gentium iure introducta est," that is, domination does not find its basis in Natural Law.

Clearly Natural Law is distinct, not only from Positive Law in the form of enactments of particular legislatures, but even from that particular kind of Positive Law which is called Constitutional Law. This is true, even if both may be described as sharing a character (repudiated in the so-called British Constitution) of being distinct, as fundamental law, from most positive law. Again, it differs from Common Law, and from that kind of local habit or custom, recognized by judges, which has never been enacted by a legislature as positive law or command at any time, and which today has been largely superseded by Statute Law and by judicial precedents established in particular cases.

Certain churchmen in the Middle Ages (and others later with the rise of nationalism, not least in Spain) sought to assimilate the *consuetudines regni* with a kind of secondary Natural Law, doubtless on the ground of their supposedly universal and primitive character within the realm and their acceptance by common understanding and consent; and also because they sought to give more respect and weight to these customs and common law.

Appeal to Natural Law provided an obvious prop in the context of the churchly thought of the times. The nexus of thought can be detected from Bracton to Fortescue. Likewise in early Hellas the *themis* might have the character of a local 'doom' or judgement or of a general divine justice. The identification, however, of local custom or convention with the fundamental demands of human nature is illegitimate and even, in some cases, an association of contradictories. 'Convention' and 'nature' can sometimes properly (as in much Greek thought) be put into opposition.

In discussing the relative positions of Natural and Positive Law, and the function of the former, it is important to permit history to rescue us from the illusions of what is merely contemporary prejudice. Positive law is not the original form of law, but a derivative and initially a subsidiary form. Nor did law originally carry the element, in its definition, of command given by some set or established human authority.

The usual Greek word for laws, *nomoi* (here like *dikē* or 'justice'), carried the meaning of an allocation, made in accordance with the sacred tradition or customs of the elders. Themselves being 'the silent ones,' their tradition, at a later stage and still with the aura of the sacred, was reduced to writing or to a code. The earliest Anglo-Saxon laws preserved are mere lists of customary penalties for offences, like a tariff. But, as in the cases of the laws of Solon, the Ten Commandments, and the Twelve Tables of Roman Law, frequently general principles were enunciated or, if already known to the elders and priests, were written down. Of this character also were the Laws of Manu.

From the point of view even of the late Greek democracies, the statute laws or enactments of the legislature, the *psephismata* or 'votes,' were subordinate in dignity to the fundamental laws, of which the most fundamental were those of rational Nature herself; and the same holds true later of the edicts and rescripts of praetors and emperors. The *responsa iuris prudentium* brought the wisdom of the more fundamental law to bear upon the interpretation of the enactments.

With the process of time and by a kind of reverse process of assimilation with positive law, the notion of command increasingly enters in. For St. Thomas indeed Natural Law can contain the element of command, as part of the *lex aeterna* decreed by God; but then God's own law is identical with that of Reason and the divine Logos. On this St. Thomas is very specific. God, by definition, cannot be supposed ever to act contrary to reason and Natural Justice. It is with the later schoolmen and the Protestant theologians, with their stress on God's arbitrary, inscrutable and Sultan-like will, that the notion of law comes to be received as primarily command—even command (in the case of God's word, and in the view of Kierkegaard) *because* it seems absurd and as a challenge—rather than primarily a formula of nature and reason.

In establishing today the notion of a Natural Law, the first issue is: what precisely do we mean by it, and is this meaning sustained by common usage? The second is whether, so meant, it is valid. From the standpoint of the Austinian lawyers Natural Law was merely a grandiose or pseudo-legal name for Morals; and this, not in the sense of *mores et consuetudines regni* such as might find their home in Common Law, but in the sense of Ethics or moral opinion, upon which every man's private or protestant conscience was the best judge. Nor could even modern systems, which, following Kant and accepting these premises, sought yet to affirm a systematic logical construction upon the ground that 'good' law, professionally speaking, could not be contradictory, of themselves escape from the objection that no reason could be shown why a sovereign legislature, which chose to enact law otherwise than by the rules of good jurisprudence, should conform to these theoretical systems.

Usually the doctrine of Natural Law of the seventeenth and eighteenth centuries, as found from Pufendorf to Vattel, lost itself among Protestant writers in a network of moral considerations of a subjective kind. In an age of individualism, Natural Laws were broken down or atomized into a multiplicity of Natural Rights of the Individual, which tended to be increased or varied according to the whim and moral preferences of the writer. Their character was not changed by calling them Human Rights. Hence, even when there was agreement upon meanings, few agreed upon what precisely the Natural Rights of Man just were, and still less about the natural laws which might underlie their diversity. The Austinians were correct in supposing that this whole version of the doctrine of Natural Law and Rights is unsatisfactory. It rests upon an ambiguity between unprovable ethical norms and validated positive commands, issuing from some human and particular validating authority—which last the Austinians held could alone be correctly described as 'law.'

We are yet entitled to insist that the same logic which provides an attack upon Natural Law also provides one upon Natural and Human Rights. It is further submitted that no doctrine of Natural or Human Rights (of which the public guarantee will have costs or obligations) can be satisfactorily based which does not rest upon a socially stated doctrine of Natural Law. There have indeed been Natural Right doctrines, as Hegel objected, which deny man's natural sociality, in a fashion contrary to the position of Aristotle and St. Thomas. Such doctrines are, on analysis, indefensible; but that the basic demand is of the concrete individual and his *psyche*, who enjoys and suffers in his flesh and soul, and not of a 'metapolitical' society, is a truism which is yet true. Even among Marxists today there is a reaction in the direction of stressing the radical revolutionary individual and the psychological factors. THE CONCRETE INDIVIDUAL IS NEVER MERELY FORCED INTO, AND LOST WITHOUT RESIDUE IN, SOCIETY (Proposition 42).

Cf. the discussion by Professor Leo Strauss of Chicago in his *Natural Right and History* (1953), which brings together natural right and law as above. "The rejection of natural right is bound to lead to disastrous consequences" (p. 3) . . . "to nihilism—nay, it is identical with nihilism." To state this is (as shown in the text) in no wise to invalidate the considerations that society is 'natural' and that "Primitive man is not a 'natural man' [meant in Hobbes' sense: although perchance the gorilla and orang-utan have this solitary and brutish quality] because he is a 'social man' in the strictest sense of the word" (Hans Kelsen, *Society and Nature*, 1946, p. 48).

The confused and contradictory (or, since Locke had a tortuous mind, perhaps we should say dishonest) lectures of John Locke on Natural Law, which he himself discreetly decided not to publish, have now been edited by Mr. W. von Leyden and published (1954). Locke in some passages here follows the admirable Hooker and in others (without acknowledging the debt) Thomas Hobbes, so that he emerges with the theme that the natural instinct or inclination of man would be, for the most part, not so much to virtue as to follow *immediate appetites* or immediate interests. Natural Law here lies rather in the long-range and *calculated public interest in civil peace.* The somewhat perfunctory criticism of Natural Law by Mr. W. von Leyden is met by Professor Strauss in his review in the *American Political Science Review* (June, 1958) of von Leyden's edition of Locke's *Essays on the Law of Nature*.

§ii. *Natural Law Restored*

To admit the defects of a doctrine of detached Natural Rights, pepper-potted around according to subjective or arbitrary taste, is not to say that Natural Law doctrine may not be restated in a satisfactory manner. Indeed, such an exponent as Professor Paul Weiss of Yale has to bring the atomic rights into relation together under some such principle as their relativity to a more fundamental "sense of proportion." It is incumbent so to restate it if International Law as such, and also all theses in law based on Natural Rights, are not to collapse. The alternative position is that the so-called 'rights of man' are authenticated only by the municipal law of some particular civil society. The Rights of Man would, then, be no more than the claims which the man of stronger might chooses to uphold, like the twelve-mile limit at sea, until a stronger yet comes and overthrows him. Civil rights are claims that national law chooses to allow and validate (cf. Proposition 12).

Any new statement, however, of Natural Law will have to be different from that current in individualistic and morally subjectivist centuries. Indeed, a strong objection to Natural Law in some quarters is that, as an arbitrary stabilization of customary subjective and ethical thinking, or as an abstract, untested, and too hasty assumption about how 'nature,' for example in economics, must work, it becomes a doctrine of conservativism or even of reaction. People talk glibly about 'what is natural,' meaning not 'what comes naturally' but what is customary, as a method of evading giving serious attention to the detailed sociological factors. Do we mean 'what comes naturally to the animal' or 'what is natural to the reasonable and fulfilled man'? The ancient antithesis between nature and convention is ignored. But indeed a sound doctrine of Natural Law, as setting up an objective basis of criticism of existing constitutions, is more likely to be challenging and revolutionary.

Is, however, a new statement, in this fashion, compatible with the original meaning of the phrase 'Natural Law'? The answer is: yes. We have already pointed out that historically the concept of law has not always been essentially connected with the concept of local command (as by the tyrant Creon in *Antigone*, whose view is there challenged); that this connection does not hold in the case of physical law; and that the use of the word 'law' in this latter sense is not a metaphor but original, and indeed the older and better founded of the two meanings. With the Stoics the notion of a Natural Law emanated from the belief in a rational order or cosmos in the divinely and *logos-*

created universe; and this notion was perpetuated by the Roman lawyers. Even if "the will of the *princeps* has the vigour of law," the law itself was other and prior, and sprang from the consensus of the people echoing the dictates of right reason concerning the social order. That order had its own intrinsic rules, dictated by the nature of reasoning man and of the basic social structure. In succeeding centuries and in a continuous grand tradition, reason recognized it in history. It was, to repeat, a *patrimonium generis humani*.

In the golden age of Scholasticism, before we pass into the epoch of post-Protestant subjectivism (which Grotius endeavoured to balance by invoking the objective authority of the Bible, the Roman lawyers, and the poets, since the poet was *vates*), St. Thomas re-enunciates the older doctrine. Like the universe itself, so all human nature is subject to an eternal law, in part revealed but in part natural and detectable by reason, in the one case a natural law of the physical or inanimate world and in the other of this human nature itself. If any restatement of Natural Law is consistent with the usage of the Stoics, the Roman Law and of St. Thomas, the restatement cannot be called a perversion of usage or radical departure from what ought to be meant by the words.

St. Thomas Aquinas (*Summa Theologica*, 1a, 2ae, q. 93, art. i) writes: "the eternal law is nothing other than the reason of the Divine Wisdom (*Divinae Sapientiae ratio* [*Hagia Sophia*]) . . . in so far as it is the directive of *all* actions and motions." The participation of the eternal law [as operative] in the rational [human] creature is called the law of nature." (q. 91, art. 2) Thus, the rational man by force of his reason is able to detect, in part, the *objective* eternal law (other parts being only made plain by revelation in the *lex divina*). Reference may here be made to the scholarly work of Professor Heinrich A. Rommen, *The Natural Law* (trans. Thomas R. Hanley, 1947); and also to the arguments in Professor John Wild's book—primarily, however, concerned with the case of Popper v. Plato—*Plato's Modern Enemies and the Theory of Natural Law* (1953) —and to Professor John Hallowell's writings.

We must, then, distinguish between those matters of choice and creativeness in which man *ought* to be guided by reason and logical consistency, as well as by revelation and due authority, and those matters of man's physical, psychological, and social structure which have their own constants and rules of function. As touching the former field we must admit that the area of strict reason is limited, of which it can be said that, whether or not a man *ought* to be himself reasonable, he *must* conform, as touching his behaviour and means, to these objective laws of logic if he is to aspire to consistency and to advance to his social and moral ends through it. This area of the rational and creative personality is obviously of final human importance, beyond challenge. It is also an area of choice, within limits set for ethics by reason.

But there is also, only very inadequately explored as yet, the other field. It may be said that the destiny of man lies in his autonomous nervous system—although such a predestinationist theory would be false in its exaggeration of the role in determining conduct played by this system. More truly it can be said that, by 'human nature and its wants,' we mean the order and wants which accord with man's higher nervous system which, even if it has evolved, remains stable for historic time. Since we propose, in discussing Natural Law, to follow the classical usage of the term, there is neither proper ground why we should discard a great tradition, from which historically much good has flowed, nor why, dividing Natural Law, we should deny to the second field, where empiric investigation is possible, also the name of Natural Law. And it is on the clarification of this field (which we need not hold to have 'changeable content,' but only variety of application) that the restatement of Natural Law rests. The proper balance of the two elements in Natural Law, rational and instinctual, maintained by the Romans, is of high practical importance. Most recent sociological and medical research, including research into the biological history of humanity, indicates that excessive domination of behaviour by the intellect, rationalization (to use Weber's term), and systematization, can be *contra naturam humanam*; and that the function of reason is to shape, but not (which ultimately would be 'irrational') to suppress or pervert, the native instincts, about which empirically we continually learn more. This also is the position of St. Thomas: grace perfects nature. St. Thomas further comments (*Ethics*, I, 3): "what pertains to moral science is known mostly through experience"—a point well stressed by Professor Rommen.

The need, incidentally, for empiric research into this natural law can scarcely be over-emphasized. Thus, with the Roman lawyers, a stock instance of natural law expressions, founded upon instinct, was 'maternal affection.' Recent medical and scientific research indicates that this can better be stated as instinctive 'parental affection,' in particular situations less evolved in the male, but still authentically present for these in a normal or healthy condition.

Catholic theorists and jurisprudents have never ceased to emphasize the importance of reason, as distinct from mere sentiment, in the first field. Nor need we suppose, if the field of human psychology is subject to law and constants, that these constants, moulding our judgements of aesthetics and of values, will not project themselves significantly into the area of creation and free choice. The work of Erich Fromm, R. B. Cattell, and R. E. Money-Kyrle (in his *Psychoanalysis and Politics*) emphasizes this. Fromm writes in *Man for Himself*: "If ethics constitutes the body of norms for achieving excellence in performing the art of living, its most general principles must follow from the nature of life in general and of human existence in particular." Richard Hooker, it is interesting to note, judiciously quotes no other than Hippocrates in discussing the character of natural law.

As Professor Morris Cohen pointed out in "Jus Naturale Redivivum" (*Philosophical Review*, vol. XXV, 1916), Stammler had shown that the Historical School of Jurisprudence had not rejected the claims of the supporters of Natural Law, and Sir Frederick Pollock also adopted this view. Cf. also J. Charmont, *La Renaissance du droit naturel* (1910). Otto von Gierke's *Das Deutsche Genossenschaftsrecht*, vol. IV (1913; in part translated by Professor Sir Ernest Barker, with Introduction, as *Natural Law and the Theory of Society*, 1934), should also be consulted.

A formal logic of law cannot be extracted from positive law, pulling itself up, as it were, by its own bootstraps; but a logic of rational justice (whatever hypothetical values we choose to assign to the term) is defensible, and is by Cohen defended, over against an Anglo-Saxon tendency to set up, conservatively, "an idealization of the prevailing system." This is not to say that we can rest satisfied with the pure formalism of del Vecchio, for example. The Roman Lawyers placed, as already said, 'instinct' along with 'reason' as a guide to Natural Law. And 'instinct' can be experimentally investigated.

However, our preferred problem is that of the whole relation of the laws of human and social nature, that is of Psychology and of Political Science, to the field of positive laws and of a satisfactory Jurisprudence. It will be noted that the argument of certain philosophers (*cf. infra*, p. 351) that there is no cognition of objective values, even were it true, would be irrelevant to a Natural Law empirically ascertainable by research into the fields of medicine and sociology. *Vide* the discussion of our theme here by Professor Andrew Hacker of Cornell University in the *Natural Law Forum* (Vol. III, no. 1, 1958). Cf. also A. Passerin d'Entrèves, *Natural Law* (1951), *passim*; and A. Cobban, *The Crisis of Our Civilization* (1941, chap. VIII).

It may, indeed, be argued that knowledge of the physiological laws of health or the sociological laws of equilibrium no more commands us to follow them than the maxim that 'drunkenness incapacitates' commands us to be sober. They do not decide our ends by command. They are not *imperative*: but *descriptive* of what will happen anyhow. This argument can readily be accepted, since it is the precise argument of this tractate. They are not *normative* in the sense of imposing a moral rule *ab externo* (although some moralists will hold that the rule of reason must be so held); but, even beyond being descriptive of 'the way things are,' they are *presumptive* of what, by a pragmatic 'must,' we must do to achieve such ends as health, human harmony, social order, compatibility with our own natures, and whatever lasting goods we may prudently choose. It may at most be said to provide a formula governing the normal, in the sense of recurrent, pattern of demand, but not an inevitable or unbroken demand. But, even more compulsively than by any command of a human legislator, which may be evaded, we are commanded by reason and the nature of things, *if* we choose to pursue health, not to swallow poison. And, *if* we would be free or have a free or consumers' political market, we must not connive at lifting tyranny into power.

The magistrate seeks to impose penalties as (within the limits of human error) certain. The modern use of law, therefore—that is, the recent development of statute law, with its appropriate courts and police—seeks (and, the jurisprudent may add, normatively *should* seek, just as good medicine follows the laws of physiology) by short-term and immediate penalties to dissuade men from doing what must conduce to long-term disasters to their physiological frame, psychological make-up, and social constitution. Here, in accordance with traditional doctrine classically expressed by Cicero, the positive law, if sound, should seek to be a local and temporary exemplar or mirror of the fundamental Natural Law. If it runs athwart it, it is *nulla et vana* in Jurisprudence, even if it continues to enjoy coercive police force at the moment. It is without that socially validating authority, in the appeal to reason, which sound jurisprudence alone gives. It is in this sense, as M. de Jouvenel points out, that the great Jesuit philosopher Suarez poses the question *utrum sit in hominibus potestas ad leges ferendas*. The only answer must be that the *potestas*, as 'authority' and not only 'power' (*potentia*), springs from conformity to a precedent, objective, real, and supra-individual law in the nature of things.

It is an error, especially of the megalomaniac Renaissance and post-Renaissance era, obsessed by notions of *dominatio*, to suppose that it adds to the dignity of law to view it as a sultan-like and arbitrary command. It is *not* the original or primitive conception of law, but develops with this notion of state sovereignty. We may choose to think with St. Thomas that the command of God to order a cosmos, the Providential Order, enters in even to physical law. But here also the fundamental dignity of law lies in its compatibility with the rational order; and without this it commands no rational moral allegiance. It is only when we can descry and describe this compatibility that we know what we *ought* temporally to command, not arbitrarily *as* command but rationally since the command would be for the social good.

In epochs of conflicts of jurisdictions and of laws, the civilians and (much more) contemporary positive lawyers, whether Austinian or pragmatic, have been reluctant for a political reason to admit a doctrine of Natural Law. The rising Leviathan State (or even the rising legal profession, in the secular courts . . .) was not admitted, as Hobbes with irritation pointed out, by exponents of Natural Law to be privileged to act as supreme adjudicator of the interpretation of this Natural Law. Its champions, therefore, asked, in the mood of Hobbes, 'who rides in front?' Maybe, said Hobbes, this Natural Law is the calculating reason that tells a man to defend himself. But what human power, said the old atheist, was to be the adjudicator or supreme interpreter? The secular politicians and lawyers smelled sedition (as it was also at first smelled in every emergent notion of a 'general will,' since "the prince is the people" and "the 'people' is but the mob").

The *reductio ad absurdum* of this pride of sovereignty is the story of the Texas legislator who proposed that π should be a neat 3:1 ratio within his state! The laws of nature exist and are not amenable to the commands of sovereigns. Cf. the statement of the canonist Pope Gregory IX (quoted by R. W. and A. J. Carlyle, *A History of Mediaeval Political Theory in the West*, vol. II, p. 32): "Si iuri naturali . . . (rescripta) contradixerint, refutantur omnino." It can appropriately be argued that, whatever may be the case with law 'made' in the courts or legislatures, a doctrine of a limiting principle of 'sound' law 'found' in nature and reality would do much to bring the practice of law into accord with the more solid conclusions of medicine, psychology, and sociology, much to the public advantage and its own progress. (Cf. Roscoe Pound, *Interpretations of Legal History*, 1923, pp. 121–52. Natural Law, Dean Pound comments on page 133, is "the great agency of the juristic development of law.")

Few indeed who have discussed Justice, save Hobbes (*Leviathan*, part II, chap. xxx), have denied that the law can be unjust and requires a criterion or that Justice is not the same thing as Law-observance. The present writer can perhaps claim to have been one of the first, in his *Thomas Hobbes*, to call attention to the criticism of this theme of Hobbes' by George Lawson, in his *Examination of the Political Part of Leviathan* (1657).

A plea may here be made for the professional sociological investigation—such as was not within the terms of reference, for example, of the British Street Offences Commission, reporting in 1959 (Wolfenden Report)—before legislation. Refusal to avail themselves of available and relevant knowledge only serves to bring legislators and law into contempt; nor are most social problems, as the destiny of the Poor Law indicates, so simple for amateurs that research by experts is a waste of money. There is no excuse for deliberate bad—that is, ignorant— law.

There are indeed many interpretations which may be put upon the Laws of Nature by political scientists and others, who may be concerned with man's physical and psychological health. As against this, it may be said that men who break the positive law will in fact—and not as any matter of divers interpretations—be subjected to the penalties of the positive law; and this law will pragmatically be such as the courts choose to enforce. This may be true but, even were it true, it would prove nothing concerning the character of Law or of Authority. Actually, if we wish to make the 'realistic' argument thorough, and if we bear in mind the challenge of President Andrew Jackson, exercising the executive power, to Chief Justice John Marshall, we must more accurately say: the penalties will be those which the police and the prison commissioners and (as the Communists appreciate full well) the Minister of the Interior choose to enforce; and the penalties will apply to those to whom these officials, but also perhaps the juries, and not only the judges, say they will apply.

There are indeed some pragmatists among the lawyers who would accept this argument and, with Mr. Justice Holmes in one of his more immoral and paradoxical moods, would say that the real issue in law is "who can kill or hang whom." But this is utterly to confound law with force, and nefariously to misunderstand the whole meaning of law, authority and, obligation. The comment of Cicero (*De re publica* iii. 22) is directly relevant: "Whoever is disobedient is fleeing from himself and denying his human nature; and by reason of this very fact he will suffer the worst penalties, even if he escapes what is commonly considered punishment." The sanction is there, unless a man *chooses* ill health, personal and social. *Non curat lex.* Likewise the criminal may opt for the course that 'lands him in jail.' He will yet find that the most perfect positive law and police are less sure and remorseless in their penalties than are the natural laws of man and society.

It may indeed be asked whether the social delinquent is not also following the impulses and passions of his 'nature.' What norm does 'nature' provide? The answer would seem to be that, although the delinquent is certainly the slave of his impulses, what is expressed is so far disproportionate and undisciplined that, if not indeed the physiological, at least the psychological and sociological, expression of the individual becomes perverted, as judged by the standards of any rational harmony with the more permanent nature of man and his society. If these delinquent patterns become prevalent the result would be patent catastrophe. The rational in man is primordial.

Professor Sir Hersch Lauterpacht has discussed with weight the importance of Natural Law doctrine in several of his books, especially his *Function of Law in the International Community* (1933) and his *International Law and Human Rights* (1950). In his *Private Law Sources and Analogies of International Law* (1927) he also quotes the remark of Sir Frederick Pollock, in his *Essays in the Law*: "We must either admit that modern international law is a law founded on the cosmopolitan principles of reason, a truly living offshoot of the Law of Nature, or ignore our most authoritative exposition of it." Lauterpacht himself writes (*International Law and Human Rights*, p. 112): "The renaissance of the law of nature at the beginning of the twentieth century was not yet another theory of the judicial function. It was the unmistakable result of the urge to find a spiritual counterpart to the growing power of the Modern State. . . . The movement towards the revival of natural law after the First World War was a manifestation of the resulting wide-spread sense of danger."

Comment has already been made (*supra*, p. 116) on the danger of confusing Power, which is a lasting potentiality of force or other forms of control, with Authority, as recognized power, whether by passive assent or by active consent. Cf. also my contribution on "Authority and Its Critics" in the symposium *Authority*, edited by C. J. Friedrich.

It will be noted that we have above stated a double position: (*a*) the creative reason, even when exercising moral choice on ends, must move in accordance with logical and intelligible laws. This does not mean that man may not frequently choose to be irrational. It does mean that it is improbable, not as a matter of 'ought' but of 'fact,' that men who have deserted their rational nature for their passionate and animal impulses can build a stable and harmonious society, whether of co-operation or even (without rational statesmanship) by domination. The argument is as old as Plato's. It holds.

However, (*b*) man indeed also has this animal and emotional nature, shaped by the instincts, and, in terms of abiding desires and the logical means thereto, follows in his behaviour certain patterns which we can formulate. Thus the Roman lawyers referred to instinct as well as to reason. This instinctive life not only tends to regularity of psychological and physical habit, despite the innumerable cultural or even chance external forms which circumstances may dictate. It also is capable of empirical investigation by physiologist, psychologist, and sociologist. Moreover, we may find that in many cases these deeper and more permanent 'drives' are only partially expressed and are in fact twisted, distorted, or malformed by particular cultural or institutional modes of expression. There is a social malfunctioning, conventional or anarchic. As a consequence a sick condition is produced, in some cases physically—for example in a society characterized by malnutrition or by the lack of facilities for young children to play in impoverished neighbourhoods—or mentally, spiritually, or socially. We can study empirically alike these impulses (and learn more about them) and these societies. We can speak of a sick society and of a sane society; and we can criticize the former normatively in terms of a Natural Law, which the scientist can understand and test.

Reference can be made here back to psychological literature already cited, but perhaps especially to the lucid and popular work of Dr. Erich Fromm, *The Sane Society* (1955). It will be noted here that we have indeed what Stammler called "Natural Law with changeable content," but not changeable, as with Stammler, because of casuistical adjustment to the *casus* of the particular circumstances or opportunities. It is changeable only in the sense that our *knowledge* of a (broadly and in historic time) unchanging human nature does greatly change with further empirical studies; and the fulness of our increasing formulations must change with it. Of human nature itself Professor Arnold Brecht (*Political Theory*, p. 90) rightly comments "Above all, in every unique situation of human history, there is always *man*, with his characteristic peculiarities that have remained fundamentally the same through all recorded history."

An unusual view of Natural Law, perhaps owing much to Stammler, is put forward by Professor Paul Weiss, of Yale, in his systematic *Our Public Life* (1959). Here Professor Weiss, with others, stresses the important function of Natural Law, but, unexpectedly, he introduces in effect more systems or levels of Natural Law than one. There is one which is normative to a particular time and place and indeed (which indicates the tone of Professor Weiss' thinking) to each existent State; "it has a different context in different states" (p. 186). Beyond this relevant Natural Law, so named, there is a wider 'Law of Civilization,' of our culture. "Natural Law stands in between positive law and the more comprehensive law, a Law of Civilization." This, in turn, has to be distinguished from the yet more universal and absolute principles of Ethics, despite the fact that there is a subjectivist emphasis in Professor Weiss' enunciation, so that Natural Law "is no substance" but is related "to the social good which *ought* to be" (p. 162). These distinctions are unorthodox and I remain, with deference, unconvinced as to how far they are useful.

One important distinction must be made clear. Is Natural Law to be understood as 'naturalistic' or as 'ethical'? Let us admit that discussion of Natural Law, which limits means, is perhaps the most apt bridge by which the student can pass over from the political science of means to the political philosophy of speculation about real ends and the values of concrete achievement. Natural Law for humanity, being the law of our own constant nature, rational and animal or instinctive —and, in the opinion of its earliest theorists, rightly continuous with the divine and natural law formulating the constants of the physical world or *cosmos*—governs both means *and* ends. For it they come together again concretely; and we do not have to ask whether the ends be or be not intermediary to further ends, not hypothetical but actual. What is contrary to it is perverse and condemned to malfunctioning; and the formulations of this as norm are futile or erroneous. The Good is not whatever is within its ambit; but, nevertheless, whatever is Good always is within its ambit and what is not within its ambit is, for our human nature, not good. Thus, as limiting the ethical, it has an essential 'ethical' bearing. It is normative in this sense.

Nevertheless, Natural Law does not command us, like Positive Law, about what we *must* do under penalty of temporal punishment but also it does not, like the principles of applied Ethics (I do not here mean a verbal analysis), make clear to our consciences an imperative concerning what we ought to choose. It is 'naturalistic' in the sense that it is the formulation of how things actually are, in all those aspects of human nature, rational, psychological, physiological, and social, to which it applies in conduct. It very much, then, does have, or rests on, a 'substance,' and moreover one capable of logical or empirical investigation. If we choose to reckon in our economic affairs that two times two equals five, it is our free choice; but our finances will be in confusion. If we choose to walk over a precipice, we may; but we shall break our neck. (We can indeed here say, if we like, that there is an inherent rationality or law of the cosmos; and that there is a divine command to the reasonable man—which command does not yet deprive him of moral freedom to choose.) If we choose to defy the natural law of our being, we are free to do so, but the consequences for us personally and socially, being what we are, will be disastrous. And, moreover, the sanction and the penalty does not depend upon men but is quite inevitable, whatever positive law, misdrawn, may decree to the contrary. *The basis of sound law lies in human nature itself.* Natural law is, then, also 'normative' in the 'naturalistic' or 'scientific' sense.

In able critical articles Professor Felix E. Oppenheim, of the University of Delaware ("The Natural Law Thesis: Affirmation or Denial?" with reply by Professor H. V. Jaffa, *American Political Science Review*, March, 1957) has sought to explode Natural Law Doctrine; but (*a*) on the basis of an interpretation, *not* here made, of Natural Law as a matter of ethical values; and (*b*) on a denial of the theory, which is itself no concern of political science, that objective values are cognizable. What is being argued is that man's nature, empirically perceptible, is objective as touching any individual; and that this nature limits what for man is valuable. We cannot adjudge that, which by hypothesis is impossible, to be humanly good. It will be noted that this is *not* to adopt the thesis of 'adjustment,' as developed from Herbert Spencer to contemporary 'organization man,' described by Mr. Whyte in his book of this title. On the contrary, it is in terms of man's abiding and fundamental nature (here primarily psychological) that we judge social convention and what invites adaptation.

§iii. *Natural Rights*

As has been mentioned, the classical and objective doctrine of Natural Law, of which the present revival is of prime theoretical importance, temporarily broke down, not so much owing to any inherent defect—although the time for empirical explanation of the rules of health, especially in the psychological and sociological fields had not yet come —but owing to the development of a mental climate that was nominalist, anthropocentric, individualist, and Protestant. Old Natural Law of the cosmos and of man (sometimes thought of as complementary) gave way to restatement as the Natural Rights of each free-born human unit. And it is of course true that the advantages both of health and of rights to health must accrue not to 'a group' or society, which has no substance, whatever metapolitical theorists of the 'social organism' may say, but to the concrete individual, even if of an individual formed as a member of some community with other members.

The heyday of Natural Rights doctrine was in the late seventeenth and in the eighteenth century. Political theorists tended, with a free hand, to distribute Natural Rights, inalienable and indefeasible, around according to their taste and partisanship, whether of 'private property' (which had earlier been denied by many classical Natural Law writers and by those Patristic writers who held property to be fundamentally a trust) or of 'the pursuit of happiness.' There was also a natural right 'to think,' (that is, to go through the mental process) which, as Hobbes said, since it could never be denied, was perhaps scarcely worth asserting. Professor Paul Weiss, in a recent book (*Our Public Life*, pp. 63–4) has provided an abstract and singularly full catalogue of such rights, including the right *to* 'believe,' to 'enjoyment,' to 'existence,' and even to 'travel,' the right *of* 'consumption,' 'the body,' 'rebellion,' and 'thought,' and the right of freedom *from* 'want.'

It may, however, be more prudent to restrict ourselves to recent historical instances. There have been contemporary laudable endeavours, while not mentioning 'natural' law or rights, to establish Laws of Civilization and Humanity, so little abstract that under them men may be hanged, and also, from the United Nations or the Council of Europe, to issue Declarations of Human Rights.

It seems to be a legitimate criticism that some of the national representatives accredited to draw up these Declarations, in what is one of the most notorious fields of political rhetoric, had no especial qualifications either as lawyers or as philosophers. For example, Sir Charles Dukes, late Lord Dukeston, the British representative, was a veteran trade unionist, an admirable man, and a good democrat; but it is open to doubt whether he had ever consciously considered a philosophical problem as such (in which he had no training) in his life. As touching the Laws of Civilization, enunciated *post factum* (or on the basis of the Kellogg Pact), Sir Winston Churchill has ruefully observed that, in an age of less courtesy or humour than earlier, it looked as if the time was coming when anybody who lost a war would be hanged by the moralists.

If we examine the United Nations 'Universal Declaration of Human

Rights' (agreed to 'in principle,' but of which a Covenant, involving enforcement, has quite failed in ratification), it is stated to express "a common standard of achievement . . . to the end that every individual . . . shall strive . . . to secure [for these rights] universal and effective recognition" (a confused sequence of phrases), one finds a succession of rights affirmed, some of which are mentioned here, with brief comment. Thus, (a) there is a 'right to life': but this does not mean avoiding conscription or following the advice of Thomas Hobbes to desert if the chances are better that way. (b) "No one shall be subjected to arbitrary . . . detention" and is "entitled . . . to a . . . public hearing" . . . with "the right to be presumed innocent . . . in a public trial": but this does not repudiate the right of a sovereign parliament to authorize detention without trial for an undefined period. The issue of detention without trial also arose in connection with the Irish Government's Proclamation (against the I.R.A.) of July, 1957, and the Lawless case thence arising, adjudicated in that Government's favour by the European Court of Human Rights on July 1, 1961. (c) "No one shall be subjected to arbitrary interference with his correspondence": but this does not prevent the legal right of the Customs, in Canada for example, to open and examine private letters in pursuit of contraband. (d) "Everyone has the right to leave any country, including his own, and to return," a freedom to which Immanuel Kant attached immense importance, as guaranteeing the freedom of the social contract. But the right to leave and return without passport or visa is usually only grudgingly admitted (the British Foreign Office does, under question, admit it). (e) "No one shall be . . . denied the right to change his nationality": but he may, in France for example, be called up for military service by his country of origin and be treated as a deserter if he does not report. (f) "Men and women of full age . . . have the right to . . . found a family": but not when there is heritable disease.

Further (g) "Everyone has the right to freedom of . . . expression . . . and to . . . impart . . . ideas through any media": but not if they are obscene, sacrilegious, or directly subversive. Incidentally, the right depends for its exercise upon editorial willingness of editors of a 'free press' to publish; or again upon the willingness of a monopoly broadcasting system (such as the British Broadcasting Corporation was until a recent campaign) to give opportunity for expression. Thus exercise of this right depends upon finding a publisher or sponsor in a very closed and costly circle. Perhaps democracy would in principle require that all chairmen of newspapers, editors, and cartoonists, being so powerful, should be elected. However, the British Press Council has recently decided that journalism is rather a trade than a profession, so presumably the choice of news can be left to the demands of the market. The same comment applies to public manifestations of religion, which should yet (sometimes) not include the Abrahamic practice of polygamy or disturb public order. Incidentally, consideration must be given to how far the elevation of some absolute rights of a free press (or free television), isolated from social responsibility, might not end by ignoring the distinction between, among newspapers, those referred to respectively, in the jargon of Fleet Street, as the money-making 'Dirties' and the (often trust-held) 'Cleanies.' We here have to beware of elevating abstractions into principles. (h) "Everyone has the right . . . to free choice of employment": but not perhaps when there is a closed shop. (i) "Everyone . . . has the right to social security . . . and the free development of his personality": but not, of course, if he feels that he develops this best by cutting up small boys, raping girls, or the like. Few rights, reference to objective reason being omitted, could be more ambiguous or philosophically questionable. The development of a man's personality, let it be reiterated yet again, must be (to use Aristotelian terminology) as an entelechy, not anarchic, and in accordance with humanism and fundamental human nature. Freedom from Want, again, may either mean a freedom from that starvation, or shortage, which is a most potent cause of revolution or it may mean freedom from want in such a human dream-contentment that all political activity would come to an end. (j) "Parents have a prior right to choose the kind of education that shall be given to their children": but, in Oregon for example, unless they choose the state schools they will be thus without aid of the funds which (as taxpayers) they pay, because Messrs. Jefferson and Paine had other views about the Constitution. They may not, for example, choose a school where religious teaching is imparted, unless they pay double. Christianity (or any other religion) and State are separate, under the ill-conceived (or dishonestly ambiguous) First Amendment. Indeed, whereas the United Kingdom is indubitably in law officially Christian, whatever may be the practices of its people, it is dubious, despite Presidential statements to the contrary, whether the United States in law, as recently interpreted, is such. But cf. Murray, *We Hold These Truths*, p. 151. One might add that no Natural Right is perhaps more patent than that of the pedestrian, on his two Nature-given feet, to the prior use of the road against a limited plutocracy of power-drunk car-owners.

The conclusion to be drawn from this examination is not, with Bentham, that Natural or Human Rights, so declared, are "bawling on paper" or baubles for children to play with. It is that they are subjective, arbitrary, unsystematic, and unproven. By hypothesis, they are not merely Liberties A, approved by the civil (or other) competent authority. But no attempt has been made to show, by connection with a general and tested Natural Law, just why these Liberties B, no less and no other, should be enjoyed. As they stand they are little more than the expression of Popular Wants. Perhaps they have been confirmed by experience and better opinion. But no attempt has been made to show that just these rights were necessary and why. The comments above, which could also in part be made on the European Convention of Human Rights (1950), will be entirely misunderstood if construed as an attack upon Natural Rights. On the contrary, they are a plea that Natural Rights are so important and are to be understood as being rooted in something more than mere subjective velleities, that it is deplorable if they are not logically thought out and properly based upon an underlying Natural Law.

As has been mentioned earlier (*supra*, p. 182) some writers, such as Professor David Spitz, have abandoned the argument that democracy arises to protect these inalienable rights and have, with brilliant ingenuity and much logic, argued that these rights, on the contrary, are not cause but consequence of Democracy D —'necessary' in the pragmatic sense that recognition of them is required for its practical working.

The arguments against Natural Rights of the neo-Hegelian school, dominant in the latter part of the last century (from T. H. Green and the Cairds) through to the third decade of this century, are ill-founded. First, it assumed that the exaggeratedly individualist Natural Rights doctrine expressed all that had still to be said about (objective) Natural Law doctrine. It, then, successfully pointed out that man, as indeed Aristotle said, was born a social animal. Hence it was concluded that the rational rights of men must not be construed individualistically or atomically, and were not ever against 'society' but within it, for the benefit of social man. Rational rights, then, would be defined by 'society' and by the State as (it was usually held) alone organized society. The vital distinction between Society in general and some particular 'society,' with its conventions of "the city of Cecrops," although as old as the Cynics and Stoics, they crassly overlooked; and that particular State Sovereigns could abuse the fundamental social nature and individual dignity of men they chose to ignore or underestimate. On these themes Professor D. G. Ritchie's *Natural Rights* (1895) still repays reading.

The conservative position here being maintained is that no doctrine of Natural Rights can be given an intellectually satisfactory base save upon, or in connection with, a doctrine of Natural Laws as formulae of the recurrent characteristics of basic human nature. We may answer indeed that some of this human nature is not only passionate but corrupt; and we may ask 'what is basic?' The reply, since Plato (and Goethe) is in terms of harmony; and that our often schizophrenic nature is co-ordinated by reason, and the co-ordination attested by what is considered to be health. Here is the canon or gnomon of reference. As Professor Paul Weiss himself emphasizes, even in judging as between legitimate natural rights, a sense of proportion has to be exercised in establishing relations and priorities and in solving conflicts. A human being too cowed to express himself, and too fearful to communicate with other human beings, either is himself somebody who cannot satisfy us medically or aesthetically or is a member of a society so diseased that it produces these perversions. The Natural Rights, so far as valid, flow from the nature of man; the Natural Law formulates the rules of that nature as part of the intelligible cosmos. To that nature we appeal in adjudicating on just ends and social values, if not to define their detail, at least to exclude what does not belong to them. Social and political institutions are made for man. There is a dangerous totalitarianism implicit in the view popular with some sociologists that men are entirely the product of their *particular* temporal and concrete society and its institutions, which their mind cannot transcend and their morals should not. The false doctrine of conditioning inevitably by 'the material dialectic' is probably less disastrous and intellectually more reputable. Man is not made to be adjusted to any one society, institution, or convention.

The connection of freedom with the instinctive nature of man we have already discussed (*supra*, p. 114). The right to have his society provide security, such as from violent death from the underworld or from foreign foes, was rightly asserted by Hobbes; and is no less clear as touching physical health endangered by such causes as bad sanitation in the neighbourhood. Ideal rights arising from what has been called 'the picture of man' and his nature we shall discuss later.

A. F. Bentley, who is often paradoxical and 'folksy,' errs when, from rightly asserting with Plato the continuum between man and his society, he wrongly proceeds (or leaves the steady impression of proceeding) to expound behaviouristically the whole study of sociology in terms of actions and group relations or (as he later chooses to put it) of "wave motions of the linguistic behaviours of men." This seems to me to be so narrow a use of 'scientifically operational tools' as to lead to distortion. If indeed there is no 'skin' or 'iron curtain' of dualism between man's psychological nature and his institutional society, then surely it logically follows that this nature is of no less interest to us than these institutions.

The present writer indeed has emphasized (*supra*, p. 61) the importance of focus on the political *act*, the relational act of control, for study. But we must not, with Bentley, throw out the baby in order to analyse the bath-water. Nor will the linguistic theory provide a thesis wide enough to be useful, however it may fit in with 'linguistic philosophies' (*supra*, p. 18). Cf., however, R. W. Taylor's contribution in the Bentley festschrift, *Life, Language, Law* (1957). There is something in Bentley, as there was in Lincoln Steffens, with his 'no illusions' attitude, of 'the great American primitive' in political science, free from European 'mind stuff'—a kind of scientific Grandma Moses.

For a detailed comment on the Declaration of Human Rights, *vide* the article by Felix S. Cohen in *ibid.*, pp. 204–9.

§iv. *Concerning State Sovereignty*

The empirical Doctrine of Natural Law, as above set out, has an obvious bearing upon the Doctrine of Sovereignty.

The Doctrine of Sovereignty as initially formulated, especially by lawyers, is a theoretical vindication of the actual claims of the New Monarchies and of the Modern States as they arose with the late Renaissance. This secular sovereignty is a more sophisticated or legalistic version of the assertion of the divine rights of the new kings against the international rights alike of the Papacy and of the Empire, the infallibility of the Pope being the sovereignty of the Pope. After the lawyers' fight and pamphleteering between the Pope's men and the Emperor's men, the turn comes of the men of the Kings, who hitherto had been dismissed as mere *reguli*, 'little kings,' such as the kings of Wessex and Sussex and the chieftains of Wales. These men, like Richard II, might claim an *'empire entire'* or, like Henry VIII, might edge up to entertain Charles V, but they were not serious Emperors or Powers. Henry II was flattered to be known as Henry FitzEmpress. A fifteenth-century Duke of Brittany could say that, if a King of France could claim to have the rights of Emperor in France, the Duke had likewise the rights of king in Brittany.

Although, from Bodin to Blackstone, assertions of sovereignty are formally qualified by homage to the traditional doctrine of Natural Law, nevertheless in many even of the earlier forms this assertion of sovereignty is singularly uncompromising and (it should be noted) without distinction between the legal, political, and philosophical aspects. One of its clearest expressions in about the second century of its maturing development, indicating the nature of the logic upon which it rests, will be found in Hobbes' graphic phrase, already referred to: "if two men ride upon a horse, one must ride in front." For Hobbes no distinction is drawn (nor could it be drawn, consistently with his philosophy) between legal, political, and moral sovereignty.

In discussions of the Modern State one of the classical problems is that of the nature of Sovereignty. In Churches insisting upon communal discipline a like problem arises. It is not confined to civil organization alone, but reappears almost precisely in ecclesiastical organization, where *decisions* on authoritative doctrine and morals have to be taken, under the caption of Infallibility. As Selden said: "The Pope is infallible, where he hath power to command . . . as is every supreme power and prince."

In society, which is plural because different social functions take different organizational forms, there are border-lines of jurisdiction between the organizations and there are the possibilities of conflicts which can break any particular society into schismatic or secessionist parts. In crisis indeed a 'monistic' organization, with centralized if not dictatorial powers, may be most successful. An authority, therefore, seems to be required in the interest of the social pattern of cohesion ('the will of the society to survive') or of civil peace, which either (*a*) will adjudicate between jurisdictions or (*b*) will reduce all other jurisdictions, in what becomes a monistic or even totalitarian society, to insignificance compared with its own. In international or world society unfortunately no such authority or sovereign at the present time exists.

The modern civil doctrine of Sovereignty takes its origin, prior to the so-called 'Divine Rights' of kings or of majorities, in the embryonic doctrine of Infallibility in directing the ecclesiastical (not the civil) field; and, in ordering the community of the faithful, outstandingly expressed in the *Unam Sanctam* of Boniface VIII. Authority must have *unum caput, non duo sicut monstrum*. This *maiestas* or *souveraineté* is, for Bodin, a power "absolved from control of the laws," *legibus soluta potestas*.

The Austinian definition of sovereignty, which is almost verbally the same as that offered by Jeremy Bentham, runs: "If a determinate human superior, not in a habit of obedience to a like superior, receive habitual obedience from the bulk of a given society, that determinate superior is sovereign in that society, and the society (including the superior) is a society political and independent." Bentham writes: "When a number of persons (whom we may style subjects) are supposed to be in a habit of obedience to a person, or an assembly of persons, of a known and certain description (whom we may call governor or governors), such persons altogether (subjects and governors) are said to be in a state of Political Society." It is 'the *relation of authority*' (and the existence of control) which constitutes distinctively any Political Society, including a church as organized.

The Austinian assumption is of one determinate superior and of a monistic society, politically delimited in terms of the writ of that superior. John Austin did not hesitate to criticize Grotius for the absolute and abstract quality of his notion of natural rights. Nevertheless, Austin endeavoured to discover such a determinate single superior in the American Constitution, without conspicuous success, not surprisingly in view of the conscious Congregationalist background of much Puritanism and its influence on American thought. Blackstone, in his *Commentaries*, speaks of "a supreme, irresistible, uncontrollable authority, in which the *iura summa imperii* or rights of sovereignty reside," although he elsewhere limits this in Natural Law terms (as does Bodin), while the theologian ·Paley talks of a power "arbitrary, despotic, and . . . alike so in all nations." Rousseau finds that the sovereign cannot impose restrictions on itself and is always what he ought to be (*Contrat Social*, II, 3.6).

A more recent statement is to be found in T. E. Holland's *The Elements of Jurisprudence* (2nd ed., p. 367): "The sovereign part of the State, as thus ascertained, is omnipotent. Since it is the source of all law, its Acts can never be illegal. As little can they be, strictly speaking, unconstitutional." For discussion cf. my *Principia*, part II, chap. VIII.

It is noteworthy that American constitutional law is chary of using the concept of Sovereignty, as was Locke (who preferred to speak more generally of 'a supreme power') and the Whigs. Sovereignty (within their 'proper' jurisdiction) is even attributed to States of the American Union. Not only have the Southern States (especially) continued to claim for themselves the attribute 'sovereign,' but in the Legislature of Mississippi there is a 'Mississippi Sovereignty Committee' for defence of State rights. Thus the Civil War is referred to as the War between the States. This, of course, is to use the word 'sovereignty' in a plural sense, in defiance of Hobbes and Austin. As will be seen (if we reject the route, advocated by H. J. Laski, of discarding the term and, instead, reduce it to the description of a function) it is not necessarily for the worse that this usage be adopted, with its plural, federal, and functional stress; although in the South it can be held to be obstructive or to threaten the community—in legal phraseology, 'the American Nation.'

As F. W. Maitland authoritatively showed, the doctrine of sovereignty is a sixteenth-century product which has no counterpart in the mutuality system of Mediaeval Feudalism (unless it be with the Papacy, under the decretal already quoted), while 'the pleasure of the prince' of the Roman Empire, tracing from the *tribunicia potestas* and *lex regia* is subject, in jurisprudence, to a concept of Natural Law. As to a power 'arbitrary and despotic,' St. Thomas (*Summa Theologica*, 2a, 2ae, q. 42) not only comments that "it is the tyrant who is seditious," but he or his continuator speaks (*De regimine*) of a name which "pompously and pretentiously takes its origin from a supreme dominion, as did the proud Nicanor."

The word 'Sovereign' (A) is sometimes used as the characteristic mark of what is called 'the Modern State' or fully developed State *du sang pur*; sometimes as a means of distinguishing some states or their governments from others, for example the Government of the United States or of Canada from that of Texas or of Quebec; and, sometimes, again, to refer to a monarch, whether absolute or constitutional, or such royal person, who could claim with Louis XIV that "*l'Etat c'est moi.*" Sometimes these last powers are referred to as 'of the Crown.'

In Britain technically the Sovereign is not the State as such, or its people, but the King-in-Parliament. Sovereignty is also (B) used in a quite different although connected sense—not 'internally' but 'externally'—of "being above orders," because 'juristically independendent' of other States.

In *A Grammar of Politics* (1925) H. J. Laski wrote: "It would be of lasting benefit to political science if the whole concept of sovereignty were surrendered. That, in fact, with which we are dealing is power." However, in *The State in Theory and Practice* (1935) he states: "It is by the possession of sovereignty that the state is distinguished from all other forms of human association." Laski, originally (in the 1914–18 war) a vehement pluralist or opponent of the theory of the 'sovereign' and of the always dominant power of a monistic or centralized state (especially a state at war), in his *Democracy in Crisis* (1933) goes rather in the Marxist direction of dictatorship and writes: "Such an administration [a government of the type approved by Laski] could not, if it sought to be effective, accept the present forms of its procedure. It would have to take vast powers and legislate under them by ordinance and decree."

As pointed out in my *Principia*, chapter VIII, were it not for reference to "subjects and governors," the type or function of obedient activity being undefined, we would not know that Bentham's definition applied to the State at all: it could apply to schoolboys. The extreme danger of leaving the word 'political' undefined, and then packing in preconceptions, shows up here. Bluntschli, in his *Lehre vom Modernen Staat*, an admirable book, yet defines the State as "the politically organised Folks-person of a definite land," but does not tell us what he means by "politically organised," which maybe, tautologically, means 'state-organized.'

Hegel and the post-Hegelians, such as Bosanquet, developed a doctrine of the moral claim to obedience held by states, e.g. Venezuela, as concrete materializations of 'the State,' as absolute. There was, as Hobhouse pointed out, much ideal metapolitics here. Earlier Hobbes, unconcerned with 'objective idealist' arguments concerning the final moral claims of State or Church (cf. Augustine), more brutally enunciated a clear doctrine of sovereignty based upon fear. The Sovereign is "one person"—natural or corporate: and Hobbes prefers a king or other autocrat as sovereign, as having natural unity of will—"said to have sovereign power," "of whose acts a great multitude, by mutual covenants one with another," or, as is almost immediately afterwards added, "by natural force" and conquest, and acts of submission, "have made themselves every one the author [i.e., prisoners of war can be 'the authors'] to the end that he [the sovereign] may use the strength and means of them all, as he shall think expedient, for their peace and common defence," the alternative being a primitive life, "solitary, poor, nasty, brutish and short." Heinrich von Treitschke, in his *Politics*, while using all the philosophical reinforcements which he can from Hegel, yet places the emphasis, like Hobbes and the royal author of the *Anti-Machiavel*, Frederick the Great of Prussia, upon power, from which he feels that recognized and legitimatized authority (the problem later of Ferrero's study) flows.

Distinct alike from the philosophical idealists and from the analysts of power is the position of the Austinian lawyers. Actually utilitarian by derivation in philosophy, when hard pressed they tend to adopt the defence that sovereignty is purely a concept in and for law, the sovereign being algebraically necessary in legal theory or jurisprudence (although not so for the Romans) as a kind of unmoved mover or *fons et origo* of legal authorization, and a determiner of which claim shall prevail in a contest of authorities. In brief, we are here playing a kind of elegant legal game, which has its rules. It is played out in what is subtly distinguished as *le pays légal*, as frontiered off from *le pays réel*. The only objection here is that this qualification is so frequently covered up—and the ensuing statements are made to appear as if they were political.

T. E. Holland, it is noteworthy, in his *Elements of Jurisprudence*, writes that the State is "a numerous assemblage of human beings, generally occupying a certain territory, amongst whom the will of the majority, or of an ascertainable class of persons, is by the strength of such a majority, or class, made to prevail against any of their number who oppose it." It will be noted that the definition of, presumably, the sovereign as a will that can 'prevail' is markedly 'realistic' and is *dictum de facto*, not *de iure*. It recalls certain of the more pragmatic observations of Mr. Justice Oliver Wendell Holmes. Professor Holland, when he speaks of sovereignty, does not distinguish sovereignty from this pragmatic will. In part his definition also recalls, to a surprising degree, the analysis of Marx and his follower, Franz Oppenheimer, in *Der Staat* (1907, translated by John M. Gitterman as *The State*, 1914). As early as 1855, Sir Henry Maine had criticized what he called "the ambiguities of the word 'sovereignty,'" which resulted in the publication of "the most incomprehensible books ever written."

Metaphysical hypostasization and the multiplication of nouns of grandeur are among the curses of political theory. It is legitimate, although dangerous, for lawyers to abstract the field of jurisprudence, for the purposes of theory of law, from that of politics (just as one might foolishly separate this, in turn, from that of sociology); and to affirm that such a juristic theory logically requires the notion of a Sovereign as source of legal authorization, all question of actual power to enforce the law in actuality apart. This position, within its self-chosen limits of postulation, cannot be assailed if its premises are granted. The only question is whether or not it is useful and realistic.

It has been noted that Locke and his successors, who shaped the American Constitution and law, while speaking of 'the supreme power,' carefully avoided the use of the word sovereignty, as put into use by Blackstone, for the purposes of a constitutional form of government. A theory, thus, was later developed of 'greater and lesser' sovereignties. The above stictly legal position must, however, be sharply distinguished from the political position of Hobbes, who both affirms the political need, if the peace-maintaining *function* of the State is to be maintained, for some person or authority to have the final word of command, "or the private sword hath place again"; and for this person to be in possession of actual and *de facto* dominant power to break down all opposition.

It was especially the work of Otto von Gierke and of his translator and introducer, F. W. Maitland, to insist that during long periods of mediaeval history no one, either in actuality or in admitted principle, corresponded to this executive or even juristic sovereign. Earlier, although the maxim *quod principi placuit legis habet vigorem* corresponds to one of sovereignty—nor is this undermined because the power by *tribunicia potestas* is formally derived from the people—nevertheless the overriding restriction of Natural Law is admitted in theory, and in the orthodox practice of Byzantium (cf. Professor Sir Ernest Barker, *Social and Political Thought in Byzantium*, Introduction). The same applies to the Papacy, even if the norm of the Pope's interpretation of law natural and divine be held by some extremists to be *in scrinio pectoris sui*.

Hence, in perhaps his most important book, *The Modern State*, R. M. MacIver insists that the social form of a State, functioning to maintain at least peace (whether or not, to use Aristotle's own distinction, also welfare), which both claims sovereign power and in practice holds a dominant force, is not so much logical, inevitable, and unalterable as recent, and a possibly transient expression of the nation in its aspect as nation-state.

It will be noted, however, that despite claims of power 'despotic' or 'irresistible and uncontrollable' or 'omnipotent,' as by Paley, Blackstone, and Holland, the actual force at the disposal of the State's Government is limited by restrictions, perhaps unwritten, but effective, as such pragmatists as Léon Duguit insisted, within the social structure and constitution, consensus, or *mores* of the country. Moreover, it will be noted that the Austinian sovereign, in many political entities such as the British Commonwealth, is almost undetectable or, as Austin himself found with the United States Constitution, cannot be detected except by a forced formula.

A comprehension of the subject involves, then, a clear distinction between philosophical meanings attached to sovereignty (as by Bosanquet) which connect with the concept of Community, sometimes as *corpus mysticum* with a head; legal meanings; and political meanings— as well as the subsidiary distinction between domestic sovereignty and that international sovereignty which by no means spells a final power, but only mutual recognition (subject to treaty and other claims) of Independence, as in the Six Principles of Nehru and Mao. From the point of view of some one particular system or metaphysic of Jurisprudence (and, as already indicated, there may be others, just as in Geometry), it is entirely legitimate to make it an axiom, beyond discussion, that Law finds its source and definition in a Sovereign. And, if indeed this is discussed or challenged, it may be said that the law says so and, as a matter of convenience to prevent other force, the law and lawyers will so enforce it. (The issue whether this does not only mean that the police will perhaps enforce it has been mentioned. In the Nuremberg Trial the international court, having the force of the victors and also claiming to be the upholder of the known Laws of Humanity and Civilization and of the sanctity of the Kellogg Pact, held that the validity of its jurisdiction was beyond challenge by the subjects of an allegedly sovereign national state, Nazi Germany.)

It will be noted that Austin himself makes a condition of the sovereign's authority that it does receive "habitual obedience from the bulk of a given society," whereas this is readily turned circularly into the argument that habitual obedience *must* be rendered, because the determinate superior is sovereign. Politically and sociologically we can, however, return to Aristotle—and are wise if we do—that "he who bids the law rule bids God and Reason rule." There is no *actual* executive political authority despotic or omnipotent save that, tempered by assassination, of a tyrant. What is actual is a Constitutional Morality or consensus that enjoins us, within a limited framework, to obey the agencies of law and especially the judicial agencies of final arbitration.

Lord Bryce, in his *Studies in History and Jurisprudence* (1901), writes of Bentham's definitions that "they are arbitrary and artificial, concealing under few words many fallacies. Human nature and human society are too complex to be thus dealt with." "The great bulk of the rules which determine the relations of individuals or groups to one another have in most countries, until comparatively recent times, rested upon Custom. . . . The definition of a law as that which the State is prepared to enforce fits a modern State," but is "not universally applicable to early communities." We may, if we choose, concur with the controversial and 'tough' statement of Mr. Justice Holmes, in 257 U.S. 432, *The Western Maid*, that "sovereignty is a question of power, and no human power is unlimited." It will yet be noted that, removing the appeal to reason, this dictum leaves the issue as one of force by "a strong man armed," and hence is anarchic in logic, awaiting the arrival of "a stronger than he." We do well to add, with Professor Henry Sidgwick, in his *Elements of Politics*, that "the power of government, then, in a modern state is limited not only by its own majority— or by the law of God, so far as it itself recognizes principles of religious duty—

but by the prevalent moral opinion of the community; especially by opinions, resting on custom and habit, as to the proper nature and limits of governmental coercion." Moreover, custom is different from any temporary majority vote of those who trouble to vote.

In brief, in the words of H. J. Laski, "unlimited power turns out to be power exercised under conditions fairly well known to each generation," even if, in accordance with the dictum, already quoted in part, of John Chipman Gray, "the real rulers of a people are undiscoverable. They are the persons who dominate the wills of their fellows. The truth is that the ideal or fictitious entity (of philosophers), the State can manifest itself only through organs, and these organs may be so limited that there are certain acts they cannot perform, and therefore there may be no one sovereign in Austin's sense, with complete powers. Such is the case in the United States of America." (*The Nature and Sources of Law*, 1909, pp. 78 ff.)

Writings about unlimited sovereign power, save as a convenient legal hypothesis divorced from political conditions, is merely a pompous form of "bawling on paper," designed to frighten the unlearned and simple, as if one should pretend by like sophistry that the Queen of the United Kingdom, because 'sovereign,' was absolute, and that all should crawl, like flunkeys, before her as before the Turkish Soldan. The first proposition is contrary to the constitutional law of the country and the second contrary to its constitutional morality.

Concerning the need for a judicial final authority to decide, between departments, the limits of their authority, the wise remarks of Mr. Justice Learned Hand in *The Bill of Rights* (1958) can be consulted with advantage.

There has been a tendency to regard the essence of sovereignty, because concerned with the fount of law, as lying in the Legislature or, because concerned with the final authority in civil matters, as lying in the Executive. But if we accept with Austin that it is conditioned by habitual obedience, and with Sidgwick that it "rests on custom and habit," and detect its function to be rather to arbitrate finally between different claimants to jurisdiction, then: WE MAY HOLD THE FUNDAMENTAL NATURE OF SOVEREIGNTY RATHER TO BE JUDICIAL THAN EXECUTIVE OR LEGISLATIVE (Proposition 43). Its competence lies in adjudicating about the competence of others, as the jurist Dr. Paul Labande maintained. It is for a connected reason that the Supreme Court of the United States is one of the greatest institutions in history. On principle a world arbitrator is required. The earlier international lawyers such as Vittoria and Ayala found this, at least for the Occident, in the Papacy; but the role has not been occupied since the unhappy sixteenth-century schism. As a consequence of these anomalies the provision of the civil goods of peace, described by Dante as once offered by the united Roman Empire, has been very imperfect in our age. Hobbes, shying away from the consequences, deliberately refused to carry through the logic of his own argument on peace and sovereignty.

President Eisenhower, in an address of 1958, admitted the need, in order to ensure peace, of a modification of already archaic national notions of sovereignty (so that we indeed may say 'the Modern State' is rather the Obsolescent State). Mr. Harold Macmillan has repeatedly emphasized the theme of "interdependence." What does emerge is that, if the function of sovereignty is not one of actual executive omnipotence (and hence in theory of tyranny, individual, or corporate), but of a judicial character in the allocation of boundaries between possibly conflicting jurisdictions, then it operates within a framework of social or cultural presumptions set by habit, custom and what we may call Constitutional Morality, whether or not shaped in sound jurisprudence by concepts of natural rights, and of that Natural Law without which natural or human 'rights' have no intelligible base in jurisprudence.

It may, in conclusion, be said that it is important that discussions of the operations of civil government, especially when they tend to drift into what Professor Hobhouse called "a Metaphysical Theory of the State" or of Sovereignty, should be conducted in close relation to the politicist's or sociologist's general theory of action and of social controls and sanctions. They cannot be just a lawyers' preserve. This prudence can save us from the error of which Guizot wrote: "It is a gross delusion to believe in the sovereign power of political machinery." It merely encourages the heady partisans of would-be dictators, impatient of constitutional morality. A recognized political pluralism (such as is always actually present in the multiplicity of political functions) and indeed the permanent balance of Church and State, small Family and great Industry, is a desirable element in social functioning and equilibrium, sustaining the interest of liberty against monopoly and contributing to the benefit of an Open Political Market.

Immanuel Kant maintained that, prior to the establishment of an impartial international arbiter, it violated fundamental maxims of ethics to describe any war as a just war. This is consonant indeed with the earlier ecclesiastical theory of the *bellum iustum* (in the Articles of incorporation of the Church of England, mistranslated simply as 'war'). However, writing in *The Times*, Lord Cecil of Chelwood truly said of the modern position that (like the right of rebellion claimed as legal by the barons of Magna Carta) "it is a recognized principle of international law that sovereign states have the right to resort to war, should they desire to do so"; and diplomatic pressures for the restriction of arms may be described, as by the late Kaiser Wilhelm II, as "a foreign assault upon our right of self-determination." Ethical principles are here invoked. For example, Professor von Martens, of Göttingen, wrote that "a sovereign government is one which *ought* not to receive command from any external source," presumably even under treaty or formal commitment to a united command.

It is probable that this especially German principle, of *absolute* domestic sovereignty as against international claims, although enshrined in certain clauses of the United Nations Charter, is today technically untenable. It is increasingly difficult to maintain that the obstinate direction of a majority by a minority on race principles, as in South Africa and South West Africa, is a purely domestic matter; or the murder, on race principles, of a minority by a majority, as in Hitler's Germany; or the diffusion of a lethal bomb fall-out which can do damage to children across the entire world. Against the last contention the Prime Minister of Canada, Mr. John Diefenbaker, has protested, not alone, in vigorous and justified terms (October, 1961). The time would seem to be approaching when some international authority must be recognized as competent to decide the competence of such rights and the validity of such claims. Practically, however, despite possible world collaboration, such an effective authority will have to begin (like the rights of the crown in France) as regional. The power will have to have focus—maybe in Washington, Ottawa and Westminster.

The comment may be added, as touching internal sovereignty A (where this is locatable), that, although we may say that "the Public of England is the sovereign of England," as does Professor Sir Ernest Barker in his article, "The Rule of Law," actually there is the keenest jealousy between the sovereignty in Britain of the Queen-in-Parliament and the voice of the Sovereign People as expressed daily in scientific plebiscites (cf. my article on "The British Constitution," *Political Science Quarterly*, 1955). *Vide supra* p. 165.

Even in the United States, as touching a suggested 'sovereignty of the people' through the power of amendment, Mr. Elihu Root, in 253 U.S., *Rhode Island* v. *Palmer*, said (perhaps controversially): "Article V of the Constitution could not be construed to confer unlimited legislative power upon the amending authorities" —a thesis of which the apparent logical conclusion is that there is no internal sovereign whatsoever within the United States and, therefore, technically no single one with which, in the Austinian sense, a foreign sovereign can negotiate —as indeed emerged in certain cases of collection of pre-Civil-War State debts.

§v. *Government and Positive Right*

The Government is the directive and administrative side of that state organization of inhabitants of an area which, as State, also includes those who are directed and administered. So also Trades Unions have their directors, conferences, and committees, together with innumerable and in effect compulsory (but often non-voting, apathetic) members. Churches have their Hierarchies, Houses of Laity, and flocks of sheep.

The directive powers can be executive, legislative, judicial, or stated in treaty undertakings—by some writers, such as Locke, called 'federative' (*foedus*). Some early writers, including Hobbes, are primarily concerned with the Executive Power to repress violence. They regard Sovereignty as necessarily inhering in the command of this power and as partaking of an actual, political nature of direct control, and depict the legislative and judicial powers as derivative (being indications of the channels of action which will be pursued or of effects upon the individual case) from this undivided and indivisible sovereign.

The objection here is final: that it is improbable that the absolute sovereign so described *ought* to exist, even for the practical reason of maintaining peace, since this is not best maintained by the apotheosis of domination (and, as Hobbes says, for him 'strong government' and 'tyranny' are merely different names for the same thing); and it is certain that, in this absolute sense of total surrender of individual wills and power, Locke rightly asserts that it *does not* exist. Nor would the political market continue in so far as it did exist. It is not sovereignty which sets finally the actual political limits but, in the last analysis, actual political and sociological limits are always set to it.

It follows that, as we have said, whatever may be convenient in an abstracted legal theory, in political theory, the quality of Sovereignty is better visualized as *of a judicial tincture*. We must turn aside from the metapolitical propositions, beloved by lawyers wandering in *le pays légal*, to weigh the rough actualities of *le pays réel*. The practical function of the sovereign, as maintained rightly by such German jurists as Labande, is that of competence to decide the areas of authority and competence of conflicting subsidiary authorities or groups. It is *Competenz-Competenz*. These decisions, however, it will be noted, command recognition, respect, and authority in custom (as of recognized utility in self-protection on the market) so far as they act within a framework—primarily that of the written Constitution, when its exists as defining the powers of government (and, as A. V. Dicey pointed out, even the British Constitution in a certain sense is 'written,' so far as it is statute) and secondarily that of what may be called the Constitutional Morality of the country, which will decide how its citizens will choose to act in critical issues. This will probably involve recognition of some fundamental civil or like rights and liberties (and obligations, costs or duties) in individuals or in other social functions and forms as significant, beside the rights (and claims) of the State and its Government. By this, as shaping support, the Government is limited in practice and in theory.

It will be noted that Sovereignty itself, even as a function of perpetual arbitration, giving finality in the otherwise infinite chain of judicial and other appeals, and—even more, if considered as the supreme executive force (with force regarded as dominant power)— is something which, from the nature of the case, cannot inhere in an unorganized body such as the People, unless the People speak juridically through 'some determinate superior,' or else in an occasionally organized and recognized body, such as the Electorate. "The will of the people," the political consumers, may be "the basis of the authority of government" (*Declaration of Human Rights*, art. 21) and without them there would be no market; but they are not the form of government.

Thomas Hobbes is here correct when he writes: "because the Multitude naturally is not One, but Many, they cannot be understood for one; but many Authors of everything their executive Representative saith or doth in their name." Again, Rousseau's own view that the People are sovereign by direct intervention in legislation, or by representation by mere delegates, is logical and is satisfactory just so far as the People is not only the directed body of the State but is (as with the Athenian assemblies and juries) the juristically recognized directing Government of the State or *polis*. Nevertheless, so far as this condition, where the whole people both produces and consumes (if indeed this ever in practice holds true, and Aristotle indicated its limits), is a primitive and undifferentiated political condition; and, as much as does Hobbes, if for the opposite reason, ignores the legitimate distinction between political Producer and Consumer.

Sovereignty, in brief, is an attribute not so much of the populace or actual people as such, as of a juristic something, articulate through the Hierarchy or Government. The opinion, however, of humanity or of the particular people, whether or not guided by reason and empiric inquiry, shapes the Constitutional Morality of a place or civilization.

In so far as sovereignty is recognized final competence in decision between claims, the Sovereign decides legal Rights (whether under civil or canon law) or recognized liberties (A), as distinct from any actual freedoms; and Rights flow (as Hobbes truly said) from its decisions. This is true even although rights, in fact preserved and unchallenged by customs, may exist without appeal to such decisions and, under common law and practice, be allowed in the courts.

When John Locke writes, as it were by way of concession (*Essays on the Law of Nature*, chap. IV. 3. 18) that "no government allows absolutely liberty," either he is saying that no government allows each man absolute freedom to do as he chooses, which is an empty truism, or he is saying that no government or State allows or ought to allow any liberties save such as it does or ought to allow (liberties being by definition what the State allows or should allow), which is a no less empty tautology.

Rights are such claims as we may hold that we are entitled to make on our neighbours, under Natural Law or by our private opinion and conscience about our moral due. They are those claims to which we hold our 'just' freedom entitles us. As Ahrens says, they flow from that principle which governs "the exercise of liberty [freedom] in the relations of human life." Legal rights are (a) such subjective claims on the State or other political body, as are objectively recognized as fit liberties *in need* of recognition, protection, and remedy for their infringement, and (b) as *iura*, such objective guarantees, which the courts will enforce, as the law sets up, not only as permission, but to assure the exercise of this class of liberties. Duties are either the subjective obligations recognized by objective reason or by private opinion as corresponding to these rights; or they are the costs objectively required by law in correspondence to the provision of goods, such as the social guarantees of rights. Legal Duties or obligations which are the converse, in costs, of such Rights and Liberties, as imposed or defined by authority, and not matters of opinion, likewise flow from the legislature and, by definition, from the sovereign.

C. S. M. Phillipps, in his *Jurisprudence* (1863), writes that there is a "fundamental axiom that one human being has no right to control for his own benefit the volition of another." But (a) the whole system of law is designed to control for the common or majority good (which is what is commonly or by majority held to be the long-range good of each) the actions of others. (b) We may agree that there is an important moral right of free choice to obey the law or to prefer to pay the penalty, and it may be argued that the law should not, by requiring uniformity, superfluously and beyond common utility challenge this claim of non-conformity. For example, should military conscription be imposed (i) under any circumstances or (ii) apart from any military emergency? Or should Sunday shop-closing or 'saluting the flag' be imposed compulsorily? (c) It cannot cogently be argued that what by law controls finally the action does not shape the will which is disposed to action. In one quite important sense, despite Kant's dogma, men are habitually used as means for what is, for some, an imposed end.

§vi. *External Sovereignty*

Sovereignty, we have said, by general usage of the term, has not only an internal aspect (A), as touching the people subject to it, but also an external aspect (B), as touching subjection to none, whether it be the Pope as supreme pontiff or the King or King-in-Parliament as being subject to none. And even where, as in the United States, a full doctrine of an internal sovereignty has been deliberately avoided by lawyers, and other theses about State power and States' rights have been advanced, a doctrine of full external sovereignty, or Absolute Independence as juristically true, has been enunciated. What Positive Rights, then, exist, in a situation where there is no Common Sovereign?

Just indeed as human beings are unavoidably born into society for distinguishable functions, so also the associations of human beings organized as States grow up in a planet where States are, whether they will or not, associated with other states. Under fortunate conditions of remoteness and of temporary lack of interest in each other's power, and of attention only to 'their own business,' these states can indeed be absolutely independent in fact, in the only intelligible sense of being in a condition of unentangled isolation.

In the highly specialized situation of Britain under Lord Salisbury, this condition of freedom from expensive entanglement was, by Sir Edward Goschen, called 'splendid.' In fact it merely was a way of saying that British naval power was not only so great (as the Roman military power had been) that, in the field which at that moment happened to interest her wishes and desires, Britain could do what she liked, but that also no Power then was other than fearful of an attempt to restrict her. In the case of post-colonial America, the power was much less great (and the Monroe Doctrine contingent on the support of the British navy and policy), but, conversely, the wishes and desires of European Powers remained, until the Spanish-American and First World Wars, not—save exceptionally—concentrated in fields which clashed with American development interests.

However, juristically, wherever treaty obligations are *bona fide* entered into, there is a limitation under International Law of External Sovereignty. We can only elude this argument by maintaining that International Law is not law in the strict sense, emanating from a sovereign authority and giving positive rights, and that the restrictions imposed under it are of the nature of provisional concessions, capable of recall by the national sovereign at the convenience of its local interest. The convenience of its people will be the supreme law; and *pacta non sunt servanda.* This argument has force so long as convenience and the gain of political goods is actually to be found in breaking the law, and indeed is an argument that also applies to the common law breaker, if moral restraints are not within the field of legal discussion but only 'realism.' Hence the issue, already discussed in my *Principia*, of the *functional* limits of state autonomy, whether the word 'State' be construed locally or nationally (federally), demands attention.

§vii. *The Functions of the Civil State*

The Civil State, which once having assumed different forms as *polis* and empire and feudal kingdom, today is usually to be found in the form of the Nation-State (with some new breeds burgeoning, indicating yet a new form), and may be discussed and analysed in juristic terms of sovereignty and of static and statutorily determined jurisdictions. However, going back to its legitimization, it can also be analysed in terms of an organization of society performing specific functions within its structure, and can be judged by its performance, its agreed end being something in conformity with the development of man's authentic nature and with Natural Law.

As Aristotle rightly lays down, the prime purpose of the Civil Organization is to maintain life. We need to turn again to Aristotle, with his analysis of function, and away from the metaphysical lawyers of sovereignty—and if American law here is relatively immune, the American system is one of those most in bondage to formal legalism in the world—and their successors in the schools. *Civil Organization is produced* propter regnum, *in order to produce particular kinds of wanted political goods.* Whether or not it is the appropriate producer of certain kinds of goods, to be settled by support in the market in relation to costs (for example, welfare goods such as public education as against war or private enterprise), there is almost universal agreement that it is the sole competent producer of some particular goods in which States have priority, to wit, goods of security which may require the application of the *vis coactiva*, coercion and physical force. One of these goods is, as Hobbes truly said, the averting of violent death (death itself it can postpone by medical aids, but never avert), whether threatened from internal or foreign quarters as crime or as war. The welfare activities of 'the good life' have to lie within this ambit of the preservation of life.

The States are fundamentally power organizations of Society, by their authority providing particular goods. For their effective functioning as against anarchy (which Hobbes recognized), they require a certain measure of assent or positive consent about means in public opinion, whether under Constitutionalism, with its agreements on the constitutional morality, or even under Dictatorship.

Clearly it is advantageous for its support and authority if the State-Society is also a Community, inspired by sentiments of like-mindedness. It was a traditional Liberal error to overlook how far variety and divergence and non-conformity, obstinately persisted in, might demolish the prospect of stability in the producer, even for Democracy itself. But, nevertheless, it must be stressed that this *homoinoia* is not essential or even, in any marked measure, characteristic of the Civil State form. Indeed the whole Liberal philosophy preferred to stress the desirability of variety, individual freedom, and individual power;

and the dangers of mental uniformity which had to it any touch of compulsion. Likewise, one conceivable philosophy (such as that of Metternich) stressed the nature of administration of men as a human need, and the mechanical relation of the civil authority to subjects, who were yet free as individuals in everything outside the state sphere. Government, *ratione peccati*, might be an evil; but it was a necessary one, and only dreamers supposed that it did not involve the use of force. *Pro tanto*, the Civil State was administration and not community, whether nationalist or otherwise.

If we assume this contention to be valid about the stigmata or characteristics of Civil Power, the *dominium civile*, and that there are prior functions which—whatever else it may do—the State cannot evade doing without deserting its purposes, certain consequences follow. Whether or not eternal peace (to use Kant's phrase) is a good thing fundamentally for civilization is not here in question. The allocated and hypothetical purpose of the State is to maintain, for its subjects or citizens, the civil peace at home and in relations abroad. The first question, therefore, whereby to test any particular one of the many forms of the Civil Power, is: does it do this? *Does* it function?

Broadly and roughly, for its provincials in a vast area from Tigris to Thames, centred on the Mediterranean, the Roman Empire did this. The *pax romana* was a reality. Equally broadly speaking the Hellenic *polis* failed to do this—perhaps in part precisely owing to its inappropriate over-attachment to the local, like-minded Community and its rich values. Despite the arguments for harmony of its philosophers, the *polis*, as Thucydides records, was broken apart by strife and *stasis* owing to the excessive loyalty, first of clans and, then, of groups and classes to their own way of life. Moreover, despite an Aeschines, the Greek, inspired by the high values of the local community and by dislike of mass-means such as those of semi-barbaric Macedon or, later, of 'Romanization' (rather as some people today fear 'Americanization'), was incapable of subordinating his local patriotism to the demands and costs of a wider structure. The patent fact of lack of power, military and economic, in view of a glorious tradition of the past he obstinately, and with the rhetoric of a Demosthenes, refused to take into account. In modern times the Spanish Empire broke owing to excessive and inept centralization, unsupported by power—a fault which also afflicted the Chinese Empire until restored by strong rulers. The British Empire—and the same comment applies to most Northern peoples such as the Dutch—was unable to transcend the toils of nationalism, even of that composite nationalism which is 'British,' and to overcome the dividing colour bar. It never developed a logical philosophy of Empire which subordinated the original nationals (for example, the English natives) to the equal claims of the equal citizens of the entire Empire. It preferred, not a legal, but an empiric approach as more politic. It could rise from being English to being British and even Anglo-Saxon, and to developing a doctrine of Trusteeship; but only awkwardly beyond—even if today, as consequence of a "fit of absent-mindedness," it is presented with the unexpected benefits of a great multiracial Commonwealth and is willing, for example, to employ hired Fijian soldiers for a defence for which its own affluent citizens (as in Rome of old) are reluctant to volunteer or be conscripted.

Hence, until the Commonwealth concept (itself not one logical in jurisprudence) was shaped, it could not rise to the policy of the Roman Empire, which broke out beyond the confines of the *populus Romanus* of the City, gave the imperial purple to a great Spaniard such as Hadrian, and could have a Philip the Arabian as Caesar Augustus of the whole, leaving a legacy (as Hobbes said, 'a ghost') in the cosmopolitan Papal concept.

What stands out is that the modern National Sovereign State, which may roughly be said to be a unit in a system recognized since the Peace of Westphalia, although reinforced by the French Revolution, has conspicuously failed to solve the prime problem of war and to perform the function of maintaining peace, although this is the major *raison d'être* of the Civil Power—and one today not less, but more, important and urgent than in the past. We have then to end the Westphalian system. Even the principle of Self-Determination raises the issues of the legitimate historical claims and security of other— perhaps more numerous—peoples; and also of who precisely are the "People" who do the self-determining—if a minority, then may it be also the minority of a minority? Natural right does not include the right of a minority to intimidate others.

It may be argued that there is no scientific need, as means to ends, to change the present system of eighty or a hundred (twenty have been added on during the preparation of this book) Sovereign National States, juristically equal and independent, since, thanks to the Balance of Power, some kind of practical stalemate and even coexistent harmony can be pragmatically worked out among them. This, it is alleged, can be done without any deliberate or serious supra-national organization, rather playing along 'by ear,' by practical diplomacy from year to year. This course, it may be argued, is the really shrewd and statesmanlike one.

Against this may be urged (*a*) that the Balance of Power—and not only in Europe (cf. E. H. Carr, *Twenty Years Crisis*)—has been discarded in recent years. It can even be argued (and by Professor Williams, in a paper read in 1959 before the International Political Science Conference in Dubrovnic, it was argued) that Sir Winston Churchill himself, until a late date in the Second World War, was a grievous offender here, "lacking in war the wisdom and statecraft of eighteenth-century diplomacy," by his acquiescence in the 'unconditional surrender' policy of January 7, 1943, with its demolition of the European Balance. At least it may be said (i) that Sir Winston became alive to the danger long before Franklin Roosevelt who, guided by Harry Hopkins (a tuberculosis expert), remained an optimist to the end; (ii) that Sir Winston had small alternative if victory, let alone security, was to be achieved and that the blame lies with the earlier obstinate and short-sighted treatment (especially French) of the Weimar Republic, which treatment Sir Winston himself is on record as condemning.

In the eighteenth century it was held that journalists were a major cause of wars. At least the moral, confirmed alike by Lloyd George and Churchill, seems to be the immense danger of allowing higher policy in war and peace-making to be deflected by popular temporary passion, whipped up by sometimes irresponsible journalists and their wealthy proprietors who are responsible to none. The history of Castlereagh, who went to the Congress of Vienna to get, along with his late enemy Talleyrand, not glory but peace, shows the true course of professional politics. The peace lasted—which is the test. Likewise great economic prosperity is not to be achieved by the absurdity of inviting the consumers to run the factories. Granted agreed popular ends there are specific efficient means.

b. In a system which essentially depends, not upon *institutions* to enforce and maintain peace, but solely upon *sentiment* and good luck, incidents and errors may occur, ending in disaster. Such incidents may be but small blazes started amid the political affairs and ambitions of small Powers or even may be caused by the mere technical errors of distraught individuals. General Omar Bradley (speaking in Washington in 1957) has not been alone among military men in warning us that errors will occur, if not sooner then later; and that, if too much explosive material is, by the negligence of politicians, left around, one day a chance match will be dropped. By the soldiers, then, we have been warned. Further, it will be noted that even professional military intelligence can be greatly wrong on facts: the duration of war in

1914; the false rumours of mobilization in 1938 and 1939; the gross misestimate of the strength of Germany in 1935, and of the Russians in 1914 and 1939. The historical facts do not warrant optimism about what can be achieved in politics without relevant institutions. It has already, in the last chapter, been emphasized that these necessary efficient institutions themselves of course rest upon a basis in sentiment and demand.

The conclusions would seem to be clear. IN THE TWENTIETH CENTURY AN EFFECTIVE SUPRA-NATIONAL INSTITUTION MUST BE CONSTITUTED, SOVEREIGN *ad hoc*, AND SUPERSEDING IN ITS OWN FUNCTIONAL FIELD THE ARCHAIC POLITICAL INVENTIONS OF THE SEVENTEENTH CENTURY (Proposition 44). The old engines are rusty and liable to explode; and the task of the engineer is to drive and not to watch for an explosion. If it be said that this is the idle philosophic dream of a Kant, talking about categorical moral imperatives such as no Senator or practical politician worries about, the answer is that this, on the contrary, is about as sure a conclusion of scientific political analysis, on the basis of power, as any professional political scientist can offer. However, a justifiable argument may be raised. Any such organization would only be tolerable if, thanks to inspection and control, we could be sure both that it would fulfil its own function and that it would not, like a tyranny, intrude into other functions. This, in turn, depends upon co-operation and confidence. And how can we have confidence? It is a mood, not an institution. The answer, as in all practical matters, lies in terms of probabilities, not proofs.

The argument is frequently used that politics being "the art of the possible," it is futile to consider changes involving sacrifice of sovereignty because the Senators and legislators of the various countries, being "in touch with the grass roots," would "never contemplate" such a sacrifice. Natural law, however, is not defied, whatever may be the pretensions of so-called sovereign parliaments or peoples. Such parliaments and electorates must take their medicine of confronting facts like the rest of mankind, and substitute responsibility for the endemic irresponsibility of which Schumpeter complains, in passages already quoted. Public opinion is reluctant to contemplate the gravity of the position. The fallibility of human nature is such and the technological developments are such that a situation can all too easily arise in which both the legislators and their constituents are liable to be dissolved in very fervent heat. *Dies irae, dies illa, solvet coelum in favilla.* The Senators will be atomized. This is a prospect so unpleasant that the mind of the common man recoils and banishes the thought from consciousness, thrusts it as an anxiety 'under the rug' of the subliminal, or turns to those who offer the conventional remedy of accumulating even more armaments or turning to circuses and amusements. As the deacon Salvian wrote, "The Roman world was laughing when it died." To this prime issue of politics we return in the next chapter.

The political scientist is under a professional obligation to examine without flinching such defects as there may be in the current functioning of the modern State and in the usual theory of State Sovereignty. On the other hand, the politician has to consider how it will be most practical to achieve reform; and a frontal attack upon 'sovereignty,' in view of its associations with the defence of the local pattern of life which charges it with emotion, may be mistaken. The objective concern is not with words, if we are not to fall into precisely those metapolitical errors which we have condemned, but with the actual functioning or malfunctioning of the present system. Rather specific changes should be demanded as the most efficient way to procure, piecemeal, goods generally demanded. In time this will produce a modification in ideologies and lawyers' doctrines, and indeed in the law itself so far as it offers obstacles.

The military experts cannot be accused of not having given adequate warning. Apart from the remarks of Field Marshal Viscount Montgomery about the need for "pooling sovereignty," on November 5, 1957, at St. Alban's School, Washington, General Omar Bradley said: "We are now speeding inexorably towards a day when even the ingenuity of our scientists may be unable to save us from the consequences of a single rash act or a lone reckless hand upon the switch of an uninterceptable missile. This irony can probably be compounded a few more years or perhaps even a few decades." In brief, thanks to military mutual 'massive deterrents,' a brief holding operation is possible, while constructive statesmanship does its work. Bradley continues: "The problem of peaceful accommodation in the world is infinitely more difficult than the conquest of space, infinitely more complex than a trip to the moon. But if we will only come to the realization that it must be worked out—whatever it may mean to such sacred traditions as absolute national sovereignty—I believe that we can somehow, somewhere, and perhaps through some as yet undiscovered world thinker and leader find a workable solution. . . . If I am sometimes discouraged it is not by the magnitude of the problem, but by our colossal indifference to it."

Again the statesmen cannot be accused of not having suggested a way out. Apart from the Ball-Fulbright Resolution and the specific campaigning on the issue by Earl Attlee, sometime Premier of Britain, the sometime Chairman of the British Conservative Party, at present Lord President, Viscount Hailsham, speaking in the House of Lords on March 9, 1960—and developing Premier Macmillan's theme for a Declaration of Interdependence—said: "When I contemplate the hideous weapons on both sides, which even in my partially informed state I know to have been invented, I regard either a world authority or total disarmament in the long run as the only rational objective." He gave priority to the first alternative as guarantee for the second. The trouble would seem to be that the consumer public demands peace with liberty; but is ready usually to be persuaded emotionally by any cheapjack or demagogue not to pay the price.

The remedy would seem to lie with the producers, the statesmen, giving their publics what they ought to have. Consumer demand can be created, with the assent of all that public which have given the matter thought. A mass demand is potential, when the necessary work of public education has been performed.

It profits little to enquire from the historians how this situation was ever allowed to grow up or to conduct a *post mortem* on past diplomacy and statesmanship. One may suggest, as contributory, the reluctance of the comfortable to confront smaller difficulties and threats in time (as in 1936), as well as genuine vacillations of judgement; a hysterical or ambitious and ever-optimistic statesmanship which totally wrecked the existing balance of power; and, complementarily, the unwillingness—a species of 'cultural lag' in thought— to substitute, for balance, such a concentration of effective military power that the League or United Nations, overwhelmingly armed, could perform what Sir Anthony Eden assigns as its proper task of 'keeping peace' or what was more emphatically called, in the days of President Taft's original committee, 'enforcing peace.'

Thanks to a built-in veto in the Security Council, which now logically appears as a 'troika' proposal in the Secretariat, the United Nations has become incompetent to enforce peace except subject to power-support by, and some kind of pragmatic *condominium* of, the Great Powers. Until this is feasible on a basis of social justice and freedom, we do well to bear in mind the words of Salvador de Madariaga, quoted by Senator William Fulbright: "The trouble today is that the Communist world understands unity but not liberty, while the free world understands liberty but not unity. Eventual victory may be won by the first of the two sides to achieve the synthesis of both liberty and unity."

Senator J. W. Fulbright, in his article "For a Concert of Free Nations," (*Foreign Affairs*, October, 1961) writes, as touching the position of the United Nations, "the real problem is one not of legalities but of power politics on a divided world." The United Nations is likely to remain ineffective for enforcing peace until an effective world tribunal is set up, such as Kant demanded in his scheme for a cosmopolitical society, with powers to penalize and fine comparable to that now held by the High Tribunal of the supra-national European Steel and Coal Authority.

Senator Fulbright wisely continues, commenting on ambitious schemes for the reform of the United Nations, "a working concept of the organic evolution of community must lead us in a different direction." Commenting favourably on the proposal of Sir Anthony Eden (Lord Avon) for "a political general staff" of Western leaders, he writes: "A realistic balancing of the need for new forms of international organization on the one hand, and our capacity to achieve them on the other, must be approached through the concept of 'community.' History has demonstrated many times that concerts of nations based solely on the negative spur of common danger are unlikely to survive when the external danger ceases to be dramatically urgent." The present writer's phrase "Commonwealth of the Free World" perhaps has merit as laying stress upon the sense of community, rather than upon constitution-making and legalism.

The interest of the political scientist is not in the historical excuses but in the current political structure. Some written constitutions are two hundred years old. The present forms and machinery of the State system (if we choose to date them from the Peace of Westphalia) are something over three hundred years old. The block to change lies in the incapacity of politicians and electors to think except in terms of the emotion-fixed stereotypes in which they were themselves educated. They are like cavalrymen attached to their horses. They fail to realize the situation. THE PRESENT STATE, IN SO FAR AS IT IS MACHINERY, IS OBSOLETE, DECREPIT, AND DANGEROUS. IT IS ITSELF PROVOCATIVE OF FRICTION AND WAR. THE TEST IS THAT, FAR FROM EFFICIENTLY PERFORMING ITS CIVIL FUNCTION OF MAINTAINING PEACE, IT CREATES EXPLOSIVE DANGERS OF ITS OWN, LIKE ANY OTHER OUTWORN ENGINE. THE APPROPRIATE FORMS NEED TO BE RETHOUGHT. (Proposition 45) In other fields of human endeavour, in medicine, engineering, economics, the argument against the obsolete would be too patent to require stress. In politics men's minds are bemused by ideas which are not criticized, which solidify as stereotypes, and which they do not allow to become fluid.

Professor Karl Loewenstein, in his *Political Power* (p. 6), writes: "Within society the State is the predominant or, at least in certain historical cases, the exclusive organization." Most textbook writers of the last century have written, almost as routine, in the same fashion, with as unqualified assurance. That this is just what is in question and, as touching the future, would have to be proved, alike internationally, ecclesiastically, and even industrially (especially to those who regard the present State as 'the executive committee of the bourgeoisie') is ignored. For an example of what has been called 'the modern political behaviour approach,' *vide* the excellent *Analysis of Political Systems* of Douglas V. Verney, especially the Introduction and pp. 206–13.

It does not at all follow that the political structure can be changed overnight in accordance with some engineering blueprint or doctrinaire abstractions—although the caution is necessary that the Anglo-Saxon mind, with its valid preference for the piecemeal approach, is inclined to underestimate what can be achieved practically by the fierce logical clarity of, for example, a Lenin, however much fired by vituperation. Even in engineering the nature of the materials has to be taken into account, and the same is even more true of politics. It may be argued that what is going to be determinant in state arrangements is not men's wishes and prejudices, but the actual distribution of military power strategically employed, together with supporting economic and human potential. Not all the passion of a Hitler could make up for shortage of manpower. In an interesting display of detachment General Charles de Gaulle, in his recent book, pays homage to the qualities of leadership of both a Hitler and a Mussolini. But neither the dedication of a de Gaulle nor the dramatic activities of a Mussolini, whatever their intentions, can in fact convert France or Italy into super-powers on the modern scale. Military power in operation, in politics, always counts. After each of two world wars, it was the great illusion of the liberal electorates, which were responsible for withdrawing their service men in a hurry, to suppose otherwise. But it would yet be an even greater illusion to suppose that only military power counts and not also the ideas and political choices which are made in sustaining and directing it.

The downfall of the Russian Empire before the Marxist idea and of the Austrian before the nationalist idea—and the skilful and positive ·reconstruction of the vast British Empire—are cases in point. New political shapes are acceptable to the Arab and the African, with their projected (if not over-satisfactory) unions, and (remarkably enough in view of ancient deep enmities) to the Western European. The reconstruction of political structure is a matter of political choice, both of means and of ends.

Granted, not *anomie* and the irresponsible encouragement of the development of each man's irrational powers (which the Germans call 'demonism'), but the existence of a certain *sentiment of community* which may be consciously, deliberately, and institutionally encouraged, then common values and a sentiment of common confidence will be engendered, first in a nucleus, then in a region, then world-wide. The daily habit of administrative, as well as of cultural, co-operation, with interchange of personnel and plans through this widest area of confidence, will issue in not only the sentiment but, in turn, the institutions of Co-operative Power. Support will be given, costs paid, power concentrated and authority built up. Thus the great cause of peace (one of our major functional concerns in this book) will be vindicated. The alternative may well be that only elsewhere, even under dictatorship, will there be a unanimity (even if by drill) of the majority of mankind about the pattern upon which peace can be enforced; and, in Hobbes' phrase, there must come "a Commonwealth of Acquisition

... that, where the Sovereign Power is acquired by Force." The choice then would be between universal empire and atomic race-dissolution. (Even here it would still remain to be debated *whose* empire.)

Mr. Nikita Khrushchev has quite properly said that it is unusual for an acquaintance, who pleads for more confidence and friendship, to initiate the relationship by asking for the latch-key of the house. The moral is that we should build up *experience* in co-operation by lending around latch-keys first among assured friends, that is, by having exhaustive schemes of inspections and international military integration among ourselves, not excluding American and other international inspection of all French arms, and British and other inspection of all German arms (which last has been actually, in certain fields, very efficiently done already). Otherwise, and without any adequate practical experience, why should submission to inquisition be expected from Russians or Chinese? Trust begins at home. Such a thesis of 'Organic Union' the present writer has advocated for some time. *Vide* Walter Lippmann: *U.S. War Aims* (1944), chap. vii, "Second Aim, 'The Atlantic Community,' §i: 'Organic Consultation' ": "There is no alternative, so it seems to me, to the conclusion that the nations of the Atlantic Community will have to stipulate with one another that they will pursue a common foreign policy . . . Such a common policy will require what Mr. George Catlin has called 'organic consultation.' " (p. 76)

More broadly, why should effective union of our sovereign units be limited to England and Scotland, or, functionally, to Western Europe; but not be extended to all Commonwealth countries, or to some other European countries also; or to an Atlantic Community or in a Free World Commonwealth, radiating out from some present nucleus of power? (Cf. my article, "Commonwealth of the Free World," *Contemporary Review*, October, 1960). Or why, drawing in from the periphery of the present 'watery,' lax, and ineffective forum of the United Nations, should not effective instruments of police power be, perchance, shaped there, at least among that majority which agrees?

The notion, mentioned above, of an 'Organic Union' (rather than any written federal constitution), involved the ready interchange of personnel and communication of plans between 'opposite number' departments at all administrative levels of the various states of the Union, engendering the habit of co-operation; and the principle of 'organic consultation,' as a normal and not an abnormal procedure. In this connection an editorial comment by the *Observer* (May 15, 1960) merits quotation: "All such factors (economic, religious, ideological) may cause *quarrels* between peoples. What turns these quarrels into wars is (as has often been said) the condition of anarchy that exists between sovereign States."

The views of the present writer on the regional organization of peace (related to the United Nations as the inner boxes are to the outer in a Chinese 'box of bricks') and on the development of community sentiment, have been expressed in his *Anglo-Saxon Tradition* (1939; in the U.S.A. published as *Anglo-Saxony and its Traditions*); *One Anglo-American Nation* (1941); *Anglo-American Union as a Nucleus of World Federation* (1942); *The Unity of Europe* (1944; commissioned by the Polish Government-in-Exile); *The Atlantic Community* (1959), and *Atlantic Union* (1961). His preoccupation with the practical issues, in the art of politics, of war and peace, dating from the First World War, is indicated in *Principia*, p. 9. Political science, like geometry, is anchored to original concern with practical matters.

If we ask—amidst such grave threats from 'the politics of nature,' the threat of destruction from man's own discoveries of power, due to natural science—why these things have not already been done, the first answer, amid the excuses, lies in a 'stereotype,' in archaic political thinking. THE STATE IN ITS PRESENT FORM MUST BE ABOLISHED. IT IS THE PRIME THREAT TODAY TO PEACE (WHATEVER ITS PAST UTILITY) AND AN INSTRUMENT OF DOMINATION MENACING PEOPLES. (Proposition 46) Because Engels happened to make the same remark, it is not thereby proved to be false.

Men's minds, however, recoil with emotional horror from the proposition. It is certainly not hereby meant that the States of Mississippi or Massachusetts should be abolished (or Scotland or Wales, which are not States). It does not, of course, mean that the national communities should be abolished. On the contrary, the theme has been to emphasize the importance of community, both national and churchly. Indeed, with Dr. Arnold Toynbee (here along with St. Augustine and Karl Marx) we may be inclined to think that the course of civilization may well move away from Civil Society to Community (despite all the great advantages of the free market and variety) and from the coercive State-form towards more non-coercive and directive forms, the element of mere force and *brutum fulmen* being reduced. The Legal-State (*Rechtsstaat*) may change its nature from the Whig conception of it. The necessary homogeneity of any community, not least a democratic one, may become one of habit, custom, culture, and cult, and not one of mental monopoly directed by law.

Patently we are not concerned to suggest that the Civil Power should be abolished, which would be absurd. In one major respect—international organs functioning for peace—the theme is to strengthen it. The particular and practical proposal touches the specific temporal *form* of civil organization, which may be as due for supersession as was, in the sixteenth century, the barony (also useful in its day), with each baron *souverain dans sa baronie*. It is that, wherever the present state administrative system, or allegiance to it or statutes defining it, conflict with functions required for the maintenance of peace for the good of mankind, such a state, and the retrospective system in which it is involved, should be eroded; allegiance should be pooled; and these statutes should be repealed. To take one specific case, it is important, in any international civil or military service, that during their terms of office the officers should owe their prime duty to the international organization, and not to their respective national organizations. If this conflicts with the doctrine of absolute National State Sovereignty, so much the worse for the latter.

We may restate the proposition by saying that all forms of an excessive, flag-waving, and pernicious national-statism are to be deplored, which certainly does not depreciate the values of national community as such. For example, in Canada such an isolationist and segregationist nationalism, fundamentally artificial, is to be deplored. For one thing, it can logically and practically lead, as a form of provincialism, to the demand for administrative nationalism for the culturally homogeneous provinces within Canada, and to a nemesis in the form of the break-up of the whole—new national flags, provincial flags, or no flags. And the opposite, and synthesizing, tendency is to be welcomed, which is more likely to appeal to those not obsessively preoccupied with psychological and 'hundred-percentist' compensations as touching ethnic origins. What is valuable, as Mr. Nehru has said, in the Commonwealth—and, more, in the Free World Commonwealth—is not the exclusion, but the inclusion, of cultural nationalities. To explain the matter more technically: POLITICAL FUNCTIONS BEING ADAPTED TO ACTUAL HUMAN WANTS AND BEING IMPROVED BY THE NEED TO FULFIL THEM, IT FOLLOWS THAT, WHERE THE PRIME FUNCTION IS THE MAINTENANCE OF ACTUAL CIVIL PEACE, ONLY A SYSTEM OF ORGANIZATION WHICH IS WIDE ENOUGH, AS SOVEREIGN ARBITER, IN FACT TO FULFIL THE FUNCTION IS RATIONAL AS TO ENDS AND TOLERABLE AS TO MEANS (Proposition 47). Granted the widespread actual market demand for civil peace, the scientific and technical conclusion as to means seems inevitably to follow. The costs of the present ineffective machinery, as with most clumsy machinery, are excessive. Those who want the ends *enough*, must accept the means. What has to be recognized is 'the permanence of change' in international as in all human affairs. The question is whether the change will be 'peaceful'—and 'just,' i.e., reasonable.

The crushing costs of military defence, under the present sovereign state system, is generally admitted. To this, however, must be added reflection on the extent to which, under the present obsolescent state system, the whole civil structure is deflected to considerations of military force. The character of the State as a war-machine, instead of as an actually effective peace organization, not only remains as a residue of the past but grows more oppressive. The economic structure is shaped to its fiscal needs, to its strategic needs, and to considerations of strategic materials. The educational system is directed towards the physical sciences for reasons concerned with research and human power, but certainly not disconnected from success in the test of arms. Much of the so-called conflict between ethics and politics arises from the embarrassments of a political system which makes demands, imperfectly justifiable functionally, for which therefore claims of dubious moral validity are urged. Religious liberty will be restrained. Spying becomes a virtue. Even under the auspices of democratic countries the facilities exist under which prisoners of war may, it is alleged, be scientifically 'brain-washed' by new techniques. (*Vide* the disturbing description of brain-washing given at the Royal Institution by Professor Alexander Kennedy of Edinburgh University, *Observer*, February 28 and March 6 and 27, 1960, and official comment in Parliament on March 16 and 17.) (*a*) It is arguable that those engaged in compulsory brain-washing could be prosecuted as offenders against the laws of Civilization and Humanity. (*b*) However, the Nuremberg Court itself was formally defective in stipulating the existence of juristic injuries without, contrary to a basic maxim of law, providing any permanent remedy. It was itself only a court *ad hoc*, not regular and co-ordinated with any permanent court of International Criminal Justice, integrated with the World Court. The conduct of the great Powers since 1945 on the World Court has been highly unsatisfactory, for which the United States has recently (1960) begun to make amends.

It may prudently be argued that men will be saved from destruction, not by their virtues, but by their vices and, specifically, by intense fear induced by the new weapons, multiplied even among the smallest Powers. However, although even a Balkan Power can still endanger peace, it is admitted that the game of effective defence in this fashion is, for the moment, too costly for all but a few Powers to play (although others, it is thought, can carry more weight with their friends by having private bombs in their pockets, as 'bargaining counters'). And even the greatest Powers, in the case of retaliation, fear to imperil their own economies by spending enough to kill the enemy more than once. The alternative technique would seem to be that of wisdom and faith, by reducing the probable area of conflict—reshaping the existent political forms and state machineries to meet ends, ultimately world-wide, and immediately regional; pooling military and economic resources and interlocking administrative areas; and displaying the resolution to penalize rebellious baronies in the style and mode once used, for the *raison d'état* of the unification of France, by the Cardinal de Richelieu. In this fashion the argument for peace by Hobbes would reach, in power terms, its logical conclusion. The World State would be Leviathan, hooked in the nose by Natural Law and maintained by effective popular demand. 'Force may be the *ultima ratio principum*; but it is precisely *not* the rational finality of politics. To say this is not to deny that, despite superficial paradox, those determined to maintain peace will require power in all forms and, in crisis, not only the prior customs of social peace but a police force effectively belligerent to enforce the rule of law.'

Once, however, we start to talk in terms of man's wants or demands (as distinct from the scientific means for their fulfilment) or what 'he' or 'I' would welcome, we pass into the area of the shaping of wants, of values, of the Good Society, of what is good; of how we know that it is good; and of how far we are entitled to direct or instruct another. Here we can but say that any political system, be it world-state or nation-state, which, owing to incompetence in its powers, does not fulfil mass demands will be exposed to heavy tensions; and that we should not wilfully make this attainment of their aims more difficult or embarrassed than it need be in a free political market, thanks to our own lack of heart or imagination. The remark of President Eisenhower (cf. *supra* p. 166), "Why not give the people what they want?" if it is not to be interpreted as the merest platitude, alternatively can only be understood as cutting to the bone—the political means must be radically readjusted to the common and agreed civil ends. We revert, then, to the discussion of the condition of man and of the wants, economic and spiritual, that flow from his own human nature.

9. Concerning Political Ends*

§i. *Philosophy and Political Philosophy*

Philosophy means, etymologically and for common sense, the love of wisdom. Minute intellectual analysis has seldom yet been held by any sane man to be synonymous with wisdom, although there have indeed been schools of philosophy, not only the Sophists but the late Scholastics such as Duns Scotus (vulgarly known as Dunce) and Occam, who have become notorious and unpopular for their addiction to it. The Humanist Renaissance was a reaction against the latter logical school, entrenched in the universities, which was ridiculed—sometimes unjustly. It may yet be argued that, if we are lovers of truth, then such exact linguistic analysis will clearly seem to us to be of high importance, and that the pursuit of truth has been and is frustrated by the introduction into common language of unwarranted ghost ideas and by that misuse of terms to which we referred at the beginning of this book.

For example, it may be argued that much primitive animism still pervades our minds; and a careful philosopher, such as Hume, can entertain a doubt, not just about the existence of God, but concerning

*On this subject the reader is also referred to the writer's Weil Lectures, in the University of North Carolina, of 1957, *On Political Goals* (St. Martin's Press, New York, 1957), published in Britain, in abbreviated form, as *What Does the West Want?* (Dent-Phoenix Press).

whether our own identity is not a superstition. If so, what folly to talk politically of cultivating to the full the powers of a personality which, in the accepted meaning, does not exist. Certainly a precise mind will always rightly feel that small progress towards truth will ever be made if we substitute enthusiasm for clarity. One of the merits of the better Scholasticism is that it did not. Likewise in political discussion of such subjects as the State and Sovereignty and Democracy, we are afflicted by uncertain definitions, such as Bentham, father of linguistic analysis, deplored. We have just as many ghosts walking in the country of secular dominion as in what Thomas Hobbes called the 'Kingdom of Spirits.'

Political Philosophy, as was stated at the beginning, is an indubitable part of Political Theory. POLITICAL PHILOSOPHY IS CONCERNED WITH THE ENDS AND VALUES MEN PURSUE (INCLUDING *pro tanto* THE INTERMEDIARY ENDS), AS DISTINCT FROM THE MEANS AS SUCH. NO POLITICAL THEORY, SINCE ITS SUBJECT MATTER IS ALSO PRACTICAL, CAN BE COMPLETE WITHOUT CONSIDERATION OF THE ENDS OF ACTION AND THE DISCUSSION OF VALUES. (Proposition 48) All discussions of social ends, hypothetical or actual (involving hence organized means), of their values and priorities, of the Good Society, of the ethical basis of Allegiance, of the respective claims of Nationalism and Internationalism, and the like are discussions appropriate for Political Philosophy, as is also the evaluation of previous speculations and their tradition. Nevertheless Philosophy, as wisdom, historically has always been also concerned to provide a synthesis or coherent perspective of human experience, including social and political experience (or several such possible syntheses). Philosophy, then, is by its nature a seamless robe, and cannot be parted into portions. Political, Social or Legal Philosophy is merely Philosophy speaking with a certain emphasis. Its method and approach will be fundamentally different from that of Political Science. There is, strictly speaking, only Philosophy as a subject, and not Political Philosophy, which is a mere distinction of emphasis and not of form. PHILOSOPHY IS ONE (Proposition 49). All ethics is of men as social; and so, for example, the state is not a separable political form, susceptible of being treated, any more than individuals, in isolation from other social forms.

It may be noted that Political Philosophy is not only part of Philosophy, but is more closely related to Ethics than is Ethics to Ontology, although these latter are always included under Philosophy strictly so called. Some philosophers contend today that the real task of philosophy is logico-scientific, to wit, to provide the natural scientists with a logical critique of scientific methods. It is not yet clear that this offer of help has been welcomed by natural and physical scientists.

It has been our contention that there is a great didactic and scientific advantage in separating, in abstraction, these two fields of Political Science and Political Philosophy as sharply as possible—even although, when it comes to practice, the abstraction must be abandoned except in the sense that the engineer retains his blue-prints, even although the actual bridge he builds will be complicated by the specific and individual difficulties of one place and one time. It may indeed be urged, not (as Professor Michael Polanyi has rightly argued) that all means, *including* those in the natural and physical sciences, are permeated by values of choice, but that, contrariwise, all ethics must be regarded scientifically, as an empiric study of the successful means towards progress in overcoming human ills. This is the theme of John Dewey. Hence there is grave practical danger in contempt for means, as distinct from a supposed ethical realm of 'ideal ends.' Nevertheless, common sense and advantage continue to make the distinction between them.

Where the two methods come together is in that philosophy rightly has to assess the value of Power itself, individual or collective, which is the core of political science. Granted indeed that we have desirable ends, it will follow that we should demand adequate means and powers. But (*a*) what are the final (not intermediate) ends to which this vast apparatus of power, held severally or collectively by the human race, should lead up? Are they one? And do we know it? And (*b*) granted that Power characterizes the entire political structure and, moreover, that Power, like Wealth, is isolable and can be directly enjoyed, and (as has been said) that "absolute power is enjoyable absolutely," are there conditions under which this is ethically justifiable? The theologian will reflect that God Almighty is absolute Power and absolute Good. What, if any, is the nexus?

Comparable to the distinction here between 'means' and 'ends,' Croce draws a distinction, not merely abstract but concrete and historical, between what he calls 'the economic' (in a specialized sense, not used here, of 'the instrumental') and 'the aesthetic.'

It is fascinating to note, at this point, the weakness in the theme of Professor John Dewey's instrumentalist or pragmatic argument. In effect, he presents us, as does also Williams James (despite, or perhaps related to, James' passionate denials of 'the bitch goddess'), with a philosophy of efficient Success which is then, more socially, represented as a philosophy of efficient Progress, 'growth,' and 'ready change.' This becomes defined, in turn, as a philosophy of struggle, overcoming the run-of-the-mill evils of humanity, ill health, bad housing, and the like. It fuses with the argument of some earnest Socialists who urge (with some small support, however, from St. James and the Parables) that, since religion is a matter of works, therefore the collective provision of milk and good housing and a 'cup of water' is not only the expression, but even the core and test of true religion.

It is yet notable that, when Professor Dewey came to discuss the positive gratifications of living, desirous like J. S. Mill to distinguish 'higher' and 'lower' pleasures, and reluctant to posit here the pattern of an equalitarian democracy with prizes awarded by plebiscite (for 'what the people want' or can be profitably persuaded to want), he slips hastily over into praise of the aesthetically excellent, without adequate explanation of how he can give high value to that which is, by definition, not instrumental and not even useful. We pass, as it were, into a separate Sabbath department. Indeed his language almost recalls Plato's famous description, in the *Symposium*, of "beholding beauty with the life of the mind."

"When the liberating of human capacity operates as a socially creative force, art will not be a luxury, a stranger to the daily occupations of making a living . . . And when the emotional force, the mystic force one might say, of communication, of the miracle of shared life and shared experience is spontaneously felt, the hardness and crudeness of contemporary life will be bathed in the light that never was on land or sea." (*Reconstruction in Philosophy*, 1920; rev. ed., 1948, p. 211).

This "light" one yet feels, for Professor Dewey, is somehow a decoration, connected with the kind of 'art' put as pictures on the wall in the Sunday parlour, along with Walt Whitman in the book-case, but which (to avoid the charge of a 'waist-high culture') Dewey would prefer to transfer to the work-day living-room. The sceptical *Modern Temper*, of Mr. Joseph Wood Krutch, is worth reading in this connection. Mr. Krutch observes that men find a value in such things as 'speed' (a 'source of power') on race-courses or highways.

It is also perhaps relevant that Lord Russell, who adopts 'a modified hedonism,' less social but perhaps broader than Dewey's, postulates in his latest works the man of 'aesthetic sensitivity' and 'imagination' (as Bentham postulated 'benevolence'). When, however, it is pointed out that the really highly intelligent hedonist will know how to cheat his fellow men who interfere with his pleasures, will be aware of the social 'ropes,' will be able to put 'sensitivity' and 'imagination' in their place as well as appreciate that it is "conscience does make cowards of us all," Lord Russell in a newspaper article admits, Hobbes-wise, that for such disconcerting hedonists the philosopher finds his response in the policeman and the gaol. Somehow, if aesthetic integrity is the core of ethics, being itself 'disinterested,' then 'intelligent self-interest,' in the service of hedonism, equalitarian, naive, or vulgar, is *not* the core. The connection (so admirably stressed by the great sociologist Durkheim) between 'the full development of individual powers'— all reference to rational, objective, and public norms omitted—and well-organized crime, as the quickest cut to the fruits of individual success, is overlooked at our peril.

Recent medical experiments on dolphins seem to indicate that, within a century, human beings, granted adequate manipulation of the brain, can be guaranteed to do anything for pleasure. But this merely transfers the moral problem of the norm of conduct to the manipulator.

§ii. *Mode of Discussion*

It will emerge that, in this writer's judgement, quite unlike Political Science, the issues of Political Philosophy are speculative, and not positivistic; can seldom be entirely decided by any empiric investigation (although there are no small reservations to this, where human means and technical methods limit achievable ends); and, further, do not in their decisions admit of proof by logic. Hence a different method and style of argument is required; and will be here adopted. While we must also describe and analyse, yet (since our concern is with choices and values) either we may overtly seek to persuade by arguing for some judgement which we hold to be preferable, although without complete demonstration either empirical or logical—not empirical because values transcend perhaps this field; and not logical because the very axiomata and premisses of logic are involved—or we must safeguard the reader against covert attempts at persuasion by forewarning him what our own values and propaganda (even used in the correct sense as in *de propaganda fide*) will be.

Despite Spinoza, there is no geometric proof, although we may think that we have arguments of objective validity, to which we can persuade the public, as the best thesis. We have to adjudge the fit limits of such propaganda in society. To use our earlier terminology, we have to decide, not only technically how much the public can be persuaded, but also what it should be persuaded, to want when we have the power to persuade it. We have to judge whether, in Lippmann's phrase, there is such a thing as a public philosophy or philosophies of our civilization which should be taught; or whether indeed the only sound public philosophy is that there is none and that the main Communist error is to think otherwise. (The same argument could also be used to the effect that it was a Christian error —although here without normal use of coercive power: a most important distinction.) We are entering the field, not of the social sciences, but where it may behove a man to be a good humanist. The vastness of the subject is such as to permit here little more than a mere outline of topics for discussion.

The word 'Humanism' is here used in the traditional sense, as finding nothing about man alien, and as opposed to the form of a scholastic verbalism as adequate. It is not used in the sense (as by F. C. S. Schiller, Irving Babbitt, and others) of attempts at a new, non-transcendent religion, or in the sense of the so-called 'scientific humanists,' which would seem either to endeavour to combine opposite emphases or to adhere to faith in the emergence of a single system of truths of value based upon material studies by natural science, which system, slowly constricting ends by empiric means, would be unitary and dogmatic. This claim is not accepted here nor is it implied in the use of the word 'Humanism' here adopted, which is that of the outlook characteristic of a Pico, Erasmus, Leibnitz, and Goethe. However, *Le Phénomène humain* (1955) by Père Pierre Teilhard de Chardin, S.J., merits consultation in this connection.

§iii. *Concerning the Varieties of Social Ends*

About the valuations of the ends which Political Philosophy discusses, we can only say that they are neither experimentally nor in logic provable, but only probable. Human affairs do not here admit of such proof. Any Public Philosophy of Politics (and a philosophy of 'society,' to be taught in society, is socially 'public') must take into account this element of probabilism in its very structure. Even revelation, as mandatory, rests upon preliminary, and various, free acts of trust or faith (the Greek word *pistis* means both). This assertion, however, does not amount, as will be shown, to a relativism or to a denial of 'absolutes' in ethics or of categorical imperatives, in the sense here used, for the individual.

This present assertion of a prudent probabilism, as a guide in public instruction and in community life, admits of a vast cultural training of the human mind, to which it is the duty of the responsible individual to submit himself, concerning what is to be accounted probable and probably good or excellent for achievement, without prating about sacrosanct rights to develop any and every personal power, however irrational and cacophonous. Here the early romantic Rousseau may mislead us, although the later Rousseau falls over backwards towards a social dogma that is almost inquisitorial.

There is a discipline—to begin with, that of History itself. Amid a variety of competent teachers, the moral and intellectual choice of decision is one of the highest accomplishments of civilized living. Even, however, in choosing our true aristocracy we shall still by history be judged. This species of judgement on ends is in no wise to be confused with that individualism or social atomism which maintains, to use a current phrase, that 'all opinions are born free and equal'; or with its even less reputable variant, largely characteristic of Australian popular civilization, that 'any opinion goes,' provided enough of other people's opinions, for whatever reasons, are in agreement with it. The ethical judgement, as considered here, is essentially a matter of cultivation, is hierarchical, and is only to be challenged by those whose genius is greater than the reason and tradition of the age.

We may yet ask: if this be so, why is the opinion on morals and the social order of simple men—and indeed of uneducated and quite primitive men—so often shown by history to be far 'healthier' than that of the educated, the cultivated, the sophisticated and (be it added) of those too often influenced by desire, picayune or megalomaniac, to hold or to acquire power? Are, for example, the 'red professors' of the Marxist academy *always* right? Or the Académie française? Or, every day, the Catholic Hierarchy? Is it not the ends that these common men choose for which the experts will be well to find the means (and Aristotle came near to this view), rather than the ends—or means— chosen by philosophers or 'the high and mighty.' We shall return to this argument, which is as old as the times of the Twelve Apostles, who were yet 'chosen' and elect by the Divinity itself.

There are some, not least in the North American continent, who have a prejudice or aesthetic valuation in favour of 'variety' *as such*, and of the beauty or virtue of maximum diversity. The new is the good unless shown to be otherwise, whereas in England the new tends to be the bad unless there is evidence to the contrary. (This variety indeed has its communal inconveniences and those who praise it most sometimes insist that the variety shall be in their own manner. It has been said that, in the Middle West, some communities are all in favour of individualism—they will consider nothing else—so long as it is displayed in their own fashion.) Tolerance of variety can follow, not so much from intellectual clarity, patience, or personal good will, but from this mental and aesthetic preference and from an easy indifference on standards. It follows that, if there are three possible moral positions, it is preferable of itself that all three positions should be held and argued than only one; and that indeed there should be three un- resolved arguments than only one; and, if three, then, better still, three hundred arguments and opinions. Nor indeed, so long as there is legitimate ground for intellectual doubt and moral integrity in com- manding tolerance, is this theoretical contention absurd. These posi- tions, it can yet also be said, are not to be judged selectively by how far they correspond to the deeper nature of man, but (as an intellectual or amusing and witty exercise) by how far they correspond to the individual opinions and autonomy of so many individuals. *Quot homines tot sententiae.* It is the most decadent civilizations which, slightly earlier, have been among the most brilliant and amusing. This judgement will also apply to the political ideals of men and to the desirable vitality of their notions of the good societies or, as it may otherwise be phrased, of 'the open society.' Whether the variety is of

the true or false is irrelevant. Who knows which is which? Nevertheless such variety provides, it may be said, the most effective and
utilitarian social check on tyranny. Tyranny can only provide sputniks
and such material achievements; but not wide-ranging Party debate
about the American Constitution.

The thesis for that 'open political market' for which indeed we have
argued—it will yet be noted that our discussion here is not of power to
obtain, but of the wants themselves and of what wants we *should*
want—can be stated more solidly. Variety in judgements, theories, and
opinions and social 'multanimity' can be regarded, with J. S. Mill, as
itself desirable in life, leading to freshness in the adventure of ideas.
So the Liberal school has held. (*a*) Intellectually this, then, rests in
part upon the correct assumption of *necessary* imperfection of human
knowledge (which possibly also offers the clue to the correct, semi-
Pelagian doctrine of human 'free will'), which only permits approximation to any total scheme of truth; and in part upon the enduring
possibility of new experience, which may, and should be allowed to,
serve to challenge a fool with power. Variety is then praised—although
the method is not at all that of the natural scientist in arriving by
selective and eliminating experiment at truth—because it connects, as
a by-product, with the growth of wisdom. There is indeed a presumption of intellectual integrity and responsibility; but we cannot
democratically be sure what integrity here is, against so many protest-
ing claimants. (*b*) Variety is also praised (and the theme defended)
because, again as an incidental quality, variety of views *may* (by no
means necessarily *must*) involve concentration, mental exercise, and
development of choices in reason and judgement, although there is no
intellectual defence indeed for the laziness of choosing the false just
in order that variety may be kept going. With the discovery of specific
truth—and, *pro tanto*, of high probability—entire free choice, as a
virtue, there ends. The determinist argument of Spinoza on rational
freedom, truth, and virtue here has force. Also, following from this
last and most forcible, (*c*) morally and pedagogically variety is
praised because the volitional or creative element in each individual,
always a challenge to deadness, monopoly and self-interested tyranny,
is emphasized, together with curiosity; and not only the rational,
abstract, and intellectual element. It is deduced that this passionate
or activist element is entitled to shape and discover for itself—which
behaviour is aesthetically pleasing and also the best pragmatic guardian
of men's interests—what is the successful solution to problems, rather
than having them provided ready-made, probably in a fashion con-

venient to the local society or culture but less so to the individual spirit.

This last view will seldom be found expressed in the classical schools of philosophy or indeed by quite recent philosophers. *Vide* the discussion on Freedom *supra* p. 105. The philosophers have (on the whole with remarkable unanimity) praised *freedom* on condition that it was sophisticated or redefined to mean *self-discipline* or even discipline by, and service to, an external authority, provided it be freely chosen. The stress has been upon Obedience by the Passionate Man or what the Moslem calls *Islam*. What marked *servitude*, as opposed to freedom, for the classical writers was the subordination of the Rational Man to the actual wishes, as dictated by passion, appetites, and wants of the individual animal. St. Clement of Alexandria dismisses with contempt any praise of freedom divorced from knowledge. For such a Puritan as John Milton (*Tenure of Kings and Magistrates*), "none can love freedom heartily but good men." Montesquieu and Spinoza have already been cited. For the nineteenth-century Liberals 'education' and 'educated men' offered a standard of guidance.

Over against this must be set the very different notion of freedom of the common 'man in the street.' It was well put by Lincoln in his Baltimore speech, of 1864 (already quoted), that freedom means 'liberty' for "each man to do as he pleases with himself." The statement is as remarkable for its simplicity as for its patent ethical weakness. It is re-expressed by Mr. Justice Brandeis: "Freedom to think *as you will* and to speak as you think are means indispensable to the discovery and spread of political truth" [and error] (quoted by S. E. Morison and H. S. Commager, *The Growth of the American Republic*, 1960, vol. II, p. 557; italics mine). Thus a Hitler not only can, but is ethically *entitled* to, say what he likes without reference to reason, to the judgement of the *validior pars* or to social responsibility—whether or not (which is another question) he can find anybody else dupe enough to believe him. If indeed he is led to believe himself to be utterly right, he is entitled to persuade others to believe him and in him. No doubt need disturb this blessed confidence.

This view springs in part from Renaissance individualism, following the success of philosophical Nominalism, and in part later from a Protestantism which, quitting the dogmatic appeal of the early religious revolutionaries to the supposed views of the Primitive Church, turned away from all such objective authority to the subjective *individual* conscience. This, it was suggested, infallibly would guide opinion to what was objectively right (or at least towards the paving stones of a good intention or will)—conscience itself now being rather identified with intuition or miraculous guidance than, as by St. Thomas, with reason. On the virtue of a sound Thomistic rationalism, a remark of Mr. Justice Frankfurter (*Felix Frankfurter Reminisces*, p. 37) is worth recalling. "You've nothing else except that poor reed of reason to lean on in order to get as far away as possible from the jungle and the earth from whence we all come and a good deal of which we have in us."

On this matter of individual and existential ethical freedom, all objective norms (for example, of civilization and communal responsibility) apart, the authority of Immanuel Kant is usually adduced. It will yet be noted: (*a*) that Kant stated indeed that the will is "a law unto itself," but this is to be understood rather ontologically than morally, the rules of conduct remaining also 'a law'; (*b*) that Kant certainly laid down *a priori* Categorical Imperatives for the will to follow which, even if schematic, arid, and often unhelpful, assuredly provided limits on 'opinion'; and (*c*) Kant specifically said that freedom was "independence of any *other* than the moral law alone," which reason, not vulgar opinion, apprehended. The opposite view rather springs from the natural *hubris*, passion, or pride of the individual who, the more ignorant he is, the more strongly holds that he cannot be wrong—as Locke says, "being sure because he is sure"—encouraged by an empirical optimism that believes, not only that if all the cards are played, the ace of trumps, called 'truth,' must turn up sooner or later, but also that even the player who has never learned what trumps are will identify it.

The political scientist has to study, as did the Benthamites, men's actual "pleasure and security"; but the political philosopher will probably detect in this false view, current in our education, about the freedoms which men *ought* to wish to have recognized as liberties, a weakness of direction. It will be remedied by a truer view of self-respect, as something to be striven for, and of conformity, not to the opinions of oneself, Smith, and Jones, but to an objective, historical, and rationally probable type of excellence. Here a current American carping against 'conformity,' while perhaps valuable and needed against a provincial or rustic conventionalism, is itself weakly based, when what is at issue are the most exacting standards of high culture. To discard this last is, not to enrich, but grossly to impoverish conduct. It should especially be noted that, whereas at critical points in his argument J. S. Mill appeals to the dicta of Wilhelm von Humboldt and, hence, to the humanistic philosophy of Goethe, Goethe himself, the great apostle of exact taste in the Hellenist tradition, makes no such error of becoming Rousseauite—in fairness to Rousseau it should be said that Jean Jacques also expressed more cautious views—and of optimistically and romantically exalting the untrained and arrogant judgement. The thesis here maintained is Goethean.

Subject to the same criticism is the current doctrine, in education and society, of 'the development of each man's powers,' the right to do evil being all part of the exercise of the moral muscles, that fails to note with von Humboldt and Goethe the rider about 'a harmonious whole'—which takes into account rational, cultural, and historical or natural law criteria of what is 'harmonious.' It is yet surely this latter which involves the strenuous intellectual life. Over against this we may quote a remark, typical of the passing mood, attributed by the press to a son of the Duke of Bedford: "After all, it's *my* life, isn't it?" There is perhaps nothing more erroneous or hurtful than the easy contemporary talk—as if it were basic and self-evident—which is now almost a cliché, about the need (unqualified) for 'the development of a man's powers,' which are not here the same as 'Man's powers. Power is neutral. There is, in this prevalent and uncritical philosophy, which is a fruitful source of Western weakness, an assumption of the natural goodness of man equally and at all times—as distinct from the perhaps sometimes exaggerated and over-coloured doctrines of sin and salvation—and a refusal to consider the place of some rational or other canon concerning *what* power should be developed and *how*.

It may, nevertheless, be argued that all appeal to reason or to any other standard providing a single norm for conduct is itself an error. It is not merely the case, as with Locke, that there *is* a truth towards which yet, even when guided "by the candle of the Lord," the individual climbs, without reaching. There is no such one truth or norm or decisive pattern, nor should it be taught. The only Public Philosophy, as has been said, is that there is No Public Philosophy; and all guiding or educating of wants is a dishonest manipulation. Men's passions will impel them to demand the education which best suits their wants and tastes—and here is meant, not that fundamental human nature, which the social physician can detect, but whatever passions the mood and advertising of the moment may stimulate. Education must be popular. In the words of a song, we must be "contemporary," while "making a stir" and "doing things big." Indeed, for success it may be held to be an asset to have a pertinaceously and toughly unpleasant disposition, provided that one has some 'private means' and that one's object and 'main chance' is simple and not dependent upon the goodwill of others—such as acquiring still more 'means.' (It is noteworthy that economic wealth is frequently described as 'means.') Passion is vital and Reason is dead.

When the Soviet leader, Mr. Nikita Khrushchev, visited Hollywood, the symbol of Western culture presented to him—in honour perhaps of Lafayette and 'the old alliance'—was the cancan. His moral Puritanism was not unnaturally offended by what the Puritan Fathers would certainly have agreed with him in regarding as a 'decadent' culture. In this culture, what matters is not the 'considerable man,' but the inferior-feeling man who demands 'to be considered,' if necessary by his noise. A quick way to this is the exhibitionism of crime. Simplicity is put to shame. The criminal has, of course, great advantages, especially in international affairs, and may be acclaimed as the successful statesman. The Press itself, instead of regarding its freedom as relative and functional to the political process, regards it as absolute, so that it claims rights, not as 'a free and responsible Press,' but as freely irresponsible, providing the public with what it wants, and dishing out from real life the daily demanded crime ration. The conclusion is the domination of the vulgarian and his master, the commercial 'adman,' and, in a permissive and neo-pagan society, the irresponsibility of Western Man. The teachers, unsure of what popular education is, abdicate their function. For the rest, in the pathetic declaration of bankruptcy of Professor G. C. Field in his *Political Theory* (1956), there can be, properly speaking, no conclusion to a book on political theory: "[we can only] clear up one or two loose ends."

There is no coherent Political Philosophy of ends; and it therefore cannot be taught. Neither is there a coherent Ethic in the sense of one without intrinsic contradictions. There may be, it can be said, or there may not be, a Political Science. What remains on the Market is a matter of Power. Only the actual wants of the market should prevail. If large masses of people want Bolshevik Communism, they are entitled to have it—or, indeed, Hitlerism—or if they want "not to be free," or to pursue a course where they have "nothing to gain but their chains," provided that they do not thereby menace their neighbours by their self-determination. And to ask that men's wants conform to some standard of what ought to be, and to make this the basis of our laws, may involve the sacrifice of what men, actually and by free vote, opine to be "indispensable to their lives as human beings."

There is a metaphysical route of defence against the objector who asks if we are to suppose that "the universe is not a cosmos, not a harmony . . . that conflicts of values may be an intrinsic, irremovable element of human life . . . the fulfilment of some of our ideals may in principle make the fulfilment of others impossible [which] is to say that the notion of total human fulfilment is a general contradiction, a metaphysical chimaera." To all this the up-to-date philosopher of integrity may reply that "the ordinary resources of empirical observation and ordinary human knowledge . . . certainly give us no warrant for supposing (or even understanding what would be meant by saying) that all good things, or all bad things for that matter, are reconcilable with each other" (Isaiah Berlin, *Two Concepts of Liberty*, 1958, being his Oxford Inaugural Lecture). To take one instance, the values of charity and of objective justice can be supposed to be so difficult to reconcile that Dr. Reinhold Niebuhr—apparently making 'true' justice subjective—puts 'true justice' and 'order,' that is, objective justice, into antithesis (*The Structure of Nations and Empires*).

Professor Berlin concludes (p. 57) his important, if controversial, Inaugural Address (one of the most important of recent statements of a fundamental position) with praise of tolerance, in the style of E. M. Forster, on the basis of a desirable, civilized, and quite essential recognition of the factor of necessary human ignorance. This is not in dispute. All dogmas are provisional. All sovereignties are provisional. History cannot be brought to a stop. Each vision may be overtaken by a developing and fuller vision. In this sense certainty is not static, but a process. The doctrine of permanent practical plurality of values, not in any Leibnitzian harmony, but as both present and final potential contradiction, is a different story. A laudable political pluralism is here in metamorphosis into a 'multanimity' (in Professor Crane Brinton's phrase) or mental pluralism of society, which is not incidental but radical.

The dialectical point can be made that, if "not all good things are compatible" —and, at a naive and haphazard level this is, of course, true—so as to be welded into one philosophy, then this assertion itself is our public philosophy and should be taught. Patently—and as we have repeatedly said—moral choice is important and costs do have to be paid. But must the choice be solely individual, be without gnomon, and be an arbitrary (and existentially 'free' or non-rational) commitment? Is freedom to choose only valuable if we cannot know what we ought to choose? Is the fun in the *Angst* and agony of guideless choices? (Cf. *Two Concepts of Liberty*, p. 54.) There is no single formula to harmonize ends. "The necessity of choosing between *absolute* claims is then an inescapable characteristic of the human condition" (italics mine). In important respects this is the faith of Kierkegaard. *Eligo quia absurdum et quia absurdus homo sum*. This is called 'the human tragedy,' and gives great satisfaction to some theologians concerned with what is also called 'the human predicament.'

Nevertheless there is here a flagrant divorce between the idea of liberty of the classical philosophers and the common idea of freedom which challenges such a rethinking as Professor Berlin has offered; and it cannot yet be said that a satisfactory reply has been made to these questions, which go to the root of the *homoinoia* of communities. The potentially evil side, however, of community thinking and the danger of supposing that man, body and mind, is merely social, of the social actuality, we have stressed.

In earlier chapters we have emphasized, as basic, that in the market hard choices may have to be made between, for example, a specific wanted freedom and a specific wanted justice. We cannot escape this. Particular powerful groups or close communities may force a monopoly and one type of goods only upon us. But still instinctively we strive to be free and to have power to do as we want. We may yet admit of advice about our wants and of counsel about probabilities. And perhaps we *ought* to admit of such professional, aristocratic, and disinterested advice and *vis directiva*. Even the Marxist, who holds that all advice tendered hitherto has been interested and class-determined asserts that his own advice is disinterested in terms of human good. We have protested with force against all 'metapolitics,' which assassinates human values for the sake of a doctrine. History has not ended with the last dictator or revolution; nor has experience or judgement. But, if we have the basic freedom to choose our advisers, is some counsel really no better than others? And why is it so? As Sir Isaiah himself wisely says: "This judgement depends on . . . our moral, religious, intellectual, economic and aesthetic values; which are in turn bound up with our conception of man and of the basic demands of his nature . . . on our vision . . . of what constitutes a fulfilled human life." Allowing for the actual and present diversity of human ends in detail in this life, let us return to our principles of the last chapter and reflect again upon the nature of man and "the basic demands of his nature." In the words (*A German of the Resistance*, 1946) of Helmuth von Moltke: "For us Europe after the war is . . . a question of how the picture of man can be restored in the breasts of our fellow citizens." Here perhaps is modest promise of a political philosophy of probabilities which we can teach.

In the argument by Berlin and others, above discussed, it is contended that there *are* certain ultimate values—indeed many of them and perhaps (according to Berlin) contradictory ones or ones incapable of synthesis—and, further, that they *remain eternally valuable*, whether or not they have social survival power (*Two Concepts of Liberty*, p. 57). They appear to have a kind of lasting aesthetic value, apart from practical considerations of social power and *interim ethik*. The great virtue is tolerance founded upon intellectual humility. However, it is possible to take a more sceptical position. In this more radical scepticism is found a reinforcement of the view that ethics must be a study of men's *actual* wishes, where the autonomy of their wills is demonstrated—not in any discovery of an ideal *nomos*, but in acknowledgement as right of each man's claim to follow his own opinions, being no worse than his neighbours. If, with some anthropologists, we equate morals more positivistically with *mores* or 'customs,' then it follows that that man is good who follows the customs of his people. Put more emphatically, what is so called 'good' is decided by Smith, Jones, and myself. This must end in praise of arrant opportunism, so that I quickly adjust my differences out of existence. Moreover, the 'good,' so established in one place, is not by any means likewise established in another. Speaking absolutely we are not entitled to call *any* act 'good' or 'bad'—these become terms of convention and convenience to mislead the herd.

The shrewd man or moderate hedonist, or the Success Man, concerned with private *success* and 'living it up,' will note that, as between groups, classes, and peoples, what will win is force or, alternatively, cunning. A great premium, whether in the arts, politics, or common life, is placed upon charlatanism. The old-fashioned Platonic distinction between Rhetoric and Philosophy, and between 'seeming' and 'being,' could scarcely be carried further—except that here 'seeming' will be all, save for the essential power-lust that burns beneath. Nothing is more actual than Power; but here (in flat contradiction of Plato's ethics) it becomes allied with 'seeming,' advertising, and 'getting across,' as against the genuine merit of unadvertised 'being,' which is lost in the busy rout. If the man involved in this race becomes 'immoderate,' he may be deterred, as Hobbes suggested, by civic punishment; but he can also be spurred, as a clever man (*deinos*, in the Greek term), to discover effective means to circumvent the laws, punishment being for the stupid. We issue in the ethics of Thrasymachus, of Callicles, and of the Sophists.

This line of argument, once much encouraged by anthropologists with their noses close to their data and arrogant about their insights, has now become less popular. During the Second World War, anthropologists dealing with race issues, such as Dr. Ruth Benedict, and with the persecution of the Jews, affirmed that there *were* certain norms for civilized nations—which raised the issue of what was 'good' or 'bad' in terms of civilization itself. The view was slowly abandoned, at least by implication, that one could not ascend above the nine-and-forty tribal ways, each adapted to its surroundings, and outside those surroundings wrong. There are not only 'cultures,' but 'culture.' (The terms, in some usages, as between 'primitive cultures' and 'high cultures' or 'human culture,' are almost antithetic.) In Chinese it is interesting that 'culture' can be translated by two words meaning either 'good manners' or 'enlightenment.' A 'primitive culture' is to the Chinese the 'uncultured'—or to use the admirable Russian phrase of the Moscow public placards: "Be cultural: spit in the can."

We may support the argument for freedom in ends as philosophically that which is 'absence of objective restraint,' and for Callicles, as against Plato, by noting the limits of intellectual reasoning. The argument of Callicles is indeed logically carried beyond the contention that every man's own opinion is best about what is good or moral (and even, with Sartre, that although there are no objective values, even in reason, yet 'freedom' itself has supreme human value, pending its arbitrary commitment). The argument of Callicles is fundamentally that it is idle to hold opinions, Protestant or Catholic, Liberal or Conservative, fundamentalist or MacLeishian, about 'the good' or 'what is best' because, save as 'my success' or 'my power,' it does not exist. We cannot touch it. Cunning is king—a position philologically sound. We may support this by showing that the logic of the intellect can prove much about effective ways and means, but nothing about ethical ultimates. Hence political science, to assure its own advances, is so wise not to engage upon these speculations.

We can show, for the medical profession, what must result if we assume that human life is a good thing. But we cannot logically prove this assumption to be true to a Buddhist who denies it. There is a difference of fundamental judgement. Also we can posit that pain is an evil, but this has to be taken in the context of surgical health or, again, of national security. Likewise, we can condemn murder, whether by the individual or state, or genocide; but we can argue that the state, by definition, can commit no murder or its agents, as such, either. On the contrary we may argue that mass killings, whether relatively painlessly in gas chambers or more slowly and painfully, in Arctic enterprises or by starvation, are for the good of society.

Thus we can reach the Nietzschean position that discomfort, pain, killings, the mass extermination of common people, may be good from the view of the ethic and advantage of the human race. Or, going further, with Netchaev we may abandon this attempt to detect some ultimate good for mankind to be reached through ruthlessness—for example, the extermination of all people who are not of the tough fibre to promise success in the venture to reach the stars—and may merely nihilistically posit the desirability of Power as end for itself, occasionally reaching incarnations or *avatars*, manifested in the success and immortality by notoriety of humanity's princes, rulers, and despots—or successful criminals.

There is, then, a clear logical case for ethical nihilism—although, of course, it would cease to be logical if it sought to establish a rule for others. It is a disease that, although not peculiar to the twentieth century, is, for reasons of a widespread demand for self-expression by no means entirely discouraging, prominent in it. Some express themselves who have nil to express. It is as much present, in the form of the thesis that all opinions must be regarded as of equal weight, with its concomitants in social atomization, as in the totalitarian systems, accepting no code superior to themselves, in Europe and Asia. In a more genial form it exists in a general tolerance, arising not from an admirable patience or humility but from a less admirable indifference. It also displays itself in a willingness to accept, as final in politics and social affairs, the decisions arising from the day-to-day fluctuations of the empiric market, with its trade between men's actual wants, whether abstractly good or bad, and whether informed or ill-informed, rational or animal. It is certainly essential that we should study these fluctuations. But what we have now to judge is whether they should be an endless 'free' affair of aimless fashions.

It can be argued that the view that each man's opinion is to count for one may be atomistic but in no way issues in the alienation of the human individual, unable to detect any accepted 'common good,' from his society. On the contrary, its tendency is to develop, if not a general will, at least a vote on the common good in which *each* man has to be heard. The answer must be that, if ninety-nine per cent vote about a common good or for a dictator, they are (on this level of argument) aware that this policy has no more validity than the wisdom of the individual votes, and they are conscious that each can himself give no clear idea why he voted as he did. The issue is mechanical and by chance; and the individual beings are alienated from that to which no one has given his mind (cf. Schumpeter, *Capitalism, Socialism and Democracy*, p. 261). The situation is changed if some common *idea* (as Hegel said in correction of Rousseau), even if not fully articulate, has captured these atoms and given them union. The correct supposition is that these are the votes or opinions of equally rational beings.

That each simple man should be heard is due to his human dignity (which yet also is not a datum, but has to be *achieved* and displayed). That each should count according to his ability placed at the service of the community is due to his intelligence and worth. Here the orthodox Communist position is both sounder and more in the tradition of Western culture than the modern bourgeois, equalitarian-democratic one.

Incidentally, what precisely is *meant* by 'human dignity' is too seldom discussed. The 'dignified man' is certainly not today the 'popular man,' who rather should be a 'good mixer,' humorous and even comic, who makes everyone feel a little superior to himself, a Chaplinesque figure. The contemporary cartoons of the little, moustachioed, goggle-eyed John Citizen of Strube or Herblock make this clear. It is almost the antithesis of the Confucian or Aristotelian or Renaissance ideal—or even of that of simple peoples, Mohawk or Zulu, or Irish Connemara peasants or Spanish herdsmen. An Abraham Lincoln had this dignity; a baby-kissing politician, anxious to please all men and women, does not. One is not automatically possessed of dignity, but only potentially so possessed. What, however, is true is that the Christian (and modern) idea of 'dignity' includes humility, imagination, sympathy, and the capacity for the individual to suffer owing to his share—no man being to himself, as Donne said, "an island"—in the universal experience, his archetype being, not 'a man,' but Man. In this aspect he must have an utterly authentic sense of fraternity.

§iv. *Reason, Instinct, and History*

Is there, then, a philosophically cogent alternative to ethical nihilism? From the lessons of political science we may be warned against any theme involving a mere transfer of power from the democratic consumer, concerned with his actual wants and sceptical about all persuasions to yield in his pleasures, across to the governmental producers (who may well be no more ethical, although more formidably avid of power) and some 'planster'-planned or monopolist polity. A rational tolerance and common experience warn against this and in favour of social balance.

The political scientist has to assume that each man, even the most recessive and masochistic, has a will; and that he will aspire to a power which he will not relinquish save under pressure or in exchange for some more wished-for power of enjoyment. The political philosopher, on the other hand, will probably not assume that the wishes of men are of equal value or merit equal powers of gratification. The political scientist will discuss the condition of the market, which will settle which wishes *will* be gratified. The political philosopher, it is arguable, will seek to educate the individuals of the society, in order to produce a rational valuation of which wishes *ought* to be satisfied. The question then traditionally arises whether the philosopher, like Plato's Philosopher-King, himself ought to impose this valuation coercively on the mass—which also the Leninists suppose—or whether he should content himself, like a Buddhist, in remaining under his bo-tree to be sought for, and then advising. How much harm are the ignorant to be permitted to do, without, as Rousseau recommended, being constrained so that the liberty they enjoy is rational? How far are we to suffer what I have termed 'an Elvis Presley civilization' or 'a Diana Dors civilization' or 'a Bardot civilization'? (I use these symbolic terms not personally but as significant because these types are deliberately encouraged, as models, by certain powers in a go-as-you-please culture which is lucrative to its exploiters.) To go further: how far is Freud right that, unrestrained by discipline and left to nature, *les bons gorilles*, who are Darwinian men, would prove not so good and would reach down to the level of a gangster civilization? Are Plato and Lenin right or is Archibald MacLeish? Or is there a third course?

The traditional Greco-Roman answer to the problems alike of moral relativism or localism, and of practical diversity in *mores* and laws, was the appeal to reason and instinct, twin bases of the *ius naturae*. The limits of reason understood in an Aristotelian sense as understanding and intellectual logic, and not in a Stoic sense as the logos of the cosmic universe, we have already indicated. Such intellectual understanding (on which William Blake made his comments) can point out contradictions, reveal coherences, outline harmony. It cannot produce, as we have said, proof in logic that even harmony or consistency itself is good, which another logic could not subvert.

When we come to the fundamental axioms and value judgements, the instincts might seem to provide a more solid basis. Moreover, although the Greeks, and their Gnostic followers even among the Christians, were prone to put into sharp antithesis in valuation the rule of reason, as archetypally human, if not indeed causing men to resemble the Divine (this also being Mind), as over against the rule of the passions, as animal, it must not be supposed (nor did Ulpian suppose) that animal passions were bad, unless disproportionate; and still less were the instincts bad which gave rise to them. Nature, says St. Thomas later, is perfected, not abrogated, by grace. Maternal love was peculiarly cited as such an instinct, approved by reason itself.

The thesis on the revival of Natural Law, argued in chapter vIII, indicates the importance to be attached to the empirical study of the human instincts, as indicating the character of the 'healthy' man and, hence, of the healthy and sane society. No defender of the importance of Natural Law, therefore, will underestimate the importance of reference to the instincts for a criterion. Nevertheless, (a) certainly not all cultural expressions of the instincts are good, and the bias to human distrust and hate, if not truly instinctive, is yet original—it is easy to appeal to what is 'natural,' but reason, science and history must show us whether we mean here the 'primitive,' the 'spontaneous,' or the 'fundamental'; (b) in many critical issues of ethics, the guidance to action offered by the instincts, even when springing from the deepest levels of the healthy individual, are often too general to provide aid for any specific decision.

Here a supplementary guide may be found, which bears directly upon the role of the history of political theory. We can turn, in our search for an ethical norm, in private and public life, to the page of History. This will, indeed, yield no logically ineluctable conclusions. It does not prove: it renders probable. It will yield a record of major probabilities in the preservation of values and the avoidance of stupidities, if perhaps with a conservative or retrospective bias, such as will appeal to the man of common sense and of the middle way. IT CAN BE ARGUED (AND IS HERE ARGUED) THAT THERE IS A GRAND TRADITION OF CIVILIZED VALUES, AS DISPLAYED IN HISTORY (Proposition 50).

The historian of ideas can detect those which the centuries—and even diverse human civilizations ranging from China to America—have reaffirmed as viable and sound, and those which, episodically occurrent as heresies from time to time and place to place, have revealed themselves as paradoxes or exaggerations which were not viable. This historical record or tradition, it must be emphasized, will *not supply* us with any original judgement, any more than of itself it can confute the possibilities of scepticism. The nature of the original judgement we have still to discuss. But this record can and should *confirm* the private judgement, which can otherwise on its own be, in detail, error. That private judgement can be initially and generally convinced by the aid of the judgements of those whom, independent of the particular case, we have judged to be judges. This aid can confirm what is probable in judgement, and the degree of its probability, about a potential certainty or absolute affirmation. In brief, we are in the process of confirming a hypothesis, not only by our own reason and experience, but by those of others competent to be heard.

Of this argument, I submit, there are only three major criticisms: (a) the stream of human valuations is not to be detected only in the history of intellectual ideas and in the lives of exceptional authors; (b) we do not rise here above probabilities, so important as a corrective but not entitling us to dogmatize against the new adventures of genius in valuation: the human race has erred in knowledge in the past and humanly may err again; (c) history can show that eminent men have in fact made certain valuations and even have, in the objective course of history, co-opted the subjective valuations of others or have been themselves co-opted, as masters and judges, thanks to the valuations of acknowledged masters, their predecessors; but this will not validate directly (or even be generally concerned with) the process by which these valuations have been reached. The accusation that occasionally occurs, that this tradition is subjective because the historian—or, in dealing with Mr. Leavis' 'Great Tradition,' the literary critic—picks out what he likes and calls this 'the tradition' is patently one of bad faith. It would only serve to show that the writer in question was a bad historian.

The present writer, in *History*, the third volume of his trilogy on method, science, and values (of which the present tractate is a review), attempted to indicate the validity of the notion of a Grand Tradition of values in high civilization (more accurately, in high culture). Professor Sir Ernest Barker, more recently, in his *Traditions of Civility*, a title taken from Patmore, stated the general argument, so necessary to a stable, rooted and confident culture, in an eminent fashion. It is interesting that he preferred the plural, 'traditions.'

If, of course, the review of the history of political ideas, however scholarly, is itself inspired by a Humean philosophy, as with the distinguished work of Professor George Sabine, clearly an analytical discussion, rather than the attempted display of such a tradition, will result. One of the more interesting speculations, not merely of private whim and caprice, but of the reiterations of history, can be how far such a *philosophia perennis*, which certainly includes the contributions of St. Thomas and of Locke, of Erasmus and of Goethe, indeed accepts the contributions of Hume (not indeed as touching detailed discussions, but as touching general impact), who, on the basis of scepticism stimulated by Hobbes, built up a defence of strong monarchical rule and of acceptance of local political habit. My judgement is adverse; but the heresy is, of course, ancient. It can be argued that, as he grew older, Hume was frightened himself by the youthful Hume—or by what men thought the younger Hume to say. At least, it frightened Kant.

It is noteworthy that Mr. Walter Lippmann, in his strenuous attempt to build up a Public Philosophy of liberalism for the West, takes his start from Sir Ernest Barker's book.

We may, then, admit that, while there is a right to disagree, protest, rebel, adventure, and take the risks, there is yet a dominant tradition of values slowly built, like coral, by the major minds (and major cults) of human civilization. How yet, we may ask, essentially have these minds arrived at their valuations? There will be those who will say, not without excuse, that most of the rational arguments of these philosophies are indeed rationalizations of prior irrational judgements. It would be better to say that they are intellectual testings, analyses, and re-examinations of intuitions.

Do we, then, end with an intuitionism of values and ethics? The answer is: in the ordinary and received sense, no. The intuitionism of the philosophic schools is generally thought, despite the contrary arguments of Sir David Ross and others, on the ground of the diversity of intuitions to be committed to subjectivism in valuation. And, for this very reason, it has to be admitted that the subjective valuations, even of those admitted to be competent (supposing that subjectivism admits of any objective test of competence), is diverse, varies—and this even to the point of contradiction. We may end where we began, if not in ethical nihilism, at least in ethical anarchy.

§v. *Concerning the Good as End*

In the Western World it is broadly true that the domination of the Hegelian school, and its various right and left deviations, which succeeded the intellectual collapse of the rule of Utilitarianism and (in France) Sociological Positivism, has been overthrown during this century, in no small measure by Logical Positivism—now modified to Logical Analysis, with a debt to Bentham—and (in France and Germany) by variations of Existentialism. The first school is nominalist-scholastic in mood and preoccupied with linguistic structure, and the second school is in revolt from the abstract and verbal schematisms of the Hegelians, but both are preoccupied with *sensibilia.*

It seems at least possible that the mood of philosophic teaching will soon again change and that, without departing from sensation (*aesthesis*), a new interest may be displayed in the aesthetic judgement, with curiosity revived about the work of Shaftesbury, Hutcheson, Schiller, and their successors, not to speak of what is here relevant in

Plato and the Cyrenaics. This may well be the philosophical school of the immediate future and, as such, might be commended to the attention and study of students now young.

If our concern is about stable values, then the aesthetic judgement, as of the moment, is categorical, when confronted by what the Stoics used to call the *kataleptikē phantasia*—according to their phrase, 'a conviction seizing a man by the hair of the head.' Moreover, the argument that the aesthetic judgement either trivializes, being pre-occupied with 'art for art's sake,' or is passive, whereas the ethical or value judgement is active and practical, is clearly false. In entering empathically into a drama, whether of art or life, the mood of the judge is not passive; nor is a pure ethical speculation active in any practical sense. The line of distinction is too facile and fades. It is, moreover, remarkable (although Kant typically uses the reverse argument) in common language and philology how many of our words of ethical appraisal or dispraisal are words of aesthetic use or origin. We shall, then, argue here that, if there be eternal values, these values owe their categorical—or what Sir Isaiah Berlin calls 'eternal'—quality primarily to the nature of the aesthetic judgement.

> The distinction drawn by Ritschl—who developed a doctrine of 'value judgement,' as distinct from 'practical judgement' (the 'economic judgement' of Croce) or rational proof, but divided it from the 'aesthetic judgement'—is here rejected, on the principle *entia non sunt multiplicanda*. We may note the dictum: 'ethics is aesthetics.' A more precise definition is given by St. Thomas. "*The beautiful coincides with the good* but is distinguishable. For since the good is 'that which all things desire,' it follows from our definition of the good that in it desire should be satisfied. But it is implied in the definition of beauty that by its very sight or recognition, desire should be satisfied." (*Summa Theologica*, 1a, 2ae, q. 1, art. xxvii) "The good is conceived as the end, for desire is a kind of impulse towards something. But beauty concerns our cognitive faculty, for those things are called beautiful whose sight pleases. So beauty consists in due proportion" (*ibid.*, I, art. v, q. 4) or harmony. St. Thomas here draws a very different distinction between the good and the beautiful from that which is usual and with which we are now concerned. Incidentally, his stress on proportion seems to be more lucid than S. T. Coleridge's declaration that beauty is "unity in variety." Were this the place, it would be interesting to raise the question why, if the good must be appropriated, it is so often discussed as a matter of *visio* and contemplation. Also we need not discuss here whether Reality or God *is* (a foolish question) but whether 'I-am-that-I-am' is One; and is Beautiful and to be loved as such . . .

It can be urged that the idea of the good involves an obligation to pursue it, whereas the idea of the beautiful does not. This would be denied (in the judgement of the writer, correctly) by Plato. The beautiful, as St. Thomas says, is that towards which in experience we turn and pursue and, moreover, is that which satisfies rational desire. It therefore not only is, but ought to be, pursued. It is that, according alike to Plato and St. Thomas himself, towards which *in se* we ought to turn, that is, towards which we have a rational obligation to turn. The only distinction is that between the conation towards, or appetition of, the good and the immediate enjoyment of the beautiful. Here surely, we must distinguish between the idea (or vision) of the good and also of the beautiful, both of which we can—and in theology are enjoined to—contemplate; and the appropriation of the value-for-us— which, no less in the case of the beautiful than of the good, is an affair of striving and pursuit. We must not be misled by the Kantian or Puritan identification of virtue with duty, as something, almost by definition, non-pleasant but intellectually compulsory. We may yet admit a valid distinction between *ultimate* goods, which are absolute and objects of vision, as is beauty also, and intermediary goods, always relative, never absolute, which (as intermediate) are means, subject to that economic and practical striving which characterizes all means. (This does not spell that the means cannot themselves, like money for the miser, be enjoyed as temporary and transitional ends; they can.) To this indeed, beauty offers no adequate parallel. But these means, as secondary, are not (despite the pragmatists) authentic objects of the ethical, any more than of the aesthetic, judgement.

In order to clarify the matter certain distinctions should be made. (*a*) Art is not the same thing as the production or reproduction of Beauty, since the most skilful art can deliberately reproduce the ugly or, in literature, produce the evil. This distinction is elementary but often ignored. Apart from the position where lauded art is merely a matter of fashion, study alike of the Greek drama, not least the Oedipus cycle, and of modern artists should warn us that Art, far from being concerned essentially and habitually with beauty, can also be the sublimation, subjected to form, for social man of the detestable, the tabu, and the outrageous in his own primitive and unreconciled nature. Thus there are art students today who make it their specialty to study *graffiti* on walls. Indeed, Professor Stuart Hampshire, who speaks without distinction of "the problems of Art and Beauty" seems to fall into this very error. There can be, in Berenson's term, "the illustrative artist." There can be men, by technical skill indubitably artists, who are motivated by exhibitionism or hate and who are disinterested in the beautiful or negative to it. How far this vitiates the rest of Hampshire's argument is controversial. It is perhaps also worth remark that Dr. Helen Knight, in the same symposium, associates even art with the concept of the good: "We commend the (artistic) works of man for their goodness." Upon the originality and importance of Professor Hampshire's work, in his *Thought and Action* (1959), for the theory of aesthetics, see Bernard Williams' "Man as Agent" (*Encounter*, November, 1960); and also Hampshire's remark in this book may be noted (p. 38): "The poverty of British aesthetics, at least among philosophers, is notorious."

b. The Beautiful patently is to be distinguished from our Judgement of the Beautiful. The Beautiful itself (whatever may be the case with Art) is not, as some have contended, a mere creation of the imagination. However, 'value' is value for somebody; and, hence, the Beautiful has value but, by the definition of value, only in relation to a perceiver and his aesthetic judgement; nor should the Beautiful, despite Socrates, be regarded as having ulterior purpose or use (as distinct from satisfaction, even if as part of an integrating whole), which would be a subject for an 'economic' or practical judgement. (*c*) Beauty is *not* subjective, in the sense of being solely subjective or solely intuitive; nor is the particular judgement of the beautiful without an objective and limiting cause, in which object the quality and form of beauty inhere.

Kant, in his *Critique of Judgement*, writes: "Now I say the Beautiful is the symbol of the morally good, and that it is only in this respect . . . that it gives pleasure *with* a claim for the agreement of every one else." It is difficult to conceive how the judgement of the symbol in its appropriateness can, in genus, be other than the judgement of that [the good] of which beauty is the symbol. Nevertheless, Kant does distinguish at least the two objects here of judgement, on the ground that the one pleases immediately in reflective intuition, stimulating the imagination, whereas the object of ethical judgements corresponds to a rational concept and indeed an *interest*, aiding *power*. Incidentally, "all our knowledge of God," he concedes, is symbolic (and aesthetic?) and not schematic.

Kant seems to err in two respects: he holds (*a*) that "our Aesthetic Judgement is itself legislative in respect of the judgement whether anything is beautiful or not," which does not indeed involve that 'beauty lies only in the eye of the [individual] beholder' (a view Kant opposes); but does seem to deny *objective* limiting factors to the sensation of that beauty which we are told is an adequate symbol; (*b*) that the Good can adequately and fully be arrived at by an *intellectual* and indeed practical or power judgement, limited by certain intellectual laws of consistency which become categorical.

Here we must make a sharp distinction. On the one side, there is the axiomatic core of the Good (or goods) which we cannot demonstrate to be good by any proof of the Understanding and which we do not arrive at by intellectual judgements. On the other side, we must grant that, if we accept certain experience or behaviour as incarnating or expressing such an axiomatic good, then our reason also compels us to judge good that which consistently conduces to and empowers us to find this good, or produces a coherent system—of purposes to ends— of the Good or (even and *pro tanto*) of the plural goods.

Thus St. Thomas rightly insists that the moral philosopher is concerned with discovering the system or schema of the good by perseverance in intellectual discussion. It is not the case that he would have held that the goodness of God could be apprehended by demonstration by reason (for, as Augustine also says, this is unutterable but more nearly apprehended by the symbol of beauty). But because the reduction of the aesthetic judgements of axiomata, or indubitable cores or foci of goodness, to a coherent intellectual scheme of activities favourable—and unfavourable—to the experience of the good and ethical presents great intellectual difficulties and involves also a rational construct of practice and purpose, hence much that, from one perspective and in political science with a hypothetical good, we may call *means*, from another perspective and with an aesthetically postulated good, we can call, owing to their consistency with the pattern, (*intermediary*) *goods* themselves. In the peculiar terminology of Croce, they are 'economic' (i.e., means) and not 'aesthetic' (i.e., ultimate) goods.

As touching the objectivity of the Beautiful, and its alleged qualities of proportion, harmony, and equilibrium (such as we accept also as a normative hypothesis in physical science), I am prepared to concede —and this would meet some of the difficulties of Kant, who regarded the actual universe as a necessary or determined order of the purposeless and amoral (and even evil and anti-free)—that the objective universe, as explored empirically and indicated in recent physical research, may not be, in its energy or substance, indifferent but may have direction. Also human beings, as part of that universe, may have actually evolved sympathetically to that harmony and may, both existentially and essentially, tend to be pleased by that harmony as beautiful. Whether we should choose (as I do not) to call this harmony 'material' or perhaps 'a direction of the cosmic electrical field,' I cannot discuss here! What we can perhaps say—I apologize for the use of the convenient Hindu terminology, which I employ for brevity's sake—is that the Beautiful-for-us is *maya*, phenomenal, the realm of Vishnu and Siva, not Brahmā; but that this 'phenomenal,' in its substantial causes, is yet 'real' and objective. It seems to have certain harmonies or equilibria (provoking, as Ogden and Richards say, 'life and vitality') which may penetrate far deeper in the cosmic and even transcendent nature of things than we can as yet demonstrate, so that a scientific restraint or admission of present ignorance is wise. Probable conjecture would seem to point yet to some natural or providential symbiosis, such as the Stoics and Gnostics long ago taught. In this case the rationalist total construct of realists, such as that posited by St. Thomas, would be warranted . . . The impressive recent speculations of the most eminent of our physicists, Dr. Niels Bohr, have been along these lines of a compatibility between cosmic harmonies or laws and human rhythm.

It is noteworthy that one of our greatest recent authorities on Aesthetics, Bernard Berenson, while he refers to the "tarantella of the cosmos," himself finds the source of great art in its relation to life and vitality, to which theme he recurs repeatedly; and insists that at least art—and surely still more beauty—has objective standards. "All, therefore, in the work of art which distinguishes it from the mere mental image . . . the more essential elements, as I believe, are above the revolutions of fashion and taste." (*The Italian Painters of the Renaissance*, rev. ed., 1952, pp. 107, 152) Berenson also stresses the notion of aesthetic education as authentic, and not merely arbitrary or fashionable (p. 144). Cf. L. Wittgenstein, *Philosophical Investigations* (1953, pp. 230, 143): "Compare a concept with a style of painting. For is even our style of painting arbitrary? . . . Understanding a sentence is much more akin to understanding a theme in music than one might think."

However, the work of M. André Malraux, *Psychologie de l'art* (1947–50) should also be consulted, especially volume III, "La Monnaie de l'absolu," with its theme of a continuum in perpetual metamorphosis in history through changing cultural forms, "monde éphémère et éternel." Cf. also Adrian Stokes, *Michelangelo* (1962).

In his interesting Wharton Address (1960) to the British Academy on "Great Poetry," the Warden of All Souls, Mr. J. H. A. Sparrow, expressed the view that certain physical juxtapositions affect the senses and, almost viscerally, the emotions: the reaction to harmony and beauty is "the luck of the senses." This statement was made in a comparison of the Arts. (It did not only relate to the sense of taste for excellent wines!) The general argument urged here is consonant with the Warden's theme.

A careful and suggestive essay by Professor Stuart Hampshire, "Logic and Appreciation" in *Aesthetics and Language* (edited by W. Elton, 1954), also demands attention. The argument put forward in the text, as against Professor Hampshire, is: (a) that aesthetic judgement and artistic criticism are distinct; (b) that aesthetic experience is necessary and, over the large area of interest, challenges every man to a judgement; (c) that the aesthetic experience is, not like that of History, individual, but, like that of Ethics, has general features; (d) hence, that we can provide a genuine education of the private aesthetic judgement —as otherwise we could not—in view of these features, which spring from our nature; (*e*) that a major cause of the 'dullness' or 'pretentiousness' of aesthetic theory may be inadequate empiric research into the psychology and even neurophysiology of the higher nervous system of that nature ('what pleases?') and, hence, to ignorance; (*f*) that, far from being 'irresponsible,' this judgement attempts answers to necessary questions of choice, and that an 'Aesthetic,' conscious or unconscious, with exclusive judgements is inevitable; (*g*) that harmony and proportion are of the essence of the final ethical judgement, as of the aesthetic judgement, and a factor in deciding what is worth attention; and (*h*) that ultimate ethical judgements can be irrespective of reasoning about purpose. We do not judge the final purpose or target, teleologically, in terms of *its* purpose, with infinite regression.

Perhaps no little of this difficulty is due to taking the meaning of Aesthetics, thanks to assimilation with Art, too superficially; and again to confusing two elements of the Ethical which should be distinguished. There are (*a*) 'teleological ethics' or that of the final end, of which the judgement is not intellectual, but is here called Aesthetics; and (*b*) 'casuistic ethics' which, as in pastoral theology, is concerned with the *casus*; with the application of the principle to the particular circumstance; *and* with the choice of the circumstance as means—hence what Croce called 'economic'—to the valued end. Here we find ourselves in the problems of Economics (in the usual sense); of the means which Aristotle tells us are necessary in Ethics; and indeed in problems of Politics.

Quality, it may be said, as much as time and space is a fundamental category of all human experience. Such quality, moreover, while not of its own abstractly separable nature characterized by extension, like space, or by duration, like time, is characterized by degrees. Such degrees need not necessarily have value, since they may be relative to the neutral in the aesthetic experience in general (*aesthesis*), and not to the aesthetic judgement of the beautiful or ugly (perhaps with specific marks of harmony and proportion). Nevertheless, all values have degrees in quality, of their nature. The high values or high qualities are those to a high degree significant, or relevant to the significant, for man and, hence, holding a focus of interest. They have what may be called a 'curtain-raising' quality of significance and vision, as over against the boredom in experience of a 'one-damn-thing-after-another' quality. In this field of Aesthetics the vital field of Power and its desires is—as Schelling saw and Schopenhauer did not—gathered up and comprehended. As quality, these values necessarily confront every man in his judging experience; and as of interest they challenge him. The *signa*, whether direct or symbolical (analogous), may be of many kinds, carrying different phases of meaning for different kinds of men. In some cases they will correspond as means to the variety of human instincts and, also, to men's cultural and economic needs.

In other cases the indubitable signs of beauty will divorce themselves from 'messages,' utilities, and human advantage and power, and will establish themselves, categorically, as 'end-satisfactions' in their own right, apart from the pleasures of advantage. An *antithesis* between beauty and advantage-as-power is not to be supposed. The theologians (who here have sometimes been more imaginative than the metaphysicians) rightly posit that the all-powerful or Almighty is the all-beautiful or Supreme Good. But: THE CRITERION OF GOODNESS LIES IN THE BEAUTY FOR US AS END-SATISFACTION IN ITSELF, AND NOT IN THE POWER (Proposition 51), although we may grant that some power-forms, as Michelangelo knew, possess satisfying beauty.

The reconciliation of Beauties beyond 'the all too human,' of so-called good and evil [advantage and power], with the Desires of human instinct, unbiased by sin, lies in the selection ethically of those desires which are in rational accord, healthy or good, concordant with the wider harmony and, as Kant said, having a universal quality which the more-than-private rational judgement dictates as congruent with the good. These desires, proportionate if instinctive or cultural or local, we call desires conforming to Natural Law, however empirically and rationally inadequate our appreciation of this may still be. But the nature of man, we may suggest, which is the foundation of Natural Law for man, is so created (or as others would say 'evolved') as always, by that nature, to desire, psychologically and perhaps even physiologically, the objectively beautiful—or objective substance of the subjectively beautiful-for-us.

> Kant maintains that in the Imagination we enjoy the conciliation of Freedom and Power; and that Beauty stimulates this. Here we must beware lest the world of Dream as Nightmare, through Imagination and Art—and also Craft—impose itself, as has happened frequently, upon the world of prosaic events! (Kant's estimate of Imagination seems not only pre-Freudian but somewhat naive.) It is indeed the theme in different ways of Schelling and of Schiller that it is Art which provides the reconcilation between the objective limitation or *power* and the subjective desire for *freedom*, in the act of creation. This is the vindication, in the widest, most Goethean sense, of this life of art, especially music.

We shall confine ourselves to saying that: IN THIS ALIGNMENT OF MEANS WITH THE PROFOUNDER HUMAN JUDGEMENT OF ENDS, WHICH IS THE CATEGORICAL AESTHETIC JUDGEMENT, LIES THE RECONCILIATION OF POWER WITH THE GOOD (Proposition 52); and that in the Good Society (which for the Greeks was rightly the beautiful society) also is to be found a paradigm of the reconciliation. What is here said is certainly not the same as the philosophy of the moral sentiments enunciated by Bishop Butler. Its emphasis upon a rational scheme is far greater. But it bears a certain family resemblance. Again, the attempt in the work of St. Thomas to reconcile an Aristotelian rationalism with a Platonic mysticism (consequently, but controversially, continued by M. Jacques Maritain as between Thomism and Spanish mysticism) has its bearing upon what is said here.

It must be added that: THE NAIVE JUDGEMENT OF BEAUTY IS CAPABLE OF EDUCATION (Proposition 53). Moreover, there is agreement that aesthetic education is not a mere matter of chance, regional culture, and local teachers, but is authentically such, so that the line, tradition, or direction of education is unlikely to reverse itself. With Plato we may agree that, in the aesthetic judgement, the teachers or masters will be those, expert, to whom men with the most sensitive genius accord this title, and, in turn, that the areopagus of masters is composed of those whose right the masters themselves through the centuries do not dispute. This is not to deny the vigour of the controversy about the detail of aesthetic taste. It certainly does not exclude diversity or even deny its vital virtue. It does establish a canon.

Further, although the aesthetic judgement of the individual (which, in the specific emphasis on the good, has often been called the absolute voice of conscience) is *categorical* or absolute within the range of the immediate experience, and not relative, yet the experience of the judge may be so enlarged that, without reversing the earlier judgement within its framework, a more experienced judgement, consonant with the critical cumulative wisdom of humanity in the wider framework, may supersede it at a new level. The judgement, absolute in mode so that the ugly is absolutely not the beautiful, can with new perspective acquire new depths and a more universal quality in content. The harmonizing reason may come to reinforce the specific direct intuitions and substitute for a single experience an entire pattern of thought (and even of behaviour and of society).

The Good Man, about whom I have written in *On Political Goals*, is then the culmination on the human plane. He excellently displays for judgement the pattern of the good life; and he also judges. The judgement of him and by him is not tentative, relative, and matter for apology as naive; but aesthetic and categorical and only naive as simple, although capable of increased rational consistency and of progressive education. To the character and behaviour of the Good Man, writ large and without any heretical antithesis, the character of the Good Society corresponds.

Here is the vindication of Aristotle's fundamental pro-democratic argument for the judgement of the common man; here is the ethical and catholic argument for the simple good man, as distinct from the able expert or the intellectual élite. We begin, however, with the individual persons, each both capable of goodness and capable, cleverness or intellect apart, of the aesthetic judgement of goodness: and this is what we here imply by what we shall term 'the Philosophy of the Good Man,' with its relations to what is sometimes called the philosophy of common sense. This does not mean that, on analysis of particulars, in some parts of his or its conduct, the man or the society is not better than in others or, being human, that in parts the man or society, which we yet judge aesthetically and categorically in its whole, is not imperfect. Nor is our judgement, because it is not logically provable, likely to be shaken. Nevertheless since each human judgement, even of the core or axioms of conduct, is fallible in content, we need to test it against the canons of Reason and Instinct and against the probable norms of the Tradition established by inspection of human History.

If I were asked to provide a concrete instance of what I meant by 'a good man,' I should be inclined to cite, not some saint or priest, but the late Gilbert Harding, a British TV figure and something of a Graham Greene character. I would choose him precisely because, he being a very ordinary man, there must be thousands of men as good as he, a self-confessed sinner, on his own statement a quarrelsome drunk, a man who had perhaps too low an opinion of his own importance, but yet a man in whose life flashes of what I choose to call beauty in conduct shone forth in entirely humble and unadvertised ways, but unmistakably illustrating the quality of the man.

In the aesthetic imagination of the individual we have, then, the reconciliation of Beauty and Power (cf. Proposition 52 *supra*). And it provides the needed canon for the cultural tradition and for the ideal tradition of the race. In practice the reconciliation will only take place when the rational network of practical conduct is connected lucidly with the pattern of the Beauty which decides what, centrally, *ought* to be considered as ends; and when, in turn, the Means of politics, which ensure power, are viewed, not abstractly and in isolation, but concretely and as in systematic accord with this rationally approved end, as the decent and good.

It is the belief of the present writer that, if the theory of absolute values is to be validated, or enlightenment thrown upon it, this will be by enquiries into Aesthetics in the sense above outlined. If the theory has to be abandoned, then we are left solely with some theory of relative and historical morals and *mores*, which need have no common element between Chinese and Spaniard, and cannot provide any intellectually convincing common rule of right between white and black. In this situation it follows that there may be opinions about philosophical topics, but a Political Philosophy, of choice and ends, there is not. (Here I refer to a synthesizing philosophy, and not to a professional puzzle or to some work of a journeyman or plumber in philosophy, only concerned to detect in detail why drains are stopped in their flow of water—about which there can be many opinions. For example, we may select to enquire with the editor of *Mind*, Professor Gilbert Ryle [*Aesthetics and Language*]: "what sort of thing is a tickle?" I do not wish to deprecate this indispensable, but different, work.) We are left therefore in Politics with technical and empiric Political Science as the sole theory; and with the issues, as finally decisive, of the market and of power. This is an old doctrine. But the transcendence of power fails.

The question can indeed be put whether it is not the duty of philosophers to concern themselves with human problems and with what is perhaps rather pretentiously called 'great issues.' This would be in accordance with that age-old tradition (to which Lord Russell has recently called attention) under which one of the philosopher's prime tasks is to provide that ever-renewed synthesis of current human experience which is called wisdom. It is arguable that, had philosophers in the admirable pursuit of truth (a word which can have different meanings in different contexts, including that of a photographic copy) not too much become late schoolmen who would have adorned the scholasticism of a Duns, discussing words, the present unhappy divorce between ethics and politics might be less grave. Differences between evil and good would be less readily held to be analogous to those between a grunt of disapproval and a clapping of hands. It is not for this writer to denigrate scholasticism. A severe critic might yet say that the philosophers should get back to doing their professional and social duty. Until this is done, the 'struggle for the minds of men' can be waged by our world no more than negatively, whereas it may be most truly said that the function of philosophy is not only to observe and to analyse but to change and to create. Here Marxist philosophy, although not in this respect unique or even untraditional, is without qualification right. So, however, is the better teaching of the major Greeks against the sophists and of the earlier Scholastics.

An excellent indication of the nature of the practical and theoretical problems where Ethics and Politics interlock will be found in George Kennan's *Russia and the West*, pp. 396–7.

A further argument is worth attention. If, in philosophy, the relativity theory is true, then truth itself is relative—including, of course, this truth. It is a matter of historical conventions, modes, or fashions. This fashionable philosophy perhaps explains the tendency of the West to turn to plans of force, since it can scarcely turn for hope to some clarion call from relative ideas, and lacks Marxist conviction. The conversionary force of relativity among the uncommitted is relatively too small. Tolerance is but the expression of a doubt, not the conclusion of confidence. All is morally ambiguous, new in the world's record, where nothing can be shown convincingly. On the other hand, if we accept this relativist philosophy, the appeal to force itself, among those with only negative ideals, must also fail where victory is not assured, for who would resist or suffer persecution himself for the sake of values that are but passing fashions? Only a naive fool would take such risks. If scepticism were relatively right, then certainty would have to be invented.

A full discussion or justification of this philosophical theme would carry us into a treatise on Ethics and Aesthetics, and beyond the self-imposed limits of the present tractate on Politics.

§vi. *Education, Culture, and Cult*

The assessment of a tradition, including a tradition in critical valuations, is not to be made solely in terms of the history of ideas, and peculiarly the ideas of the most eminent men of genius. The history must also include the history of art, of general culture, and indeed of the cultural forms adopted by the common folk. This is not to deny the superior insight of genius or that these cultural forms tend historically to be shaped by an aristocracy, whether of artists or of a priesthood, of saints or of commissars. Nevertheless, the findings of genius must be communicable. The highest genius is that which is able to strike the note, not necessarily with the momentarily widest, but with the most enduring and profound, appeal. In the last resort the great cultural forms are those which evoke response from the deepest feelings and primal images of every man, not as, for example, bourgeois or proletarian, but as man. Such a history, then, both of individual genius, in its effect in giving shape by its ideas to popular culture, but *also* a history of folk culture, drama, and religious cults as shaped during the decades by instinctive and collective genius, demands close attention, if we are trying to establish a probable and corrective canon of values.

The larger history will not be one of intellectual ideas alone. And, although it is open to any man to run contrary to this canon on the ground that, like Melchisedek, he has no spiritual ancestry but has an inspiration superior to any, nevertheless he assumes an immense responsibility unless, for that which he discards because "he can no other," he can substitute something, not megalomaniac and neurotic, but sane, inspired and yet more profoundly corresponding to basic human need.

Attention must here be called to the brilliant and suggestive, but uneven work of C. J. Jung, especially in his *Psychological Types* (1921, trans. H. Godwin Baynes, 1923), with his stress on primal images in the human mind, which are shaped to the deepest instinctive needs and have their inevitable projections in human culture. While starting important lines of thought, by no means superficial, the work of Jung involves speculations which it is beyond our task to discuss here.

Among many cultural evaluations at the present time especial consideration is due to the eminent work of Ernst Cassirer, a great political theorist, with his discussion of katharsis and of the public function of myth, in his *Myth of the State* (1946) and his *Essay on Man* (1944). *Vide* also the stimulating work of Susanne K. Langer, *Philosophy in a New Key* (1942) especially chaps. vii, ix, and x, and the discussion of symbolic meaning; and also W. T. Stace, *Time and Eternity* (1952), chap. vi. Here we are confronted with problems, as in drama and especially religious drama, far more subtle and profound, more sensitive and less obviously practical, than the usual problems of government and efficient power. We are led to review answers about the condition of man and what he is, sometimes a condition primitive and uncouth but, during the long generations of high culture, sometimes of tragedy and awe, and sometimes of beauty and fitness, of which the wisdom cannot be assessed in any tidy terms of intellectual proof.

To show that what we may call public art is not an excrescence or decoration, but fulfils a function as profoundly important as any that exists in human social life for our happiness, as creatures that have achieved the satisfaction of a meaningful good and a vision of adequate ends for our life, is Cassirer's great work. That the function, although issuing in fruits appropriated by the individual, has been yet also a *social* function and that the myth is a *public* myth is something of the first importance. Reference may well be made here to the suggestive chapter, "Religious Symbolism," in Professor Stace's *Time and Eternity* (pp. 91–115), and incidentally to Berenson's comment on ritual and aesthetic experience (*The Italian Painters of the Renaissance*, p. 242).

Religion, we may venture to say, is emphatically not just 'an affair of private life': the "Kingdom of God within" bursts into expression with our fellows in a public 'liturgy,' and does so from its essential nature as a shaping of men in a *relation* to the cosmos but also to men. No primitive example seems to occur to the contrary—nor, for that matter, does Buddhist monasticism, the Orphic rites, or the Christian *sacramentum* offer an instance, which perhaps would have to be sought for among the hermit Robinson Crusoes of the desert. (That religion is or should not be a state matter, or secularly controlled, is a quite different contention.) To maintain that religion is a matter of the private conscience *only*, or a philosophic flight of the alone to the alone and nothing else, runs quite contrary to the whole history of religion, which has always been in some aspect, *mutatis mutandis*, 'a religion of the churches,' and must be so studied by the sociologist. Salvation is normally by an ordained way, even if it be a salvation of the individual and eternal soul, beyond value in the world. And "the Kingdom of Heaven within" is not "an island" to itself, but is inspired by grace from without. Also "the Kingdom of Hell" is within us— but does not remain so.

Cf. this writer's paper for the Conference of Science, Philosophy, and Religion, in September, 1960, at New York: "The Interplay of Great Traditions and Political Conduct: The Effects of Politics upon Trends in Philosophical and Religious thought" (published as *The Ethic of Power*, 1962).

The ethical norm of ends is, then, to be discovered by the aesthetic judgement rendered coherent by reason, but also—in matters of doubt: which doubt a proper humility will always seek to inform—by the collective judgement as expressed in the historical tradition, not only of genius in philosophy and religion, but also of genius made articulate in the culture, drama, and cult of a people, of a civilization, and of humanity. The works of some geniuses here belong to all humanity and are so recognized. The ritual cults of the great world religions are also of this order and of this social binding power or influence, providing within these fields common ends, values, patterns of conduct to whole societies. Confucianism did this. So do Buddhism and Islam. So does Christianity. So, in its own fashion (not conspicuous for a folk drama, unless it be the May Day ritual) does Marxism.

If our analysis is correct, we here approach mankind's final ethical goals of direct satisfaction, both aesthetic and rational, or at least to symbols of what are ends in themselves. The Marxist ideal of the millennial classless society is end-in-itself; and it is contemplated that, in its achievement, there is the fusion of justice and power. Marxism can be taken as a challenging contemporary pattern, with the rational criticism of which (as self-contradictory) or with the aesthetic judgement of which (as aggressively hate-encouraging) we are not here concerned—this being rather a matter of 'comparative religion.' Patently one can choose more perfect and charistic forms. To put the matter generally, the religious cult is end-in-itself, or manifestation of it, and not means to further enjoyments or ends. The May Day procession is direct satisfying pleasure and also a present manifestation of a type or pattern of class power which millennially will, it is alleged, be more completely and widely satisfying. The Mass provides the immediate sense of union and glory which is, not more fully, but more amply manifested in the heavenly glory of an all-powerful Wisdom, shaping the universe and us. The cult, that is, provides the beautiful pattern of ends and duty. It presumes the desirability of its vision of the healthy man and of the sane society. Lived out, it reconciles beauty and power. The tragic quality of life and history lies in the temporal incongruity between the society of actual power and the society of ethical meetness and seemliness, *dignum et iustum*.

As an illustration, other than Marxist, one may quote a judgement on the civilization of the Middle Ages expressed in my *History*: "It was indeed a pyramid based on Revelation and upon the Neoplatonic theology of the Nicene Creed. It had no meaning unless Jesus was very God and the Bread and Wine the veils of a Reality that was immanent Deity. Upon that pyx and that belief the Platonic-Catholic concept of politics pivoted. The Reason was not abstract but incarnate, and yet did truly govern all nature and creation." The criticism of the Marxist ideal, as a fusing with reality to be achieved now, will be found, for example, in the writings of Trotsky and Djilas, quoted *supra* p. 188.

In irony Aristotle contrasted the good man, product of the society of ethical decency and, in turn, creatively shaping it, and the good citizen in a bad society where power is set against decency. Of course, the so-called 'good citizen of a bad society' is indeed a bad man and also a bad citizen, who has deserted any ideal, historically, for his fellows beyond that of passive obedience or loyal conformity. The most a good man can here be is a prudent man. A close discussion, not greatly in evidence since the Schoolmen, of the ethics of prudence is much required.

The connection of the ethical ideal for man with a social pattern, and indeed with a social cult, will here be noted. The cult can provide a *sacramentum* or oath which holds the community, as communion, together. In a society individualistic and competitive by its philosophy this can be lacking—although usually some more or less 'watery' secular religion, as of 'the flag,' will be substituted, with appropriate and compulsory ritual. On the one side, then, as has been noted before, the Community as a close co-operative, can be regarded in Political Science as a means to ulterior goods, not least security, provided for a specific kind of market. On the other side, the Community is a like-minded society in transition to be an ethical end-in-itself, of ambiguous temporal quality but, when impregnated with an adequate rational and aesthetic principle, the very terrestrial (and, as *corpus mysticum*, not only terrestrial) goal, enjoyment and *summum bonum* or present beatitude for man's life.

The solitary quality of man's ethical nature, as endowed with reason and direct aesthetic judgement, is often ignored by collectivist sociologists and apologists for a secular, civic or 'scientific humanist' religion, such as Comte and (more) Durkheim. It is, also, often not given adequate weight by sociologists, such as Charles Cooley, who lay over-emphatic stress on co-operation (the issue of central *principle* apart), 'civicism,' and 'community centres'—Community being stressed exclusively, as 'commune.'

The part of ritual in patterning the daily life of the pacific Suni Indians, as distinct from the bellicose environment-pattern of those of the American Northwest, is memorably recorded by Ruth Benedict, in her *Patterns of Culture.*

The answer, here submitted, to the false antithesis of private judgement and public philosophy is that, although every man, as Bosanquet stressed, may owe his ideas, ideals, and indeed civic virtue to the social whole in which he was brought up, nevertheless, as a rational and as a judging being, whose thoughts by their nature appear to him free, he possesses the qualifications to analyse these 'collective representations' and social conventions, to criticize, and indeed to repudiate. He is a growing and maturing man, not a good animal, by reason of these powers. The correct conclusion is *not* that the soul is not solitary—it is *not* totally subjected to society's convenience but of intrinsic and humanly immeasurable worth—*but* that the conscience, reason, or judgement must perform its function in what some call dread and *Angst* and others (more soberly) call an enlightened and religious sense of responsibility, including responsibility to quest for truth, to be informed *et caritate formanda* amid the society and tradition of other men.

As touching the possibility of regarding, not only a religious community or a nation, but even a federal union as an object of dedication, superior to interest in life, and even as a focus of mysticism—as it was to some degree for the late Lionel Curtis—attention may be called to Mr. Edmund Wilson's thesis about Abraham Lincoln, in his essay, "The Union as Religious Mysticism" (*Eight Essays*). This is something of which the consequences were very practical indeed —and relate to that 'resolution' and 'dedication' needed in the West, of which there is so much talk. It is quite certain that the physical conquest of the stars, an age-old dream of mankind, will not be achieved on the basis of hedonism or of intelligent self-interest, but of such almost suicidal dedication. The history of the world lies with those who are prepared to pay final costs. Those who are not will be ruled. The ethical and rational issue is: dedication to what?

The conclusion, then, that we have reached is that the ethical goal of mankind is discovered by an aesthetic judgement. This is related to an objective beauty of proportion, in nature or in behaviour. It is an aesthetic judgement which is not merely passive, since it approves or disapproves as touching choices. Although related to that which is objective, it is not susceptible of logical proof, although logical criticism may reveal contradictions, incoherences, and disharmonies which some will adjudge amount, in the particular, to a disproof. By reason a coherent system is wrought out, as St. Thomas maintained (we cannot be content with the morals of indignation, emotion, and high blood-pressure—"of men who are sure because they are sure"). Aided by the historical record and the consensus of recognized masters, a probability can be established, in accordance with which men may be educated. But the aesthetic intuition of goodness is direct. For the reason just given, this does not mean that the aesthetic judgement is incapable of education by those who themselves agree to be educated or instructed.

It follows that it is the duty of a conscientious man, in making ethical judgements, not to rely upon his own opinion alone but, aided by instinct and reason, to seek to inform himself what has been the judgement of those scientifically, or by competent judges, accounted more competent than himself; to consider, before he adventures his own view, the cultivated tradition in the matter and the monitions, so far as known, of Natural Law, partly empiric; and to consult about this grand tradition of civility in values, recorded in the pages of history. The history here is not merely secular or that of ideas, even if it includes the vision of intellectual genius, but also the aesthetic tradition itself, whether it be at the level of folkways or ascend, through folk drama, cults, and ritual, to those expressions and incarnations in art and religion which most fully express or symbolize externally the insights into what is most profound in the human spirit.

In so far as Political Philosophy has as its topic the Good Society, it cannot ignore consideration of these judgements and their mode. It must yet be noted that, since nothing fundamental here can be proved, therefore scepticism is intellectually defensible on the basis of inevitable human ignorance. Any propounding of a 'public philosophy,' even a liberal one, has to take this into account. Despite the immemorial quality of the aesthetic experience of what is Good, this recognition of the margins of doubt may be morally justified as vindicating the possibility and desirability of new experience which, in the particular and arising from new technical considerations of our civilization, will require new judgements and a consequent coherent revision and development, by philosophy, of old ones. This is a perpetual task for philosophers.

There have been those who have held that State and secular forms of social organization tend to pass over into forms of, in general type, a more Church character, that are rather shaped by voluntary choice. It is suggested that the present is a time of such passing-over. From what we have said in the chapter about Community, it may be held that this view is broadly acceptable. It is not enough to say 'for the domination of men is substituted the administration of things' (since men remain to be cared for, and 'administration' may also be soulless and pass into 'exploitation'). For the coercive we substitute the voluntary; for that which bears the characteristic and differentiating stamp of the *vis coactiva* we substitute that which bears the characteristic and educational stamp of the *vis directiva*.

The presupposition, however, of such a society is the enforcement of peace and the forging, by statesmen and people, of the means thereto. The study of the means of maintaining the peace, domestic and international, one of the prime functions of civil society, including the study of 'peaceful change' in the context of power and justice, is among the first professional duties of any political scientist of practical utility. Since the mere abjuring of arms does not, of itself, give any guarantee that a market of freedom and of individual choice—or of the tolerance of any even remotely individualist or personalist philosophy—will be preserved, it is idle to suppose that the problem is a simple one, requiring little thought beyond casual lay judgement. The generations would not so consistently have failed in averting war if war were easy to avert. One of the preconditions of its solution is an exact understanding of the essential issues of power. Whatever may be our ends or our picture of the ideal society, to be inscribed in the heart of man, on and beyond the allocation through the market of immediate gratification and the disputes attendant thereon, our hopes will come to disaster if we complacently fall short in the precise study of the efficient political means and of the political process and structures which condition them.

Our concern in this book has been with the problem of power and with those ends which are, not set over against, but which transcend, power since with their possession we regain satisfaction and freedom, and the motive for power lapses. In human society this transcendence of means by direct enjoyment of ends, including enjoyment of a sane community, will always be incomplete. If progress were simple and in a straight line, it would indeed be difficult to know how humanity could occupy itself, without problems, in the next two million years: it would succumb to a heavenly *ennui*. But particular goals may be newly or recurrently achieved—among which the important and traditional objective for civil society, peace, can be one—granted adequate and understood means. The task of political education is to increase this understanding of means and appreciation of ends.

The immediate task is to produce such a climate of opinion that we can see grow in our midst a community consonant with Natural Law and with the deeper spirit of man, which holds in tolerable balance an authoritative peace, justice, and the energy to explore the areas of freedom. Natural Law gives a basis for public consensus. This also means such shaping of opinion as would permit the extinction of such obsolescent parts of the traditional political structure as frustrate this growth. It means the acquisition of an international power to do these things with an inflexible determination. This will require more virility in statesmanship, if this new world is to be developed, than has hitherto been common. It is certain that, if peace is to be enforced, heavy costs for this will have to be paid. Whether the Western democracies are willing to pay these costs, rather than accept a world tyranny that enforces peace as the Caesars once did, is beyond our immediate scope. It is the problem which Alexander the Great posed to the Athenian and Hellenic world; and which that world failed to answer. As frequently in history, the more primitive people won. It has been sufficient here to analyse the structure of the market of power.

INDEX